SECOND EDITION

Programming Rust
Fast, Safe Systems Development

Jim Blandy, Jason Orendorff, and Leonora F. S. Tindall

Beijing · Boston · Farnham · Sebastopol · Tokyo

Programming Rust

by Jim Blandy, Jason Orendorff, and Leonora F. S. Tindall

Copyright © 2021 Jim Blandy, Leonora F. S. Tindall, Jason Orendorff. All rights reserved.

Published by O'Reilly Media, Inc., 1005 Gravenstein Highway North, Sebastopol, CA 95472.

O'Reilly books may be purchased for educational, business, or sales promotional use. Online editions are also available for most titles (*http://oreilly.com*). For more information, contact our corporate/institutional sales department: 800-998-9938 or *corporate@oreilly.com*.

Acquisitions Editor: Suzanne McQuade
Developmental Editor: Jeff Bleiel
Production Editor: Beth Kelly
Copyeditor: Charles Roumeliotis
Proofreader: Kim Wimpsett

Indexer: Potomac Indexing, LLC
Interior Designer: David Futato
Cover Designer: Karen Montgomery
Illustrator: Kate Dullea

June 2021:   Second Edition

Revision History for the Second Edition
2021-06-11:   First Release
2021-11-05:   Second Release

See *http://oreilly.com/catalog/errata.csp?isbn=9781492052593* for release details.

The O'Reilly logo is a registered trademark of O'Reilly Media, Inc. *Programming Rust*, the cover image, and related trade dress are trademarks of O'Reilly Media, Inc.

The views expressed in this work are those of the authors, and do not represent the publisher's views. While the publisher and the authors have used good faith efforts to ensure that the information and instructions contained in this work are accurate, the publisher and the authors disclaim all responsibility for errors or omissions, including without limitation responsibility for damages resulting from the use of or reliance on this work. Use of the information and instructions contained in this work is at your own risk. If any code samples or other technology this work contains or describes is subject to open source licenses or the intellectual property rights of others, it is your responsibility to ensure that your use thereof complies with such licenses and/or rights.

978-1-492-05259-3

[LSI]

Table of Contents

Preface... xv

1. Systems Programmers Can Have Nice Things.................................... 1
   Rust Shoulders the Load for You   2
   Parallel Programming Is Tamed   3
   And Yet Rust Is Still Fast   4
   Rust Makes Collaboration Easier   4

2. A Tour of Rust.. 5
   rustup and Cargo   6
   Rust Functions   8
   Writing and Running Unit Tests   10
   Handling Command-Line Arguments   11
   Serving Pages to the Web   15
   Concurrency   22
       What the Mandelbrot Set Actually Is   23
       Parsing Pair Command-Line Arguments   28
       Mapping from Pixels to Complex Numbers   30
       Plotting the Set   32
       Writing Image Files   33
       A Concurrent Mandelbrot Program   35
       Running the Mandelbrot Plotter   40
       Safety Is Invisible   41
   Filesystems and Command-Line Tools   42
       The Command-Line Interface   43
       Reading and Writing Files   45
       Find and Replace   46

3. Fundamental Types.. 49

Fixed-Width Numeric Types   52
   Integer Types   53
   Checked, Wrapping, Saturating, and Overflowing Arithmetic   56
   Floating-Point Types   58
The bool Type   61
Characters   61
Tuples   63
Pointer Types   65
   References   65
   Boxes   66
   Raw Pointers   66
Arrays, Vectors, and Slices   67
   Arrays   67
   Vectors   68
   Slices   71
String Types   73
   String Literals   73
   Byte Strings   74
   Strings in Memory   74
   String   76
   Using Strings   77
   Other String-Like Types   77
Type Aliases   78
Beyond the Basics   78

4. Ownership and Moves.. 79

Ownership   81
Moves   85
   More Operations That Move   90
   Moves and Control Flow   91
   Moves and Indexed Content   92
Copy Types: The Exception to Moves   94
Rc and Arc: Shared Ownership   97

5. References... 101

References to Values   102
Working with References   105
   Rust References Versus C++ References   105
   Assigning References   107
   References to References   107
   Comparing References   108

References Are Never Null	109
Borrowing References to Arbitrary Expressions	109
References to Slices and Trait Objects	110
Reference Safety	110
Borrowing a Local Variable	110
Receiving References as Function Arguments	113
Passing References to Functions	115
Returning References	116
Structs Containing References	117
Distinct Lifetime Parameters	120
Omitting Lifetime Parameters	121
Sharing Versus Mutation	123
Taking Arms Against a Sea of Objects	130

6. Expressions. **133**

An Expression Language	133
Precedence and Associativity	134
Blocks and Semicolons	137
Declarations	138
if and match	140
if let	142
Loops	142
Control Flow in Loops	144
return Expressions	145
Why Rust Has loop	146
Function and Method Calls	148
Fields and Elements	149
Reference Operators	151
Arithmetic, Bitwise, Comparison, and Logical Operators	151
Assignment	152
Type Casts	153
Closures	154
Onward	154

7. Error Handling. **157**

Panic	157
Unwinding	158
Aborting	159
Result	160
Catching Errors	160
Result Type Aliases	162
Printing Errors	163

Propagating Errors   164
Working with Multiple Error Types   166
Dealing with Errors That "Can't Happen"   168
Ignoring Errors   169
Handling Errors in main()   169
Declaring a Custom Error Type   171
Why Results?   172

8. Crates and Modules. 173
Crates   173
   Editions   176
   Build Profiles   177
Modules   178
   Nested Modules   179
   Modules in Separate Files   180
   Paths and Imports   183
   The Standard Prelude   186
   Making use Declarations pub   186
   Making Struct Fields pub   186
   Statics and Constants   187
Turning a Program into a Library   188
The src/bin Directory   189
Attributes   191
Tests and Documentation   193
   Integration Tests   196
   Documentation   197
   Doc-Tests   199
Specifying Dependencies   202
   Versions   202
   Cargo.lock   204
Publishing Crates to crates.io   205
Workspaces   207
More Nice Things   208

9. Structs. 209
Named-Field Structs   209
Tuple-Like Structs   212
Unit-Like Structs   213
Struct Layout   213
Defining Methods with impl   214
   Passing Self as a Box, Rc, or Arc   217
   Type-Associated Functions   217

Associated Consts   218
Generic Structs   219
Generic Structs with Lifetime Parameters   221
Generic Structs with Constant Parameters   222
Deriving Common Traits for Struct Types   225
Interior Mutability   225

10. Enums and Patterns... 231
Enums   232
  Enums with Data   234
  Enums in Memory   235
  Rich Data Structures Using Enums   236
  Generic Enums   238
Patterns   241
  Literals, Variables, and Wildcards in Patterns   244
  Tuple and Struct Patterns   245
  Array and Slice Patterns   246
  Reference Patterns   247
  Match Guards   249
  Matching Multiple Possibilities   250
  Binding with @ Patterns   250
  Where Patterns Are Allowed   251
  Populating a Binary Tree   252
The Big Picture   254

11. Traits and Generics.. 255
Using Traits   257
  Trait Objects   258
  Generic Functions and Type Parameters   260
  Which to Use   264
Defining and Implementing Traits   266
  Default Methods   267
  Traits and Other People's Types   268
  Self in Traits   270
  Subtraits   271
  Type-Associated Functions   272
Fully Qualified Method Calls   274
Traits That Define Relationships Between Types   275
  Associated Types (or How Iterators Work)   276
  Generic Traits (or How Operator Overloading Works)   279
  impl Trait   280
  Associated Consts   282

| | Reverse-Engineering Bounds | 283 |
| | Traits as a Foundation | 286 |

12. Operator Overloading... 287
Arithmetic and Bitwise Operators	288
Unary Operators	291
Binary Operators	292
Compound Assignment Operators	293
Equivalence Comparisons	294
Ordered Comparisons	297
Index and IndexMut	300
Other Operators	302

13. Utility Traits... 303
Drop	304
Sized	307
Clone	310
Copy	311
Deref and DerefMut	312
Default	315
AsRef and AsMut	317
Borrow and BorrowMut	318
From and Into	320
TryFrom and TryInto	323
ToOwned	324
Borrow and ToOwned at Work: The Humble Cow	325

14. Closures.. 327
Capturing Variables	329
Closures That Borrow	330
Closures That Steal	330
Function and Closure Types	332
Closure Performance	334
Closures and Safety	335
Closures That Kill	336
FnOnce	336
FnMut	338
Copy and Clone for Closures	340
Callbacks	341
Using Closures Effectively	345

15. Iterators. **347**

The Iterator and IntoIterator Traits   349

Creating Iterators   350

  iter and iter_mut Methods   350

  IntoIterator Implementations   351

  from_fn and successors   353

  drain Methods   355

  Other Iterator Sources   356

Iterator Adapters   358

  map and filter   358

  filter_map and flat_map   361

  flatten   363

  take and take_while   365

  skip and skip_while   365

  peekable   366

  fuse   367

  Reversible Iterators and rev   368

  inspect   369

  chain   370

  enumerate   371

  zip   372

  by_ref   372

  cloned, copied   373

  cycle   374

Consuming Iterators   375

  Simple Accumulation: count, sum, product   375

  max, min   376

  max_by, min_by   376

  max_by_key, min_by_key   377

  Comparing Item Sequences   377

  any and all   378

  position, rposition, and ExactSizeIterator   378

  fold and rfold   379

  try_fold and try_rfold   380

  nth, nth_back   382

  last   382

  find, rfind, and find_map   382

  Building Collections: collect and FromIterator   384

  The Extend Trait   385

  partition   386

  for_each and try_for_each   387

Implementing Your Own Iterators   388

16. Collections. **393**
    Overview 394
    Vec<T> 395
      Accessing Elements 396
      Iteration 398
      Growing and Shrinking Vectors 398
      Joining 402
      Splitting 402
      Swapping 405
      Filling 406
      Sorting and Searching 406
      Comparing Slices 408
      Random Elements 408
      Rust Rules Out Invalidation Errors 409
    VecDeque<T> 410
    BinaryHeap<T> 412
    HashMap<K, V> and BTreeMap<K, V> 413
      Entries 417
      Map Iteration 420
    HashSet<T> and BTreeSet<T> 420
      Set Iteration 422
      When Equal Values Are Different 422
      Whole-Set Operations 423
    Hashing 424
    Using a Custom Hashing Algorithm 425
    Beyond the Standard Collections 427

17. Strings and Text. **429**
    Some Unicode Background 430
      ASCII, Latin-1, and Unicode 430
      UTF-8 430
      Text Directionality 432
    Characters (char) 432
      Classifying Characters 433
      Handling Digits 434
      Case Conversion for Characters 435
      Conversions to and from Integers 436
    String and str 436
      Creating String Values 437
      Simple Inspection 438
      Appending and Inserting Text 439
      Removing and Replacing Text 440

Conventions for Searching and Iterating   441
Patterns for Searching Text   442
Searching and Replacing   443
Iterating over Text   444
Trimming   446
Case Conversion for Strings   447
Parsing Other Types from Strings   447
Converting Other Types to Strings   448
Borrowing as Other Text-Like Types   449
Accessing Text as UTF-8   449
Producing Text from UTF-8 Data   450
Putting Off Allocation   451
Strings as Generic Collections   453
Formatting Values   454
Formatting Text Values   455
Formatting Numbers   457
Formatting Other Types   458
Formatting Values for Debugging   459
Formatting Pointers for Debugging   460
Referring to Arguments by Index or Name   461
Dynamic Widths and Precisions   461
Formatting Your Own Types   462
Using the Formatting Language in Your Own Code   464
Regular Expressions   466
Basic Regex Use   466
Building Regex Values Lazily   467
Normalization   468
Normalization Forms   469
The unicode-normalization Crate   471

18. Input and Output.   473
Readers and Writers   474
Readers   475
Buffered Readers   477
Reading Lines   479
Collecting Lines   481
Writers   482
Files   483
Seeking   484
Other Reader and Writer Types   485
Binary Data, Compression, and Serialization   487
Files and Directories   488

OsStr and Path	488
Path and PathBuf Methods	490
Filesystem Access Functions	492
Reading Directories	493
Platform-Specific Features	495
Networking	496

19. Concurrency.. 499

Fork-Join Parallelism	501
spawn and join	502
Error Handling Across Threads	504
Sharing Immutable Data Across Threads	505
Rayon	507
Revisiting the Mandelbrot Set	510
Channels	512
Sending Values	513
Receiving Values	516
Running the Pipeline	517
Channel Features and Performance	519
Thread Safety: Send and Sync	521
Piping Almost Any Iterator to a Channel	523
Beyond Pipelines	525
Shared Mutable State	525
What Is a Mutex?	526
Mutex<T>	528
mut and Mutex	529
Why Mutexes Are Not Always a Good Idea	530
Deadlock	531
Poisoned Mutexes	531
Multiconsumer Channels Using Mutexes	532
Read/Write Locks (RwLock<T>)	533
Condition Variables (Condvar)	534
Atomics	535
Global Variables	537
What Hacking Concurrent Code in Rust Is Like	540

20. Asynchronous Programming............................... 541

From Synchronous to Asynchronous	543
Futures	544
Async Functions and Await Expressions	546
Calling Async Functions from Synchronous Code: block_on	549
Spawning Async Tasks	552

Async Blocks   556
Building Async Functions from Async Blocks   558
Spawning Async Tasks on a Thread Pool   559
But Does Your Future Implement Send?   560
Long Running Computations: yield_now and spawn_blocking   563
Comparing Asynchronous Designs   564
A Real Asynchronous HTTP Client   565
An Asynchronous Client and Server   566
Error and Result Types   568
The Protocol   569
Taking User Input: Asynchronous Streams   570
Sending Packets   572
Receiving Packets: More Asynchronous Streams   573
The Client's Main Function   575
The Server's Main Function   576
Handling Chat Connections: Async Mutexes   577
The Group Table: Synchronous Mutexes   580
Chat Groups: tokio's Broadcast Channels   581
Primitive Futures and Executors: When Is a Future Worth Polling Again?   584
Invoking Wakers: spawn_blocking   586
Implementing block_on   588
Pinning   590
The Two Life Stages of a Future   590
Pinned Pointers   594
The Unpin Trait   596
When Is Asynchronous Code Helpful?   597

21. Macros.   601
Macro Basics   602
Basics of Macro Expansion   603
Unintended Consequences   605
Repetition   607
Built-In Macros   609
Debugging Macros   611
Building the json! Macro   612
Fragment Types   613
Recursion in Macros   617
Using Traits with Macros   617
Scoping and Hygiene   619
Importing and Exporting Macros   622
Avoiding Syntax Errors During Matching   624
Beyond macro_rules!   625

22. Unsafe Code. **627**

Unsafe from What?   628
Unsafe Blocks   630
Example: An Efficient ASCII String Type   631
Unsafe Functions   633
Unsafe Block or Unsafe Function?   635
Undefined Behavior   636
Unsafe Traits   638
Raw Pointers   640
    Dereferencing Raw Pointers Safely   643
    Example: RefWithFlag   644
    Nullable Pointers   646
    Type Sizes and Alignments   647
    Pointer Arithmetic   647
    Moving into and out of Memory   649
    Example: GapBuffer   653
    Panic Safety in Unsafe Code   659
Reinterpreting Memory with Unions   660
Matching Unions   663
Borrowing Unions   663

23. Foreign Functions. **665**

Finding Common Data Representations   666
Declaring Foreign Functions and Variables   670
Using Functions from Libraries   671
A Raw Interface to libgit2   675
A Safe Interface to libgit2   681
Conclusion   692

Index. **693**

Preface

Rust is a language for systems programming.

This bears some explanation these days, as systems programming is unfamiliar to most working programmers. Yet it underlies everything we do.

You close your laptop. The operating system detects this, suspends all the running programs, turns off the screen, and puts the computer to sleep. Later, you open the laptop: the screen and other components are powered up again, and each program is able to pick up where it left off. We take this for granted. But systems programmers wrote a lot of code to make that happen.

Systems programming is for:

- Operating systems
- Device drivers of all kinds
- Filesystems
- Databases
- Code that runs in very cheap devices, or devices that must be extremely reliable
- Cryptography
- Media codecs (software for reading and writing audio, video, and image files)
- Media processing (for example, speech recognition or photo editing software)
- Memory management (for example, implementing a garbage collector)
- Text rendering (the conversion of text and fonts into pixels)
- Implementing higher-level programming languages (like JavaScript and Python)
- Networking
- Virtualization and software containers

- Scientific simulations
- Games

In short, systems programming is *resource-constrained* programming. It is programming when every byte and every CPU cycle counts.

The amount of systems code involved in supporting a basic app is staggering.

This book will not teach you systems programming. In fact, this book covers many details of memory management that might seem unnecessarily abstruse at first, if you haven't already done some systems programming on your own. But if you are a seasoned systems programmer, you'll find that Rust is something exceptional: a new tool that eliminates major, well-understood problems that have plagued a whole industry for decades.

Who Should Read This Book

If you're already a systems programmer and you're ready for an alternative to C++, this book is for you. If you're an experienced developer in any programming language, whether that's C#, Java, Python, JavaScript, or something else, this book is for you too.

However, you don't just need to learn Rust. To get the most out of the language, you also need to gain some experience with systems programming. We recommend reading this book while also implementing some systems programming side projects in Rust. Build something you've never built before, something that takes advantage of Rust's speed, concurrency, and safety. The list of topics at the beginning of this preface should give you some ideas.

Why We Wrote This Book

We set out to write the book we wished we had when we started learning Rust. Our goal was to tackle the big, new concepts in Rust up front and head-on, presenting them clearly and in depth so as to minimize learning by trial and error.

Navigating This Book

The first two chapters of this book introduce Rust and provide a brief tour before we move on to the fundamental data types in Chapter 3. Chapters 4 and 5 address the core concepts of ownership and references. We recommend reading these first five chapters through in order.

Chapters 6 through 10 cover the basics of the language: expressions (Chapter 6), error handling (Chapter 7), crates and modules (Chapter 8), structs (Chapter 9), and enums and patterns (Chapter 10). It's all right to skim a little here, but don't skip the chapter on error handling. Trust us.

Chapter 11 covers traits and generics, the last two big concepts you need to know. Traits are like interfaces in Java or C#. They're also the main way Rust supports integrating your types into the language itself. Chapter 12 shows how traits support operator overloading, and Chapter 13 covers many more utility traits.

Understanding traits and generics unlocks the rest of the book. Closures and iterators, two key power tools that you won't want to miss, are covered in Chapters 14 and 15, respectively. You can read the remaining chapters in any order, or just dip into them as needed. They cover the rest of the language: collections (Chapter 16), strings and text (Chapter 17), input and output (Chapter 18), concurrency (Chapter 19), asynchronous programming (Chapter 20), macros (Chapter 21), unsafe code (Chapter 22), and calling functions in other languages (Chapter 23).

Conventions Used in This Book

The following typographical conventions are used in this book:

Italic
> Indicates new terms, URLs, email addresses, filenames, and file extensions.

`Constant width`
> Used for program listings, as well as within paragraphs to refer to program elements such as variable or function names, databases, data types, environment variables, statements, and keywords.

`Constant width bold`
> Shows commands or other text that should be typed literally by the user.

`Constant width italic`
> Shows text that should be replaced with user-supplied values or by values determined by context.

 This icon signifies a general note.

Using Code Examples

Supplemental material (code examples, exercises, etc.) is available for download at *https://github.com/ProgrammingRust*.

This book is here to help you get your job done. In general, if example code is offered with this book, you may use it in your programs and documentation. You do not need to contact us for permission unless you're reproducing a significant portion of the code. For example, writing a program that uses several chunks of code from this book does not require permission. Selling or distributing examples from O'Reilly books does require permission. Answering a question by citing this book and quoting example code does not require permission. Incorporating a significant amount of example code from this book into your product's documentation does require permission.

We appreciate, but do not require, attribution. An attribution usually includes the title, author, publisher, and ISBN. For example: "*Programming Rust, Second Edition* by Jim Blandy, Jason Orendorff, and Leonora F. S. Tindall (O'Reilly). Copyright 2021 Jim Blandy, Leonora F. S. Tindall, and Jason Orendorff, 978-1-492-05259-3."

If you feel your use of code examples falls outside fair use or the permission given above, feel free to contact us at *permissions@oreilly.com*.

O'Reilly Online Learning

 For more than 40 years, *O'Reilly Media* has provided technology and business training, knowledge, and insight to help companies succeed.

Our unique network of experts and innovators share their knowledge and expertise through books, articles, conferences, and our online learning platform. O'Reilly's online learning platform gives you on-demand access to live training courses, in-depth learning paths, interactive coding environments, and a vast collection of text and video from O'Reilly and 200+ other publishers. For more information, please visit *http://oreilly.com*.

How to Contact Us

Please address comments and questions concerning this book to the publisher:

O'Reilly Media, Inc.
1005 Gravenstein Highway North
Sebastopol, CA 95472
800-998-9938 (in the United States or Canada)
707-829-0515 (international or local)
707-829-0104 (fax)

We have a web page for this book, where we list errata, examples, and any additional information. You can access this page at *https://oreil.ly/programming-rust-2e*.

Email *bookquestions@oreilly.com* to comment or ask technical questions about this book.

Visit *http://www.oreilly.com* for more information about our books and courses.

Find us on Facebook: *http://facebook.com/oreilly*

Follow us on Twitter: *http://twitter.com/oreillymedia*

Watch us on YouTube: *http://youtube.com/oreillymedia*

Acknowledgments

The book you are holding has benefited greatly from the attention of our official technical reviewers: Brian Anderson, Matt Brubeck, J. David Eisenberg, Ryan Levick, Jack Moffitt, Carol Nichols, and Erik Nordin; and our translators: Hidemoto Nakada (中田 秀基) (Japanese), Mr. Songfeng Li (Simplified Chinese), and Adam Bochenek and Krzysztof Sawka (Polish).

Many other unofficial reviewers read early drafts and provided invaluable feedback. We would like to thank Eddy Bruel, Nick Fitzgerald, Graydon Hoare, Michael Kelly, Jeffrey Lim, Jakob Olesen, Gian-Carlo Pascutto, Larry Rabinowitz, Jaroslav Šnajdr, Joe Walker, and Yoshua Wuyts for their thoughtful comments. Jeff Walden and Nicolas Pierron were especially generous with their time, reviewing almost the entire book. Like any programming venture, a programming book thrives on quality bug reports. Thank you.

Mozilla was extremely accommodating of Jim's and Jason's work on this project, even though it fell outside our official responsibilities and competed with them for our attention. We are grateful to Jim's and Jason's managers: Dave Camp, Naveed Ihsanullah, Tom Tromey, and Joe Walker, for their support. They take a long view of what Mozilla is about; we hope these results justify the faith they placed in us.

We would also like to express our appreciation for everyone at O'Reilly who helped bring this project to fruition, especially our astonishingly patient editors Jeff Bleiel and Brian MacDonald, and our acquisitions editor Zan McQuade.

Most of all, our heartfelt thanks to our families for their unwavering love, enthusiasm, and patience.

## CHAPTER 1

Systems Programmers Can Have Nice Things

In certain contexts—for example the context Rust is targeting—being 10x or even 2x faster than the competition is a make-or-break thing. It decides the fate of a system in the market, as much as it would in the hardware market.

> —Graydon Hoare (*https://oreil.ly/Akgzc*)

All computers are now parallel...
*Parallel programming **is** programming.*

> —Michael McCool et al., *Structured Parallel Programming*

TrueType parser flaw used by nation-state attacker for surveillance; all software is security-sensitive.

> —Andy Wingo (*https://oreil.ly/7dnHr*)

We chose to open our book with the three quotes above for a reason. But let's start with a mystery. What does the following C program do?

```c
int main(int argc, char **argv) {
  unsigned long a[1];
  a[3] = 0x7ffff7b36cebUL;
  return 0;
}
```

On Jim's laptop this morning, this program printed:

```
undef: Error: .netrc file is readable by others.
undef: Remove password or make file unreadable by others.
```

Then it crashed. If you try it on your machine, it may do something else. What's going on here?

The program is flawed. The array `a` is only one element long, so using `a[3]` is, according to the C programming language standard, *undefined behavior*:

> Behavior, upon use of a nonportable or erroneous program construct or of erroneous data, for which this International Standard imposes no requirements

Undefined behavior doesn't just have an unpredictable result: the standard explicitly permits the program to do *anything at all*. In our case, storing this particular value in the fourth element of this particular array happens to corrupt the function call stack such that returning from the `main` function, instead of exiting the program gracefully as it should, jumps into the midst of code from the standard C library for retrieving a password from a file in the user's home directory. It doesn't go well.

C and C++ have hundreds of rules for avoiding undefined behavior. They're mostly common sense: don't access memory you shouldn't, don't let arithmetic operations overflow, don't divide by zero, and so on. But the compiler does not enforce these rules; it has no obligation to detect even blatant violations. Indeed, the preceding program compiles without errors or warnings. The responsibility for avoiding undefined behavior falls entirely on you, the programmer.

Empirically speaking, we programmers do not have a great track record in this regard. While a student at the University of Utah, researcher Peng Li modified C and C++ compilers to make the programs they translated report whether they executed certain forms of undefined behavior. He found that nearly all programs do, including those from well-respected projects that hold their code to high standards. Assuming that you can avoid undefined behavior in C and C++ is like assuming you can win a game of chess simply because you know the rules.

The occasional strange message or crash may be a quality issue, but inadvertent undefined behavior has also been a major cause of security flaws since the 1988 Morris Worm used a variation of the technique shown earlier to propagate from one computer to another on the early Internet.

So C and C++ put programmers in an awkward position: those languages are the industry standards for systems programming, but the demands they place on programmers all but guarantee a steady stream of crashes and security problems. Answering our mystery just raises a bigger question: can't we do any better?

Rust Shoulders the Load for You

Our answer is framed by our three opening quotes. The third quote refers to reports that Stuxnet, a computer worm found breaking into industrial control equipment in 2010, gained control of the victims' computers using, among many other techniques, undefined behavior in code that parsed TrueType fonts embedded in word processing documents. It's a safe bet that the authors of that code were not expecting it to be used this way, illustrating that it's not just operating systems and servers that need to worry about security: any software that might handle data from an untrusted source could be the target of an exploit.

The Rust language makes you a simple promise: if your program passes the compiler's checks, it is free of undefined behavior. Dangling pointers, double-frees, and null pointer dereferences are all caught at compile time. Array references are secured with a mix of compile-time and run-time checks, so there are no buffer overruns: the Rust equivalent of our unfortunate C program exits safely with an error message.

Further, Rust aims to be both *safe* and *pleasant to use*. In order to make stronger guarantees about your program's behavior, Rust imposes more restrictions on your code than C and C++ do, and these restrictions take practice and experience to get used to. But the language overall is flexible and expressive. This is attested to by the breadth of code written in Rust and the range of application areas to which it is being applied.

In our experience, being able to trust the language to catch more mistakes encourages us to try more ambitious projects. Modifying large, complex programs is less risky when you know that issues of memory management and pointer validity are taken care of. And debugging is much simpler when the potential consequences of a bug don't include corrupting unrelated parts of your program.

Of course, there are still plenty of bugs that Rust cannot detect. But in practice, taking undefined behavior off the table substantially changes the character of development for the better.

Parallel Programming Is Tamed

Concurrency is notoriously difficult to use correctly in C and C++. Developers usually turn to concurrency only when single-threaded code has proven unable to achieve the performance they need. But the second opening quote argues that parallelism is too important to modern machines to treat as a method of last resort.

As it turns out, the same restrictions that ensure memory safety in Rust also ensure that Rust programs are free of data races. You can share data freely between threads, as long as it isn't changing. Data that does change can only be accessed using synchronization primitives. All the traditional concurrency tools are available: mutexes, condition variables, channels, atomics, and so on. Rust simply checks that you're using them properly.

This makes Rust an excellent language for exploiting the abilities of modern multicore machines. The Rust ecosystem offers libraries that go beyond the usual concurrency primitives and help you distribute complex loads evenly across pools of processors, use lock-free synchronization mechanisms like Read-Copy-Update, and more.

And Yet Rust Is Still Fast

This, finally, is our first opening quote. Rust shares the ambitions Bjarne Stroustrup articulates for C++ in his paper "Abstraction and the C++ Machine Model":

> In general, C++ implementations obey the zero-overhead principle: What you don't use, you don't pay for. And further: What you do use, you couldn't hand code any better.

Systems programming is often concerned with pushing the machine to its limits. For video games, the entire machine should be devoted to creating the best experience for the player. For web browsers, the efficiency of the browser sets the ceiling on what content authors can do. Within the machine's inherent limitations, as much memory and processor attention as possible must be left to the content itself. The same principle applies to operating systems: the kernel should make the machine's resources available to user programs, not consume them itself.

But when we say Rust is "fast," what does that really mean? One can write slow code in any general-purpose language. It would be more precise to say that, if you are ready to make the investment to design your program to make the best use of the underlying machine's capabilities, Rust supports you in that effort. The language is designed with efficient defaults and gives you the ability to control how memory gets used and how the processor's attention is spent.

Rust Makes Collaboration Easier

We hid a fourth quote in the title of this chapter: "Systems programmers can have nice things." This refers to Rust's support for code sharing and reuse.

Rust's package manager and build tool, Cargo, makes it easy to use libraries published by others on Rust's public package repository, the crates.io website. You simply add the library's name and required version number to a file, and Cargo takes care of downloading the library, together with whatever other libraries it uses in turn, and linking the whole lot together. You can think of Cargo as Rust's answer to NPM or RubyGems, with an emphasis on sound version management and reproducible builds. There are popular Rust libraries providing everything from off-the-shelf serialization to HTTP clients and servers and modern graphics APIs.

Going further, the language itself is also designed to support collaboration: Rust's traits and generics let you create libraries with flexible interfaces so that they can serve in many different contexts. And Rust's standard library provides a core set of fundamental types that establish shared conventions for common cases, making different libraries easier to use together.

The next chapter aims to make concrete the broad claims we've made in this chapter, with a tour of several small Rust programs that show off the language's strengths.

## CHAPTER 2

A Tour of Rust

Rust presents the authors of a book like this one with a challenge: what gives the language its character is not some specific, amazing feature that we can show off on the first page, but rather, the way all its parts are designed to work together smoothly in service of the goals we laid out in the last chapter: safe, performant systems programming. Each part of the language is best justified in the context of all the rest.

So rather than tackle one language feature at a time, we've prepared a tour of a few small but complete programs, each of which introduces some more features of the language, in context:

- As a warm-up, we have a program that does a simple calculation on its command-line arguments, with unit tests. This shows Rust's core types and introduces *traits*.

- Next, we build a web server. We'll use a third-party library to handle the details of HTTP and introduce string handling, closures, and error handling.

- Our third program plots a beautiful fractal, distributing the computation across multiple threads for speed. This includes an example of a generic function, illustrates how to handle something like a buffer of pixels, and shows off Rust's support for concurrency.

- Finally, we show a robust command-line tool that processes files using regular expressions. This presents the Rust standard library's facilities for working with files, and the most commonly used third-party regular expression library.

Rust's promise to prevent undefined behavior with minimal impact on performance influences the design of every part of the system, from the standard data structures like vectors and strings to the way Rust programs use third-party libraries. The details of how this is managed are covered throughout the book. But for now, we want to show you that Rust is a capable and pleasant language to use.

First, of course, you need to install Rust on your computer.

rustup and Cargo

The best way to install Rust is to use `rustup`. Go to *https://rustup.rs* and follow the instructions there.

You can, alternatively, go to the Rust website (*https://oreil.ly/4Q2FB*) to get pre-built packages for Linux, macOS, and Windows. Rust is also included in some operating system distributions. We prefer `rustup` because it's a tool for managing Rust installations, like RVM for Ruby or NVM for Node. For example, when a new version of Rust is released, you'll be able to upgrade with zero clicks by typing `rustup update`.

In any case, once you've completed the installation, you should have three new commands available at your command line:

```
$ cargo --version
cargo 1.49.0 (d00d64df9 2020-12-05)
$ rustc --version
rustc 1.49.0 (e1884a8e3 2020-12-29)
$ rustdoc --version
rustdoc 1.49.0 (e1884a8e3 2020-12-29)
```

Here, the `$` is the command prompt; on Windows, this would be `C:\>` or something similar. In this transcript we run the three commands we installed, asking each to report which version it is. Taking each command in turn:

- `cargo` is Rust's compilation manager, package manager, and general-purpose tool. You can use Cargo to start a new project, build and run your program, and manage any external libraries your code depends on.
- `rustc` is the Rust compiler. Usually we let Cargo invoke the compiler for us, but sometimes it's useful to run it directly.
- `rustdoc` is the Rust documentation tool. If you write documentation in comments of the appropriate form in your program's source code, `rustdoc` can build nicely formatted HTML from them. Like `rustc`, we usually let Cargo run `rustdoc` for us.

As a convenience, Cargo can create a new Rust package for us, with some standard metadata arranged appropriately:

```
$ cargo new hello
    Created binary (application) `hello` package
```

This command creates a new package directory named *hello*, ready to build a command-line executable.

Looking inside the package's top-level directory:

```
$ cd hello
$ ls -la
total 24
drwxrwxr-x.  4 jimb jimb 4096 Sep 22 21:09 .
drwx------. 62 jimb jimb 4096 Sep 22 21:09 ..
drwxrwxr-x.  6 jimb jimb 4096 Sep 22 21:09 .git
-rw-rw-r--.  1 jimb jimb    7 Sep 22 21:09 .gitignore
-rw-rw-r--.  1 jimb jimb   88 Sep 22 21:09 Cargo.toml
drwxrwxr-x.  2 jimb jimb 4096 Sep 22 21:09 src
```

We can see that Cargo has created a file *Cargo.toml* to hold metadata for the package. At the moment this file doesn't contain much:

```
[package]
name = "hello"
version = "0.1.0"
edition = "2021"

# See more keys and their definitions at
# https://doc.rust-lang.org/cargo/reference/manifest.html

[dependencies]
```

If our program ever acquires dependencies on other libraries, we can record them in this file, and Cargo will take care of downloading, building, and updating those libraries for us. We'll cover the *Cargo.toml* file in detail in Chapter 8.

Cargo has set up our package for use with the git version control system, creating a *.git* metadata subdirectory and a *.gitignore* file. You can tell Cargo to skip this step by passing --vcs none to cargo new on the command line.

The *src* subdirectory contains the actual Rust code:

```
$ cd src
$ ls -l
total 4
-rw-rw-r--. 1 jimb jimb 45 Sep 22 21:09 main.rs
```

It seems that Cargo has begun writing the program on our behalf. The *main.rs* file contains the text:

```
fn main() {
    println!("Hello, world!");
}
```

In Rust, you don't even need to write your own "Hello, World!" program. And this is the extent of the boilerplate for a new Rust program: two files, totaling thirteen lines.

We can invoke the `cargo run` command from any directory in the package to build and run our program:

```
$ cargo run
   Compiling hello v0.1.0 (/home/jimb/rust/hello)
    Finished dev [unoptimized + debuginfo] target(s) in 0.28s
     Running `/home/jimb/rust/hello/target/debug/hello`
Hello, world!
```

Here, Cargo has invoked the Rust compiler, `rustc`, and then run the executable it produced. Cargo places the executable in the *target* subdirectory at the top of the package:

```
$ ls -l ../target/debug
total 580
drwxrwxr-x. 2 jimb jimb   4096 Sep 22 21:37 build
drwxrwxr-x. 2 jimb jimb   4096 Sep 22 21:37 deps
drwxrwxr-x. 2 jimb jimb   4096 Sep 22 21:37 examples
-rwxrwxr-x. 1 jimb jimb 576632 Sep 22 21:37 hello
-rw-rw-r--. 1 jimb jimb    198 Sep 22 21:37 hello.d
drwxrwxr-x. 2 jimb jimb     68 Sep 22 21:37 incremental
$ ../target/debug/hello
Hello, world!
```

When we're through, Cargo can clean up the generated files for us:

```
$ cargo clean
$ ../target/debug/hello
bash: ../target/debug/hello: No such file or directory
```

Rust Functions

Rust's syntax is deliberately unoriginal. If you are familiar with C, C++, Java, or Java-Script, you can probably find your way through the general structure of a Rust program. Here is a function that computes the greatest common divisor of two integers, using Euclid's algorithm (*https://oreil.ly/DFpyb*). You can add this code to the end of *src/main.rs*:

```rust
fn gcd(mut n: u64, mut m: u64) -> u64 {
    assert!(n != 0 && m != 0);
    while m != 0 {
        if m < n {
            let t = m;
            m = n;
            n = t;
        }
        m = m % n;
    }
    n
}
```

The fn keyword (pronounced "fun") introduces a function. Here, we're defining a function named gcd, which takes two parameters n and m, each of which is of type u64, an unsigned 64-bit integer. The -> token precedes the return type: our function returns a u64 value. Four-space indentation is standard Rust style.

Rust's machine integer type names reflect their size and signedness: i32 is a signed 32-bit integer; u8 is an unsigned 8-bit integer (used for "byte" values), and so on. The isize and usize types hold pointer-sized signed and unsigned integers, 32 bits long on 32-bit platforms, and 64 bits long on 64-bit platforms. Rust also has two floating-point types, f32 and f64, which are the IEEE single- and double-precision floating-point types, like float and double in C and C++.

By default, once a variable is initialized, its value can't be changed, but placing the mut keyword (pronounced "mute," short for *mutable*) before the parameters n and m allows our function body to assign to them. In practice, most variables don't get assigned to; the mut keyword on those that do can be a helpful hint when reading code.

The function's body starts with a call to the assert! macro, verifying that neither argument is zero. The ! character marks this as a macro invocation, not a function call. Like the assert macro in C and C++, Rust's assert! checks that its argument is true, and if it is not, terminates the program with a helpful message including the source location of the failing check; this kind of abrupt termination is called a *panic*. Unlike C and C++, in which assertions can be skipped, Rust always checks assertions regardless of how the program was compiled. There is also a debug_assert! macro, whose assertions are skipped when the program is compiled for speed.

The heart of our function is a while loop containing an if statement and an assignment. Unlike C and C++, Rust does not require parentheses around the conditional expressions, but it does require curly braces around the statements they control.

A let statement declares a local variable, like t in our function. We don't need to write out t's type, as long as Rust can infer it from how the variable is used. In our function, the only type that works for t is u64, matching m and n. Rust only infers types within function bodies: you must write out the types of function parameters and return values, as we did before. If we wanted to spell out t's type, we could write:

```
let t: u64 = m;
```

Rust has a `return` statement, but the gcd function doesn't need one. If a function body ends with an expression that is *not* followed by a semicolon, that's the function's return value. In fact, any block surrounded by curly braces can function as an expression. For example, this is an expression that prints a message and then yields `x.cos()` as its value:

```
{
    println!("evaluating cos x");
    x.cos()
}
```

It's typical in Rust to use this form to establish the function's value when control "falls off the end" of the function, and use `return` statements only for explicit early returns from the midst of a function.

Writing and Running Unit Tests

Rust has simple support for testing built into the language. To test our gcd function, we can add this code at the end of *src/main.rs*:

```
#[test]
fn test_gcd() {
    assert_eq!(gcd(14, 15), 1);

    assert_eq!(gcd(2 * 3 * 5 * 11 * 17,
                   3 * 7 * 11 * 13 * 19),
               3 * 11);
}
```

Here we define a function named `test_gcd`, which calls gcd and checks that it returns correct values. The `#[test]` atop the definition marks `test_gcd` as a test function, to be skipped in normal compilations, but included and called automatically if we run our program with the `cargo test` command. We can have test functions scattered throughout our source tree, placed next to the code they exercise, and `cargo test` will automatically gather them up and run them all.

The `#[test]` marker is an example of an *attribute*. Attributes are an open-ended system for marking functions and other declarations with extra information, like attributes in C++ and C#, or annotations in Java. They're used to control compiler warnings and code style checks, include code conditionally (like #ifdef in C and C++), tell Rust how to interact with code written in other languages, and so on. We'll see more examples of attributes as we go.

With our `gcd` and `test_gcd` definitions added to the *hello* package we created at the beginning of the chapter, and our current directory somewhere within the package's subtree, we can run the tests as follows:

```
$ cargo test
   Compiling hello v0.1.0 (/home/jimb/rust/hello)
    Finished test [unoptimized + debuginfo] target(s) in 0.35s
     Running unittests (/home/jimb/rust/hello/target/debug/deps/hello-2375...)

running 1 test
test test_gcd ... ok

test result: ok. 1 passed; 0 failed; 0 ignored; 0 measured; 0 filtered out
```

Handling Command-Line Arguments

In order for our program to take a series of numbers as command-line arguments and print their greatest common divisor, we can replace the `main` function in *src/main.rs* with the following:

```rust
use std::str::FromStr;
use std::env;

fn main() {
    let mut numbers = Vec::new();

    for arg in env::args().skip(1) {
        numbers.push(u64::from_str(&arg)
                     .expect("error parsing argument"));
    }

    if numbers.len() == 0 {
        eprintln!("Usage: gcd NUMBER ...");
        std::process::exit(1);
    }

    let mut d = numbers[0];
    for m in &numbers[1..] {
        d = gcd(d, *m);
    }

    println!("The greatest common divisor of {:?} is {}",
             numbers, d);
}
```

This is a large block of code, so let's take it piece by piece:

```rust
use std::str::FromStr;
use std::env;
```

The first use declaration brings the standard library *trait* `FromStr` into scope. A trait is a collection of methods that types can implement. Any type that implements the `FromStr` trait has a `from_str` method that tries to parse a value of that type from a string. The u64 type implements `FromStr`, and we'll call `u64::from_str` to parse our command-line arguments. Although we never use the name `FromStr` elsewhere in the program, a trait must be in scope in order to use its methods. We'll cover traits in detail in Chapter 11.

The second use declaration brings in the `std::env` module, which provides several useful functions and types for interacting with the execution environment, including the `args` function, which gives us access to the program's command-line arguments.

Moving on to the program's `main` function:

```
fn main() {
```

Our `main` function doesn't return a value, so we can simply omit the `->` and return type that would normally follow the parameter list.

```
let mut numbers = Vec::new();
```

We declare a mutable local variable `numbers` and initialize it to an empty vector. Vec is Rust's growable vector type, analogous to C++'s `std::vector`, a Python list, or a Java-Script array. Even though vectors are designed to be grown and shrunk dynamically, we must still mark the variable `mut` for Rust to let us push numbers onto the end of it.

The type of `numbers` is Vec<u64>, a vector of u64 values, but as before, we don't need to write that out. Rust will infer it for us, in part because what we push onto the vector are u64 values, but also because we pass the vector's elements to `gcd`, which accepts only u64 values.

```
for arg in env::args().skip(1) {
```

Here we use a `for` loop to process our command-line arguments, setting the variable `arg` to each argument in turn and evaluating the loop body.

The `std::env` module's `args` function returns an *iterator*, a value that produces each argument on demand, and indicates when we're done. Iterators are ubiquitous in Rust; the standard library includes other iterators that produce the elements of a vector, the lines of a file, messages received on a communications channel, and almost anything else that makes sense to loop over. Rust's iterators are very efficient: the compiler is usually able to translate them into the same code as a handwritten loop. We'll show how this works and give examples in Chapter 15.

Beyond their use with `for` loops, iterators include a broad selection of methods you can use directly. For example, the first value produced by the iterator returned by `args` is always the name of the program being run. We want to skip that, so we call the iterator's `skip` method to produce a new iterator that omits that first value.

```
numbers.push(u64::from_str(&arg)
            .expect("error parsing argument"));
```

Here we call `u64::from_str` to attempt to parse our command-line argument `arg` as an unsigned 64-bit integer. Rather than a method we're invoking on some `u64` value we have at hand, `u64::from_str` is a function associated with the `u64` type, akin to a static method in C++ or Java. The `from_str` function doesn't return a `u64` directly, but rather a `Result` value that indicates whether the parse succeeded or failed. A `Result` value is one of two variants:

- A value written `Ok(v)`, indicating that the parse succeeded and `v` is the value produced
- A value written `Err(e)`, indicating that the parse failed and `e` is an error value explaining why

Functions that do anything that might fail, such as doing input or output or otherwise interacting with the operating system, can return `Result` types whose `Ok` variants carry successful results—the count of bytes transferred, the file opened, and so on—and whose `Err` variants carry an error code indicating what went wrong. Unlike most modern languages, Rust does not have exceptions: all errors are handled using either `Result` or panic, as outlined in Chapter 7.

We use `Result`'s `expect` method to check the success of our parse. If the result is an `Err(e)`, `expect` prints a message that includes a description of `e` and exits the program immediately. However, if the result is `Ok(v)`, `expect` simply returns `v` itself, which we are finally able to push onto the end of our vector of numbers.

```
if numbers.len() == 0 {
    eprintln!("Usage: gcd NUMBER ...");
    std::process::exit(1);
}
```

There's no greatest common divisor of an empty set of numbers, so we check that our vector has at least one element and exit the program with an error if it doesn't. We use the `eprintln!` macro to write our error message to the standard error output stream.

```
let mut d = numbers[0];
for m in &numbers[1..] {
    d = gcd(d, *m);
}
```

This loop uses `d` as its running value, updating it to stay the greatest common divisor of all the numbers we've processed so far. As before, we must mark `d` as mutable so that we can assign to it in the loop.

The `for` loop has two surprising bits to it. First, we wrote for `m in &numbers[1..]`; what is the & operator for? Second, we wrote `gcd(d, *m)`; what is the * in `*m` for? These two details are complementary to each other.

Up to this point, our code has operated only on simple values like integers that fit in fixed-size blocks of memory. But now we're about to iterate over a vector, which could be of any size whatsoever—possibly very large. Rust is cautious when handling such values: it wants to leave the programmer in control over memory consumption, making it clear how long each value lives, while still ensuring memory is freed promptly when no longer needed.

So when we iterate, we want to tell Rust that *ownership* of the vector should remain with `numbers`; we are merely *borrowing* its elements for the loop. The & operator in `&numbers[1..]` borrows a *reference* to the vector's elements from the second onward. The `for` loop iterates over the referenced elements, letting `m` borrow each element in succession. The * operator in `*m` *dereferences* `m`, yielding the value it refers to; this is the next `u64` we want to pass to `gcd`. Finally, since `numbers` owns the vector, Rust automatically frees it when `numbers` goes out of scope at the end of `main`.

Rust's rules for ownership and references are key to Rust's memory management and safe concurrency; we discuss them in detail in Chapter 4 and its companion, Chapter 5. You'll need to be comfortable with those rules to be comfortable in Rust, but for this introductory tour, all you need to know is that `&x` borrows a reference to `x`, and that `*r` is the value that the reference `r` refers to.

Continuing our walk through the program:

```
println!("The greatest common divisor of {:?} is {}",
         numbers, d);
```

Having iterated over the elements of `numbers`, the program prints the results to the standard output stream. The `println!` macro takes a template string, substitutes formatted versions of the remaining arguments for the `{...}` forms as they appear in the template string, and writes the result to the standard output stream.

Unlike C and C++, which require `main` to return zero if the program finished successfully, or a nonzero exit status if something went wrong, Rust assumes that if `main` returns at all, the program finished successfully. Only by explicitly calling functions like `expect` or `std::process::exit` can we cause the program to terminate with an error status code.

The `cargo run` command allows us to pass arguments to our program, so we can try out our command-line handling:

```
$ cargo run 42 56
   Compiling hello v0.1.0 (/home/jimb/rust/hello)
    Finished dev [unoptimized + debuginfo] target(s) in 0.22s
     Running `/home/jimb/rust/hello/target/debug/hello 42 56`
The greatest common divisor of [42, 56] is 14
$ cargo run 799459 28823 27347
    Finished dev [unoptimized + debuginfo] target(s) in 0.02s
     Running `/home/jimb/rust/hello/target/debug/hello 799459 28823 27347`
The greatest common divisor of [799459, 28823, 27347] is 41
$ cargo run 83
    Finished dev [unoptimized + debuginfo] target(s) in 0.02s
     Running `/home/jimb/rust/hello/target/debug/hello 83`
The greatest common divisor of [83] is 83
$ cargo run
    Finished dev [unoptimized + debuginfo] target(s) in 0.02s
     Running `/home/jimb/rust/hello/target/debug/hello`
Usage: gcd NUMBER ...
```

We've used a few features from Rust's standard library in this section. If you're curious about what else is available, we strongly encourage you to try out Rust's online documentation. It has a live search feature that makes exploration easy and even includes links to the source code. The `rustup` command automatically installs a copy on your computer when you install Rust itself. You can view the standard library documentation on the Rust website (*https://oreil.ly/CGsB5*), or in your browser with the command:

```
$ rustup doc --std
```

Serving Pages to the Web

One of Rust's strengths is the collection of freely available library packages published on the website crates.io. The `cargo` command makes it easy for your code to use a crates.io package: it will download the right version of the package, build it, and update it as requested. A Rust package, whether a library or an executable, is called a *crate*; Cargo and crates.io both derive their names from this term.

To show how this works, we'll put together a simple web server using the `actix-web` web framework crate, the `serde` serialization crate, and various other crates on which they depend. As shown in Figure 2-1, our website will prompt the user for two numbers and compute their greatest common divisor.

Figure 2-1. Web page offering to compute GCD

First, we'll have Cargo create a new package for us, named `actix-gcd`:

```
$ cargo new actix-gcd
      Created binary (application) `actix-gcd` package
$ cd actix-gcd
```

Then, we'll edit our new project's *Cargo.toml* file to list the packages we want to use; its contents should be as follows:

```
[package]
name = "actix-gcd"
version = "0.1.0"
edition = "2021"

# See more keys and their definitions at
# https://doc.rust-lang.org/cargo/reference/manifest.html

[dependencies]
actix-web = "1.0.8"
serde = { version = "1.0", features = ["derive"] }
```

Each line in the [dependencies] section of *Cargo.toml* gives the name of a crate on crates.io, and the version of that crate we would like to use. In this case, we want version `1.0.8` of the `actix-web` crate, and version `1.0` of the `serde` crate. There may well be versions of these crates on crates.io newer than those shown here, but by naming the specific versions we tested this code against, we can ensure the code will continue to compile even as new versions of the packages are published. We'll discuss version management in more detail in Chapter 8.

Crates can have optional features: parts of the interface or implementation that not all users need, but that nonetheless make sense to include in that crate. The `serde` crate offers a wonderfully terse way to handle data from web forms, but according to `serde`'s documentation, it is only available if we select the crate's `derive` feature, so we've requested it in our *Cargo.toml* file as shown.

Note that we need only name those crates we'll use directly; `cargo` takes care of bringing in whatever other crates those need in turn.

For our first iteration, we'll keep the web server simple: it will serve only the page that prompts the user for numbers to compute with. In *actix-gcd/src/main.rs*, we'll place the following text:

```rust
use actix_web::{web, App, HttpResponse, HttpServer};

fn main() {
    let server = HttpServer::new(|| {
        App::new()
            .route("/", web::get().to(get_index))
    });

    println!("Serving on http://localhost:3000...");
    server
        .bind("127.0.0.1:3000").expect("error binding server to address")
        .run().expect("error running server");
}

fn get_index() -> HttpResponse {
    HttpResponse::Ok()
        .content_type("text/html")
        .body(
            r#"
                <title>GCD Calculator</title>
                <form action="/gcd" method="post">
                <input type="text" name="n"/>
                <input type="text" name="m"/>
                <button type="submit">Compute GCD</button>
                </form>
            "#,
        )
}
```

We start with a use declaration to make some of the `actix-web` crate's definitions easier to get at. When we write `use actix_web::{...}`, each of the names listed inside the curly brackets becomes directly usable in our code; instead of having to spell out the full name `actix_web::HttpResponse` each time we use it, we can simply refer to it as `HttpResponse`. (We'll get to the `serde` crate in a bit.)

Our `main` function is simple: it calls `HttpServer::new` to create a server that responds to requests for a single path, `"/"`; prints a message reminding us how to connect to it; and then sets it listening on TCP port 3000 on the local machine.

The argument we pass to `HttpServer::new` is the Rust *closure* expression `|| { App::new() ... }`. A closure is a value that can be called as if it were a function. This closure takes no arguments, but if it did, their names would appear between the `||` vertical bars. The `{ ... }` is the body of the closure. When we start our server, Actix starts a pool of threads to handle incoming requests. Each thread calls our closure to get a fresh copy of the `App` value that tells it how to route and handle requests.

The closure calls `App::new` to create a new, empty `App` and then calls its `route` method to add a single route for the path `"/"`. The handler provided for that route, `web::get().to(get_index)`, treats HTTP `GET` requests by calling the function `get_index`. The `route` method returns the same `App` it was invoked on, now enhanced with the new route. Since there's no semicolon at the end of the closure's body, the `App` is the closure's return value, ready for the `HttpServer` thread to use.

The `get_index` function builds an `HttpResponse` value representing the response to an HTTP `GET` / request. `HttpResponse::Ok()` represents an HTTP `200 OK` status, indicating that the request succeeded. We call its `content_type` and `body` methods to fill in the details of the response; each call returns the `HttpResponse` it was applied to, with the modifications made. Finally, the return value from `body` serves as the return value of `get_index`.

Since the response text contains a lot of double quotes, we write it using the Rust "raw string" syntax: the letter r, zero or more hash marks (that is, the # character), a double quote, and then the contents of the string, terminated by another double quote followed by the same number of hash marks. Any character may occur within a raw string without being escaped, including double quotes; in fact, no escape sequences like \" are recognized. We can always ensure the string ends where we intend by using more hash marks around the quotes than ever appear in the text.

Having written *main.rs*, we can use the `cargo run` command to do everything needed to set it running: fetching the needed crates, compiling them, building our own program, linking everything together, and starting it up:

```
$ cargo run
    Updating crates.io index
 Downloading crates ...
  Downloaded serde v1.0.100
  Downloaded actix-web v1.0.8
  Downloaded serde_derive v1.0.100
...
   Compiling serde_json v1.0.40
   Compiling actix-router v0.1.5
   Compiling actix-http v0.2.10
   Compiling awc v0.2.7
   Compiling actix-web v1.0.8
   Compiling gcd v0.1.0 (/home/jimb/rust/actix-gcd)
    Finished dev [unoptimized + debuginfo] target(s) in 1m 24s
     Running `/home/jimb/rust/actix-gcd/target/debug/actix-gcd`
Serving on http://localhost:3000...
```

At this point, we can visit the given URL in our browser and see the page shown earlier in Figure 2-1.

Unfortunately, clicking Compute GCD doesn't do anything, other than navigate our browser to a blank page. Let's fix that next, by adding another route to our App to handle the POST request from our form.

It's finally time to use the serde crate we listed in our *Cargo.toml* file: it provides a handy tool that will help us process the form data. First, we'll need to add the following use directive to the top of *src/main.rs*:

```
use serde::Deserialize;
```

Rust programmers typically gather all their use declarations together toward the top of the file, but this isn't strictly necessary: Rust allows declarations to occur in any order, as long as they appear at the appropriate level of nesting.

Next, let's define a Rust structure type that represents the values we expect from our form:

```
#[derive(Deserialize)]
struct GcdParameters {
    n: u64,
    m: u64,
}
```

This defines a new type named GcdParameters that has two fields, n and m, each of which is a u64—the argument type our gcd function expects.

The annotation above the struct definition is an attribute, like the #[test] attribute we used earlier to mark test functions. Placing a #[derive(Deserialize)] attribute above a type definition tells the serde crate to examine the type when the program is compiled and automatically generate code to parse a value of this type from data in the format that HTML forms use for POST requests. In fact, that attribute is sufficient to let you parse a GcdParameters value from almost any sort of structured data: JSON, YAML, TOML, or any one of a number of other textual and binary formats. The serde crate also provides a Serialize attribute that generates code to do the reverse, taking Rust values and writing them out in a structured format.

With this definition in place, we can write our handler function quite easily:

```
fn post_gcd(form: web::Form<GcdParameters>) -> HttpResponse {
    if form.n == 0 || form.m == 0 {
        return HttpResponse::BadRequest()
            .content_type("text/html")
            .body("Computing the GCD with zero is boring.");
    }

    let response =
        format!("The greatest common divisor of the numbers {} and {} \
                is <b>{}</b>\n",
                form.n, form.m, gcd(form.n, form.m));

    HttpResponse::Ok()
        .content_type("text/html")
        .body(response)
}
```

For a function to serve as an Actix request handler, its arguments must all have types Actix knows how to extract from an HTTP request. Our `post_gcd` function takes one argument, `form`, whose type is `web::Form<GcdParameters>`. Actix knows how to extract a value of any type `web::Form<T>` from an HTTP request if, and only if, `T` can be deserialized from HTML form `POST` data. Since we've placed the `#[derive(Deserialize)]` attribute on our `GcdParameters` type definition, Actix can deserialize it from form data, so request handlers can expect a `web::Form<GcdParameters>` value as a parameter. These relationships between types and functions are all worked out at compile time; if you write a handler function with an argument type that Actix doesn't know how to handle, the Rust compiler lets you know of your mistake immediately.

Looking inside `post_gcd`, the function first returns an HTTP 400 BAD REQUEST error if either parameter is zero, since our `gcd` function will panic if they are. Then, it constructs a response to the request using the `format!` macro. The `format!` macro is just like the `println!` macro, except that instead of writing the text to the standard output, it returns it as a string. Once it has obtained the text of the response, `post_gcd` wraps it up in an HTTP 200 OK response, sets its content type, and returns it to be delivered to the sender.

We also have to register `post_gcd` as the handler for the form. We'll replace our `main` function with this version:

```
fn main() {
    let server = HttpServer::new(|| {
        App::new()
            .route("/", web::get().to(get_index))
            .route("/gcd", web::post().to(post_gcd))
    });

    println!("Serving on http://localhost:3000...");
    server
        .bind("127.0.0.1:3000").expect("error binding server to address")
        .run().expect("error running server");
}
```

The only change here is that we've added another call to `route`, establishing `web::post().to(post_gcd)` as the handler for the path `"/gcd"`.

The last remaining piece is the gcd function we wrote earlier, which goes in the *actix-gcd/src/main.rs* file. With that in place, you can interrupt any servers you might have left running and rebuild and restart the program:

```
$ cargo run
   Compiling actix-gcd v0.1.0 (/home/jimb/rust/actix-gcd)
    Finished dev [unoptimized + debuginfo] target(s) in 0.0 secs
     Running `target/debug/actix-gcd`
Serving on http://localhost:3000...
```

This time, by visiting *http://localhost:3000*, entering some numbers, and clicking the Compute GCD button, you should actually see some results (Figure 2-2).

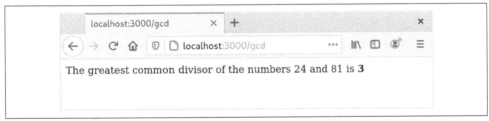

Figure 2-2. Web page showing results of computing GCD

Concurrency

One of Rust's great strengths is its support for concurrent programming. The same rules that ensure Rust programs are free of memory errors also ensure threads can share memory only in ways that avoid data races. For example:

- If you use a mutex to coordinate threads making changes to a shared data structure, Rust ensures that you can't access the data except when you're holding the lock, and releases the lock automatically when you're done. In C and C++, the relationship between a mutex and the data it protects is left to the comments.

- If you want to share read-only data among several threads, Rust ensures that you cannot modify the data accidentally. In C and C++, the type system can help with this, but it's easy to get it wrong.

- If you transfer ownership of a data structure from one thread to another, Rust makes sure you have indeed relinquished all access to it. In C and C++, it's up to you to check that nothing on the sending thread will ever touch the data again. If you don't get it right, the effects can depend on what happens to be in the processor's cache and how many writes to memory you've done recently. Not that we're bitter.

In this section, we'll walk you through the process of writing your second multi-threaded program.

You've already written your first: the Actix web framework you used to implement the Greatest Common Divisor server uses a pool of threads to run request handler functions. If the server receives simultaneous requests, it may run the get_form and post_gcd functions in several threads at once. That may come as a bit of a shock, since we certainly didn't have concurrency in mind when we wrote those functions. But Rust guarantees this is safe to do, no matter how elaborate your server gets: if your program compiles, it is free of data races. All Rust functions are thread-safe.

This section's program plots the Mandelbrot set, a fractal produced by iterating a simple function on complex numbers. Plotting the Mandelbrot set is often called an *embarrassingly parallel* algorithm, because the pattern of communication between the threads is so simple; we'll cover more complex patterns in Chapter 19, but this task demonstrates some of the essentials.

To get started, we'll create a fresh Rust project:

```
$ cargo new mandelbrot
    Created binary (application) `mandelbrot` package
$ cd mandelbrot
```

All the code will go in *mandelbrot/src/main.rs*, and we'll add some dependencies to *mandelbrot/Cargo.toml*.

Before we get into the concurrent Mandelbrot implementation, we need to describe the computation we're going to perform.

What the Mandelbrot Set Actually Is

When reading code, it's helpful to have a concrete idea of what it's trying to do, so let's take a short excursion into some pure mathematics. We'll start with a simple case and then add complicating details until we arrive at the calculation at the heart of the Mandelbrot set.

Here's an infinite loop, written using Rust's dedicated syntax for that, a `loop` statement:

```
fn square_loop(mut x: f64) {
    loop {
        x = x * x;
    }
}
```

In real life, Rust can see that x is never used for anything and so might not bother computing its value. But for the time being, assume the code runs as written. What happens to the value of x? Squaring any number smaller than 1 makes it smaller, so it approaches zero; squaring 1 yields 1; squaring a number larger than 1 makes it larger, so it approaches infinity; and squaring a negative number makes it positive, after which it behaves like one of the prior cases (Figure 2-3).

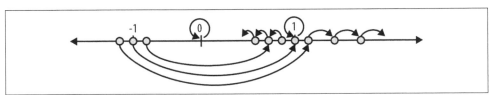

Figure 2-3. Effects of repeatedly squaring a number

So depending on the value you pass to `square_loop`, x stays at either zero or one, approaches zero, or approaches infinity.

Now consider a slightly different loop:

```
fn square_add_loop(c: f64) {
    let mut x = 0.;
    loop {
        x = x * x + c;
    }
}
```

This time, x starts at zero, and we tweak its progress in each iteration by adding in c after squaring it. This makes it harder to see how x fares, but some experimentation shows that if c is greater than 0.25 or less than –2.0, then x eventually becomes infinitely large; otherwise, it stays somewhere in the neighborhood of zero.

The next wrinkle: instead of using `f64` values, consider the same loop using complex numbers. The `num` crate on crates.io provides a complex number type we can use, so we must add a line for `num` to the [dependencies] section in our program's *Cargo.toml* file. Here's the entire file, up to this point (we'll be adding more later):

```
[package]
name = "mandelbrot"
version = "0.1.0"
edition = "2021"

# See more keys and their definitions at
# https://doc.rust-lang.org/cargo/reference/manifest.html

[dependencies]
num = "0.4"
```

Now we can write the penultimate version of our loop:

```
use num::Complex;

fn complex_square_add_loop(c: Complex<f64>) {
    let mut z = Complex { re: 0.0, im: 0.0 };
    loop {
        z = z * z + c;
    }
}
```

It's traditional to use z for complex numbers, so we've renamed our looping variable. The expression Complex { re: 0.0, im: 0.0 } is the way we write complex zero using the num crate's Complex type. Complex is a Rust structure type (or *struct*), defined like this:

```
struct Complex<T> {
    /// Real portion of the complex number
    re: T,

    /// Imaginary portion of the complex number
    im: T,
}
```

The preceding code defines a struct named Complex, with two fields, re and im. Complex is a *generic* structure: you can read the <T> after the type name as "for any type T." For example, Complex<f64> is a complex number whose re and im fields are f64 values, Complex<f32> would use 32-bit floats, and so on. Given this definition, an expression like Complex { re: 0.24, im: 0.3 } produces a Complex value with its re field initialized to 0.24, and its im field initialized to 0.3.

The num crate arranges for *, +, and other arithmetic operators to work on Complex values, so the rest of the function works just like the prior version, except that it operates on points on the complex plane, not just points along the real number line. We'll explain how you can make Rust's operators work with your own types in Chapter 12.

Finally, we've reached the destination of our pure math excursion. The Mandelbrot set is defined as the set of complex numbers c for which z does not fly out to infinity. Our original simple squaring loop was predictable enough: any number greater than 1 or less than –1 flies away. Throwing a + c into each iteration makes the behavior a little harder to anticipate: as we said earlier, values of c greater than 0.25 or less than –2 cause z to fly away. But expanding the game to complex numbers produces truly bizarre and beautiful patterns, which are what we want to plot.

Since a complex number c has both real and imaginary components c.re and c.im, we'll treat these as the x and y coordinates of a point on the Cartesian plane, and color the point black if c is in the Mandelbrot set, or a lighter color otherwise. So for each pixel in our image, we must run the preceding loop on the corresponding point on the complex plane, see whether it escapes to infinity or orbits around the origin forever, and color it accordingly.

The infinite loop takes a while to run, but there are two tricks for the impatient. First, if we give up on running the loop forever and just try some limited number of iterations, it turns out that we still get a decent approximation of the set. How many iterations we need depends on how precisely we want to plot the boundary. Second, it's been shown that, if z ever once leaves the circle of radius 2 centered at the origin, it will definitely fly infinitely far away from the origin eventually. So here's the final version of our loop, and the heart of our program:

```rust
use num::Complex;

/// Try to determine if `c` is in the Mandelbrot set, using at most `limit`
/// iterations to decide.
///
/// If `c` is not a member, return `Some(i)`, where `i` is the number of
/// iterations it took for `c` to leave the circle of radius 2 centered on the
/// origin. If `c` seems to be a member (more precisely, if we reached the
/// iteration limit without being able to prove that `c` is not a member),
/// return `None`.
fn escape_time(c: Complex<f64>, limit: usize) -> Option<usize> {
    let mut z = Complex { re: 0.0, im: 0.0 };
    for i in 0..limit {
        if z.norm_sqr() > 4.0 {
            return Some(i);
        }
        z = z * z + c;
    }

    None
}
```

This function takes the complex number c that we want to test for membership in the Mandelbrot set and a limit on the number of iterations to try before giving up and declaring c to probably be a member.

The function's return value is an Option<usize>. Rust's standard library defines the Option type as follows:

```rust
enum Option<T> {
    None,
    Some(T),
}
```

`Option` is an *enumerated type*, often called an *enum*, because its definition enumerates several variants that a value of this type could be: for any type T, a value of type `Option<T>` is either `Some(v)`, where `v` is a value of type T, or `None`, indicating no T value is available. Like the `Complex` type we discussed earlier, `Option` is a generic type: you can use `Option<T>` to represent an optional value of any type T you like.

In our case, `escape_time` returns an `Option<usize>` to indicate whether c is in the Mandelbrot set—and if it's not, how long we had to iterate to find that out. If c is not in the set, `escape_time` returns `Some(i)`, where i is the number of the iteration at which z left the circle of radius 2. Otherwise, c is apparently in the set, and `escape_time` returns `None`.

```
    for i in 0..limit {
```

The earlier examples showed `for` loops iterating over command-line arguments and vector elements; this `for` loop simply iterates over the range of integers starting with 0 and up to (but not including) `limit`.

The `z.norm_sqr()` method call returns the square of z's distance from the origin. To decide whether z has left the circle of radius 2, instead of computing a square root, we just compare the squared distance with 4.0, which is faster.

You may have noticed that we use `///` to mark the comment lines above the function definition; the comments above the members of the `Complex` structure start with `///` as well. These are *documentation comments*; the `rustdoc` utility knows how to parse them, together with the code they describe, and produce online documentation. The documentation for Rust's standard library is written in this form. We describe documentation comments in detail in Chapter 8.

The rest of the program is concerned with deciding which portion of the set to plot at what resolution and distributing the work across several threads to speed up the calculation.

Parsing Pair Command-Line Arguments

The program takes several command-line arguments controlling the resolution of the image we'll write and the portion of the Mandelbrot set the image shows. Since these command-line arguments all follow a common form, here's a function to parse them:

```rust
use std::str::FromStr;

/// Parse the string `s` as a coordinate pair, like `"400x600"` or `"1.0,0.5"`.
///
/// Specifically, `s` should have the form <left><sep><right>, where <sep> is
/// the character given by the `separator` argument, and <left> and <right> are
/// both strings that can be parsed by `T::from_str`. `separator` must be an
/// ASCII character.
///
/// If `s` has the proper form, return `Some<(x, y)>`. If it doesn't parse
/// correctly, return `None`.
fn parse_pair<T: FromStr>(s: &str, separator: char) -> Option<(T, T)> {
    match s.find(separator) {
        None => None,
        Some(index) => {
            match (T::from_str(&s[..index]), T::from_str(&s[index + 1..])) {
                (Ok(l), Ok(r)) => Some((l, r)),
                _ => None
            }
        }
    }
}

#[test]
fn test_parse_pair() {
    assert_eq!(parse_pair::<i32>("",          ','), None);
    assert_eq!(parse_pair::<i32>("10,",       ','), None);
    assert_eq!(parse_pair::<i32>(",10",       ','), None);
    assert_eq!(parse_pair::<i32>("10,20",     ','), Some((10, 20)));
    assert_eq!(parse_pair::<i32>("10,20xy",   ','), None);
    assert_eq!(parse_pair::<f64>("0.5x",      'x'), None);
    assert_eq!(parse_pair::<f64>("0.5x1.5",   'x'), Some((0.5, 1.5)));
}
```

The definition of `parse_pair` is a *generic function*:

```rust
fn parse_pair<T: FromStr>(s: &str, separator: char) -> Option<(T, T)> {
```

You can read the clause `<T: FromStr>` aloud as, "For any type T that implements the FromStr trait..." This effectively lets us define an entire family of functions at once: `parse_pair::<i32>` is a function that parses pairs of `i32` values, `parse_pair::<f64>` parses pairs of floating-point values, and so on. This is very much like a function template in C++. A Rust programmer would call T a *type parameter* of `parse_pair`. When you use a generic function, Rust will often be able to infer type parameters for you, and you won't need to write them out as we did in the test code.

Our return type is `Option<(T, T)>`: either `None` or a value `Some((v1, v2))`, where `(v1, v2)` is a tuple of two values, both of type T. The `parse_pair` function doesn't use an explicit return statement, so its return value is the value of the last (and the only) expression in its body:

```
match s.find(separator) {
    None => None,
    Some(index) => {
        ...
    }
}
```

The `String` type's `find` method searches the string for a character that matches `separator`. If `find` returns `None`, meaning that the separator character doesn't occur in the string, the entire `match` expression evaluates to `None`, indicating that the parse failed. Otherwise, we take `index` to be the separator's position in the string.

```
match (T::from_str(&s[..index]), T::from_str(&s[index + 1..])) {
    (Ok(l), Ok(r)) => Some((l, r)),
    _ => None
}
```

This begins to show off the power of the `match` expression. The argument to the match is this tuple expression:

```
(T::from_str(&s[..index]), T::from_str(&s[index + 1..]))
```

The expressions `&s[..index]` and `&s[index + 1..]` are slices of the string, preceding and following the separator. The type parameter T's associated `from_str` function takes each of these and tries to parse them as a value of type T, producing a tuple of results. This is what we match against:

```
(Ok(l), Ok(r)) => Some((l, r)),
```

This pattern matches only if both elements of the tuple are `Ok` variants of the `Result` type, indicating that both parses succeeded. If so, `Some((l, r))` is the value of the match expression and hence the return value of the function.

```
    _ => None
```

The wildcard pattern _ matches anything and ignores its value. If we reach this point, then parse_pair has failed, so we evaluate to None, again providing the return value of the function.

Now that we have parse_pair, it's easy to write a function to parse a pair of floating-point coordinates and return them as a Complex<f64> value:

```
/// Parse a pair of floating-point numbers separated by a comma as a complex
/// number.
fn parse_complex(s: &str) -> Option<Complex<f64>> {
    match parse_pair(s, ',') {
        Some((re, im)) => Some(Complex { re, im }),
        None => None
    }
}

#[test]
fn test_parse_complex() {
    assert_eq!(parse_complex("1.25,-0.0625"),
               Some(Complex { re: 1.25, im: -0.0625 }));
    assert_eq!(parse_complex(",-0.0625"), None);
}
```

The parse_complex function calls parse_pair, builds a Complex value if the coordinates were parsed successfully, and passes failures along to its caller.

If you were reading closely, you may have noticed that we used a shorthand notation to build the Complex value. It's common to initialize a struct's fields with variables of the same name, so rather than forcing you to write Complex { re: re, im: im }, Rust lets you simply write Complex { re, im }. This is modeled on similar notations in JavaScript and Haskell.

Mapping from Pixels to Complex Numbers

The program needs to work in two related coordinate spaces: each pixel in the output image corresponds to a point on the complex plane. The relationship between these two spaces depends on which portion of the Mandelbrot set we're going to plot, and the resolution of the image requested, as determined by command-line arguments. The following function converts from *image space* to *complex number space*:

```
/// Given the row and column of a pixel in the output image, return the
/// corresponding point on the complex plane.
///
/// `bounds` is a pair giving the width and height of the image in pixels.
/// `pixel` is a (column, row) pair indicating a particular pixel in that image.
/// The `upper_left` and `lower_right` parameters are points on the complex
/// plane designating the area our image covers.
fn pixel_to_point(bounds: (usize, usize),
                  pixel: (usize, usize),
                  upper_left: Complex<f64>,
                  lower_right: Complex<f64>)
    -> Complex<f64>
{
    let (width, height) = (lower_right.re - upper_left.re,
                           upper_left.im - lower_right.im);
    Complex {
        re: upper_left.re + pixel.0 as f64 * width  / bounds.0 as f64,
        im: upper_left.im - pixel.1 as f64 * height / bounds.1 as f64
        // Why subtraction here? pixel.1 increases as we go down,
        // but the imaginary component increases as we go up.
    }
}

#[test]
fn test_pixel_to_point() {
    assert_eq!(pixel_to_point((100, 200), (25, 175),
                              Complex { re: -1.0, im:  1.0 },
                              Complex { re:  1.0, im: -1.0 }),
               Complex { re: -0.5, im: -0.75 });
}
```

Figure 2-4 illustrates the calculation `pixel_to_point` performs.

The code of `pixel_to_point` is simply calculation, so we won't explain it in detail. However, there are a few things to point out. Expressions with this form refer to tuple elements:

```
pixel.0
```

This refers to the first element of the tuple `pixel`.

```
pixel.0 as f64
```

This is Rust's syntax for a type conversion: this converts `pixel.0` to an `f64` value. Unlike C and C++, Rust generally refuses to convert between numeric types implicitly; you must write out the conversions you need. This can be tedious, but being explicit about which conversions occur and when is surprisingly helpful. Implicit integer conversions seem innocent enough, but historically they have been a frequent source of bugs and security holes in real-world C and C++ code.

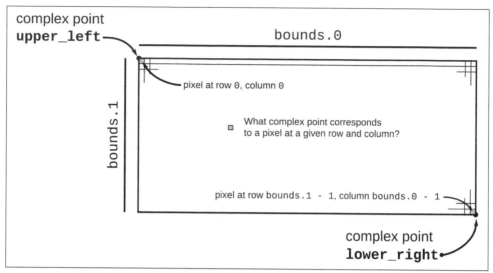

Figure 2-4. The relationship between the complex plane and the image's pixels

Plotting the Set

To plot the Mandelbrot set, for every pixel in the image, we simply apply `escape_time` to the corresponding point on the complex plane, and color the pixel depending on the result:

```
/// Render a rectangle of the Mandelbrot set into a buffer of pixels.
///
/// The `bounds` argument gives the width and height of the buffer `pixels`,
/// which holds one grayscale pixel per byte. The `upper_left` and `lower_right`
/// arguments specify points on the complex plane corresponding to the upper-
/// left and lower-right corners of the pixel buffer.
fn render(pixels: &mut [u8],
          bounds: (usize, usize),
          upper_left: Complex<f64>,
          lower_right: Complex<f64>)
{
    assert!(pixels.len() == bounds.0 * bounds.1);

    for row in 0..bounds.1 {
        for column in 0..bounds.0 {
            let point = pixel_to_point(bounds, (column, row),
                                       upper_left, lower_right);
            pixels[row * bounds.0 + column] =
                match escape_time(point, 255) {
                    None => 0,
                    Some(count) => 255 - count as u8
                };
        }
    }
}
```

This should all look pretty familiar at this point.

```
pixels[row * bounds.0 + column] =
    match escape_time(point, 255) {
        None => 0,
        Some(count) => 255 - count as u8
    };
```

If `escape_time` says that `point` belongs to the set, `render` colors the corresponding pixel black (0). Otherwise, `render` assigns darker colors to the numbers that took longer to escape the circle.

Writing Image Files

The `image` crate provides functions for reading and writing a wide variety of image formats, along with some basic image manipulation functions. In particular, it includes an encoder for the PNG image file format, which this program uses to save the final results of the calculation. In order to use `image`, add the following line to the [`dependencies`] section of *Cargo.toml*:

```
image = "0.13.0"
```

With that in place, we can write:

```
use image::ColorType;
use image::png::PNGEncoder;
use std::fs::File;

/// Write the buffer `pixels`, whose dimensions are given by `bounds`, to the
/// file named `filename`.
fn write_image(filename: &str, pixels: &[u8], bounds: (usize, usize))
    -> Result<(), std::io::Error>
{
    let output = File::create(filename)?;

    let encoder = PNGEncoder::new(output);
    encoder.encode(pixels,
                   bounds.0 as u32, bounds.1 as u32,
                   ColorType::Gray(8))?;

    Ok(())
}
```

The operation of this function is pretty straightforward: it opens a file and tries to write the image to it. We pass the encoder the actual pixel data from `pixels`, and its width and height from `bounds`, and then a final argument that says how to interpret the bytes in `pixels`: the value `ColorType::Gray(8)` indicates that each byte is an eight-bit grayscale value.

That's all straightforward. What's interesting about this function is how it copes when something goes wrong. If we encounter an error, we need to report that back to our caller. As we've mentioned before, fallible functions in Rust should return a `Result` value, which is either Ok(s) on success, where s is the successful value, or Err(e) on failure, where e is an error code. So what are write_image's success and error types?

When all goes well, our write_image function has no useful value to return; it wrote everything interesting to the file. So its success type is the *unit* type (), so called because it has only one value, also written (). The unit type is akin to void in C and C++.

When an error occurs, it's because either File::create wasn't able to create the file or encoder.encode wasn't able to write the image to it; the I/O operation returned an error code. The return type of File::create is Result<std::fs::File, std::io::Error>, while that of encoder.encode is Result<(), std::io::Error>, so both share the same error type, std::io::Error. It makes sense for our write_image function to do the same. In either case, failure should result in an immediate return, passing along the std::io::Error value describing what went wrong.

So to properly handle File::create's result, we need to match on its return value, like this:

```
let output = match File::create(filename) {
    Ok(f) => f,
    Err(e) => {
        return Err(e);
    }
};
```

On success, let output be the File carried in the Ok value. On failure, pass along the error to our own caller.

This kind of match statement is such a common pattern in Rust that the language provides the ? operator as shorthand for the whole thing. So, rather than writing out this logic explicitly every time we attempt something that could fail, you can use the following equivalent and much more legible statement:

```
let output = File::create(filename)?;
```

If File::create fails, the ? operator returns from write_image, passing along the error. Otherwise, output holds the successfully opened File.

 It's a common beginner's mistake to attempt to use ? in the main function. However, since main itself doesn't return a value, this won't work; instead, you need to use a match statement, or one of the shorthand methods like unwrap and expect. There's also the option of simply changing main to return a Result, which we'll cover later.

A Concurrent Mandelbrot Program

All the pieces are in place, and we can show you the `main` function, where we can put concurrency to work for us. First, a nonconcurrent version for simplicity:

```
use std::env;

fn main() {
    let args: Vec<String> = env::args().collect();

    if args.len() != 5 {
        eprintln!("Usage: {} FILE PIXELS UPPERLEFT LOWERRIGHT",
                  args[0]);
        eprintln!("Example: {} mandel.png 1000x750 -1.20,0.35 -1,0.20",
                  args[0]);
        std::process::exit(1);
    }

    let bounds = parse_pair(&args[2], 'x')
        .expect("error parsing image dimensions");
    let upper_left = parse_complex(&args[3])
        .expect("error parsing upper left corner point");
    let lower_right = parse_complex(&args[4])
        .expect("error parsing lower right corner point");

    let mut pixels = vec![0; bounds.0 * bounds.1];

    render(&mut pixels, bounds, upper_left, lower_right);

    write_image(&args[1], &pixels, bounds)
        .expect("error writing PNG file");
}
```

After collecting the command-line arguments into a vector of `String`s, we parse each one and then begin calculations.

```
    let mut pixels = vec![0; bounds.0 * bounds.1];
```

A macro call `vec![v; n]` creates a vector n elements long whose elements are initialized to v, so the preceding code creates a vector of zeros whose length is `bounds.0 * bounds.1`, where `bounds` is the image resolution parsed from the command line. We'll use this vector as a rectangular array of one-byte grayscale pixel values, as shown in Figure 2-5.

The next line of interest is this:

```
    render(&mut pixels, bounds, upper_left, lower_right);
```

This calls the `render` function to actually compute the image. The expression `&mut pixels` borrows a mutable reference to our pixel buffer, allowing `render` to fill it with computed grayscale values, even while `pixels` remains the vector's owner. The remaining arguments pass the image's dimensions and the rectangle of the complex plane we've chosen to plot.

```
write_image(&args[1], &pixels, bounds)
    .expect("error writing PNG file");
```

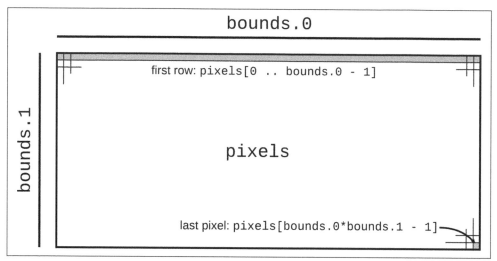

Figure 2-5. Using a vector as a rectangular array of pixels

Finally, we write the pixel buffer out to disk as a PNG file. In this case, we pass a shared (nonmutable) reference to the buffer, since `write_image` should have no need to modify the buffer's contents.

At this point, we can build and run the program in release mode, which enables many powerful compiler optimizations, and after several seconds, it will write a beautiful image to the file *mandel.png*:

```
$ cargo build --release
   Updating crates.io index
   Compiling autocfg v1.0.1
   ...
   Compiling image v0.13.0
   Compiling mandelbrot v0.1.0 ($RUSTBOOK/mandelbrot)
    Finished release [optimized] target(s) in 25.36s
$ time target/release/mandelbrot mandel.png 4000x3000 -1.20,0.35 -1,0.20
real    0m4.678s
user    0m4.661s
sys     0m0.008s
```

This command should create a file called *mandel.png*, which you can view with your system's image viewing program or in a web browser. If all has gone well, it should look like Figure 2-6.

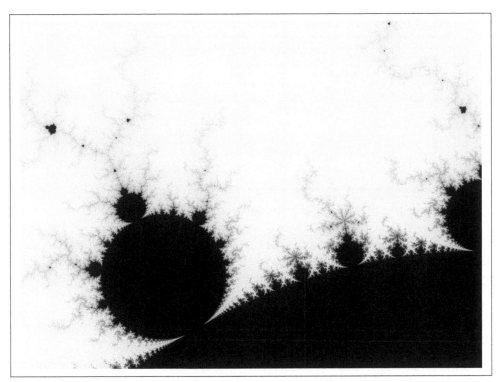

Figure 2-6. Results from parallel Mandelbrot program

In the previous transcript, we used the Unix `time` program to analyze the running time of the program: it took about five seconds total to run the Mandelbrot computation on each pixel of the image. But almost all modern machines have multiple processor cores, and this program used only one. If we could distribute the work across all the computing resources the machine has to offer, we should be able to complete the image much more quickly.

To this end, we'll divide the image into sections, one per processor, and let each processor color the pixels assigned to it. For simplicity, we'll break it into horizontal bands, as shown in Figure 2-7. When all processors have finished, we can write out the pixels to disk.

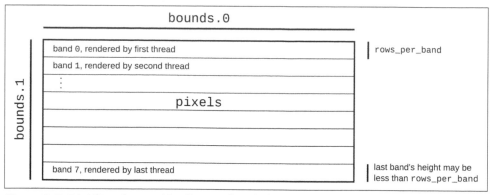

Figure 2-7. Dividing the pixel buffer into bands for parallel rendering

The `crossbeam` crate provides a number of valuable concurrency facilities, including a *scoped thread* facility that does exactly what we need here. To use it, we must add the following line to our *Cargo.toml* file:

```
crossbeam = "0.8"
```

Then we need to take out the single line calling `render` and replace it with the following:

```
let threads = 8;
let rows_per_band = bounds.1 / threads + 1;

{
    let bands: Vec<&mut [u8]> =
        pixels.chunks_mut(rows_per_band * bounds.0).collect();
    crossbeam::scope(|spawner| {
        for (i, band) in bands.into_iter().enumerate() {
            let top = rows_per_band * i;
            let height = band.len() / bounds.0;
            let band_bounds = (bounds.0, height);
            let band_upper_left =
                pixel_to_point(bounds, (0, top), upper_left, lower_right);
            let band_lower_right =
                pixel_to_point(bounds, (bounds.0, top + height),
                                upper_left, lower_right);

            spawner.spawn(move |_| {
                render(band, band_bounds, band_upper_left, band_lower_right);
            });
        }
    }).unwrap();
}
```

Breaking this down in the usual way:

```
let threads = 8;
let rows_per_band = bounds.1 / threads + 1;
```

Here we decide to use eight threads.[1] Then we compute how many rows of pixels each band should have. We round the row count upward to make sure the bands cover the entire image even if the height isn't a multiple of `threads`.

```
let bands: Vec<&mut [u8]> =
    pixels.chunks_mut(rows_per_band * bounds.0).collect();
```

Here we divide the pixel buffer into bands. The buffer's `chunks_mut` method returns an iterator producing mutable, nonoverlapping slices of the buffer, each of which encloses `rows_per_band` * `bounds.0` pixels—in other words, `rows_per_band` complete rows of pixels. The last slice that `chunks_mut` produces may contain fewer rows, but each row will contain the same number of pixels. Finally, the iterator's `collect` method builds a vector holding these mutable, nonoverlapping slices.

Now we can put the `crossbeam` library to work:

```
crossbeam::scope(|spawner| {
    ...
}).unwrap();
```

The argument `|spawner| { ... }` is a Rust closure that expects a single argument, `spawner`. Note that, unlike functions declared with `fn`, we don't need to declare the types of a closure's arguments; Rust will infer them, along with its return type. In this case, `crossbeam::scope` calls the closure, passing as the `spawner` argument a value the closure can use to create new threads. The `crossbeam::scope` function waits for all such threads to finish execution before returning itself. This behavior allows Rust to be sure that such threads will not access their portions of `pixels` after it has gone out of scope, and allows us to be sure that when `crossbeam::scope` returns, the computation of the image is complete. If all goes well, `crossbeam::scope` returns `Ok(())`, but if any of the threads we spawned panicked, it returns an `Err`. We call `unwrap` on that `Result` so that, in that case, we'll panic too, and the user will get a report.

```
for (i, band) in bands.into_iter().enumerate() {
```

Here we iterate over the pixel buffer's bands. The `into_iter()` iterator gives each iteration of the loop body exclusive ownership of one band, ensuring that only one thread can write to it at a time. We explain how this works in detail in Chapter 5. Then, the `enumerate` adapter produces tuples pairing each vector element with its index.

---

1 The `num_cpus` crate provides a function that returns the number of CPUs available on the current system.

```
let top = rows_per_band * i;
let height = band.len() / bounds.0;
let band_bounds = (bounds.0, height);
let band_upper_left =
    pixel_to_point(bounds, (0, top), upper_left, lower_right);
let band_lower_right =
    pixel_to_point(bounds, (bounds.0, top + height),
                    upper_left, lower_right);
```

Given the index and the actual size of the band (recall that the last one might be shorter than the others), we can produce a bounding box of the sort render requires, but one that refers only to this band of the buffer, not the entire image. Similarly, we repurpose the renderer's pixel_to_point function to find where the band's upper-left and lower-right corners fall on the complex plane.

```
spawner.spawn(move |_| {
    render(band, band_bounds, band_upper_left, band_lower_right);
});
```

Finally, we create a thread, running the closure move |_| { ... }. The move keyword at the front indicates that this closure takes ownership of the variables it uses; in particular, only the closure may use the mutable slice band. The argument list |_| means that the closure takes one argument, which it doesn't use (another spawner for making nested threads).

As we mentioned earlier, the crossbeam::scope call ensures that all threads have completed before it returns, meaning that it is safe to save the image to a file, which is our next action.

Running the Mandelbrot Plotter

We've used several external crates in this program: num for complex number arithmetic, image for writing PNG files, and crossbeam for the scoped thread creation primitives. Here's the final *Cargo.toml* file including all those dependencies:

```
[package]
name = "mandelbrot"
version = "0.1.0"
edition = "2021"

[dependencies]
num = "0.4"
image = "0.13"
crossbeam = "0.8"
```

With that in place, we can build and run the program:

```
$ cargo build --release
    Updating crates.io index
    Compiling crossbeam-queue v0.3.2
    Compiling crossbeam v0.8.1
    Compiling mandelbrot v0.1.0 ($RUSTBOOK/mandelbrot)
    Finished release [optimized] target(s) in #.## secs
$ time target/release/mandelbrot mandel.png 4000x3000 -1.20,0.35 -1,0.20
real    0m1.436s
user    0m4.922s
sys     0m0.011s
```

Here, we've used time again to see how long the program took to run; note that even though we still spent almost five seconds of processor time, the elapsed real time was only about 1.5 seconds. You can verify that a portion of that time is spent writing the image file by commenting out the code that does so and measuring again. On the laptop where this code was tested, the concurrent version reduces the Mandelbrot calculation time proper by a factor of almost four. We'll show how to substantially improve on this in Chapter 19.

As before, this program will have created a file called *mandel.png*. With this faster version, you can more easily explore the Mandelbrot set by changing the command-line arguments to your liking.

Safety Is Invisible

In the end, the parallel program we ended up with is not substantially different from what we might write in any other language: we apportion pieces of the pixel buffer out among the processors, let each one work on its piece separately, and when they've all finished, present the result. So what is so special about Rust's concurrency support?

What we haven't shown here is all the Rust programs we *cannot* write. The code we looked at in this chapter partitions the buffer among the threads correctly, but there are many small variations on that code that do not (and thus introduce data races); not one of those variations will pass the Rust compiler's static checks. A C or C++ compiler will cheerfully help you explore the vast space of programs with subtle data races; Rust tells you, up front, when something could go wrong.

In Chapters 4 and 5, we'll describe Rust's rules for memory safety. Chapter 19 explains how these rules also ensure proper concurrency hygiene.

Filesystems and Command-Line Tools

Rust has found a significant niche in the world of command-line tools. As a modern, safe, and fast systems programming language, it gives programmers a toolbox they can use to assemble slick command-line interfaces that replicate or extend the functionality of existing tools. For instance, the `bat` command provides a syntax-highlighting-aware `cat` alternative with built-in support for paging tools, and `hyperfine` can automatically benchmark anything that can be run with a command or pipeline.

While something that complex is out of scope for this book, Rust makes it easy to dip your toes into the world of ergonomic command-line applications. In this section, we'll show you how to build your own search-and-replace tool, complete with colorful output and friendly error messages.

To start, we'll create a new Rust project:

```
$ cargo new quickreplace
    Created binary (application) `quickreplace` package
$ cd quickreplace
```

For our program, we'll need two other crates: `text-colorizer` for creating colorful output in the terminal and `regex` for the actual search-and-replace functionality. As before, we put these crates in *Cargo.toml* to tell `cargo` that we need them:

```
[package]
name = "quickreplace"
version = "0.1.0"
edition = "2021"

# See more keys and their definitions at
# https://doc.rust-lang.org/cargo/reference/manifest.html

[dependencies]
text-colorizer = "1"
regex = "1"
```

Rust crates that have reached version `1.0`, as these have, follow the "semantic versioning" rules: until the major version number 1 changes, newer versions should always be compatible extensions of their predecessors. So if we test our program against version `1.2` of some crate, it should still work with versions `1.3`, `1.4`, and so on; but version `2.0` could introduce incompatible changes. When we simply request version `"1"` of a crate in a *Cargo.toml* file, Cargo will use the newest available version of the crate before `2.0`.

The Command-Line Interface

The interface for this program is quite simple. It takes four arguments: a string (or regular expression) to search for, a string (or regular expression) to replace it with, the name of an input file, and the name of an output file. We'll start off our *main.rs* file with a struct containing these arguments:

```
#[derive(Debug)]
struct Arguments {
    target: String,
    replacement: String,
    filename: String,
    output: String,
}
```

The `#[derive(Debug)]` attribute tells the compiler to generate some extra code that allows us to format the `Arguments` struct with `{:?}` in `println!`.

In case the user enters the wrong number of arguments, it's customary to print out a concise explanation of how to use the program. We'll do this with a simple function called `print_usage` and import everything from `text-colorizer` so we can add some color:

```
use text_colorizer::*;

fn print_usage() {
    eprintln!("{} - change occurrences of one string into another",
            "quickreplace".green());
    eprintln!("Usage: quickreplace <target> <replacement> <INPUT> <OUTPUT>");
}
```

Simply adding `.green()` to the end of a string literal produces a string wrapped in the appropriate ANSI escape codes to display as green in a terminal emulator. That string is then interpolated into the rest of the message before it is printed.

Now we can collect and process the program's arguments:

```
use std::env;

fn parse_args() -> Arguments {

    let args: Vec<String> = env::args().skip(1).collect();

    if args.len() != 4 {
        print_usage();
        eprintln!("{} wrong number of arguments: expected 4, got {}.",
            "Error:".red().bold(), args.len());
        std::process::exit(1);
    }

    Arguments {
        target: args[0].clone(),
        replacement: args[1].clone(),
        filename: args[2].clone(),
        output: args[3].clone()
    }
}
```

In order to get the arguments the user has entered, we use the same `args` iterator as in the previous examples. `.skip(1)` skips the iterator's first value (the name of the program being run) so that the result has only the command-line arguments.

The `collect()` method produces a `Vec` of arguments. We then check that the right number is present and, if not, print a message and exit with an error code. We again colorize part of the message and use `.bold()` to make the text heavier, as well. If the right number of arguments is present, we put them in an `Arguments` struct, and return it.

Then we'll add a `main` function that just calls `parse_args` and prints the output:

```
fn main() {
    let args = parse_args();
    println!("{:?}", args);
}
```

At this point, we can run the program and see that it spits out the right error message:

```
$ cargo run
 Updating crates.io index
Compiling libc v0.2.82
Compiling lazy_static v1.4.0
Compiling memchr v2.3.4
Compiling regex-syntax v0.6.22
Compiling thread_local v1.1.0
Compiling aho-corasick v0.7.15
Compiling atty v0.2.14
Compiling text-colorizer v1.0.0
Compiling regex v1.4.3
Compiling quickreplace v0.1.0 (/home/jimb/quickreplace)
Finished dev [unoptimized + debuginfo] target(s) in 6.98s
Running `target/debug/quickreplace`
quickreplace - change occurrences of one string into another
Usage: quickreplace <target> <replacement> <INPUT> <OUTPUT>
Error: wrong number of arguments: expected 4, got 0
```

If you give the program some arguments, it will instead print out a representation of the `Arguments` struct:

```
$ cargo run "find" "replace" file output
    Finished dev [unoptimized + debuginfo] target(s) in 0.01s
     Running `target/debug/quickreplace find replace file output`
Arguments { target: "find", replacement: "replace", filename: "file", output: "output" }
```

This is a very good start! The arguments are correctly picked up and placed in the correct parts of the `Arguments` struct.

Reading and Writing Files

Next, we need some way to actually get data from the filesystem so we can process it, and write it back when we're done. Rust has a robust set of tools for input and output, but the designers of the standard library know that reading and writing files is very common, and they've made it easy on purpose. All we need to do is import one module, `std::fs`, and we get access to the `read_to_string` and `write` functions:

```
use std::fs;
```

`std::fs::read_to_string` returns a `Result<String, std::io::Error>`. If the function succeeds, it produces a `String`. If it fails, it produces a `std::io::Error`, the standard library's type for representing I/O problems. Similarly, `std::fs::write` returns a `Result<(), std::io::Error>`: nothing in the success case, or the same error details if something goes wrong.

```
fn main() {
    let args = parse_args();

    let data = match fs::read_to_string(&args.filename) {
        Ok(v) => v,
        Err(e) => {
            eprintln!("{} failed to read from file '{}': {:?}",
                    "Error:".red().bold(), args.filename, e);
            std::process::exit(1);
        }
    };

    match fs::write(&args.output, &data) {
        Ok(_) => {},
        Err(e) => {
            eprintln!("{} failed to write to file '{}': {:?}",
                "Error:".red().bold(), args.filename, e);
            std::process::exit(1);
        }
    };
}
```

Here, we're using the `parse_args()` function we wrote beforehand and passing the resulting filenames to `read_to_string` and `write`. The `match` statements on those functions' outputs handle errors gracefully, printing out the filename, the provided reason for the error, and a little pop of color to get the user's attention.

With this updated `main` function, we can run the program and see that, of course, the contents of the new and old files are exactly the same:

```
$ cargo run "find" "replace" Cargo.toml Copy.toml
   Compiling quickreplace v0.1.0 (/home/jimb/rust/quickreplace)
    Finished dev [unoptimized + debuginfo] target(s) in 0.01s
     Running `target/debug/quickreplace find replace Cargo.toml Copy.toml`
```

The program *does* read in the input file *Cargo.toml*, and it *does* write to the output file *Copy.toml*, but since we haven't written any code to actually do finding and replacing, nothing in the output has changed. We can easily check by running the `diff` command, which detects no differences:

```
$ diff Cargo.toml Copy.toml
```

Find and Replace

The final touch for this program is to implement its actual functionality: finding and replacing. For this, we'll use the `regex` crate, which compiles and executes regular expressions. It provides a struct called `Regex`, which represents a compiled regular expression. `Regex` has a method `replace_all`, which does exactly what it says: it searches a string for all matches of the regular expression and replaces each one with a given replacement string. We can pull this logic out into a function:

```
use regex::Regex;
fn replace(target: &str, replacement: &str, text: &str)
    -> Result<String, regex::Error>
{
    let regex = Regex::new(target)?;
    Ok(regex.replace_all(text, replacement).to_string())
}
```

Note the return type of this function. Just like the standard library functions we used earlier, `replace` returns a `Result`, this time with an error type provided by the `regex` crate.

`Regex::new` compiles the user-provided regex, and it can fail if given an invalid string. As in the Mandelbrot program, we use ? to short-circuit in case `Regex::new` fails, but in this case the function returns an error type specific to the `regex` crate. Once the regex is compiled, its `replace_all` method replaces any matches in `text` with the given replacement string.

If `replace_all` finds matches, it returns a new `String` with those matches replaced with the text we gave it. Otherwise, `replace_all` returns a pointer to the original text, avoiding unnecessary memory allocation and copying. In this case, however, we always want an independent copy, so we use the `to_string` method to get a `String` in either case and return that string wrapped in `Result::Ok`, as in the other functions.

Now, it's time to incorporate the new function into our `main` code:

```
fn main() {
    let args = parse_args();

    let data = match fs::read_to_string(&args.filename) {
        Ok(v) => v,
        Err(e) => {
            eprintln!("{} failed to read from file '{}': {:?}",
```

```
                "Error:".red().bold(), args.filename, e);
            std::process::exit(1);
        }
    };

    let replaced_data = match replace(&args.target, &args.replacement, &data) {
        Ok(v) => v,
        Err(e) => {
            eprintln!("{} failed to replace text: {:?}",
                "Error:".red().bold(), e);
            std::process::exit(1);
        }
    };

    match fs::write(&args.output, &replaced_data) {
        Ok(v) => v,
        Err(e) => {
            eprintln!("{} failed to write to file '{}': {:?}",
                "Error:".red().bold(), args.filename, e);
            std::process::exit(1);
        }
    };
}
```

With this final touch, the program is ready, and you should be able to test it:

```
$ echo "Hello, world" > test.txt
$ cargo run "world" "Rust" test.txt test-modified.txt
   Compiling quickreplace v0.1.0 (/home/jimb/rust/quickreplace)
    Finished dev [unoptimized + debuginfo] target(s) in 0.88s
     Running `target/debug/quickreplace world Rust test.txt test-modified.txt`

$ cat test-modified.txt
Hello, Rust
```

And, of course, the error handling is also in place, gracefully reporting errors to the user:

```
$ cargo run "[[a-z]" "0" test.txt test-modified.txt
    Finished dev [unoptimized + debuginfo] target(s) in 0.01s
     Running `target/debug/quickreplace '[[a-z]' 0 test.txt test-modified.txt`
Error: failed to replace text: Syntax(
~~~~~~~~~~~~~~~~~~~~~~~~~~~~~~~~~~~~~~~~~~~~~~~~~~~~~~~~~~~~~~~~~~~~~~~~~~~~~~~~~
regex parse error:
    [[a-z]
    ^
error: unclosed character class
~~~~~~~~~~~~~~~~~~~~~~~~~~~~~~~~~~~~~~~~~~~~~~~~~~~~~~~~~~~~~~~~~~~~~~~~~~~~~~~~~
)
```

There are, of course, many features missing from this simple demonstration, but the fundamentals are there. You've seen how to read and write files, propagate and display errors, and colorize output for improved user experience in the terminal.

Future chapters will explore more advanced techniques for application development, from collections of data and functional programming with iterators to asynchronous programming techniques for extremely efficient concurrency, but first, you'll need the next chapter's solid foundation in Rust's fundamental data types.

## CHAPTER 3

Fundamental Types

There are many, many types of books in the world, which makes good sense, because there are many, many types of people, and everybody wants to read something different.

—Lemony Snicket

To a great extent, the Rust language is designed around its types. Its support for high-performance code arises from letting developers choose the data representation that best fits the situation, with the right balance between simplicity and cost. Rust's memory and thread safety guarantees also rest on the soundness of its type system, and Rust's flexibility stems from its generic types and traits.

This chapter covers Rust's fundamental types for representing values. These source-level types have concrete machine-level counterparts with predictable costs and performance. Although Rust doesn't promise it will represent things exactly as you've requested, it takes care to deviate from your requests only when it's a reliable improvement.

Compared to a dynamically typed language like JavaScript or Python, Rust requires more planning from you up front. You must spell out the types of function arguments and return values, struct fields, and a few other constructs. However, two features of Rust make this less trouble than you might expect:

- Given the types that you do spell out, Rust's *type inference* will figure out most of the rest for you. In practice, there's often only one type that will work for a given variable or expression; when this is the case, Rust lets you leave out, or *elide*, the type. For example, you could spell out every type in a function, like this:

```
fn build_vector() -> Vec<i16> {
    let mut v: Vec<i16> = Vec::<i16>::new();
    v.push(10i16);
    v.push(20i16);
    v
}
```

But this is cluttered and repetitive. Given the function's return type, it's obvious that v must be a Vec<i16>, a vector of 16-bit signed integers; no other type would work. And from that it follows that each element of the vector must be an i16. This is exactly the sort of reasoning Rust's type inference applies, allowing you to instead write:

```
fn build_vector() -> Vec<i16> {
    let mut v = Vec::new();
    v.push(10);
    v.push(20);
    v
}
```

These two definitions are exactly equivalent, and Rust will generate the same machine code either way. Type inference gives back much of the legibility of dynamically typed languages, while still catching type errors at compile time.

- Functions can be *generic*: a single function can work on values of many different types.

  In Python and JavaScript, all functions work this way naturally: a function can operate on any value that has the properties and methods the function will need. (This is the characteristic often called *duck typing*: if it quacks like a duck, it's a duck.) But it's exactly this flexibility that makes it so difficult for those languages to detect type errors early; testing is often the only way to catch such mistakes. Rust's generic functions give the language a degree of the same flexibility, while still catching all type errors at compile time.

  Despite their flexibility, generic functions are just as efficient as their nongeneric counterparts. There is no inherent performance advantage to be had from writing, say, a specific sum function for each integer over writing a generic one that handles all integers. We'll discuss generic functions in detail in Chapter 11.

The rest of this chapter covers Rust's types from the bottom up, starting with simple numeric types like integers and floating-point values then moving on to types that hold more data: boxes, tuples, arrays, and strings.

Here's a summary of the sorts of types you'll see in Rust. Table 3-1 shows Rust's primitive types, some very common types from the standard library, and some examples of user-defined types.

Table 3-1. Examples of types in Rust

Type	Description	Values
i8, i16, i32, i64, i128 u8, u16, u32, u64, u128	Signed and unsigned integers, of given bit width	42, -5i8, 0x400u16, 0o100i16, 20_922_789_888_000u64, b'*' (u8 byte literal)
isize, usize	Signed and unsigned integers, the same size as an address on the machine (32 or 64 bits)	137, -0b0101_0010isize, 0xffff_fc00usize
f32, f64	IEEE floating-point numbers, single and double precision	1.61803, 3.14f32, 6.0221e23f64
bool	Boolean	true, false
char	Unicode character, 32 bits wide	'*', '\n', '字', '\x7f', '\u{CA0}'
(char, u8, i32)	Tuple: mixed types allowed	('%', 0x7f, -1)
()	"Unit" (empty tuple)	()
struct S { x: f32, y: f32 }	Named-field struct	S { x: 120.0, y: 209.0 }
struct T (i32, char);	Tuple-like struct	T(120, 'X')
struct E;	Unit-like struct; has no fields	E
enum Attend { OnTime, Late(u32) }	Enumeration, algebraic data type	Attend::Late(5), Attend::OnTime
Box<Attend>	Box: owning pointer to value in heap	Box::new(Late(15))
&i32, &mut i32	Shared and mutable references: non-owning pointers that must not outlive their referent	&s.y, &mut v
String	UTF-8 string, dynamically sized	"ラーメン: ramen".to_string()
&str	Reference to str: non-owning pointer to UTF-8 text	"そば: soba", &s[0..12]
[f64; 4], [u8; 256]	Array, fixed length; elements all of same type	[1.0, 0.0, 0.0, 1.0], [b' '; 256]
Vec<f64>	Vector, varying length; elements all of same type	vec![0.367, 2.718, 7.389]

Type	Description	Values
&[u8],&mut [u8]	Reference to slice: reference to a portion of an array or vector, comprising pointer and length	&v[10..20],&mut a[..]
Option<&str>	Optional value: either None (absent) or Some(v) (present, with value v)	Some("Dr."), None
Result<u64, Error>	Result of operation that may fail: either a success value Ok(v), or an error Err(e)	Ok(4096), Err(Error::last_os_error())
&dyn Any, &mut dyn Read	Trait object: reference to any value that implements a given set of methods	value as &dyn Any, &mut file as &mut dyn Read
fn(&str) -> bool	Pointer to function	str::is_empty
(Closure types have no written form)	Closure	|a, b| { a*a + b*b }

Most of these types are covered in this chapter, except for the following:

- We give struct types their own chapter, Chapter 9.
- We give enumerated types their own chapter, Chapter 10.
- We describe trait objects in Chapter 11.
- We describe the essentials of String and &str here, but provide more detail in Chapter 17.
- We cover function and closure types in Chapter 14.

Fixed-Width Numeric Types

The footing of Rust's type system is a collection of fixed-width numeric types, chosen to match the types that almost all modern processors implement directly in hardware.

Fixed-width numeric types can overflow or lose precision, but they are adequate for most applications and can be thousands of times faster than representations like arbitrary-precision integers and exact rationals. If you need those sorts of numeric representations, they are supported in the num crate.

The names of Rust's numeric types follow a regular pattern, spelling out their width in bits, and the representation they use (Table 3-2).

Table 3-2. Rust numeric types

Size (bits)	Unsigned integer	Signed integer	Floating-point
8	u8	i8	
16	u16	i16	
32	u32	i32	f32
64	u64	i64	f64
128	u128	i128	
Machine word	usize	isize	

Here, a *machine word* is a value the size of an address on the machine the code runs on, 32 or 64 bits.

Integer Types

Rust's unsigned integer types use their full range to represent positive values and zero (Table 3-3).

Table 3-3. Rust unsigned integer types

Type	Range
u8	0 to 2^8-1 (0 to 255)
u16	0 to $2^{16}-1$ (0 to 65,535)
u32	0 to $2^{32}-1$ (0 to 4,294,967,295)
u64	0 to $2^{64}-1$ (0 to 18,446,744,073,709,551,615, or 18 quintillion)
u128	0 to $2^{128}-1$ (0 to around 3.4×10^{38})
usize	0 to either $2^{32}-1$ or $2^{64}-1$

Rust's signed integer types use the two's complement representation, using the same bit patterns as the corresponding unsigned type to cover a range of positive and negative values (Table 3-4).

Table 3-4. Rust signed integer types

Type	Range
i8	-2^7 to 2^7-1 (−128 to 127)
i16	-2^{15} to $2^{15}-1$ (−32,768 to 32,767)
i32	-2^{31} to $2^{31}-1$ (−2,147,483,648 to 2,147,483,647)
i64	-2^{63} to $2^{63}-1$ (−9,223,372,036,854,775,808 to 9,223,372,036,854,775,807)
i128	-2^{127} to $2^{127}-1$ (roughly -1.7×10^{38} to $+1.7 \times 10^{38}$)
isize	Either -2^{31} to $2^{31}-1$, or -2^{63} to $2^{63}-1$

Rust uses the u8 type for byte values. For example, reading data from a binary file or socket yields a stream of u8 values.

Unlike C and C++, Rust treats characters as distinct from the numeric types: a char is not a u8, nor is it a u32 (though it is 32 bits long). We describe Rust's char type in "Characters" on page 61.

The usize and isize types are analogous to size_t and ptrdiff_t in C and C++. Their precision matches the size of the address space on the target machine: they are 32 bits long on 32-bit architectures, and 64 bits long on 64-bit architectures. Rust requires array indices to be usize values. Values representing the sizes of arrays or vectors or counts of the number of elements in some data structure also generally have the usize type.

Integer literals in Rust can take a suffix indicating their type: 42u8 is a u8 value, and 1729isize is an isize. If an integer literal lacks a type suffix, Rust puts off determining its type until it finds the value being used in a way that pins it down: stored in a variable of a particular type, passed to a function that expects a particular type, compared with another value of a particular type, or something like that. In the end, if multiple types could work, Rust defaults to i32 if that is among the possibilities. Otherwise, Rust reports the ambiguity as an error.

The prefixes 0x, 0o, and 0b designate hexadecimal, octal, and binary literals.

To make long numbers more legible, you can insert underscores among the digits. For example, you can write the largest u32 value as 4_294_967_295. The exact placement of the underscores is not significant, so you can break hexadecimal or binary numbers into groups of four digits rather than three, as in 0xffff_ffff, or set off the type suffix from the digits, as in 127_u8. Some examples of integer literals are illustrated in Table 3-5.

Table 3-5. Examples of integer literals

Literal	Type	Decimal value
116i8	i8	116
0xcafeu32	u32	51966
0b0010_1010	Inferred	42
0o106	Inferred	70

Although numeric types and the char type are distinct, Rust does provide *byte literals*, character-like literals for u8 values: b'X' represents the ASCII code for the character X, as a u8 value. For example, since the ASCII code for A is 65, the literals b'A' and 65u8 are exactly equivalent. Only ASCII characters may appear in byte literals.

There are a few characters that you cannot simply place after the single quote, because that would be either syntactically ambiguous or hard to read. The characters in Table 3-6 can only be written using a stand-in notation, introduced by a backslash.

Table 3-6. Characters requiring a stand-in notation

Character	Byte literal	Numeric equivalent
Single quote, '	`b'\''`	39u8
Backslash, \	`b'\\'`	92u8
Newline	`b'\n'`	10u8
Carriage return	`b'\r'`	13u8
Tab	`b'\t'`	9u8

For characters that are hard to write or read, you can write their code in hexadecimal instead. A byte literal of the form `b'\xHH'`, where HH is any two-digit hexadecimal number, represents the byte whose value is HH. For example, you can write a byte literal for the ASCII "escape" control character as `b'\x1b'`, since the ASCII code for "escape" is 27, or 1B in hexadecimal. Since byte literals are just another notation for u8 values, consider whether a simple numeric literal might be more legible: it probably makes sense to use `b'\x1b'` instead of simply 27 only when you want to emphasize that the value represents an ASCII code.

You can convert from one integer type to another using the `as` operator. We explain how conversions work in "Type Casts" on page 153, but here are some examples:

```
assert_eq!(   10_i8  as u16,    10_u16); // in range
assert_eq!( 2525_u16 as i16,  2525_i16); // in range

assert_eq!(   -1_i16 as i32,    -1_i32); // sign-extended
assert_eq!(65535_u16 as i32, 65535_i32); // zero-extended

// Conversions that are out of range for the destination
// produce values that are equivalent to the original modulo 2^N,
// where N is the width of the destination in bits. This
// is sometimes called "truncation."
assert_eq!( 1000_i16 as  u8,   232_u8);
assert_eq!(65535_u32 as i16,    -1_i16);

assert_eq!(   -1_i8  as u8,    255_u8);
assert_eq!(  255_u8  as i8,     -1_i8);
```

The standard library provides some operations as methods on integers. For example:

```
assert_eq!(2_u16.pow(4), 16);              // exponentiation
assert_eq!((-4_i32).abs(), 4);             // absolute value
assert_eq!(0b101101_u8.count_ones(), 4);   // population count
```

You can find these in the online documentation. Note, however, that the documentation contains separate pages for the type itself under "i32 (primitive type)," and for the module dedicated to that type (search for "std::i32").

In real code, you usually won't need to write out the type suffixes as we've done here, because the context will determine the type. When it doesn't, however, the error messages can be surprising. For example, the following doesn't compile:

```
println!("{}", (-4).abs());
```

Rust complains:

```
error: can't call method `abs` on ambiguous numeric type `{integer}`
```

This can be a little bewildering: all the signed integer types have an `abs` method, so what's the problem? For technical reasons, Rust wants to know exactly which integer type a value has before it will call the type's own methods. The default of `i32` applies only if the type is still ambiguous after all method calls have been resolved, so that's too late to help here. The solution is to spell out which type you intend, either with a suffix or by using a specific type's function:

```
println!("{}", (-4_i32).abs());
println!("{}", i32::abs(-4));
```

Note that method calls have a higher precedence than unary prefix operators, so be careful when applying methods to negated values. Without the parentheses around `-4_i32` in the first statement, `-4_i32.abs()` would apply the `abs` method to the positive value 4, producing positive 4, and then negate that, producing `-4`.

Checked, Wrapping, Saturating, and Overflowing Arithmetic

When an integer arithmetic operation overflows, Rust panics, in a debug build. In a release build, the operation *wraps around*: it produces the value equivalent to the mathematically correct result modulo the range of the value. (In neither case is overflow undefined behavior, as it is in C and C++.)

For example, the following code panics in a debug build:

```
let mut i = 1;
loop {
    i *= 10; // panic: attempt to multiply with overflow
             // (but only in debug builds!)
}
```

In a release build, this multiplication wraps to a negative number, and the loop runs indefinitely.

When this default behavior isn't what you need, the integer types provide methods that let you spell out exactly what you want. For example, the following panics in any build:

```
let mut i: i32 = 1;
loop {
    // panic: multiplication overflowed (in any build)
    i = i.checked_mul(10).expect("multiplication overflowed");
}
```

These integer arithmetic methods fall in four general categories:

- *Checked* operations return an Option of the result: Some(v) if the mathematically correct result can be represented as a value of that type, or None if it cannot. For example:

```
// The sum of 10 and 20 can be represented as a u8.
assert_eq!(10_u8.checked_add(20), Some(30));

// Unfortunately, the sum of 100 and 200 cannot.
assert_eq!(100_u8.checked_add(200), None);

// Do the addition; panic if it overflows.
let sum = x.checked_add(y).unwrap();

// Oddly, signed division can overflow too, in one particular case.
// A signed n-bit type can represent -2^{n-1}, but not 2^{n-1}.
assert_eq!((-128_i8).checked_div(-1), None);
```

- *Wrapping* operations return the value equivalent to the mathematically correct result modulo the range of the value:

```
// The first product can be represented as a u16;
// the second cannot, so we get 250000 modulo 2^{16}.
assert_eq!(100_u16.wrapping_mul(200), 20000);
assert_eq!(500_u16.wrapping_mul(500), 53392);

// Operations on signed types may wrap to negative values.
assert_eq!(500_i16.wrapping_mul(500), -12144);

// In bitwise shift operations, the shift distance
// is wrapped to fall within the size of the value.
// So a shift of 17 bits in a 16-bit type is a shift
// of 1.
assert_eq!(5_i16.wrapping_shl(17), 10);
```

As explained, this is how the ordinary arithmetic operators behave in release builds. The advantage of these methods is that they behave the same way in all builds.

- *Saturating* operations return the representable value that is closest to the mathematically correct result. In other words, the result is "clamped" to the maximum and minimum values the type can represent:

  ```
  assert_eq!(32760_i16.saturating_add(10), 32767);
  assert_eq!((-32760_i16).saturating_sub(10), -32768);
  ```

  There are no saturating division, remainder, or bitwise shift methods.

- *Overflowing* operations return a tuple `(result, overflowed)`, where `result` is what the wrapping version of the function would return, and `overflowed` is a `bool` indicating whether an overflow occurred:

  ```
  assert_eq!(255_u8.overflowing_sub(2), (253, false));
  assert_eq!(255_u8.overflowing_add(2), (1, true));
  ```

  `overflowing_shl` and `overflowing_shr` deviate from the pattern a bit: they return true for `overflowed` only if the shift distance was as large or larger than the bit width of the type itself. The actual shift applied is the requested shift modulo the bit width of the type:

  ```
  // A shift of 17 bits is too large for `u16`, and 17 modulo 16 is 1.
  assert_eq!(5_u16.overflowing_shl(17), (10, true));
  ```

The operation names that follow the `checked_`, `wrapping_`, `saturating_`, or `overflowing_` prefix are shown in Table 3-7.

Table 3-7. Operation names

Operation	Name suffix	Example
Addition	add	`100_i8.checked_add(27) == Some(127)`
Subtraction	sub	`10_u8.checked_sub(11) == None`
Multiplication	mul	`128_u8.saturating_mul(3) == 255`
Division	div	`64_u16.wrapping_div(8) == 8`
Remainder	rem	`(-32768_i16).wrapping_rem(-1) == 0`
Negation	neg	`(-128_i8).checked_neg() == None`
Absolute value	abs	`(-32768_i16).wrapping_abs() == -32768`
Exponentiation	pow	`3_u8.checked_pow(4) == Some(81)`
Bitwise left shift	shl	`10_u32.wrapping_shl(34) == 40`
Bitwise right shift	shr	`40_u64.wrapping_shr(66) == 10`

Floating-Point Types

Rust provides IEEE single- and double-precision floating-point types. These types include positive and negative infinities, distinct positive and negative zero values, and a *not-a-number* value (Table 3-8).

Table 3-8. IEEE single- and double-precision floating-point types

Type	Precision	Range
f32	IEEE single precision (at least 6 decimal digits)	Roughly -3.4×10^{38} to $+3.4 \times 10^{38}$
f64	IEEE double precision (at least 15 decimal digits)	Roughly -1.8×10^{308} to $+1.8 \times 10^{308}$

Rust's f32 and f64 correspond to the float and double types in C and C++ (in implementations that support IEEE floating point) as well as Java (which always uses IEEE floating point).

Floating-point literals have the general form diagrammed in Figure 3-1.

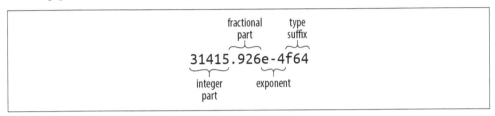

Figure 3-1. A floating-point literal

Every part of a floating-point number after the integer part is optional, but at least one of the fractional part, exponent, or type suffix must be present, to distinguish it from an integer literal. The fractional part may consist of a lone decimal point, so 5. is a valid floating-point constant.

If a floating-point literal lacks a type suffix, Rust checks the context to see how the values are used, much as it does for integer literals. If it ultimately finds that either floating-point type could fit, it chooses f64 by default.

For the purposes of type inference, Rust treats integer literals and floating-point literals as distinct classes: it will never infer a floating-point type for an integer literal, or vice versa. Table 3-9 shows some examples of floating-point literals.

Table 3-9. Examples of floating-point literals

Literal	Type	Mathematical value
-1.5625	Inferred	$-(1\,\%_{16})$
2.	Inferred	2
0.25	Inferred	¼
1e4	Inferred	10,000
40f32	f32	40
9.109_383_56e-31f64	f64	Roughly $9.10938356 \times 10^{-31}$

The types f32 and f64 have associated constants for the IEEE-required special values like INFINITY, NEG_INFINITY (negative infinity), NAN (the not-a-number value), and MIN and MAX (the largest and smallest finite values):

```
assert!((-1. / f32::INFINITY).is_sign_negative());
assert_eq!(-f32::MIN, f32::MAX);
```

The f32 and f64 types provide a full complement of methods for mathematical calculations; for example, 2f64.sqrt() is the double-precision square root of two. Some examples:

```
assert_eq!(5f32.sqrt() * 5f32.sqrt(), 5.); // exactly 5.0, per IEEE
assert_eq!((-1.01f64).floor(), -2.0);
```

Again, method calls have a higher precedence than prefix operators, so be sure to correctly parenthesize method calls on negated values.

The std::f32::consts and std::f64::consts modules provide various commonly used mathematical constants like E, PI, and the square root of two.

When searching the documentation, remember that there are pages for both the types themselves, named "f32 (primitive type)" and "f64 (primitive type)", and the modules for each type, std::f32 and std::f64.

As with integers, you usually won't need to write out type suffixes on floating-point literals in real code, but when you do, putting a type on either the literal or the function will suffice:

```
println!("{}", (2.0_f64).sqrt());
println!("{}", f64::sqrt(2.0));
```

Unlike C and C++, Rust performs almost no numeric conversions implicitly. If a function expects an f64 argument, it's an error to pass an i32 value as the argument. In fact, Rust won't even implicitly convert an i16 value to an i32 value, even though every i16 value is also an i32 value. But you can always write out *explicit* conversions using the as operator: i as f64, or x as i32.

The lack of implicit conversions sometimes makes a Rust expression more verbose than the analogous C or C++ code would be. However, implicit integer conversions have a well-established record of causing bugs and security holes, especially when the integers in question represent the size of something in memory, and an unanticipated overflow occurs. In our experience, the act of writing out numeric conversions in Rust has alerted us to problems we would otherwise have missed.

We explain exactly how conversions behave in "Type Casts" on page 153.

The bool Type

Rust's Boolean type, bool, has the usual two values for such types, true and false. Comparison operators like == and < produce bool results: the value of 2 < 5 is true.

Many languages are lenient about using values of other types in contexts that require a Boolean value: C and C++ implicitly convert characters, integers, floating-point numbers, and pointers to Boolean values, so they can be used directly as the condition in an if or while statement. Python permits strings, lists, dictionaries, and even sets in Boolean contexts, treating such values as true if they're nonempty. Rust, however, is very strict: control structures like if and while require their conditions to be bool expressions, as do the short-circuiting logical operators && and ||. You must write if x != 0 { ... }, not simply if x { ... }.

Rust's as operator can convert bool values to integer types:

```
assert_eq!(false as i32, 0);
assert_eq!(true  as i32, 1);
```

However, as won't convert in the other direction, from numeric types to bool. Instead, you must write out an explicit comparison like x != 0.

Although a bool needs only a single bit to represent it, Rust uses an entire byte for a bool value in memory, so you can create a pointer to it.

Characters

Rust's character type char represents a single Unicode character, as a 32-bit value.

Rust uses the char type for single characters in isolation, but uses the UTF-8 encoding for strings and streams of text. So, a String represents its text as a sequence of UTF-8 bytes, not as an array of characters.

Character literals are characters enclosed in single quotes, like '8' or '!'. You can use the full breadth of Unicode: '錆' is a char literal representing the Japanese kanji for *sabi* (rust).

As with byte literals, backslash escapes are required for a few characters (Table 3-10).

Table 3-10. Characters that require backslash escapes

Character	Rust character literal
Single quote, '	'\''
Backslash, \	'\\'
Newline	'\n'
Carriage return	'\r'
Tab	'\t'

If you prefer, you can write out a character's Unicode code point in hexadecimal:

- If the character's code point is in the range U+0000 to U+007F (that is, if it is drawn from the ASCII character set), then you can write the character as '\xHH', where HH is a two-digit hexadecimal number. For example, the character literals '*' and '\x2A' are equivalent, because the code point of the character * is 42, or 2A in hexadecimal.

- You can write any Unicode character as '\u{HHHHHH}', where HHHHHH is a hexadecimal number up to six digits long, with underscores allowed for grouping as usual. For example, the character literal '\u{CA0}' represents the character "ಠ", a Kannada character used in the Unicode Look of Disapproval, "ಠ_ಠ". The same literal could also be simply written as 'ಠ'.

A char always holds a Unicode code point in the range 0x0000 to 0xD7FF, or 0xE000 to 0x10FFFF. A char is never a surrogate pair half (that is, a code point in the range 0xD800 to 0xDFFF), or a value outside the Unicode codespace (that is, greater than 0x10FFFF). Rust uses the type system and dynamic checks to ensure char values are always in the permitted range.

Rust never implicitly converts between char and any other type. You can use the as conversion operator to convert a char to an integer type; for types smaller than 32 bits, the upper bits of the character's value are truncated:

```
assert_eq!('*' as i32, 42);
assert_eq!('ಠ' as u16, 0xca0);
assert_eq!('ಠ' as i8, -0x60); // U+0CA0 truncated to eight bits, signed
```

Going in the other direction, u8 is the only type the as operator will convert to char: Rust intends the as operator to perform only cheap, infallible conversions, but every integer type other than u8 includes values that are not permitted Unicode code points, so those conversions would require run-time checks. Instead, the standard library function std::char::from_u32 takes any u32 value and returns an Option<char>: if the u32 is not a permitted Unicode code point, then from_u32 returns None; otherwise, it returns Some(c), where c is the char result.

The standard library provides some useful methods on characters, which you can look up in the online documentation under "char (primitive type)," and the module "std::char." For example:

```
assert_eq!('*'.is_alphabetic(), false);
assert_eq!('β'.is_alphabetic(), true);
assert_eq!('8'.to_digit(10), Some(8));
assert_eq!('ಠ'.len_utf8(), 3);
assert_eq!(std::char::from_digit(2, 10), Some('2'));
```

Naturally, single characters in isolation are not as interesting as strings and streams of text. We'll describe Rust's standard `String` type and text handling in general in "String Types" on page 73.

Tuples

A *tuple* is a pair, or triple, quadruple, quintuple, etc. (hence, *n-tuple*, or *tuple*), of values of assorted types. You can write a tuple as a sequence of elements, separated by commas and surrounded by parentheses. For example, `("Brazil", 1985)` is a tuple whose first element is a statically allocated string, and whose second is an integer; its type is `(&str, i32)`. Given a tuple value `t`, you can access its elements as `t.0`, `t.1`, and so on.

To a certain extent, tuples resemble arrays: both types represent an ordered sequence of values. Many programming languages conflate or combine the two concepts, but in Rust, they're completely separate. For one thing, each element of a tuple can have a different type, whereas an array's elements must be all the same type. Further, tuples allow only constants as indices, like `t.4`. You can't write `t.i` or `t[i]` to get the `i`th element.

Rust code often uses tuple types to return multiple values from a function. For example, the `split_at` method on string slices, which divides a string into two halves and returns them both, is declared like this:

```
fn split_at(&self, mid: usize) -> (&str, &str);
```

The return type `(&str, &str)` is a tuple of two string slices. You can use pattern-matching syntax to assign each element of the return value to a different variable:

```
let text = "I see the eigenvalue in thine eye";
let (head, tail) = text.split_at(21);
assert_eq!(head, "I see the eigenvalue ");
assert_eq!(tail, "in thine eye");
```

This is more legible than the equivalent:

```
let text = "I see the eigenvalue in thine eye";
let temp = text.split_at(21);
let head = temp.0;
let tail = temp.1;
assert_eq!(head, "I see the eigenvalue ");
assert_eq!(tail, "in thine eye");
```

You'll also see tuples used as a sort of minimal-drama struct type. For example, in the Mandelbrot program in Chapter 2, we needed to pass the width and height of the image to the functions that plot it and write it to disk. We could declare a struct with `width` and `height` members, but that's pretty heavy notation for something so obvious, so we just used a tuple:

```
/// Write the buffer `pixels`, whose dimensions are given by `bounds`, to the
/// file named `filename`.
fn write_image(filename: &str, pixels: &[u8], bounds: (usize, usize))
    -> Result<(), std::io::Error>
{ ... }
```

The type of the bounds parameter is (usize, usize), a tuple of two usize values. Admittedly, we could just as well write out separate width and height parameters, and the machine code would be about the same either way. It's a matter of clarity. We think of the size as one value, not two, and using a tuple lets us write what we mean.

The other commonly used tuple type is the zero-tuple (). This is traditionally called the *unit type* because it has only one value, also written (). Rust uses the unit type where there's no meaningful value to carry, but context requires some sort of type nonetheless.

For example, a function that returns no value has a return type of (). The standard library's std::mem::swap function has no meaningful return value; it just exchanges the values of its two arguments. The declaration for std::mem::swap reads:

```
fn swap<T>(x: &mut T, y: &mut T);
```

The <T> means that swap is *generic*: you can use it on references to values of any type T. But the signature omits the swap's return type altogether, which is shorthand for returning the unit type:

```
fn swap<T>(x: &mut T, y: &mut T) -> ();
```

Similarly, the write_image example we mentioned before has a return type of Result<(), std::io::Error>, meaning that the function returns a std::io::Error value if something goes wrong, but returns no value on success.

If you like, you may include a comma after a tuple's last element: the types (&str, i32,) and (&str, i32) are equivalent, as are the expressions ("Brazil", 1985,) and ("Brazil", 1985). Rust consistently permits an extra trailing comma everywhere commas are used: function arguments, arrays, struct and enum definitions, and so on. This may look odd to human readers, but it can make diffs easier to read when entries are added and removed at the end of a list.

For consistency's sake, there are even tuples that contain a single value. The literal ("lonely hearts",) is a tuple containing a single string; its type is (&str,). Here, the comma after the value is necessary to distinguish the singleton tuple from a simple parenthetic expression.

Pointer Types

Rust has several types that represent memory addresses.

This is a big difference between Rust and most languages with garbage collection. In Java, if `class Rectangle` contains a field `Vector2D upperLeft;`, then `upperLeft` is a reference to another separately created `Vector2D` object. Objects never physically contain other objects in Java.

Rust is different. The language is designed to help keep allocations to a minimum. Values nest by default. The value `((0, 0), (1440, 900))` is stored as four adjacent integers. If you store it in a local variable, you've got a local variable four integers wide. Nothing is allocated in the heap.

This is great for memory efficiency, but as a consequence, when a Rust program needs values to point to other values, it must use pointer types explicitly. The good news is that the pointer types used in safe Rust are constrained to eliminate undefined behavior, so pointers are much easier to use correctly in Rust than in C++.

We'll discuss three pointer types here: references, boxes, and unsafe pointers.

References

A value of type `&String` (pronounced "ref String") is a reference to a `String` value, a `&i32` is a reference to an `i32`, and so on.

It's easiest to get started by thinking of references as Rust's basic pointer type. At run time, a reference to an `i32` is a single machine word holding the address of the `i32`, which may be on the stack or in the heap. The expression `&x` produces a reference to x; in Rust terminology, we say that it *borrows a reference to x*. Given a reference r, the expression `*r` refers to the value r points to. These are very much like the & and * operators in C and C++. And like a C pointer, a reference does not automatically free any resources when it goes out of scope.

Unlike C pointers, however, Rust references are never null: there is simply no way to produce a null reference in safe Rust. And unlike C, Rust tracks the ownership and lifetimes of values, so mistakes like dangling pointers, double frees, and pointer invalidation are ruled out at compile time.

Rust references come in two flavors:

`&T`

> An immutable, shared reference. You can have many shared references to a given value at a time, but they are read-only: modifying the value they point to is forbidden, as with `const T*` in C.

```
&mut T
```
A mutable, exclusive reference. You can read and modify the value it points to, as with a T* in C. But for as long as the reference exists, you may not have any other references of any kind to that value. In fact, the only way you may access the value at all is through the mutable reference.

Rust uses this dichotomy between shared and mutable references to enforce a "single writer *or* multiple readers" rule: either you can read and write the value, or it can be shared by any number of readers, but never both at the same time. This separation, enforced by compile-time checks, is central to Rust's safety guarantees. Chapter 5 explains Rust's rules for safe reference use.

Boxes

The simplest way to allocate a value in the heap is to use Box::new:

```
let t = (12, "eggs");
let b = Box::new(t);  // allocate a tuple in the heap
```

The type of t is (i32, &str), so the type of b is Box<(i32, &str)>. The call to Box::new allocates enough memory to contain the tuple on the heap. When b goes out of scope, the memory is freed immediately, unless b has been *moved*—by returning it, for example. Moves are essential to the way Rust handles heap-allocated values; we explain all this in detail in Chapter 4.

Raw Pointers

Rust also has the raw pointer types *mut T and *const T. Raw pointers really are just like pointers in C++. Using a raw pointer is unsafe, because Rust makes no effort to track what it points to. For example, raw pointers may be null, or they may point to memory that has been freed or that now contains a value of a different type. All the classic pointer mistakes of C++ are offered for your enjoyment.

However, you may only dereference raw pointers within an unsafe block. An unsafe block is Rust's opt-in mechanism for advanced language features whose safety is up to you. If your code has no unsafe blocks (or if those it does are written correctly), then the safety guarantees we emphasize throughout this book still hold. For details, see Chapter 22.

Arrays, Vectors, and Slices

Rust has three types for representing a sequence of values in memory:

- The type [T; N] represents an array of N values, each of type T. An array's size is a constant determined at compile time and is part of the type; you can't append new elements or shrink an array.

- The type Vec<T>, called a *vector of Ts*, is a dynamically allocated, growable sequence of values of type T. A vector's elements live on the heap, so you can resize vectors at will: push new elements onto them, append other vectors to them, delete elements, and so on.

- The types &[T] and &mut [T], called a *shared slice of Ts* and *mutable slice of Ts*, are references to a series of elements that are a part of some other value, like an array or vector. You can think of a slice as a pointer to its first element, together with a count of the number of elements you can access starting at that point. A mutable slice &mut [T] lets you read and modify elements, but can't be shared; a shared slice &[T] lets you share access among several readers, but doesn't let you modify elements.

Given a value v of any of these three types, the expression v.len() gives the number of elements in v, and v[i] refers to the ith element of v. The first element is v[0], and the last element is v[v.len() - 1]. Rust checks that i always falls within this range; if it doesn't, the expression panics. The length of v may be zero, in which case any attempt to index it will panic. i must be a usize value; you can't use any other integer type as an index.

Arrays

There are several ways to write array values. The simplest is to write a series of values within square brackets:

```
let lazy_caterer: [u32; 6] = [1, 2, 4, 7, 11, 16];
let taxonomy = ["Animalia", "Arthropoda", "Insecta"];

assert_eq!(lazy_caterer[3], 7);
assert_eq!(taxonomy.len(), 3);
```

For the common case of a long array filled with some value, you can write [*V*; *N*], where *V* is the value each element should have, and *N* is the length. For example, [true; 10000] is an array of 10,000 bool elements, all set to true:

```
let mut sieve = [true; 10000];
for i in 2..100 {
    if sieve[i] {
        let mut j = i * i;
        while j < 10000 {
            sieve[j] = false;
```

```
            j += i;
        }
    }
}

assert!(sieve[211]);
assert!(!sieve[9876]);
```

You'll see this syntax used for fixed-size buffers: [0u8; 1024] can be a one-kilobyte buffer, filled with zeros. Rust has no notation for an uninitialized array. (In general, Rust ensures that code can never access any sort of uninitialized value.)

An array's length is part of its type and fixed at compile time. If n is a variable, you can't write [true; n] to get an array of n elements. When you need an array whose length varies at run time (and you usually do), use a vector instead.

The useful methods you'd like to see on arrays—iterating over elements, searching, sorting, filling, filtering, and so on—are all provided as methods on slices, not arrays. But Rust implicitly converts a reference to an array to a slice when searching for methods, so you can call any slice method on an array directly:

```
let mut chaos = [3, 5, 4, 1, 2];
chaos.sort();
assert_eq!(chaos, [1, 2, 3, 4, 5]);
```

Here, the sort method is actually defined on slices, but since it takes its operand by reference, Rust implicitly produces a &mut [i32] slice referring to the entire array and passes that to sort to operate on. In fact, the len method we mentioned earlier is a slice method as well. We cover slices in more detail in "Slices" on page 71.

Vectors

A vector Vec<T> is a resizable array of elements of type T, allocated on the heap.

There are several ways to create vectors. The simplest is to use the vec! macro, which gives us a syntax for vectors that looks very much like an array literal:

```
let mut primes = vec![2, 3, 5, 7];
assert_eq!(primes.iter().product::<i32>(), 210);
```

But of course, this is a vector, not an array, so we can add elements to it dynamically:

```
primes.push(11);
primes.push(13);
assert_eq!(primes.iter().product::<i32>(), 30030);
```

You can also build a vector by repeating a given value a certain number of times, again using a syntax that imitates array literals:

```
fn new_pixel_buffer(rows: usize, cols: usize) -> Vec<u8> {
    vec![0; rows * cols]
}
```

The `vec!` macro is equivalent to calling `Vec::new` to create a new, empty vector and then pushing the elements onto it, which is another idiom:

```
let mut pal = Vec::new();
pal.push("step");
pal.push("on");
pal.push("no");
pal.push("pets");
assert_eq!(pal, vec!["step", "on", "no", "pets"]);
```

Another possibility is to build a vector from the values produced by an iterator:

```
let v: Vec<i32> = (0..5).collect();
assert_eq!(v, [0, 1, 2, 3, 4]);
```

You'll often need to supply the type when using `collect` (as we've done here), because it can build many different sorts of collections, not just vectors. By specifying the type of v, we've made it unambiguous which sort of collection we want.

As with arrays, you can use slice methods on vectors:

```
// A palindrome!
let mut palindrome = vec!["a man", "a plan", "a canal", "panama"];
palindrome.reverse();
// Reasonable yet disappointing:
assert_eq!(palindrome, vec!["panama", "a canal", "a plan", "a man"]);
```

Here, the `reverse` method is actually defined on slices, but the call implicitly borrows a `&mut [&str]` slice from the vector and invokes `reverse` on that.

Vec is an essential type to Rust—it's used almost anywhere one needs a list of dynamic size—so there are many other methods that construct new vectors or extend existing ones. We'll cover them in Chapter 16.

A Vec<T> consists of three values: a pointer to the heap-allocated buffer for the elements, which is created and owned by the Vec<T>; the number of elements that buffer has the capacity to store; and the number it actually contains now (in other words, its length). When the buffer has reached its capacity, adding another element to the vector entails allocating a larger buffer, copying the present contents into it, updating the vector's pointer and capacity to describe the new buffer, and finally freeing the old one.

If you know the number of elements a vector will need in advance, instead of `Vec::new` you can call `Vec::with_capacity` to create a vector with a buffer large enough to hold them all, right from the start; then, you can add the elements to the vector one at a time without causing any reallocation. The `vec!` macro uses a trick like this, since it knows how many elements the final vector will have. Note that this only establishes the vector's initial size; if you exceed your estimate, the vector simply enlarges its storage as usual.

Many library functions look for the opportunity to use `Vec::with_capacity` instead of `Vec::new`. For example, in the `collect` example, the iterator `0..5` knows in advance that it will yield five values, and the `collect` function takes advantage of this to pre-allocate the vector it returns with the correct capacity. We'll see how this works in Chapter 15.

Just as a vector's `len` method returns the number of elements it contains now, its `capacity` method returns the number of elements it could hold without reallocation:

```
let mut v = Vec::with_capacity(2);
assert_eq!(v.len(), 0);
assert_eq!(v.capacity(), 2);

v.push(1);
v.push(2);
assert_eq!(v.len(), 2);
assert_eq!(v.capacity(), 2);

v.push(3);
assert_eq!(v.len(), 3);
// Typically prints "capacity is now 4":
println!("capacity is now {}", v.capacity());
```

The capacity printed at the end isn't guaranteed to be exactly 4, but it will be at least 3, since the vector is holding three values.

You can insert and remove elements wherever you like in a vector, although these operations shift all the elements after the affected position forward or backward, so they may be slow if the vector is long:

```
let mut v = vec![10, 20, 30, 40, 50];

// Make the element at index 3 be 35.
v.insert(3, 35);
assert_eq!(v, [10, 20, 30, 35, 40, 50]);

// Remove the element at index 1.
v.remove(1);
assert_eq!(v, [10, 30, 35, 40, 50]);
```

You can use the `pop` method to remove the last element and return it. More precisely, popping a value from a `Vec<T>` returns an `Option<T>`: `None` if the vector was already empty, or `Some(v)` if its last element had been `v`:

```
let mut v = vec!["Snow Puff", "Glass Gem"];
assert_eq!(v.pop(), Some("Glass Gem"));
assert_eq!(v.pop(), Some("Snow Puff"));
assert_eq!(v.pop(), None);
```

You can use a `for` loop to iterate over a vector:

```
// Get our command-line arguments as a vector of Strings.
let languages: Vec<String> = std::env::args().skip(1).collect();
for l in languages {
    println!("{}: {}", l,
             if l.len() % 2 == 0 {
                 "functional"
             } else {
                 "imperative"
             });
}
```

Running this program with a list of programming languages is illuminating:

```
$ cargo run Lisp Scheme C C++ Fortran
   Compiling proglangs v0.1.0 (/home/jimb/rust/proglangs)
    Finished dev [unoptimized + debuginfo] target(s) in 0.36s
     Running `target/debug/proglangs Lisp Scheme C C++ Fortran`
Lisp: functional
Scheme: functional
C: imperative
C++: imperative
Fortran: imperative
$
```

Finally, a satisfying definition for the term *functional language*.

Despite its fundamental role, `Vec` is an ordinary type defined in Rust, not built into the language. We'll cover the techniques needed to implement such types in Chapter 22.

Slices

A slice, written `[T]` without specifying the length, is a region of an array or vector. Since a slice can be any length, slices can't be stored directly in variables or passed as function arguments. Slices are always passed by reference.

A reference to a slice is a *fat pointer*: a two-word value comprising a pointer to the slice's first element, and the number of elements in the slice.

Suppose you run the following code:

```
let v: Vec<f64> = vec![0.0,  0.707,  1.0,  0.707];
let a: [f64; 4] =     [0.0, -0.707, -1.0, -0.707];

let sv: &[f64] = &v;
let sa: &[f64] = &a;
```

In the last two lines, Rust automatically converts the `&Vec<f64>` reference and the `&[f64; 4]` reference to slice references that point directly to the data.

By the end, memory looks like Figure 3-2.

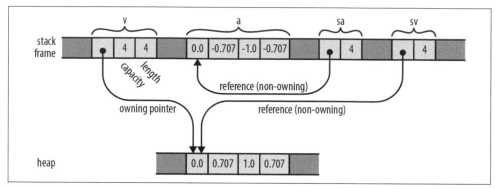

Figure 3-2. A vector v and an array a in memory, with slices sa and sv referring to each

Whereas an ordinary reference is a non-owning pointer to a single value, a reference to a slice is a non-owning pointer to a range of consecutive values in memory. This makes slice references a good choice when you want to write a function that operates on either an array or a vector. For example, here's a function that prints a slice of numbers, one per line:

```
fn print(n: &[f64]) {
    for elt in n {
        println!("{}", elt);
    }
}

print(&a);  // works on arrays
print(&v);  // works on vectors
```

Because this function takes a slice reference as an argument, you can apply it to either a vector or an array, as shown. In fact, many methods you might think of as belonging to vectors or arrays are methods defined on slices: for example, the sort and reverse methods, which sort or reverse a sequence of elements in place, are actually methods on the slice type [T].

You can get a reference to a slice of an array or vector, or a slice of an existing slice, by indexing it with a range:

```
print(&v[0..2]);   // print the first two elements of v
print(&a[2..]);    // print elements of a starting with a[2]
print(&sv[1..3]);  // print v[1] and v[2]
```

As with ordinary array accesses, Rust checks that the indices are valid. Trying to borrow a slice that extends past the end of the data results in a panic.

Since slices almost always appear behind references, we often just refer to types like &[T] or &str as "slices," using the shorter name for the more common concept.

String Types

Programmers familiar with C++ will recall that there are two string types in the language. String literals have the pointer type `const char *`. The standard library also offers a class, `std::string`, for dynamically creating strings at run time.

Rust has a similar design. In this section, we'll show all the ways to write string literals and then introduce Rust's two string types. We provide more detail about strings and text handling in Chapter 17.

String Literals

String literals are enclosed in double quotes. They use the same backslash escape sequences as `char` literals:

```
let speech = "\"Ouch!\" said the well.\n";
```

In string literals, unlike `char` literals, single quotes don't need a backslash escape, and double quotes do.

A string may span multiple lines:

```
println!("In the room the women come and go,
    Singing of Mount Abora");
```

The newline character in that string literal is included in the string and therefore in the output. So are the spaces at the beginning of the second line.

If one line of a string ends with a backslash, then the newline character and the leading whitespace on the next line are dropped:

```
println!("It was a bright, cold day in April, and \
    there were four of us—\
    more or less.");
```

This prints a single line of text. The string contains a single space between "and" and "there" because there is a space before the backslash in the program, and no space between the em dash and "more."

In a few cases, the need to double every backslash in a string is a nuisance. (The classic examples are regular expressions and Windows paths.) For these cases, Rust offers *raw strings*. A raw string is tagged with the lowercase letter r. All backslashes and whitespace characters inside a raw string are included verbatim in the string. No escape sequences are recognized:

```
let default_win_install_path = r"C:\Program Files\Gorillas";

let pattern = Regex::new(r"\d+(\.\d+)*");
```

You can't include a double-quote character in a raw string simply by putting a back-slash in front of it—remember, we said *no* escape sequences are recognized. However, there is a cure for that too. The start and end of a raw string can be marked with pound signs:

```
println!(r###"
    This raw string started with 'r###"'.
    Therefore it does not end until we reach a quote mark ('"')
    followed immediately by three pound signs ('###'):
"###);
```

You can add as few or as many pound signs as needed to make it clear where the raw string ends.

Byte Strings

A string literal with the b prefix is a *byte string*. Such a string is a slice of u8 values—that is, bytes—rather than Unicode text:

```
let method = b"GET";
assert_eq!(method, &[b'G', b'E', b'T']);
```

The type of method is &[u8; 3]: it's a reference to an array of three bytes. It doesn't have any of the string methods we'll discuss in a minute. The most string-like thing about it is the syntax we used to write it.

Byte strings can use all the other string syntax we've shown: they can span multiple lines, use escape sequences, and use backslashes to join lines. Raw byte strings start with br".

Byte strings can't contain arbitrary Unicode characters. They must make do with ASCII and \xHH escape sequences.

Strings in Memory

Rust strings are sequences of Unicode characters, but they are not stored in memory as arrays of chars. Instead, they are stored using UTF-8, a variable-width encoding. Each ASCII character in a string is stored in one byte. Other characters take up multiple bytes.

Figure 3-3 shows the String and &str values created by the following code:

```
let noodles = "noodles".to_string();
let oodles = &noodles[1..];
let poodles = "ಠ_ಠ";
```

A String has a resizable buffer holding UTF-8 text. The buffer is allocated on the heap, so it can resize its buffer as needed or requested. In the example, noodles is a String that owns an eight-byte buffer, of which seven are in use. You can think of a

`String` as a `Vec<u8>` that is guaranteed to hold well-formed UTF-8; in fact, this is how `String` is implemented.

A `&str` (pronounced "stir" or "string slice") is a reference to a run of UTF-8 text owned by someone else: it "borrows" the text. In the example, `oodles` is a `&str` referring to the last six bytes of the text belonging to `noodles`, so it represents the text "oodles." Like other slice references, a `&str` is a fat pointer, containing both the address of the actual data and its length. You can think of a `&str` as being nothing more than a `&[u8]` that is guaranteed to hold well-formed UTF-8.

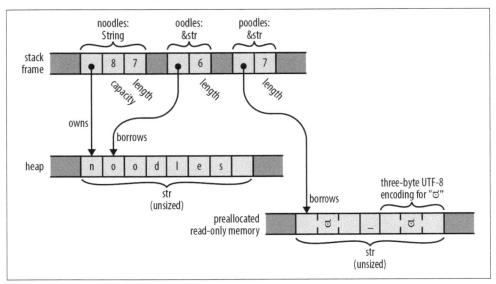

Figure 3-3. `String`, `&str`, and `str`

A string literal is a `&str` that refers to preallocated text, typically stored in read-only memory along with the program's machine code. In the preceding example, `poodles` is a string literal, pointing to seven bytes that are created when the program begins execution and that last until it exits.

A `String` or `&str`'s `.len()` method returns its length. The length is measured in bytes, not characters:

```
assert_eq!("ಠ_ಠ".len(), 7);
assert_eq!("ಠ_ಠ".chars().count(), 3);
```

It is impossible to modify a `&str`:

```
let mut s = "hello";
s[0] = 'c';       // error: `&str` cannot be modified, and other reasons
s.push('\n');     // error: no method named `push` found for reference `&str`
```

For creating new strings at run time, use `String`.

The type &mut str does exist, but it is not very useful, since almost any operation on UTF-8 can change its overall byte length, and a slice cannot reallocate its referent. In fact, the only operations available on &mut str are make_ascii_uppercase and make_ascii_lowercase, which modify the text in place and affect only single-byte characters, by definition.

String

&str is very much like &[T]: a fat pointer to some data. String is analogous to Vec<T>, as described in Table 3-11.

Table 3-11. Vec⟨T⟩ and String comparison

	Vec<T>	String
Automatically frees buffers	Yes	Yes
Growable	Yes	Yes
::new() and ::with_capacity() type-associated functions	Yes	Yes
.reserve() and .capacity() methods	Yes	Yes
.push() and .pop() methods	Yes	Yes
Range syntax v[start..stop]	Yes, returns &[T]	Yes, returns &str
Automatic conversion	&Vec<T> to &[T]	&String to &str
Inherits methods	From &[T]	From &str

Like a Vec, each String has its own heap-allocated buffer that isn't shared with any other String. When a String variable goes out of scope, the buffer is automatically freed, unless the String was moved.

There are several ways to create Strings:

- The .to_string() method converts a &str to a String. This copies the string:

    ```
    let error_message = "too many pets".to_string();
    ```

    The .to_owned() method does the same thing, and you may see it used the same way. It works for some other types as well, as we'll discuss in Chapter 13.

- The format!() macro works just like println!(), except that it returns a new String instead of writing text to stdout, and it doesn't automatically add a newline at the end:

    ```
    assert_eq!(format!("{}°{:02}′{:02}″N", 24, 5, 23),
               "24°05′23″N".to_string());
    ```

- Arrays, slices, and vectors of strings have two methods, .concat() and .join(sep), that form a new String from many strings:

```
let bits = vec!["veni", "vidi", "vici"];
assert_eq!(bits.concat(), "venividivici");
assert_eq!(bits.join(", "), "veni, vidi, vici");
```

The choice sometimes arises of which type to use: &str or String. Chapter 5 addresses this question in detail. For now it will suffice to point out that a &str can refer to any slice of any string, whether it is a string literal (stored in the executable) or a String (allocated and freed at run time). This means that &str is more appropriate for function arguments when the caller should be allowed to pass either kind of string.

Using Strings

Strings support the == and != operators. Two strings are equal if they contain the same characters in the same order (regardless of whether they point to the same location in memory):

```
assert!("ONE".to_lowercase() == "one");
```

Strings also support the comparison operators <, <=, >, and >=, as well as many useful methods and functions that you can find in the online documentation under "str (primitive type)" or the "std::str" module (or just flip to Chapter 17). Here are a few examples:

```
assert!("peanut".contains("nut"));
assert_eq!("ʊ_ʊ".replace("ʊ", "■"), "■_■");
assert_eq!("   clean\n".trim(), "clean");

for word in "veni, vidi, vici".split(", ") {
    assert!(word.starts_with("v"));
}
```

Keep in mind that, given the nature of Unicode, simple char-by-char comparison does *not* always give the expected answers. For example, the Rust strings "th\u{e9}" and "the\u{301}" are both valid Unicode representations for *thé*, the French word for tea. Unicode says they should both be displayed and processed in the same way, but Rust treats them as two completely distinct strings. Similarly, Rust's ordering operators like < use a simple lexicographical order based on character code point values. This ordering only sometimes resembles the ordering used for text in the user's language and culture. We discuss these issues in more detail in Chapter 17.

Other String-Like Types

Rust guarantees that strings are valid UTF-8. Sometimes a program really needs to be able to deal with strings that are *not* valid Unicode. This usually happens when a Rust program has to interoperate with some other system that doesn't enforce any such rules. For example, in most operating systems it's easy to create a file with a filename that isn't valid Unicode. What should happen when a Rust program comes across this sort of filename?

Rust's solution is to offer a few string-like types for these situations:

- Stick to `String` and `&str` for Unicode text.
- When working with filenames, use `std::path::PathBuf` and `&Path` instead.
- When working with binary data that isn't UTF-8 encoded at all, use `Vec<u8>` and `&[u8]`.
- When working with environment variable names and command-line arguments in the native form presented by the operating system, use `OsString` and `&OsStr`.
- When interoperating with C libraries that use null-terminated strings, use `std::ffi::CString` and `&CStr`.

Type Aliases

The `type` keyword can be used like `typedef` in C++ to declare a new name for an existing type:

```
type Bytes = Vec<u8>;
```

The type `Bytes` that we're declaring here is shorthand for this particular kind of `Vec`:

```
fn decode(data: &Bytes) {
    ...
}
```

Beyond the Basics

Types are a central part of Rust. We'll continue talking about types and introducing new ones throughout the book. In particular, Rust's user-defined types give the language much of its flavor, because that's where methods are defined. There are three kinds of user-defined types, and we'll cover them in three successive chapters: structs in Chapter 9, enums in Chapter 10, and traits in Chapter 11.

Functions and closures have their own types, covered in Chapter 14. And the types that make up the standard library are covered throughout the book. For example, Chapter 16 presents the standard collection types.

All of that will have to wait, though. Before we move on, it's time to tackle the concepts that are at the heart of Rust's safety rules.

## CHAPTER 4

Ownership and Moves

When it comes to managing memory, there are two characteristics we'd like from our programing languages:

- We'd like memory to be freed promptly, at a time of our choosing. This gives us control over the program's memory consumption.

- We never want to use a pointer to an object after it's been freed. This would be undefined behavior, leading to crashes and security holes.

But these seem to be mutually exclusive: freeing a value while pointers exist to it necessarily leaves those pointers dangling. Almost all major programming languages fall into one of two camps, depending on which of the two qualities they give up on:

- The "Safety First" camp uses garbage collection to manage memory, automatically freeing objects when all reachable pointers to them are gone. This eliminates dangling pointers by simply keeping the objects around until there are no pointers to them left to dangle. Almost all modern languages fall in this camp, from Python, JavaScript, and Ruby to Java, C#, and Haskell.

  But relying on garbage collection means relinquishing control over exactly when objects get freed to the collector. In general, garbage collectors are surprising beasts, and understanding why memory wasn't freed when you expected can be a challenge.

- The "Control First" camp leaves you in charge of freeing memory. Your program's memory consumption is entirely in your hands, but avoiding dangling pointers also becomes entirely your concern. C and C++ are the only mainstream languages in this camp.

This is great if you never make mistakes, but evidence suggests that eventually you will. Pointer misuse has been a common culprit in reported security problems for as long as that data has been collected.

Rust aims to be both safe and performant, so neither of these compromises is acceptable. But if reconciliation were easy, someone would have done it long before now. Something fundamental needs to change.

Rust breaks the deadlock in a surprising way: by restricting how your programs can use pointers. This chapter and the next are devoted to explaining exactly what these restrictions are and why they work. For now, suffice it to say that some common structures you are accustomed to using may not fit within the rules, and you'll need to look for alternatives. But the net effect of these restrictions is to bring just enough order to the chaos to allow Rust's compile-time checks to verify that your program is free of memory safety errors: dangling pointers, double frees, using uninitialized memory, and so on. At run time, your pointers are simple addresses in memory, just as they would be in C and C++. The difference is that your code has been proven to use them safely.

These same rules also form the basis of Rust's support for safe concurrent programming. Using Rust's carefully designed threading primitives, the rules that ensure your code uses memory correctly also serve to prove that it is free of data races. A bug in a Rust program cannot cause one thread to corrupt another's data, introducing hard-to-reproduce failures in unrelated parts of the system. The nondeterministic behavior inherent in multithreaded code is isolated to those features designed to handle it—mutexes, message channels, atomic values, and so on—rather than appearing in ordinary memory references. Multithreaded code in C and C++ has earned its ugly reputation, but Rust rehabilitates it quite nicely.

Rust's radical wager, the claim on which it stakes its success and that forms the root of the language, is that even with these restrictions in place, you'll find the language more than flexible enough for almost every task and that the benefits—the elimination of broad classes of memory management and concurrency bugs—will justify the adaptations you'll need to make to your style. The authors of this book are bullish on Rust exactly because of our extensive experience with C and C++. For us, Rust's deal is a no-brainer.

Rust's rules are probably unlike what you've seen in other programming languages. Learning how to work with them and turn them to your advantage is, in our opinion, the central challenge of learning Rust. In this chapter, we'll first provide insight into the logic and intent behind Rust's rules by showing how the same underlying issues play out in other languages. Then, we'll explain Rust's rules in detail, looking at what ownership means at a conceptual and mechanical level, how changes in ownership are tracked in various scenarios, and types that bend or break some of these rules in order to provide more flexibility.

Ownership

If you've read much C or C++ code, you've probably come across a comment saying that an instance of some class *owns* some other object that it points to. This generally means that the owning object gets to decide when to free the owned object: when the owner is destroyed, it destroys its possessions along with it.

For example, suppose you write the following C++ code:

```
std::string s = "frayed knot";
```

The string s is usually represented in memory as shown in Figure 4-1.

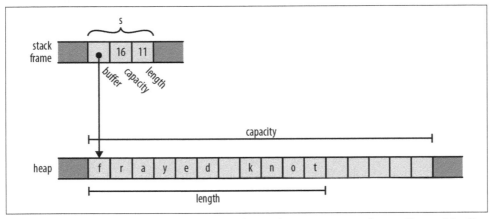

Figure 4-1. A C++ `std::string` value on the stack, pointing to its heap-allocated buffer

Here, the actual `std::string` object itself is always exactly three words long, comprising a pointer to a heap-allocated buffer, the buffer's overall capacity (that is, how large the text can grow before the string must allocate a larger buffer to hold it), and the length of the text it holds now. These are fields private to the `std::string` class, not accessible to the string's users.

A `std::string` owns its buffer: when the program destroys the string, the string's destructor frees the buffer. In the past, some C++ libraries shared a single buffer among several `std::string` values, using a reference count to decide when the buffer should be freed. Newer versions of the C++ specification effectively preclude that representation; all modern C++ libraries use the approach shown here.

In these situations it's generally understood that although it's fine for other code to create temporary pointers to the owned memory, it is that code's responsibility to make sure its pointers are gone before the owner decides to destroy the owned object. You can create a pointer to a character living in a `std::string`'s buffer, but when the string is destroyed, your pointer becomes invalid, and it's up to you to make sure you don't use it anymore. The owner determines the lifetime of the owned, and everyone else must respect its decisions.

We've used `std::string` here as an example of what ownership looks like in C++: it's just a convention that the standard library generally follows, and although the language encourages you to follow similar practices, how you design your own types is ultimately up to you.

In Rust, however, the concept of ownership is built into the language itself and enforced by compile-time checks. Every value has a single owner that determines its lifetime. When the owner is freed—*dropped*, in Rust terminology—the owned value is dropped too. These rules are meant to make it easy for you to find any given value's lifetime simply by inspecting the code, giving you the control over its lifetime that a systems language should provide.

A variable owns its value. When control leaves the block in which the variable is declared, the variable is dropped, so its value is dropped along with it. For example:

```
fn print_padovan() {
    let mut padovan = vec![1,1,1];  // allocated here
    for i in 3..10 {
        let next = padovan[i-3] + padovan[i-2];
        padovan.push(next);
    }
    println!("P(1..10) = {:?}", padovan);
}                                   // dropped here
```

The type of the variable `padovan` is `Vec<i32>`, a vector of 32-bit integers. In memory, the final value of `padovan` will look something like Figure 4-2.

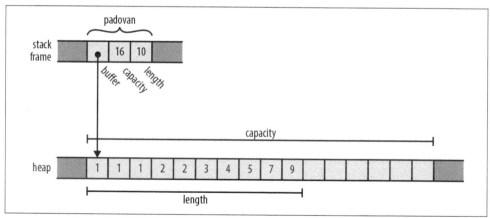

Figure 4-2. A Vec<i32> on the stack, pointing to its buffer in the heap

This is very similar to the C++ `std::string` we showed earlier, except that the elements in the buffer are 32-bit values, not characters. Note that the words holding padovan's pointer, capacity, and length live directly in the stack frame of the print_padovan function; only the vector's buffer is allocated on the heap.

As with the string s earlier, the vector owns the buffer holding its elements. When the variable padovan goes out of scope at the end of the function, the program drops the vector. And since the vector owns its buffer, the buffer goes with it.

Rust's Box type serves as another example of ownership. A Box<T> is a pointer to a value of type T stored on the heap. Calling Box::new(v) allocates some heap space, moves the value v into it, and returns a Box pointing to the heap space. Since a Box owns the space it points to, when the Box is dropped, it frees the space too.

For example, you can allocate a tuple in the heap like so:

```
{
    let point = Box::new((0.625, 0.5));  // point allocated here
    let label = format!("{:?}", point);  // label allocated here
    assert_eq!(label, "(0.625, 0.5)");
}                                        // both dropped here
```

When the program calls Box::new, it allocates space for a tuple of two f64 values on the heap, moves its argument (0.625, 0.5) into that space, and returns a pointer to it. By the time control reaches the call to assert_eq!, the stack frame looks like Figure 4-3.

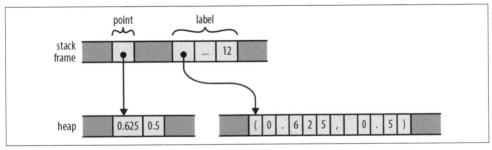

Figure 4-3. Two local variables, each owning memory in the heap

The stack frame itself holds the variables point and label, each of which refers to a heap allocation that it owns. When they are dropped, the allocations they own are freed along with them.

Just as variables own their values, structs own their fields, and tuples, arrays, and vectors own their elements:

```
struct Person { name: String, birth: i32 }

let mut composers = Vec::new();
composers.push(Person { name: "Palestrina".to_string(),
                        birth: 1525 });
composers.push(Person { name: "Dowland".to_string(),
```

```
                            birth: 1563 });
    composers.push(Person { name: "Lully".to_string(),
                            birth: 1632 });
    for composer in &composers {
        println!("{}, born {}", composer.name, composer.birth);
    }
```

Here, `composers` is a `Vec<Person>`, a vector of structs, each of which holds a string
and a number. In memory, the final value of `composers` looks like Figure 4-4.

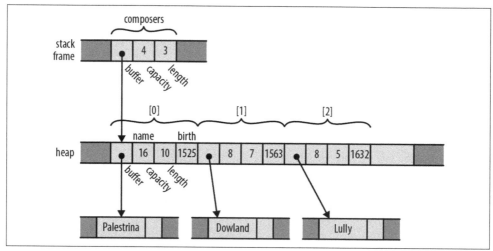

Figure 4-4. A more complex tree of ownership

There are many ownership relationships here, but each one is pretty straightforward:
`composers` owns a vector; the vector owns its elements, each of which is a `Person`
structure; each structure owns its fields; and the string field owns its text. When control leaves the scope in which `composers` is declared, the program drops its value and
takes the entire arrangement with it. If there were other sorts of collections in the picture—a `HashMap`, perhaps, or a `BTreeSet`—the story would be the same.

At this point, take a step back and consider the consequences of the ownership relations we've presented so far. Every value has a single owner, making it easy to decide
when to drop it. But a single value may own many other values: for example, the vector `composers` owns all of its elements. And those values may own other values in
turn: each element of `composers` owns a string, which owns its text.

It follows that the owners and their owned values form *trees*: your owner is your parent, and the values you own are your children. And at the ultimate root of each tree is
a variable; when that variable goes out of scope, the entire tree goes with it. We can
see such an ownership tree in the diagram for `composers`: it's not a "tree" in the sense
of a search tree data structure, or an HTML document made from DOM elements.
Rather, we have a tree built from a mixture of types, with Rust's single-owner rule

forbidding any rejoining of structure that could make the arrangement more complex than a tree. Every value in a Rust program is a member of some tree, rooted in some variable.

Rust programs don't usually explicitly drop values at all, in the way C and C++ programs would use `free` and `delete`. The way to drop a value in Rust is to remove it from the ownership tree somehow: by leaving the scope of a variable, or deleting an element from a vector, or something of that sort. At that point, Rust ensures the value is properly dropped, along with everything it owns.

In a certain sense, Rust is less powerful than other languages: every other practical programming language lets you build arbitrary graphs of objects that point to each other in whatever way you see fit. But it is exactly because Rust is less powerful that the analyses the language can carry out on your programs can be more powerful. Rust's safety guarantees are possible exactly because the relationships it may encounter in your code are more tractable. This is part of Rust's "radical wager" we mentioned earlier: in practice, Rust claims, there is usually more than enough flexibility in how one goes about solving a problem to ensure that at least a few perfectly fine solutions fall within the restrictions the language imposes.

That said, the concept of ownership as we've explained it so far is still much too rigid to be useful. Rust extends this simple idea in several ways:

- You can move values from one owner to another. This allows you to build, rearrange, and tear down the tree.
- Very simple types like integers, floating-point numbers, and characters are excused from the ownership rules. These are called `Copy` types.
- The standard library provides the reference-counted pointer types `Rc` and `Arc`, which allow values to have multiple owners, under some restrictions.
- You can "borrow a reference" to a value; references are non-owning pointers, with limited lifetimes.

Each of these strategies contributes flexibility to the ownership model, while still upholding Rust's promises. We'll explain each one in turn, with references covered in the next chapter.

Moves

In Rust, for most types, operations like assigning a value to a variable, passing it to a function, or returning it from a function don't copy the value: they *move* it. The source relinquishes ownership of the value to the destination and becomes uninitialized; the destination now controls the value's lifetime. Rust programs build up and tear down complex structures one value at a time, one move at a time.

You may be surprised that Rust would change the meaning of such fundamental operations; surely assignment is something that should be pretty well nailed down at this point in history. However, if you look closely at how different languages have chosen to handle assignment, you'll see that there's actually significant variation from one school to another. The comparison also makes the meaning and consequences of Rust's choice easier to see.

Consider the following Python code:

```python
s = ['udon', 'ramen', 'soba']
t = s
u = s
```

Each Python object carries a reference count, tracking the number of values that are currently referring to it. So after the assignment to s, the state of the program looks like Figure 4-5 (note that some fields are left out).

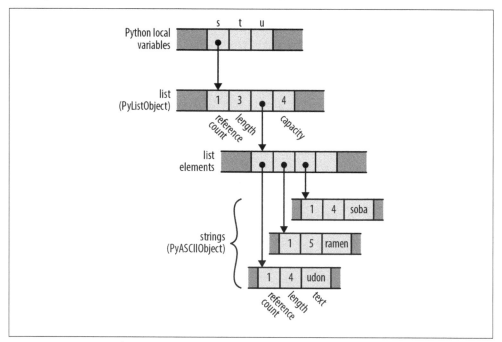

Figure 4-5. How Python represents a list of strings in memory

Since only s is pointing to the list, the list's reference count is 1; and since the list is the only object pointing to the strings, each of their reference counts is also 1.

What happens when the program executes the assignments to t and u? Python implements assignment simply by making the destination point to the same object as the
source, and incrementing the object's reference count. So the final state of the program is something like Figure 4-6.

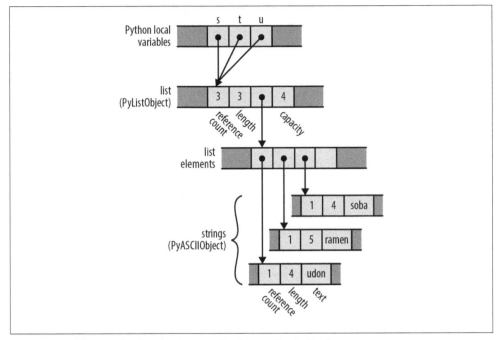

Figure 4-6. The result of assigning s to both t and u in Python

Python has copied the pointer from s into t and u and updated the list's reference
count to 3. Assignment in Python is cheap, but because it creates a new reference to
the object, we must maintain reference counts to know when we can free the value.

Now consider the analogous C++ code:

```
using namespace std;
vector<string> s = { "udon", "ramen", "soba" };
vector<string> t = s;
vector<string> u = s;
```

The original value of s looks like Figure 4-7 in memory.

What happens when the program assigns s to t and u? Assigning a `std::vector` produces a copy of the vector in C++; `std::string` behaves similarly. So by the time the
program reaches the end of this code, it has actually allocated three vectors and nine
strings (Figure 4-8).

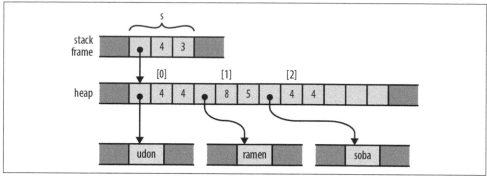

Figure 4-7. How C++ represents a vector of strings in memory

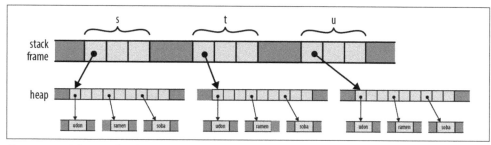

Figure 4-8. The result of assigning s to both t and u in C++

Depending on the values involved, assignment in C++ can consume unbounded amounts of memory and processor time. The advantage, however, is that it's easy for the program to decide when to free all this memory: when the variables go out of scope, everything allocated here gets cleaned up automatically.

In a sense, C++ and Python have chosen opposite trade-offs: Python makes assignment cheap, at the expense of requiring reference counting (and in the general case, garbage collection). C++ keeps the ownership of all the memory clear, at the expense of making assignment carry out a deep copy of the object. C++ programmers are often less than enthusiastic about this choice: deep copies can be expensive, and there are usually more practical alternatives.

So what would the analogous program do in Rust? Here's the code:

```
let s = vec!["udon".to_string(), "ramen".to_string(), "soba".to_string()];
let t = s;
let u = s;
```

Like C and C++, Rust puts plain string literals like "udon" in read-only memory, so for a clearer comparison with the C++ and Python examples, we call to_string here to get heap-allocated String values.

After carrying out the initialization of s, since Rust and C++ use similar representations for vectors and strings, the situation looks just as it did in C++ (Figure 4-9).

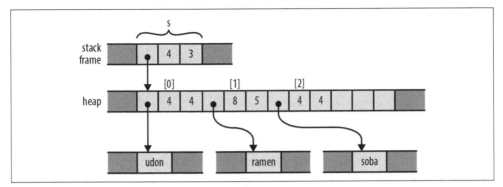

Figure 4-9. How Rust represents a vector of strings in memory

But recall that, in Rust, assignments of most types *move* the value from the source to the destination, leaving the source uninitialized. So after initializing t, the program's memory looks like Figure 4-10.

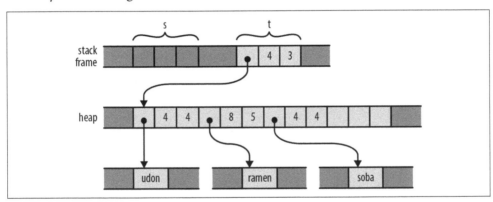

Figure 4-10. The result of assigning s to t in Rust

What has happened here? The initialization let t = s; moved the vector's three header fields from s to t; now t owns the vector. The vector's elements stayed just where they were, and nothing happened to the strings either. Every value still has a single owner, although one has changed hands. There were no reference counts to be adjusted. And the compiler now considers s uninitialized.

So what happens when we reach the initialization let u = s;? This would assign the uninitialized value s to u. Rust prudently prohibits using uninitialized values, so the compiler rejects this code with the following error:

```
error: use of moved value: `s`
  |
7 |      let s = vec!["udon".to_string(), "ramen".to_string(), "soba".to_string()];
  |          - move occurs because `s` has type `Vec<String>`,
  |            which does not implement the `Copy` trait
8 |      let t = s;
  |              - value moved here
9 |      let u = s;
  |              ^ value used here after move
```

Consider the consequences of Rust's use of a move here. Like Python, the assignment is cheap: the program simply moves the three-word header of the vector from one spot to another. But like C++, ownership is always clear: the program doesn't need reference counting or garbage collection to know when to free the vector elements and string contents.

The price you pay is that you must explicitly ask for copies when you want them. If you want to end up in the same state as the C++ program, with each variable holding an independent copy of the structure, you must call the vector's clone method, which performs a deep copy of the vector and its elements:

```
let s = vec!["udon".to_string(), "ramen".to_string(), "soba".to_string()];
let t = s.clone();
let u = s.clone();
```

You could also re-create Python's behavior by using Rust's reference-counted pointer types; we'll discuss those shortly in "Rc and Arc: Shared Ownership" on page 97.

More Operations That Move

In the examples thus far, we've shown initializations, providing values for variables as they come into scope in a let statement. Assigning to a variable is slightly different, in that if you move a value into a variable that was already initialized, Rust drops the variable's prior value. For example:

```
let mut s = "Govinda".to_string();
s = "Siddhartha".to_string(); // value "Govinda" dropped here
```

In this code, when the program assigns the string "Siddhartha" to s, its prior value "Govinda" gets dropped first. But consider the following:

```
let mut s = "Govinda".to_string();
let t = s;
s = "Siddhartha".to_string(); // nothing is dropped here
```

This time, t has taken ownership of the original string from s, so that by the time we assign to s, it is uninitialized. In this scenario, no string is dropped.

We've used initializations and assignments in the examples here because they're simple, but Rust applies move semantics to almost any use of a value. Passing arguments to functions moves ownership to the function's parameters; returning a value from a function moves ownership to the caller. Building a tuple moves the values into the tuple. And so on.

You may now have better insight into what's really going on in the examples we offered in the previous section. For example, when we were constructing our vector of composers, we wrote:

```
struct Person { name: String, birth: i32 }

let mut composers = Vec::new();
composers.push(Person { name: "Palestrina".to_string(),
                        birth: 1525 });
```

This code shows several places at which moves occur, beyond initialization and assignment:

Returning values from a function
> The call `Vec::new()` constructs a new vector and returns, not a pointer to the vector, but the vector itself: its ownership moves from `Vec::new` to the variable `composers`. Similarly, the `to_string` call returns a fresh `String` instance.

Constructing new values
> The `name` field of the new `Person` structure is initialized with the return value of `to_string`. The structure takes ownership of the string.

Passing values to a function
> The entire `Person` structure, not a pointer to it, is passed to the vector's `push` method, which moves it onto the end of the structure. The vector takes ownership of the `Person` and thus becomes the indirect owner of the name `String` as well.

Moving values around like this may sound inefficient, but there are two things to keep in mind. First, the moves always apply to the value proper, not the heap storage they own. For vectors and strings, the *value proper* is the three-word header alone; the potentially large element arrays and text buffers sit where they are in the heap. Second, the Rust compiler's code generation is good at "seeing through" all these moves; in practice, the machine code often stores the value directly where it belongs.

Moves and Control Flow

The previous examples all have very simple control flow; how do moves interact with more complicated code? The general principle is that, if it's possible for a variable to have had its value moved away and it hasn't definitely been given a new value since, it's considered uninitialized. For example, if a variable still has a value after evaluating an `if` expression's condition, then we can use it in both branches:

```
let x = vec![10, 20, 30];
if c {
    f(x); // ... ok to move from x here
} else {
    g(x); // ... and ok to also move from x here
}
h(x); // bad: x is uninitialized here if either path uses it
```

For similar reasons, moving from a variable in a loop is forbidden:

```
let x = vec![10, 20, 30];
while f() {
    g(x); // bad: x would be moved in first iteration,
          // uninitialized in second
}
```

That is, unless we've definitely given it a new value by the next iteration:

```
let mut x = vec![10, 20, 30];
while f() {
    g(x);           // move from x
    x = h();        // give x a fresh value
}
e(x);
```

Moves and Indexed Content

We've mentioned that a move leaves its source uninitialized, as the destination takes ownership of the value. But not every kind of value owner is prepared to become uninitialized. For example, consider the following code:

```
// Build a vector of the strings "101", "102", ... "105"
let mut v = Vec::new();
for i in 101 .. 106 {
    v.push(i.to_string());
}

// Pull out random elements from the vector.
let third = v[2]; // error: Cannot move out of index of Vec
let fifth = v[4]; // here too
```

For this to work, Rust would somehow need to remember that the third and fifth elements of the vector have become uninitialized, and track that information until the vector is dropped. In the most general case, vectors would need to carry around extra information with them to indicate which elements are live and which have become uninitialized. That is clearly not the right behavior for a systems programming language; a vector should be nothing but a vector. In fact, Rust rejects the preceding code with the following error:

```
error: cannot move out of index of `Vec<String>`
   |
14 |     let third = v[2];
   |                 ^^^^
   |                 |
   |                 move occurs because value has type `String`,
   |                 which does not implement the `Copy` trait
   |                 help: consider borrowing here: `&v[2]`
```

It also makes a similar complaint about the move to fifth. In the error message, Rust suggests using a reference, in case you want to access the element without moving it. This is often what you want. But what if you really do want to move an element out of a vector? You need to find a method that does so in a way that respects the limitations of the type. Here are three possibilities:

```
// Build a vector of the strings "101", "102", ... "105"
let mut v = Vec::new();
for i in 101 .. 106 {
    v.push(i.to_string());
}

// 1. Pop a value off the end of the vector:
let fifth = v.pop().expect("vector empty!");
assert_eq!(fifth, "105");

// 2. Move a value out of a given index in the vector,
// and move the last element into its spot:
let second = v.swap_remove(1);
assert_eq!(second, "102");

// 3. Swap in another value for the one we're taking out:
let third = std::mem::replace(&mut v[2], "substitute".to_string());
assert_eq!(third, "103");

// Let's see what's left of our vector.
assert_eq!(v, vec!["101", "104", "substitute"]);
```

Each one of these methods moves an element out of the vector, but does so in a way that leaves the vector in a state that is fully populated, if perhaps smaller.

Collection types like Vec also generally offer methods to consume all their elements in a loop:

```
let v = vec!["liberté".to_string(),
             "égalité".to_string(),
             "fraternité".to_string()];

for mut s in v {
    s.push('!');
    println!("{}", s);
}
```

When we pass the vector to the loop directly, as in for ... in v, this *moves* the vector out of v, leaving v uninitialized. The for loop's internal machinery takes ownership of the vector and dissects it into its elements. At each iteration, the loop moves another element to the variable s. Since s now owns the string, we're able to modify it in the loop body before printing it. And since the vector itself is no longer visible to the code, nothing can observe it mid-loop in some partially emptied state.

If you do find yourself needing to move a value out of an owner that the compiler can't track, you might consider changing the owner's type to something that can dynamically track whether it has a value or not. For example, here's a variant on the earlier example:

```
struct Person { name: Option<String>, birth: i32 }

let mut composers = Vec::new();
composers.push(Person { name: Some("Palestrina".to_string()),
                        birth: 1525 });
```

You can't do this:

```
let first_name = composers[0].name;
```

That will just elicit the same "cannot move out of index" error shown earlier. But because you've changed the type of the name field from String to Option<String>, that means that None is a legitimate value for the field to hold, so this works:

```
let first_name = std::mem::replace(&mut composers[0].name, None);
assert_eq!(first_name, Some("Palestrina".to_string()));
assert_eq!(composers[0].name, None);
```

The replace call moves out the value of composers[0].name, leaving None in its place, and passes ownership of the original value to its caller. In fact, using Option this way is common enough that the type provides a take method for this very purpose. You could write the preceding manipulation more legibly as follows:

```
let first_name = composers[0].name.take();
```

This call to take has the same effect as the earlier call to replace.

Copy Types: The Exception to Moves

The examples we've shown so far of values being moved involve vectors, strings, and other types that could potentially use a lot of memory and be expensive to copy. Moves keep ownership of such types clear and assignment cheap. But for simpler types like integers or characters, this sort of careful handling really isn't necessary.

Compare what happens in memory when we assign a `String` with what happens when we assign an `i32` value:

```
let string1 = "somnambulance".to_string();
let string2 = string1;

let num1: i32 = 36;
let num2 = num1;
```

After running this code, memory looks like Figure 4-11.

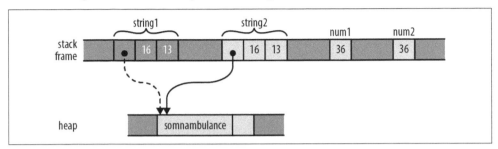

Figure 4-11. Assigning a `String` moves the value, whereas assigning an `i32` copies it

As with the vectors earlier, assignment *moves* string1 to string2 so that we don't end up with two strings responsible for freeing the same buffer. However, the situation with num1 and num2 is different. An i32 is simply a pattern of bits in memory; it doesn't own any heap resources or really depend on anything other than the bytes it comprises. By the time we've moved its bits to num2, we've made a completely independent copy of num1.

Moving a value leaves the source of the move uninitialized. But whereas it serves an essential purpose to treat string1 as valueless, treating num1 that way is pointless; no harm could result from continuing to use it. The advantages of a move don't apply here, and it's inconvenient.

Earlier we were careful to say that *most* types are moved; now we've come to the exceptions, the types Rust designates as *Copy types*. Assigning a value of a Copy type copies the value, rather than moving it. The source of the assignment remains initialized and usable, with the same value it had before. Passing Copy types to functions and constructors behaves similarly.

The standard Copy types include all the machine integer and floating-point numeric types, the char and bool types, and a few others. A tuple or fixed-size array of Copy types is itself a Copy type.

Only types for which a simple bit-for-bit copy suffices can be Copy. As we've already explained, String is not a Copy type, because it owns a heap-allocated buffer. For similar reasons, Box<T> is not Copy; it owns its heap-allocated referent. The File type, representing an operating system file handle, is not Copy; duplicating such a value would entail asking the operating system for another file handle. Similarly, the MutexGuard type, representing a locked mutex, isn't Copy: this type isn't meaningful to copy at all, as only one thread may hold a mutex at a time.

As a rule of thumb, any type that needs to do something special when a value is dropped cannot be Copy: a Vec needs to free its elements, a File needs to close its file handle, a MutexGuard needs to unlock its mutex, and so on. Bit-for-bit duplication of such types would leave it unclear which value was now responsible for the original's resources.

What about types you define yourself? By default, struct and enum types are not Copy:

```
struct Label { number: u32 }

fn print(l: Label) { println!("STAMP: {}", l.number); }

let l = Label { number: 3 };
print(l);
println!("My label number is: {}", l.number);
```

This won't compile; Rust complains:

```
error: borrow of moved value: `l`
   |
10 |     let l = Label { number: 3 };
   |         - move occurs because `l` has type `main::Label`,
   |           which does not implement the `Copy` trait
11 |     print(l);
   |           - value moved here
12 |     println!("My label number is: {}", l.number);
   |                                        ^^^^^^^^
   |                         value borrowed here after move
```

Since Label is not Copy, passing it to print moved ownership of the value to the print function, which then dropped it before returning. But this is silly; a Label is nothing but a u32 with pretensions. There's no reason passing l to print should move the value.

But user-defined types being non-Copy is only the default. If all the fields of your struct are themselves Copy, then you can make the type Copy as well by placing the attribute #[derive(Copy, Clone)] above the definition, like so:

```
#[derive(Copy, Clone)]
struct Label { number: u32 }
```

With this change, the preceding code compiles without complaint. However, if we try this on a type whose fields are not all Copy, it doesn't work. Suppose we compile the following code:

```
#[derive(Copy, Clone)]
struct StringLabel { name: String }
```

It elicits this error:

```
error: the trait `Copy` may not be implemented for this type
  |
7 | #[derive(Copy, Clone)]
  |          ^^^^
8 | struct StringLabel { name: String }
  |                      ----------- this field does not implement `Copy`
```

Why aren't user-defined types automatically Copy, assuming they're eligible? Whether a type is Copy or not has a big effect on how code is allowed to use it: Copy types are more flexible, since assignment and related operations don't leave the original uninitialized. But for a type's implementer, the opposite is true: Copy types are very limited in which types they can contain, whereas non-Copy types can use heap allocation and own other sorts of resources. So making a type Copy represents a serious commitment on the part of the implementer: if it's necessary to change it to non-Copy later, much of the code that uses it will probably need to be adapted.

While C++ lets you overload assignment operators and define specialized copy and move constructors, Rust doesn't permit this sort of customization. In Rust, every move is a byte-for-byte, shallow copy that leaves the source uninitialized. Copies are the same, except that the source remains initialized. This does mean that C++ classes can provide convenient interfaces that Rust types cannot, where ordinary-looking code implicitly adjusts reference counts, puts off expensive copies for later, or uses other sophisticated implementation tricks.

But the effect of this flexibility on C++ as a language is to make basic operations like assignment, passing parameters, and returning values from functions less predictable. For example, earlier in this chapter we showed how assigning one variable to another in C++ can require arbitrary amounts of memory and processor time. One of Rust's principles is that costs should be apparent to the programmer. Basic operations must remain simple. Potentially expensive operations should be explicit, like the calls to clone in the earlier example that make deep copies of vectors and the strings they contain.

In this section, we've talked about Copy and Clone in vague terms as characteristics a type might have. They are actually examples of *traits*, Rust's open-ended facility for categorizing types based on what you can do with them. We describe traits in general in Chapter 11, and Copy and Clone in particular in Chapter 13.

Rc and Arc: Shared Ownership

Although most values have unique owners in typical Rust code, in some cases it's difficult to find every value a single owner that has the lifetime you need; you'd like the value to simply live until everyone's done using it. For these cases, Rust provides the reference-counted pointer types Rc and Arc. As you would expect from Rust, these are entirely safe to use: you cannot forget to adjust the reference count, create other pointers to the referent that Rust doesn't notice, or stumble over any of the other sorts of problems that accompany reference-counted pointer types in C++.

The Rc and Arc types are very similar; the only difference between them is that an Arc is safe to share between threads directly—the name Arc is short for *atomic reference count*—whereas a plain Rc uses faster non-thread-safe code to update its reference count. If you don't need to share the pointers between threads, there's no reason to pay the performance penalty of an Arc, so you should use Rc; Rust will prevent you from accidentally passing one across a thread boundary. The two types are otherwise equivalent, so for the rest of this section, we'll only talk about Rc.

Earlier we showed how Python uses reference counts to manage its values' lifetimes. You can use Rc to get a similar effect in Rust. Consider the following code:

```
use std::rc::Rc;

// Rust can infer all these types; written out for clarity
let s: Rc<String> = Rc::new("shirataki".to_string());
let t: Rc<String> = s.clone();
let u: Rc<String> = s.clone();
```

For any type T, an Rc<T> value is a pointer to a heap-allocated T that has had a reference count affixed to it. Cloning an Rc<T> value does not copy the T; instead, it simply creates another pointer to it and increments the reference count. So the preceding code produces the situation illustrated in Figure 4-12 in memory.

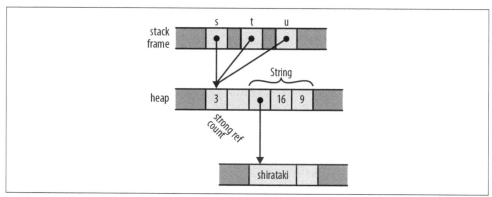

Figure 4-12. A reference-counted string with three references

Each of the three Rc<String> pointers is referring to the same block of memory, which holds a reference count and space for the String. The usual ownership rules apply to the Rc pointers themselves, and when the last extant Rc is dropped, Rust drops the String as well.

You can use any of String's usual methods directly on an Rc<String>:

```
assert!(s.contains("shira"));
assert_eq!(t.find("taki"), Some(5));
println!("{} are quite chewy, almost bouncy, but lack flavor", u);
```

A value owned by an Rc pointer is immutable. Suppose you try to add some text to the end of the string:

```
s.push_str(" noodles");
```

Rust will decline:

```
error: cannot borrow data in an `Rc` as mutable
   |
13 |     s.push_str(" noodles");
   |     ^ cannot borrow as mutable
   |
```

Rust's memory and thread-safety guarantees depend on ensuring that no value is ever simultaneously shared and mutable. Rust assumes the referent of an Rc pointer might in general be shared, so it must not be mutable. We explain why this restriction is important in Chapter 5.

One well-known problem with using reference counts to manage memory is that, if there are ever two reference-counted values that point to each other, each will hold the other's reference count above zero, so the values will never be freed (Figure 4-13).

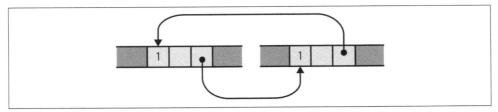

Figure 4-13. A reference-counting loop; these objects will not be freed

It is possible to leak values in Rust this way, but such situations are rare. You cannot create a cycle without, at some point, making an older value point to a newer value. This obviously requires the older value to be mutable. Since Rc pointers hold their referents immutable, it's not normally possible to create a cycle. However, Rust does provide ways to create mutable portions of otherwise immutable values; this is called *interior mutability*, and we cover it in "Interior Mutability" on page 225. If you combine those techniques with Rc pointers, you can create a cycle and leak memory.

You can sometimes avoid creating cycles of Rc pointers by using *weak pointers*, std::rc::Weak, for some of the links instead. However, we won't cover those in this book; see the standard library's documentation for details.

Moves and reference-counted pointers are two ways to relax the rigidity of the ownership tree. In the next chapter, we'll look at a third way: borrowing references to values. Once you have become comfortable with both ownership and borrowing, you will have climbed the steepest part of Rust's learning curve, and you'll be ready to take advantage of Rust's unique strengths.

## CHAPTER 5

References

Libraries cannot provide new inabilities.
—Mark Miller

All the pointer types we've seen so far—the simple `Box<T>` heap pointer, and the pointers internal to `String` and `Vec` values—are owning pointers: when the owner is dropped, the referent goes with it. Rust also has non-owning pointer types called *references*, which have no effect on their referents' lifetimes.

In fact, it's rather the opposite: references must never outlive their referents. You must make it apparent in your code that no reference can possibly outlive the value it points to. To emphasize this, Rust refers to creating a reference to some value as *borrowing* the value: what you have borrowed, you must eventually return to its owner.

If you felt a moment of skepticism when reading the phrase "You must make it apparent in your code," you're in excellent company. The references themselves are nothing special—under the hood, they're just addresses. But the rules that keep them safe are novel to Rust; outside of research languages, you won't have seen anything like them before. And although these rules are the part of Rust that requires the most effort to master, the breadth of classic, absolutely everyday bugs they prevent is surprising, and their effect on multithreaded programming is liberating. This is Rust's radical wager, again.

In this chapter, we'll walk through how references work in Rust; show how references, functions, and user-defined types all incorporate lifetime information to ensure that they're used safely; and illustrate some common categories of bugs that these efforts prevent, at compile time and without run-time performance penalties.

References to Values

As an example, let's suppose we're going to build a table of murderous Renaissance artists and the works they're known for. Rust's standard library includes a hash table type, so we can define our type like this:

```
use std::collections::HashMap;

type Table = HashMap<String, Vec<String>>;
```

In other words, this is a hash table that maps `String` values to `Vec<String>` values, taking the name of an artist to a list of the names of their works. You can iterate over the entries of a `HashMap` with a `for` loop, so we can write a function to print out a `Table`:

```
fn show(table: Table) {
    for (artist, works) in table {
        println!("works by {}:", artist);
        for work in works {
            println!("  {}", work);
        }
    }
}
```

Constructing and printing the table is straightforward:

```
fn main() {
    let mut table = Table::new();
    table.insert("Gesualdo".to_string(),
                 vec!["many madrigals".to_string(),
                      "Tenebrae Responsoria".to_string()]);
    table.insert("Caravaggio".to_string(),
                 vec!["The Musicians".to_string(),
                      "The Calling of St. Matthew".to_string()]);
    table.insert("Cellini".to_string(),
                 vec!["Perseus with the head of Medusa".to_string(),
                      "a salt cellar".to_string()]);

    show(table);
}
```

And it all works fine:

```
$ cargo run
     Running `/home/jimb/rust/book/fragments/target/debug/fragments`
works by Gesualdo:
  many madrigals
  Tenebrae Responsoria
works by Cellini:
  Perseus with the head of Medusa
  a salt cellar
works by Caravaggio:
```

```
    The Musicians
    The Calling of St. Matthew
  $
```

But if you've read the previous chapter's section on moves, this definition for show should raise a few questions. In particular, HashMap is not Copy—it can't be, since it owns a dynamically allocated table. So when the program calls show(table), the whole structure gets moved to the function, leaving the variable table uninitialized. (It also iterates over its contents in no specific order, so if you've gotten a different order, don't worry.) If the calling code tries to use table now, it'll run into trouble:

```
    ...
    show(table);
    assert_eq!(table["Gesualdo"][0], "many madrigals");
```

Rust complains that table isn't available anymore:

```
error: borrow of moved value: `table`
   |
20 |     let mut table = Table::new();
   |         --------- move occurs because `table` has type
   |                   `HashMap<String, Vec<String>>`,
   |                   which does not implement the `Copy` trait
   ...
31 |     show(table);
   |          ----- value moved here
32 |     assert_eq!(table["Gesualdo"][0], "many madrigals");
   |                ^^^^^ value borrowed here after move
```

In fact, if we look into the definition of show, the outer for loop takes ownership of the hash table and consumes it entirely; and the inner for loop does the same to each of the vectors. (We saw this behavior earlier, in the "liberté, égalité, fraternité" example.) Because of move semantics, we've completely destroyed the entire structure simply by trying to print it out. Thanks, Rust!

The right way to handle this is to use references. A reference lets you access a value without affecting its ownership. References come in two kinds:

- A *shared reference* lets you read but not modify its referent. However, you can have as many shared references to a particular value at a time as you like. The expression &e yields a shared reference to e's value; if e has the type T, then &e has the type &T, pronounced "ref T." Shared references are Copy.

- If you have a *mutable reference* to a value, you may both read and modify the value. However, you may not have any other references of any sort to that value active at the same time. The expression &mut e yields a mutable reference to e's value; you write its type as &mut T, which is pronounced "ref mute T." Mutable references are not Copy.

You can think of the distinction between shared and mutable references as a way to enforce a *multiple readers or single writer* rule at compile time. In fact, this rule doesn't apply only to references; it covers the borrowed value's owner as well. As long as there are shared references to a value, not even its owner can modify it; the value is locked down. Nobody can modify `table` while `show` is working with it. Similarly, if there is a mutable reference to a value, it has exclusive access to the value; you can't use the owner at all, until the mutable reference goes away. Keeping sharing and mutation fully separate turns out to be essential to memory safety, for reasons we'll go into later in the chapter.

The printing function in our example doesn't need to modify the table, just read its contents. So the caller should be able to pass it a shared reference to the table, as follows:

```
show(&table);
```

References are non-owning pointers, so the `table` variable remains the owner of the entire structure; `show` has just borrowed it for a bit. Naturally, we'll need to adjust the definition of `show` to match, but you'll have to look closely to see the difference:

```
fn show(table: &Table) {
    for (artist, works) in table {
        println!("works by {}:", artist);
        for work in works {
            println!("  {}", work);
        }
    }
}
```

The type of `show`'s parameter `table` has changed from `Table` to `&Table`: instead of passing the table by value (and hence moving ownership into the function), we're now passing a shared reference. That's the only textual change. But how does this play out as we work through the body?

Whereas our original outer `for` loop took ownership of the `HashMap` and consumed it, in our new version it receives a shared reference to the `HashMap`. Iterating over a shared reference to a `HashMap` is defined to produce shared references to each entry's key and value: `artist` has changed from a `String` to a `&String`, and `works` from a `Vec<String>` to a `&Vec<String>`.

The inner loop is changed similarly. Iterating over a shared reference to a vector is defined to produce shared references to its elements, so `work` is now a `&String`. No ownership changes hands anywhere in this function; it's just passing around non-owning references.

Now, if we wanted to write a function to alphabetize the works of each artist, a shared reference doesn't suffice, since shared references don't permit modification. Instead, the sorting function needs to take a mutable reference to the table:

```
fn sort_works(table: &mut Table) {
    for (_artist, works) in table {
        works.sort();
    }
}
```

And we need to pass it one:

```
sort_works(&mut table);
```

This mutable borrow grants sort_works the ability to read and modify our structure, as required by the vectors' sort method.

When we pass a value to a function in a way that moves ownership of the value to the function, we say that we have passed it *by value*. If we instead pass the function a reference to the value, we say that we have passed the value *by reference*. For example, we fixed our show function by changing it to accept the table by reference, rather than by value. Many languages draw this distinction, but it's especially important in Rust, because it spells out how ownership is affected.

Working with References

The preceding example shows a pretty typical use for references: allowing functions to access or manipulate a structure without taking ownership. But references are more flexible than that, so let's look at some examples to get a more detailed view of what's going on.

Rust References Versus C++ References

If you're familiar with references in C++, they do have something in common with Rust references. Most importantly, they're both just addresses at the machine level. But in practice, Rust's references have a very different feel.

In C++, references are created implicitly by conversion, and dereferenced implicitly too:

```
// C++ code!
int x = 10;
int &r = x;             // initialization creates reference implicitly
assert(r == 10);        // implicitly dereference r to see x's value
r = 20;                 // stores 20 in x, r itself still points to x
```

In Rust, references are created explicitly with the & operator, and dereferenced explicitly with the * operator:

```
// Back to Rust code from this point onward.
let x = 10;
let r = &x;              // &x is a shared reference to x
assert!(*r == 10);       // explicitly dereference r
```

To create a mutable reference, use the &mut operator:

```
let mut y = 32;
let m = &mut y;          // &mut y is a mutable reference to y
*m += 32;                // explicitly dereference m to set y's value
assert!(*m == 64);       // and to see y's new value
```

But you might recall that, when we fixed the show function to take the table of artists by reference instead of by value, we never had to use the * operator. Why is that?

Since references are so widely used in Rust, the . operator implicitly dereferences its left operand, if needed:

```
struct Anime { name: &'static str, bechdel_pass: bool }
let aria = Anime { name: "Aria: The Animation", bechdel_pass: true };
let anime_ref = &aria;
assert_eq!(anime_ref.name, "Aria: The Animation");

// Equivalent to the above, but with the dereference written out:
assert_eq!((*anime_ref).name, "Aria: The Animation");
```

The println! macro used in the show function expands to code that uses the . operator, so it takes advantage of this implicit dereference as well.

The . operator can also implicitly borrow a reference to its left operand, if needed for a method call. For example, Vec's sort method takes a mutable reference to the vector, so these two calls are equivalent:

```
let mut v = vec![1973, 1968];
v.sort();                // implicitly borrows a mutable reference to v
(&mut v).sort();         // equivalent, but more verbose
```

In a nutshell, whereas C++ converts implicitly between references and lvalues (that is, expressions referring to locations in memory), with these conversions appearing anywhere they're needed, in Rust you use the & and * operators to create and follow references, with the exception of the . operator, which borrows and dereferences implicitly.

Assigning References

Assigning a reference to a variable makes that variable point somewhere new:

```
let x = 10;
let y = 20;
let mut r = &x;

if b { r = &y; }

assert!(*r == 10 || *r == 20);
```

The reference r initially points to x. But if b is true, the code points it at y instead, as illustrated in Figure 5-1.

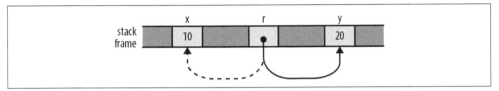

Figure 5-1. The reference r, now pointing to y instead of x

This behavior may seem too obvious to be worth mentioning: of course r now points to y, since we stored &y in it. But we point this out because C++ references behave very differently: as shown earlier, assigning a value to a reference in C++ stores the value in its referent. Once a C++ reference has been initialized, there's no way to make it point at anything else.

References to References

Rust permits references to references:

```
struct Point { x: i32, y: i32 }
let point = Point { x: 1000, y: 729 };
let r: &Point = &point;
let rr: &&Point = &r;
let rrr: &&&Point = &rr;
```

(We've written out the reference types for clarity, but you could omit them; there's nothing here Rust can't infer for itself.) The . operator follows as many references as it takes to find its target:

```
assert_eq!(rrr.y, 729);
```

In memory, the references are arranged as shown in Figure 5-2.

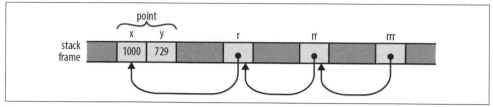

Figure 5-2. A chain of references to references

So the expression `rrr.y`, guided by the type of `rrr`, actually traverses three references to get to the `Point` before fetching its y field.

Comparing References

Like the `.` operator, Rust's comparison operators "see through" any number of references:

```
let x = 10;
let y = 10;

let rx = &x;
let ry = &y;

let rrx = &rx;
let rry = &ry;

assert!(rrx <= rry);
assert!(rrx == rry);
```

The final assertion here succeeds, even though `rrx` and `rry` point at different values (namely, `rx` and `ry`), because the `==` operator follows all the references and performs the comparison on their final targets, x and y. This is almost always the behavior you want, especially when writing generic functions. If you actually want to know whether two references point to the same memory, you can use `std::ptr::eq`, which compares them as addresses:

```
assert!(rx == ry);              // their referents are equal
assert!(!std::ptr::eq(rx, ry)); // but occupy different addresses
```

Note that the operands of a comparison must have exactly the same type, including the references:

```
assert!(rx == rrx);    // error: type mismatch: `&i32` vs `&&i32`
assert!(rx == *rrx);   // this is okay
```

References Are Never Null

Rust references are never null. There's no analogue to C's NULL or C++'s nullptr. There is no default initial value for a reference (you can't use any variable until it's been initialized, regardless of its type) and Rust won't convert integers to references (outside of unsafe code), so you can't convert zero into a reference.

C and C++ code often uses a null pointer to indicate the absence of a value: for example, the malloc function returns either a pointer to a new block of memory or nullptr if there isn't enough memory available to satisfy the request. In Rust, if you need a value that is either a reference to something or not, use the type Option<&T>. At the machine level, Rust represents None as a null pointer and Some(r), where r is a &T value, as the nonzero address, so Option<&T> is just as efficient as a nullable pointer in C or C++, even though it's safer: its type requires you to check whether it's None before you can use it.

Borrowing References to Arbitrary Expressions

Whereas C and C++ only let you apply the & operator to certain kinds of expressions, Rust lets you borrow a reference to the value of any sort of expression at all:

```
fn factorial(n: usize) -> usize {
    (1..n+1).product()
}
let r = &factorial(6);
// Arithmetic operators can see through one level of references.
assert_eq!(r + &1009, 1729);
```

In situations like this, Rust simply creates an anonymous variable to hold the expression's value and makes the reference point to that. The lifetime of this anonymous variable depends on what you do with the reference:

- If you immediately assign the reference to a variable in a let statement (or make it part of some struct or array that is being immediately assigned), then Rust makes the anonymous variable live as long as the variable the let initializes. In the preceding example, Rust would do this for the referent of r.

- Otherwise, the anonymous variable lives to the end of the enclosing statement. In our example, the anonymous variable created to hold 1009 lasts only to the end of the assert_eq! statement.

If you're used to C or C++, this may sound error-prone. But remember that Rust will never let you write code that would produce a dangling reference. If the reference could ever be used beyond the anonymous variable's lifetime, Rust will always report the problem to you at compile time. You can then fix your code to keep the referent in a named variable with an appropriate lifetime.

References to Slices and Trait Objects

The references we've shown so far are all simple addresses. However, Rust also includes two kinds of *fat pointers*, two-word values carrying the address of some value, along with some further information necessary to put the value to use.

A reference to a slice is a fat pointer, carrying the starting address of the slice and its length. We described slices in detail in Chapter 3.

Rust's other kind of fat pointer is a *trait object*, a reference to a value that implements a certain trait. A trait object carries a value's address and a pointer to the trait's implementation appropriate to that value, for invoking the trait's methods. We'll cover trait objects in detail in "Trait Objects" on page 258.

Aside from carrying this extra data, slice and trait object references behave just like the other sorts of references we've shown so far in this chapter: they don't own their referents, they are not allowed to outlive their referents, they may be mutable or shared, and so on.

Reference Safety

As we've presented them so far, references look pretty much like ordinary pointers in C or C++. But those are unsafe; how does Rust keep its references under control? Perhaps the best way to see the rules in action is to try to break them.

To convey the fundamental ideas, we'll start with the simplest cases, showing how Rust ensures references are used properly within a single function body. Then we'll look at passing references between functions and storing them in data structures. This entails giving said functions and data types *lifetime parameters*, which we'll explain. Finally, we'll present some shortcuts that Rust provides to simplify common usage patterns. Throughout, we'll be showing how Rust points out broken code and often suggests solutions.

Borrowing a Local Variable

Here's a pretty obvious case. You can't borrow a reference to a local variable and take it out of the variable's scope:

```
{
    let r;
    {
        let x = 1;
        r = &x;
    }
```

```
        assert_eq!(*r, 1);  // bad: reads memory `x` used to occupy
    }
```

The Rust compiler rejects this program, with a detailed error message:

```
error: `x` does not live long enough
    |
7   |         r = &x;
    |              ^^ borrowed value does not live long enough
8   |     }
    |     - `x` dropped here while still borrowed
9   |     assert_eq!(*r, 1);  // bad: reads memory `x` used to occupy
10  | }
```

Rust's complaint is that x lives only until the end of the inner block, whereas the reference remains alive until the end of the outer block, making it a dangling pointer, which is verboten.

While it's obvious to a human reader that this program is broken, it's worth looking at how Rust itself reached that conclusion. Even this simple example shows the logical tools Rust uses to check much more complex code.

Rust tries to assign each reference type in your program a *lifetime* that meets the constraints imposed by how it is used. A lifetime is some stretch of your program for which a reference could be safe to use: a statement, an expression, the scope of some variable, or the like. Lifetimes are entirely figments of Rust's compile-time imagination. At run time, a reference is nothing but an address; its lifetime is part of its type and has no run-time representation.

In this example, there are three lifetimes whose relationships we need to work out. The variables r and x both have a lifetime, extending from the point at which they're initialized until the point that the compiler can prove they are no longer in use. The third lifetime is that of a reference type: the type of the reference we borrow to x and store in r.

Here's one constraint that should seem pretty obvious: if you have a variable x, then a reference to x must not outlive x itself, as shown in Figure 5-3.

Beyond the point where x goes out of scope, the reference would be a dangling pointer. We say that the variable's lifetime must *contain* or *enclose* that of the reference borrowed from it.

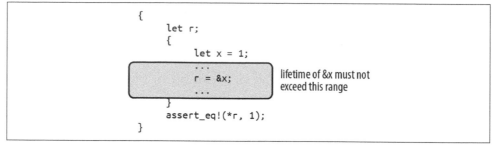

Figure 5-3. Permissible lifetimes for &x

Here's another kind of constraint: if you store a reference in a variable r, the reference's type must be good for the entire lifetime of the variable, from its initialization until its last use, as shown in Figure 5-4.

If the reference can't live at least as long as the variable does, then at some point r will be a dangling pointer. We say that the reference's lifetime must contain or enclose the variable's.

```
{
    let r;
    {
        let x = 1;
        ...
        r = &x;
        ...
    }
    assert_eq!(*r, 1);
}
```

lifetime of anything stored in
r must cover at least this range

Figure 5-4. Permissible lifetimes for reference stored in r

The first kind of constraint limits how large a reference's lifetime can be, while the second kind limits how small it can be. Rust simply tries to find a lifetime for each reference that satisfies all these constraints. In our example, however, there is no such lifetime, as shown in Figure 5-5.

```
{
    let r;
    {
        let x = 1;
        ...
        r = &x;
        ...
    }
    assert_eq!(*r, 1);
}
```

There is no lifetime that lies
entirely within this range...

...but also fully encloses this range.

Figure 5-5. A reference with contradictory constraints on its lifetime

Let's now consider a different example where things do work out. We have the same kinds of constraints: the reference's lifetime must be contained by x's, but fully enclose r's. But because r's lifetime is smaller now, there is a lifetime that meets the constraints, as shown in Figure 5-6.

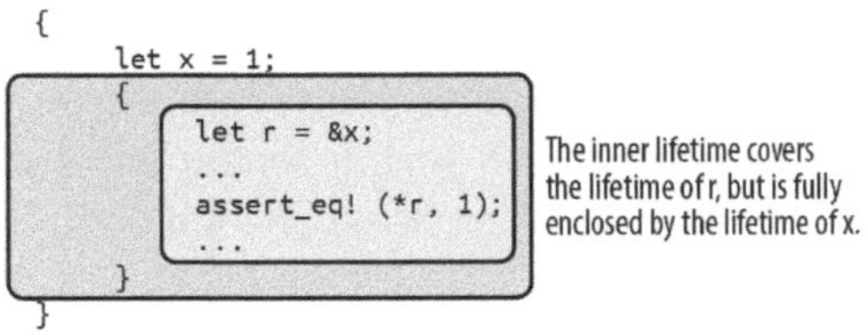

Figure 5-6. A reference with a lifetime enclosing r's scope, but within x's scope

These rules apply in a natural way when you borrow a reference to some part of some larger data structure, like an element of a vector:

```
let v = vec![1, 2, 3];
let r = &v[1];
```

Since v owns the vector, which owns its elements, the lifetime of v must enclose that of the reference type of &v[1]. Similarly, if you store a reference in some data structure, its lifetime must enclose that of the data structure. For example, if you build a vector of references, all of them must have lifetimes enclosing that of the variable that owns the vector.

This is the essence of the process Rust uses for all code. Bringing more language features into the picture—e.g., data structures and function calls—introduces new sorts of constraints, but the principle remains the same: first, understand the constraints arising from the way the program uses references; then, find lifetimes that satisfy them. This is not so different from the process C and C++ programmers impose on themselves; the difference is that Rust knows the rules and enforces them.

Receiving References as Function Arguments

When we pass a reference to a function, how does Rust make sure the function uses it safely? Suppose we have a function f that takes a reference and stores it in a global variable. We'll need to make a few revisions to this, but here's a first cut:

```
// This code has several problems, and doesn't compile.
static mut STASH: &i32;
fn f(p: &i32) { STASH = p; }
```

Rust's equivalent of a global variable is called a *static*: it's a value that's created when the program starts and lasts until it terminates. (Like any other declaration, Rust's module system controls where statics are visible, so they're only "global" in their lifetime, not their visibility.) We cover statics in Chapter 8, but for now we'll just call out a few rules that the code just shown doesn't follow:

- Every static must be initialized.

- Mutable statics are inherently not thread-safe (after all, any thread can access a static at any time), and even in single-threaded programs, they can fall prey to other sorts of reentrancy problems. For these reasons, you may access a mutable static only within an unsafe block. In this example we're not concerned with those particular problems, so we'll just throw in an unsafe block and move on.

With those revisions made, we now have the following:

```
static mut STASH: &i32 = &128;
fn f(p: &i32) { // still not good enough
    unsafe {
        STASH = p;
    }
}
```

We're almost done. To see the remaining problem, we need to write out a few things that Rust is helpfully letting us omit. The signature of f as written here is actually shorthand for the following:

```
fn f<'a>(p: &'a i32) { ... }
```

Here, the lifetime 'a (pronounced "tick A") is a *lifetime parameter* of f. You can read <'a> as "for any lifetime 'a" so when we write fn f<'a>(p: &'a i32), we're defining a function that takes a reference to an i32 with any given lifetime 'a.

Since we must allow 'a to be any lifetime, things had better work out if it's the smallest possible lifetime: one just enclosing the call to f. This assignment then becomes a point of contention:

```
STASH = p;
```

Since STASH lives for the program's entire execution, the reference type it holds must have a lifetime of the same length; Rust calls this the 'static lifetime. But the lifetime of p's reference is some 'a, which could be anything, as long as it encloses the call to f. So, Rust rejects our code:

```
error: explicit lifetime required in the type of `p`
  |
5 |         STASH = p;
  |                 ^ lifetime `'static` required
```

At this point, it's clear that our function can't accept just any reference as an argument. But as Rust points out, it ought to be able to accept a reference that has a 'static lifetime: storing such a reference in STASH can't create a dangling pointer. And indeed, the following code compiles just fine:

```
static mut STASH: &i32 = &10;

fn f(p: &'static i32) {
    unsafe {
        STASH = p;
    }
}
```

This time, f's signature spells out that p must be a reference with lifetime 'static, so there's no longer any problem storing that in STASH. We can only apply f to references to other statics, but that's the only thing that's certain not to leave STASH dangling anyway. So we can write:

```
static WORTH_POINTING_AT: i32 = 1000;
f(&WORTH_POINTING_AT);
```

Since WORTH_POINTING_AT is a static, the type of &WORTH_POINTING_AT is &'static i32, which is safe to pass to f.

Take a step back, though, and notice what happened to f's signature as we amended our way to correctness: the original f(p: &i32) ended up as f(p: &'static i32). In other words, we were unable to write a function that stashed a reference in a global variable without reflecting that intention in the function's signature. In Rust, a function's signature always exposes the body's behavior.

Conversely, if we do see a function with a signature like g(p: &i32) (or with the lifetimes written out, g<'a>(p: &'a i32)), we can tell that it *does not* stash its argument p anywhere that will outlive the call. There's no need to look into g's definition; the signature alone tells us what g can and can't do with its argument. This fact ends up being very useful when you're trying to establish the safety of a call to the function.

Passing References to Functions

Now that we've shown how a function's signature relates to its body, let's examine how it relates to the function's callers. Suppose you have the following code:

```
// This could be written more briefly: fn g(p: &i32),
// but let's write out the lifetimes for now.
fn g<'a>(p: &'a i32) { ... }

let x = 10;
g(&x);
```

From g's signature alone, Rust knows it will not save p anywhere that might outlive the call: any lifetime that encloses the call must work for 'a. So Rust chooses the smallest possible lifetime for &x: that of the call to g. This meets all constraints: it doesn't outlive x, and it encloses the entire call to g. So this code passes muster.

Note that although g takes a lifetime parameter 'a, we didn't need to mention it when calling g. You only need to worry about lifetime parameters when defining functions and types; when using them, Rust infers the lifetimes for you.

What if we tried to pass &x to our function f from earlier that stores its argument in a static?

```
fn f(p: &'static i32) { ... }

let x = 10;
f(&x);
```

This fails to compile: the reference &x must not outlive x, but by passing it to f, we constrain it to live at least as long as 'static. There's no way to satisfy everyone here, so Rust rejects the code.

Returning References

It's common for a function to take a reference to some data structure and then return a reference into some part of that structure. For example, here's a function that returns a reference to the smallest element of a slice:

```
// v should have at least one element.
fn smallest(v: &[i32]) -> &i32 {
    let mut s = &v[0];
    for r in &v[1..] {
        if *r < *s { s = r; }
    }
    s
}
```

We've omitted lifetimes from that function's signature in the usual way. When a function takes a single reference as an argument and returns a single reference, Rust assumes that the two must have the same lifetime. Writing this out explicitly would give us:

```
fn smallest<'a>(v: &'a [i32]) -> &'a i32 { ... }
```

Suppose we call smallest like this:

```
let s;
{
    let parabola = [9, 4, 1, 0, 1, 4, 9];
    s = smallest(&parabola);
}
assert_eq!(*s, 0); // bad: points to element of dropped array
```

From smallest's signature, we can see that its argument and return value must have the same lifetime, 'a. In our call, the argument &parabola must not outlive parabola itself, yet smallest's return value must live at least as long as s. There's no possible lifetime 'a that can satisfy both constraints, so Rust rejects the code:

```
error: `parabola` does not live long enough
   |
11 |          s = smallest(&parabola);
   |                       -------- borrow occurs here
12 |      }
   |      ^ `parabola` dropped here while still borrowed
13 |      assert_eq!(*s, 0); // bad: points to element of dropped array
   |                 - borrowed value needs to live until here
14 | }
```

Moving s so that its lifetime is clearly contained within parabola's fixes the problem:

```
{
    let parabola = [9, 4, 1, 0, 1, 4, 9];
    let s = smallest(&parabola);
    assert_eq!(*s, 0); // fine: parabola still alive
}
```

Lifetimes in function signatures let Rust assess the relationships between the references you pass to the function and those the function returns, and they ensure they're being used safely.

Structs Containing References

How does Rust handle references stored in data structures? Here's the same erroneous program we looked at earlier, except that we've put the reference inside a structure:

```
// This does not compile.
struct S {
    r: &i32
}

let s;
{
    let x = 10;
    s = S { r: &x };
}
assert_eq!(*s.r, 10); // bad: reads from dropped `x`
```

The safety constraints Rust places on references can't magically disappear just because we hid the reference inside a struct. Somehow, those constraints must end up applying to S as well. Indeed, Rust is skeptical:

```
error: missing lifetime specifier
   |
7  |           r: &i32
   |              ^ expected lifetime parameter
```

Whenever a reference type appears inside another type's definition, you must write out its lifetime. You can write this:

```
struct S {
    r: &'static i32
}
```

This says that r can only refer to i32 values that will last for the lifetime of the program, which is rather limiting. The alternative is to give the type a lifetime parameter 'a and use that for r:

```
struct S<'a> {
    r: &'a i32
}
```

Now the S type has a lifetime, just as reference types do. Each value you create of type S gets a fresh lifetime 'a, which becomes constrained by how you use the value. The lifetime of any reference you store in r had better enclose 'a, and 'a must outlast the lifetime of wherever you store the S.

Turning back to the preceding code, the expression S { r: &x } creates a fresh S value with some lifetime 'a. When you store &x in the r field, you constrain 'a to lie entirely within x's lifetime.

The assignment s = S { ... } stores this S in a variable whose lifetime extends to the end of the example, constraining 'a to outlast the lifetime of s. And now Rust has arrived at the same contradictory constraints as before: 'a must not outlive x, yet must live at least as long as s. No satisfactory lifetime exists, and Rust rejects the code. Disaster averted!

How does a type with a lifetime parameter behave when placed inside some other type?

```
struct D {
    s: S  // not adequate
}
```

Rust is skeptical, just as it was when we tried placing a reference in S without specifying its lifetime:

```
error: missing lifetime specifier
   |
8  |     s: S  // not adequate
   |        ^ expected named lifetime parameter
   |
```

We can't leave off S's lifetime parameter here: Rust needs to know how D's lifetime relates to that of the reference in its S in order to apply the same checks to D that it does for S and plain references.

We could give s the 'static lifetime. This works:

```
struct D {
    s: S<'static>
}
```

With this definition, the s field may only borrow values that live for the entire execution of the program. That's somewhat restrictive, but it does mean that D can't possibly borrow a local variable; there are no special constraints on D's lifetime.

The error message from Rust actually suggests another approach, which is more general:

```
help: consider introducing a named lifetime parameter
  |
7 | struct D<'a> {
8 |     s: S<'a>
  |
```

Here, we give D its own lifetime parameter and pass that to S:

```
struct D<'a> {
    s: S<'a>
}
```

By taking a lifetime parameter 'a and using it in s's type, we've allowed Rust to relate D value's lifetime to that of the reference its S holds.

We showed earlier how a function's signature exposes what it does with the references we pass it. Now we've shown something similar about types: a type's lifetime parameters always reveal whether it contains references with interesting (that is, non-'static) lifetimes and what those lifetimes can be.

For example, suppose we have a parsing function that takes a slice of bytes and returns a structure holding the results of the parse:

```
fn parse_record<'i>(input: &'i [u8]) -> Record<'i> { ... }
```

Without looking into the definition of the Record type at all, we can tell that, if we receive a Record from parse_record, whatever references it contains must point into the input buffer we passed in, and nowhere else (except perhaps at 'static values).

In fact, this exposure of internal behavior is the reason Rust requires types that contain references to take explicit lifetime parameters. There's no reason Rust couldn't simply make up a distinct lifetime for each reference in the struct and save you the trouble of writing them out. Early versions of Rust actually behaved this way, but developers found it confusing: it is helpful to know when one value borrows something from another value, especially when working through errors.

It's not just references and types like S that have lifetimes. Every type in Rust has a lifetime, including i32 and String. Most are simply 'static, meaning that values of those types can live for as long as you like; for example, a Vec<i32> is self-contained and needn't be dropped before any particular variable goes out of scope. But a type like Vec<&'a i32> has a lifetime that must be enclosed by 'a: it must be dropped while its referents are still alive.

Distinct Lifetime Parameters

Suppose you've defined a structure containing two references like this:

```
struct S<'a> {
    x: &'a i32,
    y: &'a i32
}
```

Both references use the same lifetime 'a. This could be a problem if your code wants to do something like this:

```
let x = 10;
let r;
{
    let y = 20;
    {
        let s = S { x: &x, y: &y };
        r = s.x;
    }
}
println!("{}", r);
```

This code doesn't create any dangling pointers. The reference to y stays in s, which goes out of scope before y does. The reference to x ends up in r, which doesn't outlive x.

If you try to compile this, however, Rust will complain that y does not live long enough, even though it clearly does. Why is Rust worried? If you work through the code carefully, you can follow its reasoning:

- Both fields of S are references with the same lifetime 'a, so Rust must find a single lifetime that works for both s.x and s.y.
- We assign r = s.x, requiring 'a to enclose r's lifetime.
- We initialized s.y with &y, requiring 'a to be no longer than y's lifetime.

These constraints are impossible to satisfy: no lifetime is shorter than y's scope but longer than r's. Rust balks.

The problem arises because both references in S have the same lifetime 'a. Changing the definition of S to let each reference have a distinct lifetime fixes everything:

```
struct S<'a, 'b> {
    x: &'a i32,
    y: &'b i32
}
```

With this definition, s.x and s.y have independent lifetimes. What we do with s.x has no effect on what we store in s.y, so it's easy to satisfy the constraints now: 'a can simply be r's lifetime, and 'b can be s's. (y's lifetime would work too for 'b, but Rust tries to choose the smallest lifetime that works.) Everything ends up fine.

Function signatures can have similar effects. Suppose we have a function like this:

```
fn f<'a>(r: &'a i32, s: &'a i32) -> &'a i32 { r } // perhaps too tight
```

Here, both reference parameters use the same lifetime 'a, which can unnecessarily constrain the caller in the same way we've shown previously. If this is a problem, you can let parameters' lifetimes vary independently:

```
fn f<'a, 'b>(r: &'a i32, s: &'b i32) -> &'a i32 { r } // looser
```

The downside to this is that adding lifetimes can make types and function signatures harder to read. Your authors tend to try the simplest possible definition first and then loosen restrictions until the code compiles. Since Rust won't permit the code to run unless it's safe, simply waiting to be told when there's a problem is a perfectly acceptable tactic.

Omitting Lifetime Parameters

We've shown plenty of functions so far in this book that return references or take them as parameters, but we've usually not needed to spell out which lifetime is which. The lifetimes are there; Rust is just letting us omit them when it's reasonably obvious what they should be.

In the simplest cases, you may never need to write out lifetimes for your parameters. Rust just assigns a distinct lifetime to each spot that needs one. For example:

```
struct S<'a, 'b> {
    x: &'a i32,
    y: &'b i32
}

fn sum_r_xy(r: &i32, s: S) -> i32 {
```

```
    r + s.x + s.y
}
```

This function's signature is shorthand for:

```
fn sum_r_xy<'a, 'b, 'c>(r: &'a i32, s: S<'b, 'c>) -> i32
```

If you do return references or other types with lifetime parameters, Rust still tries to make the unambiguous cases easy. If there's only a single lifetime that appears among your function's parameters, then Rust assumes any lifetimes in your return value must be that one:

```
fn first_third(point: &[i32; 3]) -> (&i32, &i32) {
    (&point[0], &point[2])
}
```

With all the lifetimes written out, the equivalent would be:

```
fn first_third<'a>(point: &'a [i32; 3]) -> (&'a i32, &'a i32)
```

If there are multiple lifetimes among your parameters, then there's no natural reason to prefer one over the other for the return value, and Rust makes you spell out what's going on.

If your function is a method on some type and takes its self parameter by reference, then that breaks the tie: Rust assumes that self's lifetime is the one to give everything in your return value. (A self parameter refers to the value the method is being called on Rust's equivalent of this in C++, Java, or JavaScript, or self in Python. We'll cover methods in "Defining Methods with impl" on page 214.)

For example, you can write the following:

```
struct StringTable {
    elements: Vec<String>,
}

impl StringTable {
    fn find_by_prefix(&self, prefix: &str) -> Option<&String> {
        for i in 0 .. self.elements.len() {
            if self.elements[i].starts_with(prefix) {
                return Some(&self.elements[i]);
            }
        }
        None
    }
}
```

The find_by_prefix method's signature is shorthand for:

```
fn find_by_prefix<'a, 'b>(&'a self, prefix: &'b str) -> Option<&'a String>
```

Rust assumes that whatever you're borrowing, you're borrowing from self.

Again, these are just abbreviations, meant to be helpful without introducing surprises. When they're not what you want, you can always write the lifetimes out explicitly.

Sharing Versus Mutation

So far, we've discussed how Rust ensures no reference will ever point to a variable that has gone out of scope. But there are other ways to introduce dangling pointers. Here's an easy case:

```
let v = vec![4, 8, 19, 27, 34, 10];
let r = &v;
let aside = v;  // move vector to aside
r[0];           // bad: uses `v`, which is now uninitialized
```

The assignment to `aside` moves the vector, leaving v uninitialized, and turns r into a dangling pointer, as shown in Figure 5-7.

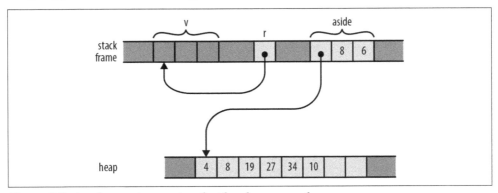

Figure 5-7. A reference to a vector that has been moved away

Although v stays in scope for r's entire lifetime, the problem here is that v's value gets moved elsewhere, leaving v uninitialized while r still refers to it. Naturally, Rust catches the error:

```
error: cannot move out of `v` because it is borrowed
    |
9   |     let r = &v;
    |             - borrow of `v` occurs here
10  |     let aside = v;  // move vector to aside
    |         ^^^^^ move out of `v` occurs here
```

Throughout its lifetime, a shared reference makes its referent read-only: you may not assign to the referent or move its value elsewhere. In this code, r's lifetime contains the attempt to move the vector, so Rust rejects the program. If you change the program as shown here, there's no problem:

```
let v = vec![4, 8, 19, 27, 34, 10];
{
    let r = &v;
    r[0];          // ok: vector is still there
}
let aside = v;
```

In this version, r goes out of scope earlier, the reference's lifetime ends before v is moved aside, and all is well.

Here's a different way to wreak havoc. Suppose we have a handy function to extend a vector with the elements of a slice:

```
fn extend(vec: &mut Vec<f64>, slice: &[f64]) {
    for elt in slice {
        vec.push(*elt);
    }
}
```

This is a less flexible (and much less optimized) version of the standard library's extend_from_slice method on vectors. We can use it to build up a vector from slices of other vectors or arrays:

```
let mut wave = Vec::new();
let head = vec![0.0, 1.0];
let tail = [0.0, -1.0];

extend(&mut wave, &head);    // extend wave with another vector
extend(&mut wave, &tail);    // extend wave with an array

assert_eq!(wave, vec![0.0, 1.0, 0.0, -1.0]);
```

So we've built up one period of a sine wave here. If we want to add another undulation, can we append the vector to itself?

```
extend(&mut wave, &wave);
assert_eq!(wave, vec![0.0, 1.0, 0.0, -1.0,
                      0.0, 1.0, 0.0, -1.0]);
```

This may look fine on casual inspection. But remember that when we add an element to a vector, if its buffer is full, it must allocate a new buffer with more space. Suppose wave starts with space for four elements and so must allocate a larger buffer when extend tries to add a fifth. Memory ends up looking like Figure 5-8.

The extend function's vec argument borrows wave (owned by the caller), which has allocated itself a new buffer with space for eight elements. But slice continues to point to the old four-element buffer, which has been dropped.

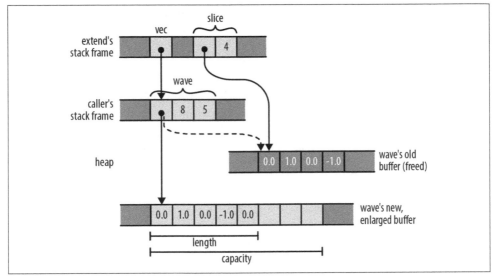

Figure 5-8. A slice turned into a dangling pointer by a vector reallocation

This sort of problem isn't unique to Rust: modifying collections while pointing into them is delicate territory in many languages. In C++, the `std::vector` specification cautions you that "reallocation [of the vector's buffer] invalidates all the references, pointers, and iterators referring to the elements in the sequence." Similarly, Java says, of modifying a `java.util.Hashtable` object:

> If the Hashtable is structurally modified at any time after the iterator is created, in any way except through the iterator's own remove method, the iterator will throw a ConcurrentModificationException.

What's especially difficult about this sort of bug is that it doesn't happen all the time. In testing, your vector might always happen to have enough space, the buffer might never be reallocated, and the problem might never come to light.

Rust, however, reports the problem with our call to `extend` at compile time:

```
error: cannot borrow `wave` as immutable because it is also
       borrowed as mutable
   |
9 |      extend(&mut wave, &wave);
   |                 ----   ^^^^- mutable borrow ends here
   |                 |      |
   |                 |      immutable borrow occurs here
   |                 mutable borrow occurs here
```

In other words, we may borrow a mutable reference to the vector, and we may borrow a shared reference to its elements, but those two references' lifetimes must not overlap. In our case, both references' lifetimes contain the call to extend, so Rust rejects the code.

These errors both stem from violations of Rust's rules for mutation and sharing:

Shared access is read-only access.

Values borrowed by shared references are read-only. Across the lifetime of a shared reference, neither its referent, nor anything reachable from that referent, can be changed *by anything*. There exist no live mutable references to anything in that structure, its owner is held read-only, and so on. It's really frozen.

Mutable access is exclusive access.

A value borrowed by a mutable reference is reachable exclusively via that reference. Across the lifetime of a mutable reference, there is no other usable path to its referent or to any value reachable from there. The only references whose lifetimes may overlap with a mutable reference are those you borrow from the mutable reference itself.

Rust reported the extend example as a violation of the second rule: since we've borrowed a mutable reference to wave, that mutable reference must be the only way to reach the vector or its elements. The shared reference to the slice is itself another way to reach the elements, violating the second rule.

But Rust could also have treated our bug as a violation of the first rule: since we've borrowed a shared reference to wave's elements, the elements and the Vec itself are all read-only. You can't borrow a mutable reference to a read-only value.

Each kind of reference affects what we can do with the values along the owning path to the referent, and the values reachable from the referent (Figure 5-9).

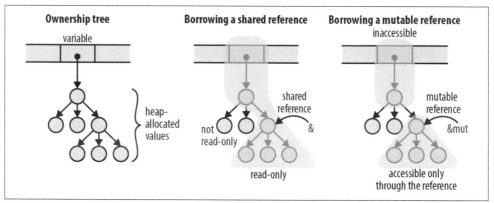

Figure 5-9. Borrowing a reference affects what you can do with other values in the same ownership tree

Note that in both cases, the path of ownership leading to the referent cannot be changed for the reference's lifetime. For a shared borrow, the path is read-only; for a mutable borrow, it's completely inaccessible. So there's no way for the program to do anything that will invalidate the reference.

Paring these principles down to the simplest possible examples:

```
let mut x = 10;
let r1 = &x;
let r2 = &x;       // ok: multiple shared borrows permitted
x += 10;           // error: cannot assign to `x` because it is borrowed
let m = &mut x;    // error: cannot borrow `x` as mutable because it is
                   // also borrowed as immutable
println!("{}, {}, {}", r1, r2, m); // the references are used here,
                                   // so their lifetimes must last
                                   // at least this long

let mut y = 20;
let m1 = &mut y;
let m2 = &mut y;   // error: cannot borrow as mutable more than once
let z = y;         // error: cannot use `y` because it was mutably borrowed
println!("{}, {}, {}", m1, m2, z); // references are used here
```

It is OK to reborrow a shared reference from a shared reference:

```
let mut w = (107, 109);
let r = &w;
let r0 = &r.0;      // ok: reborrowing shared as shared
let m1 = &mut r.1;  // error: can't reborrow shared as mutable
println!("{}", r0); // r0 gets used here
```

You can reborrow from a mutable reference:

```
let mut v = (136, 139);
let m = &mut v;
let m0 = &mut m.0;  // ok: reborrowing mutable from mutable
*m0 = 137;
let r1 = &m.1;      // ok: reborrowing shared from mutable,
                    // and doesn't overlap with m0
v.1;                // error: access through other paths still forbidden
println!("{}", r1); // r1 gets used here
```

These restrictions are pretty tight. Turning back to our attempted call extend(&mut wave, &wave), there's no quick and easy way to fix up the code to work the way we'd like. And Rust applies these rules everywhere: if we borrow, say, a shared reference to a key in a HashMap, we can't borrow a mutable reference to the HashMap until the shared reference's lifetime ends.

But there's good justification for this: designing collections to support unrestricted, simultaneous iteration and modification is difficult and often precludes simpler, more efficient implementations. Java's Hashtable and C++'s vector don't bother, and neither Python dictionaries nor JavaScript objects define exactly how such access behaves. Other collection types in JavaScript do, but require heavier implementations as a result. C++'s `std::map` promises that inserting new entries doesn't invalidate pointers to other entries in the map, but by making that promise, the standard precludes more cache-efficient designs like Rust's `BTreeMap`, which stores multiple entries in each node of the tree.

Here's another example of the kind of bug these rules catch. Consider the following C++ code, meant to manage a file descriptor. To keep things simple, we're only going to show a constructor and a copying assignment operator, and we're going to omit error handling:

```cpp
struct File {
  int descriptor;

  File(int d) : descriptor(d) { }

  File& operator=(const File &rhs) {
    close(descriptor);
    descriptor = dup(rhs.descriptor);
    return *this;
  }
};
```

The assignment operator is simple enough, but fails badly in a situation like this:

```cpp
File f(open("foo.txt", ...));
...
f = f;
```

If we assign a `File` to itself, both `rhs` and `*this` are the same object, so `operator=` closes the very file descriptor it's about to pass to `dup`. We destroy the same resource we were meant to copy.

In Rust, the analogous code would be:

```rust
struct File {
    descriptor: i32
}

fn new_file(d: i32) -> File {
    File { descriptor: d }
}

fn clone_from(this: &mut File, rhs: &File) {
    close(this.descriptor);
    this.descriptor = dup(rhs.descriptor);
}
```

(This is not idiomatic Rust. There are excellent ways to give Rust types their own constructor functions and methods, which we describe in Chapter 9, but the preceding definitions work for this example.)

If we write the Rust code corresponding to the use of `File`, we get:

```
let mut f = new_file(open("foo.txt", ...));
...
clone_from(&mut f, &f);
```

Rust, of course, refuses to even compile this code:

```
error: cannot borrow `f` as immutable because it is also
       borrowed as mutable
   |
18 |     clone_from(&mut f, &f);
   |                   -    ^- mutable borrow ends here
   |                   |    |
   |                   |    immutable borrow occurs here
   |                   mutable borrow occurs here
```

This should look familiar. It turns out that two classic C++ bugs—failure to cope with self-assignment and using invalidated iterators—are the same underlying kind of bug! In both cases, code assumes it is modifying one value while consulting another, when in fact they're both the same value. If you've ever accidentally let the source and destination of a call to `memcpy` or `strcpy` overlap in C or C++, that's yet another form the bug can take. By requiring mutable access to be exclusive, Rust has fended off a wide class of everyday mistakes.

The immiscibility of shared and mutable references really demonstrates its value when writing concurrent code. A data race is possible only when some value is both mutable and shared between threads—which is exactly what Rust's reference rules eliminate. A concurrent Rust program that avoids `unsafe` code is free of data races *by construction*. We'll cover this aspect in more detail when we talk about concurrency in Chapter 19, but in summary, concurrency is much easier to use in Rust than in most other languages.

Taking Arms Against a Sea of Objects

Since the rise of automatic memory management in the 1990s, the default architecture of all programs has been the *sea of objects*, shown in Figure 5-10.

This is what happens if you have garbage collection and you start writing a program without designing anything. We've all built systems that look like this.

This architecture has many advantages that don't show up in the diagram: initial progress is rapid, it's easy to hack stuff in, and a few years down the road, you'll have no difficulty justifying a complete rewrite. (Cue AC/DC's "Highway to Hell.")

Of course, there are disadvantages too. When everything depends on everything else like this, it's hard to test, evolve, or even think about any component in isolation.

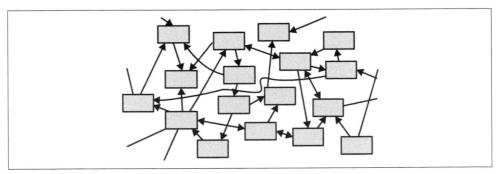

Figure 5-10. A sea of objects

One fascinating thing about Rust is that the ownership model puts a speed bump on the highway to hell. It takes a bit of effort to make a cycle in Rust—two values such that each one contains a reference pointing to the other. You have to use a smart pointer type, such as Rc, and interior mutability—a topic we haven't even covered yet. Rust prefers for pointers, ownership, and data flow to pass through the system in one direction, as shown in Figure 5-11.

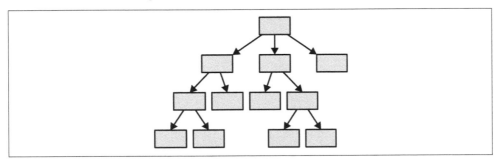

Figure 5-11. A tree of values

The reason we bring this up right now is that it would be natural, after reading this chapter, to want to run right out and create a "sea of structs," all tied together with Rc smart pointers, and re-create all the object-oriented antipatterns you're familiar with. This won't work for you right away. Rust's ownership model will give you some trouble. The cure is to do some up-front design and build a better program.

Rust is all about transferring the pain of understanding your program from the future to the present. It works unreasonably well: not only can Rust force you to understand why your program is thread-safe, it can even require some amount of high-level architectural design.

## CHAPTER 6

Expressions

LISP programmers know the value of everything, but the cost of nothing.
—Alan Perlis, epigram #55

In this chapter, we'll cover the *expressions* of Rust, the building blocks that make up the body of Rust functions and thus the majority of Rust code. Most things in Rust are expressions. In this chapter, we'll explore the power this brings and how to work with its limitations. We'll cover control flow, which in Rust is entirely expression-oriented, and how Rust's foundational operators work in isolation and combination.

A few concepts that technically fall into this category, such as closures and iterators, are deep enough that we will dedicate a whole chapter to them later. For now, we aim to cover as much syntax as possible in a few pages.

An Expression Language

Rust visually resembles the C family of languages, but this is a bit of a ruse. In C, there is a sharp distinction between *expressions*, bits of code that look something like this:

```
5 * (fahr-32) / 9
```

and *statements*, which look more like this:

```
for (; begin != end; ++begin) {
    if (*begin == target)
        break;
}
```

Expressions have values. Statements don't.

Rust is what is called an *expression language*. This means it follows an older tradition, dating back to Lisp, where expressions do all the work.

In C, if and switch are statements. They don't produce a value, and they can't be used in the middle of an expression. In Rust, if and match *can* produce values. We already saw a match expression that produces a numeric value in Chapter 2:

```
pixels[r * bounds.0 + c] =
    match escapes(Complex { re: point.0, im: point.1 }, 255) {
        None => 0,
        Some(count) => 255 - count as u8
    };
```

An if expression can be used to initialize a variable:

```
let status =
    if cpu.temperature <= MAX_TEMP {
        HttpStatus::Ok
    } else {
        HttpStatus::ServerError  // server melted
    };
```

A match expression can be passed as an argument to a function or macro:

```
println!("Inside the vat, you see {}.",
    match vat.contents {
        Some(brain) => brain.desc(),
        None => "nothing of interest"
    });
```

This explains why Rust does not have C's ternary operator (*expr1 ? expr2 : expr3*). In C, it is a handy expression-level analogue to the if statement. It would be redundant in Rust: the if expression handles both cases.

Most of the control flow tools in C are statements. In Rust, they are all expressions.

Precedence and Associativity

Table 6-1 summarizes Rust expression syntax. We will discuss all of these kinds of expressions in this chapter. Operators are listed in order of precedence, from highest to lowest. (Like most programming languages, Rust has *operator precedence* to determine the order of operations when an expression contains multiple adjacent operators. For example, in limit < 2 * broom.size + 1, the . operator has the highest precedence, so the field access happens first.)

Table 6-1. Expressions

Expression type	Example	Related traits
Array literal	`[1, 2, 3]`	
Repeat array literal	`[0; 50]`	
Tuple	`(6, "crullers")`	
Grouping	`(2 + 2)`	
Block	`{ f(); g() }`	
Control flow expressions	`if ok { f() }`	
	`if ok { 1 } else { 0 }`	
	`if let Some(x) = f() { x } else { 0 }`	
	`match x { None => 0, _ => 1 }`	
	`for v in e { f(v); }`	`std::iter::IntoIterator`
	`while ok { ok = f(); }`	
	`while let Some(x) = it.next() { f(x); }`	
	`loop { next_event(); }`	
	`break`	
	`continue`	
	`return 0`	
Macro invocation	`println!("ok")`	
Path	`std::f64::consts::PI`	
Struct literal	`Point {x: 0, y: 0}`	
Tuple field access	`pair.0`	`Deref, DerefMut`
Struct field access	`point.x`	`Deref, DerefMut`
Method call	`point.translate(50, 50)`	`Deref, DerefMut`
Function call	`stdin()`	`Fn(Arg0, ...) -> T,` `FnMut(Arg0, ...) -> T,` `FnOnce(Arg0, ...) -> T`
Index	`arr[0]`	`Index, IndexMut` `Deref, DerefMut`
Error check	`create_dir("tmp")?`	
Logical/bitwise NOT	`!ok`	`Not`
Negation	`-num`	`Neg`
Dereference	`*ptr`	`Deref, DerefMut`
Borrow	`&val`	
Type cast	`x as u32`	
Multiplication	`n * 2`	`Mul`
Division	`n / 2`	`Div`
Remainder (modulus)	`n % 2`	`Rem`
Addition	`n + 1`	`Add`

Expression type	Example	Related traits
Subtraction	`n - 1`	Sub
Left shift	`n << 1`	Shl
Right shift	`n >> 1`	Shr
Bitwise AND	`n & 1`	BitAnd
Bitwise exclusive OR	`n ^ 1`	BitXor
Bitwise OR	`n	1`	BitOr
Less than	`n < 1`	std::cmp::PartialOrd
Less than or equal	`n <= 1`	std::cmp::PartialOrd
Greater than	`n > 1`	std::cmp::PartialOrd
Greater than or equal	`n >= 1`	std::cmp::PartialOrd
Equal	`n == 1`	std::cmp::PartialEq
Not equal	`n != 1`	std::cmp::PartialEq
Logical AND	`x.ok && y.ok`	
Logical OR	`x.ok || backup.ok`	
End-exclusive range	`start .. stop`	
End-inclusive range	`start ..= stop`	
Assignment	`x = val`	
Compound assignment	`x *= 1`	MulAssign
	`x /= 1`	DivAssign
	`x %= 1`	RemAssign
	`x += 1`	AddAssign
	`x -= 1`	SubAssign
	`x <<= 1`	ShlAssign
	`x >>= 1`	ShrAssign
	`x &= 1`	BitAndAssign
	`x ^= 1`	BitXorAssign
	`x |= 1`	BitOrAssign
Closure	`|x, y| x + y`	

All of the operators that can usefully be chained are left-associative. That is, a chain of operations such as `a - b - c` is grouped as `(a - b) - c`, not `a - (b - c)`. The operators that can be chained in this way are all the ones you might expect:

```
*   /   %   +   -   <<   >>   &   ^   |   &&   ||   as
```

The comparison operators, the assignment operators, and the range operators `..` and `..=` can't be chained at all.

Blocks and Semicolons

Blocks are the most general kind of expression. A block produces a value and can be used anywhere a value is needed:

```
let display_name = match post.author() {
    Some(author) => author.name(),
    None => {
        let network_info = post.get_network_metadata()?;
        let ip = network_info.client_address();
        ip.to_string()
    }
};
```

The code after `Some(author) =>` is the simple expression `author.name()`. The code after `None =>` is a block expression. It makes no difference to Rust. The value of the block is the value of its last expression, `ip.to_string()`.

Note that there is no semicolon after the `ip.to_string()` method call. Most lines of Rust code do end with either a semicolon or curly braces, just like C or Java. And if a block looks like C code, with semicolons in all the familiar places, then it will run just like a C block, and its value will be `()`. As we mentioned in Chapter 2, when you leave the semicolon off the last line of a block, that makes the value of the block the value of its final expression, rather than the usual `()`.

In some languages, particularly JavaScript, you're allowed to omit semicolons, and the language simply fills them in for you—a minor convenience. This is different. In Rust, the semicolon actually means something:

```
let msg = {
    // let-declaration: semicolon is always required
    let dandelion_control = puffball.open();

    // expression + semicolon: method is called, return value dropped
    dandelion_control.release_all_seeds(launch_codes);

    // expression with no semicolon: method is called,
    // return value stored in `msg`
    dandelion_control.get_status()
};
```

This ability of blocks to contain declarations and also produce a value at the end is a neat feature, one that quickly comes to feel natural. The one drawback is that it leads to an odd error message when you leave out a semicolon by accident:

```
...
if preferences.changed() {
    page.compute_size()  // oops, missing semicolon
}
...
```

If you made this mistake in a C or Java program, the compiler would simply point out that you're missing a semicolon. Here's what Rust says:

```
error: mismatched types
22 |            page.compute_size()  // oops, missing semicolon
   |            ^^^^^^^^^^^^^^^^^^^- help: try adding a semicolon: `;`
   |            |
   |            expected (), found tuple
   |
   = note: expected unit type `()`
              found tuple `(u32, u32)`
```

With the semicolon missing, the block's value would be whatever `page.compute_size()` returns, but an `if` without an `else` must always return `()`. Fortunately, Rust has seen this sort of thing before and suggests adding the semicolon.

Declarations

In addition to expressions and semicolons, a block may contain any number of declarations. The most common are `let` declarations, which declare local variables:

```
let name: type = expr;
```

The type and initializer are optional. The semicolon is required. Like all identifiers in Rust, variable names must start with a letter or underscore, and can contain digits only after that first character. Rust has a broad definition of "letter": it includes Greek letters, accented Latin characters, and many more symbols—anything that Unicode Standard Annex #31 declares suitable. Emoji aren't allowed.

A `let` declaration can declare a variable without initializing it. The variable can then be initialized with a later assignment. This is occasionally useful, because sometimes a variable should be initialized from the middle of some sort of control flow construct:

```
let name;
if user.has_nickname() {
    name = user.nickname();
} else {
    name = generate_unique_name();
    user.register(&name);
}
```

Here there are two different ways the local variable `name` might be initialized, but either way it will be initialized exactly once, so `name` does not need to be declared `mut`.

It's an error to use a variable before it's initialized. (This is closely related to the error of using a value after it's been moved. Rust really wants you to use values only while they exist!)

You may occasionally see code that seems to redeclare an existing variable, like this:

```
for line in file.lines() {
    let line = line?;
    ...
}
```

The `let` declaration creates a new, second variable, of a different type. The type of the first variable `line` is `Result<String, io::Error>`. The second `line` is a `String`. Its definition supersedes the first's for the rest of the block. This is called *shadowing* and is very common in Rust programs. The code is equivalent to:

```
for line_result in file.lines() {
    let line = line_result?;
    ...
}
```

In this book, we'll stick to using a `_result` suffix in such situations so that the variables have distinct names.

A block can also contain *item declarations*. An item is simply any declaration that could appear globally in a program or module, such as a `fn`, `struct`, or `use`.

Later chapters will cover items in detail. For now, `fn` makes a sufficient example. Any block may contain an `fn`:

```
use std::io;
use std::cmp::Ordering;

fn show_files() -> io::Result<()> {
    let mut v = vec![];
    ...

    fn cmp_by_timestamp_then_name(a: &FileInfo, b: &FileInfo) -> Ordering {
        a.timestamp.cmp(&b.timestamp)      // first, compare timestamps
            .reverse()                      // newest file first
            .then(a.path.cmp(&b.path))      // compare paths to break ties
    }

    v.sort_by(cmp_by_timestamp_then_name);
    ...
}
```

When an `fn` is declared inside a block, its scope is the entire block—that is, it can be *used* throughout the enclosing block. But a nested `fn` cannot access local variables or arguments that happen to be in scope. For example, the function `cmp_by_timestamp_then_name` could not use `v` directly. (Rust also has closures, which do see into enclosing scopes. See Chapter 14.)

A block can even contain a whole module. This may seem a bit much—do we really need to be able to nest *every* piece of the language inside every other piece?—but programmers (and particularly programmers using macros) have a way of finding uses for every scrap of orthogonality the language provides.

if and match

The form of an if expression is familiar:

```
if condition1 {
    block1
} else if condition2 {
    block2
} else {
    block_n
}
```

Each *condition* must be an expression of type bool; true to form, Rust does not implicitly convert numbers or pointers to Boolean values.

Unlike C, parentheses are not required around conditions. In fact, rustc will emit a warning if unnecessary parentheses are present. The curly braces, however, are required.

The else if blocks, as well as the final else, are optional. An if expression with no else block behaves exactly as though it had an empty else block.

match expressions are something like the C switch statement, but more flexible. A simple example:

```
match code {
    0 => println!("OK"),
    1 => println!("Wires Tangled"),
    2 => println!("User Asleep"),
    _ => println!("Unrecognized Error {}", code)
}
```

This is something a switch statement could do. Exactly one of the four arms of this match expression will execute, depending on the value of code. The wildcard pattern _ matches everything. This is like the default: case in a switch statement, except that it must come last; placing a _ pattern before other patterns means that it will have precedence over them. Those patterns will never match anything (and the compiler will warn you about it).

The compiler can optimize this kind of match using a jump table, just like a switch statement in C++. A similar optimization is applied when each arm of a match produces a constant value. In that case, the compiler builds an array of those values, and the match is compiled into an array access. Apart from a bounds check, there is no branching at all in the compiled code.

The versatility of `match` stems from the variety of supported *patterns* that can be used to the left of => in each arm. Above, each pattern is simply a constant integer. We've also shown `match` expressions that distinguish the two kinds of `Option` value:

```
match params.get("name") {
    Some(name) => println!("Hello, {}!", name),
    None => println!("Greetings, stranger.")
}
```

This is only a hint of what patterns can do. A pattern can match a range of values. It can unpack tuples. It can match against individual fields of structs. It can chase references, borrow parts of a value, and more. Rust's patterns are a mini-language of their own. We'll dedicate several pages to them in Chapter 10.

The general form of a `match` expression is:

```
match value {
    pattern => expr,
    ...
}
```

The comma after an arm may be dropped if the *expr* is a block.

Rust checks the given *value* against each pattern in turn, starting with the first. When a pattern matches, the corresponding *expr* is evaluated, and the `match` expression is complete; no further patterns are checked. At least one of the patterns must match. Rust prohibits `match` expressions that do not cover all possible values:

```
let score = match card.rank {
    Jack => 10,
    Queen => 10,
    Ace => 11
}; // error: nonexhaustive patterns
```

All blocks of an `if` expression must produce values of the same type:

```
let suggested_pet =
    if with_wings { Pet::Buzzard } else { Pet::Hyena };  // ok

let favorite_number =
    if user.is_hobbit() { "eleventy-one" } else { 9 };  // error

let best_sports_team =
    if is_hockey_season() { "Predators" };  // error
```

(The last example is an error because in July, the result would be ( ).)

Similarly, all arms of a `match` expression must have the same type:

```
let suggested_pet =
    match favorites.element {
        Fire => Pet::RedPanda,
        Air => Pet::Buffalo,
```

```
        Water => Pet::Orca,
        _ => None  // error: incompatible types
    };
```

if let

There is one more if form, the if let expression:

```
if let pattern = expr {
    block1
} else {
    block2
}
```

The given *expr* either matches the *pattern*, in which case *block1* runs, or doesn't match, and *block2* runs. Sometimes this is a nice way to get data out of an Option or Result:

```
if let Some(cookie) = request.session_cookie {
    return restore_session(cookie);
}

if let Err(err) = show_cheesy_anti_robot_task() {
    log_robot_attempt(err);
    politely_accuse_user_of_being_a_robot();
} else {
    session.mark_as_human();
}
```

It's never strictly *necessary* to use if let, because match can do everything if let can do. An if let expression is shorthand for a match with just one pattern:

```
match expr {
    pattern => { block1 }
    _ => { block2 }
}
```

Loops

There are four looping expressions:

```
while condition {
    block
}

while let pattern = expr {
    block
}

loop {
    block
}
```

```
for pattern in iterable {
    block
}
```

Loops are expressions in Rust, but the value of a while or for loop is always (), so their value isn't very useful. A loop expression can produce a value if you specify one.

A while loop behaves exactly like the C equivalent, except that, again, the *condition* must be of the exact type bool.

The while let loop is analogous to if let. At the beginning of each loop iteration, the value of *expr* either matches the given *pattern*, in which case the block runs, or doesn't, in which case the loop exits.

Use loop to write infinite loops. It executes the *block* repeatedly forever (or until a break or return is reached or the thread panics).

A for loop evaluates the *iterable* expression and then evaluates the *block* once for each value in the resulting iterator. Many types can be iterated over, including all the standard collections like Vec and HashMap. The standard C for loop:

```
for (int i = 0; i < 20; i++) {
    printf("%d\n", i);
}
```

is written like this in Rust:

```
for i in 0..20 {
    println!("{}", i);
}
```

As in C, the last number printed is 19.

The .. operator produces a *range*, a simple struct with two fields: start and end. 0..20 is the same as std::ops::Range { start: 0, end: 20 }. Ranges can be used with for loops because Range is an iterable type: it implements the std::iter::IntoIterator trait, which we'll discuss in Chapter 15. The standard collections are all iterable, as are arrays and slices.

In keeping with Rust's move semantics, a for loop over a value consumes the value:

```
let strings: Vec<String> = error_messages();
for s in strings {                       // each String is moved into s here...
    println!("{}", s);
}                                        // ...and dropped here
println!("{} error(s)", strings.len()); // error: use of moved value
```

This can be inconvenient. The easy remedy is to loop over a reference to the collection instead. The loop variable, then, will be a reference to each item in the collection:

```
for rs in &strings {
    println!("String {:?} is at address {:p}.", *rs, rs);
}
```

Here the type of &strings is &Vec<String>, and the type of rs is &String.

Iterating over a mut reference provides a mut reference to each element:

```
for rs in &mut strings {  // the type of rs is &mut String
    rs.push('\n');  // add a newline to each string
}
```

Chapter 15 covers for loops in greater detail and shows many other ways to use iterators.

Control Flow in Loops

A break expression exits an enclosing loop. (In Rust, break works only in loops. It is not necessary in match expressions, which are unlike switch statements in this regard.)

Within the body of a loop, you can give break an expression, whose value becomes that of the loop:

```
// Each call to `next_line` returns either `Some(line)`, where
// `line` is a line of input, or `None`, if we've reached the end of
// the input. Return the first line that starts with "answer: ".
// Otherwise, return "answer: nothing".
let answer = loop {
    if let Some(line) = next_line() {
        if line.starts_with("answer: ") {
            break line;
        }
    } else {
        break "answer: nothing";
    }
};
```

Naturally, all the break expressions within a loop must produce values with the same type, which becomes the type of the loop itself.

A continue expression jumps to the next loop iteration:

```
// Read some data, one line at a time.
for line in input_lines {
    let trimmed = trim_comments_and_whitespace(line);
    if trimmed.is_empty() {
        // Jump back to the top of the loop and
        // move on to the next line of input.
        continue;
    }
```

```
        ...
}
```

In a `for` loop, `continue` advances to the next value in the collection. If there are no more values, the loop exits. Similarly, in a `while` loop, `continue` rechecks the loop condition. If it's now false, the loop exits.

A loop can be *labeled* with a lifetime. In the following example, `'search:` is a label for the outer `for` loop. Thus, `break 'search` exits that loop, not the inner loop:

```
'search:
for room in apartment {
    for spot in room.hiding_spots() {
        if spot.contains(keys) {
            println!("Your keys are {} in the {}.", spot, room);
            break 'search;
        }
    }
}
```

A `break` can have both a label and a value expression:

```
// Find the square root of the first perfect square
// in the series.
let sqrt = 'outer: loop {
    let n = next_number();
    for i in 1.. {
        let square = i * i;
        if square == n {
            // Found a square root.
            break 'outer i;
        }
        if square > n {
            // `n` isn't a perfect square, try the next
            break;
        }
    }
};
```

Labels can also be used with `continue`.

return Expressions

A `return` expression exits the current function, returning a value to the caller.

`return` without a value is shorthand for `return ()`:

```
fn f() {     // return type omitted: defaults to ()
    return;  // return value omitted: defaults to ()
}
```

Functions don't have to have an explicit `return` expression. The body of a function works like a block expression: if the last expression isn't followed by a semicolon, its value is the function's return value. In fact, this is the preferred way to supply a function's return value in Rust.

But this doesn't mean that `return` is useless, or merely a concession to users who aren't experienced with expression languages. Like a `break` expression, `return` can abandon work in progress. For example, in Chapter 2, we used the `?` operator to check for errors after calling a function that can fail:

```
let output = File::create(filename)?;
```

We explained that this is shorthand for a `match` expression:

```
let output = match File::create(filename) {
    Ok(f) => f,
    Err(err) => return Err(err)
};
```

This code starts by calling `File::create(filename)`. If that returns `Ok(f)`, then the whole `match` expression evaluates to `f`, so `f` is stored in `output`, and we continue with the next line of code following the `match`.

Otherwise, we'll match `Err(err)` and hit the `return` expression. When that happens, it doesn't matter that we're in the middle of evaluating a `match` expression to determine the value of the variable `output`. We abandon all of that and exit the enclosing function, returning whatever error we got from `File::create()`.

We'll cover the `?` operator more completely in "Propagating Errors" on page 164.

Why Rust Has loop

Several pieces of the Rust compiler analyze the flow of control through your program:

- Rust checks that every path through a function returns a value of the expected return type. To do this correctly, it needs to know whether it's possible to reach the end of the function.

- Rust checks that local variables are never used uninitialized. This entails checking every path through a function to make sure there's no way to reach a place where a variable is used without having already passed through code that initializes it.

- Rust warns about unreachable code. Code is unreachable if *no* path through the function reaches it.

These are called *flow-sensitive* analyses. They are nothing new; Java has had a "definite assignment" analysis, similar to Rust's, for years.

When enforcing this sort of rule, a language must strike a balance between simplicity, which makes it easier for programmers to figure out what the compiler is talking about sometimes, and cleverness, which can help eliminate false warnings and cases where the compiler rejects a perfectly safe program. Rust went for simplicity. Its flow-sensitive analyses do not examine loop conditions at all, instead simply assuming that any condition in a program can be either true or false.

This causes Rust to reject some safe programs:

```
fn wait_for_process(process: &mut Process) -> i32 {
    while true {
        if process.wait() {
            return process.exit_code();
        }
    }
}  // error: mismatched types: expected i32, found ()
```

The error here is bogus. This function only exits via the return statement, so the fact that the while loop doesn't produce an i32 is irrelevant.

The loop expression is offered as a "say-what-you-mean" solution to this problem.

Rust's type system is affected by control flow, too. Earlier we said that all branches of an if expression must have the same type. But it would be silly to enforce this rule on blocks that end with a break or return expression, an infinite loop, or a call to panic!() or std::process::exit(). What all those expressions have in common is that they never finish in the usual way, producing a value. A break or return exits the current block abruptly, an infinite loop never finishes at all, and so on.

So in Rust, these expressions don't have a normal type. Expressions that don't finish normally are assigned the special type !, and they're exempt from the rules about types having to match. You can see ! in the function signature of std::process::exit():

```
fn exit(code: i32) -> !
```

The ! means that exit() never returns. It's a *divergent function*.

You can write divergent functions of your own using the same syntax, and this is perfectly natural in some cases:

```
fn serve_forever(socket: ServerSocket, handler: ServerHandler) -> ! {
    socket.listen();
    loop {
        let s = socket.accept();
        handler.handle(s);
    }
}
```

Of course, Rust then considers it an error if the function can return normally.

With these building blocks of large-scale control flow in place, we can move on to the finer-grained expressions typically used within that flow, like function calls and arithmetic operators.

Function and Method Calls

The syntax for calling functions and methods is the same in Rust as in many other languages:

```
let x = gcd(1302, 462);  // function call

let room = player.location();  // method call
```

In the second example here, `player` is a variable of the made-up type `Player`, which has a made-up `.location()` method. (We'll show how to define your own methods when we start talking about user-defined types in Chapter 9.)

Rust usually makes a sharp distinction between references and the values they refer to. If you pass a `&i32` to a function that expects an `i32`, that's a type error. You'll notice that the `.` operator relaxes those rules a bit. In the method call `player.location()`, `player` might be a `Player`, a reference of type `&Player`, or a smart pointer of type `Box<Player>` or `Rc<Player>`. The `.location()` method might take the player either by value or by reference. The same `.location()` syntax works in all cases, because Rust's `.` operator automatically dereferences `player` or borrows a reference to it as needed.

A third syntax is used for calling type-associated functions, like `Vec::new()`:

```
let mut numbers = Vec::new();  // type-associated function call
```

These are similar to static methods in object-oriented languages: ordinary methods are called on values (like `my_vec.len()`), and type-associated functions are called on types (like `Vec::new()`).

Naturally, method calls can be chained:

```
// From the Actix-based web server in Chapter 2:
server
    .bind("127.0.0.1:3000").expect("error binding server to address")
    .run().expect("error running server");
```

One quirk of Rust syntax is that in a function call or method call, the usual syntax for generic types, `Vec<T>`, does not work:

```
return Vec<i32>::with_capacity(1000);  // error: something about chained comparisons
```

```
let ramp = (0 .. n).collect<Vec<i32>>();  // same error
```

The problem is that in expressions, < is the less-than operator. The Rust compiler helpfully suggests writing ::<T> instead of <T> in this case, and that solves the problem:

```
return Vec::<i32>::with_capacity(1000);  // ok, using ::<
```

```
let ramp = (0 .. n).collect::<Vec<i32>>();  // ok, using ::<
```

The symbol ::<...> is affectionately known in the Rust community as the *turbofish*.

Alternatively, it is often possible to drop the type parameters and let Rust infer them:

```
return Vec::with_capacity(10);  // ok, if the fn return type is Vec<i32>
```

```
let ramp: Vec<i32> = (0 .. n).collect();  // ok, variable's type is given
```

It's considered good style to omit the types whenever they can be inferred.

Fields and Elements

The fields of a struct are accessed using familiar syntax. Tuples are the same except that their fields have numbers rather than names:

```
game.black_pawns   // struct field
coords.1           // tuple element
```

If the value to the left of the dot is a reference or smart pointer type, it is automatically dereferenced, just as for method calls.

Square brackets access the elements of an array, a slice, or a vector:

```
pieces[i]          // array element
```

The value to the left of the brackets is automatically dereferenced.

Expressions like these three are called *lvalues*, because they can appear on the left side of an assignment:

```
game.black_pawns = 0x00ff0000_00000000_u64;
coords.1 = 0;
pieces[2] = Some(Piece::new(Black, Knight, coords));
```

Of course, this is permitted only if game, coords, and pieces are declared as mut variables.

Extracting a slice from an array or vector is straightforward:

```
let second_half = &game_moves[midpoint .. end];
```

Here game_moves may be either an array, a slice, or a vector; the result, regardless, is a borrowed slice of length end - midpoint. game_moves is considered borrowed for the lifetime of second_half.

The .. operator allows either operand to be omitted; it produces up to four different types of object depending on which operands are present:

```
..        // RangeFull
a ..      // RangeFrom { start: a }
.. b      // RangeTo { end: b }
a .. b    // Range { start: a, end: b }
```

The latter two forms are *end-exclusive* (or *half-open*): the end value is not included in the range represented. For example, the range 0 .. 3 includes the numbers 0, 1, and 2.

The ..= operator produces *end-inclusive* (or *closed*) ranges, which do include the end value:

```
..= b     // RangeToInclusive { end: b }
a ..= b   // RangeInclusive::new(a, b)
```

For example, the range 0 ..= 3 includes the numbers 0, 1, 2, and 3.

Only ranges that include a start value are iterable, since a loop must have somewhere to start. But in array slicing, all six forms are useful. If the start or end of the range is omitted, it defaults to the start or end of the data being sliced.

So an implementation of quicksort, the classic divide-and-conquer sorting algorithm, might look, in part, like this:

```
fn quicksort<T: Ord>(slice: &mut [T]) {
    if slice.len() <= 1 {
        return;  // Nothing to sort.
    }

    // Partition the slice into two parts, front and back.
    let pivot_index = partition(slice);

    // Recursively sort the front half of `slice`.
    quicksort(&mut slice[.. pivot_index]);

    // And the back half.
    quicksort(&mut slice[pivot_index + 1 ..]);
}
```

Reference Operators

The address-of operators, `&` and `&mut`, are covered in Chapter 5.

The unary `*` operator is used to access the value pointed to by a reference. As we've seen, Rust automatically follows references when you use the `.` operator to access a field or method, so the `*` operator is necessary only when we want to read or write the entire value that the reference points to.

For example, sometimes an iterator produces references, but the program needs the underlying values:

```
let padovan: Vec<u64> = compute_padovan_sequence(n);
for elem in &padovan {
    draw_triangle(turtle, *elem);
}
```

In this example, the type of `elem` is `&u64`, so `*elem` is a `u64`.

Arithmetic, Bitwise, Comparison, and Logical Operators

Rust's binary operators are like those in many other languages. To save time, we assume familiarity with one of those languages, and focus on the few points where Rust departs from tradition.

Rust has the usual arithmetic operators, `+`, `-`, `*`, `/`, and `%`. As mentioned in Chapter 3, integer overflow is detected, and causes a panic, in debug builds. The standard library provides methods like `a.wrapping_add(b)` for unchecked arithmetic.

Integer division rounds toward zero, and dividing an integer by zero triggers a panic even in release builds. Integers have a method `a.checked_div(b)` that returns an `Option` (`None` if `b` is zero) and never panics.

Unary `-` negates a number. It is supported for all the numeric types except unsigned integers. There is no unary `+` operator.

```
println!("{}", -100);      // -100
println!("{}", -100u32);   // error: can't apply unary `-` to type `u32`
println!("{}", +100);      // error: expected expression, found `+`
```

As in C, `a % b` computes the signed remainder, or modulus, of division rounding toward zero. The result has the same sign as the lefthand operand. Note that `%` can be used on floating-point numbers as well as integers:

```
let x = 1234.567 % 10.0;   // approximately 4.567
```

Rust also inherits C's bitwise integer operators, `&`, `|`, `^`, `<<`, and `>>`. However, Rust uses `!` instead of `~` for bitwise NOT:

```
let hi: u8 = 0xe0;
let lo = !hi;   // 0x1f
```

This means that `!n` can't be used on an integer `n` to mean "n is zero." For that, write `n == 0`.

Bit shifting is always sign-extending on signed integer types and zero-extending on unsigned integer types. Since Rust has unsigned integers, it does not need an unsigned shift operator, like Java's `>>>` operator.

Bitwise operations have higher precedence than comparisons, unlike C, so if you write `x & BIT != 0`, that means `(x & BIT) != 0`, as you probably intended. This is much more useful than C's interpretation, `x & (BIT != 0)`, which tests the wrong bit!

Rust's comparison operators are `==`, `!=`, `<`, `<=`, `>`, and `>=`. The two values being compared must have the same type.

Rust also has the two short-circuiting logical operators `&&` and `||`. Both operands must have the exact type `bool`.

Assignment

The `=` operator can be used to assign to `mut` variables and their fields or elements. But assignment is not as common in Rust as in other languages, since variables are immutable by default.

As described in Chapter 4, if the value has a non-`Copy` type, assignment *moves* it into the destination. Ownership of the value is transferred from the source to the destination. The destination's prior value, if any, is dropped.

Compound assignment is supported:

```
total += item.price;
```

This is equivalent to `total = total + item.price;`. Other operators are supported too: `-=`, `*=`, and so forth. The full list is given in Table 6-1, earlier in this chapter.

Unlike C, Rust doesn't support chaining assignment: you can't write `a = b = 3` to assign the value 3 to both `a` and `b`. Assignment is rare enough in Rust that you won't miss this shorthand.

Rust does not have C's increment and decrement operators `++` and `--`.

Type Casts

Converting a value from one type to another usually requires an explicit cast in Rust. Casts use the `as` keyword:

```
let x = 17;              // x is type i32
let index = x as usize;  // convert to usize
```

Several kinds of casts are permitted:

- Numbers may be cast from any of the built-in numeric types to any other.

  Casting an integer to another integer type is always well-defined. Converting to a narrower type results in truncation. A signed integer cast to a wider type is sign-extended, an unsigned integer is zero-extended, and so on. In short, there are no surprises.

  Converting from a floating-point type to an integer type rounds toward zero: the value of `-1.99 as i32` is `-1`. If the value is too large to fit in the integer type, the cast produces the closest value that the integer type can represent: the value of `1e6 as u8` is `255`.

- Values of type `bool` or `char`, or of a C-like `enum` type, may be cast to any integer type. (We'll cover enums in Chapter 10.)

  Casting in the other direction is not allowed, as `bool`, `char`, and `enum` types all have restrictions on their values that would have to be enforced with run-time checks. For example, casting a `u16` to type `char` is banned because some `u16` values, like `0xd800`, correspond to Unicode surrogate code points and therefore would not make valid `char` values. There is a standard method, `std::char::from_u32()`, which performs the run-time check and returns an `Option<char>`; but more to the point, the need for this kind of conversion has grown rare. We typically convert whole strings or streams at once, and algorithms on Unicode text are often nontrivial and best left to libraries.

  As an exception, a `u8` may be cast to type `char`, since all integers from 0 to 255 are valid Unicode code points for `char` to hold.

- Some casts involving unsafe pointer types are also allowed. See "Raw Pointers" on page 640.

We said that a conversion *usually* requires a cast. A few conversions involving reference types are so straightforward that the language performs them even without a cast. One trivial example is converting a `mut` reference to a non-`mut` reference.

Several more significant automatic conversions can happen, though:

- Values of type &String auto-convert to type &str without a cast.
- Values of type &Vec<i32> auto-convert to &[i32].
- Values of type &Box<Chessboard> auto-convert to &Chessboard.

These are called *deref coercions*, because they apply to types that implement the Deref built-in trait. The purpose of Deref coercion is to make smart pointer types, like Box, behave as much like the underlying value as possible. Using a Box<Chessboard> is mostly just like using a plain Chessboard, thanks to Deref.

User-defined types can implement the Deref trait, too. When you need to write your own smart pointer type, see "Deref and DerefMut" on page 312.

Closures

Rust has *closures*, lightweight function-like values. A closure usually consists of an argument list, given between vertical bars, followed by an expression:

```
let is_even = |x| x % 2 == 0;
```

Rust infers the argument types and return type. You can also write them out explicitly, as you would for a function. If you do specify a return type, then the body of the closure must be a block, for the sake of syntactic sanity:

```
let is_even = |x: u64| -> bool x % 2 == 0;   // error

let is_even = |x: u64| -> bool { x % 2 == 0 };  // ok
```

Calling a closure uses the same syntax as calling a function:

```
assert_eq!(is_even(14), true);
```

Closures are one of Rust's most delightful features, and there is a great deal more to be said about them. We shall say it in Chapter 14.

Onward

Expressions are what we think of as "running code." They're the part of a Rust program that compiles to machine instructions. Yet they are a small fraction of the whole language.

The same is true in most programming languages. The first job of a program is to run, but that's not its only job. Programs have to communicate. They have to be testable. They have to stay organized and flexible so that they can continue to evolve. They have to interoperate with code and services built by other teams. And even just to run, programs in a statically typed language like Rust need some more tools for organizing data than just tuples and arrays.

Coming up, we'll spend several chapters talking about features in this area: modules and crates, which give your program structure, and then structs and enums, which do the same for your data.

First, we'll dedicate a few pages to the important topic of what to do when things go wrong.

## CHAPTER 7

Error Handling

I knew if I stayed around long enough, something like this would happen.
—George Bernard Shaw on dying

Rust's approach to error handling is unusual enough to warrant a short chapter on the topic. There aren't any difficult ideas here, just ideas that might be new to you. This chapter covers the two different kinds of error handling in Rust: panic and `Results`.

Ordinary errors are handled using the `Result` type. `Results` typically represent problems caused by things outside the program, like erroneous input, a network outage, or a permissions problem. That such situations occur is not up to us; even a bug-free program will encounter them from time to time. Most of this chapter is dedicated to that kind of error. We'll cover panic first, though, because it's the simpler of the two.

Panic is for the other kind of error, the kind that *should never happen*.

Panic

A program panics when it encounters something so messed up that there must be a bug in the program itself. Something like:

- Out-of-bounds array access
- Integer division by zero
- Calling `.expect()` on a `Result` that happens to be `Err`
- Assertion failure

(There's also the macro panic!(), for cases where your own code discovers that it has gone wrong, and you therefore need to trigger a panic directly. panic!() accepts optional println!()-style arguments, for building an error message.)

What these conditions have in common is that they are all—not to put too fine a point on it—the programmer's fault. A good rule of thumb is: "Don't panic."

But we all make mistakes. When these errors that shouldn't happen do happen—what then? Remarkably, Rust gives you a choice. Rust can either unwind the stack when a panic happens or abort the process. Unwinding is the default.

Unwinding

When pirates divvy up the booty from a raid, the captain gets half of the loot. Ordinary crew members earn equal shares of the other half. (Pirates hate fractions, so if either division does not come out even, the result is rounded down, with the remainder going to the ship's parrot.)

```
fn pirate_share(total: u64, crew_size: usize) -> u64 {
    let half = total / 2;
    half / crew_size as u64
}
```

This may work fine for centuries until one day it transpires that the captain is the sole survivor of a raid. If we pass a crew_size of zero to this function, it will divide by zero. In C++, this would be undefined behavior. In Rust, it triggers a panic, which typically proceeds as follows:

- An error message is printed to the terminal:

    ```
    thread 'main' panicked at 'attempt to divide by zero', pirates.rs:3780
    note: Run with `RUST_BACKTRACE=1` for a backtrace.
    ```

    If you set the RUST_BACKTRACE environment variable, as the messages suggests, Rust will also dump the stack at this point.

- The stack is unwound. This is a lot like C++ exception handling.

    Any temporary values, local variables, or arguments that the current function was using are dropped, in the reverse of the order they were created. Dropping a value simply means cleaning up after it: any Strings or Vecs the program was using are freed, any open Files are closed, and so on. User-defined drop methods are called too; see "Drop" on page 304. In the particular case of pirate_share(), there's nothing to clean up.

    Once the current function call is cleaned up, we move on to its caller, dropping its variables and arguments the same way. Then we move to *that* function's caller, and so on up the stack.

- Finally, the thread exits. If the panicking thread was the main thread, then the whole process exits (with a nonzero exit code).

Perhaps *panic* is a misleading name for this orderly process. A panic is not a crash. It's not undefined behavior. It's more like a `RuntimeException` in Java or a `std::logic_error` in C++. The behavior is well-defined; it just shouldn't be happening.

Panic is safe. It doesn't violate any of Rust's safety rules; even if you manage to panic in the middle of a standard library method, it will never leave a dangling pointer or a half-initialized value in memory. The idea is that Rust catches the invalid array access, or whatever it is, *before* anything bad happens. It would be unsafe to proceed, so Rust unwinds the stack. But the rest of the process can continue running.

Panic is per thread. One thread can be panicking while other threads are going on about their normal business. In Chapter 19, we'll show how a parent thread can find out when a child thread panics and handle the error gracefully.

There is also a way to *catch* stack unwinding, allowing the thread to survive and continue running. The standard library function `std::panic::catch_unwind()` does this. We won't cover how to use it, but this is the mechanism used by Rust's test harness to recover when an assertion fails in a test. (It can also be necessary when writing Rust code that can be called from C or C++, because unwinding across non-Rust code is undefined behavior; see Chapter 22.)

Ideally, we would all have bug-free code that never panics. But nobody's perfect. You can use threads and `catch_unwind()` to handle panic, making your program more robust. One important caveat is that these tools only catch panics that unwind the stack. Not every panic proceeds this way.

Aborting

Stack unwinding is the default panic behavior, but there are two circumstances in which Rust does not try to unwind the stack.

If a `.drop()` method triggers a second panic while Rust is still trying to clean up after the first, this is considered fatal. Rust stops unwinding and aborts the whole process.

Also, Rust's panic behavior is customizable. If you compile with `-C panic=abort`, the *first* panic in your program immediately aborts the process. (With this option, Rust does not need to know how to unwind the stack, so this can reduce the size of your compiled code.)

This concludes our discussion of panic in Rust. There is not much to say, because ordinary Rust code has no obligation to handle panic. Even if you do use threads or `catch_unwind()`, all your panic-handling code will likely be concentrated in a few places. It's unreasonable to expect every function in a program to anticipate and cope with bugs in its own code. Errors caused by other factors are another kettle of fish.

Result

Rust doesn't have exceptions. Instead, functions that can fail have a return type that says so:

```
fn get_weather(location: LatLng) -> Result<WeatherReport, io::Error>
```

The Result type indicates possible failure. When we call the get_weather() function, it will return either a *success result* Ok(weather), where weather is a new WeatherReport value, or an *error result* Err(error_value), where error_value is an io::Error explaining what went wrong.

Rust requires us to write some kind of error handling whenever we call this function. We can't get at the WeatherReport without doing *something* to the Result, and you'll get a compiler warning if a Result value isn't used.

In Chapter 10, we'll see how the standard library defines Result and how you can define your own similar types. For now, we'll take a "cookbook" approach and focus on how to use Results to get the error-handling behavior you want. We'll look at how to catch, propagate, and report errors, as well as common patterns for organizing and working with Result types.

Catching Errors

The most thorough way of dealing with a Result is the way we showed in Chapter 2: use a match expression.

```
match get_weather(hometown) {
    Ok(report) => {
        display_weather(hometown, &report);
    }
    Err(err) => {
        println!("error querying the weather: {}", err);
        schedule_weather_retry();
    }
}
```

This is Rust's equivalent of try/catch in other languages. It's what you use when you want to handle errors head-on, not pass them on to your caller.

match is a bit verbose, so Result<T, E> offers a variety of methods that are useful in particular common cases. Each of these methods has a match expression in its implementation. (For the full list of Result methods, consult the online documentation. The methods listed here are the ones we use the most.)

`result.is_ok()`, `result.is_err()`

Return a `bool` telling if `result` is a success result or an error result.

`result.ok()`

Returns the success value, if any, as an `Option<T>`. If `result` is a success result, this returns `Some(success_value)`; otherwise, it returns `None`, discarding the error value.

`result.err()`

Returns the error value, if any, as an `Option<E>`.

`result.unwrap_or(fallback)`

Returns the success value, if `result` is a success result. Otherwise, it returns `fallback`, discarding the error value.

```
// A fairly safe prediction for Southern California.
const THE_USUAL: WeatherReport = WeatherReport::Sunny(72);

// Get a real weather report, if possible.
// If not, fall back on the usual.
let report = get_weather(los_angeles).unwrap_or(THE_USUAL);
display_weather(los_angeles, &report);
```

This is a nice alternative to `.ok()` because the return type is T, not `Option<T>`. Of course, it works only when there's an appropriate fallback value.

`result.unwrap_or_else(fallback_fn)`

This is the same, but instead of passing a fallback value directly, you pass a function or closure. This is for cases where it would be wasteful to compute a fallback value if you're not going to use it. The `fallback_fn` is called only if we have an error result.

```
let report =
    get_weather(hometown)
    .unwrap_or_else(|_err| vague_prediction(hometown));
```

(Chapter 14 covers closures in detail.)

`result.unwrap()`

Also returns the success value, if `result` is a success result. However, if `result` is an error result, this method panics. This method has its uses; we'll talk more about it later.

`result.expect(message)`

This the same as `.unwrap()`, but lets you provide a message that it prints in case of panic.

Lastly, methods for working with references in a `Result`:

`result.as_ref()`
> Converts a `Result<T, E>` to a `Result<&T, &E>`.

`result.as_mut()`
> This is the same, but borrows a mutable reference. The return type is `Result<&mut T, &mut E>`.

One reason these last two methods are useful is that all of the other methods listed here, except `.is_ok()` and `.is_err()`, *consume* the `result` they operate on. That is, they take the `self` argument by value. Sometimes it's quite handy to access data inside a `result` without destroying it, and this is what `.as_ref()` and `.as_mut()` do for us. For example, suppose you'd like to call `result.ok()`, but you need `result` to be left intact. You can write `result.as_ref().ok()`, which merely borrows `result`, returning an `Option<&T>` rather than an `Option<T>`.

Result Type Aliases

Sometimes you'll see Rust documentation that seems to omit the error type of a `Result`:

```
fn remove_file(path: &Path) -> Result<()>
```

This means that a `Result` type alias is being used.

A type alias is a kind of shorthand for type names. Modules often define a `Result` type alias to avoid having to repeat an error type that's used consistently by almost every function in the module. For example, the standard library's `std::io` module includes this line of code:

```
pub type Result<T> = result::Result<T, Error>;
```

This defines a public type `std::io::Result<T>`. It's an alias for `Result<T, E>`, but hardcodes `std::io::Error` as the error type. In practical terms, this means that if you write `use std::io;`, then Rust will understand `io::Result<String>` as shorthand for `Result<String, io::Error>`.

When something like `Result<()>` appears in the online documentation, you can click on the identifier `Result` to see which type alias is being used and learn the error type. In practice, it's usually obvious from context.

Printing Errors

Sometimes the only way to handle an error is by dumping it to the terminal and moving on. We already showed one way to do this:

```
println!("error querying the weather: {}", err);
```

The standard library defines several error types with boring names: `std::io::Error`, `std::fmt::Error`, `std::str::Utf8Error`, and so on. All of them implement a common interface, the `std::error::Error` trait, which means they share the following features and methods:

`println!()`

All error types are printable using this. Printing an error with the {} format specifier typically displays only a brief error message. Alternatively, you can print with the {:?} format specifier, to get a `Debug` view of the error. This is less user-friendly, but includes extra technical information.

```
// result of `println!("error: {}", err);`
error: failed to look up address information: No address associated with
hostname

// result of `println!("error: {:?}", err);`
error: Error { repr: Custom(Custom { kind: Other, error: StringError(
"failed to look up address information: No address associated with
hostname") }) }
```

`err.to_string()`

Returns an error message as a `String`.

`err.source()`

Returns an `Option` of the underlying error, if any, that caused `err`. For example, a networking error might cause a banking transaction to fail, which could in turn cause your boat to be repossessed. If `err.to_string()` is "boat was repossessed", then `err.source()` might return an error about the failed transaction. That error's `.to_string()` might be "failed to transfer $300 to United Yacht Supply", and its `.source()` might be an `io::Error` with details about the specific network outage that caused all the fuss. This third error is the root cause, so its `.source()` method would return `None`. Since the standard library only includes rather low-level features, the source of errors returned from the standard library is usually `None`.

Printing an error value does not also print out its source. If you want to be sure to print all the available information, use this function:

```
use std::error::Error;
use std::io::{Write, stderr};

/// Dump an error message to `stderr`.
///
/// If another error happens while building the error message or
/// writing to `stderr`, it is ignored.
fn print_error(mut err: &dyn Error) {
    let _ = writeln!(stderr(), "error: {}", err);
    while let Some(source) = err.source() {
        let _ = writeln!(stderr(), "caused by: {}", source);
        err = source;
    }
}
```

The writeln! macro works like println!, except that it writes the data to a stream of your choice. Here, we write the error messages to the standard error stream, std::io::stderr. We could use the eprintln! macro to do the same thing, but eprintln! panics if an error occurs. In print_error, we want to ignore errors that arise while writing the message; we explain why in "Ignoring Errors" on page 169, later in the chapter.

The standard library's error types do not include a stack trace, but the popular anyhow crate provides a ready-made error type that does, when used with an unstable version of the Rust compiler. (As of Rust 1.50, the standard library's functions for capturing backtraces were not yet stabilized.)

Propagating Errors

In most places where we try something that could fail, we don't want to catch and handle the error immediately. It is simply too much code to use a 10-line match statement every place where something could go wrong.

Instead, if an error occurs, we usually want to let our caller deal with it. We want errors to *propagate* up the call stack.

Rust has a ? operator that does this. You can add a ? to any expression that produces a Result, such as the result of a function call:

```
let weather = get_weather(hometown)?;
```

The behavior of ? depends on whether this function returns a success result or an error result:

- On success, it unwraps the `Result` to get the success value inside. The type of weather here is not `Result<WeatherReport, io::Error>` but simply `WeatherReport`.

- On error, it immediately returns from the enclosing function, passing the error result up the call chain. To ensure that this works, ? can only be used on a `Result` in functions that have a `Result` return type.

There's nothing magical about the ? operator. You can express the same thing using a `match` expression, although it's much wordier:

```
let weather = match get_weather(hometown) {
    Ok(success_value) => success_value,
    Err(err) => return Err(err)
};
```

The only differences between this and the ? operator are some fine points involving types and conversions. We'll cover those details in the next section.

In older code, you may see the `try!()` macro, which was the usual way to propagate errors until the ? operator was introduced in Rust 1.13:

```
let weather = try!(get_weather(hometown));
```

The macro expands to a `match` expression, like the one earlier.

It's easy to forget just how pervasive the possibility of errors is in a program, particularly in code that interfaces with the operating system. The ? operator sometimes shows up on almost every line of a function:

```
use std::fs;
use std::io;
use std::path::Path;

fn move_all(src: &Path, dst: &Path) -> io::Result<()> {
    for entry_result in src.read_dir()? {  // opening dir could fail
        let entry = entry_result?;         // reading dir could fail
        let dst_file = dst.join(entry.file_name());
        fs::rename(entry.path(), dst_file)?;  // renaming could fail
    }
    Ok(())  // phew!
}
```

? also works similarly with the `Option` type. In a function that returns `Option`, you can use ? to unwrap a value and return early in the case of `None`:

```
let weather = get_weather(hometown).ok()?;
```

Working with Multiple Error Types

Often, more than one thing could go wrong. Suppose we are simply reading numbers from a text file:

```
use std::io::{self, BufRead};

/// Read integers from a text file.
/// The file should have one number on each line.
fn read_numbers(file: &mut dyn BufRead) -> Result<Vec<i64>, io::Error> {
    let mut numbers = vec![];
    for line_result in file.lines() {
        let line = line_result?;          // reading lines can fail
        numbers.push(line.parse()?);      // parsing integers can fail
    }
    Ok(numbers)
}
```

Rust gives us a compiler error:

```
error: `?` couldn't convert the error to `std::io::Error`

  numbers.push(line.parse()?);       // parsing integers can fail
                         ^
            the trait `std::convert::From<std::num::ParseIntError>`
            is not implemented for `std::io::Error`

note: the question mark operation (`?`) implicitly performs a conversion
on the error value using the `From` trait
```

The terms in this error message will make more sense when we reach Chapter 11, which covers traits. For now, just note that Rust is complaining that the ? operator can't convert a std::num::ParseIntError value to the type std::io::Error.

The problem here is that reading a line from a file and parsing an integer produce two different potential error types. The type of line_result is Result<String, std::io::Error>. The type of line.parse() is Result<i64, std::num::Parse IntError>. The return type of our read_numbers() function only accommodates io::Errors. Rust tries to cope with the ParseIntError by converting it to a io::Error, but there's no such conversion, so we get a type error.

There are several ways of dealing with this. For example, the image crate that we used in Chapter 2 to create image files of the Mandelbrot set defines its own error type, ImageError, and implements conversions from io::Error and several other error types to ImageError. If you'd like to go this route, try the thiserror crate, which is designed to help you define good error types with just a few lines of code.

A simpler approach is to use what's built into Rust. All of the standard library error types can be converted to the type Box<dyn std::error::Error + Send + Sync + 'static>. This is a bit of a mouthful, but dyn std::error::Error represents "any error," and Send + Sync + 'static makes it safe to pass between threads, which you'll often want.[1] For convenience, you can define type aliases:

```
type GenericError = Box<dyn std::error::Error + Send + Sync + 'static>;
type GenericResult<T> = Result<T, GenericError>;
```

Then, change the return type of read_numbers() to GenericResult<Vec<i64>>. With this change, the function compiles. The ? operator automatically converts either type of error into a GenericError as needed.

Incidentally, the ? operator does this automatic conversion using a standard method that you can use yourself. To convert any error to the GenericError type, call GenericError::from():

```
let io_error = io::Error::new(          // make our own io::Error
    io::ErrorKind::Other, "timed out");
return Err(GenericError::from(io_error));  // manually convert to GenericError
```

We'll cover the From trait and its from() method fully in Chapter 13.

The downside of the GenericError approach is that the return type no longer communicates precisely what kinds of errors the caller can expect. The caller must be ready for anything.

If you're calling a function that returns a GenericResult and you want to handle one particular kind of error but let all others propagate out, use the generic method error.downcast_ref::<ErrorType>(). It borrows a reference to the error, *if* it happens to be the particular type of error you're looking for:

```
loop {
    match compile_project() {
        Ok(()) => return Ok(()),
        Err(err) => {
            if let Some(mse) = err.downcast_ref::<MissingSemicolonError>() {
                insert_semicolon_in_source_code(mse.file(), mse.line())?;
                continue;   // try again!
            }
            return Err(err);
        }
    }
}
```

Many languages have built-in syntax to do this, but it turns out to be rarely needed. Rust has a method for it instead.

---

1 You should also consider using the popular anyhow crate, which provides error and result types very much like our GenericError and GenericResult, but with some nice additional features.

Dealing with Errors That "Can't Happen"

Sometimes we just *know* that an error can't happen. For example, suppose we're writing code to parse a configuration file, and at one point we find that the next thing in the file is a string of digits:

```
if next_char.is_digit(10) {
    let start = current_index;
    current_index = skip_digits(&line, current_index);
    let digits = &line[start..current_index];
    ...
```

We want to convert this string of digits to an actual number. There's a standard method that does this:

```
let num = digits.parse::<u64>();
```

Now the problem: the `str.parse::<u64>()` method doesn't return a `u64`. It returns a `Result`. It can fail, because some strings aren't numeric:

```
"bleen".parse::<u64>()   // ParseIntError: invalid digit
```

But we happen to know that in this case, `digits` consists entirely of digits. What should we do?

If the code we're writing already returns a `GenericResult`, we can tack on a `?` and forget about it. Otherwise, we face the irritating prospect of having to write error-handling code for an error that can't happen. The best choice then would be to use `.unwrap()`, a `Result` method that panics if the result is an `Err`, but simply returns the success value of an `Ok`:

```
let num = digits.parse::<u64>().unwrap();
```

This is just like `?` except that if we're wrong about this error, if it *can* happen, then in that case we would panic.

In fact, we are wrong about this particular case. If the input contains a long enough string of digits, the number will be too big to fit in a `u64`:

```
"9999999999999999999999".parse::<u64>()     // overflow error
```

Using `.unwrap()` in this particular case would therefore be a bug. Bogus input shouldn't cause a panic.

That said, situations do come up where a `Result` value truly can't be an error. For example, in Chapter 18, you'll see that the `Write` trait defines a common set of methods (`.write()` and others) for text and binary output. All of those methods return `io::Result`s, but if you happen to be writing to a `Vec<u8>`, they can't fail. In such cases, it's acceptable to use `.unwrap()` or `.expect(message)` to dispense with the `Result`s.

These methods are also useful when an error would indicate a condition so severe or bizarre that panic is exactly how you want to handle it:

```
fn print_file_age(filename: &Path, last_modified: SystemTime) {
    let age = last_modified.elapsed().expect("system clock drift");
    ...
}
```

Here, the `.elapsed()` method can fail only if the system time is *earlier* than when the file was created. This can happen if the file was created recently, and the system clock was adjusted backward while our program was running. Depending on how this code is used, it's a reasonable judgment call to panic in that case, rather than handle the error or propagate it to the caller.

Ignoring Errors

Occasionally we just want to ignore an error altogether. For example, in our `print_error()` function, we had to handle the unlikely situation where printing the error triggers another error. This could happen, for example, if `stderr` is piped to another process, and that process is killed. The original error we were trying to report is probably more important to propagate, so we just want to ignore the troubles with `stderr`, but the Rust compiler warns about unused `Result` values:

```
writeln!(stderr(), "error: {}", err);  // warning: unused result
```

The idiom `let _ = ...` is used to silence this warning:

```
let _ = writeln!(stderr(), "error: {}", err);  // ok, ignore result
```

Handling Errors in main()

In most places where a `Result` is produced, letting the error bubble up to the caller is the right behavior. This is why `?` is a single character in Rust. As we've seen, in some programs it's used on many lines of code in a row.

But if you propagate an error long enough, eventually it reaches `main()`, and something has to be done with it. Normally, `main()` can't use `?` because its return type is not `Result`:

```
fn main() {
    calculate_tides()?;  // error: can't pass the buck any further
}
```

The simplest way to handle errors in `main()` is to use `.expect()`:

```
fn main() {
    calculate_tides().expect("error");  // the buck stops here
}
```

If `calculate_tides()` returns an error result, the `.expect()` method panics. Panicking in the main thread prints an error message and then exits with a nonzero exit code, which is roughly the desired behavior. We use this all the time for tiny programs. It's a start.

The error message is a little intimidating, though:

```
$ tidecalc --planet mercury
thread 'main' panicked at 'error: "moon not found"', src/main.rs:2:23
note: run with `RUST_BACKTRACE=1` environment variable to display a backtrace
```

The error message is lost in the noise. Also, RUST_BACKTRACE=1 is bad advice in this particular case.

However, you can also change the type signature of `main()` to return a `Result` type, so you can use ?:

```
fn main() -> Result<(), TideCalcError> {
    let tides = calculate_tides()?;
    print_tides(tides);
    Ok(())
}
```

This works for any error type that can be printed with the `{:?}` formatter, which all standard error types, like `std::io::Error`, can be. This technique is easy to use and gives a somewhat nicer error message, but it's not ideal:

```
$ tidecalc --planet mercury
Error: TideCalcError { error_type: NoMoon, message: "moon not found" }
```

If you have more complex error types or want to include more details in your message, it pays to print the error message yourself:

```
fn main() {
    if let Err(err) = calculate_tides() {
        print_error(&err);
        std::process::exit(1);
    }
}
```

This code uses an `if let` expression to print the error message only if the call to `calculate_tides()` returns an error result. For details about `if let` expressions, see Chapter 10. The `print_error` function is listed in "Printing Errors" on page 163.

Now the output is nice and tidy:

```
$ tidecalc --planet mercury
error: moon not found
```

Declaring a Custom Error Type

Suppose you are writing a new JSON parser, and you want it to have its own error type. (We haven't covered user-defined types yet; that's coming up in a few chapters. But error types are handy, so we'll include a bit of a sneak preview here.)

Approximately the minimum code you would write is:

```
// json/src/error.rs

#[derive(Debug, Clone)]
pub struct JsonError {
    pub message: String,
    pub line: usize,
    pub column: usize,
}
```

This struct will be called `json::error::JsonError`, and when you want to raise an error of this type, you can write:

```
return Err(JsonError {
    message: "expected ']' at end of array".to_string(),
    line: current_line,
    column: current_column
});
```

This will work fine. However, if you want your error type to work like the standard error types, as your library's users will expect, then you have a bit more work to do:

```
use std::fmt;

// Errors should be printable.
impl fmt::Display for JsonError {
    fn fmt(&self, f: &mut fmt::Formatter) -> Result<(), fmt::Error> {
        write!(f, "{} ({}:{})", self.message, self.line, self.column)
    }
}

// Errors should implement the std::error::Error trait,
// but the default definitions for the Error methods are fine.
impl std::error::Error for JsonError { }
```

Again, the meaning of the `impl` keyword, `self`, and all the rest will be explained in the next few chapters.

As with many aspects of the Rust language, crates exist to make error handling much easier and more concise. There is quite a variety, but one of the most used is `thiserror`, which does all of the previous work for you, allowing you to write errors like this:

```
use thiserror::Error;
#[derive(Error, Debug)]
#[error("{message:} ({line:}, {column})")]
```

```
pub struct JsonError {
    message: String,
    line: usize,
    column: usize,
}
```

The `#[derive(Error)]` directive tells `thiserror` to generate the code shown earlier, which can save a lot of time and effort.

Why Results?

Now we know enough to understand what Rust is getting at by choosing `Results` over exceptions. Here are the key points of the design:

- Rust requires the programmer to make some sort of decision, and record it in the code, at every point where an error could occur. This is good because otherwise it's easy to get error handling wrong through neglect.

- The most common decision is to allow errors to propagate, and that's written with a single character, ?. Thus, error plumbing does not clutter up your code the way it does in C and Go. Yet it's still visible: you can look at a chunk of code and see at a glance all places where errors are propagated.

- Since the possibility of errors is part of every function's return type, it's clear which functions can fail and which can't. If you change a function to be fallible, you're changing its return type, so the compiler will make you update that function's downstream users.

- Rust checks that `Result` values are used, so you can't accidentally let an error pass silently (a common mistake in C).

- Since `Result` is a data type like any other, it's easy to store success and error results in the same collection. This makes it easy to model partial success. For example, if you're writing a program that loads millions of records from a text file and you need a way to cope with the likely outcome that most will succeed, but some will fail, you can represent that situation in memory using a vector of `Results`.

The cost is that you'll find yourself thinking about and engineering error handling more in Rust than you would in other languages. As in many other areas, Rust's take on error handling is wound just a little tighter than what you're used to. For systems programming, it's worth it.

## CHAPTER 8

Crates and Modules

This is one note in a Rust theme: systems programmers can have nice things.
    —Robert O'Callahan, "Random Thoughts on Rust: crates.io and IDEs" (*https://oreil.ly/ Y22sV*)

Suppose you're writing a program that simulates the growth of ferns, from the level of individual cells on up. Your program, like a fern, will start out very simple, with all the code, perhaps, in a single file—just the spore of an idea. As it grows, it will start to have internal structure. Different pieces will have different purposes. It will branch out into multiple files. It may cover a whole directory tree. In time it may become a significant part of a whole software ecosystem. For any program that grows beyond a few data structures or a few hundred lines, some organization is necessary.

This chapter covers the features of Rust that help keep your program organized: crates and modules. We'll also cover other topics related to the structure and distribution of a Rust crate, including how to document and test Rust code, how to silence unwanted compiler warnings, how to use Cargo to manage project dependencies and versioning, how to publish open source libraries on Rust's public crate repository, crates.io, how Rust evolves through language editions, and more, using the fern simulator as our running example.

Crates

Rust programs are made of *crates*. Each crate is a complete, cohesive unit: all the source code for a single library or executable, plus any associated tests, examples, tools, configuration, and other junk. For your fern simulator, you might use third-party libraries for 3D graphics, bioinformatics, parallel computation, and so on. These libraries are distributed as crates (see Figure 8-1).

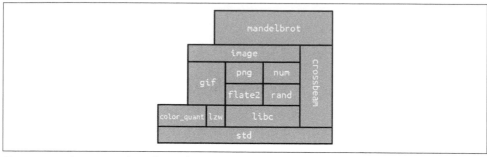

Figure 8-1. A crate and its dependencies

The easiest way to see what crates are and how they work together is to use `cargo build` with the `--verbose` flag to build an existing project that has some dependencies. We did this using "A Concurrent Mandelbrot Program" on page 35 as our example. The results are shown here:

```
$ cd mandelbrot
$ cargo clean     # delete previously compiled code
$ cargo build --verbose
    Updating registry `https://github.com/rust-lang/crates.io-index`
 Downloading autocfg v1.0.0
 Downloading semver-parser v0.7.0
 Downloading gif v0.9.0
 Downloading png v0.7.0

... (downloading and compiling many more crates)

Compiling jpeg-decoder v0.1.18
    Running `rustc
      --crate-name jpeg_decoder
      --crate-type lib
      ...
      --extern byteorder=.../libbyteorder-29efdd0b59c6f920.rmeta
      ...
   Compiling image v0.13.0
    Running `rustc
      --crate-name image
      --crate-type lib
      ...
      --extern byteorder=.../libbyteorder-29efdd0b59c6f920.rmeta
      --extern gif=.../libgif-a7006d35f1b58927.rmeta
      --extern jpeg_decoder=.../libjpeg_decoder-5c10558d0d57d300.rmeta
   Compiling mandelbrot v0.1.0 (/tmp/rustbook-test-files/mandelbrot)
    Running `rustc
      --edition=2021
      --crate-name mandelbrot
      --crate-type bin
      ...
      --extern crossbeam=.../libcrossbeam-f87b4b3d3284acc2.rlib
      --extern image=.../libimage-b5737c12bd641c43.rlib
      --extern num=.../libnum-1974e9a1dc582ba7.rlib -C link-arg=-fuse-ld=lld`
   Finished dev [unoptimized + debuginfo] target(s) in 16.94s
$
```

We reformatted the `rustc` command lines for readability, and we deleted a lot of compiler options that aren't relevant to our discussion, replacing them with an ellipsis (...).

You might recall that by the time we were done, the Mandelbrot program's *main.rs* contained several `use` declarations for items from other crates:

```
use num::Complex;
// ...
use image::ColorType;
use image::png::PNGEncoder;
```

We also specified in our *Cargo.toml* file which version of each crate we wanted:

```
[dependencies]
num = "0.4"
image = "0.13"
crossbeam = "0.8"
```

The word *dependencies* here just means other crates this project uses: code we're depending on. We found these crates on crates.io, the Rust community's site for open source crates. For example, we found out about the `image` library by going to crates.io and searching for an image library. Each crate's page on crates.io shows its *README.md* file and links to documentation and source, as well as a line of configuration like `image = "0.13"` that you can copy and add to your *Cargo.toml*. The version numbers shown here are simply the latest versions of these three packages at the time we wrote the program.

The Cargo transcript tells the story of how this information is used. When we run `cargo build`, Cargo starts by downloading source code for the specified versions of these crates from crates.io. Then, it reads those crates' *Cargo.toml* files, downloads *their* dependencies, and so on recursively. For example, the source code for version 0.13.0 of the `image` crate contains a *Cargo.toml* file that includes this:

```
[dependencies]
byteorder = "1.0.0"
num-iter = "0.1.32"
num-rational = "0.1.32"
num-traits = "0.1.32"
enum_primitive = "0.1.0"
```

Seeing this, Cargo knows that before it can use `image`, it must fetch these crates as well. Later we'll see how to tell Cargo to fetch source code from a Git repository or the local filesystem rather than crates.io.

Since `mandelbrot` depends on these crates indirectly, through its use of the `image` crate, we call them *transitive* dependencies of `mandelbrot`. The collection of all these dependency relationships, which tells Cargo everything it needs to know about what crates to build and in what order, is known as the *dependency graph* of the crate.

Cargo's automatic handling of the dependency graph and transitive dependencies is a huge win in terms of programmer time and effort.

Once it has the source code, Cargo compiles all the crates. It runs `rustc`, the Rust compiler, once for each crate in the project's dependency graph. When compiling libraries, Cargo uses the `--crate-type lib` option. This tells `rustc` not to look for a `main()` function but instead to produce an *.rlib* file containing compiled code that can be used to create binaries and other *.rlib* files.

When compiling a program, Cargo uses `--crate-type bin`, and the result is a binary executable for the target platform: *mandelbrot.exe* on Windows, for example.

With each `rustc` command, Cargo passes `--extern` options, giving the filename of each library the crate will use. That way, when `rustc` sees a line of code like `use image::png::PNGEncoder`, it can figure out that `image` is the name of another crate, and thanks to Cargo, it knows where to find that compiled crate on disk. The Rust compiler needs access to these *.rlib* files because they contain the compiled code of the library. Rust will statically link that code into the final executable. The *.rlib* also contains type information so Rust can check that the library features we're using in our code actually exist in the crate and that we're using them correctly. It also contains a copy of the crate's public inline functions, generics, and macros, features that can't be fully compiled to machine code until Rust sees how we use them.

`cargo build` supports all sorts of options, most of which are beyond the scope of this book, but we will mention one here: `cargo build --release` produces an optimized build. Release builds run faster, but they take longer to compile, they don't check for integer overflow, they skip `debug_assert!()` assertions, and the stack traces they generate on panic are generally less reliable.

Editions

Rust has extremely strong compatibility guarantees. Any code that compiled on Rust 1.0 must compile just as well on Rust 1.50 or, if it's ever released, Rust 1.900.

But sometimes there are compelling proposals for extensions to the language that would cause older code to no longer compile. For example, after much discussion, Rust settled on a syntax for asynchronous programming support that repurposes the identifiers `async` and `await` as keywords (see Chapter 20). But this language change would break any existing code that uses `async` or `await` as the name of a variable.

To evolve without breaking existing code, Rust uses *editions*. The 2015 edition of Rust is compatible with Rust 1.0. The 2018 edition changed `async` and `await` into keywords and streamlined the module system, while the 2021 edition improved array ergonomics and made some widely-used library definitions available everywhere by default. These were all important improvements to the language, but would have broken existing code. To avoid this, each crate indicates which edition of Rust it is written in with a line like this in the [`package`] section atop its *Cargo.toml* file:

```
edition = "2021"
```

If that keyword is absent, the 2015 edition is assumed, so old crates don't have to change at all. But if you want to use asynchronous functions or the new module system, you'll need `edition = "2018"` or later in your *Cargo.toml* file.

Rust promises that the compiler will always accept all extant editions of the language, and programs can freely mix crates written in different editions. It's even fine for a 2015 edition crate to depend on a 2021 edition crate. In other words, a crate's edition only affects how its source code is construed; edition distinctions are gone by the time the code has been compiled. This means there's no pressure to update old crates just to continue to participate in the modern Rust ecosystem. Similarly, there's no pressure to keep your crate on an older edition to avoid inconveniencing its users. You only need to change editions when you want to use new language features in your own code.

Editions don't come out every year, only when the Rust project decides one is necessary. For example, there's no 2020 edition. Setting `edition` to `"2020"` causes an error. The Rust Edition Guide (*https://oreil.ly/bKEO7*) covers the changes introduced in each edition and provides good background on the edition system.

It's almost always a good idea to use the latest edition, especially for new code. `cargo new` creates new projects on the latest edition by default. This book uses the 2021 edition throughout.

If you have a crate written in an older edition of Rust, the `cargo fix` command may be able to help you automatically upgrade your code to the newer edition. The Rust Edition Guide explains the `cargo fix` command in detail.

Build Profiles

There are several configuration settings you can put in your *Cargo.toml* file that affect the `rustc` command lines that `cargo` generates (Table 8-1).

Table 8-1. Cargo.toml configuration setting sections

Command line	Cargo.toml section used
`cargo build`	`[profile.dev]`
`cargo build --release`	`[profile.release]`
`cargo test`	`[profile.test]`

The defaults are usually fine, but one exception we've found is when you want to use a profiler—a tool that measures where your program is spending its CPU time. To get the best data from a profiler, you need both optimizations (usually enabled only in release builds) and debug symbols (usually enabled only in debug builds). To enable both, add this to your *Cargo.toml*:

```
[profile.release]
debug = true  # enable debug symbols in release builds
```

The debug setting controls the -g option to rustc. With this configuration, when you type cargo build --release, you'll get a binary with debug symbols. The optimization settings are unaffected.

The Cargo documentation (*https://oreil.ly/mTNiN*) lists many other settings you can adjust in *Cargo.toml*.

Modules

Whereas crates are about code sharing between projects, *modules* are about code organization *within* a project. They act as Rust's namespaces, containers for the functions, types, constants, and so on that make up your Rust program or library. A module looks like this:

```
mod spores {
    use cells::{Cell, Gene};

    /// A cell made by an adult fern. It disperses on the wind as part of
    /// the fern life cycle. A spore grows into a prothallus -- a whole
    /// separate organism, up to 5mm across -- which produces the zygote
    /// that grows into a new fern. (Plant sex is complicated.)
    pub struct Spore {
        ...
    }

    /// Simulate the production of a spore by meiosis.
    pub fn produce_spore(factory: &mut Sporangium) -> Spore {
        ...
    }

    /// Extract the genes in a particular spore.
    pub(crate) fn genes(spore: &Spore) -> Vec<Gene> {
        ...
    }

    /// Mix genes to prepare for meiosis (part of interphase).
    fn recombine(parent: &mut Cell) {
        ...
    }

    ...
}
```

A module is a collection of *items*, named features like the Spore struct and the two functions in this example. The pub keyword makes an item public, so it can be accessed from outside the module.

One function is marked pub(crate), meaning that it is available anywhere inside this crate, but isn't exposed as part of the external interface. It can't be used by other crates, and it won't show up in this crate's documentation.

Anything that isn't marked pub is private and can only be used in the same module in which it is defined, or any child modules:

```
let s = spores::produce_spore(&mut factory);  // ok

spores::recombine(&mut cell);  // error: `recombine` is private
```

Marking an item as pub is often known as "exporting" that item.

The rest of this section covers the details you'll need to know to make full use of modules:

- We show how to nest modules and distribute them across different files and directories, if needed.
- We explain the path syntax Rust uses to refer to items from other modules and show how to import items so that you can use them without having to write out their full paths.
- We touch on Rust's fine-grained control for struct fields.
- We introduce *prelude* modules, which reduce boilerplate by gathering together common imports that almost any user will need.
- We present *constants* and *statics*, two ways to define named values, for clarity and consistency.

Nested Modules

Modules can nest, and it's fairly common to see a module that's just a collection of submodules:

```
mod plant_structures {
    pub mod roots {
        ...
    }
    pub mod stems {
        ...
    }
    pub mod leaves {
        ...
    }
}
```

If you want an item in a nested module to be visible to other crates, be sure to mark it *and all enclosing modules* as public. Otherwise you may see a warning like this:

```
warning: function is never used: `is_square`
  |
```

```
23 | /       pub fn is_square(root: &Root) -> bool {
24 | |           root.cross_section_shape().is_square()
25 | |       }
   | |_____^
   |
```

Perhaps this function really is dead code at the moment. But if you meant to use it in other crates, Rust is letting you know that it's not actually visible to them. You should make sure its enclosing modules are all pub as well.

It's also possible to specify pub(super), making an item visible to the parent module only, and pub(in <path>), which makes it visible in a specific parent module and its descendants. This is especially useful with deeply nested modules:

```
mod plant_structures {
    pub mod roots {
        pub mod products {
            pub(in crate::plant_structures::roots) struct Cytokinin {
                ...
            }
        }

        use products::Cytokinin; // ok: in `roots` module
    }

    use roots::products::Cytokinin; // error: `Cytokinin` is private
}

// error: `Cytokinin` is private
use plant_structures::roots::products::Cytokinin;
```

In this way, we could write out a whole program, with a huge amount of code and a whole hierarchy of modules, related in whatever ways we wanted, all in a single source file.

Actually working that way is a pain, though, so there's an alternative.

Modules in Separate Files

A module can also be written like this:

```
mod spores;
```

Earlier, we included the body of the spores module, wrapped in curly braces. Here, we're instead telling the Rust compiler that the spores module lives in a separate file, called *spores.rs*:

```
// spores.rs

/// A cell made by an adult fern...
pub struct Spore {
    ...
```

```
}

/// Simulate the production of a spore by meiosis.
pub fn produce_spore(factory: &mut Sporangium) -> Spore {
    ...
}

/// Extract the genes in a particular spore.
pub(crate) fn genes(spore: &Spore) -> Vec<Gene> {
    ...
}

/// Mix genes to prepare for meiosis (part of interphase).
fn recombine(parent: &mut Cell) {
    ...
}
```

spores.rs contains only the items that make up the module. It doesn't need any kind of boilerplate to declare that it's a module.

The location of the code is the *only* difference between this `spores` module and the version we showed in the previous section. The rules about what's public and what's private are exactly the same either way. And Rust never compiles modules separately, even if they're in separate files: when you build a Rust crate, you're recompiling all of its modules.

A module can have its own directory. When Rust sees `mod spores;`, it checks for both *spores.rs* and *spores/mod.rs*; if neither file exists, or both exist, that's an error. For this example, we used *spores.rs*, because the `spores` module did not have any submodules. But consider the `plant_structures` module we wrote out earlier. If we decide to split that module and its three submodules into their own files, the resulting project would look like this:

```
fern_sim/
├─ Cargo.toml
└─ src/
    ├─ main.rs
    ├─ spores.rs
    └─ plant_structures/
        ├─ mod.rs
        ├─ leaves.rs
        ├─ roots.rs
        └─ stems.rs
```

In *main.rs*, we declare the `plant_structures` module:

```
pub mod plant_structures;
```

This causes Rust to load *plant_structures/mod.rs*, which declares the three submodules:

```
// in plant_structures/mod.rs
pub mod roots;
pub mod stems;
pub mod leaves;
```

The content of those three modules is stored in separate files named *leaves.rs*, *roots.rs*, and *stems.rs*, located alongside *mod.rs* in the *plant_structures* directory.

It's also possible to use a file and directory with the same name to make up a module. For instance, if stems needed to include modules called xylem and phloem, we could choose to keep stems in *plant_structures/stems.rs* and add a *stems* directory:

```
fern_sim/
├── Cargo.toml
└── src/
    ├── main.rs
    ├── spores.rs
    └── plant_structures/
        ├── mod.rs
        ├── leaves.rs
        ├── roots.rs
        ├── stems/
        │   ├── phloem.rs
        │   └── xylem.rs
        └── stems.rs
```

Then, in *stems.rs*, we declare the two new submodules:

```
// in plant_structures/stems.rs
pub mod xylem;
pub mod phloem;
```

These three options—modules in their own file, modules in their own directory with a *mod.rs*, and modules in their own file with a supplementary directory containing submodules—give the module system enough flexibility to support almost any project structure you might desire.

Paths and Imports

The `::` operator is used to access features of a module. Code anywhere in your project can refer to any standard library feature by writing out its path:

```
if s1 > s2 {
    std::mem::swap(&mut s1, &mut s2);
}
```

`std` is the name of the standard library. The path `std` refers to the top-level module of the standard library. `std::mem` is a submodule within the standard library, and `std::mem::swap` is a public function in that module.

You could write all your code this way, spelling out `std::f64::consts::PI` and `std::collections::HashMap::new` every time you want a circle or a dictionary, but it would be tedious to type and hard to read. The alternative is to *import* features into the modules where they're used:

```
use std::mem;

if s1 > s2 {
    mem::swap(&mut s1, &mut s2);
}
```

The `use` declaration causes the name `mem` to be a local alias for `std::mem` throughout the enclosing block or module.

We could write `use std::mem::swap;` to import the `swap` function itself instead of the `mem` module. However, what we did earlier is generally considered the best style: import types, traits, and modules (like `std::mem`) and then use relative paths to access the functions, constants, and other members within.

Several names can be imported at once:

```
use std::collections::{HashMap, HashSet};  // import both

use std::fs::{self, File}; // import both `std::fs` and `std::fs::File`.

use std::io::prelude::*;  // import everything
```

This is just shorthand for writing out all the individual imports:

```
use std::collections::HashMap;
use std::collections::HashSet;

use std::fs;
use std::fs::File;

// all the public items in std::io::prelude:
use std::io::prelude::Read;
use std::io::prelude::Write;
```

```
use std::io::prelude::BufRead;
use std::io::prelude::Seek;
```

You can use as to import an item but give it a different name locally:

```
use std::io::Result as IOResult;

// This return type is just another way to write `std::io::Result<()>`:
fn save_spore(spore: &Spore) -> IOResult<()>
    ...
```

Modules do *not* automatically inherit names from their parent modules. For example, suppose we have this in our *proteins/mod.rs*:

```
// proteins/mod.rs
pub enum AminoAcid { ... }
pub mod synthesis;
```

Then the code in *synthesis.rs* does not automatically see the type AminoAcid:

```
// proteins/synthesis.rs
pub fn synthesize(seq: &[AminoAcid])  // error: can't find type `AminoAcid`
    ...
```

Instead, each module starts with a blank slate and must import the names it uses:

```
// proteins/synthesis.rs
use super::AminoAcid;  // explicitly import from parent

pub fn synthesize(seq: &[AminoAcid])  // ok
    ...
```

By default, paths are relative to the current module:

```
// in proteins/mod.rs

// import from a submodule
use synthesis::synthesize;
```

self is also a synonym for the current module, so we could write either:

```
// in proteins/mod.rs

// import names from an enum,
// so we can write `Lys` for lysine, rather than `AminoAcid::Lys`
use self::AminoAcid::*;
```

or simply:

```
// in proteins/mod.rs

use AminoAcid::*;
```

(The AminoAcid example here is, of course, a departure from the style rule we mentioned earlier about only importing types, traits, and modules. If our program includes long amino acid sequences, this is justified under Orwell's Sixth Rule: "Break any of these rules sooner than say anything outright barbarous.")

The keywords `super` and `crate` have a special meaning in paths: `super` refers to the parent module, and `crate` refers to the crate containing the current module.

Using paths relative to the crate root rather than the current module makes it easier to move code around the project, since all the imports won't break if the path of the current module changes. For example, we could write *synthesis.rs* using `crate`:

```
// proteins/synthesis.rs
use crate::proteins::AminoAcid;  // explicitly import relative to crate root

pub fn synthesize(seq: &[AminoAcid])  // ok
    ...
```

Submodules can access private items in their parent modules with `use super::*`.

If you have a module with the same name as a crate that you are using, then referring to their contents takes some care. For example, if your program lists the `image` crate as a dependency in its *Cargo.toml* file, but also has a module named `image`, then paths starting with `image` are ambiguous:

```
mod image {
    pub struct Sampler {
        ...
    }
}

// error: Does this refer to our `image` module, or the `image` crate?
use image::Pixels;
```

Even though the `image` module has no `Pixels` type, the ambiguity is still considered an error: it would be confusing if adding such a definition later could silently change what paths elsewhere in the program refer to.

To resolve the ambiguity, Rust has a special kind of path called an *absolute path*, starting with `::`, which always refers to an external crate. To refer to the `Pixels` type in the `image` crate, you can write:

```
use ::image::Pixels;        // the `image` crate's `Pixels`
```

To refer to your own module's `Sampler` type, you can write:

```
use self::image::Sampler;   // the `image` module's `Sampler`
```

Modules aren't the same thing as files, but there is a natural analogy between modules and the files and directories of a Unix filesystem. The `use` keyword creates aliases, just as the `ln` command creates links. Paths, like filenames, come in absolute and relative forms. `self` and `super` are like the . and .. special directories.

The Standard Prelude

We said a moment ago that each module starts with a "blank slate," as far as imported names are concerned. But the slate is not *completely* blank.

For one thing, the standard library `std` is automatically linked with every project. This means you can always go with `use std::whatever` or refer to `std` items by name, like `std::mem::swap()` inline in your code. Furthermore, a few particularly handy names, like `Vec` and `Result`, are included in the *standard prelude* and automatically imported. Rust behaves as though every module, including the root module, started with the following import:

```
use std::prelude::v1::*;
```

The standard prelude contains a few dozen commonly used traits and types.

In Chapter 2, we mentioned that libraries sometimes provide modules named `prelude`. But `std::prelude::v1` is the only prelude that is ever imported automatically. Naming a module `prelude` is just a convention that tells users it's meant to be imported using *.

Making use Declarations pub

Even though `use` declarations are just aliases, they can be public:

```
// in plant_structures/mod.rs
...
pub use self::leaves::Leaf;
pub use self::roots::Root;
```

This means that `Leaf` and `Root` are public items of the `plant_structures` module. They are still simple aliases for `plant_structures::leaves::Leaf` and `plant_structures::roots::Root`.

The standard prelude is written as just such a series of pub imports.

Making Struct Fields pub

A module can include user-defined struct types, introduced using the `struct` keyword. We cover these in detail in Chapter 9, but this is a good point to mention how modules interact with the visibility of struct fields.

A simple struct looks like this:

```
pub struct Fern {
    pub roots: RootSet,
    pub stems: StemSet
}
```

A struct's fields, even private fields, are accessible throughout the module where the struct is declared, and its submodules. Outside the module, only public fields are accessible.

It turns out that enforcing access control by module, rather than by class as in Java or C++, is surprisingly helpful for software design. It cuts down on boilerplate "getter" and "setter" methods, and it largely eliminates the need for anything like C++ `friend` declarations. A single module can define several types that work closely together, such as perhaps `frond::LeafMap` and `frond::LeafMapIter`, accessing each other's private fields as needed, while still hiding those implementation details from the rest of your program.

Statics and Constants

In addition to functions, types, and nested modules, modules can also define *constants* and *statics*.

The `const` keyword introduces a constant. The syntax is just like `let` except that it may be marked `pub`, and the type is required. Also, `UPPERCASE_NAMES` are conventional for constants:

```
pub const ROOM_TEMPERATURE: f64 = 20.0;  // degrees Celsius
```

The `static` keyword introduces a static item, which is nearly the same thing:

```
pub static ROOM_TEMPERATURE: f64 = 68.0;  // degrees Fahrenheit
```

A constant is a bit like a C++ `#define`: the value is compiled into your code every place it's used. A static is a variable that's set up before your program starts running and lasts until it exits. Use constants for magic numbers and strings in your code. Use statics for larger amounts of data, or any time you need to borrow a reference to the constant value.

There are no `mut` constants. Statics can be marked `mut`, but as discussed in Chapter 5, Rust has no way to enforce its rules about exclusive access on `mut` statics. They are, therefore, inherently non-thread-safe, and safe code can't use them at all:

```
static mut PACKETS_SERVED: usize = 0;

println!("{} served", PACKETS_SERVED);  // error: use of mutable static
```

Rust discourages global mutable state. For a discussion of the alternatives, see "Global Variables" on page 537.

Turning a Program into a Library

As your fern simulator starts to take off, you decide you need more than a single program. Suppose you've got one command-line program that runs the simulation and saves results in a file. Now, you want to write other programs for performing scientific analysis of the saved results, displaying 3D renderings of the growing plants in real time, rendering photorealistic pictures, and so on. All these programs need to share the basic fern simulation code. You need to make a library.

The first step is to factor your existing project into two parts: a library crate, which contains all the shared code, and an executable, which contains the code that's only needed for your existing command-line program.

To show how you can do this, let's use a grossly simplified example program:

```
struct Fern {
    size: f64,
    growth_rate: f64
}

impl Fern {
    /// Simulate a fern growing for one day.
    fn grow(&mut self) {
        self.size *= 1.0 + self.growth_rate;
    }
}

/// Run a fern simulation for some number of days.
fn run_simulation(fern: &mut Fern, days: usize) {
    for _ in 0 .. days {
        fern.grow();
    }
}

fn main() {
    let mut fern = Fern {
        size: 1.0,
        growth_rate: 0.001
    };
    run_simulation(&mut fern, 1000);
    println!("final fern size: {}", fern.size);
}
```

We'll assume that this program has a trivial *Cargo.toml* file:

```
[package]
name = "fern_sim"
version = "0.1.0"
authors = ["You <you@example.com>"]
edition = "2021"
```

Turning this program into a library is easy. Here are the steps:

1. Rename the file *src/main.rs* to *src/lib.rs*.

2. Add the `pub` keyword to items in *src/lib.rs* that will be public features of our library.

3. Move the `main` function to a temporary file somewhere. We'll come back to it in a minute.

The resulting *src/lib.rs* file looks like this:

```
pub struct Fern {
    pub size: f64,
    pub growth_rate: f64
}

impl Fern {
    /// Simulate a fern growing for one day.
    pub fn grow(&mut self) {
        self.size *= 1.0 + self.growth_rate;
    }
}

/// Run a fern simulation for some number of days.
pub fn run_simulation(fern: &mut Fern, days: usize) {
    for _ in 0 .. days {
        fern.grow();
    }
}
```

Note that we didn't need to change anything in *Cargo.toml*. This is because our minimal *Cargo.toml* file leaves Cargo to its default behavior. By default, `cargo build` looks at the files in our source directory and figures out what to build. When it sees the file *src/lib.rs*, it knows to build a library.

The code in *src/lib.rs* forms the *root module* of the library. Other crates that use our library can only access the public items of this root module.

The src/bin Directory

Getting the original command-line `fern_sim` program working again is also straightforward: Cargo has some built-in support for small programs that live in the same crate as a library.

In fact, Cargo itself is written this way. The bulk of the code is in a Rust library. The `cargo` command-line program that we've been using throughout this book is a thin wrapper program that calls out to the library for all the heavy lifting. Both the library and the command-line program live in the same source repository (*https://oreil.ly/ aJKOk*).

We can keep our program and our library in the same crate, too. Put this code into a file named *src/bin/efern.rs*:

```
use fern_sim::{Fern, run_simulation};

fn main() {
    let mut fern = Fern {
        size: 1.0,
        growth_rate: 0.001
    };
    run_simulation(&mut fern, 1000);
    println!("final fern size: {}", fern.size);
}
```

The `main` function is the one we set aside earlier. We've added a `use` declaration for some items from the `fern_sim` crate, `Fern` and `run_simulation`. In other words, we're using that crate as a library.

Because we've put this file into *src/bin*, Cargo will compile both the `fern_sim` library and this program the next time we run `cargo build`. We can run the `efern` program using `cargo run --bin efern`. Here's what it looks like, using `--verbose` to show the commands Cargo is running:

```
$ cargo build --verbose
   Compiling fern_sim v0.1.0 (file:///.../fern_sim)
     Running `rustc src/lib.rs --crate-name fern_sim --crate-type lib ...`
     Running `rustc src/bin/efern.rs --crate-name efern --crate-type bin ...`
$ cargo run --bin efern --verbose
       Fresh fern_sim v0.1.0 (file:///.../fern_sim)
     Running `target/debug/efern`
final fern size: 2.7169239322355985
```

We still didn't have to make any changes to *Cargo.toml*, because, again, Cargo's default is to look at your source files and figure things out. It automatically treats *.rs* files in *src/bin* as extra programs to build.

We can also build larger programs in the *src/bin* directory using subdirectories. Suppose we want to provide a second program that draws a fern on the screen, but the drawing code is large and modular, so it belongs in its own file. We can give the second program its own subdirectory:

```
fern_sim/
├── Cargo.toml
└── src/
    └── bin/
        ├── efern.rs
        └── draw_fern/
```

```
├── main.rs
└── draw.rs
```

This has the advantage of letting larger binaries have their own submodules without cluttering up either the library code or the *src/bin* directory.

Of course, now that `fern_sim` is a library, we also have another option. We could have put this program in its own isolated project, in a completely separate directory, with its own *Cargo.toml* listing `fern_sim` as a dependency:

```
[dependencies]
fern_sim = { path = "../fern_sim" }
```

Perhaps that is what you'll do for other fern-simulating programs down the road. The *src/bin* directory is just right for simple programs like `efern` and `draw_fern`.

Attributes

Any item in a Rust program can be decorated with *attributes*. Attributes are Rust's catchall syntax for writing miscellaneous instructions and advice to the compiler. For example, suppose you're getting this warning:

```
libgit2.rs: warning: type `git_revspec` should have a camel case name
    such as `GitRevspec`, #[warn(non_camel_case_types)] on by default
```

But you chose this name for a reason, and you wish Rust would shut up about it. You can disable the warning by adding an `#[allow]` attribute on the type:

```
#[allow(non_camel_case_types)]
pub struct git_revspec {
    ...
}
```

Conditional compilation is another feature that's written using an attribute, namely, `#[cfg]`:

```
// Only include this module in the project if we're building for Android.
#[cfg(target_os = "android")]
mod mobile;
```

The full syntax of `#[cfg]` is specified in the Rust Reference (*https://oreil.ly/F7gqB*); the most commonly used options are listed in Table 8-2.

Table 8-2. Most commonly used #[cfg] options

`#[cfg(...)]` option	Enabled when
`test`	Tests are enabled (compiling with `cargo test` or `rustc --test`).
`debug_assertions`	Debug assertions are enabled (typically in nonoptimized builds).
`unix`	Compiling for Unix, including macOS.

#[cfg(...)] option	Enabled when
windows	Compiling for Windows.
target_pointer_width = "64"	Targeting a 64-bit platform. The other possible value is "32".
target_arch = "x86_64"	Targeting x86-64 in particular. Other values: "x86", "arm", "aarch64", "powerpc", "powerpc64", "mips".
target_os = "macos"	Compiling for macOS. Other values: "windows", "ios", "android", "linux", "freebsd", "openbsd", "netbsd", "dragonfly".
feature = "robots"	The user-defined feature named "robots" is enabled (compiling with cargo build --feature robots or rustc --cfg feature='"robots"'). Features are declared in the [features] section of *Cargo.toml* (*https://oreil.ly/IfEpj*).
not(A)	A is not satisfied. To provide two different implementations of a function, mark one with #[cfg(X)] and the other with #[cfg(not(X))].
all(A,B)	Both A and B are satisfied (the equivalent of &&).
any(A,B)	Either A or B is satisfied (the equivalent of ||).

Occasionally, we need to micromanage the inline expansion of functions, an optimization that we're usually happy to leave to the compiler. We can use the #[inline] attribute for that:

```
/// Adjust levels of ions etc. in two adjacent cells
/// due to osmosis between them.
#[inline]
fn do_osmosis(c1: &mut Cell, c2: &mut Cell) {
    ...
}
```

There's one situation where inlining *won't* happen without #[inline]. When a function or method defined in one crate is called in another crate, Rust won't inline it unless it's generic (it has type parameters) or it's explicitly marked #[inline].

Otherwise, the compiler treats #[inline] as a suggestion. Rust also supports the more insistent #[inline(always)], to request that a function be expanded inline at every call site, and #[inline(never)], to ask that a function never be inlined.

Some attributes, like #[cfg] and #[allow], can be attached to a whole module and apply to everything in it. Others, like #[test] and #[inline], must be attached to individual items. As you might expect for a catchall feature, each attribute is custom-made and has its own set of supported arguments. The Rust Reference documents the full set of supported attributes (*https://oreil.ly/FtJWN*) in detail.

To attach an attribute to a whole crate, add it at the top of the *main.rs* or *lib.rs* file, before any items, and write #! instead of #, like this:

```
// libgit2_sys/lib.rs
#![allow(non_camel_case_types)]

pub struct git_revspec {
    ...
}

pub struct git_error {
    ...
}
```

The #! tells Rust to attach an attribute to the enclosing item rather than whatever comes next: in this case, the #![allow] attribute attaches to the whole libgit2_sys crate, not just struct git_revspec.

#! can also be used inside functions, structs, and so on, but it's only typically used at the beginning of a file, to attach an attribute to the whole module or crate. Some attributes always use the #! syntax because they can only be applied to a whole crate.

For example, the #![feature] attribute is used to turn on *unstable* features of the Rust language and libraries, features that are experimental, and therefore might have bugs or might be changed or removed in the future. For instance, as we're writing this, Rust has experimental support for tracing the expansion of macros like assert!, but since this support is experimental, you can only use it by (1) installing the nightly version of Rust and (2) explicitly declaring that your crate uses macro tracing:

```
#![feature(trace_macros)]

fn main() {
    // I wonder what actual Rust code this use of assert_eq!
    // gets replaced with!
    trace_macros!(true);
    assert_eq!(10*10*10 + 9*9*9, 12*12*12 + 1*1*1);
    trace_macros!(false);
}
```

Over time, the Rust team sometimes *stabilizes* an experimental feature so that it becomes a standard part of the language. The #![feature] attribute then becomes superfluous, and Rust generates a warning advising you to remove it.

Tests and Documentation

As we saw in "Writing and Running Unit Tests" on page 10, a simple unit testing framework is built into Rust. Tests are ordinary functions marked with the #[test] attribute:

```
#[test]
fn math_works() {
    let x: i32 = 1;
    assert!(x.is_positive());
    assert_eq!(x + 1, 2);
}
```

`cargo test` runs all the tests in your project:

```
$ cargo test
   Compiling math_test v0.1.0 (file:///.../math_test)
     Running target/release/math_test-e31ed91ae51ebf22

running 1 test
test math_works ... ok

test result: ok. 1 passed; 0 failed; 0 ignored; 0 measured; 0 filtered out
```

(You'll also see some output about "doc-tests," which we'll get to in a minute.)

This works the same whether your crate is an executable or a library. You can run specific tests by passing arguments to Cargo: `cargo test math` runs all tests that contain `math` somewhere in their name.

Tests commonly use the `assert!` and `assert_eq!` macros from the Rust standard library. `assert!(expr)` succeeds if `expr` is true. Otherwise, it panics, which causes the test to fail. `assert_eq!(v1, v2)` is just like `assert!(v1 == v2)` except that if the assertion fails, the error message shows both values.

You can use these macros in ordinary code, to check invariants, but note that `assert!` and `assert_eq!` are included even in release builds. Use `debug_assert!` and `debug_assert_eq!` instead to write assertions that are checked only in debug builds.

To test error cases, add the `#[should_panic]` attribute to your test:

```
/// This test passes only if division by zero causes a panic,
/// as we claimed in the previous chapter.
#[test]
#[allow(unconditional_panic, unused_must_use)]
#[should_panic(expected="divide by zero")]
fn test_divide_by_zero_error() {
    1 / 0;  // should panic!
}
```

In this case, we also need to add an `allow` attribute to tell the compiler to let us do things that it can statically prove will panic, and perform divisions and just throw away the answer, because normally, it tries to stop that kind of silliness.

You can also return a `Result<(), E>` from your tests. As long as the error variant is `Debug`, which is usually the case, you can simply return a `Result` by using `?` to throw away the `Ok` variant:

```
use std::num::ParseIntError;

/// This test will pass if "1024" is a valid number, which it is.
#[test]
fn main() -> Result<(), ParseIntError> {
  i32::from_str_radix("1024", 10)?;
  Ok(())
}
```

Functions marked with #[test] are compiled conditionally. A plain `cargo build` or `cargo build --release` skips the testing code. But when you run `cargo test`, Cargo builds your program twice: once in the ordinary way and once with your tests and the test harness enabled. This means your unit tests can live right alongside the code they test, accessing internal implementation details if they need to, and yet there's no run-time cost. However, it can result in some warnings. For example:

```
fn roughly_equal(a: f64, b: f64) -> bool {
    (a - b).abs() < 1e-6
}

#[test]
fn trig_works() {
    use std::f64::consts::PI;
    assert!(roughly_equal(PI.sin(), 0.0));
}
```

In builds that omit the test code, `roughly_equal` appears unused, and Rust will complain:

```
$ cargo build
   Compiling math_test v0.1.0 (file:///.../math_test)
warning: function is never used: `roughly_equal`
  |
7 | / fn roughly_equal(a: f64, b: f64) -> bool {
8 | |     (a - b).abs() < 1e-6
9 | | }
  | |_^
  |
  = note: #[warn(dead_code)] on by default
```

So the convention, when your tests get substantial enough to require support code, is to put them in a `tests` module and declare the whole module to be testing-only using the #[cfg] attribute:

```
#[cfg(test)]   // include this module only when testing
mod tests {
    fn roughly_equal(a: f64, b: f64) -> bool {
        (a - b).abs() < 1e-6
    }

    #[test]
    fn trig_works() {
```

```
        use std::f64::consts::PI;
        assert!(roughly_equal(PI.sin(), 0.0));
    }
}
```

Rust's test harness uses multiple threads to run several tests at a time, a nice side benefit of your Rust code being thread-safe by default. To disable this, either run a single test, cargo test *testname*, or run cargo test -- --test-threads 1. (The first -- ensures that cargo test passes the --test-threads option through to the test executable.) This means that, technically, the Mandelbrot program we showed in Chapter 2 was not the second multithreaded program in that chapter, but the third! The cargo test run in "Writing and Running Unit Tests" on page 10 was the first.

Normally, the test harness only shows the output of tests that failed. To show the output from tests that pass too, run cargo test -- --no-capture.

Integration Tests

Your fern simulator continues to grow. You've decided to put all the major functionality into a library that can be used by multiple executables. It would be nice to have some tests that link with the library the way an end user would, using *fern_sim.rlib* as an external crate. Also, you have some tests that start by loading a saved simulation from a binary file, and it is awkward having those large test files in your *src* directory. Integration tests help with these two problems.

Integration tests are *.rs* files that live in a *tests* directory alongside your project's *src* directory. When you run cargo test, Cargo compiles each integration test as a separate, standalone crate, linked with your library and the Rust test harness. Here is an example:

```
// tests/unfurl.rs - Fiddleheads unfurl in sunlight

use fern_sim::Terrarium;
use std::time::Duration;

#[test]
fn test_fiddlehead_unfurling() {
    let mut world = Terrarium::load("tests/unfurl_files/fiddlehead.tm");
    assert!(world.fern(0).is_furled());
    let one_hour = Duration::from_secs(60 * 60);
    world.apply_sunlight(one_hour);
    assert!(world.fern(0).is_fully_unfurled());
}
```

Integration tests are valuable in part because they see your crate from the outside, just as a user would. They test the crate's public API.

`cargo test` runs both unit tests and integration tests. To run only the integration tests in a particular file—for example, *tests/unfurl.rs*—use the command `cargo test --test unfurl`.

Documentation

The command `cargo doc` creates HTML documentation for your library:

```
$ cargo doc --no-deps --open
    Documenting fern_sim v0.1.0 (file:///.../fern_sim)
```

The `--no-deps` option tells Cargo to generate documentation only for `fern_sim` itself, and not for all the crates it depends on.

The `--open` option tells Cargo to open the documentation in your browser afterward.

You can see the result in Figure 8-2. Cargo saves the new documentation files in *target/doc*. The starting page is *target/doc/fern_sim/index.html*.

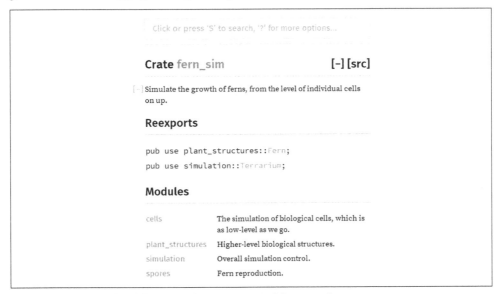

Figure 8-2. Example of documentation generated by `rustdoc`

The documentation is generated from the pub features of your library, plus any *doc comments* you've attached to them. We've seen a few doc comments in this chapter already. They look like comments:

```
/// Simulate the production of a spore by meiosis.
pub fn produce_spore(factory: &mut Sporangium) -> Spore {
    ...
}
```

But when Rust sees comments that start with three slashes, it treats them as a #[doc] attribute instead. Rust treats the preceding example exactly the same as this:

```
#[doc = "Simulate the production of a spore by meiosis."]
pub fn produce_spore(factory: &mut Sporangium) -> Spore {
    ...
}
```

When you compile a library or binary, these attributes don't change anything, but when you generate documentation, doc comments on public features are included in the output.

Likewise, comments starting with //! are treated as #![doc] attributes and are attached to the enclosing feature, typically a module or crate. For example, your *fern_sim/src/lib.rs* file might begin like this:

```
//! Simulate the growth of ferns, from the level of
//! individual cells on up.
```

The content of a doc comment is treated as Markdown, a shorthand notation for simple HTML formatting. Asterisks are used for *italics* and **bold type**, a blank line is treated as a paragraph break, and so on. You can also include HTML tags, which are copied verbatim into the formatted documentation.

One special feature of doc comments in Rust is that Markdown links can use Rust item paths, like leaves::Leaf, instead of relative URLs, to indicate what they refer to. Cargo will look up what the path refers to and substitute a link to the right place in the right documentation page. For example, the documentation generated from this code links to the documentation pages for VascularPath, Leaf, and Root:

```
/// Create and return a [`VascularPath`] which represents the path of
/// nutrients from the given [`Root`][r] to the given [`Leaf`](leaves::Leaf).
///
/// [r]: roots::Root
pub fn trace_path(leaf: &leaves::Leaf, root: &roots::Root) -> VascularPath {
    ...
}
```

You can also add search aliases to make it easier to find things using the built-in search feature. Searching for either "path" or "route" in this crate's documentation will lead to VascularPath:

```
#[doc(alias = "route")]
pub struct VascularPath {
    ...
}
```

For longer blocks of documentation, or to streamline your workflow, you can include external files in your documentation. For example, if your repository's *README.md* file holds the same text you'd like to use as your crate's top-level documentation, you could put this at the top of lib.rs or main.rs:

```
#![doc = include_str!("../README.md")]
```

You can use `backticks` to set off bits of code in the middle of running text. In the output, these snippets will be formatted in a fixed-width font. Larger code samples can be added by indenting four spaces:

```
/// A block of code in a doc comment:
///
///     if samples::everything().works() {
///         println!("ok");
///     }
```

You can also use Markdown-fenced code blocks. This has exactly the same effect:

```
/// Another snippet, the same code, but written differently:
///
/// ```
/// if samples::everything().works() {
///     println!("ok");
/// }
/// ```
```

Whichever format you use, an interesting thing happens when you include a block of code in a doc comment. Rust automatically turns it into a test.

Doc-Tests

When you run tests in a Rust library crate, Rust checks that all the code that appears in your documentation actually runs and works. It does this by taking each block of code that appears in a doc comment, compiling it as a separate executable crate, linking it with your library, and running it.

Here is a standalone example of a doc-test. Create a new project by running `cargo new --lib ranges` (the `--lib` flag tells Cargo we're creating a library crate, not an executable crate) and put the following code in *ranges/src/lib.rs*:

```
use std::ops::Range;

/// Return true if two ranges overlap.
///
///     assert_eq!(ranges::overlap(0..7, 3..10), true);
///     assert_eq!(ranges::overlap(1..5, 101..105), false);
///
/// If either range is empty, they don't count as overlapping.
///
///     assert_eq!(ranges::overlap(0..0, 0..10), false);
///
pub fn overlap(r1: Range<usize>, r2: Range<usize>) -> bool {
    r1.start < r1.end && r2.start < r2.end &&
```

```
        r1.start < r2.end && r2.start < r1.end
}
```

The two small blocks of code in the doc comment appear in the documentation generated by `cargo doc`, as shown in Figure 8-3.

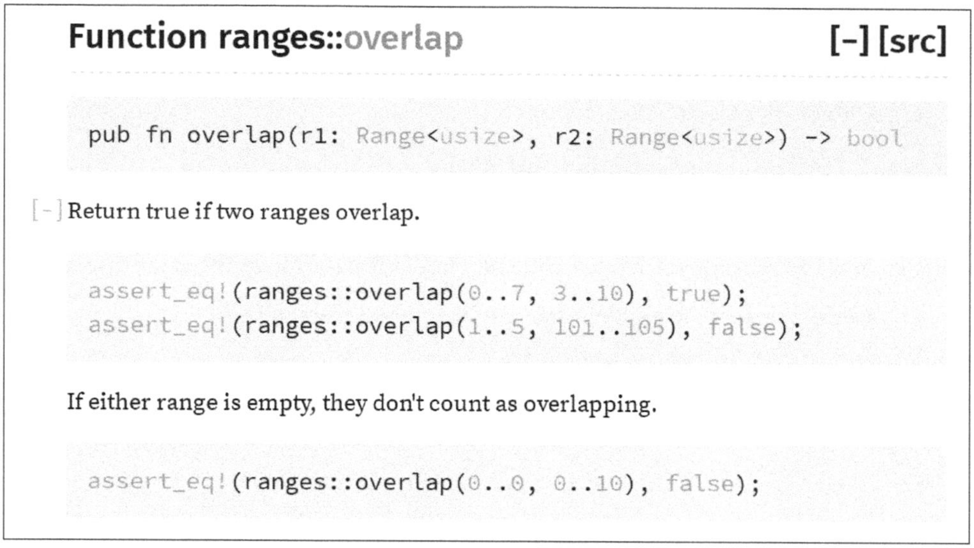

```
Function ranges::overlap                          [–] [src]
```

```
    pub fn overlap(r1: Range<usize>, r2: Range<usize>) -> bool
```

[–] Return true if two ranges overlap.

```
    assert_eq!(ranges::overlap(0..7, 3..10), true);
    assert_eq!(ranges::overlap(1..5, 101..105), false);
```

If either range is empty, they don't count as overlapping.

```
    assert_eq!(ranges::overlap(0..0, 0..10), false);
```

Figure 8-3. Documentation showing some doc-tests

They also become two separate tests:

```
$ cargo test
   Compiling ranges v0.1.0 (file:///.../ranges)
...
   Doc-tests ranges

running 2 tests
test overlap_0 ... ok
test overlap_1 ... ok

test result: ok. 2 passed; 0 failed; 0 ignored; 0 measured; 0 filtered out
```

If you pass the `--verbose` flag to Cargo, you'll see that it's using `rustdoc --test` to
run these two tests. `rustdoc` stores each code sample in a separate file, adding a few
lines of boilerplate code, to produce two programs. Here's the first:

```
use ranges;
fn main() {
    assert_eq!(ranges::overlap(0..7, 3..10), true);
    assert_eq!(ranges::overlap(1..5, 101..105), false);
}
```

And here's the second:

```
use ranges;
fn main() {
    assert_eq!(ranges::overlap(0..0, 0..10), false);
}
```

The tests pass if these programs compile and run successfully.

These two code samples contain assertions, but that's just because in this case, the assertions make decent documentation. The idea behind doc-tests is not to put all your tests into comments. Rather, you write the best possible documentation, and Rust makes sure the code samples in your documentation actually compile and run.

Very often a minimal working example includes some details, such as imports or setup code, that are necessary to make the code compile, but just aren't important enough to show in the documentation. To hide a line of a code sample, put a # followed by a space at the beginning of that line:

```
/// Let the sun shine in and run the simulation for a given
/// amount of time.
///
///      # use fern_sim::Terrarium;
///      # use std::time::Duration;
///      # let mut tm = Terrarium::new();
///      tm.apply_sunlight(Duration::from_secs(60));
///
pub fn apply_sunlight(&mut self, time: Duration) {
    ...
}
```

Sometimes it's helpful to show a complete sample program in documentation, including a main function. Obviously, if those pieces of code appear in your code sample, you do not also want rustdoc to add them automatically. The result wouldn't compile. rustdoc therefore treats any code block containing the exact string fn main as a complete program and doesn't add anything to it.

Testing can be disabled for specific blocks of code. To tell Rust to compile your example, but stop short of actually running it, use a fenced code block with the no_run annotation:

```
/// Upload all local terrariums to the online gallery.
///
/// ```no_run
/// let mut session = fern_sim::connect();
/// session.upload_all();
/// ```
pub fn upload_all(&mut self) {
    ...
}
```

If the code isn't even expected to compile, use `ignore` instead of `no_run`. Blocks marked with `ignore` don't show up in the output of `cargo run`, but `no_run` tests show up as having passed if they compile. If the code block isn't Rust code at all, use the name of the language, like `c++` or `sh`, or `text` for plain text. `rustdoc` doesn't know the names of hundreds of programming languages; rather, it treats any annotation it doesn't recognize as indicating that the code block isn't Rust. This disables code highlighting as well as doc-testing.

Specifying Dependencies

We've seen one way of telling Cargo where to get source code for crates your project depends on: by version number.

```
image = "0.6.1"
```

There are several ways to specify dependencies, and some rather nuanced things you might want to say about which versions to use, so it's worth spending a few pages on this.

First of all, you may want to use dependencies that aren't published on crates.io at all. One way to do this is by specifying a Git repository URL and revision:

```
image = { git = "https://github.com/Piston/image.git", rev = "528f19c" }
```

This particular crate is open source, hosted on GitHub, but you could just as easily point to a private Git repository hosted on your corporate network. As shown here, you can specify the particular `rev`, `tag`, or `branch` to use. (These are all ways of telling Git which revision of the source code to check out.)

Another alternative is to specify a directory that contains the crate's source code:

```
image = { path = "vendor/image" }
```

This is convenient when your team has a single version control repository that contains source code for several crates, or perhaps the entire dependency graph. Each crate can specify its dependencies using relative paths.

Having this level of control over your dependencies is powerful. If you ever decide that any of the open source crates you use isn't exactly to your liking, you can trivially fork it: just hit the Fork button on GitHub and change one line in your *Cargo.toml* file. Your next `cargo build` will seamlessly use your fork of the crate instead of the official version.

Versions

When you write something like `image = "0.13.0"` in your *Cargo.toml* file, Cargo interprets this rather loosely. It uses the most recent version of `image` that is considered compatible with version 0.13.0.

The compatibility rules are adapted from Semantic Versioning (*http://semver.org*).

- A version number that starts with 0.0 is so raw that Cargo never assumes it's compatible with any other version.

- A version number that starts with 0.*x*, where *x* is nonzero, is considered compatible with other point releases in the 0.*x* series. We specified `image` version 0.6.1, but Cargo would use 0.6.3 if available. (This is not what the Semantic Versioning standard says about 0.*x* version numbers, but the rule proved too useful to leave out.)

- Once a project reaches 1.0, only new major versions break compatibility. So if you ask for version 2.0.1, Cargo might use 2.17.99 instead, but not 3.0.

Version numbers are flexible by default because otherwise the problem of which version to use would quickly become overconstrained. Suppose one library, `libA`, used `num = "0.1.31"` while another, `libB`, used `num = "0.1.29"`. If version numbers required exact matches, no project would be able to use those two libraries together. Allowing Cargo to use any compatible version is a much more practical default.

Still, different projects have different needs when it comes to dependencies and versioning. You can specify an exact version or range of versions by using operators, as illustrated in Table 8-3.

Table 8-3. Specifying versions in a Cargo.toml file

Cargo.toml line	Meaning
`image = "=0.10.0"`	Use only the exact version 0.10.0
`image = ">=1.0.5"`	Use 1.0.5 or *any* higher version (even 2.9, if it's available)
`image = ">1.0.5 <1.1.9"`	Use a version that's higher than 1.0.5, but lower than 1.1.9
`image = "<=2.7.10"`	Use any version up to 2.7.10

Another version specification you'll occasionally see is the wildcard *. This tells Cargo that any version will do. Unless some other *Cargo.toml* file contains a more specific constraint, Cargo will use the latest available version. The Cargo documentation at *doc.crates.io* (*https://oreil.ly/gI1Lq*) covers version specifications in even more detail.

Note that the compatibility rules mean that version numbers can't be chosen purely for marketing reasons. They actually mean something. They're a contract between a crate's maintainers and its users. If you maintain a crate that's at version 1.7 and you decide to remove a function or make any other change that isn't fully backward compatible, you must bump your version number to 2.0. If you were to call it 1.8, you'd be claiming that the new version is compatible with 1.7, and your users might find themselves with broken builds.

Cargo.lock

The version numbers in *Cargo.toml* are deliberately flexible, yet we don't want Cargo to upgrade us to the latest library versions every time we build. Imagine being in the middle of an intense debugging session when suddenly `cargo build` upgrades you to a new version of a library. This could be incredibly disruptive. Anything changing in the middle of debugging is bad. In fact, when it comes to libraries, there's never a good time for an unexpected change.

Cargo therefore has a built-in mechanism to prevent this. The first time you build a project, Cargo outputs a *Cargo.lock* file that records the exact version of every crate it used. Later builds will consult this file and continue to use the same versions. Cargo upgrades to newer versions only when you tell it to, either by manually bumping up the version number in your *Cargo.toml* file or by running `cargo update`:

```
$ cargo update
    Updating registry `https://github.com/rust-lang/crates.io-index`
    Updating libc v0.2.7 -> v0.2.11
    Updating png v0.4.2 -> v0.4.3
```

`cargo update` only upgrades to the latest versions that are compatible with what you've specified in *Cargo.toml*. If you've specified `image = "0.6.1"`, and you want to upgrade to version 0.10.0, you'll have to change that in *Cargo.toml*. The next time you build, Cargo will update to the new version of the `image` library and store the new version number in *Cargo.lock*.

The preceding example shows Cargo updating two crates that are hosted on crates.io. Something very similar happens for dependencies that are stored in Git. Suppose our *Cargo.toml* file contains this:

```
image = { git = "https://github.com/Piston/image.git", branch = "master" }
```

`cargo build` will not pull new changes from the Git repository if it sees that we've got a *Cargo.lock* file. Instead, it reads *Cargo.lock* and uses the same revision as last time. But `cargo update` will pull from `master` so that our next build uses the latest revision.

Cargo.lock is automatically generated for you, and you normally won't edit it by hand. Nonetheless, if your project is an executable, you should commit *Cargo.lock* to version control. That way, everyone who builds your project will consistently get the same versions. The history of your *Cargo.lock* file will record your dependency updates.

If your project is an ordinary Rust library, don't bother committing *Cargo.lock*. Your library's downstream users will have *Cargo.lock* files that contain version information for their entire dependency graph; they will ignore your library's *Cargo.lock* file. In the rare case that your project is a shared library (i.e., the output is a *.dll*, *.dylib*, or *.so* file), there is no such downstream `cargo` user, and you should therefore commit *Cargo.lock*.

Cargo.toml's flexible version specifiers make it easy to use Rust libraries in your project and maximize compatibility among libraries. *Cargo.lock*'s bookkeeping supports consistent, reproducible builds across machines. Together, they go a long way toward helping you avoid dependency hell.

Publishing Crates to crates.io

You've decided to publish your fern-simulating library as open source software. Congratulations! This part is easy.

First, make sure Cargo can pack the crate for you.

```
$ cargo package
warning: manifest has no description, license, license-file, documentation,
homepage or repository. See http://doc.crates.io/manifest.html#package-metadata
for more info.
    Packaging fern_sim v0.1.0 (file:///.../fern_sim)
    Verifying fern_sim v0.1.0 (file:///.../fern_sim)
    Compiling fern_sim v0.1.0 (file:///.../fern_sim/target/package/fern_sim-0.1.0)
```

The `cargo package` command creates a file (in this case, *target/package/fern_sim-0.1.0.crate*) containing all your library's source files, including *Cargo.toml*. This is the file that you'll upload to crates.io to share with the world. (You can use `cargo package --list` to see which files are included.) Cargo then double-checks its work by building your library from the *.crate* file, just as your eventual users will.

Cargo warns that the [`package`] section of *Cargo.toml* is missing some information that will be important to downstream users, such as the license under which you're distributing the code. The URL in the warning is an excellent resource, so we won't explain all the fields in detail here. In short, you can fix the warning by adding a few lines to *Cargo.toml*:

```
[package]
name = "fern_sim"
version = "0.1.0"
edition = "2021"
authors = ["You <you@example.com>"]
license = "MIT"
homepage = "https://fernsim.example.com/"
repository = "https://gitlair.com/sporeador/fern_sim"
documentation = "http://fernsim.example.com/docs"
description = """
Fern simulation, from the cellular level up.
"""
```

Once you publish this crate on crates.io, anyone who downloads your crate can see the *Cargo.toml* file. So if the authors field contains an email address that you'd rather keep private, now is the time to change it.

Another problem that sometimes arises at this stage is that your *Cargo.toml* file might be specifying the location of other crates by path, as shown in "Specifying Dependencies" on page 202:

```
image = { path = "vendor/image" }
```

For you and your team, this might work fine. But naturally, when other people download the fern_sim library, they will not have the same files and directories on their computer that you have. Cargo therefore *ignores* the path key in automatically downloaded libraries, and this can cause build errors. The fix, however, is straightforward: if your library is going to be published on crates.io, its dependencies should be on crates.io too. Specify a version number instead of a path:

```
image = "0.13.0"
```

If you prefer, you can specify both a path, which takes precedence for your own local builds, and a version for all other users:

```
image = { path = "vendor/image", version = "0.13.0" }
```

Of course, in that case it's your responsibility to make sure that the two stay in sync.

Lastly, before publishing a crate, you'll need to log in to crates.io and get an API key. This step is straightforward: once you have an account on crates.io, your "Account Settings" page will show a cargo login command, like this one:

```
$ cargo login 5j0dV54BjlXBpUUbfIj7G9DvNl1vsWW1
```

Cargo saves the key in a configuration file, and the API key should be kept secret, like a password. So run this command only on a computer you control.

That done, the final step is to run cargo publish:

```
$ cargo publish
    Updating registry `https://github.com/rust-lang/crates.io-index`
    Uploading fern_sim v0.1.0 (file:///.../fern_sim)
```

With this, your library joins thousands of others on crates.io.

Workspaces

As your project continues to grow, you end up writing many crates. They live side by side in a single source repository:

```
fernsoft/
├── .git/...
├── fern_sim/
│   ├── Cargo.toml
│   ├── Cargo.lock
│   ├── src/...
│   └── target/...
├── fern_img/
│   ├── Cargo.toml
│   ├── Cargo.lock
│   ├── src/...
│   └── target/...
└── fern_video/
    ├── Cargo.toml
    ├── Cargo.lock
    ├── src/...
    └── target/...
```

The way Cargo works, each crate has its own build directory, `target`, which contains a separate build of all that crate's dependencies. These build directories are completely independent. Even if two crates have a common dependency, they can't share any compiled code. This is wasteful.

You can save compilation time and disk space by using a Cargo *workspace*, a collection of crates that share a common build directory and *Cargo.lock* file.

All you need to do is create a *Cargo.toml* file in your repository's root directory and put these lines in it:

```
[workspace]
members = ["fern_sim", "fern_img", "fern_video"]
```

Here `fern_sim` etc. are the names of the subdirectories containing your crates. Delete any leftover *Cargo.lock* files and *target* directories that exist in those subdirectories.

Once you've done this, `cargo build` in any crate will automatically create and use a shared build directory under the root directory (in this case, *fernsoft/target*). The command `cargo build --workspace` builds all crates in the current workspace. `cargo test` and `cargo doc` accept the `--workspace` option as well.

More Nice Things

In case you're not delighted yet, the Rust community has a few more odds and ends for you:

- When you publish an open source crate on crates.io, your documentation is automatically rendered and hosted on *docs.rs* thanks to Onur Aslan.

- If your project is on GitHub, Travis CI can build and test your code on every push. It's surprisingly easy to set up; see travis-ci.org for details. If you're already familiar with Travis, this *.travis.yml* file will get you started:

  ```
  language: rust
  rust:
    - stable
  ```

- You can generate a *README.md* file from your crate's top-level doc-comment. This feature is offered as a third-party Cargo plug-in by Livio Ribeiro. Run `cargo install cargo-readme` to install the plug-in, then `cargo readme --help` to learn how to use it.

We could go on.

Rust is new, but it's designed to support large, ambitious projects. It has great tools and an active community. System programmers *can* have nice things.

## CHAPTER 9

Structs

Long ago, when shepherds wanted to see if two herds of sheep were isomorphic, they would look for an explicit isomorphism.

—John C. Baez and James Dolan, "Categorification" (*https://oreil.ly/EpGpb*)

Rust structs, sometimes called *structures*, resemble `struct` types in C and C++, classes in Python, and objects in JavaScript. A struct assembles several values of assorted types together into a single value so you can deal with them as a unit. Given a struct, you can read and modify its individual components. And a struct can have methods associated with it that operate on its components.

Rust has three kinds of struct types, *named-field*, *tuple-like*, and *unit-like*, which differ in how you refer to their components: a named-field struct gives a name to each component, whereas a tuple-like struct identifies them by the order in which they appear. Unit-like structs have no components at all; these are not common, but more useful than you might think.

In this chapter, we'll explain each kind in detail and show what they look like in memory. We'll cover how to add methods to them, how to define generic struct types that work with many different component types, and how to ask Rust to generate implementations of common handy traits for your structs.

Named-Field Structs

The definition of a named-field struct type looks like this:

```
/// A rectangle of eight-bit grayscale pixels.
struct GrayscaleMap {
    pixels: Vec<u8>,
    size: (usize, usize)
}
```

This declares a type GrayscaleMap with two fields named pixels and size, of the given types. The convention in Rust is for all types, structs included, to have names that capitalize the first letter of each word, like GrayscaleMap, a convention called *CamelCase* (or *PascalCase*). Fields and methods are lowercase, with words separated by underscores. This is called *snake_case*.

You can construct a value of this type with a *struct expression*, like this:

```
let width = 1024;
let height = 576;
let image = GrayscaleMap {
    pixels: vec![0; width * height],
    size: (width, height)
};
```

A struct expression starts with the type name (GrayscaleMap) and lists the name and value of each field, all enclosed in curly braces. There's also shorthand for populating fields from local variables or arguments with the same name:

```
fn new_map(size: (usize, usize), pixels: Vec<u8>) -> GrayscaleMap {
    assert_eq!(pixels.len(), size.0 * size.1);
    GrayscaleMap { pixels, size }
}
```

The struct expression GrayscaleMap { pixels, size } is short for GrayscaleMap { pixels: pixels, size: size }. You can use key: value syntax for some fields and shorthand for others in the same struct expression.

To access a struct's fields, use the familiar . operator:

```
assert_eq!(image.size, (1024, 576));
assert_eq!(image.pixels.len(), 1024 * 576);
```

Like all other items, structs are private by default, visible only in the module where they're declared and its submodules. You can make a struct visible outside its module by prefixing its definition with pub. The same goes for each of its fields, which are also private by default:

```
/// A rectangle of eight-bit grayscale pixels.
pub struct GrayscaleMap {
    pub pixels: Vec<u8>,
    pub size: (usize, usize)
}
```

Even if a struct is declared pub, its fields can be private:

```
/// A rectangle of eight-bit grayscale pixels.
pub struct GrayscaleMap {
    pixels: Vec<u8>,
    size: (usize, usize)
}
```

Other modules can use this struct and any public associated functions it might have, but can't access the private fields by name or use struct expressions to create new GrayscaleMap values. That is, creating a struct value requires all the struct's fields to be visible. This is why you can't write a struct expression to create a new String or Vec. These standard types are structs, but all their fields are private. To create one, you must use public type-associated functions like Vec::new().

When creating a named-field struct value, you can use another struct of the same type to supply values for fields you omit. In a struct expression, if the named fields are followed by .. EXPR, then any fields not mentioned take their values from EXPR, which must be another value of the same struct type. Suppose we have a struct representing a monster in a game:

```
// In this game, brooms are monsters. You'll see.
struct Broom {
    name: String,
    height: u32,
    health: u32,
    position: (f32, f32, f32),
    intent: BroomIntent
}

/// Two possible alternatives for what a `Broom` could be working on.
#[derive(Copy, Clone)]
enum BroomIntent { FetchWater, DumpWater }
```

The best fairy tale for programmers is *The Sorcerer's Apprentice*: a novice magician enchants a broom to do his work for him, but doesn't know how to stop it when the job is done. Chopping the broom in half with an axe just produces two brooms, each of half the size, but continuing the task with the same blind dedication as the original:

```
// Receive the input Broom by value, taking ownership.
fn chop(b: Broom) -> (Broom, Broom) {
    // Initialize `broom1` mostly from `b`, changing only `height`. Since
    // `String` is not `Copy`, `broom1` takes ownership of `b`'s name.
    let mut broom1 = Broom { height: b.height / 2, .. b };

    // Initialize `broom2` mostly from `broom1`. Since `String` is not
    // `Copy`, we must clone `name` explicitly.
    let mut broom2 = Broom { name: broom1.name.clone(), .. broom1 };

    // Give each fragment a distinct name.
    broom1.name.push_str(" I");
    broom2.name.push_str(" II");

    (broom1, broom2)
}
```

With that definition in place, we can create a broom, chop it in two, and see what we get:

```
let hokey = Broom {
    name: "Hokey".to_string(),
    height: 60,
    health: 100,
    position: (100.0, 200.0, 0.0),
    intent: BroomIntent::FetchWater
};

let (hokey1, hokey2) = chop(hokey);
assert_eq!(hokey1.name, "Hokey I");
assert_eq!(hokey1.height, 30);
assert_eq!(hokey1.health, 100);

assert_eq!(hokey2.name, "Hokey II");
assert_eq!(hokey2.height, 30);
assert_eq!(hokey2.health, 100);
```

The new `hokey1` and `hokey2` brooms have received adjusted names, half the height, and all the health of the original.

Tuple-Like Structs

The second kind of struct type is called a *tuple-like struct*, because it resembles a tuple:

```
struct Bounds(usize, usize);
```

You construct a value of this type much as you would construct a tuple, except that you must include the struct name:

```
let image_bounds = Bounds(1024, 768);
```

The values held by a tuple-like struct are called *elements*, just as the values of a tuple are. You access them just as you would a tuple's:

```
assert_eq!(image_bounds.0 * image_bounds.1, 786432);
```

Individual elements of a tuple-like struct may be public or not:

```
pub struct Bounds(pub usize, pub usize);
```

The expression `Bounds(1024, 768)` looks like a function call, and in fact it is: defining the type also implicitly defines a function:

```
fn Bounds(elem0: usize, elem1: usize) -> Bounds { ... }
```

At the most fundamental level, named-field and tuple-like structs are very similar. The choice of which to use comes down to questions of legibility, ambiguity, and brevity. If you will use the `.` operator to get at a value's components much at all, identifying fields by name provides the reader more information and is probably more robust against typos. If you will usually use pattern matching to find the elements, tuple-like structs can work nicely.

Tuple-like structs are good for *newtypes*, structs with a single component that you define to get stricter type checking. For example, if you are working with ASCII-only text, you might define a newtype like this:

```
struct Ascii(Vec<u8>);
```

Using this type for your ASCII strings is much better than simply passing around Vec<u8> buffers and explaining what they are in the comments. The newtype helps Rust catch mistakes where some other byte buffer is passed to a function expecting ASCII text. We'll give an example of using newtypes for efficient type conversions in Chapter 22.

Unit-Like Structs

The third kind of struct is a little obscure: it declares a struct type with no elements at all:

```
struct Onesuch;
```

A value of such a type occupies no memory, much like the unit type (). Rust doesn't bother actually storing unit-like struct values in memory or generating code to operate on them, because it can tell everything it might need to know about the value from its type alone. But logically, an empty struct is a type with values like any other—or more precisely, a type of which there is only a single value:

```
let o = Onesuch;
```

You've already encountered a unit-like struct when reading about the .. range operator in "Fields and Elements" on page 149. Whereas an expression like 3..5 is shorthand for the struct value Range { start: 3, end: 5 }, the expression .., a range omitting both endpoints, is shorthand for the unit-like struct value RangeFull.

Unit-like structs can also be useful when working with traits, which we'll describe in Chapter 11.

Struct Layout

In memory, both named-field and tuple-like structs are the same thing: a collection of values, of possibly mixed types, laid out in a particular way in memory. For example, earlier in the chapter we defined this struct:

```
struct GrayscaleMap {
    pixels: Vec<u8>,
    size: (usize, usize)
}
```

A `GrayscaleMap` value is laid out in memory as diagrammed in Figure 9-1.

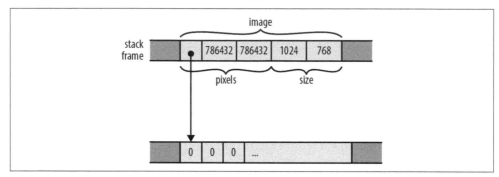

Figure 9-1. A GrayscaleMap structure in memory

Unlike C and C++, Rust doesn't make specific promises about how it will order a struct's fields or elements in memory; this diagram shows only one possible arrangement. However, Rust does promise to store fields' values directly in the struct's block of memory. Whereas JavaScript, Python, and Java would put the `pixels` and `size` values each in their own heap-allocated blocks and have `GrayscaleMap`'s fields point at them, Rust embeds `pixels` and `size` directly in the `GrayscaleMap` value. Only the heap-allocated buffer owned by the `pixels` vector remains in its own block.

You can ask Rust to lay out structures in a way compatible with C and C++, using the `#[repr(C)]` attribute. We'll cover this in detail in Chapter 23.

Defining Methods with impl

Throughout the book we've been calling methods on all sorts of values. We've pushed elements onto vectors with `v.push(e)`, fetched their length with `v.len()`, checked `Result` values for errors with `r.expect("msg")`, and so on. You can define methods on your own struct types as well. Rather than appearing inside the struct definition, as in C++ or Java, Rust methods appear in a separate `impl` block.

An `impl` block is simply a collection of `fn` definitions, each of which becomes a method on the struct type named at the top of the block. Here, for example, we define a public struct `Queue`, and then give it two public methods, push and pop:

```
/// A first-in, first-out queue of characters.
pub struct Queue {
    older: Vec<char>,   // older elements, eldest last.
    younger: Vec<char>  // younger elements, youngest last.
}

impl Queue {
    /// Push a character onto the back of a queue.
    pub fn push(&mut self, c: char) {
```

```
        self.younger.push(c);
    }

    /// Pop a character off the front of a queue. Return `Some(c)` if there
    /// was a character to pop, or `None` if the queue was empty.
    pub fn pop(&mut self) -> Option<char> {
        if self.older.is_empty() {
            if self.younger.is_empty() {
                return None;
            }

            // Bring the elements in younger over to older, and put them in
            // the promised order.
            use std::mem::swap;
            swap(&mut self.older, &mut self.younger);
            self.older.reverse();
        }

        // Now older is guaranteed to have something. Vec's pop method
        // already returns an Option, so we're set.
        self.older.pop()
    }
}
```

Functions defined in an impl block are called *associated functions*, since they're associated with a specific type. The opposite of an associated function is a *free function*, one that is not defined as an impl block's item.

Rust passes a method the value it's being called on as its first argument, which must have the special name self. Since self's type is obviously the one named at the top of the impl block, or a reference to that, Rust lets you omit the type, and write self, &self, or &mut self as shorthand for self: Queue, self: &Queue, or self: &mut Queue. You can use the longhand forms if you like, but almost all Rust code uses the shorthand, as shown before.

In our example, the push and pop methods refer to the Queue's fields as self.older and self.younger. Unlike C++ and Java, where the members of the "this" object are directly visible in method bodies as unqualified identifiers, a Rust method must explicitly use self to refer to the value it was called on, similar to the way Python methods use self, and the way JavaScript methods use this.

Since push and pop need to modify the Queue, they both take &mut self. However, when you call a method, you don't need to borrow the mutable reference yourself; the ordinary method call syntax takes care of that implicitly. So with these definitions in place, you can use Queue like this:

```
let mut q = Queue { older: Vec::new(), younger: Vec::new() };

q.push('0');
q.push('1');
assert_eq!(q.pop(), Some('0'));

q.push('∞');
assert_eq!(q.pop(), Some('1'));
assert_eq!(q.pop(), Some('∞'));
assert_eq!(q.pop(), None);
```

Simply writing q.push(...) borrows a mutable reference to q, as if you had written (&mut q).push(...), since that's what the push method's self requires.

If a method doesn't need to modify its self, then you can define it to take a shared reference instead. For example:

```
impl Queue {
    pub fn is_empty(&self) -> bool {
        self.older.is_empty() && self.younger.is_empty()
    }
}
```

Again, the method call expression knows which sort of reference to borrow:

```
assert!(q.is_empty());
q.push('⊙');
assert!(!q.is_empty());
```

Or, if a method wants to take ownership of self, it can take self by value:

```
impl Queue {
    pub fn split(self) -> (Vec<char>, Vec<char>) {
        (self.older, self.younger)
    }
}
```

Calling this split method looks like the other method calls:

```
let mut q = Queue { older: Vec::new(), younger: Vec::new() };

q.push('P');
q.push('D');
assert_eq!(q.pop(), Some('P'));
q.push('X');

let (older, younger) = q.split();
// q is now uninitialized.
assert_eq!(older, vec!['D']);
assert_eq!(younger, vec!['X']);
```

But note that, since `split` takes its `self` by value, this *moves* the Queue out of q, leaving q uninitialized. Since `split`'s `self` now owns the queue, it's able to move the individual vectors out of it and return them to the caller.

Sometimes, taking `self` by value like this, or even by reference, isn't enough, so Rust also lets you pass `self` via smart pointer types.

Passing Self as a Box, Rc, or Arc

A method's `self` argument can also be a `Box<Self>`, `Rc<Self>`, or `Arc<Self>`. Such a method can only be called on a value of the given pointer type. Calling the method passes ownership of the pointer to it.

You won't usually need to do this. A method that expects `self` by reference works fine when called on any of those pointer types:

```
let mut bq = Box::new(Queue::new());

// `Queue::push` expects a `&mut Queue`, but `bq` is a `Box<Queue>`.
// This is fine: Rust borrows a `&mut Queue` from the `Box` for the
// duration of the call.
bq.push('■');
```

For method calls and field access, Rust automatically borrows a reference from pointer types like `Box`, `Rc`, and `Arc`, so `&self` and `&mut self` are almost always the right thing in a method signature, along with the occasional `self`.

But if it does come to pass that some method needs ownership of a pointer to `Self`, and its callers have such a pointer handy, Rust will let you pass it as the method's `self` argument. To do so, you must spell out the type of `self`, as if it were an ordinary parameter:

```
impl Node {
    fn append_to(self: Rc<Self>, parent: &mut Node) {
        parent.children.push(self);
    }
}
```

Type-Associated Functions

An `impl` block for a given type can also define functions that don't take `self` as an argument at all. These are still associated functions, since they're in an `impl` block, but they're not methods, since they don't take a `self` argument. To distinguish them from methods, we call them *type-associated functions*.

They're often used to provide constructor functions, like this:

```
impl Queue {
    pub fn new() -> Queue {
```

```
            Queue { older: Vec::new(), younger: Vec::new() }
        }
    }
```

To use this function, we refer to it as `Queue::new`: the type name, a double colon, and then the function name. Now our example code becomes a bit more svelte:

```
let mut q = Queue::new();

q.push('*');
...
```

It's conventional in Rust for constructor functions to be named `new`; we've already seen `Vec::new`, `Box::new`, `HashMap::new`, and others. But there's nothing special about the name `new`. It's not a keyword, and types often have other associated functions that serve as constructors, like `Vec::with_capacity`.

Although you can have many separate `impl` blocks for a single type, they must all be in the same crate that defines that type. However, Rust does let you attach your own methods to other types; we'll explain how in Chapter 11.

If you're used to C++ or Java, separating a type's methods from its definition may seem unusual, but there are several advantages to doing so:

- It's always easy to find a type's data members. In large C++ class definitions, you might need to skim hundreds of lines of member function definitions to be sure you haven't missed any of the class's data members; in Rust, they're all in one place.

- Although one can imagine fitting methods into the syntax for named-field structs, it's not so neat for tuple-like and unit-like structs. Pulling methods out into an `impl` block allows a single syntax for all three. In fact, Rust uses this same syntax for defining methods on types that are not structs at all, such as `enum` types and primitive types like `i32`. (The fact that any type can have methods is one reason Rust doesn't use the term *object* much, preferring to call everything a *value*.)

- The same `impl` syntax also serves neatly for implementing traits, which we'll go into in Chapter 11.

Associated Consts

Another feature of languages like C# and Java that Rust adopts in its type system is the idea of values associated with a type, rather than a specific instance of that type. In Rust, these are known as *associated consts*.

As the name implies, associated consts are constant values. They're often used to specify commonly used values of a type. For instance, you could define a two-dimensional vector for use in linear algebra with an associated unit vector:

```
pub struct Vector2 {
    x: f32,
    y: f32,
}

impl Vector2 {
    const ZERO: Vector2 = Vector2 { x: 0.0, y: 0.0 };
    const UNIT: Vector2 = Vector2 { x: 1.0, y: 0.0 };
}
```

These values are associated with the type itself, and you can use them without referring to another instance of Vector2. Much like associated functions, they are accessed
by naming the type with which they're associated, followed by their name:

```
let scaled = Vector2::UNIT.scaled_by(2.0);
```

Nor does an associated const have to be of the same type as the type it's associated
with; we could use this feature to add IDs or names to types. For example, if there
were several types similar to Vector2 that needed to be written to a file and then
loaded into memory later, an associated const could be used to add names or numeric
IDs that could be written next to the data to identify its type:

```
impl Vector2 {
    const NAME: &'static str = "Vector2";
    const ID: u32 = 18;
}
```

Generic Structs

Our earlier definition of Queue is unsatisfying: it is written to store characters, but
there's nothing about its structure or methods that is specific to characters at all. If we
were to define another struct that held, say, String values, the code could be identical, except that char would be replaced with String. That would be a waste of time.

Fortunately, Rust structs can be *generic*, meaning that their definition is a template
into which you can plug whatever types you like. For example, here's a definition for
Queue that can hold values of any type:

```
pub struct Queue<T> {
    older: Vec<T>,
    younger: Vec<T>
}
```

You can read the <T> in Queue<T> as "for any element type T...". So this definition
reads, "For any type T, a Queue<T> is two fields of type Vec<T>." For example, in
Queue<String>, T is String, so older and younger have type Vec<String>. In
Queue<char>, T is char, and we get a struct identical to the char-specific definition we
started with. In fact, Vec itself is a generic struct, defined in just this way.

In generic struct definitions, the type names used in <angle brackets> are called *type parameters*. An `impl` block for a generic struct looks like this:

```
impl<T> Queue<T> {
    pub fn new() -> Queue<T> {
        Queue { older: Vec::new(), younger: Vec::new() }
    }

    pub fn push(&mut self, t: T) {
        self.younger.push(t);
    }

    pub fn is_empty(&self) -> bool {
        self.older.is_empty() && self.younger.is_empty()
    }

    ...
}
```

You can read the line `impl<T> Queue<T>` as something like, "for any type T, here are some associated functions available on `Queue<T>`." Then, you can use the type parameter T as a type in the associated function definitions.

The syntax may look a bit redundant, but the `impl<T>` makes it clear that the `impl` block covers any type T, which distinguishes it from an `impl` block written for one specific kind of `Queue`, like this one:

```
impl Queue<f64> {
    fn sum(&self) -> f64 {
        ...
    }
}
```

This `impl` block header reads, "Here are some associated functions specifically for `Queue<f64>`." This gives `Queue<f64>` a `sum` method, available on no other kind of `Queue`.

We've used Rust's shorthand for `self` parameters in the preceding code; writing out `Queue<T>` everywhere becomes a mouthful and a distraction. As another shorthand, every `impl` block, generic or not, defines the special type parameter `Self` (note the `CamelCase` name) to be whatever type we're adding methods to. In the preceding code, `Self` would be `Queue<T>`, so we can abbreviate `Queue::new`'s definition a bit further:

```
pub fn new() -> Self {
    Queue { older: Vec::new(), younger: Vec::new() }
}
```

You might have noticed that, in the body of `new`, we didn't need to write the type parameter in the construction expression; simply writing `Queue { ... }` was good enough. This is Rust's type inference at work: since there's only one type that works for that function's return value—namely, Queue<T>—Rust supplies the parameter for us. However, you'll always need to supply type parameters in function signatures and type definitions. Rust doesn't infer those; instead, it uses those explicit types as the basis from which it infers types within function bodies.

Self can also be used in this way; we could have written Self { ... } instead. It's up to you to decide which you find easiest to understand.

For associated function calls, you can supply the type parameter explicitly using the ::<> (turbofish) notation:

```
let mut q = Queue::<char>::new();
```

But in practice, you can usually just let Rust figure it out for you:

```
let mut q = Queue::new();
let mut r = Queue::new();

q.push("CAD");  // apparently a Queue<&'static str>
r.push(0.74);   // apparently a Queue<f64>

q.push("BTC");    // Bitcoins per USD, 2019-6
r.push(13764.0); // Rust fails to detect irrational exuberance
```

In fact, this is exactly what we've been doing with Vec, another generic struct type, throughout the book.

It's not just structs that can be generic. Enums can take type parameters as well, with a very similar syntax. We'll show that in detail in "Enums" on page 232.

Generic Structs with Lifetime Parameters

As we discussed in "Structs Containing References" on page 117, if a struct type contains references, you must name those references' lifetimes. For example, here's a structure that might hold references to the greatest and least elements of some slice:

```
struct Extrema<'elt> {
    greatest: &'elt i32,
    least: &'elt i32
}
```

Earlier, we invited you to think of a declaration like struct Queue<T> as meaning that, given any specific type T, you can make a Queue<T> that holds that type. Similarly, you can think of struct Extrema<'elt> as meaning that, given any specific lifetime 'elt, you can make an Extrema<'elt> that holds references with that lifetime.

Here's a function to scan a slice and return an Extrema value whose fields refer to its elements:

```
fn find_extrema<'s>(slice: &'s [i32]) -> Extrema<'s> {
    let mut greatest = &slice[0];
    let mut least = &slice[0];

    for i in 1..slice.len() {
        if slice[i] < *least    { least    = &slice[i]; }
        if slice[i] > *greatest { greatest = &slice[i]; }
    }
    Extrema { greatest, least }
}
```

Here, since `find_extrema` borrows elements of `slice`, which has lifetime `'s`, the `Extrema` struct we return also uses `'s` as the lifetime of its references. Rust always infers lifetime parameters for calls, so calls to `find_extrema` needn't mention them:

```
let a = [0, -3, 0, 15, 48];
let e = find_extrema(&a);
assert_eq!(*e.least, -3);
assert_eq!(*e.greatest, 48);
```

Because it's so common for the return type to use the same lifetime as an argument, Rust lets us omit the lifetimes when there's one obvious candidate. We could also have written `find_extrema`'s signature like this, with no change in meaning:

```
fn find_extrema(slice: &[i32]) -> Extrema {
    ...
}
```

Granted, we *might* have meant `Extrema<'static>`, but that's pretty unusual. Rust provides a shorthand for the common case.

Generic Structs with Constant Parameters

A generic struct can also take parameters that are constant values. For example, you could define a type representing polynomials of arbitrary degree like so:

```
/// A polynomial of degree N - 1.
struct Polynomial<const N: usize> {
    /// The coefficients of the polynomial.
    ///
    /// For a polynomial a + bx + cx² + ... + zxⁿ⁻¹,
    /// the `i`'th element is the coefficient of xⁱ.
    coefficients: [f64; N]
}
```

With this definition, `Polynomial<3>` is a quadratic polynomial, for example. The `<const N: usize>` clause says that the `Polynomial` type expects a `usize` value as its generic parameter, which it uses to decide how many coefficients to store.

Unlike `Vec`, which has fields holding its length and capacity and stores its elements in the heap, `Polynomial` stores its coefficients directly in the value, and nothing else.

The length is given by the type. (The capacity isn't needed, because `Polynomial`s can't grow dynamically.)

We can use the parameter N in the type's associated functions:

```
impl<const N: usize> Polynomial<N> {
    fn new(coefficients: [f64; N]) -> Polynomial<N> {
        Polynomial { coefficients }
    }

    /// Evaluate the polynomial at `x`.
    fn eval(&self, x: f64) -> f64 {
        // Horner's method is numerically stable, efficient, and simple:
        // c₀ + x(c₁ + x(c₂ + x(c₃ + ... x(c[n-1] + x c[n])))))
        let mut sum = 0.0;
        for i in (0..N).rev() {
            sum = self.coefficients[i] + x * sum;
        }

        sum
    }
}
```

Here, the `new` function accepts an array of length N, and takes its elements as the coefficients of a fresh `Polynomial` value. The `eval` method iterates over the range `0..N` to find the value of the polynomial at a given point x.

As with type and lifetime parameters, Rust can often infer the right values for constant parameters:

```
use std::f64::consts::FRAC_PI_2;    // π/2

// Approximate the `sin` function: sin x ≅ x - 1/6 x³ + 1/120 x⁵
// Around zero, it's pretty accurate!
let sine_poly = Polynomial::new([0.0, 1.0, 0.0, -1.0/6.0, 0.0,
                                 1.0/120.0]);
assert_eq!(sine_poly.eval(0.0), 0.0);
assert!((sine_poly.eval(FRAC_PI_2) - 1.).abs() < 0.005);
```

Since we pass `Polynomial::new` an array with six elements, Rust knows we must be constructing a `Polynomial<6>`. The `eval` method knows how many iterations the for loop should run simply by consulting its `Self` type. Since the length is known at compile time, the compiler will probably replace the loop entirely with straight-line code.

A `const` generic parameter may be any integer type, `char`, or `bool`. Floating-point numbers, enums, and other types are not permitted.

If the struct takes other kinds of generic parameters, lifetime parameters must come first, followed by types, followed by any `const` values. For example, a type that holds an array of references could be declared like this:

```
struct LumpOfReferences<'a, T, const N: usize> {
    the_lump: [&'a T; N]
}
```

Constant generic parameters are a relatively new addition to Rust, and their use is somewhat restricted for now. For example, it would have been nicer to define Polynomial like this:

```
/// A polynomial of degree N.
struct Polynomial<const N: usize> {
    coefficients: [f64; N + 1]
}
```

However, Rust rejects this definition:

```
error: generic parameters may not be used in const operations
  |
6 |     coefficients: [f64; N + 1]
  |                         ^ cannot perform const operation using `N`
  |
  = help: const parameters may only be used as standalone arguments, i.e. `N`
```

While it's fine to say [f64; N], a type like [f64; N + 1] is apparently too risqué for Rust. But Rust imposes this restriction for the time being to avoid confronting issues like this:

```
struct Ketchup<const N: usize> {
    tomayto: [i32; N & !31],
    tomahto: [i32; N - (N % 32)],
}
```

As it turns out, N & !31 and N - (N % 32) are equal for all values of N, so tomayto and tomahto always have the same type. It should be permitted to assign one to the other, for example. But teaching Rust's type checker the bit-fiddling algebra it would need to be able to recognize this fact risks introducing confusing corner cases to an aspect of the language that is already quite complicated. Of course, simple expressions like N + 1 are much more well-behaved, and there is work underway to teach Rust to handle those smoothly.

Since the concern here is with the type checker's behavior, this restriction applies only to constant parameters appearing in types, like the length of an array. In an ordinary expression, you can use N however you like: N + 1 and N & !31 are perfectly acceptable.

If the value you want to supply for a const generic parameter is not simply a literal or a single identifier, then you must wrap it in braces, as in Polynomial<{5 + 1}>. This rule allows Rust to report syntax errors more accurately.

Deriving Common Traits for Struct Types

Structs can be very easy to write:

```
struct Point {
    x: f64,
    y: f64
}
```

However, if you were to start using this `Point` type, you would quickly notice that it's a bit of a pain. As written, `Point` is not copyable or cloneable. You can't print it with `println!("{:?}", point);` and it does not support the `==` and `!=` operators.

Each of these features has a name in Rust—`Copy`, `Clone`, `Debug`, and `PartialEq`. They are called *traits*. In Chapter 11, we'll show how to implement traits by hand for your own structs. But in the case of these standard traits, and several others, you don't need to implement them by hand unless you want some kind of custom behavior. Rust can automatically implement them for you, with mechanical accuracy. Just add a `#[derive]` attribute to the struct:

```
#[derive(Copy, Clone, Debug, PartialEq)]
struct Point {
    x: f64,
    y: f64
}
```

Each of these traits can be implemented automatically for a struct, provided that each of its fields implements the trait. We can ask Rust to derive `PartialEq` for `Point` because its two fields are both of type `f64`, which already implements `PartialEq`.

Rust can also derive `PartialOrd`, which would add support for the comparison operators `<`, `>`, `<=`, and `>=`. We haven't done so here, because comparing two points to see if one is "less than" the other is actually a pretty weird thing to do. There's no one conventional order on points. So we choose not to support those operators for `Point` values. Cases like this are one reason that Rust makes us write the `#[derive]` attribute rather than automatically deriving every trait it can. Another reason is that implementing a trait is automatically a public feature, so copyability, cloneability, and so forth are all part of your struct's public API and should be chosen deliberately.

We'll describe Rust's standard traits in detail and explain which ones are `#[derive]`able in Chapter 13.

Interior Mutability

Mutability is like anything else: in excess, it causes problems, but you often want just a little bit of it. For example, say your spider robot control system has a central struct,

SpiderRobot, that contains settings and I/O handles. It's set up when the robot boots, and the values never change:

```
pub struct SpiderRobot {
    species: String,
    web_enabled: bool,
    leg_devices: [fd::FileDesc; 8],
    ...
}
```

Every major system of the robot is handled by a different struct, and each one has a pointer back to the SpiderRobot:

```
use std::rc::Rc;

pub struct SpiderSenses {
    robot: Rc<SpiderRobot>,  // <-- pointer to settings and I/O
    eyes: [Camera; 32],
    motion: Accelerometer,
    ...
}
```

The structs for web construction, predation, venom flow control, and so forth also all have an Rc<SpiderRobot> smart pointer. Recall that Rc stands for reference counting, and a value in an Rc box is always shared and therefore always immutable.

Now suppose you want to add a little logging to the SpiderRobot struct, using the standard File type. There's a problem: a File has to be mut. All the methods for writing to it require a mut reference.

This sort of situation comes up fairly often. What we need is a little bit of mutable data (a File) inside an otherwise immutable value (the SpiderRobot struct). This is called *interior mutability*. Rust offers several flavors of it; in this section, we'll discuss the two most straightforward types: Cell<T> and RefCell<T>, both in the std::cell module.

A Cell<T> is a struct that contains a single private value of type T. The only special thing about a Cell is that you can get and set the field even if you don't have mut access to the Cell itself:

Cell::new(value)
> Creates a new Cell, moving the given value into it.

cell.get()
> Returns a copy of the value in the cell.

cell.set(value)
> Stores the given value in the cell, dropping the previously stored value.

This method takes self as a non-mut reference:

```
fn set(&self, value: T)     // note: not `&mut self`
```

This is, of course, unusual for methods named set. By now, Rust has trained us to expect that we need mut access if we want to make changes to data. But by the same token, this one unusual detail is the whole point of Cells. They're simply a safe way of bending the rules on immutability—no more, no less.

Cells also have a few other methods, which you can read about in the documentation (*https://oreil.ly/WqRrt*).

A Cell would be handy if you were adding a simple counter to your SpiderRobot. You could write:

```
use std::cell::Cell;

pub struct SpiderRobot {
    ...
    hardware_error_count: Cell<u32>,
    ...
}
```

Then even non-mut methods of SpiderRobot can access that u32, using the .get() and .set() methods:

```
impl SpiderRobot {
    /// Increase the error count by 1.
    pub fn add_hardware_error(&self) {
        let n = self.hardware_error_count.get();
        self.hardware_error_count.set(n + 1);
    }

    /// True if any hardware errors have been reported.
    pub fn has_hardware_errors(&self) -> bool {
        self.hardware_error_count.get() > 0
    }
}
```

This is easy enough, but it doesn't solve our logging problem. Cell does *not* let you call mut methods on a shared value. The .get() method returns a copy of the value in the cell, so it works only if T implements the Copy trait. For logging, we need a mutable File, and File isn't copyable.

The right tool in this case is a RefCell. Like Cell<T>, RefCell<T> is a generic type that contains a single value of type T. Unlike Cell, RefCell supports borrowing references to its T value:

RefCell::new(value)
Creates a new RefCell, moving value into it.

`ref_cell.borrow()`
> Returns a `Ref<T>`, which is essentially just a shared reference to the value stored in `ref_cell`.
>
> This method panics if the value is already mutably borrowed; see details to follow.

`ref_cell.borrow_mut()`
> Returns a `RefMut<T>`, essentially a mutable reference to the value in `ref_cell`.
>
> This method panics if the value is already borrowed; see details to follow.

`ref_cell.try_borrow()`, `ref_cell.try_borrow_mut()`
> Work just like `borrow()` and `borrow_mut()`, but return a `Result`. Instead of panicking if the value is already mutably borrowed, they return an `Err` value.

Again, `RefCell` has a few other methods, which you can find in the documentation (*https://oreil.ly/FtnIO*).

The two `borrow` methods panic only if you try to break the Rust rule that `mut` references are exclusive references. For example, this would panic:

```
use std::cell::RefCell;

let ref_cell: RefCell<String> = RefCell::new("hello".to_string());

let r = ref_cell.borrow();       // ok, returns a Ref<String>
let count = r.len();             // ok, returns "hello".len()
assert_eq!(count, 5);

let mut w = ref_cell.borrow_mut();  // panic: already borrowed
w.push_str(" world");
```

To avoid panicking, you could put these two borrows into separate blocks. That way, r would be dropped before you try to borrow w.

This is a lot like how normal references work. The only difference is that normally, when you borrow a reference to a variable, Rust checks *at compile time* to ensure that you're using the reference safely. If the checks fail, you get a compiler error. `RefCell` enforces the same rule using run-time checks. So if you're breaking the rules, you get a panic (or an `Err`, for `try_borrow` and `try_borrow_mut`).

Now we're ready to put `RefCell` to work in our `SpiderRobot` type:

```
pub struct SpiderRobot {
    ...
    log_file: RefCell<File>,
    ...
}
```

```
impl SpiderRobot {
    /// Write a line to the log file.
    pub fn log(&self, message: &str) {
        let mut file = self.log_file.borrow_mut();
        // `writeln!` is like `println!`, but sends
        // output to the given file.
        writeln!(file, "{}", message).unwrap();
    }
}
```

The variable `file` has type `RefMut<File>`. It can be used just like a mutable reference to a `File`. For details about writing to files, see Chapter 18.

Cells are easy to use. Having to call `.get()` and `.set()` or `.borrow()` and `.borrow_mut()` is slightly awkward, but that's just the price we pay for bending the rules. The other drawback is less obvious and more serious: cells—and any types that contain them—are not thread-safe. Rust therefore will not allow multiple threads to access them at once. We'll describe thread-safe flavors of interior mutability in Chapter 19, when we discuss "Mutex<T>" on page 528, "Atomics" on page 535, and "Global Variables" on page 537.

Whether a struct has named fields or is tuple-like, it is an aggregation of other values: if I have a `SpiderSenses` struct, then I have an `Rc` pointer to a shared `SpiderRobot` struct, and I have eyes, and I have an accelerometer, and so on. So the essence of a struct is the word "and": I have an X *and* a Y. But what if there were another kind of type built around the word "or"? That is, when you have a value of such a type, you'd have *either* an X *or* a Y? Such types turn out to be so useful that they're ubiquitous in Rust, and they are the subject of the next chapter.

## CHAPTER 10

Enums and Patterns

Surprising how much computer stuff makes sense viewed as tragic deprivation of sum types (cf. deprivation of lambdas).
—Graydon Hoare (*https://oreil.ly/cyYQc*)

The first topic of this chapter is potent, as old as the hills, happy to help you get a lot done in short order (for a price), and known by many names in many cultures. But it's not the devil. It's a kind of user-defined data type, long known to ML and Haskell hackers as sum types, discriminated unions, or algebraic data types. In Rust, they are called *enumerations*, or simply *enums*. Unlike the devil, they are quite safe, and the price they ask is no great privation.

C++ and C# have enums; you can use them to define your own type whose values are a set of named constants. For example, you might define a type named `Color` with values `Red`, `Orange`, `Yellow`, and so on. This kind of enum works in Rust, too. But Rust takes enums much further. A Rust enum can also contain data, even data of varying types. For example, Rust's `Result<String, io::Error>` type is an enum; such a value is either an `Ok` value containing a `String` or an `Err` value containing an `io::Error`. This is beyond what C++ and C# enums can do. It's more like a C `union` —but unlike unions, Rust enums are type-safe.

Enums are useful whenever a value might be either one thing or another. The "price" of using them is that you must access the data safely, using pattern matching, our topic for the second half of this chapter.

Patterns, too, may be familiar if you've used unpacking in Python or destructuring in JavaScript, but Rust takes patterns further. Rust patterns are a little like regular expressions for all your data. They're used to test whether or not a value has a particular desired shape. They can extract several fields from a struct or tuple into local variables all at once. And like regular expressions, they are concise, typically doing it all in a single line of code.

This chapter starts with the basics of enums, showing how data can be associated with enum variants and how enums are stored in memory. Then we'll show how Rust's patterns and `match` statements can concisely specify logic based on enums, structs, arrays, and slices. Patterns can also include references, moves, and `if` conditions, making them even more capable.

Enums

Simple, C-style enums are straightforward:

```
enum Ordering {
    Less,
    Equal,
    Greater,
}
```

This declares a type `Ordering` with three possible values, called *variants* or *constructors*: `Ordering::Less`, `Ordering::Equal`, and `Ordering::Greater`. This particular enum is part of the standard library, so Rust code can import it, either by itself:

```
use std::cmp::Ordering;

fn compare(n: i32, m: i32) -> Ordering {
    if n < m {
        Ordering::Less
    } else if n > m {
        Ordering::Greater
    } else {
        Ordering::Equal
    }
}
```

or with all its constructors:

```
use std::cmp::Ordering::{self, *};    // `*` to import all children

fn compare(n: i32, m: i32) -> Ordering {
    if n < m {
        Less
    } else if n > m {
        Greater
    } else {
        Equal
    }
}
```

After importing the constructors, we can write `Less` instead of `Ordering::Less`, and so on, but because this is less explicit, it's generally considered better style *not* to import them except when it makes your code much more readable.

To import the constructors of an enum declared in the current module, use a `self` import:

```
enum Pet {
    Orca,
    Giraffe,
    ...
}

use self::Pet::*;
```

In memory, values of C-style enums are stored as integers. Occasionally it's useful to tell Rust which integers to use:

```
enum HttpStatus {
    Ok = 200,
    NotModified = 304,
    NotFound = 404,
    ...
}
```

Otherwise Rust will assign the numbers for you, starting at 0.

By default, Rust stores C-style enums using the smallest built-in integer type that can accommodate them. Most fit in a single byte:

```
use std::mem::size_of;
assert_eq!(size_of::<Ordering>(), 1);
assert_eq!(size_of::<HttpStatus>(), 2);  // 404 doesn't fit in a u8
```

You can override Rust's choice of in-memory representation by adding a `#[repr]` attribute to the enum. For details, see "Finding Common Data Representations" on page 666.

Casting a C-style enum to an integer is allowed:

```
assert_eq!(HttpStatus::Ok as i32, 200);
```

However, casting in the other direction, from the integer to the enum, is not. Unlike C and C++, Rust guarantees that an enum value is only ever one of the values spelled out in the `enum` declaration. An unchecked cast from an integer type to an enum type could break this guarantee, so it's not allowed. You can either write your own checked conversion:

```
fn http_status_from_u32(n: u32) -> Option<HttpStatus> {
    match n {
        200 => Some(HttpStatus::Ok),
        304 => Some(HttpStatus::NotModified),
        404 => Some(HttpStatus::NotFound),
```

```
    ...
    _ => None,
        }
    }
```

or use the `enum_primitive` crate (*https://oreil.ly/8BGLH*). It contains a macro that autogenerates this kind of conversion code for you.

As with structs, the compiler will implement features like the == operator for you, but you have to ask:

```
#[derive(Copy, Clone, Debug, PartialEq, Eq)]
enum TimeUnit {
    Seconds, Minutes, Hours, Days, Months, Years,
}
```

Enums can have methods, just like structs:

```
impl TimeUnit {
    /// Return the plural noun for this time unit.
    fn plural(self) -> &'static str {
        match self {
            TimeUnit::Seconds => "seconds",
            TimeUnit::Minutes => "minutes",
            TimeUnit::Hours => "hours",
            TimeUnit::Days => "days",
            TimeUnit::Months => "months",
            TimeUnit::Years => "years",
        }
    }

    /// Return the singular noun for this time unit.
    fn singular(self) -> &'static str {
        self.plural().trim_end_matches('s')
    }
}
```

So much for C-style enums. The more interesting sort of Rust enum is the kind whose variants hold data. We'll show how these are stored in memory, how to make them generic by adding type parameters, and how to build complex data structures from enums.

Enums with Data

Some programs always need to display full dates and times down to the millisecond, but for most applications, it's more user-friendly to use a rough approximation, like "two months ago." We can write an enum to help with that, using the enum defined earlier:

```
/// A timestamp that has been deliberately rounded off, so our program
/// says "6 months ago" instead of "February 9, 2016, at 9:49 AM".
#[derive(Copy, Clone, Debug, PartialEq)]
```

```
enum RoughTime {
    InThePast(TimeUnit, u32),
    JustNow,
    InTheFuture(TimeUnit, u32),
}
```

Two of the variants in this enum, `InThePast` and `InTheFuture`, take arguments. These are called *tuple variants*. Like tuple structs, these constructors are functions that create new `RoughTime` values:

```
let four_score_and_seven_years_ago =
    RoughTime::InThePast(TimeUnit::Years, 4 * 20 + 7);

let three_hours_from_now =
    RoughTime::InTheFuture(TimeUnit::Hours, 3);
```

Enums can also have *struct variants*, which contain named fields, just like ordinary structs:

```
enum Shape {
    Sphere { center: Point3d, radius: f32 },
    Cuboid { corner1: Point3d, corner2: Point3d },
}

let unit_sphere = Shape::Sphere {
    center: ORIGIN,
    radius: 1.0,
};
```

In all, Rust has three kinds of enum variant, echoing the three kinds of struct we showed in the previous chapter. Variants with no data correspond to unit-like structs. Tuple variants look and function just like tuple structs. Struct variants have curly braces and named fields. A single enum can have variants of all three kinds:

```
enum RelationshipStatus {
    Single,
    InARelationship,
    ItsComplicated(Option<String>),
    ItsExtremelyComplicated {
        car: DifferentialEquation,
        cdr: EarlyModernistPoem,
    },
}
```

All constructors and fields of an enum share the same visibility as the enum itself.

Enums in Memory

In memory, enums with data are stored as a small integer *tag*, plus enough memory to hold all the fields of the largest variant. The tag field is for Rust's internal use. It tells which constructor created the value and therefore which fields it has.

As of Rust 1.50, RoughTime fits in 8 bytes, as shown in Figure 10-1.

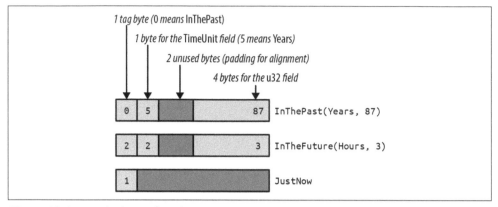

Figure 10-1. RoughTime values in memory

Rust makes no promises about enum layout, however, in order to leave the door open for future optimizations. In some cases, it would be possible to pack an enum more efficiently than the figure suggests. For instance, some generic structs can be stored without a tag at all, as we'll see later.

Rich Data Structures Using Enums

Enums are also useful for quickly implementing tree-like data structures. For example, suppose a Rust program needs to work with arbitrary JSON data. In memory, any JSON document can be represented as a value of this Rust type:

```
use std::collections::HashMap;

enum Json {
    Null,
    Boolean(bool),
    Number(f64),
    String(String),
    Array(Vec<Json>),
    Object(Box<HashMap<String, Json>>),
}
```

The explanation of this data structure in English can't improve much upon the Rust code. The JSON standard specifies the various data types that can appear in a JSON document: null, Boolean values, numbers, strings, arrays of JSON values, and objects with string keys and JSON values. The Json enum simply spells out these types.

This is not a hypothetical example. A very similar enum can be found in serde_json, a serialization library for Rust structs that is one of the most-downloaded crates on crates.io.

The `Box` around the `HashMap` that represents an `Object` serves only to make all `Json` values more compact. In memory, values of type `Json` take up four machine words. `String` and `Vec` values are three words, and Rust adds a tag byte. `Null` and `Boolean` values don't have enough data in them to use up all that space, but all `Json` values must be the same size. The extra space goes unused. Figure 10-2 shows some examples of how `Json` values actually look in memory.

A `HashMap` is larger still. If we had to leave room for it in every `Json` value, they would be quite large, eight words or so. But a `Box<HashMap>` is a single word: it's just a pointer to heap-allocated data. We could make `Json` even more compact by boxing more fields.

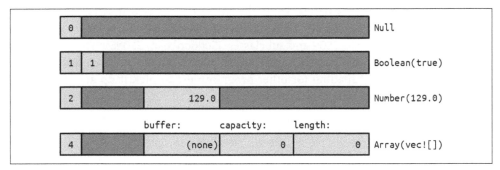

Figure 10-2. `Json` values in memory

What's remarkable here is how easy it was to set this up. In C++, one might write a class for this:

```
class JSON {
private:
    enum Tag {
        Null, Boolean, Number, String, Array, Object
    };
    union Data {
        bool boolean;
        double number;
        shared_ptr<string> str;
        shared_ptr<vector<JSON>> array;
        shared_ptr<unordered_map<string, JSON>> object;

        Data() {}
        ~Data() {}
        ...
    };

    Tag tag;
    Data data;

public:
```

```
        bool is_null() const { return tag == Null; }
        bool is_boolean() const { return tag == Boolean; }
        bool get_boolean() const {
            assert(is_boolean());
            return data.boolean;
        }
        void set_boolean(bool value) {
            this->~JSON();  // clean up string/array/object value
            tag = Boolean;
            data.boolean = value;
        }
        ...
    };
```

At 30 lines of code, we have barely begun the work. This class will need constructors, a destructor, and an assignment operator. An alternative would be to create a class hierarchy with a base class JSON and subclasses JSONBoolean, JSONString, and so on. Either way, when it's done, our C++ JSON library will have more than a dozen methods. It will take a bit of reading for other programmers to pick it up and use it. The entire Rust enum is eight lines of code.

Generic Enums

Enums can be generic. Two examples from the standard library are among the most-used data types in the language:

```
enum Option<T> {
    None,
    Some(T),
}

enum Result<T, E> {
    Ok(T),
    Err(E),
}
```

These types are familiar enough by now, and the syntax for generic enums is the same as for generic structs.

One unobvious detail is that Rust can eliminate the tag field of Option<T> when the type T is a reference, Box, or other smart pointer type. Since none of those pointer types is allowed to be zero, Rust can represent Option<Box<i32>>, say, as a single machine word: 0 for None and nonzero for Some pointer. This makes such Option types close analogues to C or C++ pointer values that could be null. The difference is that Rust's type system requires you to check that an Option is Some before you can use its contents. This effectively eliminates null pointer dereferences.

Generic data structures can be built with just a few lines of code:

```
// An ordered collection of `T`s.
enum BinaryTree<T> {
    Empty,
    NonEmpty(Box<TreeNode<T>>),
}

// A part of a BinaryTree.
struct TreeNode<T> {
    element: T,
    left: BinaryTree<T>,
    right: BinaryTree<T>,
}
```

These few lines of code define a BinaryTree type that can store any number of values of type T.

A great deal of information is packed into these two definitions, so we will take the time to translate the code word for word into English. Each BinaryTree value is either Empty or NonEmpty. If it's Empty, then it contains no data at all. If NonEmpty, then it has a Box, a pointer to a heap-allocated TreeNode.

Each TreeNode value contains one actual element, as well as two more BinaryTree values. This means a tree can contain subtrees, and thus a NonEmpty tree can have any number of descendants.

A sketch of a value of type BinaryTree<&str> is shown in Figure 10-3. As with Option<Box<T>>, Rust eliminates the tag field, so a BinaryTree value is just one machine word.

Building any particular node in this tree is straightforward:

```
use self::BinaryTree::*;
let jupiter_tree = NonEmpty(Box::new(TreeNode {
    element: "Jupiter",
    left: Empty,
    right: Empty,
}));
```

Larger trees can be built from smaller ones:

```
let mars_tree = NonEmpty(Box::new(TreeNode {
    element: "Mars",
    left: jupiter_tree,
    right: mercury_tree,
}));
```

Naturally, this assignment transfers ownership of jupiter_node and mercury_node to their new parent node.

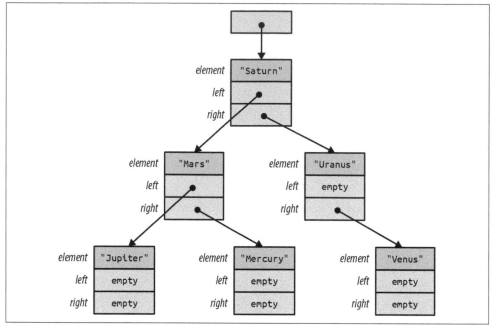

Figure 10-3. A `BinaryTree` containing six strings

The remaining parts of the tree follow the same patterns. The root node is no different from the others:

```
let tree = NonEmpty(Box::new(TreeNode {
    element: "Saturn",
    left: mars_tree,
    right: uranus_tree,
}));
```

Later in this chapter, we'll show how to implement an add method on the `BinaryTree` type so that we can instead write:

```
let mut tree = BinaryTree::Empty;
for planet in planets {
    tree.add(planet);
}
```

No matter what language you're coming from, creating data structures like `BinaryTree` in Rust will likely take some practice. It won't be obvious at first where to put the `Box`es. One way to find a design that will work is to draw a picture like Figure 10-3 that shows how you want things laid out in memory. Then work backward from the picture to the code. Each collection of rectangles is a struct or tuple; each arrow is a `Box` or other smart pointer. Figuring out the type of each field is a bit of a puzzle, but a manageable one. The reward for solving the puzzle is control over your program's memory usage.

Now comes the "price" we mentioned in the introduction. The tag field of an enum costs a little memory, up to eight bytes in the worst case, but that is usually negligible. The real downside to enums (if it can be called that) is that Rust code cannot throw caution to the wind and try to access fields regardless of whether they are actually present in the value:

```
let r = shape.radius;  // error: no field `radius` on type `Shape`
```

The only way to access the data in an enum is the safe way: using patterns.

Patterns

Recall the definition of our `RoughTime` type from earlier in this chapter:

```
enum RoughTime {
    InThePast(TimeUnit, u32),
    JustNow,
    InTheFuture(TimeUnit, u32),
}
```

Suppose you have a `RoughTime` value and you'd like to display it on a web page. You need to access the `TimeUnit` and `u32` fields inside the value. Rust doesn't let you access them directly, by writing `rough_time.0` and `rough_time.1`, because after all, the value might be `RoughTime::JustNow`, which has no fields. But then, how can you get the data out?

You need a `match` expression:

```
 1  fn rough_time_to_english(rt: RoughTime) -> String {
 2      match rt {
 3          RoughTime::InThePast(units, count) =>
 4              format!("{} {} ago", count, units.plural()),
 5          RoughTime::JustNow =>
 6              format!("just now"),
 7          RoughTime::InTheFuture(units, count) =>
 8              format!("{} {} from now", count, units.plural()),
 9      }
10  }
```

`match` performs pattern matching; in this example, the *patterns* are the parts that appear before the => symbol on lines 3, 5, and 7. Patterns that match `RoughTime` values look just like the expressions used to create `RoughTime` values. This is no coincidence. Expressions *produce* values; patterns *consume* values. The two use a lot of the same syntax.

Let's step through what happens when this `match` expression runs. Suppose `rt` is the value `RoughTime::InTheFuture(TimeUnit::Months, 1)`. Rust first tries to match this value against the pattern on line 3. As you can see in Figure 10-4, it doesn't match.

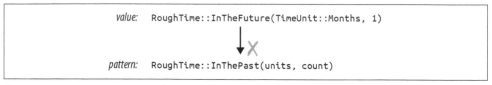

Figure 10-4. A RoughTime value and pattern that do not match

Pattern matching an enum, struct, or tuple works as though Rust is doing a simple left-to-right scan, checking each component of the pattern to see if the value matches it. If it doesn't, Rust moves on to the next pattern.

The patterns on lines 3 and 5 fail to match. But the pattern on line 7 succeeds (Figure 10-5).

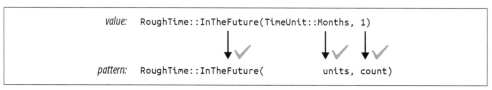

Figure 10-5. A successful match

When a pattern contains simple identifiers like `units` and `count`, those become local variables in the code following the pattern. Whatever is present in the value is copied or moved into the new variables. Rust stores `TimeUnit::Months` in `units` and 1 in `count`, runs line 8, and returns the string `"1 months from now"`.

That output has a minor grammatical issue, which can be fixed by adding another arm to the `match`:

```
RoughTime::InTheFuture(unit, 1) =>
    format!("a {} from now", unit.singular()),
```

This arm matches only if the `count` field is exactly 1. Note that this new code must be added before line 7. If we add it at the end, Rust will never get to it, because the pattern on line 7 matches all `InTheFuture` values. The Rust compiler will warn about an "unreachable pattern" if you make this kind of mistake.

Even with the new code, `RoughTime::InTheFuture(TimeUnit::Hours, 1)` still presents a problem: the result `"a hour from now"` is not quite right. Such is the English language. This too can be fixed by adding another arm to the `match`.

As this example shows, pattern matching works hand in hand with enums and can even test the data they contain, making `match` a powerful, flexible replacement for C's `switch` statement. So far, we've only seen patterns that match enum values. There's more to it than that. Rust patterns are their own little language, summarized in

Table 10-1. We'll spend most of the rest of the chapter on the features shown in this table.

Table 10-1. Patterns

Pattern type	Example	Notes
Literal	`100` `"name"`	Matches an exact value; the name of a `const` is also allowed

Range	`0 ..= 100`
	`'a' ..= 'k'`
	`256..`
		Matches any value in range, including the end value if given

Wildcard	`_`	Matches any value and ignores it
Variable	`name` `mut count`	Like `_` but moves or copies the value into a new local variable
`ref` variable	`ref field` `ref mut field`	Borrows a reference to the matched value instead of moving or copying it
Binding with subpattern	`val @ 0 ..= 99` `ref circle @ Shape::Circle { .. }`	Matches the pattern to the right of @, using the variable name to the left

Enum pattern	`Some(value)`
	`None`
	`Pet::Orca`	

Tuple pattern	`(key, value)` `(r, g, b)`	
Array pattern	`[a, b, c, d, e, f, g]` `[heading, carom, correction]`	

Slice pattern	`[first, second]`
	`[first, _, third]`
	`[first, .., nth]`
	`[]`	

Struct pattern	`Color(r, g, b)`
	`Point { x, y }`
	`Card { suit: Clubs, rank: n }`
	`Account { id, name, .. }`	

Reference	`&value` `&(k, v)`	Matches only reference values
Or patterns	`'a'	'A'` `Some("left" | "right")`	
Guard expression	`x if x * x <= r2`	In `match` only (not valid in `let`, etc.)

Literals, Variables, and Wildcards in Patterns

So far, we've shown `match` expressions working with enums. Other types can be matched too. When you need something like a C `switch` statement, use `match` with an integer value. Integer literals like 0 and 1 can serve as patterns:

```
match meadow.count_rabbits() {
    0 => {}  // nothing to say
    1 => println!("A rabbit is nosing around in the clover."),
    n => println!("There are {} rabbits hopping about in the meadow", n),
}
```

The pattern 0 matches if there are no rabbits in the meadow. 1 matches if there is just one. If there are two or more rabbits, we reach the third pattern, n. This pattern is just a variable name. It can match any value, and the matched value is moved or copied into a new local variable. So in this case, the value of `meadow.count_rabbits()` is stored in a new local variable n, which we then print.

Other literals can be used as patterns too, including Booleans, characters, and even strings:

```
let calendar = match settings.get_string("calendar") {
    "gregorian" => Calendar::Gregorian,
    "chinese" => Calendar::Chinese,
    "ethiopian" => Calendar::Ethiopian,
    other => return parse_error("calendar", other),
};
```

In this example, `other` serves as a catchall pattern like n in the previous example. These patterns play the same role as a `default` case in a `switch` statement, matching values that don't match any of the other patterns.

If you need a catchall pattern, but you don't care about the matched value, you can use a single underscore _ as a pattern, the *wildcard pattern*:

```
let caption = match photo.tagged_pet() {
    Pet::Tyrannosaur => "RRRAAAAAHHHHHH",
    Pet::Samoyed => "*dog thoughts*",
    _ => "I'm cute, love me", // generic caption, works for any pet
};
```

The wildcard pattern matches any value, but without storing it anywhere. Since Rust requires every `match` expression to handle all possible values, a wildcard is often required at the end. Even if you're very sure the remaining cases can't occur, you must at least add a fallback arm, perhaps one that panics:

```
// There are many Shapes, but we only support "selecting"
// either some text, or everything in a rectangular area.
// You can't select an ellipse or trapezoid.
match document.selection() {
    Shape::TextSpan(start, end) => paint_text_selection(start, end),
```

```
        Shape::Rectangle(rect) => paint_rect_selection(rect),
        _ => panic!("unexpected selection type"),
    }
```

Tuple and Struct Patterns

Tuple patterns match tuples. They're useful any time you want to get multiple pieces of data involved in a single match:

```
fn describe_point(x: i32, y: i32) -> &'static str {
    use std::cmp::Ordering::*;
    match (x.cmp(&0), y.cmp(&0)) {
        (Equal, Equal) => "at the origin",
        (_, Equal) => "on the x axis",
        (Equal, _) => "on the y axis",
        (Greater, Greater) => "in the first quadrant",
        (Less, Greater) => "in the second quadrant",
        _ => "somewhere else",
    }
}
```

Struct patterns use curly braces, just like struct expressions. They contain a subpattern for each field:

```
match balloon.location {
    Point { x: 0, y: height } =>
        println!("straight up {} meters", height),
    Point { x: x, y: y } =>
        println!("at ({}m, {}m)", x, y),
}
```

In this example, if the first arm matches, then balloon.location.y is stored in the new local variable height.

Suppose balloon.location is Point { x: 30, y: 40 }. As always, Rust checks each component of each pattern in turn Figure 10-6.

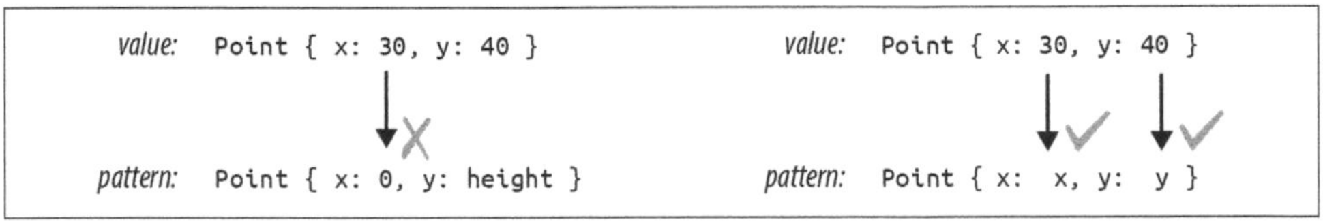

Figure 10-6. Pattern matching with structs

The second arm matches, so the output would be at (30m, 40m).

Patterns like Point { x: x, y: y } are common when matching structs, and the redundant names are visual clutter, so Rust has a shorthand for this: Point {x, y}. The meaning is the same. This pattern still stores a point's x field in a new local x and its y field in a new local y.

Even with the shorthand, it is cumbersome to match a large struct when we only care about a few fields:

```
match get_account(id) {
    ...
    Some(Account {
            name, language,  // <--- the 2 things we care about
            id: _, status: _, address: _, birthday: _, eye_color: _,
            pet: _, security_question: _, hashed_innermost_secret: _,
            is_adamantium_preferred_customer: _, }) =>
        language.show_custom_greeting(name),
}
```

To avoid this, use .. to tell Rust you don't care about any of the other fields:

```
Some(Account { name, language, .. }) =>
    language.show_custom_greeting(name),
```

Array and Slice Patterns

Array patterns match arrays. They're often used to filter out some special-case values and are useful any time you're working with arrays whose values have a different meaning based on position.

For example, when converting hue, saturation, and lightness (HSL) color values to red, green, blue (RGB) color values, colors with zero lightness or full lightness are just black or white. We could use a match expression to deal with those cases simply.

```
fn hsl_to_rgb(hsl: [u8; 3]) -> [u8; 3] {
    match hsl {
        [_, _, 0] => [0, 0, 0],
        [_, _, 255] => [255, 255, 255],
        ...
    }
}
```

Slice patterns are similar, but unlike arrays, slices have variable lengths, so slice patterns match not only on values but also on length. .. in a slice pattern matches any number of elements:

```
fn greet_people(names: &[&str]) {
    match names {
        [] => { println!("Hello, nobody.") },
        [a] => { println!("Hello, {}.", a) },
        [a, b] => { println!("Hello, {} and {}.", a, b) },
        [a, .., b] => { println!("Hello, everyone from {} to {}.", a, b) }
    }
}
```

Reference Patterns

Rust patterns support two features for working with references. `ref` patterns borrow parts of a matched value. `&` patterns match references. We'll cover `ref` patterns first.

Matching a noncopyable value moves the value. Continuing with the account example, this code would be invalid:

```
match account {
    Account { name, language, .. } => {
        ui.greet(&name, &language);
        ui.show_settings(&account);  // error: borrow of moved value: `account`
    }
}
```

Here, the fields `account.name` and `account.language` are moved into local variables `name` and `language`. The rest of `account` is dropped. That's why we can't borrow a reference to it afterward.

If `name` and `language` were both copyable values, Rust would copy the fields instead of moving them, and this code would be fine. But suppose these are `String`s. What can we do?

We need a kind of pattern that *borrows* matched values instead of moving them. The `ref` keyword does just that:

```
match account {
    Account { ref name, ref language, .. } => {
        ui.greet(name, language);
        ui.show_settings(&account);  // ok
    }
}
```

Now the local variables `name` and `language` are references to the corresponding fields in `account`. Since `account` is only being borrowed, not consumed, it's OK to continue calling methods on it.

You can use `ref mut` to borrow `mut` references:

```
match line_result {
    Err(ref err) => log_error(err),  // `err` is &Error (shared ref)
    Ok(ref mut line) => {            // `line` is &mut String (mut ref)
        trim_comments(line);         // modify the String in place
        handle(line);
    }
}
```

The pattern `Ok(ref mut line)` matches any success result and borrows a `mut` reference to the success value stored inside it.

The opposite kind of reference pattern is the & pattern. A pattern starting with & matches a reference:

```
match sphere.center() {
    &Point3d { x, y, z } => ...
}
```

In this example, suppose `sphere.center()` returns a reference to a private field of `sphere`, a common pattern in Rust. The value returned is the address of a `Point3d`. If the center is at the origin, then `sphere.center()` returns `&Point3d { x: 0.0, y: 0.0, z: 0.0 }`.

Pattern matching proceeds as shown in Figure 10-7.

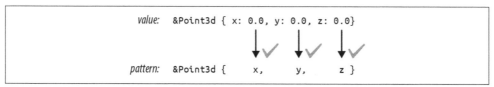

Figure 10-7. Pattern matching with references

This is a bit tricky because Rust is following a pointer here, an action we usually associate with the * operator, not the & operator. The thing to remember is that patterns and expressions are natural opposites. The expression (x, y) makes two values into a new tuple, but the pattern (x, y) does the opposite: it matches a tuple and breaks out the two values. It's the same with &. In an expression, & creates a reference. In a pattern, & matches a reference.

Matching a reference follows all the rules we've come to expect. Lifetimes are enforced. You can't get mut access via a shared reference. And you can't move a value out of a reference, even a mut reference. When we match &Point3d { x, y, z }, the variables x, y, and z receive copies of the coordinates, leaving the original Point3d value intact. It works because those fields are copyable. If we try the same thing on a struct with noncopyable fields, we'll get an error:

```
match friend.borrow_car() {
    Some(&Car { engine, .. }) =>  // error: can't move out of borrow
        ...
    None => {}
}
```

Scrapping a borrowed car for parts is not nice, and Rust won't stand for it. You can use a ref pattern to borrow a reference to a part. You just don't own it:

```
Some(&Car { ref engine, .. }) =>  // ok, engine is a reference
```

Let's look at one more example of an & pattern. Suppose we have an iterator `chars` over the characters in a string, and it has a method `chars.peek()` that returns an `Option<&char>`: a reference to the next character, if any. (Peekable iterators do in fact return an `Option<&ItemType>`, as we'll see in Chapter 15.)

A program can use an & pattern to get the pointed-to character:

```
match chars.peek() {
    Some(&c) => println!("coming up: {:?}", c),
    None => println!("end of chars"),
}
```

Match Guards

Sometimes a match arm has additional conditions that must be met before it can be considered a match. Suppose we're implementing a board game with hexagonal spaces, and the player just clicked to move a piece. To confirm that the click was valid, we might try something like this:

```
fn check_move(current_hex: Hex, click: Point) -> game::Result<Hex> {
    match point_to_hex(click) {
        None =>
            Err("That's not a game space."),
        Some(current_hex) =>  // try to match if user clicked the current_hex
                              // (it doesn't work: see explanation below)
            Err("You are already there! You must click somewhere else."),
        Some(other_hex) =>
            Ok(other_hex)
    }
}
```

This fails because identifiers in patterns introduce *new* variables. The pattern `Some(current_hex)` here creates a new local variable `current_hex`, shadowing the argument `current_hex`. Rust emits several warnings about this code—in particular, the last arm of the `match` is unreachable. One way to fix this is simply to use an `if` expression in the match arm:

```
match point_to_hex(click) {
    None => Err("That's not a game space."),
    Some(hex) => {
        if hex == current_hex {
            Err("You are already there! You must click somewhere else")
        } else {
            Ok(hex)
        }
    }
}
```

But Rust also provides *match guards*, extra conditions that must be true in order for a match arm to apply, written as `if` CONDITION, between the pattern and the arm's => token:

```
match point_to_hex(click) {
    None => Err("That's not a game space."),
    Some(hex) if hex == current_hex =>
        Err("You are already there! You must click somewhere else"),
    Some(hex) => Ok(hex)
}
```

If the pattern matches, but the condition is false, matching continues with the next arm.

Matching Multiple Possibilities

A pattern of the form *pat1* | *pat2* matches if either subpattern matches:

```
let at_end = match chars.peek() {
    Some(&'\r' | &'\n') | None => true,
    _ => false,
};
```

In an expression, | is the bitwise OR operator, but here it works more like the | symbol in a regular expression. at_end is set to true if chars.peek() is None, or a Some holding a carriage return or line feed.

Use ..= to match a whole range of values. Range patterns include the begin and end values, so '0' ..= '9' matches all the ASCII digits:

```
match next_char {
    '0'..='9' => self.read_number(),
    'a'..='z' | 'A'..='Z' => self.read_word(),
    ' ' | '\t' | '\n' => self.skip_whitespace(),
    _ => self.handle_punctuation(),
}
```

Rust also permits range patterns like x.., which match any value from x up to the maximum value of the type. However, the other varieties of end-exclusive ranges, like 0..100 or ..100, and unbounded ranges like .. aren't allowed in patterns yet.

Binding with @ Patterns

Finally, *x* @ *pattern* matches exactly like the given *pattern*, but on success, instead of creating variables for parts of the matched value, it creates a single variable *x* and moves or copies the whole value into it. For example, say you have this code:

```
match self.get_selection() {
    Shape::Rect(top_left, bottom_right) => {
        optimized_paint(&Shape::Rect(top_left, bottom_right))
    }
```

```
        other_shape => {
            paint_outline(other_shape.get_outline())
        }
    }
```

Note that the first case unpacks a `Shape::Rect` value, only to rebuild an identical `Shape::Rect` value on the next line. This can be rewritten to use an @ pattern:

```
    rect @ Shape::Rect(..) => {
        optimized_paint(&rect)
    }
```

@ patterns are also useful with ranges:

```
    match chars.next() {
        Some(digit @ '0'..='9') => read_number(digit, chars),
        ...
    },
```

Where Patterns Are Allowed

Although patterns are most prominent in `match` expressions, they are also allowed in several other places, typically in place of an identifier. The meaning is always the same: instead of just storing a value in a single variable, Rust uses pattern matching to take the value apart.

This means patterns can be used to...

```
    // ...unpack a struct into three new local variables
    let Track { album, track_number, title, .. } = song;

    // ...unpack a function argument that's a tuple
    fn distance_to((x, y): (f64, f64)) -> f64 { ... }

    // ...iterate over keys and values of a HashMap
    for (id, document) in &cache_map {
        println!("Document #{}: {}", id, document.title);
    }

    // ...automatically dereference an argument to a closure
    // (handy because sometimes other code passes you a reference
    // when you'd rather have a copy)
    let sum = numbers.fold(0, |a, &num| a + num);
```

Each of these saves two or three lines of boilerplate code. The same concept exists in some other languages: in JavaScript, it's called *destructuring*, while in Python, it's *unpacking*.

Note that in all four examples, we use patterns that are guaranteed to match. The pattern `Point3d { x, y, z }` matches every possible value of the `Point3d` struct type, `(x, y)` matches any `(f64, f64)` pair, and so on. Patterns that always match are special in Rust. They're called *irrefutable patterns*, and they're the only patterns allowed in the four places shown here (after let, in function arguments, after for, and in closure arguments).

A *refutable pattern* is one that might not match, like Ok(x), which doesn't match an error result, or '0' ..= '9', which doesn't match the character 'Q'. Refutable patterns can be used in match arms, because match is designed for them: if one pattern fails to match, it's clear what happens next. The four preceding examples are places in Rust programs where a pattern can be handy, but the language doesn't allow for match failure.

Refutable patterns are also allowed in if let and while let expressions, which can be used to...

```
// ...handle just one enum variant specially
if let RoughTime::InTheFuture(_, _) = user.date_of_birth() {
    user.set_time_traveler(true);
}

// ...run some code only if a table lookup succeeds
if let Some(document) = cache_map.get(&id) {
    return send_cached_response(document);
}

// ...repeatedly try something until it succeeds
while let Err(err) = present_cheesy_anti_robot_task() {
    log_robot_attempt(err);
    // let the user try again (it might still be a human)
}

// ...manually loop over an iterator
while let Some(_) = lines.peek() {
    read_paragraph(&mut lines);
}
```

For details about these expressions, see "if let" on page 142 and "Loops" on page 142.

Populating a Binary Tree

Earlier we promised to show how to implement a method, BinaryTree::add(), that adds a node to a BinaryTree of this type:

```
// An ordered collection of `T`s.
enum BinaryTree<T> {
    Empty,
    NonEmpty(Box<TreeNode<T>>),
}

// A part of a BinaryTree.
struct TreeNode<T> {
    element: T,
    left: BinaryTree<T>,
```

```
        right: BinaryTree<T>,
    }
```

You now know enough about patterns to write this method. An explanation of binary search trees is beyond the scope of this book, but for readers already familiar with the topic, it's worth seeing how it plays out in Rust.

```
 1  impl<T: Ord> BinaryTree<T> {
 2      fn add(&mut self, value: T) {
 3          match *self {
 4              BinaryTree::Empty => {
 5                  *self = BinaryTree::NonEmpty(Box::new(TreeNode {
 6                      element: value,
 7                      left: BinaryTree::Empty,
 8                      right: BinaryTree::Empty,
 9                  }))
10              }
11              BinaryTree::NonEmpty(ref mut node) => {
12                  if value <= node.element {
13                      node.left.add(value);
14                  } else {
15                      node.right.add(value);
16                  }
17              }
18          }
19      }
20  }
```

Line 1 tells Rust that we're defining a method on `BinaryTrees` of ordered types. This is exactly the same syntax we use to define methods on generic structs, explained in "Defining Methods with impl" on page 214.

If the existing tree `*self` is empty, that's the easy case. Lines 5–9 run, changing the `Empty` tree to a `NonEmpty` one. The call to `Box::new()` here allocates a new `TreeNode` in the heap. When we're done, the tree contains one element. Its left and right subtrees are both `Empty`.

If `*self` is not empty, we match the pattern on line 11:

```
BinaryTree::NonEmpty(ref mut node) => {
```

This pattern borrows a mutable reference to the `Box<TreeNode<T>>`, so we can access and modify data in that tree node. That reference is named `node`, and it's in scope from line 12 to line 16. Since there's already an element in this node, the code must recursively call `.add()` to add the new element to either the left or the right subtree.

The new method can be used like this:

```
let mut tree = BinaryTree::Empty;
tree.add("Mercury");
tree.add("Venus");
...
```

The Big Picture

Rust's enums may be new to systems programming, but they are not a new idea. Traveling under various academic-sounding names, like *algebraic data types*, they've been used in functional programming languages for more than forty years. It's unclear why so few other languages in the C tradition have ever had them. Perhaps it is simply that for a programming language designer, combining variants, references, mutability, and memory safety is extremely challenging. Functional programming languages dispense with mutability. C unions, by contrast, have variants, pointers, and mutability —but are so spectacularly unsafe that even in C, they're a last resort. Rust's borrow checker is the magic that makes it possible to combine all four without compromise.

Programming is data processing. Getting data into the right shape can be the difference between a small, fast, elegant program and a slow, gigantic tangle of duct tape and virtual method calls.

This is the problem space enums address. They are a design tool for getting data into the right shape. For cases when a value may be one thing, or another thing, or perhaps nothing at all, enums are better than class hierarchies on every axis: faster, safer, less code, easier to document.

The limiting factor is flexibility. End users of an enum can't extend it to add new variants. Variants can be added only by changing the enum declaration. And when that happens, existing code breaks. Every `match` expression that individually matches each variant of the enum must be revisited—it needs a new arm to handle the new variant. In some cases, trading flexibility for simplicity is just good sense. After all, the structure of JSON is not expected to change. And in some cases, revisiting all uses of an enum when it changes is exactly what we want. For example, when an `enum` is used in a compiler to represent the various operators of a programming language, adding a new operator *should* involve touching all code that handles operators.

But sometimes more flexibility is needed. For those situations, Rust has traits, the topic of our next chapter.

## CHAPTER 11

Traits and Generics

[A] computer scientist tends to be able to deal with nonuniform structures—case 1, case 2, case 3—while a mathematician will tend to want one unifying axiom that governs an entire system.

> —Donald Knuth

One of the great discoveries in programming is that it's possible to write code that operates on values of many different types, *even types that haven't been invented yet*. Here are two examples:

- Vec<T> is generic: you can create a vector of any type of value, including types defined in your program that the authors of Vec never anticipated.

- Many things have .write() methods, including Files and TcpStreams. Your code can take a writer by reference, any writer, and send data to it. Your code doesn't have to care what type of writer it is. Later, if someone adds a new type of writer, your code will already support it.

Of course, this capability is hardly new with Rust. It's called *polymorphism*, and it was the hot new programming language technology of the 1970s. By now it's effectively universal. Rust supports polymorphism with two related features: traits and generics. These concepts will be familiar to many programmers, but Rust takes a fresh approach inspired by Haskell's typeclasses.

Traits are Rust's take on interfaces or abstract base classes. At first, they look just like interfaces in Java or C#. The trait for writing bytes is called std::io::Write, and its definition in the standard library starts out like this:

```
trait Write {
    fn write(&mut self, buf: &[u8]) -> Result<usize>;
    fn flush(&mut self) -> Result<()>;
```

```
    fn write_all(&mut self, buf: &[u8]) -> Result<()> { ... }
    ...
}
```

This trait offers several methods; we've shown only the first three.

The standard types `File` and `TcpStream` both implement `std::io::Write`. So does `Vec<u8>`. All three types provide methods named `.write()`, `.flush()`, and so on. Code that uses a writer without caring about its type looks like this:

```
use std::io::Write;

fn say_hello(out: &mut dyn Write) -> std::io::Result<()> {
    out.write_all(b"hello world\n")?;
    out.flush()
}
```

The type of `out` is `&mut dyn Write`, meaning "a mutable reference to any value that implements the `Write` trait." We can pass `say_hello` a mutable reference to any such value:

```
use std::fs::File;
let mut local_file = File::create("hello.txt")?;
say_hello(&mut local_file)?;  // works

let mut bytes = vec![];
say_hello(&mut bytes)?;  // also works
assert_eq!(bytes, b"hello world\n");
```

This chapter begins by showing how traits are used, how they work, and how to define your own. But there is more to traits than we've hinted at so far. We'll use them to add extension methods to existing types, even built-in types like `str` and `bool`. We'll explain why adding a trait to a type costs no extra memory and how to use traits without virtual method call overhead. We'll see that built-in traits are the hook into the language that Rust provides for operator overloading and other features. And we'll cover the `Self` type, associated functions, and associated types, three features Rust lifted from Haskell that elegantly solve problems that other languages address with workarounds and hacks.

Generics are the other flavor of polymorphism in Rust. Like a C++ template, a generic function or type can be used with values of many different types:

```
/// Given two values, pick whichever one is less.
fn min<T: Ord>(value1: T, value2: T) -> T {
    if value1 <= value2 {
        value1
    } else {
        value2
    }
}
```

The `<T: Ord>` in this function means that `min` can be used with arguments of any type T that implements the `Ord` trait—that is, any ordered type. A requirement like this is called a *bound*, because it sets limits on which types T could possibly be. The compiler generates custom machine code for each type T that you actually use.

Generics and traits are closely related: generic functions use traits in bounds to spell out what types of arguments they can be applied to. So we'll also talk about how `&mut dyn Write` and `<T: Write>` are similar, how they're different, and how to choose between these two ways of using traits.

Using Traits

A trait is a feature that any given type may or may not support. Most often, a trait represents a capability: something a type can do.

- A value that implements `std::io::Write` can write out bytes.

- A value that implements `std::iter::Iterator` can produce a sequence of values.

- A value that implements `std::clone::Clone` can make clones of itself in memory.

- A value that implements `std::fmt::Debug` can be printed using `println!()` with the `{:?}` format specifier.

Those four traits are all part of Rust's standard library, and many standard types implement them. For example:

- `std::fs::File` implements the `Write` trait; it writes bytes to a local file. `std::net::TcpStream` writes to a network connection. `Vec<u8>` also implements `Write`. Each `.write()` call on a vector of bytes appends some data to the end.

- `Range<i32>` (the type of `0..10`) implements the `Iterator` trait, as do some iterator types associated with slices, hash tables, and so on.

- Most standard library types implement `Clone`. The exceptions are mainly types like `TcpStream` that represent more than just data in memory.

- Likewise, most standard library types support `Debug`.

There is one unusual rule about trait methods: the trait itself must be in scope. Otherwise, all its methods are hidden:

```
let mut buf: Vec<u8> = vec![];
buf.write_all(b"hello")?;  // error: no method named `write_all`
```

In this case, the compiler prints a friendly error message that suggests adding `use std::io::Write;` and indeed that fixes the problem:

```
use std::io::Write;

let mut buf: Vec<u8> = vec![];
buf.write_all(b"hello")?;  // ok
```

Rust has this rule because, as we'll see later in this chapter, you can use traits to add new methods to any type—even standard library types like u32 and str. Third-party crates can do the same thing. Clearly, this could lead to naming conflicts! But since Rust makes you import the traits you plan to use, crates are free to take advantage of this superpower. To get a conflict, you'd have to import two traits that add a method with the same name to the same type. This is rare in practice. (If you do run into a conflict, you can spell out what you want using fully qualified method syntax, covered later in the chapter.)

The reason `Clone` and `Iterator` methods work without any special imports is that they're always in scope by default: they're part of the standard prelude, names that Rust automatically imports into every module. In fact, the prelude is mostly a carefully chosen selection of traits. We'll cover many of them in Chapter 13.

C++ and C# programmers will already have noticed that trait methods are like virtual methods. Still, calls like the one shown above are fast, as fast as any other method call. Simply put, there's no polymorphism here. It's obvious that buf is a vector, not a file or a network connection. The compiler can emit a simple call to `Vec<u8>::write()`. It can even inline the method. (C++ and C# will often do the same, although the possibility of subclassing sometimes precludes this.) Only calls through &mut dyn Write incur the overhead of a dynamic dispatch, also known as a virtual method call, which is indicated by the dyn keyword in the type. dyn Write is known as a *trait object*; we'll look at the technical details of trait objects, and how they compare to generic functions, in the following sections.

Trait Objects

There are two ways of using traits to write polymorphic code in Rust: trait objects and generics. We'll present trait objects first and turn to generics in the next section.

Rust doesn't permit variables of type dyn Write:

```
use std::io::Write;

let mut buf: Vec<u8> = vec![];
let writer: dyn Write = buf;  // error: `Write` does not have a constant size
```

A variable's size has to be known at compile time, and types that implement Write can be any size.

This may be surprising if you're coming from C# or Java, but the reason is simple. In Java, a variable of type `OutputStream` (the Java standard interface analogous to `std::io::Write`) is a reference to any object that implements `OutputStream`. The fact that it's a reference goes without saying. It's the same with interfaces in C# and most other languages.

What we want in Rust is the same thing, but in Rust, references are explicit:

```
let mut buf: Vec<u8> = vec![];
let writer: &mut dyn Write = &mut buf;  // ok
```

A reference to a trait type, like `writer`, is called a *trait object*. Like any other reference, a trait object points to some value, it has a lifetime, and it can be either `mut` or shared.

What makes a trait object different is that Rust usually doesn't know the type of the referent at compile time. So a trait object includes a little extra information about the referent's type. This is strictly for Rust's own use behind the scenes: when you call `writer.write(data)`, Rust needs the type information to dynamically call the right `write` method depending on the type of `*writer`. You can't query the type information directly, and Rust does not support downcasting from the trait object `&mut dyn Write` back to a concrete type like `Vec<u8>`.

Trait object layout

In memory, a trait object is a fat pointer consisting of a pointer to the value, plus a pointer to a table representing that value's type. Each trait object therefore takes up two machine words, as shown in Figure 11-1.

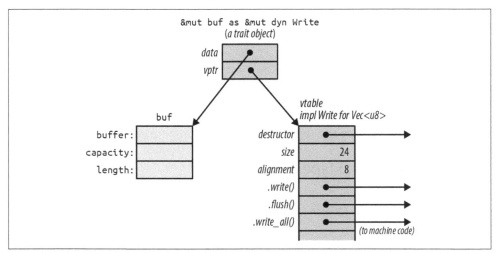

Figure 11-1. Trait objects in memory

C++ has this kind of run-time type information as well. It's called a *virtual table*, or *vtable*. In Rust, as in C++, the vtable is generated once, at compile time, and shared by all objects of the same type. Everything shown in the darker shade in Figure 11-1, including the vtable, is a private implementation detail of Rust. Again, these aren't fields and data structures that you can access directly. Instead, the language automatically uses the vtable when you call a method of a trait object, to determine which implementation to call.

Seasoned C++ programmers will notice that Rust and C++ use memory a bit differently. In C++, the vtable pointer, or *vptr*, is stored as part of the struct. Rust uses fat pointers instead. The struct itself contains nothing but its fields. This way, a struct can implement dozens of traits without containing dozens of vptrs. Even types like i32, which aren't big enough to accommodate a vptr, can implement traits.

Rust automatically converts ordinary references into trait objects when needed. This is why we're able to pass &mut local_file to say_hello in this example:

```
let mut local_file = File::create("hello.txt")?;
say_hello(&mut local_file)?;
```

The type of &mut local_file is &mut File, and the type of the argument to say_hello is &mut dyn Write. Since a File is a kind of writer, Rust allows this, automatically converting the plain reference to a trait object.

Likewise, Rust will happily convert a Box<File> to a Box<dyn Write>, a value that owns a writer in the heap:

```
let w: Box<dyn Write> = Box::new(local_file);
```

Box<dyn Write>, like &mut dyn Write, is a fat pointer: it contains the address of the writer itself and the address of the vtable. The same goes for other pointer types, like Rc<dyn Write>.

This kind of conversion is the only way to create a trait object. What the compiler is actually doing here is very simple. At the point where the conversion happens, Rust knows the referent's true type (in this case, File), so it just adds the address of the appropriate vtable, turning the regular pointer into a fat pointer.

Generic Functions and Type Parameters

At the beginning of this chapter, we showed a say_hello() function that took a trait object as an argument. Let's rewrite that function as a generic function:

```
fn say_hello<W: Write>(out: &mut W) -> std::io::Result<()> {
    out.write_all(b"hello world\n")?;
    out.flush()
}
```

Only the type signature has changed:

```
fn say_hello(out: &mut dyn Write)      // plain function

fn say_hello<W: Write>(out: &mut W)    // generic function
```

The phrase `<W: Write>` is what makes the function generic. This is a *type parameter*. It means that throughout the body of this function, W stands for some type that implements the `Write` trait. Type parameters are usually single uppercase letters, by convention.

Which type W stands for depends on how the generic function is used:

```
say_hello(&mut local_file)?; // calls say_hello::<File>
say_hello(&mut bytes)?;      // calls say_hello::<Vec<u8>>
```

When you pass `&mut local_file` to the generic `say_hello()` function, you're calling `say_hello::<File>()`. Rust generates machine code for this function that calls `File::write_all()` and `File::flush()`. When you pass `&mut bytes`, you're calling `say_hello::<Vec<u8>>()`. Rust generates separate machine code for this version of the function, calling the corresponding `Vec<u8>` methods. In both cases, Rust infers the type W from the type of the argument. This process is known as *monomorphization*, and the compiler handles it all automatically.

You can always spell out the type parameters:

```
say_hello::<File>(&mut local_file)?;
```

This is seldom necessary, because Rust can usually deduce the type parameters by looking at the arguments. Here, the `say_hello` generic function expects a `&mut W` argument, and we're passing it a `&mut File`, so Rust infers that `W = File`.

If the generic function you're calling doesn't have any arguments that provide useful clues, you may have to spell it out:

```
// calling a generic method collect<C>() that takes no arguments
let v1 = (0 .. 1000).collect();  // error: can't infer type
let v2 = (0 .. 1000).collect::<Vec<i32>>(); // ok
```

Sometimes we need multiple abilities from a type parameter. For example, if we want to print out the top ten most common values in a vector, we'll need for those values to be printable:

```
use std::fmt::Debug;

fn top_ten<T: Debug>(values: &Vec<T>) { ... }
```

But this isn't good enough. How are we planning to determine which values are the most common? The usual way is to use the values as keys in a hash table. That means the values need to support the `Hash` and `Eq` operations. The bounds on T must include these as well as `Debug`. The syntax for this uses the + sign:

```
use std::hash::Hash;
use std::fmt::Debug;

fn top_ten<T: Debug + Hash + Eq>(values: &Vec<T>) { ... }
```

Some types implement Debug, some implement Hash, some support Eq, and a few, like u32 and String, implement all three, as shown in Figure 11-2.

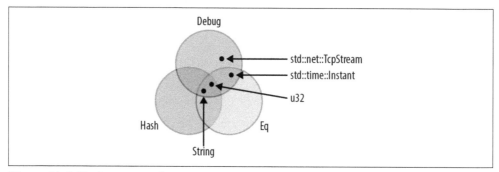

Figure 11-2. Traits as sets of types

It's also possible for a type parameter to have no bounds at all, but you can't do much with a value if you haven't specified any bounds for it. You can move it. You can put it into a box or vector. That's about it.

Generic functions can have multiple type parameters:

```
/// Run a query on a large, partitioned data set.
/// See <http://research.google.com/archive/mapreduce.html>.
fn run_query<M: Mapper + Serialize, R: Reducer + Serialize>(
    data: &DataSet, map: M, reduce: R) -> Results
{ ... }
```

As this example shows, the bounds can get to be so long that they are hard on the eyes. Rust provides an alternative syntax using the keyword where:

```
fn run_query<M, R>(data: &DataSet, map: M, reduce: R) -> Results
    where M: Mapper + Serialize,
          R: Reducer + Serialize
{ ... }
```

The type parameters M and R are still declared up front, but the bounds are moved to separate lines. This kind of where clause is also allowed on generic structs, enums, type aliases, and methods—anywhere bounds are permitted.

Of course, an alternative to where clauses is to keep it simple: find a way to write the program without using generics quite so intensively.

"Receiving References as Function Arguments" on page 113 introduced the syntax for lifetime parameters. A generic function can have both lifetime parameters and type parameters. Lifetime parameters come first:

```
/// Return a reference to the point in `candidates` that's
/// closest to the `target` point.
fn nearest<'t, 'c, P>(target: &'t P, candidates: &'c [P]) -> &'c P
    where P: MeasureDistance
{
    ...
}
```

This function takes two arguments, `target` and `candidates`. Both are references, and we give them distinct lifetimes `'t` and `'c` (as discussed in "Distinct Lifetime Parameters" on page 120). Furthermore, the function works with any type P that implements the `MeasureDistance` trait, so we might use it on `Point2d` values in one program and `Point3d` values in another.

Lifetimes never have any impact on machine code. Two calls to `nearest()` using the same type P, but different lifetimes, will call the same compiled function. Only differing types cause Rust to compile multiple copies of a generic function.

In addition to types and lifetimes, generic functions can take constant parameters as well, like the `Polynomial` struct we presented in "Generic Structs with Constant Parameters" on page 222:

```
fn dot_product<const N: usize>(a: [f64; N], b: [f64; N]) -> f64 {
    let mut sum = 0.;
    for i in 0..N {
        sum += a[i] * b[i];
    }
    sum
}
```

Here, the phrase `<const N: usize>` indicates that the function `dot_product` expects a generic parameter N, which must be a `usize`. Given N, the function takes two arguments of type `[f64; N]`, and adds up the products of their corresponding elements. What distinguishes N from an ordinary `usize` argument is that you can use it in the types in `dot_product`'s signature or body.

As with type parameters, you can either provide constant parameters explicitly, or let Rust infer them:

```
// Explicitly provide `3` as the value for `N`.
dot_product::<3>([0.2, 0.4, 0.6], [0., 0., 1.])

// Let Rust infer that `N` must be `2`.
dot_product([3., 4.], [-5., 1.])
```

Of course, functions are not the only kind of generic code in Rust:

- We've already covered generic types in "Generic Structs" on page 219 and "Generic Enums" on page 238.

- An individual method can be generic, even if the type it's defined on is not generic:

```
impl PancakeStack {
    fn push<T: Topping>(&mut self, goop: T) -> PancakeResult<()> {
        goop.pour(&self);
        self.absorb_topping(goop)
    }
}
```

- Type aliases can be generic, too:

```
type PancakeResult<T> = Result<T, PancakeError>;
```

- We'll cover generic traits later in this chapter.

All the features introduced in this section—bounds, `where` clauses, lifetime parameters, and so forth—can be used on all generic items, not just functions.

Which to Use

The choice of whether to use trait objects or generic code is subtle. Since both features are based on traits, they have a lot in common.

Trait objects are the right choice whenever you need a collection of values of mixed types, all together. It is technically possible to make generic salad:

```
trait Vegetable {
    ...
}

struct Salad<V: Vegetable> {
    veggies: Vec<V>
}
```

However, this is a rather severe design. Each such salad consists entirely of a single type of vegetable. Not everyone is cut out for this sort of thing. One of your authors once paid $14 for a `Salad<IcebergLettuce>` and has never quite gotten over the experience.

How can we build a better salad? Since `Vegetable` values can be all different sizes, we can't ask Rust for a `Vec<dyn Vegetable>`:

```
struct Salad {
    veggies: Vec<dyn Vegetable>  // error: `dyn Vegetable` does
                                 // not have a constant size
}
```

Trait objects are the solution:

```
struct Salad {
    veggies: Vec<Box<dyn Vegetable>>
}
```

Each Box<dyn Vegetable> can own any type of vegetable, but the box itself has a constant size—two pointers—suitable for storing in a vector. Apart from the unfortunate mixed metaphor of having boxes in one's food, this is precisely what's called for, and it would work out just as well for shapes in a drawing app, monsters in a game, pluggable routing algorithms in a network router, and so on.

Another possible reason to use trait objects is to reduce the total amount of compiled code. Rust may have to compile a generic function many times, once for each type it's used with. This could make the binary large, a phenomenon called *code bloat* in C++ circles. These days, memory is plentiful, and most of us have the luxury of ignoring code size; but constrained environments do exist.

Outside of situations involving salad or low-resource environments, generics have three important advantages over trait objects, with the result that in Rust, generics are the more common choice.

The first advantage is speed. Note the absence of the dyn keyword in generic function signatures. Because you specify the types at compile time, either explicitly or through type inference, the compiler knows exactly which write method to call. The dyn keyword isn't used because there are no trait objects—and thus no dynamic dispatch—involved.

The generic min() function shown in the introduction is just as fast as if we had written separate functions min_u8, min_i64, min_string, and so on. The compiler can inline it, like any other function, so in a release build, a call to min::<i32> is likely just two or three instructions. A call with constant arguments, like min(5, 3), will be even faster: Rust can evaluate it at compile time, so that there's no run-time cost at all.

Or consider this generic function call:

```
let mut sink = std::io::sink();
say_hello(&mut sink)?;
```

std::io::sink() returns a writer of type Sink that quietly discards all bytes written to it.

When Rust generates machine code for this, it could emit code that calls Sink::write_all, checks for errors, and then calls Sink::flush. That's what the body of the generic function says to do.

Or, Rust could look at those methods and realize the following:

- Sink::write_all() does nothing.
- Sink::flush() does nothing.

- Neither method ever returns an error.

In short, Rust has all the information it needs to optimize away this function call entirely.

Compare that to the behavior with trait objects. Rust never knows what type of value a trait object points to until run time. So even if you pass a `Sink`, the overhead of calling virtual methods and checking for errors still applies.

The second advantage of generics is that not every trait can support trait objects. Traits support several features, such as associated functions, that work only with generics: they rule out trait objects entirely. We'll point out these features as we come to them.

The third advantage of generics is that it's easy to bound a generic type parameter with several traits at once, as our `top_ten` function did when it required its `T` parameter to implement `Debug + Hash + Eq`. Trait objects can't do this: types like `&mut (dyn Debug + Hash + Eq)` aren't supported in Rust. (You can work around this with subtraits, defined later in this chapter, but it's a bit involved.)

Defining and Implementing Traits

Defining a trait is simple. Give it a name and list the type signatures of the trait methods. If we're writing a game, we might have a trait like this:

```
/// A trait for characters, items, and scenery -
/// anything in the game world that's visible on screen.
trait Visible {
    /// Render this object on the given canvas.
    fn draw(&self, canvas: &mut Canvas);

    /// Return true if clicking at (x, y) should
    /// select this object.
    fn hit_test(&self, x: i32, y: i32) -> bool;
}
```

To implement a trait, use the syntax `impl TraitName for Type`:

```
impl Visible for Broom {
    fn draw(&self, canvas: &mut Canvas) {
        for y in self.y - self.height - 1 .. self.y {
            canvas.write_at(self.x, y, '|');
        }
        canvas.write_at(self.x, self.y, 'M');
    }

    fn hit_test(&self, x: i32, y: i32) -> bool {
        self.x == x
        && self.y - self.height - 1 <= y
        && y <= self.y
```

```
        }
    }
```

Note that this impl contains an implementation for each method of the Visible trait, and nothing else. Everything defined in a trait impl must actually be a feature of the trait; if we wanted to add a helper method in support of Broom::draw(), we would have to define it in a separate impl block:

```
impl Broom {
    /// Helper function used by Broom::draw() below.
    fn broomstick_range(&self) -> Range<i32> {
        self.y - self.height - 1 .. self.y
    }
}
```

These helper functions can be used within the trait impl blocks:

```
impl Visible for Broom {
    fn draw(&self, canvas: &mut Canvas) {
        for y in self.broomstick_range() {
            ...
        }
        ...
    }
    ...
}
```

Default Methods

The Sink writer type we discussed earlier can be implemented in a few lines of code. First, we define the type:

```
/// A Writer that ignores whatever data you write to it.
pub struct Sink;
```

Sink is an empty struct, since we don't need to store any data in it. Next, we provide an implementation of the Write trait for Sink:

```
use std::io::{Write, Result};

impl Write for Sink {
    fn write(&mut self, buf: &[u8]) -> Result<usize> {
        // Claim to have successfully written the whole buffer.
        Ok(buf.len())
    }

    fn flush(&mut self) -> Result<()> {
        Ok(())
    }
}
```

So far, this is very much like the Visible trait. But we have also seen that the Write trait has a write_all method:

```
let mut out = Sink;
out.write_all(b"hello world\n")?;
```

Why does Rust let us impl Write for Sink without defining this method? The answer is that the standard library's definition of the Write trait contains a *default implementation* for write_all:

```
trait Write {
    fn write(&mut self, buf: &[u8]) -> Result<usize>;
    fn flush(&mut self) -> Result<()>;

    fn write_all(&mut self, buf: &[u8]) -> Result<()> {
        let mut bytes_written = 0;
        while bytes_written < buf.len() {
            bytes_written += self.write(&buf[bytes_written..])?;
        }
        Ok(())
    }

    ...
}
```

The write and flush methods are the basic methods that every writer must implement. A writer may also implement write_all, but if not, the default implementation shown earlier will be used.

Your own traits can include default implementations using the same syntax.

The most dramatic use of default methods in the standard library is the Iterator trait, which has one required method (.next()) and dozens of default methods. Chapter 15 explains why.

Traits and Other People's Types

Rust lets you implement any trait on any type, as long as either the trait or the type is introduced in the current crate.

This means that any time you want to add a method to any type, you can use a trait to do it:

```
trait IsEmoji {
    fn is_emoji(&self) -> bool;
}

/// Implement IsEmoji for the built-in character type.
impl IsEmoji for char {
    fn is_emoji(&self) -> bool {
        ...
```

```
        }
    }

    assert_eq!('$'.is_emoji(), false);
```

Like any other trait method, this new `is_emoji` method is only visible when `IsEmoji` is in scope.

The sole purpose of this particular trait is to add a method to an existing type, `char`. This is called an *extension trait*. Of course, you can add this trait to types, too, by writing `impl IsEmoji for str { ... }` and so forth.

You can even use a generic `impl` block to add an extension trait to a whole family of types at once. This trait could be implemented on any type:

```
use std::io::{self, Write};

/// Trait for values to which you can send HTML.
trait WriteHtml {
    fn write_html(&mut self, html: &HtmlDocument) -> io::Result<()>;
}
```

Implementing the trait for all writers makes it an extension trait, adding a method to all Rust writers:

```
/// You can write HTML to any std::io writer.
impl<W: Write> WriteHtml for W {
    fn write_html(&mut self, html: &HtmlDocument) -> io::Result<()> {
        ...
    }
}
```

The line `impl<W: Write> WriteHtml for W` means "for every type W that implements `Write`, here's an implementation of `WriteHtml` for W."

The `serde` library offers a nice example of how useful it can be to implement user-defined traits on standard types. `serde` is a serialization library. That is, you can use it to write Rust data structures to disk and reload them later. The library defines a trait, `Serialize`, that's implemented for every data type the library supports. So in the `serde` source code, there is code implementing `Serialize` for `bool`, `i8`, `i16`, `i32`, array and tuple types, and so on, through all the standard data structures like `Vec` and `HashMap`.

The upshot of all this is that `serde` adds a `.serialize()` method to all these types. It can be used like this:

```
use serde::Serialize;
use serde_json;

pub fn save_configuration(config: &HashMap<String, String>)
    -> std::io::Result<()>
```

```
{
    // Create a JSON serializer to write the data to a file.
    let writer = File::create(config_filename())?;
    let mut serializer = serde_json::Serializer::new(writer);

    // The serde `.serialize()` method does the rest.
    config.serialize(&mut serializer)?;

    Ok(())
}
```

We said earlier that when you implement a trait, either the trait or the type must be new in the current crate. This is called the *orphan rule*. It helps Rust ensure that trait implementations are unique. Your code can't impl Write for u8, because both Write and u8 are defined in the standard library. If Rust let crates do that, there could be multiple implementations of Write for u8, in different crates, and Rust would have no reasonable way to decide which implementation to use for a given method call.

(C++ has a similar uniqueness restriction: the One Definition Rule. In typical C++ fashion, it isn't enforced by the compiler, except in the simplest cases, and you get undefined behavior if you break it.)

Self in Traits

A trait can use the keyword Self as a type. The standard Clone trait, for example, looks like this (slightly simplified):

```
pub trait Clone {
    fn clone(&self) -> Self;
    ...
}
```

Using Self as the return type here means that the type of x.clone() is the same as the type of x, whatever that might be. If x is a String, then the type of x.clone() is String—not dyn Clone or any other cloneable type.

Likewise, if we define this trait:

```
pub trait Spliceable {
    fn splice(&self, other: &Self) -> Self;
}
```

with two implementations:

```
impl Spliceable for CherryTree {
    fn splice(&self, other: &Self) -> Self {
        ...
    }
}

impl Spliceable for Mammoth {
```

```
    fn splice(&self, other: &Self) -> Self {
        ...
    }
}
```

then inside the first `impl`, `Self` is simply an alias for `CherryTree`, and in the second, it's an alias for `Mammoth`. This means that we can splice together two cherry trees or two mammoths, not that we can create a mammoth-cherry hybrid. The type of `self` and the type of `other` must match.

A trait that uses the `Self` type is incompatible with trait objects:

```
// error: the trait `Spliceable` cannot be made into an object
fn splice_anything(left: &dyn Spliceable, right: &dyn Spliceable) {
    let combo = left.splice(right);
    // ...
}
```

The reason is something we'll see again and again as we dig into the advanced features of traits. Rust rejects this code because it has no way to type-check the call `left.splice(right)`. The whole point of trait objects is that the type isn't known until run time. Rust has no way to know at compile time if `left` and `right` will be the same type, as required.

Trait objects are really intended for the simplest kinds of traits, the kinds that could be implemented using interfaces in Java or abstract base classes in C++. The more advanced features of traits are useful, but they can't coexist with trait objects because with trait objects, you lose the type information Rust needs to type-check your program.

Now, had we wanted genetically improbable splicing, we could have designed a trait-object-friendly trait:

```
pub trait MegaSpliceable {
    fn splice(&self, other: &dyn MegaSpliceable) -> Box<dyn MegaSpliceable>;
}
```

This trait is compatible with trait objects. There's no problem type-checking calls to this `.splice()` method because the type of the argument `other` is not required to match the type of `self`, as long as both types are `MegaSpliceable`.

Subtraits

We can declare that a trait is an extension of another trait:

```
/// Someone in the game world, either the player or some other
/// pixie, gargoyle, squirrel, ogre, etc.
trait Creature: Visible {
    fn position(&self) -> (i32, i32);
    fn facing(&self) -> Direction;
```

```
    ...
}
```

The phrase `trait Creature: Visible` means that all creatures are visible. Every type that implements `Creature` must also implement the `Visible` trait:

```
impl Visible for Broom {
    ...
}

impl Creature for Broom {
    ...
}
```

We can implement the two traits in either order, but it's an error to implement `Creature` for a type without also implementing `Visible`. Here, we say that `Creature` is a *subtrait* of `Visible`, and that `Visible` is `Creature`'s *supertrait*.

Subtraits resemble subinterfaces in Java or C#, in that users can assume that any value that implements a subtrait implements its supertrait as well. But in Rust, a subtrait does not inherit the associated items of its supertrait; each trait still needs to be in scope if you want to call its methods.

In fact, Rust's subtraits are really just a shorthand for a bound on `Self`. A definition of `Creature` like this is exactly equivalent to the one shown earlier:

```
trait Creature where Self: Visible {
    ...
}
```

Type-Associated Functions

In most object-oriented languages, interfaces can't include static methods or constructors, but traits can include type-associated functions, Rust's analog to static methods:

```
trait StringSet {
    /// Return a new empty set.
    fn new() -> Self;

    /// Return a set that contains all the strings in `strings`.
    fn from_slice(strings: &[&str]) -> Self;

    /// Find out if this set contains a particular `value`.
    fn contains(&self, string: &str) -> bool;

    /// Add a string to this set.
    fn add(&mut self, string: &str);
}
```

Every type that implements the `StringSet` trait must implement these four associated functions. The first two, `new()` and `from_slice()`, don't take a `self` argument. They serve as constructors. In nongeneric code, these functions can be called using `::` syntax, just like any other type-associated function:

```
// Create sets of two hypothetical types that impl StringSet:
let set1 = SortedStringSet::new();
let set2 = HashedStringSet::new();
```

In generic code, it's the same, except the type is often a type variable, as in the call to `S::new()` shown here:

```
/// Return the set of words in `document` that aren't in `wordlist`.
fn unknown_words<S: StringSet>(document: &[String], wordlist: &S) -> S {
    let mut unknowns = S::new();
    for word in document {
        if !wordlist.contains(word) {
            unknowns.add(word);
        }
    }
    unknowns
}
```

Like Java and C# interfaces, trait objects don't support type-associated functions. If you want to use `&dyn StringSet` trait objects, you must change the trait, adding the bound `where Self: Sized` to each associated function that doesn't take a `self` argument by reference:

```
trait StringSet {
    fn new() -> Self
        where Self: Sized;

    fn from_slice(strings: &[&str]) -> Self
        where Self: Sized;

    fn contains(&self, string: &str) -> bool;

    fn add(&mut self, string: &str);
}
```

This bound tells Rust that trait objects are excused from supporting this particular associated function. With these additions, `StringSet` trait objects are allowed; they still don't support `new` or `from_slice`, but you can create them and use them to call `.contains()` and `.add()`. The same trick works for any other method that is incompatible with trait objects. (We will forgo the rather tedious technical explanation of why this works, but the `Sized` trait is covered in Chapter 13.)

Fully Qualified Method Calls

All the ways for calling trait methods we've seen so far rely on Rust filling in some missing pieces for you. For example, suppose you write the following:

```
"hello".to_string()
```

It's understood that `to_string` refers to the `to_string` method of the `ToString` trait, of which we're calling the `str` type's implementation. So there are four players in this game: the trait, the method of that trait, the implementation of that method, and the value to which that implementation is being applied. It's great that we don't have to spell all that out every time we want to call a method. But in some cases you need a way to say exactly what you mean. Fully qualified method calls fit the bill.

First of all, it helps to know that a method is just a special kind of function. These two calls are equivalent:

```
"hello".to_string()

str::to_string("hello")
```

The second form looks exactly like a associated function call. This works even though the `to_string` method takes a `self` argument. Simply pass `self` as the function's first argument.

Since `to_string` is a method of the standard `ToString` trait, there are two more forms you can use:

```
ToString::to_string("hello")

<str as ToString>::to_string("hello")
```

All four of these method calls do exactly the same thing. Most often, you'll just write `value.method()`. The other forms are *qualified* method calls. They specify the type or trait that a method is associated with. The last form, with the angle brackets, specifies both: a *fully qualified* method call.

When you write `"hello".to_string()`, using the `.` operator, you don't say exactly which `to_string` method you're calling. Rust has a method lookup algorithm that figures this out, depending on the types, deref coercions, and so on. With fully qualified calls, you can say exactly which method you mean, and that can help in a few odd cases:

- When two methods have the same name. The classic hokey example is the `Outlaw` with two `.draw()` methods from two different traits, one for drawing it on the screen and one for interacting with the law:

```
    outlaw.draw();  // error: draw on screen or draw pistol?

    Visible::draw(&outlaw);   // ok: draw on screen
    HasPistol::draw(&outlaw);  // ok: corral
```

Usually you're better off renaming one of the methods, but sometimes you can't.

- When the type of the self argument can't be inferred:

```
    let zero = 0;  // type unspecified; could be `i8`, `u8`, ...

    zero.abs();  // error: can't call method `abs`
                 // on ambiguous numeric type

    i64::abs(zero);  // ok
```

- When using the function itself as a function value:

```
    let words: Vec<String> =
        line.split_whitespace()  // iterator produces &str values
            .map(ToString::to_string)  // ok
            .collect();
```

- When calling trait methods in macros. We'll explain in Chapter 21.

Fully qualified syntax also works for associated functions. In the previous section, we wrote S::new() to create a new set in a generic function. We could also have written StringSet::new() or <S as StringSet>::new().

Traits That Define Relationships Between Types

So far, every trait we've looked at stands alone: a trait is a set of methods that types can implement. Traits can also be used in situations where there are multiple types that have to work together. They can describe relationships between types.

- The std::iter::Iterator trait relates each iterator type with the type of value it produces.

- The std::ops::Mul trait relates types that can be multiplied. In the expression a * b, the values a and b can be either the same type, or different types.

- The rand crate includes both a trait for random number generators (rand::Rng) and a trait for types that can be randomly generated (rand::Distribution). The traits themselves define exactly how these types work together.

You won't need to create traits like these every day, but you'll come across them throughout the standard library and in third-party crates. In this section, we'll show how each of these examples is implemented, picking up relevant Rust language features as we need them. The key skill here is the ability to read traits and method signatures and figure out what they say about the types involved.

Associated Types (or How Iterators Work)

We'll start with iterators. By now every object-oriented language has some sort of built-in support for iterators, objects that represent the traversal of some sequence of values.

Rust has a standard `Iterator` trait, defined like this:

```
pub trait Iterator {
    type Item;

    fn next(&mut self) -> Option<Self::Item>;
    ...
}
```

The first feature of this trait, `type Item;`, is an *associated type*. Each type that implements `Iterator` must specify what type of item it produces.

The second feature, the `next()` method, uses the associated type in its return value. `next()` returns an `Option<Self::Item>`: either `Some(item)`, the next value in the sequence, or `None` when there are no more values to visit. The type is written as `Self::Item`, not just plain `Item`, because `Item` is a feature of each type of iterator, not a standalone type. As always, `self` and the `Self` type show up explicitly in the code everywhere their fields, methods, and so on are used.

Here's what it looks like to implement `Iterator` for a type:

```
// (code from the std::env standard library module)
impl Iterator for Args {
    type Item = String;

    fn next(&mut self) -> Option<String> {
        ...
    }
    ...
}
```

`std::env::Args` is the type of iterator returned by the standard library function `std::env::args()` that we used in Chapter 2 to access command-line arguments. It produces `String` values, so the `impl` declares `type Item = String;`.

Generic code can use associated types:

```
/// Loop over an iterator, storing the values in a new vector.
fn collect_into_vector<I: Iterator>(iter: I) -> Vec<I::Item> {
    let mut results = Vec::new();
    for value in iter {
        results.push(value);
```

```
    }
    results
}
```

Inside the body of this function, Rust infers the type of `value` for us, which is nice; but we must spell out the return type of `collect_into_vector`, and the `Item` associated type is the only way to do that. (`Vec<I>` would be simply wrong: we would be claiming to return a vector of iterators!)

The preceding example is not code that you would write out yourself, because after reading Chapter 15, you'll know that iterators already have a standard method that does this: `iter.collect()`. So let's look at one more example before moving on:

```
/// Print out all the values produced by an iterator
fn dump<I>(iter: I)
    where I: Iterator
{
    for (index, value) in iter.enumerate() {
        println!("{}: {:?}", index, value);    // error
    }
}
```

This almost works. There is just one problem: `value` might not be a printable type.

```
error: `<I as Iterator>::Item` doesn't implement `Debug`
  |
8 |         println!("{}: {:?}", index, value);    // error
  |                                     ^^^^^
  |                      `<I as Iterator>::Item` cannot be formatted
  |                      using `{:?}` because it doesn't implement `Debug`
  |
  = help: the trait `Debug` is not implemented for `<I as Iterator>::Item`
  = note: required by `std::fmt::Debug::fmt`
help: consider further restricting the associated type
  |
5 |     where I: Iterator, <I as Iterator>::Item: Debug
  |                        ^^^^^^^^^^^^^^^^^^^^^^^^^^^^^^
```

The error message is slightly obfuscated by Rust's use of the syntax `<I as Iterator>::Item`, which is an explicit but verbose way of saying `I::Item`. This is valid Rust syntax, but you'll rarely actually need to write a type out that way.

The gist of the error message is that to make this generic function compile, we must ensure that `I::Item` implements the `Debug` trait, the trait for formatting values with `{:?}`. As the error message suggests, we can do this by placing a bound on `I::Item`:

```
use std::fmt::Debug;

fn dump<I>(iter: I)
    where I: Iterator, I::Item: Debug
{
```

```
    ...
}
```

Or, we could write, "I must be an iterator over `String` values":

```
fn dump<I>(iter: I)
    where I: Iterator<Item=String>
{
    ...
}
```

`Iterator<Item=String>` is itself a trait. If you think of `Iterator` as the set of all iterator types, then `Iterator<Item=String>` is a subset of `Iterator`: the set of iterator types that produce `String`s. This syntax can be used anywhere the name of a trait can be used, including trait object types:

```
fn dump(iter: &mut dyn Iterator<Item=String>) {
    for (index, s) in iter.enumerate() {
        println!("{}: {:?}", index, s);
    }
}
```

Traits with associated types, like `Iterator`, are compatible with trait methods, but only if all the associated types are spelled out, as shown here. Otherwise, the type of `s` could be anything, and again, Rust would have no way to type-check this code.

We've shown a lot of examples involving iterators. It's hard not to; they're by far the most prominent use of associated types. But associated types are generally useful whenever a trait needs to cover more than just methods:

- In a thread pool library, a `Task` trait, representing a unit of work, could have an associated `Output` type.

- A `Pattern` trait, representing a way of searching a string, could have an associated `Match` type, representing all the information gathered by matching the pattern to the string:

  ```
  trait Pattern {
      type Match;

      fn search(&self, string: &str) -> Option<Self::Match>;
  }

  /// You can search a string for a particular character.
  impl Pattern for char {
      /// A "match" is just the location where the
      /// character was found.
      type Match = usize;

      fn search(&self, string: &str) -> Option<usize> {
          ...
  ```

```
        }
    }
```

If you're familiar with regular expressions, it's easy to see how `impl Pattern for RegExp` would have a more elaborate `Match` type, probably a struct that would include the start and length of the match, the locations where parenthesized groups matched, and so on.

- A library for working with relational databases might have a `Database Connection` trait with associated types representing transactions, cursors, prepared statements, and so on.

Associated types are perfect for cases where each implementation has *one* specific related type: each type of `Task` produces a particular type of `Output`; each type of `Pattern` looks for a particular type of `Match`. However, as we'll see, some relationships among types are not like this.

Generic Traits (or How Operator Overloading Works)

Multiplication in Rust uses this trait:

```
/// std::ops::Mul, the trait for types that support `*`.
pub trait Mul<RHS> {
    /// The resulting type after applying the `*` operator
    type Output;

    /// The method for the `*` operator
    fn mul(self, rhs: RHS) -> Self::Output;
}
```

`Mul` is a generic trait. The type parameter, RHS, is short for *righthand side*.

The type parameter here means the same thing that it means on a struct or function: `Mul` is a generic trait, and its instances `Mul<f64>`, `Mul<String>`, `Mul<Size>`, etc., are all different traits, just as `min::<i32>` and `min::<String>` are different functions and `Vec<i32>` and `Vec<String>` are different types.

A single type—say, `WindowSize`—can implement both `Mul<f64>` and `Mul<i32>`, and many more. You would then be able to multiply a `WindowSize` by many other types. Each implementation would have its own associated `Output` type.

Generic traits get a special dispensation when it comes to the orphan rule: you can implement a foreign trait for a foreign type, so long as one of the trait's type parameters is a type defined in the current crate. So, if you've defined `WindowSize` yourself, you can implement `Mul<WindowSize>` for `f64`, even though you didn't define either `Mul` or `f64`. These implementations can even be generic, such as `impl<T> Mul<WindowSize> for Vec<T>`. This works because there's no way any other crate could define `Mul<WindowSize>` on anything, and thus no way a conflict among imple-

---

mentations could arise. (We introduced the orphan rule back in "Traits and Other People's Types" on page 268.) This is how crates like nalgebra define arithmetic operations on vectors.

The trait shown earlier is missing one minor detail. The real Mul trait looks like this:

```
pub trait Mul<RHS=Self> {
    ...
}
```

The syntax RHS=Self means that RHS defaults to Self. If I write impl Mul for Complex, without specifying Mul's type parameter, it means impl Mul<Complex> for Complex. In a bound, if I write where T: Mul, it means where T: Mul<T>.

In Rust, the expression lhs * rhs is shorthand for Mul::mul(lhs, rhs). So overloading the * operator in Rust is as simple as implementing the Mul trait. We'll show examples in the next chapter.

impl Trait

As you might imagine, combinations of many generic types can get messy. For example, combining just a few iterators using standard library combinators rapidly turns your return type into an eyesore:

```
use std::iter;
use std::vec::IntoIter;
fn cyclical_zip(v: Vec<u8>, u: Vec<u8>) ->
    iter::Cycle<iter::Chain<IntoIter<u8>, IntoIter<u8>>> {
        v.into_iter().chain(u.into_iter()).cycle()
}
```

We could easily replace this hairy return type with a trait object:

```
fn cyclical_zip(v: Vec<u8>, u: Vec<u8>) -> Box<dyn Iterator<Item=u8>> {
    Box::new(v.into_iter().chain(u.into_iter()).cycle())
}
```

However, taking the overhead of dynamic dispatch and an unavoidable heap allocation every time this function is called just to avoid an ugly type signature doesn't seem like a good trade, in most cases.

Rust has a feature called impl Trait designed for precisely this situation. impl Trait allows us to "erase" the type of a return value, specifying only the trait or traits it implements, without dynamic dispatch or a heap allocation:

```
fn cyclical_zip(v: Vec<u8>, u: Vec<u8>) -> impl Iterator<Item=u8> {
    v.into_iter().chain(u.into_iter()).cycle()
}
```

Now, rather than specifying a particular nested type of iterator combinator structs, cyclical_zip's signature just states that it returns some kind of iterator over u8. The return type expresses the intent of the function, rather than its implementation details.

This has definitely cleaned up the code and made it more readable, but `impl Trait` is more than just a convenient shorthand. Using `impl Trait` means that you can change the actual type being returned in the future as long as it still implements `Iterator<Item=u8>`, and any code calling the function will continue to compile without an issue. This provides a lot of flexibility for library authors, because only the relevant functionality is encoded in the type signature.

For example, if the first version of a library uses iterator combinators as in the preceding, but a better algorithm for the same process is discovered, the library author can use different combinators or even make a custom type that implements `Iterator`, and users of the library can get the performance improvements without changing their code at all.

It might be tempting to use `impl Trait` to approximate a statically dispatched version of the factory pattern that's commonly used in object-oriented languages. For example, you might define a trait like this:

```
trait Shape {
    fn new() -> Self;
    fn area(&self) -> f64;
}
```

After implementing it for a few types, you might want to use different `Shapes` depending on a run-time value, like a string that a user enters. This doesn't work with `impl Shape` as the return type:

```
fn make_shape(shape: &str) -> impl Shape {
    match shape {
        "circle" => Circle::new(),
        "triangle" => Triangle::new(), // error: incompatible types
        "shape" => Rectangle::new(),
    }
}
```

From the perspective of the caller, a function like this doesn't make much sense. `impl Trait` is a form of static dispatch, so the compiler has to know the type being returned from the function at compile time in order to allocate the right amount of space on the stack and correctly access fields and methods on that type. Here, it could be `Circle`, `Triangle`, or `Rectangle`, which could all take up different amounts of space and all have different implementations of `area()`.

It's important to note that Rust doesn't allow trait methods to use `impl Trait` return values. Supporting this will require some improvements in the languages's type system. Until that work is done, only free functions and functions associated with specific types can use `impl Trait` returns.

`impl Trait` can also be used in functions that take generic arguments. For instance, consider this simple generic function:

```
fn print<T: Display>(val: T) {
    println!("{}", val);
}
```

It is identical to this version using `impl Trait`:

```
fn print(val: impl Display) {
    println!("{}", val);
}
```

There is one important exception. Using generics allows callers of the function to specify the type of the generic arguments, like `print::<i32>(42)`, while using `impl Trait` does not.

Each `impl Trait` argument is assigned its own anonymous type parameter, so `impl Trait` for arguments is limited to only the simplest generic functions, with no relationships between the types of arguments.

Associated Consts

Like structs and enums, traits can have associated constants. You can declare a trait with an associated constant using the same syntax as for a struct or enum:

```
trait Greet {
    const GREETING: &'static str = "Hello";
    fn greet(&self) -> String;
}
```

Associated consts in traits have a special power, though. Like associated types and functions, you can declare them but not give them a value:

```
trait Float {
    const ZERO: Self;
    const ONE: Self;
}
```

Then, implementors of the trait can define these values:

```
impl Float for f32 {
    const ZERO: f32 = 0.0;
    const ONE: f32 = 1.0;
}

impl Float for f64 {
    const ZERO: f64 = 0.0;
    const ONE: f64 = 1.0;
}
```

This allows you to write generic code that uses these values:

```
fn add_one<T: Float + Add<Output=T>>(value: T) -> T {
    value + T::ONE
}
```

Note that associated constants can't be used with trait objects, since the compiler relies on type information about the implementation in order to pick the right value at compile time.

Even a simple trait with no behavior at all, like `Float`, can give enough information about a type, in combination with a few operators, to implement common mathematical functions like Fibonacci:

```
fn fib<T: Float + Add<Output=T>>(n: usize) -> T {
    match n {
        0 => T::ZERO,
        1 => T::ONE,
        n => fib::<T>(n - 1) + fib::<T>(n - 2)
    }
}
```

In the last two sections, we've shown different ways traits can describe relationships between types. All of these can also be seen as ways of avoiding virtual method overhead and downcasts, since they allow Rust to know more concrete types at compile time.

Reverse-Engineering Bounds

Writing generic code can be a real slog when there's no single trait that does everything you need. Suppose we have written this nongeneric function to do some computation:

```
fn dot(v1: &[i64], v2: &[i64]) -> i64 {
    let mut total = 0;
    for i in 0 .. v1.len() {
        total = total + v1[i] * v2[i];
    }
    total
}
```

Now we want to use the same code with floating-point values. We might try something like this:

```
fn dot<N>(v1: &[N], v2: &[N]) -> N {
    let mut total: N = 0;
    for i in 0 .. v1.len() {
        total = total + v1[i] * v2[i];
    }
    total
}
```

No such luck: Rust complains about the use of * and the type of 0. We can require N to be a type that supports + and * using the Add and Mul traits. Our use of 0 needs to change, though, because 0 is always an integer in Rust; the corresponding floating-point value is 0.0. Fortunately, there is a standard Default trait for types that have default values. For numeric types, the default is always 0:

```
use std::ops::{Add, Mul};

fn dot<N: Add + Mul + Default>(v1: &[N], v2: &[N]) -> N {
    let mut total = N::default();
    for i in 0 .. v1.len() {
        total = total + v1[i] * v2[i];
    }
    total
}
```

This is closer, but still does not quite work:

```
error: mismatched types
  |
5 | fn dot<N: Add + Mul + Default>(v1: &[N], v2: &[N]) -> N {
  |        - this type parameter
...
8 |         total = total + v1[i] * v2[i];
  |                         ^^^^^^^^^^^^^ expected type parameter `N`,
  |                                       found associated type
  |
  = note: expected type parameter `N`
             found associated type `<N as Mul>::Output`
help: consider further restricting this bound
  |
5 | fn dot<N: Add + Mul + Default + Mul<Output = N>>(v1: &[N], v2: &[N]) -> N {
  |                               ^^^^^^^^^^^^^^^^^^
```

Our new code assumes that multiplying two values of type N produces another value of type N. This isn't necessarily the case. You can overload the multiplication operator to return whatever type you want. We need to somehow tell Rust that this generic function only works with types that have the normal flavor of multiplication, where multiplying N * N returns an N. The suggestion in the error message is *almost* right: we can do this by replacing Mul with Mul<Output=N>, and the same for Add:

```
fn dot<N: Add<Output=N> + Mul<Output=N> + Default>(v1: &[N], v2: &[N]) -> N
{
    ...
}
```

At this point, the bounds are starting to pile up, making the code hard to read. Let's move the bounds into a where clause:

```
fn dot<N>(v1: &[N], v2: &[N]) -> N
    where N: Add<Output=N> + Mul<Output=N> + Default
```

```
{
    ...
}
```

Great. But Rust still complains about this line of code:

```
error: cannot move out of type `[N]`, a non-copy slice
   |
8  |            total = total + v1[i] * v2[i];
   |                            ^^^^^
   |                            |
   |                            cannot move out of here
   |                            move occurs because `v1[_]` has type `N`,
   |                            which does not implement the `Copy` trait
```

Since we haven't required N to be a copyable type, Rust interprets v1[i] as an attempt to move a value out of the slice, which is forbidden. But we don't want to modify the slice at all; we just want to copy the values out to operate on them. Fortunately, all of Rust's built-in numeric types implement Copy, so we can simply add that to our constraints on N:

```
where N: Add<Output=N> + Mul<Output=N> + Default + Copy
```

With this, the code compiles and runs. The final code looks like this:

```
use std::ops::{Add, Mul};

fn dot<N>(v1: &[N], v2: &[N]) -> N
    where N: Add<Output=N> + Mul<Output=N> + Default + Copy
{
    let mut total = N::default();
    for i in 0 .. v1.len() {
        total = total + v1[i] * v2[i];
    }
    total
}

#[test]
fn test_dot() {
    assert_eq!(dot(&[1, 2, 3, 4], &[1, 1, 1, 1]), 10);
    assert_eq!(dot(&[53.0, 7.0], &[1.0, 5.0]), 88.0);
}
```

This occasionally happens in Rust: there is a period of intense arguing with the compiler, at the end of which the code looks rather nice, as if it had been a breeze to write, and runs beautifully.

What we've been doing here is reverse-engineering the bounds on N, using the compiler to guide and check our work. The reason it was a bit of a pain is that there wasn't a single Number trait in the standard library that included all the operators and methods we wanted to use. As it happens, there's a popular open source crate called num that defines such a trait! Had we known, we could have added num to our *Cargo.toml* and written:

```
use num::Num;

fn dot<N: Num + Copy>(v1: &[N], v2: &[N]) -> N {
    let mut total = N::zero();
    for i in 0 .. v1.len() {
        total = total + v1[i] * v2[i];
    }
    total
}
```

Just as in object-oriented programming, the right interface makes everything nice, in generic programming, the right trait makes everything nice.

Still, why go to all this trouble? Why didn't Rust's designers make the generics more like C++ templates, where the constraints are left implicit in the code, à la "duck typing"?

One advantage of Rust's approach is forward compatibility of generic code. You can change the implementation of a public generic function or method, and if you didn't change the signature, you haven't broken any of its users.

Another advantage of bounds is that when you do get a compiler error, at least the compiler can tell you where the trouble is. C++ compiler error messages involving templates can be much longer than Rust's, pointing at many different lines of code, because the compiler has no way to tell who's to blame for a problem: the template, or its caller, which might also be a template, or *that* template's caller...

Perhaps the most important advantage of writing out the bounds explicitly is simply that they are there, in the code and in the documentation. You can look at the signature of a generic function in Rust and see exactly what kind of arguments it accepts. The same can't be said for templates. The work that goes into fully documenting argument types in C++ libraries like Boost is even *more* arduous than what we went through here. The Boost developers don't have a compiler that checks their work.

Traits as a Foundation

Traits are one of the main organizing features in Rust, and with good reason. There's nothing better to design a program or library around than a good interface.

This chapter was a blizzard of syntax, rules, and explanations. Now that we've laid a foundation, we can start talking about the many ways traits and generics are used in Rust code. The fact is, we've only begun to scratch the surface. The next two chapters cover common traits provided by the standard library. Upcoming chapters cover closures, iterators, input/output, and concurrency. Traits and generics play a central role in all of these topics.

## CHAPTER 12

Operator Overloading

In the Mandelbrot set plotter we showed in Chapter 2, we used the `num` crate's `Complex` type to represent a number on the complex plane:

```
#[derive(Clone, Copy, Debug)]
struct Complex<T> {
    /// Real portion of the complex number
    re: T,

    /// Imaginary portion of the complex number
    im: T,
}
```

We were able to add and multiply `Complex` numbers just like any built-in numeric type, using Rust's + and * operators:

```
z = z * z + c;
```

You can make your own types support arithmetic and other operators, too, just by implementing a few built-in traits. This is called *operator overloading*, and the effect is much like operator overloading in C++, C#, Python, and Ruby.

The traits for operator overloading fall into a few categories depending on what part of the language they support, as shown in Table 12-1. In this chapter, we'll cover each category. Our goal is not just to help you integrate your own types nicely into the language, but also to give you a better sense of how to write generic functions like the dot product function described in "Reverse-Engineering Bounds" on page 283 that operate on types most naturally used via these operators. The chapter should also give some insight into how some features of the language itself are implemented.

Table 12-1. Summary of traits for operator overloading

Category	Trait	Operator
Unary operators	`std::ops::Neg`	`-x`
	`std::ops::Not`	`!x`
Arithmetic operators	`std::ops::Add`	`x + y`
	`std::ops::Sub`	`x - y`
	`std::ops::Mul`	`x * y`
	`std::ops::Div`	`x / y`
	`std::ops::Rem`	`x % y`
Bitwise operators	`std::ops::BitAnd`	`x & y`
	`std::ops::BitOr`	`x | y`
	`std::ops::BitXor`	`x ^ y`
	`std::ops::Shl`	`x << y`
	`std::ops::Shr`	`x >> y`
Compound assignment arithmetic operators	`std::ops::AddAssign`	`x += y`
	`std::ops::SubAssign`	`x -= y`
	`std::ops::MulAssign`	`x *= y`
	`std::ops::DivAssign`	`x /= y`
	`std::ops::RemAssign`	`x %= y`
Compound assignment bitwise operators	`std::ops::BitAndAssign`	`x &= y`
	`std::ops::BitOrAssign`	`x |= y`
	`std::ops::BitXorAssign`	`x ^= y`
	`std::ops::ShlAssign`	`x <<= y`
	`std::ops::ShrAssign`	`x >>= y`
Comparison	`std::cmp::PartialEq`	`x == y, x != y`
	`std::cmp::PartialOrd`	`x < y, x <= y, x > y, x >= y`
Indexing	`std::ops::Index`	`x[y], &x[y]`
	`std::ops::IndexMut`	`x[y] = z, &mut x[y]`

Arithmetic and Bitwise Operators

In Rust, the expression `a + b` is actually shorthand for `a.add(b)`, a call to the `add` method of the standard library's `std::ops::Add` trait. Rust's standard numeric types all implement `std::ops::Add`. To make the expression `a + b` work for `Complex` values, the `num` crate implements this trait for `Complex` as well. Similar traits cover the other operators: `a * b` is shorthand for `a.mul(b)`, a method from the `std::ops::Mul` trait, `std::ops::Neg` covers the prefix `-` negation operator, and so on.

If you want to try writing out `z.add(c)`, you'll need to bring the `Add` trait into scope so that its method is visible. That done, you can treat all arithmetic as function calls:[1]

```
use std::ops::Add;

assert_eq!(4.125f32.add(5.75), 9.875);
assert_eq!(10.add(20), 10 + 20);
```

Here's the definition of `std::ops::Add`:

```
trait Add<Rhs = Self> {
    type Output;
    fn add(self, rhs: Rhs) -> Self::Output;
}
```

In other words, the trait `Add<T>` is the ability to add a `T` value to yourself. For example, if you want to be able to add `i32` and `u32` values to your type, your type must implement both `Add<i32>` and `Add<u32>`. The trait's type parameter `Rhs` defaults to `Self`, so if you're implementing addition between two values of the same type, you can simply write `Add` for that case. The associated type `Output` describes the result of the addition.

For example, to be able to add `Complex<i32>` values together, `Complex<i32>` must implement `Add<Complex<i32>>`. Since we're adding a type to itself, we just write `Add`:

```
use std::ops::Add;

impl Add for Complex<i32> {
    type Output = Complex<i32>;
    fn add(self, rhs: Self) -> Self {
        Complex {
            re: self.re + rhs.re,
            im: self.im + rhs.im,
        }
    }
}
```

Of course, we shouldn't have to implement `Add` separately for `Complex<i32>`, `Complex<f32>`, `Complex<f64>`, and so on. All the definitions would look exactly the same except for the types involved, so we should be able to write a single generic implementation that covers them all, as long as the type of the complex components themselves supports addition:

---

1 Lisp programmers rejoice! The expression `<i32 as Add>::add` is the + operator on `i32`, captured as a function value.

```
use std::ops::Add;

impl<T> Add for Complex<T>
where
    T: Add<Output = T>,
{
    type Output = Self;
    fn add(self, rhs: Self) -> Self {
        Complex {
            re: self.re + rhs.re,
            im: self.im + rhs.im,
        }
    }
}
```

By writing where T: Add<Output=T>, we restrict T to types that can be added to themselves, yielding another T value. This is a reasonable restriction, but we could loosen things still further: the Add trait doesn't require both operands of + to have the same type, nor does it constrain the result type. So a maximally generic implementation would let the left- and righthand operands vary independently and produce a Complex value of whatever component type that addition produces:

```
use std::ops::Add;

impl<L, R> Add<Complex<R>> for Complex<L>
where
    L: Add<R>,
{
    type Output = Complex<L::Output>;
    fn add(self, rhs: Complex<R>) -> Self::Output {
        Complex {
            re: self.re + rhs.re,
            im: self.im + rhs.im,
        }
    }
}
```

In practice, however, Rust tends to avoid supporting mixed-type operations. Since our type parameter L must implement Add<R>, it usually follows that L and R are going to be the same type: there simply aren't that many types available for L that implement anything else. So in the end, this maximally generic version may not be much more useful than the prior, simpler generic definition.

Rust's built-in traits for arithmetic and bitwise operators come in three groups: unary operators, binary operators, and compound assignment operators. Within each group, the traits and their methods all have the same form, so we'll cover one example from each.

Unary Operators

Aside from the dereferencing operator *, which we'll cover separately in "Deref and DerefMut" on page 312, Rust has two unary operators that you can customize, shown in Table 12-2.

Table 12-2. Built-in traits for unary operators

Trait name	Expression	Equivalent expression
std::ops::Neg	-x	x.neg()
std::ops::Not	!x	x.not()

All of Rust's signed numeric types implement std::ops::Neg, for the unary negation operator -; the integer types and bool implement std::ops::Not, for the unary complement operator !. There are also implementations for references to those types.

Note that ! complements bool values and performs a bitwise complement (that is, flips the bits) when applied to integers; it plays the role of both the ! and ~ operators from C and C++.

These traits' definitions are simple:

```
trait Neg {
    type Output;
    fn neg(self) -> Self::Output;
}

trait Not {
    type Output;
    fn not(self) -> Self::Output;
}
```

Negating a complex number simply negates each of its components. Here's how we might write a generic implementation of negation for Complex values:

```
use std::ops::Neg;

impl<T> Neg for Complex<T>
where
    T: Neg<Output = T>,
{
    type Output = Complex<T>;
    fn neg(self) -> Complex<T> {
        Complex {
            re: -self.re,
            im: -self.im,
        }
    }
}
```

Binary Operators

Rust's binary arithmetic and bitwise operators and their corresponding built-in traits appear in Table 12-3.

Table 12-3. Built-in traits for binary operators

Category	Trait name	Expression	Equivalent expression
Arithmetic operators	`std::ops::Add`	`x + y`	`x.add(y)`
	`std::ops::Sub`	`x - y`	`x.sub(y)`
	`std::ops::Mul`	`x * y`	`x.mul(y)`
	`std::ops::Div`	`x / y`	`x.div(y)`
	`std::ops::Rem`	`x % y`	`x.rem(y)`
Bitwise operators	`std::ops::BitAnd`	`x & y`	`x.bitand(y)`
	`std::ops::BitOr`	`x | y`	`x.bitor(y)`
	`std::ops::BitXor`	`x ^ y`	`x.bitxor(y)`
	`std::ops::Shl`	`x << y`	`x.shl(y)`
	`std::ops::Shr`	`x >> y`	`x.shr(y)`

All of Rust's numeric types implement the arithmetic operators. Rust's integer types and `bool` implement the bitwise operators. There are also implementations that accept references to those types as either or both operands.

All of the traits here have the same general form. The definition of `std::ops::BitXor`, for the `^` operator, looks like this:

```
trait BitXor<Rhs = Self> {
    type Output;
    fn bitxor(self, rhs: Rhs) -> Self::Output;
}
```

At the beginning of this chapter, we also showed `std::ops::Add`, another trait in this category, along with several sample implementations.

You can use the `+` operator to concatenate a `String` with a `&str` slice or another `String`. However, Rust does not permit the left operand of `+` to be a `&str`, to discourage building up long strings by repeatedly concatenating small pieces on the left. (This performs poorly, requiring time quadratic in the final length of the string.) Generally, the `write!` macro is better for building up strings piece by piece; we show how to do this in "Appending and Inserting Text" on page 439.

Compound Assignment Operators

A compound assignment expression is one like x += y or x &= y: it takes two operands, performs some operation on them like addition or a bitwise AND, and stores the result back in the left operand. In Rust, the value of a compound assignment expression is always ( ), never the value stored.

Many languages have operators like these and usually define them as shorthand for expressions like x = x + y or x = x & y. However, Rust doesn't take that approach. Instead, x += y is shorthand for the method call x.add_assign(y), where add_assign is the sole method of the std::ops::AddAssign trait:

```
trait AddAssign<Rhs = Self> {
    fn add_assign(&mut self, rhs: Rhs);
}
```

Table 12-4 shows all of Rust's compound assignment operators and the built-in traits that implement them.

Table 12-4. Built-in traits for compound assignment operators

Category	Trait name	Expression	Equivalent expression
Arithmetic operators	std::ops::AddAssign	x += y	x.add_assign(y)
	std::ops::SubAssign	x -= y	x.sub_assign(y)
	std::ops::MulAssign	x *= y	x.mul_assign(y)
	std::ops::DivAssign	x /= y	x.div_assign(y)
	std::ops::RemAssign	x %= y	x.rem_assign(y)
Bitwise operators	std::ops::BitAndAssign	x &= y	x.bitand_assign(y)
	std::ops::BitOrAssign	x |= y	x.bitor_assign(y)
	std::ops::BitXorAssign	x ^= y	x.bitxor_assign(y)
	std::ops::ShlAssign	x <<= y	x.shl_assign(y)
	std::ops::ShrAssign	x >>= y	x.shr_assign(y)

All of Rust's numeric types implement the arithmetic compound assignment operators. Rust's integer types and bool implement the bitwise compound assignment operators.

A generic implementation of AddAssign for our Complex type is straightforward:

```
use std::ops::AddAssign;

impl<T> AddAssign for Complex<T>
where
    T: AddAssign<T>,
{
    fn add_assign(&mut self, rhs: Complex<T>) {
        self.re += rhs.re;
```

```
        self.im += rhs.im;
    }
}
```

The built-in trait for a compound assignment operator is completely independent of the built-in trait for the corresponding binary operator. Implementing `std::ops::Add` does not automatically implement `std::ops::AddAssign`; if you want Rust to permit your type as the lefthand operand of a `+=` operator, you must implement `AddAssign` yourself.

Equivalence Comparisons

Rust's equality operators, `==` and `!=`, are shorthand for calls to the `std::cmp::PartialEq` trait's `eq` and `ne` methods:

```
assert_eq!(x == y, x.eq(&y));
assert_eq!(x != y, x.ne(&y));
```

Here's the definition of `std::cmp::PartialEq`:

```
trait PartialEq<Rhs = Self>
where
    Rhs: ?Sized,
{
    fn eq(&self, other: &Rhs) -> bool;
    fn ne(&self, other: &Rhs) -> bool {
        !self.eq(other)
    }
}
```

Since the `ne` method has a default definition, you only need to define `eq` to implement the `PartialEq` trait, so here's a complete implementation for `Complex`:

```
impl<T: PartialEq> PartialEq for Complex<T> {
    fn eq(&self, other: &Complex<T>) -> bool {
        self.re == other.re && self.im == other.im
    }
}
```

In other words, for any component type `T` that itself can be compared for equality, this implements comparison for `Complex<T>`. Assuming we've also implemented `std::ops::Mul` for `Complex` somewhere along the line, we can now write:

```
let x = Complex { re: 5, im: 2 };
let y = Complex { re: 2, im: 5 };
assert_eq!(x * y, Complex { re: 0, im: 29 });
```

Implementations of `PartialEq` are almost always of the form shown here: they compare each field of the left operand to the corresponding field of the right. These get tedious to write, and equality is a common operation to support, so if you ask, Rust will generate an implementation of `PartialEq` for you automatically. Simply add `PartialEq` to the type definition's `derive` attribute like so:

```
#[derive(Clone, Copy, Debug, PartialEq)]
struct Complex<T> {
    ...
}
```

Rust's automatically generated implementation is essentially identical to our handwritten code, comparing each field or element of the type in turn. Rust can derive `PartialEq` implementations for `enum` types as well. Naturally, each of the values the type holds (or might hold, in the case of an `enum`) must itself implement `PartialEq`.

Unlike the arithmetic and bitwise traits, which take their operands by value, `PartialEq` takes its operands by reference. This means that comparing non-`Copy` values like `Strings`, `Vecs`, or `HashMaps` doesn't cause them to be moved, which would be troublesome:

```
let s = "d\x6fv\x65t\x61i\x6c".to_string();
let t = "\x64o\x76e\x74a\x69l".to_string();
assert!(s == t);  // s and t are only borrowed...

// ... so they still have their values here.
assert_eq!(format!("{} {}", s, t), "dovetail dovetail");
```

This leads us to the trait's bound on the `Rhs` type parameter, which is of a kind we haven't seen before:

```
where
    Rhs: ?Sized,
```

This relaxes Rust's usual requirement that type parameters must be sized types, letting us write traits like `PartialEq<str>` or `PartialEq<[T]>`. The `eq` and `ne` methods take parameters of type `&Rhs`, and comparing something with a `&str` or a `&[T]` is completely reasonable. Since `str` implements `PartialEq<str>`, the following assertions are equivalent:

```
assert!("ungula" != "ungulate");
assert!("ungula".ne("ungulate"));
```

Here, both `Self` and `Rhs` would be the unsized type `str`, making `ne`'s `self` and `rhs` parameters both `&str` values. We'll discuss sized types, unsized types, and the `Sized` trait in detail in "Sized" on page 307.

Why is this trait called `PartialEq`? The traditional mathematical definition of an *equivalence relation*, of which equality is one instance, imposes three requirements. For any values x and y:

- If x == y is true, then y == x must be true as well. In other words, swapping the two sides of an equality comparison doesn't affect the result.

- If x == y and y == z, then it must be the case that x == z. Given any chain of values, each equal to the next, each value in the chain is directly equal to every other. Equality is contagious.

- It must always be true that x == x.

That last requirement might seem too obvious to be worth stating, but this is exactly where things go awry. Rust's f32 and f64 are IEEE standard floating-point values. According to that standard, expressions like 0.0/0.0 and others with no appropriate value must produce special *not-a-number* values, usually referred to as NaN values. The standard further requires that a NaN value be treated as unequal to every other value—including itself. For example, the standard requires all the following behaviors:

```
assert!(f64::is_nan(0.0 / 0.0));
assert_eq!(0.0 / 0.0 == 0.0 / 0.0, false);
assert_eq!(0.0 / 0.0 != 0.0 / 0.0, true);
```

Furthermore, any ordered comparison with a NaN value must return false:

```
assert_eq!(0.0 / 0.0 < 0.0 / 0.0, false);
assert_eq!(0.0 / 0.0 > 0.0 / 0.0, false);
assert_eq!(0.0 / 0.0 <= 0.0 / 0.0, false);
assert_eq!(0.0 / 0.0 >= 0.0 / 0.0, false);
```

So while Rust's == operator meets the first two requirements for equivalence relations, it clearly doesn't meet the third when used on IEEE floating-point values. This is called a *partial equivalence relation*, so Rust uses the name PartialEq for the == operator's built-in trait. If you write generic code with type parameters known only to be PartialEq, you may assume the first two requirements hold, but you should not assume that values always equal themselves.

That can be a bit counterintuitive and may lead to bugs if you're not vigilant. If you'd prefer your generic code to require a full equivalence relation, you can instead use the std::cmp::Eq trait as a bound, which represents a full equivalence relation: if a type implements Eq, then x == x must be true for every value x of that type. In practice, almost every type that implements PartialEq should implement Eq as well; f32 and f64 are the only types in the standard library that are PartialEq but not Eq.

The standard library defines Eq as an extension of PartialEq, adding no new methods:

```
trait Eq: PartialEq<Self> {}
```

If your type is PartialEq and you would like it to be Eq as well, you must explicitly implement Eq, even though you need not actually define any new functions or types to do so. So implementing Eq for our Complex type is quick:

```
impl<T: Eq> Eq for Complex<T> {}
```

We could implement it even more succinctly by just including Eq in the derive attribute on the Complex type definition:

```
#[derive(Clone, Copy, Debug, Eq, PartialEq)]
struct Complex<T> {
    ...
}
```

Derived implementations on a generic type may depend on the type parameters. With the derive attribute, Complex<i32> would implement Eq, because i32 does, but Complex<f32> would only implement PartialEq, since f32 doesn't implement Eq.

When you implement std::cmp::PartialEq yourself, Rust can't check that your definitions for the eq and ne methods actually behave as required for partial or full equivalence. They could do anything you like. Rust simply takes your word that you've implemented equality in a way that meets the expectations of the trait's users.

Although the definition of PartialEq provides a default definition for ne, you can provide your own implementation if you like. However, you must ensure that ne and eq are exact complements of each other. Users of the PartialEq trait will assume this is so.

Ordered Comparisons

Rust specifies the behavior of the ordered comparison operators <, >, <=, and >= all in terms of a single trait, std::cmp::PartialOrd:

```
trait PartialOrd<Rhs = Self>: PartialEq<Rhs>
where
    Rhs: ?Sized,
{
    fn partial_cmp(&self, other: &Rhs) -> Option<Ordering>;

    fn lt(&self, other: &Rhs) -> bool { ... }
    fn le(&self, other: &Rhs) -> bool { ... }
    fn gt(&self, other: &Rhs) -> bool { ... }
    fn ge(&self, other: &Rhs) -> bool { ... }
}
```

Note that PartialOrd<Rhs> extends PartialEq<Rhs>: you can do ordered comparisons only on types that you can also compare for equality.

The only method of PartialOrd you must implement yourself is partial_cmp. When partial_cmp returns Some(o), then o indicates self's relationship to other:

```
enum Ordering {
    Less,       // self < other
    Equal,      // self == other
    Greater,    // self > other
}
```

But if `partial_cmp` returns `None`, that means `self` and `other` are unordered with respect to each other: neither is greater than the other, nor are they equal. Among all of Rust's primitive types, only comparisons between floating-point values ever return `None`: specifically, comparing a NaN (not-a-number) value with anything else returns `None`. We give some more background on NaN values in "Equivalence Comparisons" on page 294.

Like the other binary operators, to compare values of two types `Left` and `Right`, `Left` must implement `PartialOrd<Right>`. Expressions like `x < y` or `x >= y` are shorthand for calls to `PartialOrd` methods, as shown in Table 12-5.

Table 12-5. Ordered comparison operators and `PartialOrd` methods

Expression	Equivalent method call	Default definition
x < y	x.lt(y)	x.partial_cmp(&y) == Some(Less)
x > y	x.gt(y)	x.partial_cmp(&y) == Some(Greater)
x <= y	x.le(y)	matches!(x.partial_cmp(&y), Some(Less | Equal))
x >= y	x.ge(y)	matches!(x.partial_cmp(&y), Some(Greater | Equal))

As in prior examples, the equivalent method call code shown assumes that `std::cmp::PartialOrd` and `std::cmp::Ordering` are in scope.

If you know that values of two types are always ordered with respect to each other, then you can implement the stricter `std::cmp::Ord` trait:

```
trait Ord: Eq + PartialOrd<Self> {
    fn cmp(&self, other: &Self) -> Ordering;
}
```

The `cmp` method here simply returns an `Ordering`, instead of an `Option<Ordering>` like `partial_cmp`: `cmp` always declares its arguments equal or indicates their relative order. Almost all types that implement `PartialOrd` should also implement `Ord`. In the standard library, `f32` and `f64` are the only exceptions to this rule.

Since there's no natural ordering on complex numbers, we can't use our `Complex` type from the previous sections to show a sample implementation of `PartialOrd`. Instead, suppose you're working with the following type, representing the set of numbers falling within a given half-open interval:

```
#[derive(Debug, PartialEq)]
struct Interval<T> {
    lower: T, // inclusive
    upper: T, // exclusive
}
```

You'd like to make values of this type partially ordered: one interval is less than another if it falls entirely before the other, with no overlap. If two unequal intervals overlap, they're unordered: some element of each side is less than some element of the other. And two equal intervals are simply equal. The following implementation of PartialOrd implements those rules:

```
use std::cmp::{Ordering, PartialOrd};

impl<T: PartialOrd> PartialOrd<Interval<T>> for Interval<T> {
    fn partial_cmp(&self, other: &Interval<T>) -> Option<Ordering> {
        if self == other {
            Some(Ordering::Equal)
        } else if self.lower >= other.upper {
            Some(Ordering::Greater)
        } else if self.upper <= other.lower {
            Some(Ordering::Less)
        } else {
            None
        }
    }
}
```

With that implementation in place, you can write the following:

```
assert!(Interval { lower: 10, upper: 20 } <  Interval { lower: 20, upper: 40 });
assert!(Interval { lower: 7,  upper: 8  } >= Interval { lower: 0,  upper: 1  });
assert!(Interval { lower: 7,  upper: 8  } <= Interval { lower: 7,  upper: 8  });

// Overlapping intervals aren't ordered with respect to each other.
let left  = Interval { lower: 10, upper: 30 };
let right = Interval { lower: 20, upper: 40 };
assert!(!(left < right));
assert!(!(left >= right));
```

While PartialOrd is what you'll usually see, total orderings defined with Ord are necessary in some cases, such as the sorting methods implemented in the standard library. For example, sorting intervals isn't possible with only a PartialOrd implementation. If you do want to sort them, you'll have to fill in the gaps of the unordered cases. You might want to sort by upper bound, for instance, and it's easy to do that with sort_by_key:

```
intervals.sort_by_key(|i| i.upper);
```

The Reverse wrapper type takes advantage of this by implementing Ord with a method that simply inverts any ordering. For any type T that implements Ord, std::cmp::Reverse<T> implements Ord too, but with reversed ordering. For example, sorting our intervals from high to low by lower bound is simple:

```
use std::cmp::Reverse;
intervals.sort_by_key(|i| Reverse(i.lower));
```

Index and IndexMut

You can specify how an indexing expression like a[i] works on your type by implementing the std::ops::Index and std::ops::IndexMut traits. Arrays support the [] operator directly, but on any other type, the expression a[i] is normally shorthand for *a.index(i), where index is a method of the std::ops::Index trait. However, if the expression is being assigned to or borrowed mutably, it's instead shorthand for *a.index_mut(i), a call to the method of the std::ops::IndexMut trait.

Here are the traits' definitions:

```
trait Index<Idx> {
    type Output: ?Sized;
    fn index(&self, index: Idx) -> &Self::Output;
}

trait IndexMut<Idx>: Index<Idx> {
    fn index_mut(&mut self, index: Idx) -> &mut Self::Output;
}
```

Note that these traits take the type of the index expression as a parameter. You can index a slice with a single usize, referring to a single element, because slices implement Index<usize>. But you can refer to a subslice with an expression like a[i..j] because they also implement Index<Range<usize>>. That expression is shorthand for:

```
*a.index(std::ops::Range { start: i, end: j })
```

Rust's HashMap and BTreeMap collections let you use any hashable or ordered type as the index. The following code works because HashMap<&str, i32> implements Index<&str>:

```
use std::collections::HashMap;
let mut m = HashMap::new();
m.insert("十", 10);
m.insert("百", 100);
m.insert("千", 1000);
m.insert("万", 1_0000);
m.insert("億", 1_0000_0000);

assert_eq!(m["十"], 10);
assert_eq!(m["千"], 1000);
```

Those indexing expressions are equivalent to:

```
use std::ops::Index;
assert_eq!(*m.index("十"), 10);
assert_eq!(*m.index("千"), 1000);
```

The Index trait's associated type Output specifies what type an indexing expression produces: for our HashMap, the Index implementation's Output type is i32.

The `IndexMut` trait extends `Index` with an `index_mut` method that takes a mutable reference to `self`, and returns a mutable reference to an `Output` value. Rust automatically selects `index_mut` when the indexing expression occurs in a context where it's necessary. For example, suppose we write the following:

```
let mut desserts =
    vec!["Howalon".to_string(), "Soan papdi".to_string()];
desserts[0].push_str(" (fictional)");
desserts[1].push_str(" (real)");
```

Because the `push_str` method operates on `&mut self`, those last two lines are equivalent to:

```
use std::ops::IndexMut;
(*desserts.index_mut(0)).push_str(" (fictional)");
(*desserts.index_mut(1)).push_str(" (real)");
```

One limitation of `IndexMut` is that, by design, it must return a mutable reference to some value. This is why you can't use an expression like `m["+"] = 10;` to insert a value into the `HashMap` m: the table would need to create an entry for `"+"` first, with some default value, and return a mutable reference to that. But not all types have cheap default values, and some may be expensive to drop; it would be a waste to create such a value only to be immediately dropped by the assignment. (There are plans to improve this in later versions of the language.)

The most common use of indexing is for collections. For example, suppose we are working with bitmapped images, like the ones we created in the Mandelbrot set plotter in Chapter 2. Recall that our program contained code like this:

```
pixels[row * bounds.0 + column] = ...;
```

It would be nicer to have an `Image<u8>` type that acts like a two-dimensional array, allowing us to access pixels without having to write out all the arithmetic:

```
image[row][column] = ...;
```

To do this, we'll need to declare a struct:

```
struct Image<P> {
    width: usize,
    pixels: Vec<P>,
}

impl<P: Default + Copy> Image<P> {
    /// Create a new image of the given size.
    fn new(width: usize, height: usize) -> Image<P> {
        Image {
            width,
            pixels: vec![P::default(); width * height],
        }
    }
}
```

And here are implementations of `Index` and `IndexMut` that would fit the bill:

```
impl<P> std::ops::Index<usize> for Image<P> {
    type Output = [P];
    fn index(&self, row: usize) -> &[P] {
        let start = row * self.width;
        &self.pixels[start..start + self.width]
    }
}

impl<P> std::ops::IndexMut<usize> for Image<P> {
    fn index_mut(&mut self, row: usize) -> &mut [P] {
        let start = row * self.width;
        &mut self.pixels[start..start + self.width]
    }
}
```

When you index into an `Image`, you get back a slice of pixels; indexing the slice gives you an individual pixel.

Note that when we write `image[row][column]`, if `row` is out of bounds, our `.index()` method will try to index `self.pixels` out of range, triggering a panic. This is how `Index` and `IndexMut` implementations are supposed to behave: out-of-bounds access is detected and causes a panic, the same as when you index an array, slice, or vector out of bounds.

Other Operators

Not all operators can be overloaded in Rust. As of Rust 1.50, the error-checking `?` operator works only with `Result` and `Option` values, though work is in progress to expand this to user-defined types as well. Similarly, the logical operators `&&` and `||` are limited to Boolean values only. The `..` and `..=` operators always create a struct representing the range's bounds, the `&` operator always borrows references, and the `=` operator always moves or copies values. None of them can be overloaded.

The dereferencing operator, `*val`, and the dot operator for accessing fields and calling methods, as in `val.field` and `val.method()`, can be overloaded using the `Deref` and `DerefMut` traits, which are covered in the next chapter. (We did not include them here because these traits do more than just overload a few operators.)

Rust does not support overloading the function call operator, `f(x)`. Instead, when you need a callable value, you'll typically just write a closure. We'll explain how this works and cover the `Fn`, `FnMut`, and `FnOnce` special traits in Chapter 14.

## CHAPTER 13

Utility Traits

Science is nothing else than the search to discover unity in the wild variety of nature—or, more exactly, in the variety of our experience. Poetry, painting, the arts are the same search, in Coleridge's phrase, for unity in variety.

—Jacob Bronowski

This chapter describes what we call Rust's "utility" traits, a grab bag of various traits from the standard library that have enough of an impact on the way Rust is written that you'll need to be familiar with them in order to write idiomatic code and design public interfaces for your crates that users will judge to be properly "Rustic." They fall into three broad categories:

Language extension traits

Just as the operator overloading traits we covered in the previous chapter make it possible for you to use Rust's expression operators on your own types, there are several other standard library traits that serve as Rust extension points, allowing you to integrate your own types more closely with the language. These include `Drop`, `Deref` and `DerefMut`, and the conversion traits `From` and `Into`. We'll describe those in this chapter.

Marker traits

These are traits mostly used to bound generic type variables to express constraints you can't capture otherwise. These include `Sized` and `Copy`.

Public vocabulary traits

These don't have any magical compiler integration; you could define equivalent traits in your own code. But they serve the important goal of setting down conventional solutions for common problems. These are especially valuable in public interfaces between crates and modules: by reducing needless variation, they make interfaces easier to understand, but they also increase the likelihood that features from different crates can simply be plugged together directly, without boilerplate or custom glue code. These include `Default`, the reference-borrowing traits `AsRef`, `AsMut`, `Borrow` and `BorrowMut`; the fallible conversion traits `TryFrom` and `TryInto`; and the `ToOwned` trait, a generalization of `Clone`.

These are summarized in Table 13-1.

Table 13-1. Summary of utility traits

Trait	Description
Drop	Destructors. Cleanup code that Rust runs automatically whenever a value is dropped.
Sized	Marker trait for types with a fixed size known at compile time, as opposed to types (such as slices) that are dynamically sized.
Clone	Types that support cloning values.
Copy	Marker trait for types that can be cloned simply by making a byte-for-byte copy of the memory containing the value.
Deref and DerefMut	Traits for smart pointer types.
Default	Types that have a sensible "default value."
AsRef and AsMut	Conversion traits for borrowing one type of reference from another.
Borrow and BorrowMut	Conversion traits, like AsRef/AsMut, but additionally guaranteeing consistent hashing, ordering, and equality.
From and Into	Conversion traits for transforming one type of value into another.
TryFrom and TryInto	Conversion traits for transforming one type of value into another, for transformations that might fail.
ToOwned	Conversion trait for converting a reference to an owned value.

There are other important standard library traits as well. We'll cover `Iterator` and `IntoIterator` in Chapter 15. The `Hash` trait, for computing hash codes, is covered in Chapter 16. And a pair of traits that mark thread-safe types, `Send` and `Sync`, are covered in Chapter 19.

Drop

When a value's owner goes away, we say that Rust *drops* the value. Dropping a value entails freeing whatever other values, heap storage, and system resources the value owns. Drops occur under a variety of circumstances: when a variable goes out of scope; at the end of an expression statement; when you truncate a vector, removing elements from its end; and so on.

For the most part, Rust handles dropping values for you automatically. For example, suppose you define the following type:

```
struct Appellation {
    name: String,
    nicknames: Vec<String>
}
```

An `Appellation` owns heap storage for the strings' contents and the vector's buffer of elements. Rust takes care of cleaning all that up whenever an `Appellation` is dropped, without any further coding necessary on your part. However, if you want, you can customize how Rust drops values of your type by implementing the `std::ops::Drop` trait:

```
trait Drop {
    fn drop(&mut self);
}
```

An implementation of `Drop` is analogous to a destructor in C++, or a finalizer in other languages. When a value is dropped, if it implements `std::ops::Drop`, Rust calls its drop method, before proceeding to drop whatever values its fields or elements own, as it normally would. This implicit invocation of `drop` is the only way to call that method; if you try to invoke it explicitly yourself, Rust flags that as an error.

Because Rust calls `Drop::drop` on a value before dropping its fields or elements, the value the method receives is always still fully initialized. An implementation of `Drop` for our `Appellation` type can make full use of its fields:

```
impl Drop for Appellation {
    fn drop(&mut self) {
        print!("Dropping {}", self.name);
        if !self.nicknames.is_empty() {
            print!(" (AKA {})", self.nicknames.join(", "));
        }
        println!("");
    }
}
```

Given that implementation, we can write the following:

```
{
    let mut a = Appellation {
        name: "Zeus".to_string(),
        nicknames: vec!["cloud collector".to_string(),
                        "king of the gods".to_string()]
    };

    println!("before assignment");
    a = Appellation { name: "Hera".to_string(), nicknames: vec![] };
    println!("at end of block");
}
```

When we assign the second `Appellation` to `a`, the first is dropped, and when we leave the scope of `a`, the second is dropped. This code prints the following:

```
before assignment
Dropping Zeus (AKA cloud collector, king of the gods)
at end of block
Dropping Hera
```

Since our `std::ops::Drop` implementation for `Appellation` does nothing but print a message, how, exactly, does its memory get cleaned up? The `Vec` type implements `Drop`, dropping each of its elements and then freeing the heap-allocated buffer they occupied. A `String` uses a `Vec<u8>` internally to hold its text, so `String` need not implement `Drop` itself; it lets its `Vec` take care of freeing the characters. The same principle extends to `Appellation` values: when one gets dropped, in the end it is `Vec`'s implementation of `Drop` that actually takes care of freeing each of the strings' contents, and finally freeing the buffer holding the vector's elements. As for the memory that holds the `Appellation` value itself, it too has some owner, perhaps a local variable or some data structure, which is responsible for freeing it.

If a variable's value gets moved elsewhere, so that the variable is uninitialized when it goes out of scope, then Rust will not try to drop that variable: there is no value in it to drop.

This principle holds even when a variable may or may not have had its value moved away, depending on the flow of control. In cases like this, Rust keeps track of the variable's state with an invisible flag indicating whether the variable's value needs to be dropped or not:

```
let p;
{
    let q = Appellation { name: "Cardamine hirsuta".to_string(),
                          nicknames: vec!["shotweed".to_string(),
                                          "bittercress".to_string()] };
    if complicated_condition() {
        p = q;
    }
}
println!("Sproing! What was that?");
```

Depending on whether `complicated_condition` returns `true` or `false`, either `p` or `q` will end up owning the `Appellation`, with the other uninitialized. Where it lands determines whether it is dropped before or after the `println!`, since `q` goes out of scope before the `println!`, and `p` after. Although a value may be moved from place to place, Rust drops it only once.

You usually won't need to implement `std::ops::Drop` unless you're defining a type that owns resources Rust doesn't already know about. For example, on Unix systems,

Rust's standard library uses the following type internally to represent an operating system file descriptor:

```
struct FileDesc {
    fd: c_int,
}
```

The fd field of a FileDesc is simply the number of the file descriptor that should be closed when the program is done with it; c_int is an alias for i32. The standard library implements Drop for FileDesc as follows:

```
impl Drop for FileDesc {
    fn drop(&mut self) {
        let _ = unsafe { libc::close(self.fd) };
    }
}
```

Here, libc::close is the Rust name for the C library's close function. Rust code may call C functions only within unsafe blocks, so the library uses one here.

If a type implements Drop, it cannot implement the Copy trait. If a type is Copy, that means that simple byte-for-byte duplication is sufficient to produce an independent copy of the value. But it is typically a mistake to call the same drop method more than once on the same data.

The standard prelude includes a function to drop a value, drop, but its definition is anything but magical:

```
fn drop<T>(_x: T) { }
```

In other words, it receives its argument by value, taking ownership from the caller— and then does nothing with it. Rust drops the value of _x when it goes out of scope, as it would for any other variable.

Sized

A *sized type* is one whose values all have the same size in memory. Almost all types in Rust are sized: every u64 takes eight bytes, every (f32, f32, f32) tuple twelve. Even enums are sized: no matter which variant is actually present, an enum always occupies enough space to hold its largest variant. And although a Vec<T> owns a heap-allocated buffer whose size can vary, the Vec value itself is a pointer to the buffer, its capacity, and its length, so Vec<T> is a sized type.

All sized types implement the std::marker::Sized trait, which has no methods or associated types. Rust implements it automatically for all types to which it applies; you can't implement it yourself. The only use for Sized is as a bound for type variables: a bound like T: Sized requires T to be a type whose size is known at compile time. Traits of this sort are called *marker traits*, because the Rust language itself uses them to mark certain types as having characteristics of interest.

However, Rust also has a few *unsized types* whose values are not all the same size. For example, the string slice type `str` (note, without an `&`) is unsized. The string literals `"diminutive"` and `"big"` are references to `str` slices that occupy ten and three bytes. Both are shown in Figure 13-1. Array slice types like `[T]` (again, without an `&`) are unsized, too: a shared reference like `&[u8]` can point to a `[u8]` slice of any size. Because the `str` and `[T]` types denote sets of values of varying sizes, they are unsized types.

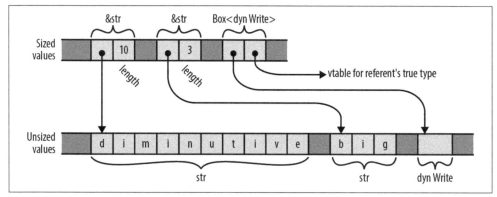

Figure 13-1. References to unsized values

The other common kind of unsized type in Rust is a dyn type, the referent of a trait object. As we explained in "Trait Objects" on page 258, a trait object is a pointer to some value that implements a given trait. For example, the types `&dyn std::io::Write` and `Box<dyn std::io::Write>` are pointers to some value that implements the `Write` trait. The referent might be a file or a network socket or some type of your own for which you have implemented `Write`. Since the set of types that implement `Write` is open-ended, `dyn Write` considered as a type is unsized: its values have various sizes.

Rust can't store unsized values in variables or pass them as arguments. You can only deal with them through pointers like `&str` or `Box<dyn Write>`, which themselves are sized. As shown in Figure 13-1, a pointer to an unsized value is always a *fat pointer*, two words wide: a pointer to a slice also carries the slice's length, and a trait object also carries a pointer to a vtable of method implementations.

Trait objects and pointers to slices are nicely symmetrical. In both cases, the type lacks information necessary to use it: you can't index a `[u8]` without knowing its length, nor can you invoke a method on a `Box<dyn Write>` without knowing the implementation of `Write` appropriate to the specific value it refers to. And in both cases, the fat pointer fills in the information missing from the type, carrying a length or a vtable pointer. The omitted static information is replaced with dynamic information.

Since unsized types are so limited, most generic type variables should be restricted to Sized types. In fact, this is necessary so often that it is the implicit default in Rust: if you write struct S<T> { ... }, Rust understands you to mean struct S<T: Sized> { ... }. If you do not want to constrain T this way, you must explicitly opt out, writing struct S<T: ?Sized> { ... }. The ?Sized syntax is specific to this case and means "not necessarily Sized." For example, if you write struct S<T: ?Sized> { b: Box<T> }, then Rust will allow you to write S<str> and S<dyn Write>, where the box becomes a fat pointer, as well as S<i32> and S<String>, where the box is an ordinary pointer.

Despite their restrictions, unsized types make Rust's type system work more smoothly. Reading the standard library documentation, you will occasionally come across a ?Sized bound on a type variable; this almost always means that the given type is only pointed to, and allows the associated code to work with slices and trait objects as well as ordinary values. When a type variable has the ?Sized bound, people often say it is *questionably sized*: it might be Sized, or it might not.

Aside from slices and trait objects, there is one more kind of unsized type. A struct type's last field (but only its last) may be unsized, and such a struct is itself unsized. For example, an Rc<T> reference-counted pointer is implemented internally as a pointer to the private type RcBox<T>, which stores the reference count alongside the T. Here's a simplified definition of RcBox:

```
struct RcBox<T: ?Sized> {
    ref_count: usize,
    value: T,
}
```

The value field is the T to which Rc<T> is counting references; Rc<T> dereferences to a pointer to this field. The ref_count field holds the reference count.

The real RcBox is just an implementation detail of the standard library and isn't available for public use. But suppose we are working with the preceding definition. You can use this RcBox with sized types, like RcBox<String>; the result is a sized struct type. Or you can use it with unsized types, like RcBox<dyn std::fmt::Display> (where Display is the trait for types that can be formatted by println! and similar macros); RcBox<dyn Display> is an unsized struct type.

You can't build an RcBox<dyn Display> value directly. Instead, you first need to create an ordinary, sized RcBox whose value type implements Display, like RcBox<String>. Rust then lets you convert a reference &RcBox<String> to a fat reference &RcBox<dyn Display>:

```
let boxed_lunch: RcBox<String> = RcBox {
    ref_count: 1,
    value: "lunch".to_string()
};

use std::fmt::Display;
let boxed_displayable: &RcBox<dyn Display> = &boxed_lunch;
```

This conversion happens implicitly when passing values to functions, so you can pass an &RcBox<String> to a function that expects an &RcBox<dyn Display>:

```
fn display(boxed: &RcBox<dyn Display>) {
    println!("For your enjoyment: {}", &boxed.value);
}

display(&boxed_lunch);
```

This would produce the following output:

```
For your enjoyment: lunch
```

Clone

The std::clone::Clone trait is for types that can make copies of themselves. Clone is defined as follows:

```
trait Clone: Sized {
    fn clone(&self) -> Self;
    fn clone_from(&mut self, source: &Self) {
        *self = source.clone()
    }
}
```

The clone method should construct an independent copy of self and return it. Since this method's return type is Self and functions may not return unsized values, the Clone trait itself extends the Sized trait: this has the effect of bounding implementations' Self types to be Sized.

Cloning a value usually entails allocating copies of anything it owns, as well, so a clone can be expensive, in both time and memory. For example, cloning a Vec<String> not only copies the vector, but also copies each of its String elements. This is why Rust doesn't just clone values automatically, but instead requires you to make an explicit method call. The reference-counted pointer types like Rc<T> and Arc<T> are exceptions: cloning one of these simply increments the reference count and hands you a new pointer.

The clone_from method modifies self into a copy of source. The default definition of clone_from simply clones source and then moves that into *self. This always works, but for some types, there is a faster way to get the same effect. For example, suppose s and t are Strings. The statement s = t.clone(); must clone t, drop the old value of s, and then move the cloned value into s; that's one heap allocation and one heap deallocation. But if the heap buffer belonging to the original s has enough capacity to hold t's contents, no allocation or deallocation is necessary: you can simply copy t's text into s's buffer and adjust the length. In generic code, you should use clone_from whenever possible to take advantage of optimized implementations when present.

If your Clone implementation simply applies clone to each field or element of your type and then constructs a new value from those clones, and the default definition of clone_from is good enough, then Rust will implement that for you: simply put #[derive(Clone)] above your type definition.

Pretty much every type in the standard library that makes sense to copy implements Clone. Primitive types like bool and i32 do. Container types like String, Vec<T>, and HashMap do, too. Some types don't make sense to copy, like std::sync::Mutex; those don't implement Clone. Some types like std::fs::File can be copied, but the copy might fail if the operating system doesn't have the necessary resources; these types don't implement Clone, since clone must be infallible. Instead, std::fs::File provides a try_clone method, which returns a std::io::Result<File>, which can report a failure.

Copy

In Chapter 4, we explained that, for most types, assignment moves values, rather than copying them. Moving values makes it much simpler to track the resources they own. But in "Copy Types: The Exception to Moves" on page 94, we pointed out the exception: simple types that don't own any resources can be Copy types, where assignment makes a copy of the source, rather than moving the value and leaving the source uninitialized.

At that time, we left it vague exactly what Copy was, but now we can tell you: a type is Copy if it implements the std::marker::Copy marker trait, which is defined as follows:

```
trait Copy: Clone { }
```

This is certainly easy to implement for your own types:

```
impl Copy for MyType { }
```

But because Copy is a marker trait with special meaning to the language, Rust permits a type to implement Copy only if a shallow byte-for-byte copy is all it needs. Types that own any other resources, like heap buffers or operating system handles, cannot implement Copy.

Any type that implements the Drop trait cannot be Copy. Rust presumes that if a type needs special cleanup code, it must also require special copying code and thus can't be Copy.

As with Clone, you can ask Rust to derive Copy for you, using #[derive(Copy)]. You will often see both derived at once, with #[derive(Copy, Clone)].

Think carefully before making a type Copy. Although doing so makes the type easier to use, it places heavy restrictions on its implementation. Implicit copies can also be expensive. We explain these factors in detail in "Copy Types: The Exception to Moves" on page 94.

Deref and DerefMut

You can specify how dereferencing operators like * and . behave on your types by implementing the std::ops::Deref and std::ops::DerefMut traits. Pointer types like Box<T> and Rc<T> implement these traits so that they can behave as Rust's built-in pointer types do. For example, if you have a Box<Complex> value b, then *b refers to the Complex value that b points to, and b.re refers to its real component. If the context assigns or borrows a mutable reference to the referent, Rust uses the DerefMut ("dereference mutably") trait; otherwise, read-only access is enough, and it uses Deref.

The traits are defined like this:

```
trait Deref {
    type Target: ?Sized;
    fn deref(&self) -> &Self::Target;
}

trait DerefMut: Deref {
    fn deref_mut(&mut self) -> &mut Self::Target;
}
```

The deref and deref_mut methods take a &Self reference and return a &Self::Target reference. Target should be something that Self contains, owns, or refers to: for Box<Complex> the Target type is Complex. Note that DerefMut extends Deref: if you can dereference something and modify it, certainly you should be able to borrow a shared reference to it as well. Since the methods return a reference with the same lifetime as &self, self remains borrowed for as long as the returned reference lives.

The Deref and DerefMut traits play another role as well. Since deref takes a &Self reference and returns a &Self::Target reference, Rust uses this to automatically convert references of the former type into the latter. In other words, if inserting a deref call would prevent a type mismatch, Rust inserts one for you. Implementing

`DerefMut` enables the corresponding conversion for mutable references. These are called the *deref coercions*: one type is being "coerced" into behaving as another.

Although the deref coercions aren't anything you couldn't write out explicitly yourself, they're convenient:

- If you have some `Rc<String>` value `r` and want to apply `String::find` to it, you can simply write `r.find('?')`, instead of `(*r).find('?')`: the method call implicitly borrows `r`, and `&Rc<String>` coerces to `&String`, because `Rc<T>` implements `Deref<Target=T>`.

- You can use methods like `split_at` on `String` values, even though `split_at` is a method of the `str` slice type, because `String` implements `Deref<Target=str>`. There's no need for `String` to reimplement all of `str`'s methods, since you can coerce a `&str` from a `&String`.

- If you have a vector of bytes `v` and you want to pass it to a function that expects a byte slice `&[u8]`, you can simply pass `&v` as the argument, since `Vec<T>` implements `Deref<Target=[T]>`.

Rust will apply several deref coercions in succession if necessary. For example, using the coercions mentioned before, you can apply `split_at` directly to an `Rc<String>`, since `&Rc<String>` dereferences to `&String`, which dereferences to `&str`, which has the `split_at` method.

For example, suppose you have the following type:

```
struct Selector<T> {
    /// Elements available in this `Selector`.
    elements: Vec<T>,

    /// The index of the "current" element in `elements`. A `Selector`
    /// behaves like a pointer to the current element.
    current: usize
}
```

To make the `Selector` behave as the doc comment claims, you must implement `Deref` and `DerefMut` for the type:

```
use std::ops::{Deref, DerefMut};

impl<T> Deref for Selector<T> {
    type Target = T;
    fn deref(&self) -> &T {
        &self.elements[self.current]
    }
}

impl<T> DerefMut for Selector<T> {
```

```
    fn deref_mut(&mut self) -> &mut T {
        &mut self.elements[self.current]
    }
}
```

Given those implementations, you can use a `Selector` like this:

```
let mut s = Selector { elements: vec!['x', 'y', 'z'],
                       current: 2 };

// Because `Selector` implements `Deref`, we can use the `*` operator to
// refer to its current element.
assert_eq!(*s, 'z');

// Assert that 'z' is alphabetic, using a method of `char` directly on a
// `Selector`, via deref coercion.
assert!(s.is_alphabetic());

// Change the 'z' to a 'w', by assigning to the `Selector`'s referent.
*s = 'w';

assert_eq!(s.elements, ['x', 'y', 'w']);
```

The `Deref` and `DerefMut` traits are designed for implementing smart pointer types, like `Box`, `Rc`, and `Arc`, and types that serve as owning versions of something you would also frequently use by reference, the way `Vec<T>` and `String` serve as owning versions of `[T]` and `str`. You should not implement `Deref` and `DerefMut` for a type just to make the `Target` type's methods appear on it automatically, the way a C++ base class's methods are visible on a subclass. This will not always work as you expect and can be confusing when it goes awry.

The deref coercions come with a caveat that can cause some confusion: Rust applies them to resolve type conflicts, but not to satisfy bounds on type variables. For example, the following code works fine:

```
let s = Selector { elements: vec!["good", "bad", "ugly"],
                   current: 2 };

fn show_it(thing: &str) { println!("{}", thing); }
show_it(&s);
```

In the call `show_it(&s)`, Rust sees an argument of type `&Selector<&str>` and a parameter of type `&str`, finds the `Deref<Target=str>` implementation, and rewrites the call as `show_it(s.deref())`, just as needed.

However, if you change `show_it` into a generic function, Rust is suddenly no longer cooperative:

```
use std::fmt::Display;
fn show_it_generic<T: Display>(thing: T) { println!("{}", thing); }
show_it_generic(&s);
```

Rust complains:

```
error: `Selector<&str>` doesn't implement `std::fmt::Display`
   |
31 |    show_it_generic(&s);
   |                    ^^
   |                    |
   |                    `Selector<&str>` cannot be formatted with
   |                    the default formatter
   |                    help: consider adding dereference here: `&*s`
   |
note: required by a bound in `show_it_generic`
   |
30 |    fn show_it_generic<T: Display>(thing: T) { println!("{}", thing); }
   |                       ^^^^^^^ required by this bound
   |                               in `show_it_generic`
```

This can be bewildering: How could making a function generic introduce an error? True, `Selector<&str>` does not implement `Display` itself, but it dereferences to `&str`, which certainly does.

Since you're passing an argument of type `&Selector<&str>` and the function's parameter type is `&T`, the type variable `T` must be `Selector<&str>`. Then, Rust checks whether the bound `T: Display` is satisfied: since it does not apply deref coercions to satisfy bounds on type variables, this check fails.

To work around this problem, you can spell out the coercion using the `as` operator:

```
show_it_generic(&s as &str);
```

Or, as the compiler suggests, you can force the coercion with `&*`:

```
show_it_generic(&*s);
```

Default

Some types have a reasonably obvious default value: the default vector or string is empty, the default number is zero, the default `Option` is `None`, and so on. Types like this can implement the `std::default::Default` trait:

```
trait Default {
    fn default() -> Self;
}
```

The `default` method simply returns a fresh value of type `Self`. `String`'s implementation of `Default` is straightforward:

```
impl Default for String {
    fn default() -> String {
        String::new()
    }
}
```

All of Rust's collection types—Vec, HashMap, BinaryHeap, and so on—implement Default, with default methods that return an empty collection. This is helpful when you need to build a collection of values but want to let your caller decide exactly what sort of collection to build. For example, the Iterator trait's partition method splits the values the iterator produces into two collections, using a closure to decide where each value goes:

```
use std::collections::HashSet;
let squares = [4, 9, 16, 25, 36, 49, 64];
let (powers_of_two, impure): (HashSet<i32>, HashSet<i32>)
    = squares.iter().partition(|&n| n & (n-1) == 0);

assert_eq!(powers_of_two.len(), 3);
assert_eq!(impure.len(), 4);
```

The closure |&n| n & (n-1) == 0 uses some bit fiddling to recognize numbers that are powers of two, and partition uses that to produce two HashSets. But of course, partition isn't specific to HashSets; you can use it to produce any sort of collection you like, as long as the collection type implements Default, to produce an empty collection to start with, and Extend<T>, to add a T to the collection. String implements Default and Extend<char>, so you can write:

```
let (upper, lower): (String, String)
    = "Great Teacher Onizuka".chars().partition(|&c| c.is_uppercase());
assert_eq!(upper, "GTO");
assert_eq!(lower, "reat eacher nizuka");
```

Another common use of Default is to produce default values for structs that represent a large collection of parameters, most of which you won't usually need to change. For example, the glium crate provides Rust bindings for the powerful and complex OpenGL graphics library. The glium::DrawParameters struct includes 24 fields, each controlling a different detail of how OpenGL should render some bit of graphics. The glium draw function expects a DrawParameters struct as an argument. Since DrawParameters implements Default, you can create one to pass to draw, mentioning only those fields you want to change:

```
let params = glium::DrawParameters {
    line_width: Some(0.02),
    point_size: Some(0.02),
    .. Default::default()
};

target.draw(..., &params).unwrap();
```

This calls Default::default() to create a DrawParameters value initialized with the default values for all its fields and then uses the .. syntax for structs to create a new one with the line_width and point_size fields changed, ready for you to pass it to target.draw.

If a type T implements `Default`, then the standard library implements `Default` automatically for `Rc<T>`, `Arc<T>`, `Box<T>`, `Cell<T>`, `RefCell<T>`, `Cow<T>`, `Mutex<T>`, and `RwLock<T>`. The default value for the type `Rc<T>`, for example, is an `Rc` pointing to the default value for type T.

If all the element types of a tuple type implement `Default`, then the tuple type does too, defaulting to a tuple holding each element's default value.

Rust does not implicitly implement `Default` for struct types, but if all of a struct's fields implement `Default`, you can implement `Default` for the struct automatically using `#[derive(Default)]`.

AsRef and AsMut

When a type implements `AsRef<T>`, that means you can borrow a `&T` from it efficiently. `AsMut` is the analogue for mutable references. Their definitions are as follows:

```
trait AsRef<T: ?Sized> {
    fn as_ref(&self) -> &T;
}

trait AsMut<T: ?Sized> {
    fn as_mut(&mut self) -> &mut T;
}
```

So, for example, `Vec<T>` implements `AsRef<[T]>`, and `String` implements `AsRef<str>`. You can also borrow a `String`'s contents as an array of bytes, so `String` implements `AsRef<[u8]>` as well.

`AsRef` is typically used to make functions more flexible in the argument types they accept. For example, the `std::fs::File::open` function is declared like this:

```
fn open<P: AsRef<Path>>(path: P) -> Result<File>
```

What `open` really wants is a `&Path`, the type representing a filesystem path. But with this signature, `open` accepts anything it can borrow a `&Path` from—that is, anything that implements `AsRef<Path>`. Such types include `String` and `str`, the operating system interface string types `OsString` and `OsStr`, and of course `PathBuf` and `Path`; see the library documentation for the full list. This is what allows you to pass string literals to `open`:

```
let dot_emacs = std::fs::File::open("/home/jimb/.emacs")?;
```

All of the standard library's filesystem access functions accept path arguments this way. For callers, the effect resembles that of an overloaded function in C++, although Rust takes a different approach toward establishing which argument types are acceptable.

But this can't be the whole story. A string literal is a &str, but the type that implements AsRef<Path> is str, without an &. And as we explained in "Deref and Deref-Mut" on page 312, Rust doesn't try deref coercions to satisfy type variable bounds, so they won't help here either.

Fortunately, the standard library includes the blanket implementation:

```
impl<'a, T, U> AsRef<U> for &'a T
    where T: AsRef<U>,
          T: ?Sized, U: ?Sized
{
    fn as_ref(&self) -> &U {
        (*self).as_ref()
    }
}
```

In other words, for any types T and U, if T: AsRef<U>, then &T: AsRef<U> as well: simply follow the reference and proceed as before. In particular, since str: AsRef<Path>, then &str: AsRef<Path> as well. In a sense, this is a way to get a limited form of deref coercion in checking AsRef bounds on type variables.

You might assume that if a type implements AsRef<T>, it should also implement AsMut<T>. However, there are cases where this isn't appropriate. For example, we've mentioned that String implements AsRef<[u8]>; this makes sense, as each String certainly has a buffer of bytes that can be useful to access as binary data. However, String further guarantees that those bytes are a well-formed UTF-8 encoding of Unicode text; if String implemented AsMut<[u8]>, that would let callers change the String's bytes to anything they wanted, and you could no longer trust a String to be well-formed UTF-8. It only makes sense for a type to implement AsMut<T> if modifying the given T cannot violate the type's invariants.

Although AsRef and AsMut are pretty simple, providing standard, generic traits for reference conversion avoids the proliferation of more specific conversion traits. You should avoid defining your own AsFoo traits when you could just implement AsRef<Foo>.

Borrow and BorrowMut

The std::borrow::Borrow trait is similar to AsRef: if a type implements Borrow<T>, then its borrow method efficiently borrows a &T from it. But Borrow imposes more restrictions: a type should implement Borrow<T> only when a &T hashes and compares the same way as the value it's borrowed from. (Rust doesn't enforce this; it's just the documented intent of the trait.) This makes Borrow valuable in dealing with keys in hash tables and trees or when dealing with values that will be hashed or compared for some other reason.

This distinction matters when borrowing from `String`s, for example: `String` implements `AsRef<str>`, `AsRef<[u8]>`, and `AsRef<Path>`, but those three target types will generally have different hash values. Only the `&str` slice is guaranteed to hash like the equivalent `String`, so `String` implements only `Borrow<str>`.

`Borrow`'s definition is identical to that of `AsRef`; only the names have been changed:

```
trait Borrow<Borrowed: ?Sized> {
    fn borrow(&self) -> &Borrowed;
}
```

`Borrow` is designed to address a specific situation with generic hash tables and other associative collection types. For example, suppose you have a `std::collections::HashMap<String, i32>`, mapping strings to numbers. This table's keys are `String`s; each entry owns one. What should the signature of the method that looks up an entry in this table be? Here's a first attempt:

```
impl<K, V> HashMap<K, V> where K: Eq + Hash
{
    fn get(&self, key: K) -> Option<&V> { ... }
}
```

This makes sense: to look up an entry, you must provide a key of the appropriate type for the table. But in this case, `K` is `String`; this signature would force you to pass a `String` by value to every call to `get`, which is clearly wasteful. You really just need a reference to the key:

```
impl<K, V> HashMap<K, V> where K: Eq + Hash
{
    fn get(&self, key: &K) -> Option<&V> { ... }
}
```

This is slightly better, but now you have to pass the key as a `&String`, so if you wanted to look up a constant string, you'd have to write:

```
hashtable.get(&"twenty-two".to_string())
```

This is ridiculous: it allocates a `String` buffer on the heap and copies the text into it, just so it can borrow it as a `&String`, pass it to `get`, and then drop it.

It should be good enough to pass anything that can be hashed and compared with our key type; a `&str` should be perfectly adequate, for example. So here's the final iteration, which is what you'll find in the standard library:

```
impl<K, V> HashMap<K, V> where K: Eq + Hash
{
    fn get<Q: ?Sized>(&self, key: &Q) -> Option<&V>
        where K: Borrow<Q>,
              Q: Eq + Hash
    { ... }
}
```

In other words, if you can borrow an entry's key as an &Q and the resulting reference hashes and compares just the way the key itself would, then clearly &Q ought to be an acceptable key type. Since `String` implements `Borrow<str>` and `Borrow<String>`, this final version of `get` allows you to pass either `&String` or `&str` as a key, as needed.

`Vec<T>` and `[T: N]` implement `Borrow<[T]>`. Every string-like type allows borrowing its corresponding slice type: `String` implements `Borrow<str>`, `PathBuf` implements `Borrow<Path>`, and so on. And all the standard library's associative collection types use `Borrow` to decide which types can be passed to their lookup functions.

The standard library includes a blanket implementation so that every type `T` can be borrowed from itself: `T: Borrow<T>`. This ensures that `&K` is always an acceptable type for looking up entries in a `HashMap<K, V>`.

As a convenience, every `&mut T` type also implements `Borrow<T>`, returning a shared reference `&T` as usual. This allows you to pass mutable references to collection lookup functions without having to reborrow a shared reference, emulating Rust's usual implicit coercion from mutable references to shared references.

The `BorrowMut` trait is the analogue of `Borrow` for mutable references:

```
trait BorrowMut<Borrowed: ?Sized>: Borrow<Borrowed> {
    fn borrow_mut(&mut self) -> &mut Borrowed;
}
```

The same expectations described for `Borrow` apply to `BorrowMut` as well.

From and Into

The `std::convert::From` and `std::convert::Into` traits represent conversions that consume a value of one type and return a value of another. Whereas the `AsRef` and `AsMut` traits borrow a reference of one type from another, `From` and `Into` take ownership of their argument, transform it, and then return ownership of the result back to the caller.

Their definitions are nicely symmetrical:

```
trait Into<T>: Sized {
    fn into(self) -> T;
}

trait From<T>: Sized {
    fn from(other: T) -> Self;
}
```

The standard library automatically implements the trivial conversion from each type to itself: every type `T` implements `From<T>` and `Into<T>`.

Although the traits simply provide two ways to do the same thing, they lend themselves to different uses.

You generally use `Into` to make your functions more flexible in the arguments they accept. For example, if you write:

```
use std::net::Ipv4Addr;
fn ping<A>(address: A) -> std::io::Result<bool>
    where A: Into<Ipv4Addr>
{
    let ipv4_address = address.into();
    ...
}
```

then `ping` can accept not just an `Ipv4Addr` as an argument, but also a `u32` or a `[u8; 4]` array, since those types both conveniently happen to implement `Into<Ipv4Addr>`. (It's sometimes useful to treat an IPv4 address as a single 32-bit value, or an array of 4 bytes.) Because the only thing `ping` knows about `address` is that it implements `Into<Ipv4Addr>`, there's no need to specify which type you want when you call `into`; there's only one that could possibly work, so type inference fills it in for you.

As with `AsRef` in the previous section, the effect is much like that of overloading a function in C++. With the definition of `ping` from before, we can make any of these calls:

```
println!("{:?}", ping(Ipv4Addr::new(23, 21, 68, 141))); // pass an Ipv4Addr
println!("{:?}", ping([66, 146, 219, 98]));              // pass a [u8; 4]
println!("{:?}", ping(0xd076eb94_u32));                  // pass a u32
```

The `From` trait, however, plays a different role. The `from` method serves as a generic constructor for producing an instance of a type from some other single value. For example, rather than `Ipv4Addr` having two methods named `from_array` and `from_u32`, it simply implements `From<[u8;4]>` and `From<u32>`, allowing us to write:

```
let addr1 = Ipv4Addr::from([66, 146, 219, 98]);
let addr2 = Ipv4Addr::from(0xd076eb94_u32);
```

We can let type inference sort out which implementation applies.

Given an appropriate `From` implementation, the standard library automatically implements the corresponding `Into` trait. When you define your own type, if it has single-argument constructors, you should write them as implementations of `From<T>` for the appropriate types; you'll get the corresponding `Into` implementations for free.

Because the `from` and `into` conversion methods take ownership of their arguments, a conversion can reuse the original value's resources to construct the converted value. For example, suppose you write:

```
let text = "Beautiful Soup".to_string();
let bytes: Vec<u8> = text.into();
```

The implementation of `Into<Vec<u8>>` for `String` simply takes the `String`'s heap buffer and repurposes it, unchanged, as the returned vector's element buffer. The conversion has no need to allocate or copy the text. This is another case where moves enable efficient implementations.

These conversions also provide a nice way to relax a value of a constrained type into something more flexible, without weakening the constrained type's guarantees. For example, a `String` guarantees that its contents are always valid UTF-8; its mutating methods are carefully restricted to ensure that nothing you can do will ever introduce bad UTF-8. But this example efficiently "demotes" a `String` to a block of plain bytes that you can do anything you like with: perhaps you're going to compress it, or combine it with other binary data that isn't UTF-8. Because `into` takes its argument by value, `text` is no longer initialized after the conversion, meaning that we can freely access the former `String`'s buffer without being able to corrupt any extant `String`.

However, cheap conversions are not part of `Into` and `From`'s contract. Whereas `AsRef` and `AsMut` conversions are expected to be cheap, `From` and `Into` conversions may allocate, copy, or otherwise process the value's contents. For example, `String` implements `From<&str>`, which copies the string slice into a new heap-allocated buffer for the `String`. And `std::collections::BinaryHeap<T>` implements `From<Vec<T>>`, which compares and reorders the elements according to its algorithm's requirements.

The `?` operator uses `From` and `Into` to help clean up code in functions that could fail in multiple ways by automatically converting from specific error types to general ones when needed.

For instance, imagine a system that needs to read binary data and convert some portion of it from base-10 numbers written out as UTF-8 text. That means using `std::str::from_utf8` and the `FromStr` implementation for `i32`, which can each return errors of different types. Assuming we use the `GenericError` and `GenericResult` types we defined in Chapter 7 when discussing error handling, the `?` operator will do the conversion for us:

```
type GenericError = Box<dyn std::error::Error + Send + Sync + 'static>;
type GenericResult<T> = Result<T, GenericError>;

fn parse_i32_bytes(b: &[u8]) -> GenericResult<i32> {
        Ok(std::str::from_utf8(b)?.parse::<i32>()?)
}
```

Like most error types, `Utf8Error` and `ParseIntError` implement the `Error` trait, and the standard library gives us a blanket `From` impl for converting from anything that implements `Error` to a `Box<dyn Error>`, which `?` automatically uses:

```
impl<'a, E: Error + Send + Sync + 'a> From<E>
  for Box<dyn Error + Send + Sync + 'a> {
    fn from(err: E) -> Box<dyn Error + Send + Sync + 'a> {
```

```
        Box::new(err)
    }
}
```

This turns what would have been a fairly large function with two `match` statements into a one-liner.

Before `From` and `Into` were added to the standard library, Rust code was full of ad hoc conversion traits and construction methods, each specific to a single type. `From` and `Into` codify conventions that you can follow to make your types easier to use, since your users are already familiar with them. Other libraries and the language itself can also rely on these traits as a canonical, standardized way to encode conversions.

`From` and `Into` are infallible traits—their API requires that conversions will not fail. Unfortunately, many conversions are more complex than that. For example, large integers like `i64` can store numbers far larger than `i32`, and converting a number like `2_000_000_000_000i64` into `i32` doesn't make much sense without some additional information. Doing a simple bitwise conversion, in which the first 32 bits are thrown out, doesn't often yield the result we would hope for:

```
let huge = 2_000_000_000_000i64;
let smaller = huge as i32;
println!("{}", smaller); // -1454759936
```

There are many options for handling this situation. Depending on the context, such a "wrapping" conversion might be appropriate. On the other hand, applications such as digital signal processing and control systems can often make do with a "saturating" conversion, in which numbers larger than the maximum possible value are limited to that maximum.

TryFrom and TryInto

Since it's not clear how such a conversion should behave, Rust doesn't implement `From<i64>` for `i32`, or any other conversion between numerical types that would lose information. Instead, `i32` implements `TryFrom<i64>`. `TryFrom` and `TryInto` are the fallible cousins of `From` and `Into` and are similarly reciprocal; implementing `TryFrom` means that `TryInto` is implemented as well.

Their definitions are only a little more complex than `From` and `Into`.

```
pub trait TryFrom<T>: Sized {
    type Error;
    fn try_from(value: T) -> Result<Self, Self::Error>;
}

pub trait TryInto<T>: Sized {
    type Error;
```

```
        fn try_into(self) -> Result<T, Self::Error>;
    }
```

The try_into() method gives us a Result, so we can choose what to do in the exceptional case, such as a number that's too large to fit in the resulting type:

```
// Saturate on overflow, rather than wrapping
let smaller: i32 = huge.try_into().unwrap_or(i32::MAX);
```

If we want to also handle the negative case, we can use the unwrap_or_else()
method of Result:

```
let smaller: i32 = huge.try_into().unwrap_or_else(|_|{
    if huge >= 0 {
        i32::MAX
    } else {
        i32::MIN
    }
});
```

Implementing fallible conversions for your own types is easy, too. The Error type can be as simple, or as complex, as a particular application demands. The standard library uses an empty struct, providing no information beyond the fact that an error occurred, since the only possible error is an overflow. On the other hand, conversions between more complex types might want to return more information:

```
impl TryInto<LinearShift> for Transform {
    type Error = TransformError;

    fn try_into(self) -> Result<LinearShift, Self::Error> {
        if !self.normalized() {
            return Err(TransformError::NotNormalized);
        }
        ...
    }
}
```

Where From and Into relate types with simple conversions, TryFrom and TryInto extend the simplicity of From and Into conversions with the expressive error handling afforded by Result. These four traits can be used together to relate many types in a single crate.

ToOwned

Given a reference, the usual way to produce an owned copy of its referent is to call clone, assuming the type implements std::clone::Clone. But what if you want to clone a &str or a &[i32]? What you probably want is a String or a Vec<i32>, but Clone's definition doesn't permit that: by definition, cloning a &T must always return a value of type T, and str and [u8] are unsized; they aren't even types that a function could return.

The std::borrow::ToOwned trait provides a slightly looser way to convert a reference to an owned value:

```
trait ToOwned {
    type Owned: Borrow<Self>;
    fn to_owned(&self) -> Self::Owned;
}
```

Unlike clone, which must return exactly Self, to_owned can return anything you could borrow a &Self from: the Owned type must implement Borrow<Self>. You can borrow a &[T] from a Vec<T>, so [T] can implement ToOwned<Owned=Vec<T>>, as long as T implements Clone, so that we can copy the slice's elements into the vector. Similarly, str implements ToOwned<Owned=String>, Path implements ToOwned<Owned=PathBuf>, and so on.

Borrow and ToOwned at Work: The Humble Cow

Making good use of Rust involves thinking through questions of ownership, like whether a function should receive a parameter by reference or by value. Usually you can settle on one approach or the other, and the parameter's type reflects your decision. But in some cases you cannot decide whether to borrow or own until the program is running; the std::borrow::Cow type (for "clone on write") provides one way to do this.

Its definition is shown here:

```
enum Cow<'a, B: ?Sized>
    where B: ToOwned
{
    Borrowed(&'a B),
    Owned(<B as ToOwned>::Owned),
}
```

A Cow<B> either borrows a shared reference to a B or owns a value from which we could borrow such a reference. Since Cow implements Deref, you can call methods on it as if it were a shared reference to a B: if it's Owned, it borrows a shared reference to the owned value; and if it's Borrowed, it just hands out the reference it's holding.

You can also get a mutable reference to a Cow's value by calling its to_mut method, which returns a &mut B. If the Cow happens to be Cow::Borrowed, to_mut simply calls the reference's to_owned method to get its own copy of the referent, changes the Cow into a Cow::Owned, and borrows a mutable reference to the newly owned value. This is the "clone on write" behavior the type's name refers to.

Similarly, `Cow` has an `into_owned` method that promotes the reference to an owned value, if necessary, and then returns it, moving ownership to the caller and consuming the `Cow` in the process.

One common use for `Cow` is to return either a statically allocated string constant or a computed string. For example, suppose you need to convert an error enum to a message. Most of the variants can be handled with fixed strings, but some of them have additional data that should be included in the message. You can return a `Cow<'static, str>`:

```
use std::path::PathBuf;
use std::borrow::Cow;
fn describe(error: &Error) -> Cow<'static, str> {
    match *error {
        Error::OutOfMemory => "out of memory".into(),
        Error::StackOverflow => "stack overflow".into(),
        Error::MachineOnFire => "machine on fire".into(),
        Error::Unfathomable => "machine bewildered".into(),
        Error::FileNotFound(ref path) => {
            format!("file not found: {}", path.display()).into()
        }
    }
}
```

This code uses `Cow`'s implementation of `Into` to construct the values. Most arms of this `match` statement return a `Cow::Borrowed` referring to a statically allocated string. But when we get a `FileNotFound` variant, we use `format!` to construct a message incorporating the given filename. This arm of the `match` statement produces a `Cow::Owned` value.

Callers of `describe` that don't need to change the value can simply treat the `Cow` as a `&str`:

```
println!("Disaster has struck: {}", describe(&error));
```

Callers who do need an owned value can readily produce one:

```
let mut log: Vec<String> = Vec::new();
...
log.push(describe(&error).into_owned());
```

Using `Cow` helps `describe` and its callers put off allocation until the moment it becomes necessary.

## CHAPTER 14

Closures

Save the environment! Create a closure today!
    —Cormac Flanagan

Sorting a vector of integers is easy:

```
integers.sort();
```

It is, therefore, a sad fact that when we want some data sorted, it's hardly ever a vector of integers. We typically have records of some kind, and the built-in `sort` method typically does not work:

```
struct City {
    name: String,
    population: i64,
    country: String,
    ...
}

fn sort_cities(cities: &mut Vec<City>) {
    cities.sort();  // error: how do you want them sorted?
}
```

Rust complains that `City` does not implement `std::cmp::Ord`. We need to specify the sort order, like this:

```
/// Helper function for sorting cities by population.
fn city_population_descending(city: &City) -> i64 {
    -city.population
}

fn sort_cities(cities: &mut Vec<City>) {
    cities.sort_by_key(city_population_descending);  // ok
}
```

The helper function, `city_population_descending`, takes a `City` record and extracts the *key*, the field by which we want to sort our data. (It returns a negative number because `sort` arranges numbers in increasing order, and we want decreasing order: the most populous city first.) The `sort_by_key` method takes this key-function as a parameter.

This works fine, but it's more concise to write the helper function as a *closure*, an anonymous function expression:

```
fn sort_cities(cities: &mut Vec<City>) {
    cities.sort_by_key(|city| -city.population);
}
```

The closure here is `|city| -city.population`. It takes an argument `city` and returns `-city.population`. Rust infers the argument type and return type from how the closure is used.

Other examples of standard library features that accept closures include:

- `Iterator` methods such as `map` and `filter`, for working with sequential data. We'll cover these methods in Chapter 15.

- Threading APIs like `thread::spawn`, which starts a new system thread. Concurrency is all about moving work to other threads, and closures conveniently represent units of work. We'll cover these features in Chapter 19.

- Some methods that conditionally need to compute a default value, like the `or_insert_with` method of `HashMap` entries. This method either gets or creates an entry in a `HashMap`, and it's used when the default value is expensive to compute. The default value is passed in as a closure that is called only if a new entry must be created.

Of course, anonymous functions are everywhere these days, even in languages like Java, C#, Python, and C++ that didn't originally have them. From now on we'll assume you've seen anonymous functions before and focus on what makes Rust's closures a little different. In this chapter, you'll learn the three types of closures, how to use closures with standard library methods, how a closure can "capture" variables in its scope, how to write your own functions and methods that take closures as arguments, and how to store closures for later use as callbacks. We'll also explain how Rust closures are implemented and why they're faster than you might expect.

Capturing Variables

A closure can use data that belongs to an enclosing function. For example:

```
/// Sort by any of several different statistics.
fn sort_by_statistic(cities: &mut Vec<City>, stat: Statistic) {
    cities.sort_by_key(|city| -city.get_statistic(stat));
}
```

The closure here uses `stat`, which is owned by the enclosing function, `sort_by_statistic`. We say that the closure "captures" `stat`. This is one of the classic features of closures, so naturally, Rust supports it; but in Rust, this feature comes with a string attached.

In most languages with closures, garbage collection plays an important role. For example, consider this JavaScript code:

```
// Start an animation that rearranges the rows in a table of cities.
function startSortingAnimation(cities, stat) {
    // Helper function that we'll use to sort the table.
    // Note that this function refers to stat.
    function keyfn(city) {
        return city.get_statistic(stat);
    }

    if (pendingSort)
        pendingSort.cancel();

    // Now kick off an animation, passing keyfn to it.
    // The sorting algorithm will call keyfn later.
    pendingSort = new SortingAnimation(cities, keyfn);
}
```

The closure `keyfn` is stored in the new `SortingAnimation` object. It's meant to be called after `startSortingAnimation` returns. Now, normally when a function returns, all its variables and arguments go out of scope and are discarded. But here, the Java-Script engine must keep `stat` around somehow, since the closure uses it. Most Java-Script engines do this by allocating `stat` in the heap and letting the garbage collector reclaim it later.

Rust doesn't have garbage collection. How will this work? To answer this question, we'll look at two examples.

Closures That Borrow

First, let's repeat the opening example of this section:

```
/// Sort by any of several different statistics.
fn sort_by_statistic(cities: &mut Vec<City>, stat: Statistic) {
    cities.sort_by_key(|city| -city.get_statistic(stat));
}
```

In this case, when Rust creates the closure, it automatically borrows a reference to stat. It stands to reason: the closure refers to stat, so it must have a reference to it.

The rest is simple. The closure is subject to the rules about borrowing and lifetimes that we described in Chapter 5. In particular, since the closure contains a reference to stat, Rust won't let it outlive stat. Since the closure is only used during sorting, this example is fine.

In short, Rust ensures safety by using lifetimes instead of garbage collection. Rust's way is faster: even a fast GC allocation will be slower than storing stat on the stack, as Rust does in this case.

Closures That Steal

The second example is trickier:

```
use std::thread;

fn start_sorting_thread(mut cities: Vec<City>, stat: Statistic)
    -> thread::JoinHandle<Vec<City>>
{
    let key_fn = |city: &City| -> i64 { -city.get_statistic(stat) };

    thread::spawn(|| {
        cities.sort_by_key(key_fn);
        cities
    })
}
```

This is a bit more like what our JavaScript example was doing: thread::spawn takes a closure and calls it in a new system thread. Note that || is the closure's empty argument list.

The new thread runs in parallel with the caller. When the closure returns, the new thread exits. (The closure's return value is sent back to the calling thread as a JoinHandle value. We'll cover that in Chapter 19.)

Again, the closure `key_fn` contains a reference to `stat`. But this time, Rust can't guarantee that the reference is used safely. Rust therefore rejects this program:

```
error: closure may outlive the current function, but it borrows `stat`,
       which is owned by the current function
   |
33 | let key_fn = |city: &City| -> i64 { -city.get_statistic(stat) };
   |              ^^^^^^^^^^^^^^^^^^^^^^                  ^^^^
   |              |                                      `stat` is borrowed here
   |              may outlive borrowed value `stat`
```

In fact, there are two problems here, because `cities` is shared unsafely as well. Quite simply, the new thread created by `thread::spawn` can't be expected to finish its work before `cities` and `stat` are destroyed at the end of the function.

The solution to both problems is the same: tell Rust to *move* `cities` and `stat` into the closures that use them instead of borrowing references to them.

```
fn start_sorting_thread(mut cities: Vec<City>, stat: Statistic)
    -> thread::JoinHandle<Vec<City>>
{
    let key_fn = move |city: &City| -> i64 { -city.get_statistic(stat) };

    thread::spawn(move || {
        cities.sort_by_key(key_fn);
        cities
    })
}
```

The only thing we've changed is to add the `move` keyword before each of the two closures. The `move` keyword tells Rust that a closure doesn't borrow the variables it uses: it steals them.

The first closure, `key_fn`, takes ownership of `stat`. Then the second closure takes ownership of both `cities` and `key_fn`.

Rust thus offers two ways for closures to get data from enclosing scopes: moves and borrowing. Really there is nothing more to say than that; closures follow the same rules about moves and borrowing that we already covered in Chapters 4 and 5. A few cases in point:

- Just as everywhere else in the language, if a closure would move a value of a copyable type, like `i32`, it copies the value instead. So if `Statistic` happened to be a copyable type, we could keep using `stat` even after creating a move closure that uses it.

- Values of noncopyable types, like `Vec<City>`, really are moved: the preceding code transfers `cities` to the new thread, by way of the `move` closure. Rust would not let us access `cities` by name after creating the closure.

- As it happens, this code doesn't need to use `cities` after the point where the closure moves it. If we did, though, the workaround would be easy: we could tell Rust to clone `cities` and store the copy in a different variable. The closure would only steal one of the copies—whichever one it refers to.

We get something important by accepting Rust's strict rules: thread safety. It is precisely because the vector is moved, rather than being shared across threads, that we know the old thread won't free the vector while the new thread is modifying it.

Function and Closure Types

Throughout this chapter, we've seen functions and closures used as values. Naturally, this means that they have types. For example:

```
fn city_population_descending(city: &City) -> i64 {
    -city.population
}
```

This function takes one argument (a `&City`) and returns an `i64`. It has the type `fn(&City) -> i64`.

You can do all the same things with functions that you do with other values. You can store them in variables. You can use all the usual Rust syntax to compute function values:

```
let my_key_fn: fn(&City) -> i64 =
    if user.prefs.by_population {
        city_population_descending
    } else {
        city_monster_attack_risk_descending
    };

cities.sort_by_key(my_key_fn);
```

Structs may have function-typed fields. Generic types like `Vec` can store scads of functions, as long as they all share the same `fn` type. And function values are tiny: a `fn` value is the memory address of the function's machine code, just like a function pointer in C++.

A function can take another function as an argument. For example:

```
/// Given a list of cities and a test function,
/// return how many cities pass the test.
fn count_selected_cities(cities: &Vec<City>,
                         test_fn: fn(&City) -> bool) -> usize
{
    let mut count = 0;
    for city in cities {
        if test_fn(city) {
            count += 1;
```

```
        }
    }
    count
}

/// An example of a test function. Note that the type of
/// this function is `fn(&City) -> bool`, the same as
/// the `test_fn` argument to `count_selected_cities`.
fn has_monster_attacks(city: &City) -> bool {
    city.monster_attack_risk > 0.0
}

// How many cities are at risk for monster attack?
let n = count_selected_cities(&my_cities, has_monster_attacks);
```

If you're familiar with function pointers in C/C++, you'll see that Rust's function values are exactly the same thing.

After all this, it may come as a surprise that closures do *not* have the same type as functions:

```
let limit = preferences.acceptable_monster_risk();
let n = count_selected_cities(
    &my_cities,
    |city| city.monster_attack_risk > limit);   // error: type mismatch
```

The second argument causes a type error. To support closures, we must change the type signature of this function. It needs to look like this:

```
fn count_selected_cities<F>(cities: &Vec<City>, test_fn: F) -> usize
    where F: Fn(&City) -> bool
{
    let mut count = 0;
    for city in cities {
        if test_fn(city) {
            count += 1;
        }
    }
    count
}
```

We have changed only the type signature of count_selected_cities, not the body. The new version is generic. It takes a test_fn of any type F as long as F implements the special trait Fn(&City) -> bool. This trait is automatically implemented by all functions and most closures that take a single &City as an argument and return a Boolean value:

```
fn(&City) -> bool    // fn type (functions only)
Fn(&City) -> bool    // Fn trait (both functions and closures)
```

This special syntax is built into the language. The -> and return type are optional; if omitted, the return type is ().

The new version of `count_selected_cities` accepts either a function or a closure:

```
count_selected_cities(
    &my_cities,
    has_monster_attacks);  // ok

count_selected_cities(
    &my_cities,
    |city| city.monster_attack_risk > limit);  // also ok
```

Why didn't our first attempt work? Well, a closure is callable, but it's not a `fn`. The closure `|city| city.monster_attack_risk > limit` has its own type that's not a `fn` type.

In fact, every closure you write has its own type, because a closure may contain data: values either borrowed or stolen from enclosing scopes. This could be any number of variables, in any combination of types. So every closure has an ad hoc type created by the compiler, large enough to hold that data. No two closures have exactly the same type. But every closure implements an `Fn` trait; the closure in our example implements `Fn(&City) -> i64`.

Since every closure has its own type, code that works with closures usually needs to be generic, like `count_selected_cities`. It's a little clunky to spell out the generic types each time, but to see the advantages of this design, just read on.

Closure Performance

Rust's closures are designed to be fast: faster than function pointers, fast enough that you can use them even in red-hot, performance-sensitive code. If you're familiar with C++ lambdas, you'll find that Rust closures are just as fast and compact, but safer.

In most languages, closures are allocated in the heap, dynamically dispatched, and garbage collected. So creating, calling, and collecting each of them costs a tiny bit of extra CPU time. Worse, closures tend to rule out *inlining*, a key technique compilers use to eliminate function call overhead and enable a raft of other optimizations. All told, closures are slow enough in these languages that it can be worth manually removing them from tight inner loops.

Rust closures have none of these performance drawbacks. They're not garbage collected. Like everything else in Rust, they aren't allocated on the heap unless you put them in a `Box`, `Vec`, or other container. And since each closure has a distinct type, whenever the Rust compiler knows the type of the closure you're calling, it can inline the code for that particular closure. This makes it OK to use closures in tight loops, and Rust programs often do so, enthusiastically, as you'll see in Chapter 15.

Figure 14-1 shows how Rust closures are laid out in memory. At the top of the figure, we show a couple of local variables that our closures will refer to: a string `food` and a simple enum `weather`, whose numeric value happens to be 27.

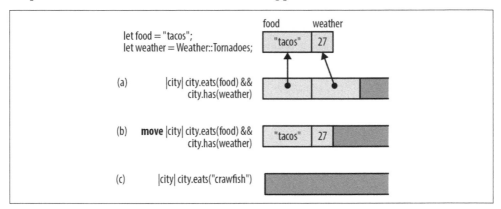

Figure 14-1. Layout of closures in memory

Closure (a) uses both variables. Apparently we're looking for cities that have both tacos and tornadoes. In memory, this closure looks like a small struct containing references to the variables it uses.

Note that it doesn't contain a pointer to its code! That's not necessary: as long as Rust knows the closure's type, it knows which code to run when you call it.

Closure (b) is exactly the same, except it's a `move` closure, so it contains values instead of references.

Closure (c) doesn't use any variables from its environment. The struct is empty, so this closure does not take up any memory at all.

As the figure shows, these closures don't take up much space. But even those few bytes are not always needed in practice. Often, the compiler can inline all calls to a closure, and then even the small structs shown in this figure are optimized away.

In "Callbacks" on page 341, we'll show how to allocate closures in the heap and call them dynamically, using trait objects. That is a bit slower, but it is still as fast as any other trait object method.

Closures and Safety

Throughout the chapter so far, we've talked about how Rust ensures that closures respect the language's safety rules when they borrow or move variables from the surrounding code. But there are some further consequences that are not exactly obvious. In this section, we'll explain a bit more about what happens when a closure drops or modifies a captured value.

Closures That Kill

We have seen closures that borrow values and closures that steal them; it was only a matter of time before they went all the way bad.

Of course, *kill* is not really the right terminology. In Rust, we *drop* values. The most straightforward way to do it is to call `drop()`:

```
let my_str = "hello".to_string();
let f = || drop(my_str);
```

When f is called, my_str is dropped.

So what happens if we call it twice?

```
f();
f();
```

Let's think it through. The first time we call f, it drops my_str, which means the memory where the string is stored is freed, returned to the system. The second time we call f, the same thing happens. It's a *double free*, a classic mistake in C++ programming that triggers undefined behavior.

Dropping a `String` twice would be an equally bad idea in Rust. Fortunately, Rust can't be fooled so easily:

```
f();  // ok
f();  // error: use of moved value
```

Rust knows this closure can't be called twice.

A closure that can be called only once may seem like a rather extraordinary thing, but we've been talking throughout this book about ownership and lifetimes. The idea of values being used up (that is, moved) is one of the core concepts in Rust. It works the same with closures as with everything else.

FnOnce

Let's try once more to trick Rust into dropping a `String` twice. This time, we'll use this generic function:

```
fn call_twice<F>(closure: F) where F: Fn() {
    closure();
    closure();
}
```

This generic function may be passed any closure that implements the trait `Fn()`: that is, closures that take no arguments and return (). (As with functions, the return type can be omitted if it's (); `Fn()` is shorthand for `Fn() -> ()`.)

Now what happens if we pass our unsafe closure to this generic function?

```
let my_str = "hello".to_string();
let f = || drop(my_str);
call_twice(f);
```

Again, the closure will drop my_str when it's called. Calling it twice would be a double free. But again, Rust is not fooled:

```
error: expected a closure that implements the `Fn` trait, but
      this closure only implements `FnOnce`
  |
8 |  let f = || drop(my_str);
  |          ^^^^^^^^^.......^
  |              |       |
  |              |       |    closure is `FnOnce` because it moves the variable `my_str`
  |              |       |    out of its environment
  |              |   this closure implements `FnOnce`, not `Fn`
9 |  call_twice(f);
  |  ---------- the requirement to implement `Fn` derives from here
```

This error message tells us more about how Rust handles "closures that kill." They could have been banned from the language entirely, but cleanup closures are useful sometimes. So instead, Rust restricts their use. Closures that drop values, like f, are not allowed to have Fn. They are, quite literally, no Fn at all. They implement a less powerful trait, FnOnce, the trait of closures that can be called once.

The first time you call a FnOnce closure, *the closure itself is used up.* It's as though the two traits, Fn and FnOnce, were defined like this:

```
// Pseudocode for `Fn` and `FnOnce` traits with no arguments.
trait Fn() -> R {
    fn call(&self) -> R;
}

trait FnOnce() -> R {
    fn call_once(self) -> R;
}
```

Just as an arithmetic expression like a + b is shorthand for a method call, Add::add(a, b), Rust treats closure() as shorthand for one of the two trait methods shown in the preceding example. For an Fn closure, closure() expands to closure.call(). This method takes self by reference, so the closure is not moved. But if the closure is only safe to call once, then closure() expands to closure.call_once(). That method takes self by value, so the closure is used up.

Of course we've been deliberately stirring up trouble here by using drop(). In practice, you'll mostly get into this situation by accident. It doesn't happen often, but once in a great while you'll write some closure code that unintentionally uses up a value:

```
let dict = produce_glossary();
let debug_dump_dict = || {
    for (key, value) in dict {  // oops!
        println!("{:?} - {:?}", key, value);
    }
};
```

Then, when you call `debug_dump_dict()` more than once, you'll get an error message like this:

```
error: use of moved value: `debug_dump_dict`
    |
19 |        debug_dump_dict();
    |        ----------------- `debug_dump_dict` moved due to this call
20 |        debug_dump_dict();
    |        ^^^^^^^^^^^^^^^^^ value used here after move
    |
note: closure cannot be invoked more than once because it moves the variable
`dict` out of its environment
    |
13 |            for (key, value) in dict {
    |                                ^^^^
```

To debug this, we have to figure out why the closure is an `FnOnce`. Which value is being used up here? The compiler helpfully points out that it's `dict`, which in this case is the only one we're referring to at all. Ah, there's the bug: we're using up `dict` by iterating over it directly. We should be looping over `&dict`, rather than plain `dict`, to access the values by reference:

```
let debug_dump_dict = || {
    for (key, value) in &dict {  // does not use up dict
        println!("{:?} - {:?}", key, value);
    }
};
```

This fixes the error; the function is now an `Fn` and can be called any number of times.

FnMut

There is one more kind of closure, the kind that contains mutable data or `mut` references.

Rust considers non-`mut` values safe to share across threads. But it wouldn't be safe to share non-`mut` closures that contain `mut` data: calling such a closure from multiple threads could lead to all sorts of race conditions as multiple threads try to read and write the same data at the same time.

Therefore, Rust has one more category of closure, `FnMut`, the category of closures that write. `FnMut` closures are called by `mut` reference, as if they were defined like this:

```
// Pseudocode for `Fn`, `FnMut`, and `FnOnce` traits.
trait Fn() -> R {
    fn call(&self) -> R;
}

trait FnMut() -> R {
    fn call_mut(&mut self) -> R;
}

trait FnOnce() -> R {
    fn call_once(self) -> R;
}
```

Any closure that requires mut access to a value, but doesn't drop any values, is an FnMut closure. For example:

```
let mut i = 0;
let incr = || {
    i += 1;  // incr borrows a mut reference to i
    println!("Ding! i is now: {}", i);
};
call_twice(incr);
```

The way we wrote call_twice, it requires an Fn. Since incr is an FnMut and not an Fn, this code fails to compile. There's an easy fix, though. To understand the fix, let's take a step back and summarize what you've learned about the three categories of Rust closures.

- Fn is the family of closures and functions that you can call multiple times without restriction. This highest category also includes all fn functions.

- FnMut is the family of closures that can be called multiple times if the closure itself is declared mut.

- FnOnce is the family of closures that can be called once, if the caller owns the closure.

Every Fn meets the requirements for FnMut, and every FnMut meets the requirements for FnOnce. As shown in Figure 14-2, they're not three separate categories.

Instead, Fn() is a subtrait of FnMut(), which is a subtrait of FnOnce(). This makes Fn the most exclusive and most powerful category. FnMut and FnOnce are broader categories that include closures with usage restrictions.

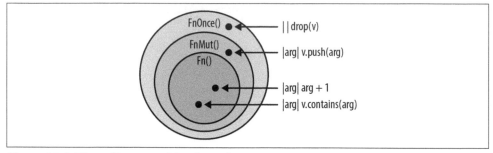

Figure 14-2. Venn diagram of the three closure categories

Now that we've organized what we know, it's clear that to accept the widest possible swath of closures, our `call_twice` function really ought to accept all `FnMut` closures, like this:

```
fn call_twice<F>(mut closure: F) where F: FnMut() {
    closure();
    closure();
}
```

The bound on the first line was `F: Fn()`, and now it's `F: FnMut()`. With this change, we still accept all `Fn` closures, and we additionally can use `call_twice` on closures that mutate data:

```
let mut i = 0;
call_twice(|| i += 1);   // ok!
assert_eq!(i, 2);
```

Copy and Clone for Closures

Just as Rust automatically figures out which closures can be called only once, it can figure out which closures can implement `Copy` and `Clone`, and which cannot.

As we explained earlier, closures are represented as structs that contain either the values (for `move` closures) or references to the values (for non-`move` closures) of the variables they capture. The rules for `Copy` and `Clone` on closures are just like the `Copy` and `Clone` rules for regular structs. A non-`move` closure that doesn't mutate variables holds only shared references, which are both `Clone` and `Copy`, so that closure is both `Clone` and `Copy` as well:

```
let y = 10;
let add_y = |x| x + y;
let copy_of_add_y = add_y;              // This closure is `Copy`, so...
assert_eq!(add_y(copy_of_add_y(22)), 42); // ... we can call both.
```

On the other hand, a non-move closure that *does* mutate values has mutable references within its internal representation. Mutable references are neither `Clone` nor `Copy`, so neither is a closure that uses them:

```
let mut x = 0;
let mut add_to_x = |n| { x += n; x };

let copy_of_add_to_x = add_to_x;        // this moves, rather than copies
assert_eq!(add_to_x(copy_of_add_to_x(1)), 2); // error: use of moved value
```

For a move closure, the rules are even simpler. If everything a move closure captures is `Copy`, it's `Copy`. If everything it captures is `Clone`, it's `Clone`. For instance:

```
let mut greeting = String::from("Hello, ");
let greet = move |name| {
    greeting.push_str(name);
    println!("{}", greeting);
};
greet.clone()("Alfred");
greet.clone()("Bruce");
```

This `.clone()(...)` syntax is a little weird, but it just means that we clone the closure and then call the clone. This program outputs:

```
Hello, Alfred
Hello, Bruce
```

When `greeting` is used in `greet`, it's moved into the struct that represents `greet` internally, because it's a move closure. So, when we clone `greet`, everything inside it is cloned, too. There are two copies of `greeting`, which are each modified separately when the clones of `greet` are called. This isn't so useful on its own, but when you need to pass the same closure into more than one function, it can be very helpful.

Callbacks

A lot of libraries use *callbacks* as part of their API: functions provided by the user, for the library to call later. In fact, you've seen some APIs like that already in this book. Back in Chapter 2, we used the `actix-web` framework to write a simple web server. One important part of that program was the router, which looked like this:

```
App::new()
    .route("/", web::get().to(get_index))
    .route("/gcd", web::post().to(post_gcd))
```

The purpose of the router is to route incoming requests from the internet to the bit of Rust code that handles that particular kind of request. In this example, `get_index` and `post_gcd` were the names of functions that we declared elsewhere in the program, using the `fn` keyword. But we could have passed closures instead, like this:

```
App::new()
    .route("/", web::get().to(|| {
        HttpResponse::Ok()
            .content_type("text/html")
            .body("<title>GCD Calculator</title>...")
    }))
    .route("/gcd", web::post().to(|form: web::Form<GcdParameters>| {
        HttpResponse::Ok()
            .content_type("text/html")
            .body(format!("The GCD of {} and {} is {}.",
                          form.n, form.m, gcd(form.n, form.m)))
    }))
```

This is because `actix-web` was written to accept any thread-safe `Fn` as an argument.

How can we do that in our own programs? Let's try writing our own very simple router from scratch, without using any code from `actix-web`. We can begin by declaring a few types to represent HTTP requests and responses:

```
struct Request {
    method: String,
    url: String,
    headers: HashMap<String, String>,
    body: Vec<u8>
}

struct Response {
    code: u32,
    headers: HashMap<String, String>,
    body: Vec<u8>
}
```

Now the job of a router is simply to store a table that maps URLs to callbacks so that the right callback can be called on demand. (For simplicity's sake, we'll only allow users to create routes that match a single exact URL.)

```
struct BasicRouter<C> where C: Fn(&Request) -> Response {
    routes: HashMap<String, C>
}

impl<C> BasicRouter<C> where C: Fn(&Request) -> Response {
    /// Create an empty router.
    fn new() -> BasicRouter<C> {
        BasicRouter { routes: HashMap::new() }
    }

    /// Add a route to the router.
    fn add_route(&mut self, url: &str, callback: C) {
        self.routes.insert(url.to_string(), callback);
    }
}
```

Unfortunately, we've made a mistake. Did you notice it?

This router works fine as long as we add only one route to it:

```
let mut router = BasicRouter::new();
router.add_route("/", |_| get_form_response());
```

This much compiles and runs. Unfortunately, if we add another route:

```
router.add_route("/gcd", |req| get_gcd_response(req));
```

then we get errors:

```
error: mismatched types
   |
41 |        router.add_route("/gcd", |req| get_gcd_response(req));
   |                                 ^^^^^^^^^^^^^^^^^^^^^^^^^^^^^
   |                                 expected closure, found a different closure
   |
   = note: expected type `[closure@closures_bad_router.rs:40:27: 40:50]`
              found type `[closure@closures_bad_router.rs:41:30: 41:57]`
note: no two closures, even if identical, have the same type
help: consider boxing your closure and/or using it as a trait object
```

Our mistake was in how we defined the BasicRouter type:

```
struct BasicRouter<C> where C: Fn(&Request) -> Response {
    routes: HashMap<String, C>
}
```

We unwittingly declared that each BasicRouter has a single callback type C, and all the callbacks in the HashMap are of that type. Back in "Which to Use" on page 264, we showed a Salad type that had the same problem:

```
struct Salad<V: Vegetable> {
    veggies: Vec<V>
}
```

The solution here is the same as for the salad: since we want to support a variety of types, we need to use boxes and trait objects:

```
type BoxedCallback = Box<dyn Fn(&Request) -> Response>;

struct BasicRouter {
    routes: HashMap<String, BoxedCallback>
}
```

Each box can contain a different type of closure, so a single HashMap can contain all sorts of callbacks. Note that the type parameter C is gone.

This requires a few adjustments to the methods:

```
impl BasicRouter {
    // Create an empty router.
    fn new() -> BasicRouter {
        BasicRouter { routes: HashMap::new() }
    }

    // Add a route to the router.
    fn add_route<C>(&mut self, url: &str, callback: C)
        where C: Fn(&Request) -> Response + 'static
    {
        self.routes.insert(url.to_string(), Box::new(callback));
    }
}
```

 Note the two bounds on C in the type signature for add_route: a particular Fn trait and the 'static lifetime. Rust makes us add this 'static bound. Without it, the call to Box::new(callback) would be an error, because it's not safe to store a closure if it contains borrowed references to variables that are about to go out of scope.

Finally, our simple router is ready to handle incoming requests:

```
impl BasicRouter {
    fn handle_request(&self, request: &Request) -> Response {
        match self.routes.get(&request.url) {
            None => not_found_response(),
            Some(callback) => callback(request)
        }
    }
}
```

At the cost of some flexibility, we could also write a more space-efficient version of this router that, rather than storing trait objects, uses *function pointers*, or fn types. These types, such as fn(u32) -> u32, act a lot like closures:

```
fn add_ten(x: u32) -> u32 {
    x + 10
}

let fn_ptr: fn(u32) -> u32 = add_ten;
let eleven = fn_ptr(1); //11
```

In fact, closures that don't capture anything from their environment are identical to function pointers, since they don't need to hold any extra information about captured variables. If you specify the appropriate fn type, either in a binding or in a function signature, the compiler is happy to let you use them that way:

```
let closure_ptr: fn(u32) -> u32 = |x| x + 1;
let two = closure_ptr(1); // 2
```

Unlike capturing closures, these function pointers take up only a single `usize`.

A routing table that holds function pointers would look like this:

```
struct FnPointerRouter {
    routes: HashMap<String, fn(&Request) -> Response>
}
```

Here, the `HashMap` is storing just a single `usize` per `String`, and critically, there's no `Box`. Aside from the `HashMap` itself, there's no dynamic allocation at all. Of course, the methods need to be adjusted as well:

```
impl FnPointerRouter {
    // Create an empty router.
    fn new() -> FnPointerRouter {
        FnPointerRouter { routes: HashMap::new() }
    }

    // Add a route to the router.
    fn add_route(&mut self, url: &str, callback: fn(&Request) -> Response)
    {
        self.routes.insert(url.to_string(), callback);
    }
}
```

As laid out in Figure 14-1, closures have unique types because each one captures different variables, so among other things, they're each a different size. If they don't capture anything, though, there's nothing to store. By using `fn` pointers in functions that take callbacks, you can restrict a caller to use only these noncapturing closures, gaining some perfomance and flexibility within the code using callbacks at the cost of flexibility for the users of your API.

Using Closures Effectively

As we've seen, Rust's closures are different from closures in most other languages. The biggest difference is that in languages with GC, you can use local variables in a closure without having to think about lifetimes or ownership. Without GC, things are different. Some design patterns that are commonplace in Java, C#, and JavaScript won't work in Rust without changes.

For example, take the Model-View-Controller design pattern (MVC for short), illustrated in Figure 14-3. For every element of a user interface, an MVC framework creates three objects: a *model* representing that UI element's state, a *view* that's responsible for its appearance, and a *controller* that handles user interaction. Countless variations on MVC have been implemented over the years, but the general idea is that three objects divvy up the UI responsibilities somehow.

Here's the problem. Typically, each object has a reference to one or both of the others, directly or through a callback, as shown in Figure 14-3. Whenever anything happens to one of the objects, it notifies the others, so everything updates promptly. The question of which object "owns" the others never comes up.

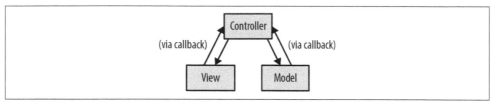

Figure 14-3. The Model-View-Controller design pattern

You can't implement this pattern in Rust without making some changes. Ownership must be made explicit, and reference cycles must be eliminated. The model and the controller can't have direct references to each other.

Rust's radical wager is that good alternative designs exist. Sometimes you can fix a problem with closure ownership and lifetimes by having each closure receive the references it needs as arguments. Sometimes you can assign each thing in the system a number and pass around the numbers instead of references. Or you can implement one of the many variations on MVC where the objects don't all have references to each other. Or model your toolkit after a non-MVC system with unidirectional data flow, like Facebook's Flux architecture, shown in Figure 14-4.

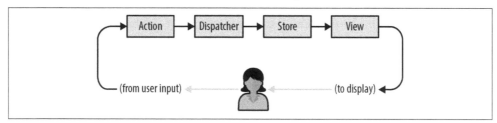

Figure 14-4. The Flux architecture, an alternative to MVC

In short, if you try to use Rust closures to make a "sea of objects," you're going to have a hard time. But there are alternatives. In this case, it seems software engineering as a discipline is already gravitating to the alternatives anyway, because they're simpler.

In the next chapter, we turn to a topic where closures really shine. We'll be writing a kind of code that takes full advantage of the concision, speed, and efficiency of Rust closures and that's fun to write, easy to read, and eminently practical. Up next: Rust iterators.

## CHAPTER 15

Iterators

It was the end of a very long day.
    —Phil

An *iterator* is a value that produces a sequence of values, typically for a loop to operate on. Rust's standard library provides iterators that traverse vectors, strings, hash tables, and other collections, but also iterators to produce lines of text from an input stream, connections arriving at a network server, values received from other threads over a communications channel, and so on. And of course, you can implement iterators for your own purposes. Rust's for loop provides a natural syntax for using iterators, but iterators themselves also provide a rich set of methods for mapping, filtering, joining, collecting, and so on.

Rust's iterators are flexible, expressive, and efficient. Consider the following function, which returns the sum of the first n positive integers (often called the *nth triangle number*):

```
fn triangle(n: i32) -> i32 {
    let mut sum = 0;
    for i in 1..=n {
        sum += i;
    }
    sum
}
```

The expression 1..=n is a RangeInclusive<i32> value. A RangeInclusive<i32> is an iterator that produces the integers from its start value to its end value (both inclusive), so you can use it as the operand of the for loop to sum the values from 1 to n.

But iterators also have a `fold` method, which you can use in the equivalent definition:

```
fn triangle(n: i32) -> i32 {
    (1..=n).fold(0, |sum, item| sum + item)
}
```

Starting with `0` as the running total, `fold` takes each value that `1..=n` produces and applies the closure `|sum, item| sum + item` to the running total and the value. The closure's return value is taken as the new running total. The last value it returns is what `fold` itself returns—in this case, the total of the entire sequence. This may look strange if you're used to `for` and `while` loops, but once you've gotten used to it, `fold` is a legible and concise alternative.

This is pretty standard fare for functional programming languages, which put a premium on expressiveness. But Rust's iterators were carefully designed to ensure that the compiler can translate them into excellent machine code as well. In a release build of the second definition shown before, Rust knows the definition of `fold` and inlines it into `triangle`. Next, the closure `|sum, item| sum + item` is inlined into that. Finally, Rust examines the combined code and recognizes that there's a simpler way to sum the numbers from one to n: the sum is always equal to `n * (n+1) / 2`. Rust translates the entire body of `triangle`, loop, closure, and all, into a single multiplication instruction and a few other bits of arithmetic.

This example happens to involve simple arithmetic, but iterators also perform well when put to heavier use. They're another example of Rust providing flexible abstractions that impose little or no overhead in typical use.

In this chapter, we'll explain:

- The `Iterator` and `IntoIterator` traits, which are the foundation of Rust's iterators
- The three stages of a typical iterator pipeline: creating an iterator from some sort of value source; adapting one sort of iterator into another by selecting or processing values as they go by; and then consuming the values the iterator produces
- How to implement iterators for your own types

There are a lot of methods, so it's fine to skim a section once you've got the general idea. But iterators are very common in idiomatic Rust, and being familiar with the tools that come with them is essential to mastering the language.

The Iterator and IntoIterator Traits

An iterator is any value that implements the `std::iter::Iterator` trait:

```
trait Iterator {
    type Item;
    fn next(&mut self) -> Option<Self::Item>;
    ... // many default methods
}
```

`Item` is the type of value the iterator produces. The `next` method either returns `Some(v)`, where `v` is the iterator's next value, or returns `None` to indicate the end of the sequence. Here we've omitted `Iterator`'s many default methods; we'll cover them individually throughout the rest of this chapter.

If there's a natural way to iterate over some type, that type can implement `std::iter::IntoIterator`, whose `into_iter` method takes a value and returns an iterator over it:

```
trait IntoIterator where Self::IntoIter: Iterator<Item=Self::Item> {
    type Item;
    type IntoIter: Iterator;
    fn into_iter(self) -> Self::IntoIter;
}
```

`IntoIter` is the type of the iterator value itself, and `Item` is the type of value it produces. We call any type that implements `IntoIterator` an *iterable*, because it's something you could iterate over if you asked.

Rust's for loop brings all these parts together nicely. To iterate over a vector's elements, you can write:

```
println!("There's:");
let v = vec!["antimony", "arsenic", "aluminum", "selenium"];

for element in &v {
    println!("{}", element);
}
```

Under the hood, every for loop is just shorthand for calls to `IntoIterator` and `Iterator` methods:

```
let mut iterator = (&v).into_iter();
while let Some(element) = iterator.next() {
    println!("{}", element);
}
```

The for loop uses `IntoIterator::into_iter` to convert its operand `&v` into an iterator and then calls `Iterator::next` repeatedly. Each time that returns `Some(element)`, the for loop executes its body; and if it returns `None`, the loop finishes.

With this example in mind, here's some terminology for iterators:

- As we've said, an *iterator* is any type that implements `Iterator`.
- An *iterable* is any type that implements `IntoIterator`: you can get an iterator over it by calling its `into_iter` method. The vector reference `&v` is the iterable in this case.
- An iterator *produces* values.
- The values an iterator produces are *items*. Here, the items are `"antimony"`, `"arsenic"`, and so on.
- The code that receives the items an iterator produces is the *consumer*. In this example, the `for` loop is the consumer.

Although a `for` loop always calls `into_iter` on its operand, you can also pass iterators to `for` loops directly; this occurs when you loop over a `Range`, for example. All iterators automatically implement `IntoIterator`, with an `into_iter` method that simply returns the iterator.

If you call an iterator's `next` method again after it has returned `None`, the `Iterator` trait doesn't specify what it should do. Most iterators will just return `None` again, but not all. (If this causes problems, the `fuse` adapter covered in "fuse" on page 367 can help.)

Creating Iterators

The Rust standard library documentation explains in detail what sort of iterators each type provides, but the library follows some general conventions to help you get oriented and find what you need.

iter and iter_mut Methods

Most collection types provide `iter` and `iter_mut` methods that return the natural iterators over the type, producing a shared or mutable reference to each item. Array slices like `&[T]` and `&mut [T]` have `iter` and `iter_mut` methods too. These methods are the most common way to get an iterator, if you're not going to let a `for` loop take care of it for you:

```
let v = vec![4, 20, 12, 8, 6];
let mut iterator = v.iter();
assert_eq!(iterator.next(), Some(&4));
assert_eq!(iterator.next(), Some(&20));
assert_eq!(iterator.next(), Some(&12));
assert_eq!(iterator.next(), Some(&8));
assert_eq!(iterator.next(), Some(&6));
assert_eq!(iterator.next(), None);
```

This iterator's item type is &i32: each call to `next` produces a reference to the next element, until we reach the end of the vector.

Each type is free to implement `iter` and `iter_mut` in whatever way makes the most sense for its purpose. The `iter` method on `std::path::Path` returns an iterator that produces one path component at a time:

```
use std::ffi::OsStr;
use std::path::Path;

let path = Path::new("C:/Users/JimB/Downloads/Fedora.iso");
let mut iterator = path.iter();
assert_eq!(iterator.next(), Some(OsStr::new("C:")));
assert_eq!(iterator.next(), Some(OsStr::new("Users")));
assert_eq!(iterator.next(), Some(OsStr::new("JimB")));
...
```

This iterator's item type is `&std::ffi::OsStr`, a borrowed slice of a string of the sort accepted by operating system calls.

If there's more than one common way to iterate over a type, the type usually provides specific methods for each sort of traversal, since a plain `iter` method would be ambiguous. For example, there is no `iter` method on the `&str` string slice type. Instead, if `s` is a `&str`, then `s.bytes()` returns an iterator that produces each byte of `s`, whereas `s.chars()` interprets the contents as UTF-8 and produces each Unicode character.

IntoIterator Implementations

When a type implements `IntoIterator`, you can call its `into_iter` method yourself, just as a `for` loop would:

```
// You should usually use HashSet, but its iteration order is
// nondeterministic, so BTreeSet works better in examples.
use std::collections::BTreeSet;
let mut favorites = BTreeSet::new();
favorites.insert("Lucy in the Sky With Diamonds".to_string());
favorites.insert("Liebesträume No. 3".to_string());

let mut it = favorites.into_iter();
assert_eq!(it.next(), Some("Liebesträume No. 3".to_string()));
assert_eq!(it.next(), Some("Lucy in the Sky With Diamonds".to_string()));
assert_eq!(it.next(), None);
```

Most collections actually provide several implementations of `IntoIterator`, for shared references (&T), mutable references (&mut T), and moves (T):

- Given a *shared reference* to the collection, `into_iter` returns an iterator that produces shared references to its items. For example, in the preceding code, `(&favorites).into_iter()` would return an iterator whose `Item` type is `&String`.

- Given a *mutable reference* to the collection, `into_iter` returns an iterator that produces mutable references to the items. For example, if `vector` is some `Vec<String>`, the call `(&mut vector).into_iter()` returns an iterator whose `Item` type is `&mut String`.

- When passed the collection *by value*, `into_iter` returns an iterator that takes ownership of the collection and returns items by value; the items' ownership moves from the collection to the consumer, and the original collection is consumed in the process. For example, the call `favorites.into_iter()` in the preceding code returns an iterator that produces each string by value; the consumer receives ownership of each string. When the iterator is dropped, any elements remaining in the `BTreeSet` are dropped too, and the set's now-empty husk is disposed of.

Since a `for` loop applies `IntoIterator::into_iter` to its operand, these three implementations are what create the following idioms for iterating over shared or mutable references to a collection, or consuming the collection and taking ownership of its elements:

```
for element in &collection { ... }
for element in &mut collection { ... }
for element in collection { ... }
```

Each of these simply results in a call to one of the `IntoIterator` implementations listed here.

Not every type provides all three implementations. For example, `HashSet`, `BTreeSet`, and `BinaryHeap` don't implement `IntoIterator` on mutable references, since modifying their elements would probably violate the type's invariants: the modified value might have a different hash value, or be ordered differently with respect to its neighbors, so modifying it would leave it incorrectly placed. Other types do support mutation, but only partially. For example, `HashMap` and `BTreeMap` produce mutable reference to their entries' values, but only shared references to their keys, for similar reasons to those given earlier.

The general principle is that iteration should be efficient and predictable, so rather than providing implementations that are expensive or could exhibit surprising behavior (for example, rehashing modified `HashSet` entries and potentially encountering them again later in the iteration), Rust omits them entirely.

Slices implement two of the three `IntoIterator` variants; since they don't own their elements, there is no "by value" case. Instead, `into_iter` for `&[T]` and `&mut [T]` returns an iterator that produces shared and mutable references to the elements. If you imagine the underlying slice type `[T]` as a collection of some sort, this fits neatly into the overall pattern.

You may have noticed that the first two `IntoIterator` variants, for shared and mutable references, are equivalent to calling `iter` or `iter_mut` on the referent. Why does Rust provide both?

`IntoIterator` is what makes `for` loops work, so that's obviously necessary. But when you're not using a `for` loop, it's clearer to write `favorites.iter()` than `(&favorites).into_iter()`. Iteration by shared reference is something you'll need frequently, so `iter` and `iter_mut` are still valuable for their ergonomics.

`IntoIterator` can also be useful in generic code: you can use a bound like `T: IntoIterator` to restrict the type variable `T` to types that can be iterated over. Or, you can write `T: IntoIterator<Item=U>` to further require the iteration to produce a particular type `U`. For example, this function dumps values from any iterable whose items are printable with the `"{:?}"` format:

```
use std::fmt::Debug;

fn dump<T, U>(t: T)
    where T: IntoIterator<Item=U>,
          U: Debug
{
    for u in t {
        println!("{:?}", u);
    }
}
```

You can't write this generic function using `iter` and `iter_mut`, since they're not methods of any trait: most iterable types just happen to have methods by those names.

from_fn and successors

One simple and general way to produce a sequence of values is to provide a closure that returns them.

Given a function returning `Option<T>`, `std::iter::from_fn` returns an iterator that simply calls the function to produce its items. For example:

```
use rand::random; // In Cargo.toml dependencies: rand = "0.7"
use std::iter::from_fn;

// Generate the lengths of 1000 random line segments whose endpoints
// are uniformly distributed across the interval [0, 1]. (This isn't a
// distribution you're going to find in the `rand_distr` crate, but
// it's easy to make yourself.)
let lengths: Vec<f64> =
    from_fn(|| Some((random::<f64>() - random::<f64>()).abs()))
    .take(1000)
    .collect();
```

This calls `from_fn` to make an iterator producing random numbers. Since the iterator always returns `Some`, the sequence never ends, but we call `take(1000)` to limit it to the first 1,000 elements. Then `collect` builds the vector from the resulting iteration. This is an efficient way of constructing initialized vectors; we explain why in "Building Collections: collect and FromIterator" on page 384, later in this chapter.

If each item depends on the one before, the `std::iter::successors` function works nicely. You provide an initial item and a function that takes one item and returns an `Option` of the next. If it returns `None`, the iteration ends. For example, here's another way to write the `escape_time` function from our Mandelbrot set plotter in Chapter 2:

```
use num::Complex;
use std::iter::successors;

fn escape_time(c: Complex<f64>, limit: usize) -> Option<usize> {
    let zero = Complex { re: 0.0, im: 0.0 };
    successors(Some(zero), |&z| { Some(z * z + c) })
        .take(limit)
        .enumerate()
        .find(|(_i, z)| z.norm_sqr() > 4.0)
        .map(|(i, _z)| i)
}
```

Starting with zero, the `successors` call produces a sequence of points on the complex plane by repeatedly squaring the last point and adding the parameter `c`. When plotting the Mandelbrot set, we want to see whether this sequence orbits near the origin forever or flies away to infinity. The call `take(limit)` establishes a limit on how long we'll chase the sequence, and `enumerate` numbers each point, turning each point `z` into a tuple `(i, z)`. We use `find` to look for the first point that gets far enough away from the origin to escape. The `find` method returns an `Option`: `Some((i, z))` if one exists, or `None` otherwise. The call to `Option::map` turns `Some((i, z))` into `Some(i)`, but returns `None` unchanged: this is exactly the return value we want.

Both from_fn and successors accept FnMut closures, so your closures can capture and modify variables from the surrounding scopes. For example, this fibonacci function uses a move closure to capture a variable and use it as its running state:

```
fn fibonacci() -> impl Iterator<Item=usize> {
    let mut state = (0, 1);
    std::iter::from_fn(move || {
        state = (state.1, state.0 + state.1);
        Some(state.0)
    })
}

assert_eq!(fibonacci().take(8).collect::<Vec<_>>(),
           vec![1, 1, 2, 3, 5, 8, 13, 21]);
```

A note of caution: the from_fn and successors methods are flexible enough that you could turn pretty much any use of iterators into a single call to one or the other, passing complex closures to get the behavior you need. But doing so neglects the opportunity that iterators provide to clarify how data flows through the computation and use standard names for common patterns. Make sure you've familiarized yourself with the other iterator methods in this chapter before you lean on these two; there are often nicer ways to get the job done.

drain Methods

Many collection types provide a drain method that takes a mutable reference to the collection and returns an iterator that passes ownership of each element to the consumer. However, unlike the into_iter() method, which takes the collection by value and consumes it, drain merely borrows a mutable reference to the collection, and when the iterator is dropped, it removes any remaining elements from the collection and leaves it empty.

On types that can be indexed by a range, like Strings, vectors, and VecDeques, the drain method takes a range of elements to remove, rather than draining the entire sequence:

```
let mut outer = "Earth".to_string();
let inner = String::from_iter(outer.drain(1..4));

assert_eq!(outer, "Eh");
assert_eq!(inner, "art");
```

If you do need to drain the entire sequence, use the full range, .., as the argument.

Other Iterator Sources

The previous sections are mostly concerned with collection types like vectors and
HashMap, but there are many other types in the standard library that support iteration.
Table 15-1 summarizes the more interesting ones, but there are many more. We cover
some of these methods in more detail in the chapters dedicated to the specific types
(namely, Chapters 16, 17, and 18).

Table 15-1. Other iterators in the standard library

Type or trait	Expression	Notes
std::ops::Range	1..10	Endpoints must be an integer type to be iterable. Range includes start value and excludes end value.
	(1..10).step_by(2)	Produces 1, 3, 5, 7, 9.
std::ops::RangeFrom	1..	Unbounded iteration. Start must be an integer. May panic or overflow if the value reaches the limit of the type.
std::ops::RangeInclusive	1..=10	Like Range, but includes end value.
Option<T>	Some(10).iter()	Behaves like a vector whose length is either 0 (None) or 1 (Some(v)).
Result<T, E>	Ok("blah").iter()	Similar to Option, producing Ok values.
Vec<T>, &[T]	v.windows(16)	Produces every contiguous slice of the given length, from left to right. The windows overlap.
	v.chunks(16)	Produces nonoverlapping, contiguous slices of the given length, from left to right.
	v.chunks_mut(1024)	Like chunks, but slices are mutable.
	v.split(|byte| byte & 1 != 0)	Produces slices separated by elements that match the given predicate.
	v.split_mut(...)	As above, but produces mutable slices.
	v.rsplit(...)	Like split, but produces slices from right to left.
	v.splitn(n, ...)	Like split, but produces at most n slices.

Type or trait	Expression	Notes
String, &str	s.bytes()	Produces the bytes of the UTF-8 form.
	s.chars()	Produces the chars the UTF-8 represents.
	s.split_whitespace()	Splits string by whitespace, and produces slices of nonspace characters.
	s.lines()	Produces slices of the lines of the string.
	s.split('/')	Splits string on a given pattern, producing the slices between matches. Patterns can be many things: characters, strings, closures.
	s.matches(char::is_numeric)	Produces slices matching the given pattern.
std::collections::HashMap, std::collections::BTreeMap	map.keys(), map.values()	Produces shared references to keys or values of the map.
	map.values_mut()	Produces mutable references to entries' values.
std::collections::HashSet, std::collections::BTreeSet	set1.union(set2)	Produces shared references to elements of union of set1 and set2.
	set1.intersection(set2)	Produces shared references to elements of intersection of set1 and set2.
std::sync::mpsc::Receiver	recv.iter()	Produces values sent from another thread on the corresponding Sender.
std::io::Read	stream.bytes()	Produces bytes from an I/O stream.
	stream.chars()	Parses stream as UTF-8 and produces chars.
std::io::BufRead	bufstream.lines()	Parses stream as UTF-8, produces lines as Strings.
	bufstream.split(0)	Splits stream on given byte, produces inter-byte Vec<u8> buffers.
std::fs::ReadDir	std::fs::read_dir(path)	Produces directory entries.
std::net::TcpListener	listener.incoming()	Produces incoming network connections.

Type or trait	Expression	Notes
Free functions	`std::iter::empty()`	Returns None immediately.
	`std::iter::once(5)`	Produces the given value and then ends.
	`std::iter::repeat("#9")`	Produces the given value forever.

Iterator Adapters

Once you have an iterator in hand, the `Iterator` trait provides a broad selection of *adapter methods*, or simply *adapters*, that consume one iterator and build a new one with useful behaviors. To see how adapters work, we'll start with two of the most popular adapters, `map` and `filter`. Then we'll cover the rest of the adapter toolbox, covering almost any way you can imagine to make sequences of values from other sequences: truncation, skipping, combination, reversal, concatenation, repetition, and more.

map and filter

The `Iterator` trait's `map` adapter lets you transform an iterator by applying a closure to its items. The `filter` adapter lets you filter out items from an iterator, using a closure to decide which to keep and which to drop.

For example, suppose you're iterating over lines of text and want to omit leading and trailing whitespace from each line. The standard library's `str::trim` method drops leading and trailing whitespace from a single `&str`, returning a new, trimmed `&str` that borrows from the original. You can use the `map` adapter to apply `str::trim` to each line from the iterator:

```
let text = "  ponies  \n   giraffes\niguanas  \nsquid".to_string();
let v: Vec<&str> = text.lines()
    .map(str::trim)
    .collect();
assert_eq!(v, ["ponies", "giraffes", "iguanas", "squid"]);
```

The `text.lines()` call returns an iterator that produces the string's lines. Calling `map` on that iterator returns a second iterator that applies `str::trim` to each line and produces the results as its items. Finally, `collect` gathers those items into a vector.

The iterator that `map` returns is, of course, itself a candidate for further adaptation. If you want to exclude iguanas from the result, you can write the following:

```
let text = "  ponies \n   giraffes\niguanas  \nsquid".to_string();
let v: Vec<&str> = text.lines()
    .map(str::trim)
    .filter(|s| *s != "iguanas")
    .collect();
assert_eq!(v, ["ponies", "giraffes", "squid"]);
```

Here, `filter` returns a third iterator that produces only those items from the `map` iterator for which the closure `|s| *s != "iguanas"` returns `true`. A chain of iterator adapters is like a pipeline in the Unix shell: each adapter has a single purpose, and it's clear how the sequence is being transformed as one reads from left to right.

These adapters' signatures are as follows:

```
fn map<B, F>(self, f: F) -> impl Iterator<Item=B>
    where Self: Sized, F: FnMut(Self::Item) -> B;

fn filter<P>(self, predicate: P) -> impl Iterator<Item=Self::Item>
    where Self: Sized, P: FnMut(&Self::Item) -> bool;
```

In the standard library, `map` and `filter` actually return specific opaque `struct` types named `std::iter::Map` and `std::iter::Filter`. However, just seeing their names is not very informative, so in this book, we're just going to write `-> impl Iterator<Item=...>` instead, since that tells us what we really want to know: the method returns an `Iterator` that produces items of the given type.

Since most adapters take `self` by value, they require `Self` to be `Sized` (which all common iterators are).

A `map` iterator passes each item to its closure by value and, in turn, passes along ownership of the closure's result to its consumer. A `filter` iterator passes each item to its closure by shared reference, retaining ownership in case the item is selected to be passed on to its consumer. This is why the example must dereference `s` to compare it with `"iguanas"`: the `filter` iterator's item type is `&str`, so the type of the closure's argument `s` is `&&str`.

There are two important points to notice about iterator adapters.

First, simply calling an adapter on an iterator doesn't consume any items; it just returns a new iterator, ready to produce its own items by drawing from the first iterator as needed. In a chain of adapters, the only way to make any work actually get done is to call `next` on the final iterator.

So in our earlier example, the method call `text.lines()` itself doesn't actually parse any lines from the string; it just returns an iterator that *would* parse lines if asked. Similarly, `map` and `filter` just return new iterators that *would* map or filter if asked. No work takes place until `collect` starts calling `next` on the `filter` iterator.

This point is especially important if you use adapters that have side effects. For example, this code prints nothing at all:

```
["earth", "water", "air", "fire"]
    .iter().map(|elt| println!("{}", elt));
```

The `iter` call returns an iterator over the array's elements, and the `map` call returns a second iterator that applies the closure to each value the first produces. But there is nothing here that ever actually demands a value from the whole chain, so no `next` method ever runs. In fact, Rust will warn you about this:

```
warning: unused `std::iter::Map` that must be used
  |
7 | /     ["earth", "water", "air", "fire"]
8 | |         .iter().map(|elt| println!("{}", elt));
  | |_____^
  |
  = note: iterators are lazy and do nothing unless consumed
```

The term "lazy" in the error message is not a disparaging term; it's just jargon for any mechanism that puts off a computation until its value is needed. It is Rust's convention that iterators should do the minimum work necessary to satisfy each call to `next`; in the example, there are no such calls at all, so no work takes place.

The second important point is that iterator adapters are a zero-overhead abstraction. Since `map`, `filter`, and their companions are generic, applying them to an iterator specializes their code for the specific iterator type involved. This means that Rust has enough information to inline each iterator's `next` method into its consumer and then translate the entire arrangement into machine code as a unit. So the `lines`/`map`/ `filter` chain of iterators we showed before is as efficient as the code you would probably write by hand:

```
for line in text.lines() {
    let line = line.trim();
    if line != "iguanas" {
        v.push(line);
    }
}
```

The rest of this section covers the various adapters available on the `Iterator` trait.

filter_map and flat_map

The map adapter is fine in situations where each incoming item produces one outgoing item. But what if you want to delete certain items from the iteration instead of processing them or replace single items with zero or more items? The filter_map and flat_map adapters grant you this flexibility.

The filter_map adapter is similar to map except that it lets its closure either transform the item into a new item (as map does) or drop the item from the iteration. Thus, it's a bit like a combination of filter and map. Its signature is as follows:

```
fn filter_map<B, F>(self, f: F) -> impl Iterator<Item=B>
    where Self: Sized, F: FnMut(Self::Item) -> Option<B>;
```

This is the same as map's signature, except that here the closure returns Option<B>, not simply B. When the closure returns None, the item is dropped from the iteration; when it returns Some(b), then b is the next item the filter_map iterator produces.

For example, suppose you want to scan a string for whitespace-separated words that can be parsed as numbers, and process the numbers, dropping the other words. You can write:

```
use std::str::FromStr;

let text = "1\nfrond .25  289\n3.1415 estuary\n";
for number in text
    .split_whitespace()
    .filter_map(|w| f64::from_str(w).ok())
{
    println!("{:4.2}", number.sqrt());
}
```

This prints the following:

```
1.00
0.50
17.00
1.77
```

The closure given to filter_map tries to parse each whitespace-separated slice using f64::from_str. That returns a Result<f64, ParseFloatError>, which .ok() turns into an Option<f64>: a parse error becomes None, whereas a successful parse result becomes Some(v). The filter_map iterator drops all the None values and produces the value v for each Some(v).

But what's the point in fusing map and filter into a single operation like this, instead of just using those adapters directly? The filter_map adapter shows its value in situations like the one just shown, when the best way to decide whether to include the item in the iteration is to actually try to process it. You can do the same thing with only `filter` and `map`, but it's a bit ungainly:

```
text.split_whitespace()
    .map(|w| f64::from_str(w))
    .filter(|r| r.is_ok())
    .map(|r| r.unwrap())
```

You can think of the `flat_map` adapter as continuing in the same vein as `map` and `filter_map`, except that now the closure can return not just one item (as with `map`) or zero or one items (as with `filter_map`), but a sequence of any number of items. The `flat_map` iterator produces the concatenation of the sequences the closure returns.

The signature of `flat_map` is shown here:

```
fn flat_map<U, F>(self, f: F) -> impl Iterator<Item=U::Item>
    where F: FnMut(Self::Item) -> U, U: IntoIterator;
```

The closure passed to `flat_map` must return an iterable, but any sort of iterable will do.[1]

For example, suppose we have a table mapping countries to their major cities. Given a list of countries, how can we iterate over their major cities?

```
use std::collections::HashMap;

let mut major_cities = HashMap::new();
major_cities.insert("Japan", vec!["Tokyo", "Kyoto"]);
major_cities.insert("The United States", vec!["Portland", "Nashville"]);
major_cities.insert("Brazil", vec!["São Paulo", "Brasília"]);
major_cities.insert("Kenya", vec!["Nairobi", "Mombasa"]);
major_cities.insert("The Netherlands", vec!["Amsterdam", "Utrecht"]);

let countries = ["Japan", "Brazil", "Kenya"];

for &city in countries.iter().flat_map(|country| &major_cities[country]) {
    println!("{}", city);
}
```

This prints the following:

```
Tokyo
Kyoto
São Paulo
Brasília
Nairobi
Mombasa
```

---

1 In fact, since `Option` is an iterable behaving like a sequence of zero or one items, `iterator.filter_map` (closure) is equivalent to `iterator.flat_map(closure)`, assuming closure returns an `Option<T>`.

One way to look at this would be to say that, for each country, we retrieve the vector of its cities, concatenate all the vectors together into a single sequence, and print that.

But remember that iterators are lazy: it's only the for loop's calls to the flat_map iterator's next method that cause work to be done. The full concatenated sequence is never constructed in memory. Instead, what we have here is a little state machine that draws from the city iterator, one item at a time, until it's exhausted, and only then produces a new city iterator for the next country. The effect is that of a nested loop, but packaged up for use as an iterator.

flatten

The flatten adapter concatenates an iterator's items, assuming each item is itself an iterable:

```
use std::collections::BTreeMap;

// A table mapping cities to their parks: each value is a vector.
let mut parks = BTreeMap::new();
parks.insert("Portland",  vec!["Mt. Tabor Park", "Forest Park"]);
parks.insert("Kyoto",     vec!["Tadasu-no-Mori Forest", "Maruyama Koen"]);
parks.insert("Nashville", vec!["Percy Warner Park", "Dragon Park"]);

// Build a vector of all parks. `values` gives us an iterator producing
// vectors, and then `flatten` produces each vector's elements in turn.
let all_parks: Vec<_> = parks.values().flatten().cloned().collect();

assert_eq!(all_parks,
           vec!["Tadasu-no-Mori Forest", "Maruyama Koen", "Percy Warner Park",
                "Dragon Park", "Mt. Tabor Park", "Forest Park"]);
```

The name "flatten" comes from the image of flattening a two-level structure into a one-level structure: the BTreeMap and its Vecs of names are flattened into an iterator producing all the names.

The signature of flatten is as follows:

```
fn flatten(self) -> impl Iterator<Item=Self::Item::Item>
    where Self::Item: IntoIterator;
```

In other words, the underlying iterator's items must themselves implement IntoIterator so that it is effectively a sequence of sequences. The flatten method then returns an iterator over the concatenation of those sequences. Of course, this is done lazily, drawing a new item from self only when we're done iterating over the last one.

The flatten method gets used in a few surprising ways. If you have a Vec<Option<...>> and you want to iterate over only the Some values, flatten works beautifully:

```
assert_eq!(vec![None, Some("day"), None, Some("one")]
            .into_iter()
            .flatten()
            .collect::<Vec<_>>(),
        vec!["day", "one"]);
```

This works because Option itself implements IntoIterator, representing a sequence of either zero or one elements. The None elements contribute nothing to the iteration, whereas each Some element contributes a single value. Similarly, you can use flatten to iterate over Option<Vec<...>> values: None behaves the same as an empty vector.

Result also implements IntoIterator, with Err representing an empty sequence, so applying flatten to an iterator of Result values effectively squeezes out all the Errs and throws them away, resulting in a stream of the unwrapped success values. We do not recommend ignoring errors in your code, but this is a neat trick people use when they think they know what's going on.

You may find yourself reaching for flatten when what you actually need is flat_map. For example, the standard library's str::to_uppercase method, which converts a string to uppercase, works something like this:

```
fn to_uppercase(&self) -> String {
    self.chars()
        .map(char::to_uppercase)
        .flatten() // there's a better way
        .collect()
}
```

The reason the flatten is necessary is that ch.to_uppercase() returns not a single character, but an iterator producing one or more characters. Mapping each character to its uppercase equivalent results in an iterator of iterators of characters, and the flatten takes care of splicing them all together into something we can finally collect into a String.

But this combination of map and flatten is so common that Iterator provides the flat_map adapter for just that case. (In fact, flat_map was added to the standard library before flatten.) So the preceding code could instead be written:

```
fn to_uppercase(&self) -> String {
    self.chars()
        .flat_map(char::to_uppercase)
        .collect()
}
```

take and take_while

The `Iterator` trait's `take` and `take_while` adapters let you end an iteration after a certain number of items or when a closure decides to cut things off. Their signatures are as follows:

```
fn take(self, n: usize) -> impl Iterator<Item=Self::Item>
    where Self: Sized;

fn take_while<P>(self, predicate: P) -> impl Iterator<Item=Self::Item>
    where Self: Sized, P: FnMut(&Self::Item) -> bool;
```

Both take ownership of an iterator and return a new iterator that passes along items from the first one, possibly ending the sequence earlier. The `take` iterator returns `None` after producing at most n items. The `take_while` iterator applies `predicate` to each item and returns `None` in place of the first item for which `predicate` returns `false` and on every subsequent call to `next`.

For example, given an email message with a blank line separating the headers from the message body, you can use `take_while` to iterate over only the headers:

```
let message = "To: jimb\r\n\
               From: superego <editor@oreilly.com>\r\n\
               \r\n\
               Did you get any writing done today?\r\n\
               When will you stop wasting time plotting fractals?\r\n";
for header in message.lines().take_while(|l| !l.is_empty()) {
    println!("{}" , header);
}
```

Recall from "String Literals" on page 73 that when a line in a string ends with a backslash, Rust doesn't include the indentation of the next line in the string, so none of the lines in the string has any leading whitespace. This means that the third line of `message` is blank. The `take_while` adapter terminates the iteration as soon as it sees that blank line, so this code prints only the two lines:

```
To: jimb
From: superego <editor@oreilly.com>
```

skip and skip_while

The `Iterator` trait's `skip` and `skip_while` methods are the complement of `take` and `take_while`: they drop a certain number of items from the beginning of an iteration, or drop items until a closure finds one acceptable, and then pass the remaining items through unchanged. Their signatures are as follows:

```
fn skip(self, n: usize) -> impl Iterator<Item=Self::Item>
    where Self: Sized;
```

```
fn skip_while<P>(self, predicate: P) -> impl Iterator<Item=Self::Item>
    where Self: Sized, P: FnMut(&Self::Item) -> bool;
```

One common use for the `skip` adapter is to skip the command name when iterating over a program's command-line arguments. In Chapter 2, our greatest common denominator calculator used the following code to loop over its command-line arguments:

```
for arg in std::env::args().skip(1) {
    ...
}
```

The `std::env::args` function returns an iterator that produces the program's arguments as `String`s, the first item being the name of the program itself. That's not a string we want to process in this loop. Calling `skip(1)` on that iterator returns a new iterator that drops the program name the first time it's called and then produces all the subsequent arguments.

The `skip_while` adapter uses a closure to decide how many items to drop from the beginning of the sequence. You can iterate over the body lines of the message from the previous section like this:

```
for body in message.lines()
    .skip_while(|l| !l.is_empty())
    .skip(1) {
    println!("{}" , body);
}
```

This uses `skip_while` to skip nonblank lines, but that iterator does produce the blank line itself—after all, the closure returned `false` for that line. So we use the `skip` method as well to drop that, giving us an iterator whose first item will be the message body's first line. Taken together with the declaration of `message` from the previous section, this code prints:

```
Did you get any writing done today?
When will you stop wasting time plotting fractals?
```

peekable

A peekable iterator lets you peek at the next item that will be produced without actually consuming it. You can turn any iterator into a peekable iterator by calling the `Iterator` trait's `peekable` method:

```
fn peekable(self) -> std::iter::Peekable<Self>
    where Self: Sized;
```

Here, `Peekable<Self>` is a `struct` that implements `Iterator<Item=Self::Item>`, and `Self` is the type of the underlying iterator.

A Peekable iterator has an additional method peek that returns an Option<&Item>: None if the underlying iterator is done and otherwise Some(r), where r is a shared reference to the next item. (Note that if the iterator's item type is already a reference to something, this ends up being a reference to a reference.)

Calling peek tries to draw the next item from the underlying iterator, and if there is one, caches it until the next call to next. All the other Iterator methods on Peekable know about this cache: for example, iter.last() on a peekable iterator iter knows to check the cache after exhausting the underlying iterator.

Peekable iterators are essential when you can't decide how many items to consume from an iterator until you've gone too far. For example, if you're parsing numbers from a stream of characters, you can't decide where the number ends until you've seen the first nonnumber character following it:

```
use std::iter::Peekable;

fn parse_number<I>(tokens: &mut Peekable<I>) -> u32
    where I: Iterator<Item=char>
{
    let mut n = 0;
    loop {
        match tokens.peek() {
            Some(r) if r.is_digit(10) => {
                n = n * 10 + r.to_digit(10).unwrap();
            }
            _ => return n
        }
        tokens.next();
    }
}

let mut chars = "226153980,1766319049".chars().peekable();
assert_eq!(parse_number(&mut chars), 226153980);
// Look, `parse_number` didn't consume the comma! So we will.
assert_eq!(chars.next(), Some(','));
assert_eq!(parse_number(&mut chars), 1766319049);
assert_eq!(chars.next(), None);
```

The parse_number function uses peek to check the next character and consumes it only if it is a digit. If it isn't a digit or the iterator is exhausted (that is, if peek returns None), we return the number we've parsed and leave the next character in the iterator, ready to be consumed.

fuse

Once an Iterator has returned None, the trait doesn't specify how it ought to behave if you call its next method again. Most iterators just return None again, but not all. If your code counts on that behavior, you may be in for a surprise.

The fuse adapter takes any iterator and produces one that will definitely continue to return None once it has done so the first time:

```
struct Flaky(bool);

impl Iterator for Flaky {
    type Item = &'static str;
    fn next(&mut self) -> Option<Self::Item> {
        if self.0 {
            self.0 = false;
            Some("totally the last item")
        } else {
            self.0 = true; // D'oh!
            None
        }
    }
}

let mut flaky = Flaky(true);
assert_eq!(flaky.next(), Some("totally the last item"));
assert_eq!(flaky.next(), None);
assert_eq!(flaky.next(), Some("totally the last item"));

let mut not_flaky = Flaky(true).fuse();
assert_eq!(not_flaky.next(), Some("totally the last item"));
assert_eq!(not_flaky.next(), None);
assert_eq!(not_flaky.next(), None);
```

The fuse adapter is probably most useful in generic code that needs to work with iterators of uncertain origin. Rather than hoping that every iterator you'll have to deal with will be well-behaved, you can use fuse to make sure.

Reversible Iterators and rev

Some iterators are able to draw items from both ends of the sequence. You can reverse such iterators by using the rev adapter. For example, an iterator over a vector could just as easily draw items from the end of the vector as from the start. Such iterators can implement the std::iter::DoubleEndedIterator trait, which extends Iterator:

```
trait DoubleEndedIterator: Iterator {
    fn next_back(&mut self) -> Option<Self::Item>;
}
```

You can think of a double-ended iterator as having two fingers marking the current front and back of the sequence. Drawing items from either end advances that finger toward the other; when the two meet, the iteration is done:

```
let bee_parts = ["head", "thorax", "abdomen"];

let mut iter = bee_parts.iter();
```

```
assert_eq!(iter.next(),       Some(&"head"));
assert_eq!(iter.next_back(), Some(&"abdomen"));
assert_eq!(iter.next(),       Some(&"thorax"));

assert_eq!(iter.next_back(), None);
assert_eq!(iter.next(),       None);
```

The structure of an iterator over a slice makes this behavior easy to implement: it is literally a pair of pointers to the start and end of the range of elements we haven't yet produced; next and next_back simply draw an item from the one or the other. Iterators for ordered collections like BTreeSet and BTreeMap are double-ended too: their next_back method draws the greatest elements or entries first. In general, the standard library provides double-ended iteration whenever it's practical.

But not all iterators can do this so easily: an iterator producing values from other threads arriving at a channel's Receiver has no way to anticipate what the last value received might be. In general, you'll need to check the standard library's documentation to see which iterators implement DoubleEndedIterator and which don't.

If an iterator is double-ended, you can reverse it with the rev adapter:

```
fn rev(self) -> impl Iterator<Item=Self>
    where Self: Sized + DoubleEndedIterator;
```

The returned iterator is also double-ended: its next and next_back methods are simply exchanged:

```
let meals = ["breakfast", "lunch", "dinner"];

let mut iter = meals.iter().rev();
assert_eq!(iter.next(), Some(&"dinner"));
assert_eq!(iter.next(), Some(&"lunch"));
assert_eq!(iter.next(), Some(&"breakfast"));
assert_eq!(iter.next(), None);
```

Most iterator adapters, if applied to a reversible iterator, return another reversible iterator. For example, map and filter preserve reversibility.

inspect

The inspect adapter is handy for debugging pipelines of iterator adapters, but it isn't used much in production code. It simply applies a closure to a shared reference to each item and then passes the item through. The closure can't affect the items, but it can do things like print them or make assertions about them.

This example shows a case in which converting a string to uppercase changes its length:

```
let upper_case: String = "große".chars()
    .inspect(|c| println!("before: {:?}", c))
    .flat_map(|c| c.to_uppercase())
    .inspect(|c| println!(" after:    {:?}", c))
    .collect();
assert_eq!(upper_case, "GROSSE");
```

The uppercase equivalent of the lowercase German letter "ß" is "SS," which is why char::to_uppercase returns an iterator over characters, not a single replacement character. The preceding code uses flat_map to concatenate all the sequences that to_uppercase returns into a single String, printing the following as it does so:

```
before: 'g'
 after:       'G'
before: 'r'
 after:       'R'
before: 'o'
 after:       'O'
before: 'ß'
 after:       'S'
 after:       'S'
before: 'e'
 after:       'E'
```

chain

The chain adapter appends one iterator to another. More precisely, i1.chain(i2) returns an iterator that draws items from i1 until it's exhausted and then draws items from i2.

The chain adapter's signature is as follows:

```
fn chain<U>(self, other: U) -> impl Iterator<Item=Self::Item>
    where Self: Sized, U: IntoIterator<Item=Self::Item>;
```

In other words, you can chain an iterator together with any iterable that produces the same item type.

For example:

```
let v: Vec<i32> = (1..4).chain([20, 30, 40]).collect();
assert_eq!(v, [1, 2, 3, 20, 30, 40]);
```

A chain iterator is reversible, if both of its underlying iterators are:

```
let v: Vec<i32> = (1..4).chain([20, 30, 40]).rev().collect();
assert_eq!(v, [40, 30, 20, 3, 2, 1]);
```

A `chain` iterator keeps track of whether each of the two underlying iterators has returned `None` and directs `next` and `next_back` calls to one or the other as appropriate.

enumerate

The `Iterator` trait's `enumerate` adapter attaches a running index to the sequence, taking an iterator that produces items `A, B, C, ...` and returning an iterator that produces pairs `(0, A), (1, B), (2, C), ....` It looks trivial at first glance, but it's used surprisingly often.

Consumers can use that index to distinguish one item from another and establish the context in which to process each one. For example, the Mandelbrot set plotter in Chapter 2 splits the image into eight horizontal bands and assigns each one to a different thread. That code uses `enumerate` to tell each thread which portion of the image its band corresponds to.

It starts with a rectangular buffer of pixels:

```
let mut pixels = vec![0; columns * rows];
```

Next, it uses `chunks_mut` to split the image into horizontal bands, one per thread:

```
let threads = 8;
let band_rows = rows / threads + 1;
...
let bands: Vec<&mut [u8]> = pixels.chunks_mut(band_rows * columns).collect();
```

And then it iterates over the bands, starting a thread for each one:

```
for (i, band) in bands.into_iter().enumerate() {
    let top = band_rows * i;
    // start a thread to render rows `top..top + band_rows`
    ...
}
```

Each iteration gets a pair `(i, band)`, where `band` is the `&mut [u8]` slice of the pixel buffer the thread should draw into, and `i` is the index of that band in the overall image, courtesy of the `enumerate` adapter. Given the boundaries of the plot and the size of the bands, this is enough information for the thread to determine which portion of the image it has been assigned and thus what to draw into `band`.

You can think of the `(index, item)` pairs that `enumerate` produces as analogous to the `(key, value)` pairs that you get when iterating over a `HashMap` or other associative collection. If you're iterating over a slice or vector, the `index` is the "key" under which the `item` appears.

zip

The `zip` adapter combines two iterators into a single iterator that produces pairs holding one value from each iterator, like a zipper joining its two sides into a single seam. The zipped iterator ends when either of the two underlying iterators ends.

For example, you can get the same effect as the `enumerate` adapter by zipping the unbounded-end range `0..` with the other iterator:

```
let v: Vec<_> = (0..).zip("ABCD".chars()).collect();
assert_eq!(v, vec![(0, 'A'), (1, 'B'), (2, 'C'), (3, 'D')]);
```

In this sense, you can think of `zip` as a generalization of `enumerate`: whereas `enumerate` attaches indices to the sequence, `zip` attaches any arbitrary iterator's items. We suggested before that `enumerate` can help provide context for processing items; `zip` is a more flexible way to do the same.

The argument to `zip` doesn't need to be an iterator itself; it can be any iterable:

```
use std::iter::repeat;

let endings = ["once", "twice", "chicken soup with rice"];
let rhyme: Vec<_> = repeat("going")
    .zip(endings)
    .collect();
assert_eq!(rhyme, vec![("going", "once"),
                       ("going", "twice"),
                       ("going", "chicken soup with rice")]);
```

by_ref

Throughout this section, we've been attaching adapters to iterators. Once you've done so, can you ever take the adapter off again? Usually, no: adapters take ownership of the underlying iterator and provide no method to give it back.

An iterator's `by_ref` method borrows a mutable reference to the iterator so that you can apply adapters to the reference. When you're done consuming items from these adapters, you drop them, the borrow ends, and you regain access to your original iterator.

For example, earlier in the chapter we showed how to use `take_while` and `skip_while` to process the header lines and body of a mail message. But what if you want to do both, using the same underlying iterator? Using `by_ref`, we can use `take_while` to handle the headers, and when that's done, get the underlying iterator back, which `take_while` has left exactly in position to handle the message body:

```
let message = "To: jimb\r\n\
               From: id\r\n\
               \r\n\
```

```
                Oooooh, donuts!!\r\n";

    let mut lines = message.lines();

    println!("Headers:");
    for header in lines.by_ref().take_while(|l| !l.is_empty()) {
        println!("{}" , header);
    }

    println!("\nBody:");
    for body in lines {
        println!("{}" , body);
    }
```

The call `lines.by_ref()` borrows a mutable reference to the iterator, and it is this reference that the `take_while` iterator takes ownership of. That iterator goes out of scope at the end of the first `for` loop, meaning that the borrow has ended, so you can use `lines` again in the second `for` loop. This prints the following:

```
Headers:
To: jimb
From: id

Body:
Oooooh, donuts!!
```

The `by_ref` adapter's definition is trivial: it returns a mutable reference to the iterator. Then, the standard library includes this strange little implementation:

```
impl<'a, I: Iterator + ?Sized> Iterator for &'a mut I {
    type Item = I::Item;
    fn next(&mut self) -> Option<I::Item> {
        (**self).next()
    }
    fn size_hint(&self) -> (usize, Option<usize>) {
        (**self).size_hint()
    }
}
```

In other words, if I is some iterator type, then `&mut I` is an iterator too, whose `next` and `size_hint` methods defer to its referent. When you call an adapter on a mutable reference to an iterator, the adapter takes ownership of the *reference*, not the iterator itself. That's just a borrow that ends when the adapter goes out of scope.

cloned, copied

The `cloned` adapter takes an iterator that produces references and returns an iterator that produces values cloned from those references, much like `iter.map(|item| item.clone())`. Naturally, the referent type must implement `Clone`. For example:

```
let a = ['1', '2', '3', '∞'];

assert_eq!(a.iter().next(),          Some(&'1'));
assert_eq!(a.iter().cloned().next(), Some('1'));
```

The `copied` adapter is the same idea, but more restrictive: the referent type must implement `Copy`. A call like `iter.copied()` is roughly the same as `iter.map(|r| *r)`. Since every type that implements `Copy` also implements `Clone`, `cloned` is strictly more general, but depending on the item type, a `clone` call can do arbitrary amounts of allocation and copying. If you're assuming that would never happen because your item type is something simple, it's best to use `copied` to make the type checker check your assumptions.

cycle

The `cycle` adapter returns an iterator that endlessly repeats the sequence produced by the underlying iterator. The underlying iterator must implement `std::clone::Clone` so that `cycle` can save its initial state and reuse it each time the cycle starts again.

For example:

```
let dirs = ["North", "East", "South", "West"];
let mut spin = dirs.iter().cycle();
assert_eq!(spin.next(), Some(&"North"));
assert_eq!(spin.next(), Some(&"East"));
assert_eq!(spin.next(), Some(&"South"));
assert_eq!(spin.next(), Some(&"West"));
assert_eq!(spin.next(), Some(&"North"));
assert_eq!(spin.next(), Some(&"East"));
```

Or, for a really gratuitous use of iterators:

```
use std::iter::{once, repeat};

let fizzes = repeat("").take(2).chain(once("fizz")).cycle();
let buzzes = repeat("").take(4).chain(once("buzz")).cycle();
let fizzes_buzzes = fizzes.zip(buzzes);

let fizz_buzz = (1..100).zip(fizzes_buzzes)
    .map(|tuple|
        match tuple {
            (i, ("", "")) => i.to_string(),
            (_, (fizz, buzz)) => format!("{}{}", fizz, buzz)
        });

for line in fizz_buzz {
    println!("{}", line);
}
```

This plays a children's word game, now sometimes used as a job interview question for coders, in which the players take turns counting, replacing any number divisible by three with the word `fizz`, and any number divisible by five with `buzz`. Numbers divisible by both become `fizzbuzz`.

Consuming Iterators

So far we've covered creating iterators and adapting them into new iterators; here we finish off the process by showing ways to consume them.

Of course, you can consume an iterator with a `for` loop, or call `next` explicitly, but there are many common tasks that you shouldn't have to write out again and again. The `Iterator` trait provides a broad selection of methods to cover many of these.

Simple Accumulation: count, sum, product

The `count` method draws items from an iterator until it returns `None` and tells you how many it got. Here's a short program that counts the number of lines on its standard input:

```
use std::io::prelude::*;

fn main() {
    let stdin = std::io::stdin();
    println!("{}", stdin.lock().lines().count());
}
```

The `sum` and `product` methods compute the sum or product of the iterator's items, which must be integers or floating-point numbers:

```
fn triangle(n: u64) -> u64 {
    (1..=n).sum()
}
assert_eq!(triangle(20), 210);

fn factorial(n: u64) -> u64 {
    (1..=n).product()
}
assert_eq!(factorial(20), 2432902008176640000);
```

(You can extend `sum` and `product` to work with other types by implementing the `std::iter::Sum` and `std::iter::Product` traits, which we won't describe in this book.)

max, min

The `min` and `max` methods on `Iterator` return the least or greatest item the iterator produces. The iterator's item type must implement `std::cmp::Ord` so that items can be compared with one another. For example:

```
assert_eq!([-2, 0, 1, 0, -2, -5].iter().max(), Some(&1));
assert_eq!([-2, 0, 1, 0, -2, -5].iter().min(), Some(&-5));
```

These methods return an `Option<Self::Item>` so that they can return `None` if the iterator produces no items.

As explained in "Equivalence Comparisons" on page 294, Rust's floating-point types `f32` and `f64` implement only `std::cmp::PartialOrd`, not `std::cmp::Ord`, so you can't use the `min` and `max` methods to compute the least or greatest of a sequence of floating-point numbers. This is not a popular aspect of Rust's design, but it is deliberate: it's not clear what such functions should do with IEEE NaN values. Simply ignoring them would risk masking more serious problems in the code.

If you know how you would like to handle NaN values, you can use the `max_by` and `min_by` iterator methods instead, which let you supply your own comparison function.

max_by, min_by

The `max_by` and `min_by` methods return the maximum or minimum item the iterator produces, as determined by a comparison function you provide:

```
use std::cmp::Ordering;

// Compare two f64 values. Panic if given a NaN.
fn cmp(lhs: &f64, rhs: &f64) -> Ordering {
    lhs.partial_cmp(rhs).unwrap()
}

let numbers = [1.0, 4.0, 2.0];
assert_eq!(numbers.iter().copied().max_by(cmp), Some(4.0));
assert_eq!(numbers.iter().copied().min_by(cmp), Some(1.0));

let numbers = [1.0, 4.0, std::f64::NAN, 2.0];
assert_eq!(numbers.iter().copied().max_by(cmp), Some(4.0)); // panics
```

The `max_by` and `min_by` methods pass items to the comparison function by reference so that they can work efficiently with any sort of iterator, so `cmp` expects to take its arguments by reference, even though we've used `copied` to get an iterator that produces `f64` items.

max_by_key, min_by_key

The max_by_key and min_by_key methods on Iterator let you select the maximum or minimum item as determined by a closure applied to each item. The closure can select some field of the item or perform a computation on the items. Since you're often interested in data associated with some minimum or maximum, not just the extremum itself, these functions are often more useful than min and max. Their signatures are as follows:

```
fn min_by_key<B: Ord, F>(self, f: F) -> Option<Self::Item>
    where Self: Sized, F: FnMut(&Self::Item) -> B;

fn max_by_key<B: Ord, F>(self, f: F) -> Option<Self::Item>
    where Self: Sized, F: FnMut(&Self::Item) -> B;
```

That is, given a closure that takes an item and returns any ordered type B, return the item for which the closure returned the maximum or minimum B, or None if no items were produced.

For example, if you need to scan a hash table of cities to find the cities with the largest and smallest populations, you could write:

```
use std::collections::HashMap;

let mut populations = HashMap::new();
populations.insert("Portland",   583_776);
populations.insert("Fossil",         449);
populations.insert("Greenhorn",        2);
populations.insert("Boring",       7_762);
populations.insert("The Dalles", 15_340);

assert_eq!(populations.iter().max_by_key(|&(_name, pop)| pop),
           Some((&"Portland", &583_776)));
assert_eq!(populations.iter().min_by_key(|&(_name, pop)| pop),
           Some((&"Greenhorn", &2)));
```

The closure |&(_name, pop)| pop gets applied to each item the iterator produces and returns the value to use for comparison—in this case, the city's population. The value returned is the entire item, not just the value the closure returns. (Naturally, if you were making queries like this often, you'd probably want to arrange for a more efficient way to find the entries than making a linear search through the table.)

Comparing Item Sequences

You can use the < and == operators to compare strings, vectors, and slices, assuming their individual elements can be compared. Although iterators do not support Rust's comparison operators, they do provide methods like eq and lt that do the same job, drawing pairs of items from the iterators and comparing them until a decision can be reached. For example:

```
let packed =    "Helen of Troy";
let spaced =    "Helen    of      Troy";
let obscure = "Helen of Sandusky"; // nice person, just not famous

assert!(packed != spaced);
assert!(packed.split_whitespace().eq(spaced.split_whitespace()));

// This is true because ' ' < 'o'.
assert!(spaced < obscure);

// This is true because 'Troy' > 'Sandusky'.
assert!(spaced.split_whitespace().gt(obscure.split_whitespace()));
```

The calls to `split_whitespace` return iterators over the whitespace-separated words of the string. Using the `eq` and `gt` methods on these iterators performs a word-by-word comparison, instead of a character-by-character comparison. These are all possible because `&str` implements `PartialOrd` and `PartialEq`.

Iterators provide the `eq` and `ne` methods for equality comparisons, and `lt`, `le`, `gt`, and `ge` methods for ordered comparisons. The `cmp` and `partial_cmp` methods behave like the corresponding methods of the `Ord` and `PartialOrd` traits.

any and all

The `any` and `all` methods apply a closure to each item the iterator produces and return `true` if the closure returns `true` for any item, or for all the items:

```
let id = "Iterator";

assert!( id.chars().any(char::is_uppercase));
assert!(!id.chars().all(char::is_uppercase));
```

These methods consume only as many items as they need to determine the answer. For example, if the closure ever returns `true` for a given item, then `any` returns `true` immediately, without drawing any more items from the iterator.

position, rposition, and ExactSizeIterator

The `position` method applies a closure to each item from the iterator and returns the index of the first item for which the closure returns `true`. More precisely, it returns an `Option` of the index: if the closure returns `true` for no item, `position` returns `None`. It stops drawing items as soon as the closure returns `true`. For example:

```
let text = "Xerxes";
assert_eq!(text.chars().position(|c| c == 'e'), Some(1));
assert_eq!(text.chars().position(|c| c == 'z'), None);
```

The `rposition` method is the same, except that it searches from the right. For example:

```
let bytes = b"Xerxes";
assert_eq!(bytes.iter().rposition(|&c| c == b'e'), Some(4));
assert_eq!(bytes.iter().rposition(|&c| c == b'X'), Some(0));
```

The rposition method requires a reversible iterator so that it can draw items from the right end of the sequence. It also requires an exact-size iterator so that it can assign indices the same way position would, starting with 0 at the left. An exact-size iterator is one that implements the std::iter::ExactSizeIterator trait:

```
trait ExactSizeIterator: Iterator {
    fn len(&self) -> usize { ... }
    fn is_empty(&self) -> bool { ... }
}
```

The len method returns the number of items remaining, and the is_empty method returns true if iteration is complete.

Naturally, not every iterator knows how many items it will produce in advance. For example, the str::chars iterator used earlier does not (since UTF-8 is a variable-width encoding), so you can't use rposition on strings. But an iterator over an array of bytes certainly knows the array's length, so it can implement ExactSizeIterator.

fold and rfold

The fold method is a very general tool for accumulating some sort of result over the entire sequence of items an iterator produces. Given an initial value, which we'll call the *accumulator*, and a closure, fold repeatedly applies the closure to the current accumulator and the next item from the iterator. The value the closure returns is taken as the new accumulator, to be passed to the closure with the next item. The final accumulator value is what fold itself returns. If the sequence is empty, fold simply returns the initial accumulator.

Many of the other methods for consuming an iterator's values can be written as uses of fold:

```
let a = [5, 6, 7, 8, 9, 10];

assert_eq!(a.iter().fold(0, |n, _| n+1), 6);        // count
assert_eq!(a.iter().fold(0, |n, i| n+i), 45);       // sum
assert_eq!(a.iter().fold(1, |n, i| n*i), 151200);   // product

// max
assert_eq!(a.iter().cloned().fold(i32::min_value(), std::cmp::max),
           10);
```

The fold method's signature is as follows:

```
fn fold<A, F>(self, init: A, f: F) -> A
    where Self: Sized, F: FnMut(A, Self::Item) -> A;
```

Here, A is the accumulator type. The `init` argument is an A, as is the closure's first argument and return value, and the return value of `fold` itself.

Note that the accumulator values are moved into and out of the closure, so you can use `fold` with non-Copy accumulator types:

```
let a = ["Pack", "my", "box", "with",
        "five", "dozen", "liquor", "jugs"];

// See also: the `join` method on slices, which won't
// give you that extra space at the end.
let pangram = a.iter()
    .fold(String::new(), |s, w| s + w + " ");
assert_eq!(pangram, "Pack my box with five dozen liquor jugs ");
```

The `rfold` method is the same as `fold`, except that it requires a double-ended iterator, and processes its items from last to first:

```
let weird_pangram = a.iter()
    .rfold(String::new(), |s, w| s + w + " ");
assert_eq!(weird_pangram, "jugs liquor dozen five with box my Pack ");
```

try_fold and try_rfold

The `try_fold` method is the same as `fold`, except that iteration can exit early, without consuming all the values from the iterator. The value returned by the closure you pass to `try_fold` indicates whether it should return immediately, or continue folding the iterator's items.

Your closure can return any one of several types, indicating how folding should proceed:

- If your closure returns `Result<T, E>`, perhaps because it does I/O or carries out some other fallible operation, then returning `Ok(v)` tells `try_fold` to continue folding, with v as the new accumulator value. Returning `Err(e)` causes folding to stop immediately. The fold's final value is a `Result` carrying the final accumulator value, or the error returned by the closure.

- If your closure returns `Option<T>`, then `Some(v)` indicates that folding should continue with v as the new accumulator value, and `None` indicates that iteration should stop immediately. The fold's final value is also an `Option`.

- Finally, the closure can return a `std::ops::ControlFlow` value. This type is an enum with two variants, `Continue(c)` and `Break(b)`, meaning to continue with new accumulator value c, or stop early. The result of the fold is a `ControlFlow` value: `Continue(v)` if the fold consumed the entire iterator, yielding the final accumulator value v; or `Break(b)`, if the closure returned that value.

`Continue(c)` and `Break(b)` behave exactly like `Ok(c)` and `Err(b)`. The advantage of using `ControlFlow` instead of `Result` is that it makes your code a little more legible when an early exit doesn't indicate an error, but merely that the answer is ready early. We show an example of this below.

Here's a program that sums numbers read from its standard input:

```rust
use std::error::Error;
use std::io::prelude::*;
use std::str::FromStr;

fn main() -> Result<(), Box<dyn Error>> {
    let stdin = std::io::stdin();
    let sum = stdin.lock()
        .lines()
        .try_fold(0, |sum, line| -> Result<u64, Box<dyn Error>> {
            Ok(sum + u64::from_str(&line?.trim())?)
        })?;
    println!("{}", sum);
    Ok(())
}
```

The `lines` iterator on buffered input streams produces items of type `Result<String, std::io::Error>`, and parsing the `String` as an integer may fail as well. Using `try_fold` here lets the closure return `Result<u64, ...>`, so we can use the `?` operator to propagate failures from the closure out to the `main` function.

Because `try_fold` is so flexible, it is used to implement many of `Iterator`'s other consumer methods. For example, here's an implementation of `all`:

```rust
fn all<P>(&mut self, mut predicate: P) -> bool
    where P: FnMut(Self::Item) -> bool,
          Self: Sized
{
    use std::ops::ControlFlow::*;
    self.try_fold((), |_, item| {
        if predicate(item) { Continue(()) } else { Break(()) }
    }) == Continue(())
}
```

Note that this cannot be written with ordinary `fold`: `all` promises to stop consuming items from the underlying iterator as soon as `predicate` returns false, but `fold` always consumes the entire iterator.

If you are implementing your own iterator type, it's worth investigating whether your iterator could implement `try_fold` more efficiently than the default definition from the `Iterator` trait. If you can speed up `try_fold`, all the other methods built on it will benefit as well.

The `try_rfold` method, as its name suggests, is the same as `try_fold`, except that it draws values from the back, instead of the front, and requires a double-ended iterator.

nth, nth_back

The `nth` method takes an index n, skips that many items from the iterator, and returns the next item, or None if the sequence ends before that point. Calling .nth(0) is equivalent to .next().

It doesn't take ownership of the iterator the way an adapter would, so you can call it many times:

```
let mut squares = (0..10).map(|i| i*i);

assert_eq!(squares.nth(4), Some(16));
assert_eq!(squares.nth(0), Some(25));
assert_eq!(squares.nth(6), None);
```

Its signature is shown here:

```
fn nth(&mut self, n: usize) -> Option<Self::Item>
    where Self: Sized;
```

The `nth_back` method is much the same, except that it draws from the back of a double-ended iterator. Calling .nth_back(0) is equivalent to .next_back(): it returns the last item, or None if the iterator is empty.

last

The `last` method returns the last item the iterator produces, or None if it's empty. Its signature is as follows:

```
fn last(self) -> Option<Self::Item>;
```

For example:

```
let squares = (0..10).map(|i| i*i);
assert_eq!(squares.last(), Some(81));
```

This consumes all the iterator's items starting from the front, even if the iterator is reversible. If you have a reversible iterator and don't need to consume all its items, you should instead just write `iter.next_back()`.

find, rfind, and find_map

The `find` method draws items from an iterator, returning the first item for which the given closure returns true, or None if the sequence ends before a suitable item is found. Its signature is:

```
fn find<P>(&mut self, predicate: P) -> Option<Self::Item>
    where Self: Sized,
          P: FnMut(&Self::Item) -> bool;
```

The `rfind` method is similar, but it requires a double-ended iterator and searches values from back to front, returning the *last* item for which the closure returns `true`.

For example, using the table of cities and populations from "max_by_key, min_by_key" on page 377, you could write:

```
assert_eq!(populations.iter().find(|&(_name, &pop)| pop > 1_000_000),
           None);
assert_eq!(populations.iter().find(|&(_name, &pop)| pop > 500_000),
           Some((&"Portland", &583_776)));
```

None of the cities in the table has a population above a million, but there is one city with half a million people.

Sometimes your closure isn't just a simple predicate casting a Boolean judgment on each item and moving on: it might be something more complex that produces an interesting value in its own right. In this case, `find_map` is just what you want. Its signature is:

```
fn find_map<B, F>(&mut self, f: F) -> Option<B> where
    F: FnMut(Self::Item) -> Option<B>;
```

This is just like `find`, except that instead of returning `bool`, the closure should return an `Option` of some value. `find_map` returns the first `Option` that is `Some`.

For example, if we have a database of each city's parks, we might want to see if any of them are volcanoes and provide the name of the park if so:

```
let big_city_with_volcano_park = populations.iter()
    .find_map(|(&city, _)| {
        if let Some(park) = find_volcano_park(city, &parks) {
            // find_map returns this value, so our caller knows
            // *which* park we found.
            return Some((city, park.name));
        }

        // Reject this item, and continue the search.
        None
    });

assert_eq!(big_city_with_volcano_park,
           Some(("Portland", "Mt. Tabor Park")));
```

Building Collections: collect and FromIterator

Throughout the book, we've been using the `collect` method to build vectors holding an iterator's items. For example, in Chapter 2, we called `std::env::args()` to get an iterator over the program's command-line arguments and then called that iterator's `collect` method to gather them into a vector:

```
let args: Vec<String> = std::env::args().collect();
```

But `collect` isn't specific to vectors: in fact, it can build any kind of collection from Rust's standard library, as long as the iterator produces a suitable item type:

```
use std::collections::{HashSet, BTreeSet, LinkedList, HashMap, BTreeMap};

let args: HashSet<String> = std::env::args().collect();
let args: BTreeSet<String> = std::env::args().collect();
let args: LinkedList<String> = std::env::args().collect();

// Collecting a map requires (key, value) pairs, so for this example,
// zip the sequence of strings with a sequence of integers.
let args: HashMap<String, usize> = std::env::args().zip(0..).collect();
let args: BTreeMap<String, usize> = std::env::args().zip(0..).collect();

// and so on
```

Naturally, `collect` itself doesn't know how to construct all these types. Rather, when some collection type like `Vec` or `HashMap` knows how to construct itself from an iterator, it implements the `std::iter::FromIterator` trait, for which `collect` is just a convenient veneer:

```
trait FromIterator<A>: Sized {
    fn from_iter<T: IntoIterator<Item=A>>(iter: T) -> Self;
}
```

If a collection type implements `FromIterator<A>`, then its type-associated function `from_iter` builds a value of that type from an iterable producing items of type A.

In the simplest case, the implementation could simply construct an empty collection and then add the items from the iterator one by one. For example, `std::collections::LinkedList`'s implementation of `FromIterator` works this way.

However, some types can do better than that. For example, constructing a vector from some iterator `iter` could be as simple as:

```
let mut vec = Vec::new();
for item in iter {
    vec.push(item)
}
vec
```

But this isn't ideal: as the vector grows, it may need to expand its buffer, requiring a call to the heap allocator and a copy of the extant elements. Vectors do take algorithmic measures to keep this overhead low, but if there were some way to simply allocate a buffer of the right size to begin with, there would be no need to resize at all.

This is where the `Iterator` trait's `size_hint` method comes in:

```
trait Iterator {
    ...
    fn size_hint(&self) -> (usize, Option<usize>) {
        (0, None)
    }
}
```

This method returns a lower bound and optional upper bound on the number of items the iterator will produce. The default definition returns zero as the lower bound and declines to name an upper bound, saying, in effect, "I have no idea," but many iterators can do better than this. An iterator over a `Range`, for example, knows exactly how many items it will produce, as does an iterator over a `Vec` or `HashMap`. Such iterators provide their own specialized definitions for `size_hint`.

These bounds are exactly the information that `Vec`'s implementation of `FromIterator` needs to size the new vector's buffer correctly from the start. Insertions still check that the buffer is large enough, so even if the hint is incorrect, only performance is affected, not safety. Other types can take similar steps: for example, `HashSet` and `HashMap` also use `Iterator::size_hint` to choose an appropriate initial size for their hash table.

One note about type inference: at the top of this section, it's a bit strange to see the same call, `std::env::args().collect()`, produce four different kinds of collections depending on its context. The return type of `collect` is its type parameter, so the first two calls are equivalent to the following:

```
let args = std::env::args().collect::<Vec<String>>();
let args = std::env::args().collect::<HashSet<String>>();
```

But as long as there's only one type that could possibly work as `collect`'s argument, Rust's type inference will supply it for you. When you spell out the type of `args`, you ensure this is the case.

The Extend Trait

If a type implements the `std::iter::Extend` trait, then its `extend` method adds an iterable's items to the collection:

```
let mut v: Vec<i32> = (0..5).map(|i| 1 << i).collect();
v.extend([31, 57, 99, 163]);
assert_eq!(v, [1, 2, 4, 8, 16, 31, 57, 99, 163]);
```

All of the standard collections implement Extend, so they all have this method; so does String. Arrays and slices, which have a fixed length, do not.

The trait's definition is as follows:

```
trait Extend<A> {
    fn extend<T>(&mut self, iter: T)
        where T: IntoIterator<Item=A>;
}
```

Obviously, this is very similar to std::iter::FromIterator: that creates a new collection, whereas Extend extends an existing collection. In fact, several implementations of FromIterator in the standard library simply create a new empty collection and then call extend to populate it. For example, the implementation of FromIterator for std::collections::LinkedList works this way:

```
impl<T> FromIterator<T> for LinkedList<T> {
    fn from_iter<I: IntoIterator<Item = T>>(iter: I) -> Self {
        let mut list = Self::new();
        list.extend(iter);
        list
    }
}
```

partition

The partition method divides an iterator's items among two collections, using a closure to decide where each item belongs:

```
let things = ["doorknob", "mushroom", "noodle", "giraffe", "grapefruit"];

// Amazing fact: the name of a living thing always starts with an
// odd-numbered letter.
let (living, nonliving): (Vec<&str>, Vec<&str>)
    = things.iter().partition(|name| name.as_bytes()[0] & 1 != 0);

assert_eq!(living,    vec!["mushroom", "giraffe", "grapefruit"]);
assert_eq!(nonliving, vec!["doorknob", "noodle"]);
```

Like collect, partition can make any sort of collections you like, although both must be of the same type. And like collect, you'll need to specify the return type: the preceding example writes out the type of living and nonliving and lets type inference choose the right type parameters for the call to partition.

The signature of partition is as follows:

```
fn partition<B, F>(self, f: F) -> (B, B)
    where Self: Sized,
          B: Default + Extend<Self::Item>,
          F: FnMut(&Self::Item) -> bool;
```

Whereas `collect` requires its result type to implement `FromIterator`, `partition` instead requires `std::default::Default`, which all Rust collections implement by returning an empty collection, and `std::default::Extend`.

Other languages offer `partition` operations that just split the iterator into two iterators, instead of building two collections. But this isn't a good fit for Rust: items drawn from the underlying iterator but not yet drawn from the appropriate partitioned iterator would need to be buffered somewhere; you would end up building a collection of some sort internally, anyway.

for_each and try_for_each

The `for_each` method simply applies a closure to each item:

```
["doves", "hens", "birds"].iter()
    .zip(["turtle", "french", "calling"])
    .zip(2..5)
    .rev()
    .map(|((item, kind), quantity)| {
        format!("{} {} {}", quantity, kind, item)
    })
    .for_each(|gift| {
        println!("You have received: {}", gift);
    });
```

This prints:

```
You have received: 4 calling birds
You have received: 3 french hens
You have received: 2 turtle doves
```

This is very similar to a simple `for` loop, in which you could also use control structures like `break` and `continue`. But long chains of adapter calls like this are a little awkward in `for` loops:

```
for gift in ["doves", "hens", "birds"].iter()
    .zip(["turtle", "french", "calling"])
    .zip(2..5)
    .rev()
    .map(|((item, kind), quantity)| {
        format!("{} {} {}", quantity, kind, item)
    })
{
    println!("You have received: {}", gift);
}
```

The pattern being bound, `gift`, can end up quite far away from the loop body in which it is used.

If your closure needs to be fallible or exit early, you can use `try_for_each`:

```
...
    .try_for_each(|gift| {
        writeln!(&mut output_file, "You have received: {}", gift)
    })?;
```

Implementing Your Own Iterators

You can implement the IntoIterator and Iterator traits for your own types, making all the adapters and consumers shown in this chapter available for use, along with lots of other library and crate code written to work with the standard iterator interface. In this section, we'll show a simple iterator over a range type and then a more complex iterator over a binary tree type.

Suppose we have the following range type (simplified from the standard library's std::ops::Range<T> type):

```
struct I32Range {
    start: i32,
    end: i32
}
```

Iterating over an I32Range requires two pieces of state: the current value and the limit at which the iteration should end. This happens to be a nice fit for the I32Range type itself, using start as the next value, and end as the limit. So you can implement Iterator like so:

```
impl Iterator for I32Range {
    type Item = i32;
    fn next(&mut self) -> Option<i32> {
        if self.start >= self.end {
            return None;
        }
        let result = Some(self.start);
        self.start += 1;
        result
    }
}
```

This iterator produces i32 items, so that's the Item type. If the iteration is complete, next returns None; otherwise, it produces the next value and updates its state to prepare for the next call.

Of course, a for loop uses IntoIterator::into_iter to convert its operand into an iterator. But the standard library provides a blanket implementation of IntoIterator for every type that implements Iterator, so I32Range is ready for use:

```
let mut pi = 0.0;
let mut numerator = 1.0;

for k in (I32Range { start: 0, end: 14 }) {
    pi += numerator / (2*k + 1) as f64;
    numerator /= -3.0;
}
pi *= f64::sqrt(12.0);

// IEEE 754 specifies this result exactly.
assert_eq!(pi as f32, std::f32::consts::PI);
```

But `I32Range` is a special case, in that the iterable and iterator are the same type. Many cases aren't so simple. For example, here's the binary tree type from Chapter 10:

```
enum BinaryTree<T> {
    Empty,
    NonEmpty(Box<TreeNode<T>>)
}

struct TreeNode<T> {
    element: T,
    left: BinaryTree<T>,
    right: BinaryTree<T>
}
```

The classic way to walk a binary tree is to recurse, using the stack of function calls to keep track of your place in the tree and the nodes yet to be visited. But when implementing `Iterator` for `BinaryTree<T>`, each call to `next` must produce exactly one value and return. To keep track of the tree nodes it has yet to produce, the iterator must maintain its own stack. Here's one possible iterator type for `BinaryTree`:

```
use self::BinaryTree::*;

// The state of an in-order traversal of a `BinaryTree`.
struct TreeIter<'a, T> {
    // A stack of references to tree nodes. Since we use `Vec`'s
    // `push` and `pop` methods, the top of the stack is the end of the
    // vector.
    //
    // The node the iterator will visit next is at the top of the stack,
    // with those ancestors still unvisited below it. If the stack is empty,
    // the iteration is over.
    unvisited: Vec<&'a TreeNode<T>>
}
```

When we create a new `TreeIter`, its initial state should be about to produce the left-most leaf node in the tree. According to the rules for the `unvisited` stack, it should thus have that leaf on the top, followed by its unvisited ancestors: the nodes along the left edge of the tree. We can initialize `unvisited` by walking the left edge of the tree from root to leaf and pushing each node we encounter, so we'll define a method on TreeIter to do that:

```
impl<'a, T: 'a> TreeIter<'a, T> {
    fn push_left_edge(&mut self, mut tree: &'a BinaryTree<T>) {
        while let NonEmpty(ref node) = *tree {
            self.unvisited.push(node);
            tree = &node.left;
        }
    }
}
```

Writing mut tree lets the loop change which node tree points to as it walks down the left edge, but since tree is a shared reference, it can't mutate the nodes themselves.

With this helper method in place, we can give BinaryTree an iter method that returns an iterator over the tree:

```
impl<T> BinaryTree<T> {
    fn iter(&self) -> TreeIter<T> {
        let mut iter = TreeIter { unvisited: Vec::new() };
        iter.push_left_edge(self);
        iter
    }
}
```

The iter method constructs a TreeIter with an empty unvisited stack and then calls push_left_edge to initialize it. The leftmost node ends up on the top, as required by the unvisited stack's rules.

Following the standard library's practices, we can then implement IntoIterator on a shared reference to a tree with a call to BinaryTree::iter:

```
impl<'a, T: 'a> IntoIterator for &'a BinaryTree<T> {
    type Item = &'a T;
    type IntoIter = TreeIter<'a, T>;
    fn into_iter(self) -> Self::IntoIter {
        self.iter()
    }
}
```

The IntoIter definition establishes TreeIter as the iterator type for a &BinaryTree.

Finally, in the Iterator implementation, we get to actually walk the tree. Like BinaryTree's iter method, the iterator's next method is guided by the stack's rules:

```
impl<'a, T> Iterator for TreeIter<'a, T> {
    type Item = &'a T;
    fn next(&mut self) -> Option<&'a T> {
        // Find the node this iteration must produce,
        // or finish the iteration. (Use the `?` operator
```

```
        // to return immediately if it's `None`.)
        let node = self.unvisited.pop()?;

        // After `node`, the next thing we produce must be the leftmost
        // child in `node`'s right subtree, so push the path from here
        // down. Our helper method turns out to be just what we need.
        self.push_left_edge(&node.right);

        // Produce a reference to this node's value.
        Some(&node.element)
    }
}
```

If the stack is empty, the iteration is complete. Otherwise, node is a reference to the node to visit now; this call will return a reference to its element field. But first, we must advance the iterator's state to the next node. If this node has a right subtree, the next node to visit is the subtree's leftmost node, and we can use push_left_edge to push it, and its unvisited ancestors, onto the stack. But if this node has no right subtree, push_left_edge has no effect, which is just what we want: we can count on the new top of the stack to be node's first unvisited ancestor, if any.

With IntoIterator and Iterator implementations in place, we can finally use a for loop to iterate over a BinaryTree by reference. Using the add method on BinaryTree from "Populating a Binary Tree" on page 252:

```
// Build a small tree.
let mut tree = BinaryTree::Empty;
tree.add("jaeger");
tree.add("robot");
tree.add("droid");
tree.add("mecha");

// Iterate over it.
let mut v = Vec::new();
for kind in &tree {
    v.push(*kind);
}
assert_eq!(v, ["droid", "jaeger", "mecha", "robot"]);
```

Figure 15-1 shows how the unvisited stack behaves as we iterate through a sample tree. At every step, the next node to be visited is at the top of the stack, with all its unvisited ancestors below it.

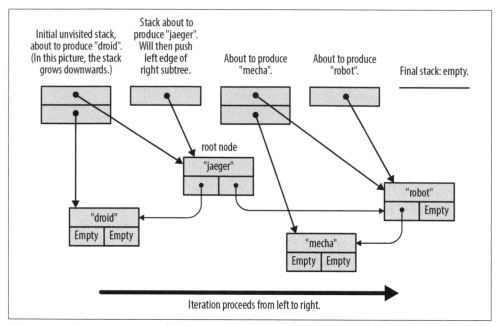

Figure 15-1. Iterating over a binary tree

All the usual iterator adapters and consumers are ready for use on our trees:

```
assert_eq!(tree.iter()
           .map(|name| format!("mega-{}", name))
           .collect::<Vec<_>>(),
           vec!["mega-droid", "mega-jaeger",
                "mega-mecha", "mega-robot"]);
```

Iterators are the embodiment of Rust's philosophy of providing powerful, zero-cost abstractions that improve the expressiveness and readability of code. Iterators don't replace loops entirely, but they do provide a capable primitive with built-in lazy evaluation and excellent performance.

## CHAPTER 16

Collections

We all behave like Maxwell's demon. Organisms organize. In everyday experience lies the reason sober physicists across two centuries kept this cartoon fantasy alive. We sort the mail, build sand castles, solve jigsaw puzzles, separate wheat from chaff, rearrange chess pieces, collect stamps, alphabetize books, create symmetry, compose sonnets and sonatas, and put our rooms in order, and all this we do requires no great energy, as long as we can apply intelligence.

—James Gleick, *The Information: A History, a Theory, a Flood*

The Rust standard library contains several *collections*, generic types for storing data in memory. We've already been using collections, such as Vec and HashMap, throughout this book. In this chapter, we'll cover the methods of these two types in detail, along with the other half-dozen standard collections. Before we begin, let's address a few systematic differences between Rust's collections and those in other languages.

First, moves and borrowing are everywhere. Rust uses moves to avoid deep-copying values. That's why the method Vec<T>::push(item) takes its argument by value, not by reference. The value is moved into the vector. The diagrams in Chapter 4 show how this works out in practice: pushing a Rust String to a Vec<String> is quick, because Rust doesn't have to copy the string's character data, and ownership of the string is always clear.

Second, Rust doesn't have invalidation errors—the kind of dangling-pointer bug where a collection is resized, or otherwise changed, while the program is holding a pointer to data inside it. Invalidation errors are another source of undefined behavior in C++, and they cause the occasional ConcurrentModificationException even in memory-safe languages. Rust's borrow checker rules them out at compile time.

Finally, Rust does not have null, so we'll see Options in places where other languages would use null.

Apart from these differences, Rust's collections are about what you'd expect. If you're an experienced programmer in a hurry, you can skim here, but don't miss "Entries" on page 417.

Overview

Table 16-1 shows Rust's eight standard collections. All of them are generic types.

Table 16-1. Summary of the standard collections

Collection	Description	Similar collection type in...		
		C++	Java	Python
Vec<T>	Growable array	vector	ArrayList	list
VecDeque<T>	Double-ended queue (growable ring buffer)	deque	ArrayDeque	collections .deque
LinkedList<T>	Doubly linked list	list	LinkedList	—
BinaryHeap<T> where T: Ord	Max heap	priority_queue	PriorityQueue	heapq
HashMap<K, V> where K: Eq + Hash	Key-value hash table	unordered_map	HashMap	dict
BTreeMap<K, V> where K: Ord	Sorted key-value table	map	TreeMap	—
HashSet<T> where T: Eq + Hash	Unordered, hash-based set	unordered_set	HashSet	set
BTreeSet<T> where T: Ord	Sorted set	set	TreeSet	—

Vec<T>, HashMap<K, V>, and HashSet<T> are the most generally useful collection types. The rest have niche uses. This chapter discusses each collection type in turn:

Vec<T>
> A growable, heap-allocated array of values of type T. About half of this chapter is dedicated to Vec and its many useful methods.

VecDeque<T>
> Like Vec<T>, but better for use as a first-in-first-out queue. It supports efficiently adding and removing values at the front of the list as well as the back. This comes at the cost of making all other operations slightly slower.

BinaryHeap<T>

A priority queue. The values in a BinaryHeap are organized so that it's always efficient to find and remove the maximum value.

HashMap<K, V>

A table of key-value pairs. Looking up a value by its key is fast. The entries are stored in an arbitrary order.

BTreeMap<K, V>

Like HashMap<K, V>, but it keeps the entries sorted by key. A BTreeMap<String, i32> stores its entries in String comparison order. Unless you need the entries to stay sorted, a HashMap is faster.

HashSet<T>

A set of values of type T. Adding and removing values is fast, and it's fast to ask whether a given value is in the set or not.

BTreeSet<T>

Like HashSet<T>, but it keeps the elements sorted by value. Again, unless you need the data sorted, a HashSet is faster.

Because LinkedList is rarely used (and there are better alternatives, both in performance and interface, for most use cases), we do not describe it here.

Vec<T>

We'll assume some familiarity with Vec, since we've been using it throughout the book. For an introduction, see "Vectors" on page 68. Here we'll finally describe its methods and its inner workings in depth.

The easiest way to create a vector is to use the vec! macro:

```
// Create an empty vector
let mut numbers: Vec<i32> = vec![];

// Create a vector with given contents
let words = vec!["step", "on", "no", "pets"];
let mut buffer = vec![0u8; 1024];  // 1024 zeroed-out bytes
```

As described in Chapter 4, a vector has three fields: the length, the capacity, and a pointer to a heap allocation where the elements are stored. Figure 16-1 shows how the preceding vectors would appear in memory. The empty vector, numbers, initially has a capacity of 0. No heap memory is allocated for it until the first element is added.

Like all collections, Vec implements std::iter::FromIterator, so you can create a vector from any iterator using the iterator's .collect() method, as described in "Building Collections: collect and FromIterator" on page 384:

```
// Convert another collection to a vector.
let my_vec = my_set.into_iter().collect::<Vec<String>>();
```

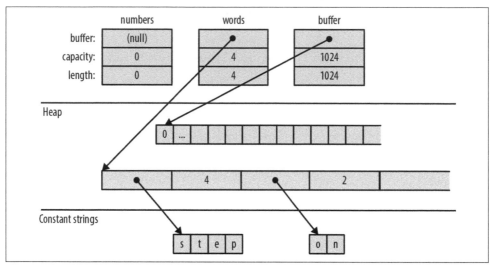

Figure 16-1. Vector layout in memory: each element of words is a &str value consisting of a pointer and a length

Accessing Elements

Getting elements of an array, slice, or vector by index is straightforward:

```
// Get a reference to an element
let first_line = &lines[0];

// Get a copy of an element
let fifth_number = numbers[4];      // requires Copy
let second_line = lines[1].clone(); // requires Clone

// Get a reference to a slice
let my_ref = &buffer[4..12];

// Get a copy of a slice
let my_copy = buffer[4..12].to_vec();  // requires Clone
```

All of these forms panic if an index is out of bounds.

Rust is picky about numeric types, and it makes no exceptions for vectors. Vector lengths and indices are of type usize. Trying to use a u32, u64, or isize as a vector index is an error. You can use an n as usize cast to convert as needed; see "Type Casts" on page 153.

Several methods provide easy access to particular elements of a vector or slice (note that all slice methods are available on arrays and vectors too):

`slice.first()`

Returns a reference to the first element of `slice`, if any.

The return type is `Option<&T>`, so the return value is `None` if `slice` is empty and `Some(&slice[0])` if it's not empty:

```
if let Some(item) = v.first() {
    println!("We got one! {}", item);
}
```

`slice.last()`

Similar but returns a reference to the last element.

`slice.get(index)`

Returns `Some` reference to `slice[index]`, if it exists. If `slice` has fewer than index+1 elements, this returns `None`:

```
let slice = [0, 1, 2, 3];
assert_eq!(slice.get(2), Some(&2));
assert_eq!(slice.get(4), None);
```

`slice.first_mut()`, `slice.last_mut()`, `slice.get_mut(index)`

Variations of the preceding that borrow `mut` references:

```
let mut slice = [0, 1, 2, 3];
{
    let last = slice.last_mut().unwrap();    // type of last: &mut i32
    assert_eq!(*last, 3);
    *last = 100;
}
assert_eq!(slice, [0, 1, 2, 100]);
```

Because returning a T by value would mean moving it, methods that access elements in place typically return those elements by reference.

An exception is the `.to_vec()` method, which makes copies:

`slice.to_vec()`

Clones a whole slice, returning a new vector:

```
let v = [1, 2, 3, 4, 5, 6, 7, 8, 9];
assert_eq!(v.to_vec(),
           vec![1, 2, 3, 4, 5, 6, 7, 8, 9]);
assert_eq!(v[0..6].to_vec(),
           vec![1, 2, 3, 4, 5, 6]);
```

This method is available only if the elements are cloneable, that is, where `T: Clone`.

Iteration

Vectors, arrays, and slices are iterable, either by value or by reference, following the pattern described in "IntoIterator Implementations" on page 351:

- Iterating over a `Vec<T>` or array `[T; N]` produces items of type `T`. The elements are moved out of the vector or array one by one, consuming it.

- Iterating over a value of type `&[T; N]`, `&[T]`, or `&Vec<T>`—that is, a reference to an array, slice, or vector—produces items of type `&T`, references to the individual elements, which are not moved.

- Iterating over a value of type `&mut [T; N]`, `&mut [T]`, or `&mut Vec<T>` produces items of type `&mut T`.

Arrays, slices, and vectors also have `.iter()` and `.iter_mut()` methods (described in "iter and iter_mut Methods" on page 350) for creating iterators that produce references to their elements.

We'll cover some fancier ways to iterate over a slice in "Splitting" on page 402.

Growing and Shrinking Vectors

The *length* of an array, slice, or vector is the number of elements it contains:

`slice.len()`
    Returns a `slice`'s length, as a `usize`.

`slice.is_empty()`
    Is true if `slice` contains no elements (that is, `slice.len() == 0`).

The remaining methods in this section are about growing and shrinking vectors. They are not present on arrays and slices, which can't be resized once created.

All of a vector's elements are stored in a contiguous, heap-allocated chunk of memory. The *capacity* of a vector is the maximum number of elements that would fit in this chunk. `Vec` normally manages the capacity for you, automatically allocating a larger buffer and moving the elements into it when more space is needed. There are also a few methods for managing capacity explicitly:

`Vec::with_capacity(n)`
    Creates a new, empty vector with capacity n.

`vec.capacity()`
    Returns `vec`'s capacity, as a `usize`. It's always true that `vec.capacity() >= vec.len()`.

`vec.reserve(n)`

> Makes sure the vector has at least enough spare capacity for n more elements: that is, `vec.capacity()` is at least `vec.len() + n`. If there's already enough room, this does nothing. If not, this allocates a larger buffer and moves the vector's contents into it.

`vec.reserve_exact(n)`

> Like `vec.reserve(n)`, but tells `vec` not to allocate any extra capacity for future growth, beyond n. Afterward, `vec.capacity()` is exactly `vec.len() + n`.

`vec.shrink_to_fit()`

> Tries to free up the extra memory if `vec.capacity()` is greater than `vec.len()`.

Vec<T> has many methods that add or remove elements, changing the vector's length. Each of these takes its `self` argument by `mut` reference.

These two methods add or remove a single value at the end of a vector:

`vec.push(value)`

> Adds the given `value` to the end of `vec`.

`vec.pop()`

> Removes and returns the last element. The return type is `Option<T>`. This returns `Some(x)` if the popped element is x and `None` if the vector was already empty.

Note that `.push()` takes its argument by value, not by reference. Likewise, `.pop()` returns the popped value, not a reference. The same is true of most of the remaining methods in this section. They move values in and out of vectors.

These two methods add or remove a value anywhere in a vector:

`vec.insert(index, value)`

> Inserts the given `value` at `vec[index]`, sliding any existing values in `vec[index..]` one spot to the right to make room.
>
> Panics if `index > vec.len()`.

`vec.remove(index)`

> Removes and returns `vec[index]`, sliding any existing values in `vec[index+1..]` one spot to the left to close the gap.
>
> Panics if `index >= vec.len()`, since in that case there is no element `vec[index]` to remove.
>
> The longer the vector, the slower this operation gets. If you find yourself doing `vec.remove(0)` a lot, consider using a VecDeque (explained in "VecDeque<T>" on page 410) instead of a Vec.

Both .insert() and .remove() are slower the more elements have to be shifted.

Four methods change the length of a vector to a specific value:

vec.resize(new_len, value)
    Sets vec's length to new_len. If this increases vec's length, copies of value are added to fill the new space. The element type must implement the Clone trait.

vec.resize_with(new_len, closure)
    Just like vec.resize, but calls the closure to construct each new element. It can be used with vectors of elements that are not Clone.

vec.truncate(new_len)
    Reduces the length of vec to new_len, dropping any elements that were in the range vec[new_len..].

    If vec.len() is already less than or equal to new_len, nothing happens.

vec.clear()
    Removes all elements from vec. It's the same as vec.truncate(0).

Four methods add or remove many values at once:

vec.extend(iterable)
    Adds all items from the given iterable value at the end of vec, in order. It's like a multivalue version of .push(). The iterable argument can be anything that implements IntoIterator<Item=T>.

    This method is so useful that there's a standard trait for it, the Extend trait, which all standard collections implement. Unfortunately, this causes rustdoc to lump .extend() with other trait methods in a big pile at the bottom of the generated HTML, so it's hard to find when you need it. You just have to remember it's there! See "The Extend Trait" on page 385 for more.

vec.split_off(index)
    Like vec.truncate(index), except that it returns a Vec<T> containing the values removed from the end of vec. It's like a multivalue version of .pop().

vec.append(&mut vec2)
    This moves all elements from vec2 into vec, where vec2 is another vector of type Vec<T>. Afterward, vec2 is empty.

    This is like vec.extend(vec2) except that vec2 still exists afterward, with its capacity unaffected.

`vec.drain(range)`

> This removes the `range` `vec[range]` from `vec` and returns an iterator over the removed elements, where `range` is a range value, like `..` or `0..4`.

There are also a few oddball methods for selectively removing some of a vector's elements:

`vec.retain(test)`

> Removes all elements that don't pass the given test. The `test` argument is a function or closure that implements `FnMut(&T) -> bool`. For each element of `vec`, this calls `test(&element)`, and if it returns `false`, the element is removed from the vector and dropped.
>
> Apart from performance, this is like writing:
>
> ```
> vec = vec.into_iter().filter(test).collect();
> ```

`vec.dedup()`

> Drops repeated elements. It's like the Unix `uniq` shell utility. It scans `vec` for places where adjacent elements are equal and drops the extra equal values so that only one is left:
>
> ```
> let mut byte_vec = b"Misssssssissippi".to_vec();
> byte_vec.dedup();
> assert_eq!(&byte_vec, b"Misisipi");
> ```

Note that there are still two `'s'` characters in the output. This method only removes *adjacent* duplicates. To eliminate all duplicates, you have three options: sort the vector before calling `.dedup()`, move the data into a set, or (to keep the elements in their original order) use this `.retain()` trick:

```
let mut byte_vec = b"Misssssssissippi".to_vec();

let mut seen = HashSet::new();
byte_vec.retain(|r| seen.insert(*r));

assert_eq!(&byte_vec, b"Misp");
```

This works because `.insert()` returns `false` when the set already contains the item we're inserting.

`vec.dedup_by(same)`

> The same as `vec.dedup()`, but it uses the function or closure `same(&mut elem1, &mut elem2)`, instead of the `==` operator, to check whether two elements should be considered equal.

```
vec.dedup_by_key(key)
```
The same as vec.dedup(), but it treats two elements as equal if key(&mut elem1)
== key(&mut elem2).

For example, if errors is a Vec<Box<dyn Error>>, you can write:

```
// Remove errors with redundant messages.
errors.dedup_by_key(|err| err.to_string());
```

Of all the methods covered in this section, only .resize() ever clones values. The
others work by moving values from one place to another.

Joining

Two methods work on *arrays of arrays*, by which we mean any array, slice, or vector
whose elements are themselves arrays, slices, or vectors:

```
slices.concat()
```
Returns a new vector made by concatenating all the slices:

```
assert_eq!([[1, 2], [3, 4], [5, 6]].concat(),
           vec![1, 2, 3, 4, 5, 6]);
```

```
slices.join(&separator)
```
The same, except a copy of the value separator is inserted between slices:

```
assert_eq!([[1, 2], [3, 4], [5, 6]].join(&0),
           vec![1, 2, 0, 3, 4, 0, 5, 6]);
```

Splitting

It's easy to get many non-mut references into an array, slice, or vector at once:

```
let v = vec![0, 1, 2, 3];
let a = &v[i];
let b = &v[j];

let mid = v.len() / 2;
let front_half = &v[..mid];
let back_half = &v[mid..];
```

Getting multiple mut references is not so easy:

```
let mut v = vec![0, 1, 2, 3];
let a = &mut v[i];
let b = &mut v[j];   // error: cannot borrow `v` as mutable
                     //        more than once at a time

*a = 6;              // references `a` and `b` get used here,
*b = 7;              // so their lifetimes must overlap
```

Rust forbids this because if i == j, then a and b would be two mut references to the same integer, in violation of Rust's safety rules. (See "Sharing Versus Mutation" on page 123.)

Rust has several methods that can borrow mut references to two or more parts of an array, slice, or vector at once. Unlike the preceding code, these methods are safe, because by design, they always split the data into *nonoverlapping* regions. Many of these methods are also handy for working with non-mut slices, so there are mut and non-mut versions of each.

Figure 16-2 illustrates these methods.

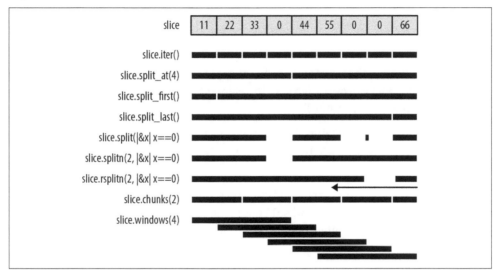

Figure 16-2. Splitting methods illustrated (note: the little rectangle in the output of `slice.split()` is an empty slice caused by the two adjacent separators, and `rsplitn` produces its output in end-to-start order, unlike the others)

None of these methods directly modifies an array, slice, or vector; they merely return new references to parts of the data inside:

`slice.iter()`, `slice.iter_mut()`
    Produce a reference to each element of slice. We covered them in "Iteration" on page 398.

`slice.split_at(index)`, `slice.split_at_mut(index)`
    Break a slice in two, returning a pair. `slice.split_at(index)` is equivalent to (`&slice[..index]`, `&slice[index..]`). These methods panic if index is out of bounds.

`slice.split_first()`, `slice.split_first_mut()`
:   Also return a pair: a reference to the first element (`slice[0]`) and a slice reference to all the rest (`slice[1..]`).

    The return type of `.split_first()` is `Option<(&T, &[T])>`; the result is `None` if `slice` is empty.

`slice.split_last()`, `slice.split_last_mut()`
:   These are analogous but split off the last element rather than the first.

    The return type of `.split_last()` is `Option<(&T, &[T])>`.

`slice.split(is_sep)`, `slice.split_mut(is_sep)`
:   Split `slice` into one or more subslices, using the function or closure `is_sep` to figure out where to split. They return an iterator over the subslices.

    As you consume the iterator, it calls `is_sep(&element)` for each element in the slice. If `is_sep(&element)` is `true`, the element is a separator. Separators are not included in any output subslice.

    The output always contains at least one subslice, plus one per separator. Empty subslices are included whenever separators appear adjacent to each other or to the ends of `slice`.

`slice.split_inclusive(is_sep)`, `slice.split_inclusive_mut(is_sep)`
:   These work just like `split` and `split_mut`, but include the separator at the end of the previous subslice rather than excluding it.

`slice.rsplit(is_sep)`, `slice.rsplit_mut(is_sep)`
:   Just like `slice` and `slice_mut`, but start at the end of the slice.

`slice.splitn(n, is_sep)`, `slice.splitn_mut(n, is_sep)`
:   The same but they produce at most n subslices. After the first n-1 slices are found, `is_sep` is not called again. The last subslice contains all the remaining elements.

`slice.rsplitn(n, is_sep)`, `slice.rsplitn_mut(n, is_sep)`
:   Just like `.splitn()` and `.splitn_mut()` except that the slice is scanned in reverse order. That is, these methods split on the *last* n-1 separators in the slice, rather than the first, and the subslices are produced starting from the end.

`slice.chunks(n)`, `slice.chunks_mut(n)`
:   Return an iterator over nonoverlapping subslices of length n. If n doesn't divide `slice.len()` exactly, the last chunk will contain fewer than n elements.

`slice.rchunks(n)`, `slice.rchunks_mut(n)`
:   Just like `slice.chunks` and `slice.chunks_mut`, but start at the end of the slice.

`slice.chunks_exact(n)`, `slice.chunks_exact_mut(n)`

Return an iterator over nonoverlapping subslices of length n. If n doesn't divide `slice.len()`, the last chunk (with less than n elements) is available in the result's `remainder()` method.

`slice.rchunks_exact(n)`, `slice.rchunks_exact_mut(n)`

Just like `slice.chunks_exact` and `slice.chunks_exact_mut`, but start at the end of the slice.

There's one more method for iterating over subslices:

`slice.windows(n)`

Returns an iterator that behaves like a "sliding window" over the data in `slice`. It produces subslices that span n consecutive elements of `slice`. The first value produced is `&slice[0..n]`, the second is `&slice[1..n+1]`, and so on.

If n is greater than the length of `slice`, then no slices are produced. If n is 0, the method panics.

For example, if `days.len()` == 31, then we can produce all seven-day spans in days by calling `days.windows(7)`.

A sliding window of size 2 is handy for exploring how a data series changes from one data point to the next:

```
let changes = daily_high_temperatures
                  .windows(2)              // get adjacent days' temps
                  .map(|w| w[1] - w[0])    // how much did it change?
                  .collect::<Vec<_>>();
```

Because the subslices overlap, there is no variation of this method that returns `mut` references.

Swapping

There are convenience methods for swapping the contents of slices:

`slice.swap(i, j)`

Swaps the two elements `slice[i]` and `slice[j]`.

`slice_a.swap(&mut slice_b)`

Swaps the entire contents of `slice_a` and `slice_b`. `slice_a` and `slice_b` must be the same length.

Vectors have a related method for efficiently removing any element:

`vec.swap_remove(i)`
> Removes and returns `vec[i]`. This is like `vec.remove(i)` except that instead of sliding the rest of the vector's elements over to close the gap, it simply moves vec's last element into the gap. It's useful when you don't care about the order of the items left in the vector.

Filling

There are two convenience methods for replacing the contents of mutable slices:

`slice.fill(value)`
> Fills the slice with clones of `value`.

`slice.fill_with(function)`
> Fills the slice with values made by calling the given function. This is especially useful for types that implement `Default`, but are not `Clone`, like `Option<T>` or `Vec<T>` when T is not `Clone`.

Sorting and Searching

Slices offer three methods for sorting:

`slice.sort()`
> Sorts the elements into increasing order. This method is present only when the element type implements `Ord`.

`slice.sort_by(cmp)`
> Sorts the elements of `slice` using a function or closure `cmp` to specify the sort order. `cmp` must implement `Fn(&T, &T) -> std::cmp::Ordering`.
>
> Hand-implementing `cmp` is a pain, unless you delegate to a `.cmp()` method:
>
> ```
> students.sort_by(|a, b| a.last_name.cmp(&b.last_name));
> ```
>
> To sort by one field, using a second field as a tiebreaker, compare tuples:
>
> ```
> students.sort_by(|a, b| {
>     let a_key = (&a.last_name, &a.first_name);
>     let b_key = (&b.last_name, &b.first_name);
>     a_key.cmp(&b_key)
> });
> ```

`slice.sort_by_key(key)`
> Sorts the elements of `slice` into increasing order by a sort key, given by the function or closure key. The type of key must implement `Fn(&T) -> K where K: Ord`.

This is useful when T contains one or more ordered fields, so that it could be sorted multiple ways:

```
// Sort by grade point average, lowest first.
students.sort_by_key(|s| s.grade_point_average());
```

Note that these sort-key values are not cached during sorting, so the key function may be called more than *n* times.

For technical reasons, `key(element)` can't return any references borrowed from the element. This won't work:

```
students.sort_by_key(|s| &s.last_name);  // error: can't infer lifetime
```

Rust can't figure out the lifetimes. But in these cases, it's easy enough to fall back on `.sort_by()`.

All three methods perform a stable sort.

To sort in reverse order, you can use `sort_by` with a `cmp` closure that swaps the two arguments. Taking arguments `|b, a|` rather than `|a, b|` effectively produces the opposite order. Or, you can just call the `.reverse()` method after sorting:

`slice.reverse()`
Reverses a slice in place.

Once a slice is sorted, it can be efficiently searched:

`slice.binary_search(&value)`, `slice.binary_search_by(&value, cmp)`,
`slice.binary_search_by_key(&value, key)`
All search for `value` in the given sorted `slice`. Note that `value` is passed by reference.

The return type of these methods is `Result<usize, usize>`. They return `Ok(index)` if `slice[index]` equals `value` under the specified sort order. If there is no such index, then they return `Err(insertion_point)` such that inserting `value` at `insertion_point` would preserve the order.

Of course, a binary search only works if the slice is in fact sorted in the specified order. Otherwise, the results are arbitrary—garbage in, garbage out.

Since `f32` and `f64` have NaN values, they do not implement `Ord` and can't be used directly as keys with the sorting and binary search methods. To get similar methods that work on floating-point data, use the `ord_subset` crate.

There's one method for searching a vector that is not sorted:

```
slice.contains(&value)
```
Returns `true` if any element of `slice` is equal to `value`. This simply checks each element of the slice until a match is found. Again, `value` is passed by reference.

To find the location of a value in a slice, like `array.indexOf(value)` in JavaScript, use an iterator:

```
slice.iter().position(|x| *x == value)
```

This returns an `Option<usize>`.

Comparing Slices

If a type `T` supports the `==` and `!=` operators (the `PartialEq` trait, described in "Equivalence Comparisons" on page 294), then arrays `[T; N]`, slices `[T]`, and vectors `Vec<T>` support them too. Two slices are equal if they're the same length and their corresponding elements are equal. The same goes for arrays and vectors.

If `T` supports the operators `<`, `<=`, `>`, and `>=` (the `PartialOrd` trait, described in "Ordered Comparisons" on page 297), then arrays, slices, and vectors of `T` do too. Slice comparisons are lexicographical.

Two convenience methods perform common slice comparisons:

```
slice.starts_with(other)
```
Returns `true` if `slice` starts with a sequence of values that are equal to the elements of the slice `other`:

```
assert_eq!([1, 2, 3, 4].starts_with(&[1, 2]), true);
assert_eq!([1, 2, 3, 4].starts_with(&[2, 3]), false);
```

```
slice.ends_with(other)
```
Similar but checks the end of `slice`:

```
assert_eq!([1, 2, 3, 4].ends_with(&[3, 4]), true);
```

Random Elements

Random numbers are not built into the Rust standard library. The `rand` crate, which provides them, offers these two methods for getting random output from an array, slice, or vector:

```
slice.choose(&mut rng)
```
Returns a reference to a random element of a slice. Like `slice.first()` and `slice.last()`, this returns an `Option<&T>` that is `None` only if the slice is empty.

```
slice.shuffle(&mut rng)
```
Randomly reorders the elements of a slice in place. The slice must be passed by `mut` reference.

These are methods of the `rand::Rng` trait, so you need a `Rng`, a random number generator, in order to call them. Fortunately, it's easy to get one by calling `rand::thread_rng()`. To shuffle the vector `my_vec`, we can write:

```
use rand::seq::SliceRandom;
use rand::thread_rng;

my_vec.shuffle(&mut thread_rng());
```

Rust Rules Out Invalidation Errors

Most mainstream programming languages have collections and iterators, and they all have some variation on this rule: don't modify a collection while you're iterating over it. For example, the Python equivalent of a vector is a list:

```
my_list = [1, 3, 5, 7, 9]
```

Suppose we try to remove all values greater than 4 from `my_list`:

```
for index, val in enumerate(my_list):
    if val > 4:
        del my_list[index]  # bug: modifying list while iterating

print(my_list)
```

(The `enumerate` function is Python's equivalent of Rust's `.enumerate()` method, described in "enumerate" on page 371.)

This program, surprisingly, prints `[1, 3, 7]`. But seven is greater than four. How did that slip through? This is an invalidation error: the program modifies data while iterating over it, *invalidating* the iterator. In Java, the result would be an exception; in C++ it is undefined behavior. In Python, while the behavior is well-defined, it's unintuitive: the iterator skips an element. `val` is never 7.

Let's try to reproduce this bug in Rust:

```
fn main() {
    let mut my_vec = vec![1, 3, 5, 7, 9];

    for (index, &val) in my_vec.iter().enumerate() {
        if val > 4 {
            my_vec.remove(index);  // error: can't borrow `my_vec` as mutable
        }
    }
    println!("{:?}", my_vec);
}
```

Naturally, Rust rejects this program at compile time. When we call `my_vec.iter()`, it borrows a shared (non-mut) reference to the vector. The reference lives as long as the iterator, to the end of the `for` loop. We can't modify the vector by calling `my_vec.remove(index)` while a non-mut reference exists.

Having an error pointed out to you is nice, but of course, you still need to find a way to get the desired behavior! The easiest fix here is to write:

```
my_vec.retain(|&val| val <= 4);
```

Or, you can do what you'd do in Python or any other language: create a new vector using a `filter`.

VecDeque<T>

Vec supports efficiently adding and removing elements only at the end. When a program needs a place to store values that are "waiting in line," Vec can be slow.

Rust's `std::collections::VecDeque<T>` is a *deque* (pronounced "deck"), a double-ended queue. It supports efficient add and remove operations at both the front and the back:

`deque.push_front(value)`
    Adds a value at the front of the queue.

`deque.push_back(value)`
    Adds a value at the end. (This method is used much more than `.push_front()`, because the usual convention for queues is that values are added at the back and removed at the front, like people waiting in a line.)

`deque.pop_front()`
    Removes and returns the front value of the queue, returning an `Option<T>` that is `None` if the queue is empty, like `vec.pop()`.

`deque.pop_back()`
    Removes and returns the value at the back, again returning an `Option<T>`.

`deque.front()`, `deque.back()`
    Work like `vec.first()` and `vec.last()`. They return a reference to the front or back element of the queue. The return value is an `Option<&T>` that is `None` if the queue is empty.

`deque.front_mut()`, `deque.back_mut()`
    Work like `vec.first_mut()` and `vec.last_mut()`, returning `Option<&mut T>`.

The implementation of VecDeque is a ring buffer, as shown in Figure 16-3.

Like a Vec, it has a single heap allocation where elements are stored. Unlike Vec, the data does not always start at the beginning of this region, and it can "wrap around" the end, as shown. The elements of this deque, in order, are ['A', 'B', 'C', 'D', 'E']. VecDeque has private fields, labeled start and stop in the figure, that it uses to remember where in the buffer the data begins and ends.

Adding a value to the queue, on either end, means claiming one of the unused slots, illustrated as the darker blocks, wrapping around or allocating a bigger chunk of memory if needed.

VecDeque manages wrapping, so you don't have to think about it. Figure 16-3 is a behind-the-scenes view of how Rust makes .pop_front() fast.

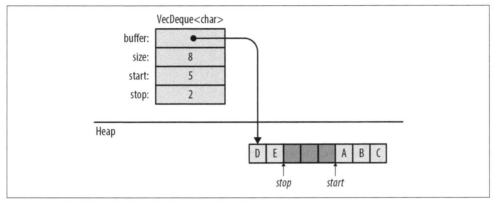

Figure 16-3. How a VecDeque is stored in memory

Oftentimes, when you need a deque, .push_back() and .pop_front() are the only two methods that you'll need. The type-associated functions VecDeque::new() and VecDeque::with_capacity(n), for creating queues, are just like their counterparts in Vec. Many Vec methods are also implemented for VecDeque: .len() and .is_empty(), .insert(index, value), .remove(index), .extend(iterable), and so on.

Deques, like vectors, can be iterated by value, by shared reference, or by mut reference. They have the three iterator methods .into_iter(), .iter(), and .iter_mut(). They can be indexed in the usual way: deque[index].

Because deques don't store their elements contiguously in memory, they can't inherit all the methods of slices. But if you're willing to pay the cost of shifting the contents around, VecDeque provides a method that will fix that:

deque.make_contiguous()
> Takes &mut self and rearranges the VecDeque into contiguous memory, returning &mut [T].

Vecs and VecDeques are closely related, and the standard library provides two trait implementations for easily converting between the two:

`Vec::from(deque)`
Vec<T> implements From<VecDeque<T>>, so this turns a deque into a vector. This costs O(n) time, since it may require rearranging the elements.

`VecDeque::from(vec)`
VecDeque<T> implements From<Vec<T>>, so this turns a vector into a deque. This is also O(n), but it's usually fast, even if the vector is large, because the vector's heap allocation can simply be moved to the new deque.

This method makes it easy to create a deque with specified elements, even though there is no standard vec_deque![] macro:

```
use std::collections::VecDeque;

let v = VecDeque::from(vec![1, 2, 3, 4]);
```

BinaryHeap<T>

A BinaryHeap is a collection whose elements are kept loosely organized so that the greatest value always bubbles up to the front of the queue. Here are the three most commonly used BinaryHeap methods:

`heap.push(value)`
Adds a value to the heap.

`heap.pop()`
Removes and returns the greatest value from the heap. It returns an Option<T> that is None if the heap was empty.

`heap.peek()`
Returns a reference to the greatest value in the heap. The return type is Option<&T>.

`heap.peek_mut()`
Returns a PeekMut<T>, which acts as a mutable reference to the greatest value in the heap and provides the type-associated function pop() to pop this value from the heap. Using this method, we can choose to pop or not pop from the heap based on the maximum value:

```
use std::collections::binary_heap::PeekMut;

if let Some(top) = heap.peek_mut() {
    if *top > 10 {
        PeekMut::pop(top);
```

```
        }
    }
```

BinaryHeap also supports a subset of the methods on Vec, including BinaryHeap::new(), .len(), .is_empty(), .capacity(), .clear(), and .append(&mut heap2).

For example, suppose we populate a BinaryHeap with a bunch of numbers:

```
use std::collections::BinaryHeap;

let mut heap = BinaryHeap::from(vec![2, 3, 8, 6, 9, 5, 4]);
```

The value 9 is at the top of the heap:

```
assert_eq!(heap.peek(), Some(&9));
assert_eq!(heap.pop(), Some(9));
```

Removing the value 9 also rearranges the other elements slightly so that 8 is now at the front, and so on:

```
assert_eq!(heap.pop(), Some(8));
assert_eq!(heap.pop(), Some(6));
assert_eq!(heap.pop(), Some(5));
...
```

Of course, BinaryHeap is not limited to numbers. It can hold any type of value that implements the Ord built-in trait.

This makes BinaryHeap useful as a work queue. You can define a task struct that implements Ord on the basis of priority so that higher-priority tasks are Greater than lower-priority tasks. Then, create a BinaryHeap to hold all pending tasks. Its .pop() method will always return the most important item, the task your program should work on next.

Note: BinaryHeap is iterable, and it has an .iter() method, but the iterators produce the heap's elements in an arbitrary order, not from greatest to least. To consume values from a BinaryHeap in order of priority, use a while loop:

```
while let Some(task) = heap.pop() {
    handle(task);
}
```

HashMap<K, V> and BTreeMap<K, V>

A *map* is a collection of key-value pairs (called *entries*). No two entries have the same key, and the entries are kept organized so that if you have a key, you can efficiently look up the corresponding value in a map. In short, a map is a lookup table.

Rust offers two map types: HashMap<K, V> and BTreeMap<K, V>. The two share many of the same methods; the difference is in how the two keep entries arranged for fast lookup.

A HashMap stores the keys and values in a hash table, so it requires a key type K that implements Hash and Eq, the standard traits for hashing and equality.

Figure 16-4 shows how a HashMap is arranged in memory. Darker regions are unused. All keys, values, and cached hash codes are stored in a single heap-allocated table. Adding entries eventually forces the HashMap to allocate a larger table and move all the data into it.

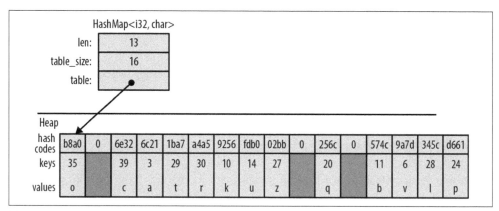

Figure 16-4. A HashMap in memory

A BTreeMap stores the entries in order by key, in a tree structure, so it requires a key type K that implements Ord. Figure 16-5 shows a BTreeMap. Again, the darker regions are unused spare capacity.

A BTreeMap stores its entries in *nodes*. Most nodes in a BTreeMap contain only key-value pairs. Nonleaf nodes, like the root node shown in this figure, also have room for pointers to child nodes. The pointer between (20, 'q') and (30, 'r') points to a child node containing keys between 20 and 30. Adding entries often requires sliding some of a node's existing entries to the right, to keep them sorted, and occasionally involves allocating new nodes.

This picture is a bit simplified to fit on the page. For example, real BTreeMap nodes have room for 11 entries, not 4.

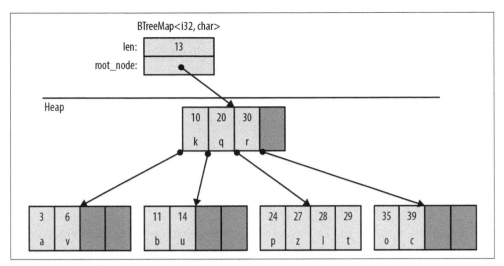

Figure 16-5. A BTreeMap in memory

The Rust standard library uses B-trees rather than balanced binary trees because B-trees are faster on modern hardware. A binary tree may use fewer comparisons per search than a B-tree, but searching a B-tree has better *locality*—that is, the memory accesses are grouped together rather than scattered across the whole heap. This makes CPU cache misses rarer. It's a significant speed boost.

There are several ways to create a map:

`HashMap::new(), BTreeMap::new()`
Create new, empty maps.

`iter.collect()`
Can be used to create and populate a new HashMap or BTreeMap from key-value pairs. `iter` must be an `Iterator<Item=(K, V)>`.

`HashMap::with_capacity(n)`
Creates a new, empty hash map with room for at least *n* entries. HashMaps, like vectors, store their data in a single heap allocation, so they have a capacity and the related methods `hash_map.capacity()`, `hash_map.reserve(additional)`, and `hash_map.shrink_to_fit()`. BTreeMaps do not.

HashMaps and BTreeMaps have the same core methods for working with keys and values:

`map.len()`
Returns the number of entries.

`map.is_empty()`

Returns `true` if `map` has no entries.

`map.contains_key(&key)`

Returns `true` if the map has an entry for the given key.

`map.get(&key)`

Searches `map` for an entry with the given key. If a matching entry is found, this returns `Some(r)`, where `r` is a reference to the corresponding value. Otherwise, this returns `None`.

`map.get_mut(&key)`

Similar, but it returns a `mut` reference to the value.

In general, maps let you have `mut` access to the values stored inside them, but not the keys. The values are yours to modify however you like. The keys belong to the map itself; it needs to ensure that they don't change, because the entries are organized by their keys. Modifying a key in-place would be a bug.

`map.insert(key, value)`

Inserts the entry (`key, value`) into `map` and returns the old value, if any. The return type is `Option<V>`. If there's already an entry for key in the map, the newly inserted `value` overwrites the old one.

`map.extend(iterable)`

Iterates over the (`K, V`) items of `iterable` and inserts each of those key-value pairs into `map`.

`map.append(&mut map2)`

Moves all entries from `map2` into `map`. Afterward, `map2` is empty.

`map.remove(&key)`

Finds and removes any entry with the given key from `map`, returning the removed value, if any. The return type is `Option<V>`.

`map.remove_entry(&key)`

Finds and removes any entry with the given key from `map`, returning the removed key and value, if any. The return type is `Option<(K, V)>`.

`map.retain(test)`

Removes all elements that don't pass the given test. The `test` argument is a function or closure that implements `FnMut(&K, &mut V) -> bool`. For each element of `map`, this calls `test(&key, &mut value)`, and if it returns `false`, the element is removed from the map and dropped.

Apart from performance, this is like writing:

```
map = map.into_iter().filter(test).collect();
```

`map.clear()`

Removes all entries.

A map can also be queried using square brackets: `map[&key]`. That is, maps implement the `Index` built-in trait. However, this panics if there is not already an entry for the given key, like an out-of-bounds array access, so use this syntax only if the entry you're looking up is sure to be populated.

The key argument to `.contains_key()`, `.get()`, `.get_mut()`, and `.remove()` does not have to have the exact type `&K`. These methods are generic over types that can be borrowed from K. It's OK to call `fish_map.contains_key("conger")` on a `HashMap<String, Fish>`, even though `"conger"` isn't exactly a `String`, because `String` implements `Borrow<&str>`. For details, see "Borrow and BorrowMut" on page 318.

Because a `BTreeMap<K, V>` keeps its entries sorted by key, it supports an additional operation:

`btree_map.split_off(&key)`

Splits `btree_map` in two. Entries with keys less than `key` are left in `btree_map`. Returns a new `BTreeMap<K, V>` containing the other entries.

Entries

Both `HashMap` and `BTreeMap` have a corresponding `Entry` type. The point of entries is to eliminate redundant map lookups. For example, here's some code to get or create a student record:

```
// Do we already have a record for this student?
if !student_map.contains_key(name) {
    // No: create one.
    student_map.insert(name.to_string(), Student::new());
}
// Now a record definitely exists.
let record = student_map.get_mut(name).unwrap();
...
```

This works fine, but it accesses `student_map` two or three times, doing the same lookup each time.

The idea with entries is that we do the lookup just once, producing an `Entry` value that is then used for all subsequent operations. This one-liner is equivalent to all the preceding code, except that it does the lookup only once:

```
let record = student_map.entry(name.to_string()).or_insert_with(Student::new);
```

The `Entry` value returned by `student_map.entry(name.to_string())` acts like a mutable reference to a place within the map that's either *occupied* by a key-value pair, or *vacant*, meaning there's no entry there yet. If vacant, the entry's `.or_insert_with()` method inserts a new `Student`. Most uses of entries are like this: short and sweet.

All `Entry` values are created by the same method:

`map.entry(key)`
> Returns an `Entry` for the given key. If there's no such key in the map, this returns a vacant `Entry`.
>
> This method takes its `self` argument by `mut` reference and returns an `Entry` with a matching lifetime:
>
> ```
> pub fn entry<'a>(&'a mut self, key: K) -> Entry<'a, K, V>
> ```
>
> The `Entry` type has a lifetime parameter `'a` because it's effectively a fancy kind of borrowed `mut` reference to the map. As long as the `Entry` exists, it has exclusive access to the map.
>
> Back in "Structs Containing References" on page 117, we saw how to store references in a type and how that affects lifetimes. Now we're seeing what that looks like from a user's perspective. That's what's going on with `Entry`.
>
> Unfortunately, it is not possible to pass a reference of type `&str` to this method if the map has `String` keys. The `.entry()` method, in that case, requires a real `String`.

Entry values provide three methods to deal with vacant entries:

`map.entry(key).or_insert(value)`
> Ensures that `map` contains an entry with the given key, inserting a new entry with the given `value` if needed. It returns a `mut` reference to the new or existing value.
>
> Suppose we need to count votes. We can write:
>
> ```
> let mut vote_counts: HashMap<String, usize> = HashMap::new();
> for name in ballots {
>     let count = vote_counts.entry(name).or_insert(0);
>     *count += 1;
> }
> ```
>
> `.or_insert()` returns a `mut` reference, so the type of `count` is `&mut usize`.

`map.entry(key).or_default()`
> Ensures that `map` contains an entry with the given key, inserting a new entry with the value returned by `Default::default()` if needed. This only works for types

that implement `Default`. Like `or_insert`, this method returns a `mut` reference to the new or existing value.

`map.entry(key).or_insert_with(default_fn)`

> This is the same, except that if it needs to create a new entry, it calls `default_fn()` to produce the default value. If there's already an entry for key in the map, then `default_fn` is not used.

> Suppose we want to know which words appear in which files. We can write:

```
// This map contains, for each word, the set of files it appears in.
let mut word_occurrence: HashMap<String, HashSet<String>> =
    HashMap::new();
for file in files {
    for word in read_words(file)? {
        let set = word_occurrence
            .entry(word)
            .or_insert_with(HashSet::new);
        set.insert(file.clone());
    }
}
```

Entry also provides a convenient way to modify only extant fields.

`map.entry(key).and_modify(closure)`

> Calls `closure` if an entry with the key key exists, passing in a mutable reference to the value. It returns the `Entry`, so it can be chained with other methods.

> For instance, we could use this to count the number of occurrences of words in a string:

```
// This map contains all the words in a given string,
// along with the number of times they occur.
let mut word_frequency: HashMap<&str, u32> = HashMap::new();
for c in text.split_whitespace() {
    word_frequency.entry(c)
        .and_modify(|count| *count += 1)
        .or_insert(1);
}
```

The `Entry` type is an enum, defined like this for `HashMap` (and similarly for `BTreeMap`):

```
// (in std::collections::hash_map)
pub enum Entry<'a, K, V> {
    Occupied(OccupiedEntry<'a, K, V>),
    Vacant(VacantEntry<'a, K, V>)
}
```

The `OccupiedEntry` and `VacantEntry` types have methods for inserting, removing, and accessing entries without repeating the initial lookup. You can find them in the online documentation. The extra methods can occasionally be used to eliminate a redundant lookup or two, but .or_insert() and .or_insert_with() cover the common cases.

Map Iteration

There are several ways to iterate over a map:

- Iterating by value (for (k, v) in map) produces (K, V) pairs. This consumes the map.

- Iterating over a shared reference (for (k, v) in &map) produces (&K, &V) pairs.

- Iterating over a mut reference (for (k, v) in &mut map) produces (&K, &mut V) pairs. (Again, there's no way to get mut access to keys stored in a map, because the entries are organized by their keys.)

Like vectors, maps have .iter() and .iter_mut() methods that return by-reference iterators, just like iterating over &map or &mut map. In addition:

map.keys()
> Returns an iterator over just the keys, by reference.

map.values()
> Returns an iterator over the values, by reference.

map.values_mut()
> Returns an iterator over the values, by mut reference.

map.into_iter(), map.into_keys(), map.into_values()
> Consume the map, returning an iterator over tuples (K, V) of keys and values, keys, or values, respectively.

All HashMap iterators visit the map's entries in an arbitrary order. BTreeMap iterators visit them in order by key.

HashSet\<T> and BTreeSet\<T>

Sets are collections of values arranged for fast membership testing:

```
let b1 = large_vector.contains(&"needle");    // slow, checks every element
let b2 = large_hash_set.contains(&"needle");  // fast, hash lookup
```

A set never contains multiple copies of the same value.

Maps and sets have different methods, but behind the scenes, a set is like a map with only keys, rather than key-value pairs. In fact, Rust's two set types, HashSet\<T> and

BTreeSet<T>, are implemented as thin wrappers around HashMap<T, ()> and BTreeMap<T, ()>.

HashSet::new(), BTreeSet::new()
   Create new sets.

iter.collect()
   Can be used to create a new set from any iterator. If iter produces any values more than once, the duplicates are dropped.

HashSet::with_capacity(n)
   Creates an empty HashSet with room for at least n values.

HashSet<T> and BTreeSet<T> have all the basic methods in common:

set.len()
   Returns the number of values in set.

set.is_empty()
   Returns true if the set contains no elements.

set.contains(&value)
   Returns true if the set contains the given value.

set.insert(value)
   Adds a value to the set. Returns true if a value was added, false if it was already a member of the set.

set.remove(&value)
   Removes a value from the set. Returns true if a value was removed, false if it already wasn't a member of the set.

set.retain(test)
   Removes all elements that don't pass the given test. The test argument is a function or closure that implements FnMut(&T) -> bool. For each element of set, this calls test(&value), and if it returns false, the element is removed from the set and dropped.

   Apart from performance, this is like writing:

   ```
   set = set.into_iter().filter(test).collect();
   ```

As with maps, the methods that look up a value by reference are generic over types that can be borrowed from T. For details, see "Borrow and BorrowMut" on page 318.

Set Iteration

There are two ways to iterate over sets:

- Iterating by value ("for v in set") produces the members of the set (and consumes the set).

- Iterating by shared reference ("for v in &set") produces shared references to the members of the set.

Iterating over a set by mut reference is not supported. There's no way to get a mut reference to a value stored in a set.

set.iter()
>   Returns an iterator over the members of set by reference.

HashSet iterators, like HashMap iterators, produce their values in an arbitrary order. BTreeSet iterators produce values in order, like a sorted vector.

When Equal Values Are Different

Sets have a few odd methods that you need to use only if you care about differences between "equal" values.

Such differences do often exist. Two identical String values, for example, store their characters in different locations in memory:

```
let s1 = "hello".to_string();
let s2 = "hello".to_string();
println!("{:p}", &s1 as &str);  // 0x7f8b32060008
println!("{:p}", &s2 as &str);  // 0x7f8b32060010
```

Usually, we don't care.

But in case you ever do, you can get access to the actual values stored inside a set by using the following methods. Each one returns an Option that's None if set did not contain a matching value:

set.get(&value)
>   Returns a shared reference to the member of set that's equal to value, if any. Returns an Option<&T>.

set.take(&value)
>   Like set.remove(&value), but it returns the removed value, if any. Returns an Option<T>.

```
set.replace(value)
```
Like `set.insert(value)`, but if `set` already contains a value that's equal to `value`, this replaces and returns the old value. Returns an `Option<T>`.

Whole-Set Operations

So far, most of the set methods we've seen are focused on a single value in a single set. Sets also have methods that operate on whole sets:

```
set1.intersection(&set2)
```
Returns an iterator over all values that are in both `set1` and `set2`.

For example, if we want to print the names of all students who are taking both brain surgery and rocket science classes, we could write:

```
for student in &brain_class {
    if rocket_class.contains(student) {
        println!("{}", student);
    }
}
```

Or, shorter:

```
for student in brain_class.intersection(&rocket_class) {
    println!("{}", student);
}
```

Amazingly, there's an operator for this.

`&set1 & &set2` returns a new set that's the intersection of `set1` and `set2`. This is the binary bitwise AND operator, applied to two references. This finds values that are in both `set1` *and* `set2`:

```
let overachievers = &brain_class & &rocket_class;
```

```
set1.union(&set2)
```
Returns an iterator over values that are in either `set1` or `set2`, or both.

`&set1 | &set2` returns a new set containing all those values. It finds values that are in either `set1` *or* `set2`.

```
set1.difference(&set2)
```
Returns an iterator over values that are in `set1` but not in `set2`.

`&set1 - &set2` returns a new set containing all those values.

```
set1.symmetric_difference(&set2)
```
Returns an iterator over values that are in either `set1` or `set2`, but not both.

`&set1 ^ &set2` returns a new set containing all those values.

And there are three methods for testing relationships between sets:

`set1.is_disjoint(set2)`
> True if `set1` and `set2` have no values in common—the intersection between them is empty.

`set1.is_subset(set2)`
> True if `set1` is a subset of `set2`—that is, all values in `set1` are also in `set2`.

`set1.is_superset(set2)`
> This is the reverse: it's true if `set1` is a superset of `set2`.

Sets also support equality testing with `==` and `!=`; two sets are equal if they contain the same values.

Hashing

`std::hash::Hash` is the standard library trait for hashable types. `HashMap` keys and `HashSet` elements must implement both `Hash` and `Eq`.

Most built-in types that implement `Eq` also implement `Hash`. The integer types, `char`, and `String` are all hashable; so are tuples, arrays, slices, and vectors, as long as their elements are hashable.

One principle of the standard library is that a value should have the same hash code regardless of where you store it or how you point to it. Therefore, a reference has the same hash code as the value it refers to, and a `Box` has the same hash code as the boxed value. A vector `vec` has the same hash code as the slice containing all its data, `&vec[..]`. A `String` has the same hash code as a `&str` with the same characters.

Structs and enums don't implement `Hash` by default, but an implementation can be derived:

```
/// The ID number for an object in the British Museum's collection.
#[derive(Clone, PartialEq, Eq, Hash)]
enum MuseumNumber {
    ...
}
```

This works as long as the type's fields are all hashable.

If you implement `PartialEq` by hand for a type, you should also implement `Hash` by hand. For example, suppose we have a type that represents priceless historical treasures:

```
struct Artifact {
    id: MuseumNumber,
    name: String,
    cultures: Vec<Culture>,
```

```
        date: RoughTime,
        ...
    }
```

Two `Artifacts` are considered equal if they have the same ID:

```
impl PartialEq for Artifact {
    fn eq(&self, other: &Artifact) -> bool {
        self.id == other.id
    }
}

impl Eq for Artifact {}
```

Since we compare artifacts purely on the basis of their ID, we must hash them the
same way:

```
use std::hash::{Hash, Hasher};

impl Hash for Artifact {
    fn hash<H: Hasher>(&self, hasher: &mut H) {
        // Delegate hashing to the MuseumNumber.
        self.id.hash(hasher);
    }
}
```

(Otherwise, `HashSet<Artifact>` would not work properly; like all hash tables, it
requires that `hash(a) == hash(b)` if `a == b`.)

This allows us to create a `HashSet` of `Artifacts`:

```
let mut collection = HashSet::<Artifact>::new();
```

As this code shows, even when you implement `Hash` by hand, you don't need to know
anything about hashing algorithms. `.hash()` receives a reference to a `Hasher`, which
represents the hashing algorithm. You simply feed this `Hasher` all the data that's relevant to the == operator. The `Hasher` computes a hash code from whatever you give it.

Using a Custom Hashing Algorithm

The `hash` method is generic, so the `Hash` implementations shown earlier can feed data
to any type that implements `Hasher`. This is how Rust supports pluggable hashing
algorithms.

A third trait, `std::hash::BuildHasher`, is the trait for types that represent the initial
state of a hashing algorithm. Each `Hasher` is single use, like an iterator: you use it
once and throw it away. A `BuildHasher` is reusable.

Every `HashMap` contains a `BuildHasher` that it uses each time it needs to compute a hash code. The `BuildHasher` value contains the key, initial state, or other parameters that the hashing algorithm needs every time it runs.

The complete protocol for computing a hash code looks like this:

```
use std::hash::{Hash, Hasher, BuildHasher};

fn compute_hash<B, T>(builder: &B, value: &T) -> u64
    where B: BuildHasher, T: Hash
{
    let mut hasher = builder.build_hasher();  // 1. start the algorithm
    value.hash(&mut hasher);                  // 2. feed it data
    hasher.finish()                           // 3. finish, producing a u64
}
```

`HashMap` calls these three methods every time it needs to compute a hash code. All the methods are inlineable, so it's very fast.

Rust's default hashing algorithm is a well-known algorithm called SipHash-1-3. SipHash is fast, and it's very good at minimizing hash collisions. In fact, it's a cryptographic algorithm: there's no known efficient way to generate SipHash-1-3 collisions. As long as a different, unpredictable key is used for each hash table, Rust is secure against a kind of denial-of-service attack called HashDoS, where attackers deliberately use hash collisions to trigger worst-case performance in a server.

But perhaps you don't need that for your application. If you're storing many small keys, such as integers or very short strings, it is possible to implement a faster hash function, at the expense of HashDoS security. The `fnv` crate implements one such algorithm, the Fowler–Noll–Vo (FNV) hash. To try it, add this line to your *Cargo.toml*:

```
[dependencies]
fnv = "1.0"
```

Then import the map and set types from `fnv`:

```
use fnv::{FnvHashMap, FnvHashSet};
```

You can use these two types as drop-in replacements for `HashMap` and `HashSet`. A peek inside the `fnv` source code reveals how they're defined:

```
/// A `HashMap` using a default FNV hasher.
pub type FnvHashMap<K, V> = HashMap<K, V, FnvBuildHasher>;

/// A `HashSet` using a default FNV hasher.
pub type FnvHashSet<T> = HashSet<T, FnvBuildHasher>;
```

The standard `HashMap` and `HashSet` collections accept an optional extra type parameter specifying the hashing algorithm; `FnvHashMap` and `FnvHashSet` are generic type aliases for `HashMap` and `HashSet`, specifying an FNV hasher for that parameter.

Beyond the Standard Collections

Creating a new, custom collection type in Rust is much the same as in any other language. You arrange data by combining the parts the language provides: structs and enums, standard collections, `Options`, `Boxes`, and so on. For an example, see the `BinaryTree<T>` type defined in "Generic Enums" on page 238.

If you're used to implementing data structures in C++, using raw pointers, manual memory management, placement `new`, and explicit destructor calls to get the best possible performance, you'll undoubtedly find safe Rust rather limiting. All of those tools are inherently unsafe. They are available in Rust, but only if you opt in to unsafe code. Chapter 22 shows how; it includes an example that uses some unsafe code to implement a safe custom collection.

For now, we'll just bask in the warm glow of the standard collections and their safe, efficient APIs. Like much of the Rust standard library, they're designed to ensure that the need to write `unsafe` is as rare as possible.

## CHAPTER 17

Strings and Text

The string is a stark data structure and everywhere it is passed there is much duplication of process. It is a perfect vehicle for hiding information.
—Alan Perlis, epigram #34

We've been using Rust's main textual types, `String`, `str`, and `char`, throughout the book. In "String Types" on page 73, we described the syntax for character and string literals and showed how strings are represented in memory. In this chapter, we cover text handling in more detail.

In this chapter:

- We give you some background on Unicode that should help you make sense of the standard library's design.

- We describe the `char` type, representing a single Unicode code point.

- We describe the `String` and `str` types, representing owned and borrowed sequences of Unicode characters. These have a broad variety of methods for building, searching, modifying, and iterating over their contents.

- We cover Rust's string formatting facilities, like the `println!` and `format!` macros. You can write your own macros that work with formatting strings and extend them to support your own types.

- We give an overview of Rust's regular expression support.

- Finally, we talk about why Unicode normalization matters and show how to do it in Rust.

Some Unicode Background

This book is about Rust, not Unicode, which has entire books devoted to it already. But Rust's character and string types are designed around Unicode. Here are a few bits of Unicode that help explain Rust.

ASCII, Latin-1, and Unicode

Unicode and ASCII match for all of ASCII's code points, from 0 to 0x7f: for example, both assign the character * the code point 42. Similarly, Unicode assigns 0 through 0xff to the same characters as the ISO/IEC 8859-1 character set, an eight-bit superset of ASCII for use with Western European languages. Unicode calls this range of code points the *Latin-1 code block*, so we'll refer to ISO/IEC 8859-1 by the more evocative name *Latin-1*.

Since Unicode is a superset of Latin-1, converting Latin-1 to Unicode doesn't even require a table:

```
fn latin1_to_char(latin1: u8) -> char {
    latin1 as char
}
```

The reverse conversion is trivial as well, assuming the code points fall in the Latin-1 range:

```
fn char_to_latin1(c: char) -> Option<u8> {
    if c as u32 <= 0xff {
        Some(c as u8)
    } else {
        None
    }
}
```

UTF-8

The Rust `String` and `str` types represent text using the UTF-8 encoding form. UTF-8 encodes a character as a sequence of one to four bytes (Figure 17-1).

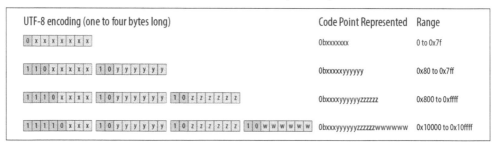

Figure 17-1. The UTF-8 encoding

There are two restrictions on well-formed UTF-8 sequences. First, only the shortest encoding for any given code point is considered well-formed; you can't spend four bytes encoding a code point that would fit in three. This rule ensures that there is exactly one UTF-8 encoding for a given code point. Second, well-formed UTF-8 must not encode numbers from `0xd800` through `0xdfff` or beyond `0x10ffff`: those are either reserved for noncharacter purposes or outside Unicode's range entirely.

Figure 17-2 shows some examples.

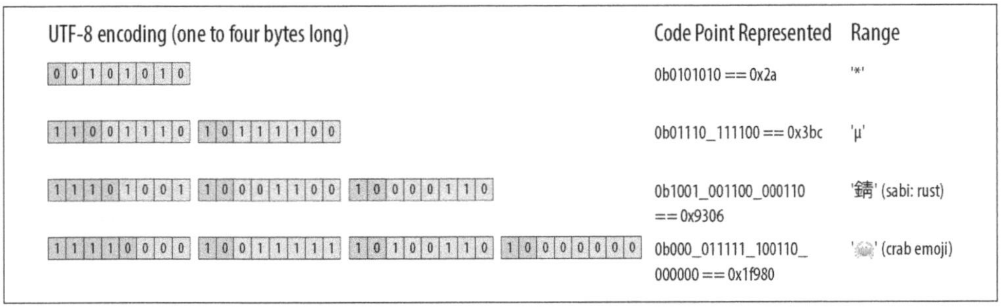

Figure 17-2. UTF-8 examples

Note that, even though the crab emoji has an encoding whose leading byte contributes only zeros to the code point, it still needs a four-byte encoding: three-byte UTF-8 encodings can only convey 16-bit code points, and `0x1f980` is 17 bits long.

Here's a quick example of a string containing characters with encodings of varying lengths:

```
assert_eq!("うどん: udon".as_bytes(),
        &[0xe3, 0x81, 0x86, // う
          0xe3, 0x81, 0xa9, // ど
          0xe3, 0x82, 0x93, // ん
          0x3a, 0x20, 0x75, 0x64, 0x6f, 0x6e // : udon
        ]);
```

Figure 17-2 also shows some very helpful properties of UTF-8:

- Since UTF-8 encodes code points 0 through `0x7f` as nothing more than the bytes 0 through `0x7f`, a range of bytes holding ASCII text is valid UTF-8. And if a string of UTF-8 includes only characters from ASCII, the reverse is also true: the UTF-8 encoding is valid ASCII.

  The same is not true for Latin-1: for example, Latin-1 encodes é as the byte `0xe9`, which UTF-8 would interpret as the first byte of a three-byte encoding.

- From looking at any byte's upper bits, you can immediately tell whether it is the start of some character's UTF-8 encoding or a byte from the midst of one.

- An encoding's first byte alone tells you the encoding's full length, via its leading bits.

- Since no encoding is longer than four bytes, UTF-8 processing never requires unbounded loops, which is nice when working with untrusted data.

- In well-formed UTF-8, you can always tell unambiguously where characters' encodings begin and end, even if you start from an arbitrary point in the midst of the bytes. UTF-8 first bytes and following bytes are always distinct, so one encoding cannot start in the midst of another. The first byte determines the encoding's total length, so no encoding can be a prefix of another. This has a lot of nice consequences. For example, searching a UTF-8 string for an ASCII delimiter character requires only a simple scan for the delimiter's byte. It can never appear as any part of a multibyte encoding, so there's no need to keep track of the UTF-8 structure at all. Similarly, algorithms that search for one byte string in another will work without modification on UTF-8 strings, even though some don't even examine every byte of the text being searched.

Although variable-width encodings are more complicated than fixed-width encodings, these characteristics make UTF-8 more comfortable to work with than you might expect. The standard library handles most aspects for you.

Text Directionality

Whereas scripts like Latin, Cyrillic, and Thai are written from left to right, other scripts like Hebrew and Arabic are written from right to left. Unicode stores characters in the order in which they would normally be written or read, so the initial bytes of a string holding, say, Hebrew text encode the character that would be written at the right:

```
assert_eq!("ערב טוב".chars().next(), Some('ע'));
```

Characters (char)

A Rust char is a 32-bit value holding a Unicode code point. A char is guaranteed to fall in the range from 0 to 0xd7ff or in the range 0xe000 to 0x10ffff; all the methods for creating and manipulating char values ensure that this is true. The char type implements Copy and Clone, along with all the usual traits for comparison, hashing, and formatting.

A string slice can produce an iterator over its characters with slice.chars():

```
assert_eq!("カ二".chars().next(), Some('カ'));
```

In the descriptions that follow, the variable ch is always of type char.

Classifying Characters

The `char` type has methods for classifying characters into a few common categories, as listed in Table 17-1. These all draw their definitions from Unicode.

Table 17-1. Classification methods for char type

Method	Description	Examples

`ch.is_numeric()`	A numeric character. This includes the Unicode general categories "Number; digit" and "Number; letter" but not "Number; other".	`'4'.is_numeric()`
		`'๔'.is_numeric()`
		`'⑧'.is_numeric()`

`ch.is_alphabetic()`	An alphabetic character: Unicode's "Alphabetic" derived property.	`'q'.is_alphabetic()` `'七'.is_alphabetic()`

`ch.is_alphanumeric()`	Either numeric or alphabetic, as defined earlier.	`'9'.is_alphanumeric()`
		`'饂'.is_alphanumeric()`
		`!'*'.is_alphanumeric()`

`ch.is_whitespace()`	A whitespace character: Unicode character property "WSpace=Y".	`' '.is_whitespace()`
		`'\n'.is_whitespace()`
		`'\u{A0}'.is_whitespace()`

`ch.is_control()`	A control character: Unicode's "Other, control" general category.	`'\n'.is_control()` `'\u{85}'.is_control()`

A parallel set of methods restricts itself to ASCII only, returning `false` for any non-ASCII `char` (Table 17-2).

Table 17-2. ASCII classification methods for char

Method	Description	Examples
`ch.is_ascii()`	An ASCII character: one whose code point falls between 0 and 127 inclusive.	`'n'.is_ascii()` `!'ñ'.is_ascii()`

`ch.is_ascii_alphabetic()`	An upper- or lowercase ASCII letter, in the range `'A'..='Z'` or `'a'..='z'`.	`'n'.is_ascii_alphabetic()`
		`!'1'.is_ascii_alphabetic()`
		`!'ñ'.is_ascii_alphabetic()`

`ch.is_ascii_digit()`	An ASCII digit, in the range `'0'..='9'`.	`'8'.is_ascii_digit()`
		`!'-'.is_ascii_digit()`
		`!'⑧'.is_ascii_digit()`

`ch.is_ascii_hexdigit()`	Any character in the ranges `'0'..='9'`, `'A'..='F'`, or `'a'..='f'`.	
`ch.is_ascii_alphanumeric()`	An ASCII digit or upper- or lowercase letter.	`'q'.is_ascii_alphanumeric()` `'0'.is_ascii_alphanumeric()`
`ch.is_ascii_control()`	An ASCII control character, including 'DEL'.	`'\n'.is_ascii_control()` `'\x7f'.is_ascii_control()`

Method	Description	Examples

`ch.is_ascii_graphic()`	Any ASCII character that leaves ink on the page: neither a space nor a control character.	`'Q'.is_ascii_graphic()`
		 `'~'.is_ascii_graphic()`
		 `!' '.is_ascii_graphic()`

`ch.is_ascii_uppercase(),` `ch.is_ascii_lowercase()`	ASCII uppercase and lowercase letters.	`'z'.is_ascii_lowercase()` `'Z'.is_ascii_uppercase()`
`ch.is_ascii_punctuation()`	Any ASCII graphic character that is neither alphabetic nor a digit.	

`ch.is_ascii_whitespace()`	An ASCII whitespace character: a space, horizonal tab, line feed, form feed, or carriage return.	`' '.is_ascii_whitespace()`
		 `'\n'.is_ascii_whitespace()`
		 `!'\u{A0}'.is_ascii_whitespace()`

All the `is_ascii_...` methods are also available on the u8 byte type:

```
assert!(32u8.is_ascii_whitespace());
assert!(b'9'.is_ascii_digit());
```

Take care when using these functions to implement an existing specification like a programming language standard or file format, since classifications can differ in surprising ways. For example, note that `is_whitespace` and `is_ascii_whitespace` differ in their treatment of certain characters:

```
let line_tab = '\u{000b}'; // 'line tab', AKA 'vertical tab'
assert_eq!(line_tab.is_whitespace(), true);
assert_eq!(line_tab.is_ascii_whitespace(), false);
```

The `char::is_ascii_whitespace` function implements a definition of whitespace common to many web standards, whereas `char::is_whitespace` follows the Unicode standard.

Handling Digits

For handling digits, you can use the following methods:

`ch.to_digit(radix)`

Decides whether `ch` is a digit in base `radix`. If it is, it returns `Some(num)`, where `num` is a u32. Otherwise, it returns `None`. This recognizes only ASCII digits, not the broader class of characters covered by `char::is_numeric`. The `radix` parameter can range from 2 to 36. For radixes larger than 10, ASCII letters of either case are considered digits with values from 10 through 35.

`std::char::from_digit(num, radix)`

A free function that converts the u32 digit value `num` to a `char` if possible. If `num` can be represented as a single digit in `radix`, `from_digit` returns `Some(ch)`, where `ch` is the digit. When `radix` is greater than 10, `ch` may be a lowercase letter. Otherwise, it returns `None`.

This is the reverse of `to_digit`. If `std::char::from_digit(num, radix)` is `Some(ch)`, then `ch.to_digit(radix)` is `Some(num)`. If ch is an ASCII digit or lowercase letter, the converse holds as well.

`ch.is_digit(radix)`

Returns `true` if ch is an ASCII digit in base `radix`. This is equivalent to `ch.to_digit(radix) != None`.

So, for example:

```
assert_eq!('F'.to_digit(16), Some(15));
assert_eq!(std::char::from_digit(15, 16), Some('f'));
assert!(char::is_digit('f', 16));
```

Case Conversion for Characters

For handling character case:

`ch.is_lowercase()`, `ch.is_uppercase()`

Indicate whether ch is a lower- or uppercase alphabetic character. These follow Unicode's Lowercase and Uppercase derived properties, so they cover non-Latin alphabets like Greek and Cyrillic and give the expected results for ASCII as well.

`ch.to_lowercase()`, `ch.to_uppercase()`

Return iterators that produce the characters of the lower- and uppercase equivalents of ch, according to the Unicode Default Case Conversion algorithms:

```
let mut upper = 's'.to_uppercase();
assert_eq!(upper.next(), Some('S'));
assert_eq!(upper.next(), None);
```

These methods return an iterator instead of a single character because case conversion in Unicode isn't always a one-to-one process:

```
// The uppercase form of the German letter "sharp S" is "SS":
let mut upper = 'ß'.to_uppercase();
assert_eq!(upper.next(), Some('S'));
assert_eq!(upper.next(), Some('S'));
assert_eq!(upper.next(), None);

// Unicode says to lowercase Turkish dotted capital 'İ' to 'i'
// followed by `'\u{307}'`, COMBINING DOT ABOVE, so that a
// subsequent conversion back to uppercase preserves the dot.
let ch = 'İ'; // `'\u{130}'`
let mut lower = ch.to_lowercase();
assert_eq!(lower.next(), Some('i'));
assert_eq!(lower.next(), Some('\u{307}'));
assert_eq!(lower.next(), None);
```

As a convenience, these iterators implement the `std::fmt::Display` trait, so you can pass them directly to a `println!` or `write!` macro.

Conversions to and from Integers

Rust's `as` operator will convert a `char` to any integer type, silently masking off any upper bits:

```
assert_eq!('B' as u32, 66);
assert_eq!('饂' as u8, 66);    // upper bits truncated
assert_eq!('二' as i8, -116); // same
```

The `as` operator will convert any u8 value to a `char`, and `char` implements `From<u8>` as well, but wider integer types can represent invalid code points, so for those you must use `std::char::from_u32`, which returns `Option<char>`:

```
assert_eq!(char::from(66), 'B');
assert_eq!(std::char::from_u32(0x9942), Some('饂'));
assert_eq!(std::char::from_u32(0xd800), None); // reserved for UTF-16
```

String and str

Rust's `String` and `str` types are guaranteed to hold only well-formed UTF-8. The library ensures this by restricting the ways you can create `String` and `str` values and the operations you can perform on them, such that the values are well-formed when introduced and remain so as you work with them. All their methods protect this guarantee: no safe operation on them can introduce ill-formed UTF-8. This simplifies code that works with the text.

Rust places text-handling methods on either `str` or `String` depending on whether the method needs a resizable buffer or is content just to use the text in place. Since `String` dereferences to `&str`, every method defined on `str` is directly available on `String` as well. This section presents methods from both types, grouped by rough function.

These methods index text by byte offsets and measure its length in bytes, rather than characters. In practice, given the nature of Unicode, indexing by character is not as useful as it may seem, and byte offsets are faster and simpler. If you try to use a byte offset that lands in the midst of some character's UTF-8 encoding, the method panics, so you can't introduce ill-formed UTF-8 this way.

A `String` is implemented as a wrapper around a `Vec<u8>` that ensures the vector's contents are always well-formed UTF-8. Rust will never change `String` to use a more complicated representation, so you can assume that `String` shares `Vec`'s performance characteristics.

In these explanations, the variables have the types given in Table 17-3.

Table 17-3. Types of variables used in explanations

Variable	Presumed type
`string`	`String`
`slice`	`&str` or something that dereferences to one, like `String` or `Rc<String>`
`ch`	`char`
`n`	`usize`, a length
`i, j`	`usize`, a byte offset
`range`	A range of `usize` byte offsets, either fully bounded like `i..j`, or partly bounded like `i..`, `..j`, or `..`
`pattern`	Any pattern type: `char`, `String`, `&str`, `&[char]`, or `FnMut(char) -> bool`

We describe pattern types in "Patterns for Searching Text" on page 442.

Creating String Values

There are a few common ways to create `String` values:

`String::new()`
> Returns a fresh, empty string. This has no heap-allocated buffer, but will allocate one as needed.

`String::with_capacity(n)`
> Returns a fresh, empty string with a buffer pre-allocated to hold at least n bytes. If you know the length of the string you're building in advance, this constructor lets you get the buffer sized correctly from the start, instead of resizing the buffer as you build the string. The string will still grow its buffer as needed if its length exceeds n bytes. Like vectors, strings have `capacity`, `reserve`, and `shrink_to_fit` methods, but usually the default allocation logic is fine.

`str_slice.to_string()`
> Allocates a fresh `String` whose contents are a copy of `str_slice`. We've been using expressions like `"literal text".to_string()` throughout the book to make `String`s from string literals.

`iter.collect()`
> Constructs a string by concatenating an iterator's items, which can be `char`, `&str`, or `String` values. For example, to remove all spaces from a string, you can write:
>
> ```
> let spacey = "man hat tan";
> let spaceless: String =
>     spacey.chars().filter(|c| !c.is_whitespace()).collect();
> assert_eq!(spaceless, "manhattan");
> ```

Using `collect` this way takes advantage of `String`'s implementation of the `std::iter::FromIterator` trait.

`slice.to_owned()`

Returns a copy of slice as a freshly allocated `String`. The `str` type cannot implement `Clone`: the trait would require `clone` on a `&str` to return a `str` value, but `str` is unsized. However, `&str` does implement `ToOwned`, which lets the implementer specify its owned equivalent.

Simple Inspection

These methods get basic information from string slices:

`slice.len()`

The length of `slice`, in bytes.

`slice.is_empty()`

True if `slice.len() == 0`.

`slice[range]`

Returns a slice borrowing the given portion of `slice`. Partially bounded and unbounded ranges are OK; for example:

```
let full = "bookkeeping";
assert_eq!(&full[..4], "book");
assert_eq!(&full[5..], "eeping");
assert_eq!(&full[2..4], "ok");
assert_eq!(full[..].len(), 11);
assert_eq!(full[5..].contains("boo"), false);
```

Note that you cannot index a string slice with a single position, like `slice[i]`. Fetching a single character at a given byte offset is a bit clumsy: you must produce a `chars` iterator over the slice, and ask it to parse one character's UTF-8:

```
let parenthesized = "Rust (鏽)";
assert_eq!(parenthesized[6..].chars().next(), Some('鏽'));
```

However, you should rarely need to do this. Rust has much nicer ways to iterate over slices, which we describe in "Iterating over Text" on page 444.

`slice.split_at(i)`

Returns a tuple of two shared slices borrowed from `slice`: the portion up to byte offset `i`, and the portion after it. In other words, this returns (`slice[..i]`, `slice[i..]`).

`slice.is_char_boundary(i)`

True if the byte offset `i` falls between character boundaries and is thus suitable as an offset into `slice`.

Naturally, slices can be compared for equality, ordered, and hashed. Ordered comparison simply treats the string as a sequence of Unicode code points and compares them in lexicographic order.

Appending and Inserting Text

The following methods add text to a `String`:

`string.push(ch)`
 Appends the character `ch` to the end `string`.

`string.push_str(slice)`
 Appends the full contents of `slice`.

`string.extend(iter)`
 Appends the items produced by the iterator `iter` to the string. The iterator can produce `char`, `str`, or `String` values. These are `String`'s implementations of `std::iter::Extend`:

```
let mut also_spaceless = "con".to_string();
also_spaceless.extend("tri but ion".split_whitespace());
assert_eq!(also_spaceless, "contribution");
```

`string.insert(i, ch)`
 Inserts the single character `ch` at byte offset `i` in `string`. This entails shifting over any characters after `i` to make room for `ch`, so building up a string this way can require time quadratic in the length of the string.

`string.insert_str(i, slice)`
 This does the same for `slice`, with the same performance caveat.

`String` implements `std::fmt::Write`, meaning that the `write!` and `writeln!` macros can append formatted text to `String`s:

```
use std::fmt::Write;

let mut letter = String::new();
writeln!(letter, "Whose {} these are I think I know", "rutabagas")?;
writeln!(letter, "His house is in the village though;")?;
assert_eq!(letter, "Whose rutabagas these are I think I know\n\
                    His house is in the village though;\n");
```

Since `write!` and `writeln!` are designed for writing to output streams, they return a `Result`, which Rust complains if you ignore. This code uses the `?` operator to handle it, but writing to a `String` is actually infallible, so in this case calling `.unwrap()` would be OK too.

Since `String` implements `Add<&str>` and `AddAssign<&str>`, you can write code like this:

```
let left = "partners".to_string();
let mut right = "crime".to_string();
assert_eq!(left + " in " + &right, "partners in crime");

right += " doesn't pay";
assert_eq!(right, "crime doesn't pay");
```

When applied to strings, the + operator takes its left operand by value, so it can actually reuse that `String` as the result of the addition. As a consequence, if the left operand's buffer is large enough to hold the result, no allocation is needed.

In an unfortunate lack of symmetry, the left operand of + cannot be a `&str`, so you cannot write:

```
let parenthetical = "(" + string + ")";
```

You must instead write:

```
let parenthetical = "(".to_string() + &string + ")";
```

However, this restriction does discourage building up strings from the end backward. That approach performs poorly because the text must be repeatedly shifted toward the end of the buffer.

Building strings from beginning to end by appending small pieces, however, is efficient. A `String` behaves the way a vector does, always at least doubling its buffer's size when it needs more capacity. This keeps recopying overhead proportional to the final size. Even so, using `String::with_capacity` to create strings with the right buffer size to begin with avoids resizing at all and can reduce the number of calls to the heap allocator.

Removing and Replacing Text

`String` has a few methods for removing text (these do not affect the string's capacity; use `shrink_to_fit` if you need to free memory):

`string.clear()`
 Resets `string` to the empty string.

`string.truncate(n)`
 Discards all characters after the byte offset n, leaving `string` with a length of at most n. If `string` is shorter than n bytes, this has no effect.

`string.pop()`
 Removes the last character from `string`, if any, and returns it as an `Option<char>`.

`string.remove(i)`

Removes the character at byte offset `i` from `string` and returns it, shifting any following characters toward the front. This takes time linear in the number of following characters.

`string.drain(range)`

Returns an iterator over the given range of byte indices and removes the characters once the iterator is dropped. Characters after the range are shifted toward the front:

```
let mut choco = "chocolate".to_string();
assert_eq!(choco.drain(3..6).collect::<String>(), "col");
assert_eq!(choco, "choate");
```

If you just want to remove the range, you can just drop the iterator immediately, without drawing any items from it:

```
let mut winston = "Churchill".to_string();
winston.drain(2..6);
assert_eq!(winston, "Chill");
```

`string.replace_range(range, replacement)`

Replaces the given range in `string` with the given replacement string slice. The slice doesn't have to be the same length as the range being replaced, but unless the range being replaced goes to the end of `string`, that will require moving all the bytes after the end of the range:

```
let mut beverage = "a piña colada".to_string();
beverage.replace_range(2..7, "kahlua"); // 'ñ' is two bytes!
assert_eq!(beverage, "a kahlua colada");
```

Conventions for Searching and Iterating

Rust's standard library functions for searching text and iterating over text follow some naming conventions to make them easier to remember:

`r`

Most operations process text from start to end, but operations with names starting with `r` work from end to start. For example, `rsplit` is the end-to-start version of `split`. In some cases changing direction can affect not only the order in which values are produced but also the values themselves. See the diagram in Figure 17-3 for an example of this.

`n`

Iterators with names ending in `n` limit themselves to a given number of matches.

`_indices`

Iterators with names ending in `_indices` produce, together with their usual iteration values, the byte offsets in the slice at which they appear.

The standard library doesn't provide all combinations for every operation. For example, many operations don't need an `n` variant, as it's easy enough to simply end the iteration early.

Patterns for Searching Text

When a standard library function needs to search, match, split, or trim text, it accepts several different types to represent what to look for:

```
let haystack = "One fine day, in the middle of the night";

assert_eq!(haystack.find(','), Some(12));
assert_eq!(haystack.find("night"), Some(35));
assert_eq!(haystack.find(char::is_whitespace), Some(3));
```

These types are called *patterns*, and most operations support them:

```
assert_eq!("## Elephants"
            .trim_start_matches(|ch: char| ch == '#' || ch.is_whitespace()),
            "Elephants");
```

The standard library supports four main kinds of patterns:

- A `char` as a pattern matches that character.

- A `String` or `&str` or `&&str` as a pattern matches a substring equal to the pattern.

- A `FnMut(char) -> bool` closure as a pattern matches a single character for which the closure returns true.

- A `&[char]` as a pattern (not a `&str`, but a slice of `char` values) matches any single character that appears in the list. Note that if you write out the list as an array literal, you may need to call `as_ref()` to get the type right:

    ```
    let code = "\t    function noodle() { ";
    assert_eq!(code.trim_start_matches([' ', '\t'].as_ref()),
                "function noodle() { ");
    // Shorter equivalent: &[' ', '\t'][..]
    ```

    Otherwise, Rust will be confused by the fixed-size array type `&[char; 2]`, which is unfortunately not a pattern type.

In the library's own code, a pattern is any type that implements the `std::str::Pattern` trait. The details of `Pattern` are not yet stable, so you can't implement it for your own types in stable Rust, but the door is open to permit regular expressions and other sophisticated patterns in the future. Rust does guarantee that the pattern types supported now will continue to work in the future.

Searching and Replacing

Rust has a few methods for searching for patterns in slices and possibly replacing them with new text:

`slice.contains(pattern)`
> Returns true if `slice` contains a match for `pattern`.

`slice.starts_with(pattern)`, `slice.ends_with(pattern)`
> Return true if `slice`'s initial or final text matches `pattern`:
> ```
> assert!("2017".starts_with(char::is_numeric));
> ```

`slice.find(pattern)`, `slice.rfind(pattern)`
> Return `Some(i)` if `slice` contains a match for `pattern`, where `i` is the byte offset at which the pattern appears. The `find` method returns the first match, `rfind` the last:
> ```
> let quip = "We also know there are known unknowns";
> assert_eq!(quip.find("know"), Some(8));
> assert_eq!(quip.rfind("know"), Some(31));
> assert_eq!(quip.find("ya know"), None);
> assert_eq!(quip.rfind(char::is_uppercase), Some(0));
> ```

`slice.replace(pattern, replacement)`
> Returns a new `String` formed by eagerly replacing all matches for `pattern` with `replacement`:
> ```
> assert_eq!("The only thing we have to fear is fear itself"
>             .replace("fear", "spin"),
>            "The only thing we have to spin is spin itself");
>
> assert_eq!("`Borrow` and `BorrowMut`"
>             .replace(|ch:char| !ch.is_alphanumeric(), ""),
>            "BorrowandBorrowMut");
> ```
>
> Because the replacement is done eagerly, `.replace()`'s behavior on overlapping matches can be surprising. Here, there are four instances of the pattern, `"aba"`, but the second and fourth no longer match after the first and third are replaced:
> ```
> assert_eq!("cababababababbage"
>             .replace("aba", "***"),
>            "c***b***babbage")
> ```

`slice.replacen(pattern, replacement, n)`
> This does the same, but replaces at most the first n matches.

Iterating over Text

The standard library provides several ways to iterate over a slice's text. Figure 17-3 shows examples of some.

You can think of the split and match families as being complements of each other: splits are the ranges between matches.

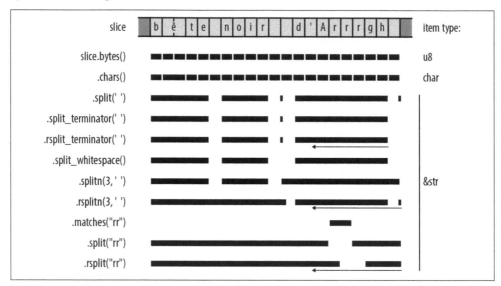

Figure 17-3. Some ways to iterate over a slice

Most of these methods return iterators that are reversible (that is, they implement DoubleEndedIterator): calling their .rev() adapter method gives you an iterator that produces the same items, but in reverse order.

slice.chars()

    Returns an iterator over slice's characters.

slice.char_indices()

    Returns an iterator over slice's characters and their byte offsets:

```
assert_eq!("élan".char_indices().collect::<Vec<_>>(),
           vec![(0, 'é'), // has a two-byte UTF-8 encoding
                (2, 'l'),
                (3, 'a'),
                (4, 'n')]);
```

Note that this is not equivalent to .chars().enumerate(), since it supplies each character's byte offset within the slice, instead of just numbering the characters.

`slice.bytes()`

Returns an iterator over the individual bytes of `slice`, exposing the UTF-8 encoding:

```
assert_eq!("élan".bytes().collect::<Vec<_>>(),
          vec![195, 169, b'l', b'a', b'n']);
```

`slice.lines()`

Returns an iterator over the lines of `slice`. Lines are terminated by "\n" or "\r\n". Each item produced is a `&str` borrowing from `slice`. The items do not include the lines' terminating characters.

`slice.split(pattern)`

Returns an iterator over the portions of `slice` separated by matches of `pattern`. This produces empty strings between immediately adjacent matches, as well as for matches at the beginning and end of `slice`.

The returned iterator is not reversible if `pattern` is a `&str`. Such patterns can produce different sequences of matches depending on which direction you scan from, which reversible iterators are forbidden to do. Instead, you may be able to use the `rsplit` method, described next.

`slice.rsplit(pattern)`

This method is the same, but scans `slice` from end to start, producing matches in that order.

`slice.split_terminator(pattern)`, `slice.rsplit_terminator(pattern)`

These are similar, except that the pattern is treated as a terminator, not a separator: if `pattern` matches at the very end of `slice`, the iterators do not produce an empty slice representing the empty string between that match and the end of the slice, as `split` and `rsplit` do. For example:

```
// The ':' characters are separators here. Note the final "".
assert_eq!("jimb:1000:Jim Blandy:".split(':').collect::<Vec<_>>(),
          vec!["jimb", "1000", "Jim Blandy", ""]);

// The '\n' characters are terminators here.
assert_eq!("127.0.0.1  localhost\n\
            127.0.0.1  www.reddit.com\n"
           .split_terminator('\n').collect::<Vec<_>>(),
          vec!["127.0.0.1  localhost",
               "127.0.0.1  www.reddit.com"]);
          // Note, no final ""!
```

`slice.splitn(n, pattern)`, `slice.rsplitn(n, pattern)`

These are like `split` and `rsplit`, except that they split the string into at most `n` slices, at the first or last `n-1` matches for `pattern`.

`slice.split_whitespace()`, `slice.split_ascii_whitespace()`

Return an iterator over the whitespace-separated portions of `slice`. A run of multiple whitespace characters is considered a single separator. Trailing whitespace is ignored.

The `split_whitespace` method uses the Unicode definition of whitespace, as implemented by the `is_whitespace` method on `char`. The `split_ascii_whitespace` method uses `char::is_ascii_whitespace` instead, which recognizes only ASCII whitespace characters.

```
let poem = "This  is  just  to say\n\
            I have eaten\n\
            the plums\n\
            again\n";

assert_eq!(poem.split_whitespace().collect::<Vec<_>>(),
           vec!["This", "is", "just", "to", "say",
                "I", "have", "eaten", "the", "plums",
                "again"]);
```

`slice.matches(pattern)`

Returns an iterator over the matches for `pattern` in `slice`. `slice.rmatches(pattern)` is the same, but iterates from end to start.

`slice.match_indices(pattern)`, `slice.rmatch_indices(pattern)`

These are similar, except that the items produced are `(offset, match)` pairs, where `offset` is the byte offset at which the match begins, and `match` is the matching slice.

Trimming

To *trim* a string is to remove text, usually whitespace, from the beginning or end of the string. It's often useful in cleaning up input read from a file where the user might have indented text for legibility or accidentally left trailing whitespace on a line.

`slice.trim()`

Returns a subslice of `slice` that omits any leading and trailing whitespace. `slice.trim_start()` omits only leading whitespace, `slice.trim_end()` only trailing whitespace:

```
assert_eq!("\t*.rs  ".trim(), "*.rs");
assert_eq!("\t*.rs  ".trim_start(), "*.rs  ");
assert_eq!("\t*.rs  ".trim_end(), "\t*.rs");
```

`slice.trim_matches(pattern)`

Returns a subslice of `slice` that omits all matches of `pattern` from the beginning and end. The `trim_start_matches` and `trim_end_matches` methods do the same for only leading or trailing matches:

```
assert_eq!("001990".trim_start_matches('0'), "1990");
```

`slice.strip_prefix(pattern)`, `slice.strip_suffix(pattern)`

If `slice` begins with `pattern`, `strip_prefix` returns `Some` holding the slice with the matching text removed. Otherwise, it returns `None`. The `strip_suffix` method is similar, but checks for a match at the end of the string.

These are like `trim_start_matches` and `trim_end_matches`, except that they return an `Option`, and only one copy of `pattern` is removed:

```
let slice = "banana";
assert_eq!(slice.strip_suffix("na"),
           Some("bana"))
```

Case Conversion for Strings

The methods `slice.to_uppercase()` and `slice.to_lowercase()` return a freshly allocated string holding the text of `slice` converted to uppercase or lowercase. The result may not be the same length as `slice`; see "Case Conversion for Characters" on page 435 for details.

Parsing Other Types from Strings

Rust provides standard traits for both parsing values from strings and producing textual representations of values.

If a type implements the `std::str::FromStr` trait, then it provides a standard way to parse a value from a string slice:

```
pub trait FromStr: Sized {
    type Err;
    fn from_str(s: &str) -> Result<Self, Self::Err>;
}
```

All the usual machine types implement `FromStr`:

```
use std::str::FromStr;

assert_eq!(usize::from_str("3628800"), Ok(3628800));
assert_eq!(f64::from_str("128.5625"), Ok(128.5625));
assert_eq!(bool::from_str("true"), Ok(true));

assert!(f64::from_str("not a float at all").is_err());
assert!(bool::from_str("TRUE").is_err());
```

The char type also implements `FromStr`, for strings with just one character:

```
assert_eq!(char::from_str("é"), Ok('é'));
assert!(char::from_str("abcdefg").is_err());
```

The `std::net::IpAddr` type, an `enum` holding either an IPv4 or an IPv6 internet address, implements `FromStr` too:

```
use std::net::IpAddr;

let address = IpAddr::from_str("fe80::0000:3ea9:f4ff:fe34:7a50")?;
assert_eq!(address,
           IpAddr::from([0xfe80, 0, 0, 0, 0x3ea9, 0xf4ff, 0xfe34, 0x7a50]));
```

String slices have a `parse` method that parses the slice into whatever type you like, assuming it implements `FromStr`. As with `Iterator::collect`, you will sometimes need to spell out which type you want, so `parse` is not always much more legible than calling `from_str` directly:

```
let address = "fe80::0000:3ea9:f4ff:fe34:7a50".parse::<IpAddr>()?;
```

Converting Other Types to Strings

There are three main ways to convert nontextual values to strings:

- Types that have a natural human-readable printed form can implement the `std::fmt::Display` trait, which lets you use the `{}` format specifier in the `format!` macro:

```
assert_eq!(format!("{}, wow", "doge"), "doge, wow");
assert_eq!(format!("{}", true), "true");
assert_eq!(format!("({:.3}, {:.3})", 0.5, f64::sqrt(3.0)/2.0),
           "(0.500, 0.866)");

// Using `address` from above.
let formatted_addr: String = format!("{}", address);
assert_eq!(formatted_addr, "fe80::3ea9:f4ff:fe34:7a50");
```

All Rust's machine numeric types implement `Display`, as do characters, strings, and slices. The smart pointer types `Box<T>`, `Rc<T>`, and `Arc<T>` implement `Display` if `T` itself does: their displayed form is simply that of their referent. Containers like `Vec` and `HashMap` do not implement `Display`, as there's no single natural human-readable form for those types.

- If a type implements `Display`, the standard library automatically implements the `std::str::ToString` trait for it, whose sole method `to_string` can be more convenient when you don't need the flexibility of `format!`:

```
// Continued from above.
assert_eq!(address.to_string(), "fe80::3ea9:f4ff:fe34:7a50");
```

The ToString trait predates the introduction of Display and is less flexible. For your own types, you should generally implement Display instead of ToString.

- Every public type in the standard library implements std::fmt::Debug, which takes a value and formats it as a string in a way helpful to programmers. The easiest way to use Debug to produce a string is via the format! macro's {:?} format specifier:

```
// Continued from above.
let addresses = vec![address,
                     IpAddr::from_str("192.168.0.1")?];
assert_eq!(format!("{:?}", addresses),
           "[fe80::3ea9:f4ff:fe34:7a50, 192.168.0.1]");
```

This takes advantage of a blanket implementation of Debug for Vec<T>, for any T that itself implements Debug. All of Rust's collection types have such implementations.

You should implement Debug for your own types, too. Usually it's best to let Rust derive an implementation, as we did for the Complex type in Chapter 12:

```
#[derive(Copy, Clone, Debug)]
struct Complex { re: f64, im: f64 }
```

The Display and Debug formatting traits are just two among several that the format! macro and its relatives use to format values as text. We'll cover the others, and explain how to implement them all, in "Formatting Values" on page 454.

Borrowing as Other Text-Like Types

You can borrow a slice's contents in several different ways:

- Slices and Strings implement AsRef<str>, AsRef<[u8]>, AsRef<Path>, and AsRef<OsStr>. Many standard library functions use these traits as bounds on their parameter types, so you can pass slices and strings to them directly, even when what they really want is some other type. See "AsRef and AsMut" on page 317 for a more detailed explanation.

- Slices and strings also implement the std::borrow::Borrow<str> trait. HashMap and BTreeMap use Borrow to make Strings work nicely as keys in a table. See "Borrow and BorrowMut" on page 318 for details.

Accessing Text as UTF-8

There are two main ways to get at the bytes representing text, depending on whether you want to take ownership of the bytes or just borrow them:

`slice.as_bytes()`

Borrows `slice`'s bytes as a `&[u8]`. Since this is not a mutable reference, `slice` can assume its bytes will remain well-formed UTF-8.

`string.into_bytes()`

Takes ownership of `string` and returns a `Vec<u8>` of the string's bytes by value. This is a cheap conversion, as it simply hands over the `Vec<u8>` that the string had been using as its buffer. Since `string` no longer exists, there's no need for the bytes to continue to be well-formed UTF-8, and the caller is free to modify the `Vec<u8>` as it pleases.

Producing Text from UTF-8 Data

If you have a block of bytes that you believe contains UTF-8 data, you have a few options for converting them into `String`s or slices, depending on how you want to handle errors:

`str::from_utf8(byte_slice)`

Takes a `&[u8]` slice of bytes and returns a `Result`: either `Ok(&str)` if `byte_slice` contains well-formed UTF-8 or an error otherwise.

`String::from_utf8(vec)`

Tries to construct a string from a `Vec<u8>` passed by value. If `vec` holds well-formed UTF-8, `from_utf8` returns `Ok(string)`, where `string` has taken ownership of `vec` for use as its buffer. No heap allocation or copying of the text takes place.

If the bytes are not valid UTF-8, this returns `Err(e)`, where `e` is a `FromUtf8Error` error value. The call `e.into_bytes()` gives you back the original vector `vec`, so it is not lost when the conversion fails:

```
let good_utf8: Vec<u8> = vec![0xe9, 0x8c, 0x86];
assert_eq!(String::from_utf8(good_utf8).ok(), Some("錆".to_string()));

let bad_utf8:  Vec<u8> = vec![0x9f, 0xf0, 0xa6, 0x80];
let result = String::from_utf8(bad_utf8);
assert!(result.is_err());
// Since String::from_utf8 failed, it didn't consume the original
// vector, and the error value hands it back to us unharmed.
assert_eq!(result.unwrap_err().into_bytes(),
           vec![0x9f, 0xf0, 0xa6, 0x80]);
```

`String::from_utf8_lossy(byte_slice)`

Tries to construct a `String` or `&str` from a `&[u8]` shared slice of bytes. This conversion always succeeds, replacing any ill-formed UTF-8 with Unicode replacement characters. The return value is a `Cow<str>` that either borrows a `&str`

directly from `byte_slice` if it contains well-formed UTF-8 or owns a freshly allocated `String` with replacement characters substituted for the ill-formed bytes. Hence, when `byte_slice` is well-formed, no heap allocation or copying takes place. We discuss `Cow<str>` in more detail in "Putting Off Allocation" on page 451.

`String::from_utf8_unchecked`

If you know for a fact that your `Vec<u8>` contains well-formed UTF-8, then you can call the unsafe function. This simply wraps the `Vec<u8>` up as a `String` and returns it, without examining the bytes at all. You are responsible for making sure you haven't introduced ill-formed UTF-8 into the system, which is why this function is marked `unsafe`.

`str::from_utf8_unchecked`

Similarly, this takes a `&[u8]` and returns it as a `&str`, without checking to see if it holds well-formed UTF-8. As with `String::from _utf8_unchecked`, you are responsible for making sure this is safe.

Putting Off Allocation

Suppose you want your program to greet the user. On Unix, you could write:

```
fn get_name() -> String {
    std::env::var("USER") // Windows uses "USERNAME"
        .unwrap_or("whoever you are".to_string())
}

println!("Greetings, {}!", get_name());
```

For Unix users, this greets them by username. For Windows users and the tragically unnamed, it provides alternative stock text.

The `std::env::var` function returns a `String`—and has good reasons to do so that we won't go into here. But that means the alternative stock text must also be returned as a `String`. This is disappointing: when `get_name` returns a static string, no allocation should be necessary at all.

The nub of the problem is that sometimes the return value of `get_name` should be an owned `String`, sometimes it should be a `&'static str`, and we can't know which one it will be until we run the program. This dynamic character is the hint to consider using `std::borrow::Cow`, the clone-on-write type that can hold either owned or borrowed data.

As explained in "Borrow and ToOwned at Work: The Humble Cow" on page 325, `Cow<'a, T>` is an enum with two variants: `Owned` and `Borrowed`. `Borrowed` holds a reference `&'a T`, and `Owned` holds the owning version of `&T`: `String` for `&str`, `Vec<i32>`

for &[i32], and so on. Whether Owned or Borrowed, a Cow<'a, T> can always produce a &T for you to use. In fact, Cow<'a, T> dereferences to &T, behaving as a kind of smart pointer.

Changing get_name to return a Cow results in the following:

```
use std::borrow::Cow;

fn get_name() -> Cow<'static, str> {
    std::env::var("USER")
        .map(|v| Cow::Owned(v))
        .unwrap_or(Cow::Borrowed("whoever you are"))
}
```

If this succeeds in reading the "USER" environment variable, the map returns the resulting String as a Cow::Owned. If it fails, the unwrap_or returns its static &str as a Cow::Borrowed. The caller can remain unchanged:

```
println!("Greetings, {}!", get_name());
```

As long as T implements the std::fmt::Display trait, displaying a Cow<'a, T> produces the same results as displaying a T.

Cow is also useful when you may or may not need to modify some text you've borrowed. When no changes are necessary, you can continue to borrow it. But the namesake clone-on-write behavior of Cow can give you an owned, mutable copy of the value on demand. Cow's to_mut method makes sure the Cow is Cow::Owned, applying the value's ToOwned implementation if necessary, and then returns a mutable reference to the value.

So if you find that some of your users, but not all, have titles by which they would prefer to be addressed, you can say:

```
fn get_title() -> Option<&'static str> { ... }

let mut name = get_name();
if let Some(title) = get_title() {
    name.to_mut().push_str(", ");
    name.to_mut().push_str(title);
}

println!("Greetings, {}!", name);
```

This might produce output like the following:

```
$ cargo run
Greetings, jimb, Esq.!
$
```

What's nice here is that, if `get_name()` returns a static string and `get_title` returns None, the Cow simply carries the static string all the way through to the `println!`. You've managed to put off allocation unless it's really necessary, while still writing straightforward code.

Since Cow is frequently used for strings, the standard library has some special support for `Cow<'a, str>`. It provides `From` and `Into` conversions from both `String` and `&str`, so you can write `get_name` more tersely:

```
fn get_name() -> Cow<'static, str> {
    std::env::var("USER")
        .map(|v| v.into())
        .unwrap_or("whoever you are".into())
}
```

`Cow<'a, str>` also implements `std::ops::Add` and `std::ops::AddAssign`, so to add the title to the name, you could write:

```
if let Some(title) = get_title() {
    name += ", ";
    name += title;
}
```

Or, since a `String` can be a `write!` macro's destination:

```
use std::fmt::Write;

if let Some(title) = get_title() {
    write!(name.to_mut(), ", {}", title).unwrap();
}
```

As before, no allocation occurs until you try to modify the Cow.

Keep in mind that not every `Cow<..., str>` must be `'static`: you can use Cow to borrow previously computed text until the moment a copy becomes necessary.

Strings as Generic Collections

String implements both `std::default::Default` and `std::iter::Extend`: default returns an empty string, and `extend` can append characters, string slices, `Cow<..., str>`s, or strings to the end of a string. This is the same combination of traits implemented by Rust's other collection types like Vec and HashMap for generic construction patterns such as `collect` and `partition`.

The `&str` type also implements `Default`, returning an empty slice. This is handy in some corner cases; for example, it lets you derive `Default` for structures containing string slices.

Formatting Values

Throughout the book, we've been using text formatting macros like `println!`:

```
println!("{:.3}µs: relocated {} at {:#x} to {:#x}, {} bytes",
         0.84391, "object",
         140737488346304_usize, 6299664_usize, 64);
```

That call produces the following output:

```
0.844µs: relocated object at 0x7fffffffdcc0 to 0x602010, 64 bytes
```

The string literal serves as a template for the output: each {...} in the template gets replaced by the formatted form of one of the following arguments. The template string must be a constant so that Rust can check it against the types of the arguments at compile time. Each argument must be used; Rust reports a compile-time error otherwise.

Several standard library features share this little language for formatting strings:

- The `format!` macro uses it to build `String`s.
- The `println!` and `print!` macros write formatted text to the standard output stream.
- The `writeln!` and `write!` macros write it to a designated output stream.
- The `panic!` macro uses it to build an (ideally informative) expression of terminal dismay.

Rust's formatting facilities are designed to be open-ended. You can extend these macros to support your own types by implementing the `std::fmt` module's formatting traits. And you can use the `format_args!` macro and the `std::fmt::Arguments` type to make your own functions and macros support the formatting language.

Formatting macros always borrow shared references to their arguments; they never take ownership of them or mutate them.

The template's {...} forms are called *format parameters* and have the form {*which*:*how*}. Both parts are optional; {} is frequently used.

The *which* value selects which argument following the template should take the parameter's place. You can select arguments by index or by name. Parameters with no *which* value are simply paired with arguments from left to right.

The *how* value says how the argument should be formatted: how much padding, to which precision, in which numeric radix, and so on. If *how* is present, the colon before it is required. Table 17-4 presents some examples.

Table 17-4. Formatted string examples

Template string	Argument list	Result
`"number of {}: {}"`	`"elephants", 19`	`"number of elephants: 19"`
`"from {1} to {0}"`	`"the grave", "the cradle"`	`"from the cradle to the grave"`
`"v = {:?}"`	`vec![0,1,2,5,12,29]`	`"v = [0, 1, 2, 5, 12, 29]"`
`"name = {:?}"`	`"Nemo"`	`"name = \"Nemo\""`
`"{:8.2} km/s"`	`11.186`	`"    11.19 km/s"`
`"{:20} {:02x} {:02x}"`	`"adc #42", 105, 42`	`"adc #42              69 2a"`
`"{1:02x} {2:02x}   {0}"`	`"adc #42", 105, 42`	`"69 2a  adc #42"`
`"{lsb:02x} {msb:02x} {insn}"`	`insn="adc #42", lsb=105, msb=42`	`"69 2a  adc #42"`
`"{:02?}"`	`[110, 11, 9]`	`"[110, 11, 09]"`
`"{:02x?}"`	`[110, 11, 9]`	`"[6e, 0b, 09]"`

If you want to include { or } characters in your output, double the characters in the template:

```
assert_eq!(format!("{{a, c}} ⊂ {{a, b, c}}"),
           "{a, c} ⊂ {a, b, c}");
```

Formatting Text Values

When formatting a textual type like `&str` or `String` (`char` is treated like a single-character string), the *how* value of a parameter has several parts, all optional:

- A *text length limit*. Rust truncates your argument if it is longer than this. If you specify no limit, Rust uses the full text.

- A *minimum field width*. After any truncation, if your argument is shorter than this, Rust pads it on the right (by default) with spaces (by default) to make a field of this width. If omitted, Rust doesn't pad your argument.

- An *alignment*. If your argument needs to be padded to meet the minimum field width, this says where your text should be placed within the field. <, ^, and > put your text at the start, middle, and end, respectively.

- A *padding* character to use in this padding process. If omitted, Rust uses spaces. If you specify the padding character, you must also specify the alignment.

Table 17-5 illustrates some examples showing how to write things out and their effects. All are using the same eight-character argument, `"bookends"`.

Table 17-5. Format string directives for text

Features in use	Template string	Result
Default	`"{}"`	`"bookends"`
Minimum field width	`"{:4}"`	`"bookends"`
	`"{:12}"`	`"bookends    "`
Text length limit	`"{:.4}"`	`"book"`
	`"{:.12}"`	`"bookends"`
Field width, length limit	`"{:12.20}"`	`"bookends    "`
	`"{:4.20}"`	`"bookends"`
	`"{:4.6}"`	`"booken"`
	`"{:6.4}"`	`"book  "`
Aligned left, width	`"{:<12}"`	`"bookends    "`
Centered, width	`"{:^12}"`	`"  bookends  "`
Aligned right, width	`"{:>12}"`	`"    bookends"`
Pad with '=', centered, width	`"{:=^12}"`	`"==bookends=="`
Pad '*', aligned right, width, limit	`"{:*>12.4}"`	`"********book"`

Rust's formatter has a naïve understanding of width: it assumes each character occupies one column, with no regard for combining characters, half-width katakana, zero-width spaces, or the other messy realities of Unicode. For example:

```
assert_eq!(format!("{:4}", "th\u{e9}"),    "th\u{e9} ");
assert_eq!(format!("{:4}", "the\u{301}"), "the\u{301}");
```

Although Unicode says these strings are both equivalent to `"thé"`, Rust's formatter doesn't know that characters like `'\u{301}'`, COMBINING ACUTE ACCENT, need special treatment. It pads the first string correctly, but assumes the second is four columns wide and adds no padding. Although it's easy to see how Rust could improve in this specific case, true multilingual text formatting for all of Unicode's scripts is a monumental task, best handled by relying on your platform's user interface toolkits, or perhaps by generating HTML and CSS and making a web browser sort it all out. There is a popular crate, `unicode-width`, that handles some aspects of this.

Along with `&str` and `String`, you can also pass formatting macros smart pointer types with textual referents, like `Rc<String>` or `Cow<'a, str>`, without ceremony.

Since filename paths are not necessarily well-formed UTF-8, `std::path::Path` isn't quite a textual type; you can't pass a `std::path::Path` directly to a formatting macro. However, a `Path`'s `display` method returns a value you can format that sorts things out in a platform-appropriate way:

```
println!("processing file: {}", path.display());
```

Formatting Numbers

When the formatting argument has a numeric type like `usize` or `f64`, the parameter's *how* value has the following parts, all optional:

- A *padding* and *alignment*, which work as they do with textual types.

- A + character, requesting that the number's sign always be shown, even when the argument is positive.

- A # character, requesting an explicit radix prefix like `0x` or `0b`. See the "notation" bullet point that concludes this list.

- A 0 character, requesting that the minimum field width be satisfied by including leading zeros in the number, instead of the usual padding approach.

- A *minimum field width*. If the formatted number is not at least this wide, Rust pads it on the left (by default) with spaces (by default) to make a field of the given width.

- A *precision* for floating-point arguments, indicating how many digits Rust should include after the decimal point. Rust rounds or zero-extends as necessary to produce exactly this many fractional digits. If the precision is omitted, Rust tries to accurately represent the value using as few digits as possible. For arguments of integer type, the precision is ignored.

- A *notation*. For integer types, this can be b for binary, o for octal, or x or X for hexadecimal with lower- or uppercase letters. If you included the # character, these include an explicit Rust-style radix prefix, `0b`, `0o`, `0x`, or `0X`. For floating-point types, a radix of e or E requests scientific notation, with a normalized coefficient, using e or E for the exponent. If you don't specify any notation, Rust formats numbers in decimal.

Table 17-6 shows some examples of formatting the `i32` value 1234.

Table 17-6. Format string directives for integers

Features in use	Template string	Result
Default	`"{}"`	`"1234"`
Forced sign	`"{:+}"`	`"+1234"`
Minimum field width	`"{:12}"`	`"        1234"`
	`"{:2}"`	`"1234"`
Sign, width	`"{:+12}"`	`"       +1234"`
Leading zeros, width	`"{:012}"`	`"000000001234"`
Sign, zeros, width	`"{:+012}"`	`"+00000001234"`
Aligned left, width	`"{:<12}"`	`"1234        "`
Centered, width	`"{:^12}"`	`"    1234    "`

Features in use	Template string	Result
Aligned right, width	`"{:>12}"`	`"        1234"`
Aligned left, sign, width	`"{:<+12}"`	`"+1234       "`
Centered, sign, width	`"{:^+12}"`	`"   +1234    "`
Aligned right, sign, width	`"{:>+12}"`	`"       +1234"`
Padded with '=', centered, width	`"{:=^12}"`	`"====1234===="`
Binary notation	`"{:b}"`	`"10011010010"`
Width, octal notation	`"{:12o}"`	`"        2322"`
Sign, width, hexadecimal notation	`"{:+12x}"`	`"        +4d2"`
Sign, width, hex with capital digits	`"{:+12X}"`	`"        +4D2"`
Sign, explicit radix prefix, width, hex	`"{:+#12x}"`	`"      +0x4d2"`
Sign, radix, zeros, width, hex	`"{:+#012x}"`	`"+0x0000004d2"`
	`"{:+#06x}"`	`"+0x4d2"`

As the last two examples show, the minimum field width applies to the entire number, sign, radix prefix, and all.

Negative numbers always include their sign. The results are like those shown in the "forced sign" examples.

When you request leading zeros, alignment and padding characters are simply ignored, since the zeros expand the number to fill the entire field.

Using the argument `1234.5678`, we can show effects specific to floating-point types (Table 17-7).

Table 17-7. Format string directives for floating-point numbers

Features in use	Template string	Result
Default	`"{}"`	`"1234.5678"`
Precision	`"{:.2}"`	`"1234.57"`
	`"{:.6}"`	`"1234.567800"`
Minimum field width	`"{:12}"`	`"   1234.5678"`
Minimum, precision	`"{:12.2}"`	`"     1234.57"`
	`"{:12.6}"`	`" 1234.567800"`
Leading zeros, minimum, precision	`"{:012.6}"`	`"01234.567800"`
Scientific	`"{:e}"`	`"1.2345678e3"`
Scientific, precision	`"{:.3e}"`	`"1.235e3"`
Scientific, minimum, precision	`"{:12.3e}"`	`"     1.235e3"`
	`"{:12.3E}"`	`"     1.235E3"`

Formatting Other Types

Beyond strings and numbers, you can format several other standard library types:

- Error types can all be formatted directly, making it easy to include them in error messages. Every error type should implement the `std::error::Error` trait, which extends the default formatting trait `std::fmt::Display`. As a consequence, any type that implements `Error` is ready to format.

- You can format internet protocol address types like `std::net::IpAddr` and `std::net::SocketAddr`.

- The Boolean `true` and `false` values can be formatted, although these are usually not the best strings to present directly to end users.

You should use the same sorts of format parameters that you would for strings. Length limit, field width, and alignment controls work as expected.

Formatting Values for Debugging

To help with debugging and logging, the `{:?}` parameter formats any public type in the Rust standard library in a way meant to be helpful to programmers. You can use this to inspect vectors, slices, tuples, hash tables, threads, and hundreds of other types.

For example, you can write the following:

```
use std::collections::HashMap;
let mut map = HashMap::new();
map.insert("Portland", (45.5237606,-122.6819273));
map.insert("Taipei",   (25.0375167, 121.5637));
println!("{:?}", map);
```

This prints:

```
{"Taipei": (25.0375167, 121.5637), "Portland": (45.5237606, -122.6819273)}
```

The `HashMap` and `(f64, f64)` types already know how to format themselves, with no effort required on your part.

If you include the `#` character in the format parameter, Rust will pretty-print the value. Changing this code to say `println!("{:#?}", map)` leads to this output:

```
{
    "Taipei": (
        25.0375167,
        121.5637
    ),
    "Portland": (
        45.5237606,
        -122.6819273
    )
}
```

These exact forms aren't guaranteed and do sometimes change from one Rust release to the next.

Debugging formatting usually prints numbers in decimal, but you can put an x or X before the question mark to request hexadecimal instead. Leading zero and field width syntax is also respected. For example, you can write:

```
println!("ordinary: {:02?}", [9, 15, 240]);
println!("hex:      {:02x?}", [9, 15, 240]);
```

This prints:

```
ordinary: [09, 15, 240]
hex:      [09, 0f, f0]
```

As we've mentioned, you can use the #[derive(Debug)] syntax to make your own types work with {:?}:

```
#[derive(Copy, Clone, Debug)]
struct Complex { re: f64, im: f64 }
```

With this definition in place, we can use a {:?} format to print Complex values:

```
let third = Complex { re: -0.5, im: f64::sqrt(0.75) };
println!("{:?}", third);
```

This prints:

```
Complex { re: -0.5, im: 0.8660254037844386 }
```

This is fine for debugging, but it might be nice if {} could print them in a more traditional form, like -0.5 + 0.8660254037844386i. In "Formatting Your Own Types" on page 462, we'll show how to do exactly that.

Formatting Pointers for Debugging

Normally, if you pass any sort of pointer to a formatting macro—a reference, a Box, an Rc—the macro simply follows the pointer and formats its referent; the pointer itself is not of interest. But when you're debugging, it's sometimes helpful to see the pointer: an address can serve as a rough "name" for an individual value, which can be illuminating when examining structures with cycles or sharing.

The {:p} notation formats references, boxes, and other pointer-like types as addresses:

```
use std::rc::Rc;
let original = Rc::new("mazurka".to_string());
let cloned = original.clone();
let impostor = Rc::new("mazurka".to_string());
println!("text:     {}, {}, {}",       original, cloned, impostor);
println!("pointers: {:p}, {:p}, {:p}", original, cloned, impostor);
```

This code prints:

```
text:     mazurka, mazurka, mazurka
pointers: 0x7f99af80e000, 0x7f99af80e000, 0x7f99af80e030
```

Of course, the specific pointer values will vary from run to run, but even so, comparing the addresses makes it clear that the first two are references to the same `String`, whereas the third points to a distinct value.

Addresses do tend to look like hexadecimal soup, so more refined visualizations can be worthwhile, but the `{:p}` style can still be an effective quick-and-dirty solution.

Referring to Arguments by Index or Name

A format parameter can explicitly select which argument it uses. For example:

```
assert_eq!(format!("{1},{0},{2}", "zeroth", "first", "second"),
           "first,zeroth,second");
```

You can include format parameters after a colon:

```
assert_eq!(format!("{2:#06x},{1:b},{0:=>10}", "first", 10, 100),
           "0x0064,1010,=====first");
```

You can also select arguments by name. This makes complex templates with many parameters much more legible. For example:

```
assert_eq!(format!("{description:.<25}{quantity:2} @ {price:5.2}",
                   price=3.25,
                   quantity=3,
                   description="Maple Turmeric Latte"),
           "Maple Turmeric Latte..... 3 @  3.25");
```

(The named arguments here resemble keyword arguments in Python, but this is just a special feature of the formatting macros, not part of Rust's function call syntax.)

You can mix indexed, named, and positional (that is, no index or name) parameters together in a single formatting macro use. The positional parameters are paired with arguments from left to right as if the indexed and named parameters weren't there:

```
assert_eq!(format!("{mode} {2} {} {}",
                   "people", "eater", "purple", mode="flying"),
           "flying purple people eater");
```

Named arguments must appear at the end of the list.

Dynamic Widths and Precisions

A parameter's minimum field width, text length limit, and numeric precision need not always be fixed values; you can choose them at run time.

We've been looking at cases like this expression, which gives you the string `content` right-justified in a field 20 characters wide:

```
format!("{:>20}", content)
```

But if you'd like to choose the field width at run time, you can write:

```
format!("{:>1$}", content, get_width())
```

Writing `1$` for the minimum field width tells `format!` to use the value of the second argument as the width. The cited argument must be a `usize`. You can also refer to the argument by name:

```
format!("{:>width$}", content, width=get_width())
```

The same approach works for the text length limit as well:

```
format!("{:>width$.limit$}", content,
        width=get_width(), limit=get_limit())
```

In place of the text length limit or floating-point precision, you can also write `*`, which says to take the next positional argument as the precision. The following clips `content` to at most `get_limit()` characters:

```
format!("{:.*}", get_limit(), content)
```

The argument taken as the precision must be a `usize`. There is no corresponding syntax for the field width.

Formatting Your Own Types

The formatting macros use a set of traits defined in the `std::fmt` module to convert values to text. You can make Rust's formatting macros format your own types by implementing one or more of these traits yourself.

The notation of a format parameter indicates which trait its argument's type must implement, as illustrated in Table 17-8.

Table 17-8. Format string directive notation

Notation	Example	Trait	Purpose
none	{}	std::fmt::Display	Text, numbers, errors: the catchall trait
b	{bits:#b}	std::fmt::Binary	Numbers in binary
o	{:#5o}	std::fmt::Octal	Numbers in octal
x	{:4x}	std::fmt::LowerHex	Numbers in hexadecimal, lowercase digits
X	{:016X}	std::fmt::UpperHex	Numbers in hexadecimal, uppercase digits
e	{:.3e}	std::fmt::LowerExp	Floating-point numbers in scientific notation
E	{:.3E}	std::fmt::UpperExp	Same, uppercase E
?	{:#?}	std::fmt::Debug	Debugging view, for developers
p	{:p}	std::fmt::Pointer	Pointer as address, for developers

When you put the `#[derive(Debug)]` attribute on a type definition so that you can use the `{:?}` format parameter, you are simply asking Rust to implement the `std::fmt::Debug` trait for you.

The formatting traits all have the same structure, differing only in their names. We'll use `std::fmt::Display` as a representative:

```
trait Display {
    fn fmt(&self, dest: &mut std::fmt::Formatter)
        -> std::fmt::Result;
}
```

The `fmt` method's job is to produce a properly formatted representation of `self` and write its characters to `dest`. In addition to serving as an output stream, the `dest` argument also carries details parsed from the format parameter, like the alignment and minimum field width.

For example, earlier in this chapter we suggested that it would be nice if `Complex` values printed themselves in the usual `a + bi` form. Here's a `Display` implementation that does that:

```
use std::fmt;

impl fmt::Display for Complex {
    fn fmt(&self, dest: &mut fmt::Formatter) -> fmt::Result {
        let im_sign = if self.im < 0.0 { '-' } else { '+' };
        write!(dest, "{} {} {}i", self.re, im_sign, f64::abs(self.im))
    }
}
```

This takes advantage of the fact that `Formatter` is itself an output stream, so the `write!` macro can do most of the work for us. With this implementation in place, we can write the following:

```
let one_twenty = Complex { re: -0.5, im: 0.866 };
assert_eq!(format!("{}", one_twenty),
           "-0.5 + 0.866i");

let two_forty = Complex { re: -0.5, im: -0.866 };
assert_eq!(format!("{}", two_forty),
           "-0.5 - 0.866i");
```

It's sometimes helpful to display complex numbers in polar form: if you imagine a line drawn on the complex plane from the origin to the number, the polar form gives the line's length, and its clockwise angle to the positive x-axis. The `#` character in a format parameter typically selects some alternate display form; the `Display` implementation could treat it as a request to use polar form:

```
impl fmt::Display for Complex {
    fn fmt(&self, dest: &mut fmt::Formatter) -> fmt::Result {
        let (re, im) = (self.re, self.im);
```

```
        if dest.alternate() {
            let abs = f64::sqrt(re * re + im * im);
            let angle = f64::atan2(im, re) / std::f64::consts::PI * 180.0;
            write!(dest, "{} ∠ {}°", abs, angle)
        } else {
            let im_sign = if im < 0.0 { '-' } else { '+' };
            write!(dest, "{} {} {}i", re, im_sign, f64::abs(im))
        }
    }
}
```

Using this implementation:

```
let ninety = Complex { re: 0.0, im: 2.0 };
assert_eq!(format!("{}", ninety),
          "0 + 2i");
assert_eq!(format!("{:#}", ninety),
          "2 ∠ 90°");
```

Although the formatting traits' fmt methods return an fmt::Result value (a typical module-specific Result type), you should propagate failures only from operations on the Formatter, as the fmt::Display implementation does with its calls to write!; your formatting functions must never originate errors themselves. This allows macros like format! to simply return a String instead of a Result<String, ...>, since appending the formatted text to a String never fails. It also ensures that any errors you do get from write! or writeln! reflect real problems from the underlying I/O stream, not formatting issues.

Formatter has plenty of other helpful methods, including some for handling structured data like maps, lists, and so on, which we won't cover here; consult the online documentation for the full details.

Using the Formatting Language in Your Own Code

You can write your own functions and macros that accept format templates and arguments by using Rust's format_args! macro and the std::fmt::Arguments type. For example, suppose your program needs to log status messages as it runs, and you'd like to use Rust's text formatting language to produce them. The following would be a start:

```
fn logging_enabled() -> bool { ... }

use std::fs::OpenOptions;
use std::io::Write;

fn write_log_entry(entry: std::fmt::Arguments) {
    if logging_enabled() {
        // Keep things simple for now, and just
        // open the file every time.
        let mut log_file = OpenOptions::new()
```

```
            .append(true)
            .create(true)
            .open("log-file-name")
            .expect("failed to open log file");

        log_file.write_fmt(entry)
            .expect("failed to write to log");
    }
}
```

You can call `write_log_entry` like so:

```
write_log_entry(format_args!("Hark! {:?}\n", mysterious_value));
```

At compile time, the `format_args!` macro parses the template string and checks it against the arguments' types, reporting an error if there are any problems. At run time, it evaluates the arguments and builds an `Arguments` value carrying all the information necessary to format the text: a pre-parsed form of the template, along with shared references to the argument values.

Constructing an `Arguments` value is cheap: it's just gathering up some pointers. No formatting work takes place yet, only the collection of the information needed to do so later. This can be important: if logging is not enabled, any time spent converting numbers to decimal, padding values, and so on would be wasted.

The `File` type implements the `std::io::Write` trait, whose `write_fmt` method takes an `Argument` and does the formatting. It writes the results to the underlying stream.

That call to `write_log_entry` isn't pretty. This is where a macro can help:

```
macro_rules! log { // no ! needed after name in macro definitions
    ($format:tt, $($arg:expr),*) => (
        write_log_entry(format_args!($format, $($arg),*))
    )
}
```

We cover macros in detail in Chapter 21. For now, take it on faith that this defines a new `log!` macro that passes its arguments along to `format_args!` and then calls your `write_log_entry` function on the resulting `Arguments` value. The formatting macros like `println!`, `writeln!`, and `format!` are all roughly the same idea.

You can use `log!` like so:

```
log!("O day and night, but this is wondrous strange! {:?}\n",
    mysterious_value);
```

Ideally, this looks a little better.

Regular Expressions

The external `regex` crate is Rust's official regular expression library. It provides the usual searching and matching functions. It has good support for Unicode, but it can search byte strings as well. Although it doesn't support some features you'll often find in other regular expression packages, like backreferences and look-around patterns, those simplifications allow `regex` to ensure that searches take time linear in the size of the expression and in the length of the text being searched. These guarantees, among others, make `regex` safe to use even with untrusted expressions searching untrusted text.

In this book, we'll provide only an overview of `regex`; you should consult its online documentation for details.

Although the `regex` crate is not in `std`, it is maintained by the Rust library team, the same group responsible for `std`. To use `regex`, put the following line in the `[dependencies]` section of your crate's *Cargo.toml* file:

```
regex = "1"
```

In the following sections, we'll assume that you have this change in place.

Basic Regex Use

A `Regex` value represents a parsed regular expression ready to use. The `Regex::new` constructor tries to parse a `&str` as a regular expression, and returns a `Result`:

```
use regex::Regex;

// A semver version number, like 0.2.1.
// May contain a pre-release version suffix, like 0.2.1-alpha.
// (No build metadata suffix, for brevity.)
//
// Note use of r"..." raw string syntax, to avoid backslash blizzard.
let semver = Regex::new(r"(\d+)\.(\d+)\.(\d+)(-[-.[:alnum:]]*)?")?;

// Simple search, with a Boolean result.
let haystack = r#"regex = "0.2.5""#;
assert!(semver.is_match(haystack));
```

The `Regex::captures` method searches a string for the first match and returns a `regex::Captures` value holding match information for each group in the expression:

```
// You can retrieve capture groups:
let captures = semver.captures(haystack)
    .ok_or("semver regex should have matched")?;
assert_eq!(&captures[0], "0.2.5");
assert_eq!(&captures[1], "0");
assert_eq!(&captures[2], "2");
assert_eq!(&captures[3], "5");
```

Indexing a `Captures` value panics if the requested group didn't match. To test whether a particular group matched, you can call `Captures::get`, which returns an `Option<regex::Match>`. A `Match` value records a single group's match:

```
assert_eq!(captures.get(4), None);
assert_eq!(captures.get(3).unwrap().start(), 13);
assert_eq!(captures.get(3).unwrap().end(), 14);
assert_eq!(captures.get(3).unwrap().as_str(), "5");
```

You can iterate over all the matches in a string:

```
let haystack = "In the beginning, there was 1.0.0. \
                For a while, we used 1.0.1-beta, \
                but in the end, we settled on 1.2.4.";

let matches: Vec<&str> = semver.find_iter(haystack)
    .map(|match_| match_.as_str())
    .collect();
assert_eq!(matches, vec!["1.0.0", "1.0.1-beta", "1.2.4"]);
```

The `find_iter` iterator produces a `Match` value for each nonoverlapping match of the expression, working from the start of the string to the end. The `captures_iter` method is similar, but produces `Captures` values recording all capture groups. Searching is slower when capture groups must be reported, so if you don't need them, it's best to use one of the methods that doesn't return them.

Building Regex Values Lazily

The `Regex::new` constructor can be expensive: constructing a `Regex` for a 1,200-character regular expression can take almost a millisecond on a fast developer machine, and even a trivial expression takes microseconds. It's best to keep `Regex` construction out of heavy computational loops; instead, you should construct your `Regex` once and then reuse the same one.

The `lazy_static` crate provides a nice way to construct static values lazily the first time they are used. To start with, note the dependency in your *Cargo.toml* file:

```
[dependencies]
lazy_static = "1"
```

This crate provides a macro to declare such variables:

```
use lazy_static::lazy_static;

lazy_static! {
    static ref SEMVER: Regex
        = Regex::new(r"(\d+)\.(\d+)\.(\d+)(-[-.[:alnum:]]*)?")
                .expect("error parsing regex");
}
```

The macro expands to a declaration of a static variable named SEMVER, but its type is not exactly Regex. Instead, it's a macro-generated type that implements Deref<Target=Regex> and therefore exposes all the same methods as a Regex. The first time SEMVER is dereferenced, the initializer is evaluated, and the value is saved for later use. Since SEMVER is a static variable, not just a local variable, the initializer runs at most once per program execution.

With this declaration in place, using SEMVER is straightforward:

```
use std::io::BufRead;

let stdin = std::io::stdin();
for line_result in stdin.lock().lines() {
    let line = line_result?;
    if let Some(match_) = SEMVER.find(&line) {
        println!("{}", match_.as_str());
    }
}
```

You can put the lazy_static! declaration in a module, or even inside the function that uses the Regex, if that's the most appropriate scope. The regular expression is still always compiled only once per program execution.

Normalization

Most users would consider the French word for tea, *thé*, to be three characters long. However, Unicode actually has two ways to represent this text:

- In the *composed* form, *"thé"* comprises the three characters 't', 'h', and 'é', where 'é' is a single Unicode character with code point 0xe9.
- In the *decomposed* form, *"thé"* comprises the four characters 't', 'h', 'e', and '\u{301}', where the 'e' is the plain ASCII character, without an accent, and code point 0x301 is the "COMBINING ACUTE ACCENT" character, which adds an acute accent to whatever character it follows.

Unicode does not consider either the composed or the decomposed form of *é* to be the "correct" one; rather, it considers them both equivalent representations of the same abstract character. Unicode says both forms should be displayed in the same way, and text input methods are permitted to produce either, so users will generally not know which form they are viewing or typing. (Rust lets you use Unicode characters directly in string literals, so you can simply write "thé" if you don't care which encoding you get. Here we'll use the \u escapes for clarity.)

However, considered as Rust `&str` or `String` values, `"th\u{e9}"` and `"the\u{301}"` are completely distinct. They have different lengths, compare as unequal, have different hash values, and order themselves differently with respect to other strings:

```
assert!("th\u{e9}" != "the\u{301}");
assert!("th\u{e9}" >  "the\u{301}");

// A Hasher is designed to accumulate the hash of a series of values,
// so hashing just one is a bit clunky.
use std::hash::{Hash, Hasher};
use std::collections::hash_map::DefaultHasher;
fn hash<T: ?Sized + Hash>(t: &T) -> u64 {
    let mut s = DefaultHasher::new();
    t.hash(&mut s);
    s.finish()
}

// These values may change in future Rust releases.
assert_eq!(hash("th\u{e9}"),    0x53e2d0734eb1dff3);
assert_eq!(hash("the\u{301}"), 0x90d837f0a0928144);
```

Clearly, if you intend to compare user-supplied text or use it as a key in a hash table or B-tree, you will need to put each string in some canonical form first.

Fortunately, Unicode specifies *normalized* forms for strings. Whenever two strings should be treated as equivalent according to Unicode's rules, their normalized forms are character-for-character identical. When encoded with UTF-8, they are byte-for-byte identical. This means you can compare normalized strings with ==, use them as keys in a `HashMap` or `HashSet`, and so on, and you'll get Unicode's notion of equality.

Failure to normalize can even have security consequences. For example, if your website normalizes usernames in some cases but not others, you could end up with two distinct users named bananasflambé, which some parts of your code treat as the same user, but others distinguish, resulting in one's privileges being extended incorrectly to the other. Of course, there are many ways to avoid this sort of problem, but history shows there are also many ways not to.

Normalization Forms

Unicode defines four normalized forms, each of which is appropriate for different uses. There are two questions to answer:

- First, do you prefer characters to be as *composed* as possible or as *decomposed* as possible?

  For example, the most composed representation of the Vietnamese word *Phở* is the three-character string `"Ph\u{1edf}"`, where both the tonal mark ˀ and the vowel mark ʾ are applied to the base character "o" in a single Unicode character,

'\u{1edf}', which Unicode dutifully names LATIN SMALL LETTER O WITH HORN AND HOOK ABOVE.

The most decomposed representation splits out the base letter and its two marks into three separate Unicode characters: 'o', '\u{31b}' (COMBINING HORN), and '\u{309}' (COMBINING HOOK ABOVE), resulting in "Pho\u{31b}\u{309}". (Whenever combining marks appear as separate characters, rather than as part of a composed character, all normalized forms specify a fixed order in which they must appear, so normalization is well specified even when characters have multiple accents.)

The composed form generally has fewer compatibility problems, since it more closely matches the representations most languages used for their text before Unicode became established. It may also work better with naïve string formatting features like Rust's `format!` macro. The decomposed form, on the other hand, may be better for displaying text or searching, since it makes the detailed structure of the text more explicit.

- The second question is: if two character sequences represent the same fundamental text but differ in the way that text should be formatted, do you want to treat them as equivalent or keep them distinct?

  Unicode has separate characters for the ordinary digit 5, the superscript digit [5] (or '\u{2075}'), and the circled digit ⑤ (or '\u{2464}'), but declares all three to be *compatibility equivalent*. Similarly, Unicode has a single character for the ligature *ffi* ('\u{fb03}'), but declares this to be compatibility equivalent to the three-character sequence ffi.

  Compatibility equivalence makes sense for searches: a search for "difficult", using only ASCII characters, ought to match the string "di\u{fb03}cult", which uses the *ffi* ligature. Applying compatibility decomposition to the latter string would replace the ligature with the three plain letters "ffi", making the search easier. But normalizing text to a compatibility equivalent form can lose essential information, so it should not be applied carelessly. For example, it would be incorrect in most contexts to store "2[5]" as "25".

Unicode Normalization Form C and Normalization Form D (NFC and NFD) use the maximally composed and maximally decomposed forms of each character, but do not try to unify compatibility equivalent sequences. The NFKC and NFKD normalization forms are like NFC and NFD, but normalize all compatibility equivalent sequences to some simple representative of their class.

The World Wide Web Consortium's "Character Model For the World Wide Web" recommends using NFC for all content. The Unicode Identifier and Pattern Syntax annex suggests using NFKC for identifiers in programming languages and offers principles for adapting the form when necessary.

The unicode-normalization Crate

Rust's `unicode-normalization` crate provides a trait that adds methods to `&str` to put the text in any of the four normalized forms. To use it, add the following line to the [`dependencies`] section of your *Cargo.toml* file:

```
unicode-normalization = "0.1.17"
```

With this declaration in place, a `&str` has four new methods that return iterators over a particular normalized form of the string:

```
use unicode_normalization::UnicodeNormalization;

// No matter what representation the left-hand string uses
// (you shouldn't be able to tell just by looking),
// these assertions will hold.
assert_eq!("Phở".nfd().collect::<String>(), "Pho\u{31b}\u{309}");
assert_eq!("Phở".nfc().collect::<String>(), "Ph\u{1edf}");

// The left-hand side here uses the "ffi" ligature character.
assert_eq!("① Di\u{fb03}culty".nfkc().collect::<String>(), "1 Difficulty");
```

Taking a normalized string and normalizing it again in the same form is guaranteed to return identical text.

Although any substring of a normalized string is itself normalized, the concatenation of two normalized strings is not necessarily normalized: for example, the second string might start with combining characters that should be placed before combining characters at the end of the first string.

As long as a text uses no unassigned code points when it is normalized, Unicode promises that its normalized form will not change in future versions of the standard. This means that normalized forms are generally safe to use in persistent storage, even as the Unicode standard evolves.

## CHAPTER 18

Input and Output

Doolittle: What concrete evidence do you have that you exist?

Bomb #20: Hmmmm... well... I think, therefore I am.

Doolittle: That's good. That's very good. But how do you know that anything else exists?

Bomb #20: My sensory apparatus reveals it to me.

    —Dark Star

Rust's standard library features for input and output are organized around three traits, `Read`, `BufRead`, and `Write`:

- Values that implement `Read` have methods for byte-oriented input. They're called *readers*.

- Values that implement `BufRead` are *buffered* readers. They support all the methods of `Read`, plus methods for reading lines of text and so forth.

- Values that implement `Write` support both byte-oriented and UTF-8 text output. They're called *writers*.

Figure 18-1 shows these three traits and some examples of reader and writer types.

In this chapter, we'll explain how to use these traits and their methods, cover the reader and writer types shown in the figure, and show other ways to interact with files, the terminal, and the network.

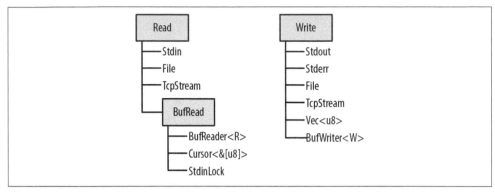

Figure 18-1. Rust's three main I/O traits and selected types that implement them

Readers and Writers

Readers are values that your program can read bytes from. Examples include:

- Files opened using `std::fs::File::open(filename)`
- `std::net::TcpStream`s, for receiving data over the network
- `std::io::stdin()`, for reading from the process's standard input stream
- `std::io::Cursor<&[u8]>` and `std::io::Cursor<Vec<u8>>` values, which are readers that "read" from a byte array or vector that's already in memory

Writers are values that your program can write bytes to. Examples include:

- Files opened using `std::fs::File::create(filename)`
- `std::net::TcpStream`s, for sending data over the network
- `std::io::stdout()` and `std::io:stderr()`, for writing to the terminal
- `Vec<u8>`, a writer whose `write` methods append to the vector
- `std::io::Cursor<Vec<u8>>`, which is similar but lets you both read and write data, and seek to different positions within the vector
- `std::io::Cursor<&mut [u8]>`, which is much like `std::io::Cursor<Vec<u8>>`, except that it can't grow the buffer, since it's just a slice of some existing byte array

Since there are standard traits for readers and writers (`std::io::Read` and `std::io::Write`), it's quite common to write generic code that works across a variety of input or output channels. For example, here's a function that copies all bytes from any reader to any writer:

```
use std::io::{self, Read, Write, ErrorKind};

const DEFAULT_BUF_SIZE: usize = 8 * 1024;

pub fn copy<R: ?Sized, W: ?Sized>(reader: &mut R, writer: &mut W)
    -> io::Result<u64>
    where R: Read, W: Write
{
    let mut buf = [0; DEFAULT_BUF_SIZE];
    let mut written = 0;
    loop {
        let len = match reader.read(&mut buf) {
            Ok(0) => return Ok(written),
            Ok(len) => len,
            Err(ref e) if e.kind() == ErrorKind::Interrupted => continue,
            Err(e) => return Err(e),
        };
        writer.write_all(&buf[..len])?;
        written += len as u64;
    }
}
```

This is the implementation of `std::io::copy()` from Rust's standard library. Since it's generic, you can use it to copy data from a `File` to a `TcpStream`, from `Stdin` to an in-memory `Vec<u8>`, etc.

If the error-handling code here is unclear, revisit Chapter 7. We'll be using the `Result` type constantly in the pages ahead; it's important to have a good grasp of how it works.

The three `std::io` traits `Read`, `BufRead`, and `Write`, along with `Seek`, are so commonly used that there's a `prelude` module containing only those traits:

```
use std::io::prelude::*;
```

You'll see this once or twice in this chapter. We also make a habit of importing the `std::io` module itself:

```
use std::io::{self, Read, Write, ErrorKind};
```

The `self` keyword here declares `io` as an alias to the `std::io` module. That way, `std::io::Result` and `std::io::Error` can be written more concisely as `io::Result` and `io::Error`, and so on.

Readers

`std::io::Read` has several methods for reading data. All of them take the reader itself by `mut` reference.

`reader.read(&mut buffer)`

Reads some bytes from the data source and stores them in the given `buffer`. The type of the `buffer` argument is `&mut [u8]`. This reads up to `buffer.len()` bytes.

The return type is `io::Result<u64>`, which is a type alias for `Result<u64, io::Error>`. On success, the `u64` value is the number of bytes read—which may be equal to or less than `buffer.len()`, *even if there's more data to come,* at the whim of the data source. `Ok(0)` means there is no more input to read.

On error, `.read()` returns `Err(err)`, where `err` is an `io::Error` value. An `io::Error` is printable, for the benefit of humans; for programs, it has a `.kind()` method that returns an error code of type `io::ErrorKind`. The members of this enum have names like `PermissionDenied` and `ConnectionReset`. Most indicate serious errors that can't be ignored, but one kind of error should be handled specially. `io::ErrorKind::Interrupted` corresponds to the Unix error code `EINTR`, which means the read happened to be interrupted by a signal. Unless the program is designed to do something clever with signals, it should just retry the read. The code for `copy()`, in the preceding section, shows an example of this.

As you can see, the `.read()` method is very low level, even inheriting quirks of the underlying operating system. If you're implementing the `Read` trait for a new type of data source, this gives you a lot of leeway. If you're trying to read some data, it's a pain. Therefore, Rust provides several higher-level convenience methods. All of them have default implementations in terms of `.read()`. They all handle `ErrorKind::Interrupted`, so you don't have to.

`reader.read_to_end(&mut byte_vec)`

Reads all remaining input from this reader, appending it to `byte_vec`, which is a `Vec<u8>`. Returns an `io::Result<usize>`, the number of bytes read.

There is no limit on the amount of data this method will pile into the vector, so don't use it on an untrusted source. (You can impose a limit using the `.take()` method, described in the next list.)

`reader.read_to_string(&mut string)`

This is the same, but appends the data to the given `String`. If the stream isn't valid UTF-8, this returns an `ErrorKind::InvalidData` error.

In some programming languages, byte input and character input are handled by different types. These days, UTF-8 is so dominant that Rust acknowledges this de facto standard and supports UTF-8 everywhere. Other character sets are supported with the open source `encoding` crate.

```
reader.read_exact(&mut buf)
```
Reads exactly enough data to fill the given buffer. The argument type is &[u8]. If the reader runs out of data before reading buf.len() bytes, this returns an ErrorKind::UnexpectedEof error.

Those are the main methods of the Read trait. In addition, there are three adapter methods that take the reader by value, transforming it into an iterator or a different reader:

```
reader.bytes()
```
Returns an iterator over the bytes of the input stream. The item type is io::Result<u8>, so an error check is required for every byte. Furthermore, this calls reader.read() once per byte, which will be very inefficient if the reader is not buffered.

```
reader.chain(reader2)
```
Returns a new reader that produces all the input from reader, followed by all the input from reader2.

```
reader.take(n)
```
Returns a new reader that reads from the same source as reader, but is limited to n bytes of input.

There is no method for closing a reader. Readers and writers typically implement Drop so that they are closed automatically.

Buffered Readers

For efficiency, readers and writers can be *buffered*, which simply means they have a chunk of memory (a buffer) that holds some input or output data in memory. This saves on system calls, as shown in Figure 18-2. The application reads data from the BufReader, in this example by calling its .read_line() method. The BufReader in turn gets its input in larger chunks from the operating system.

This picture is not to scale. The actual default size of a BufReader's buffer is several kilobytes, so a single system read can serve hundreds of .read_line() calls. This matters because system calls are slow.

(As the picture shows, the operating system has a buffer too, for the same reason: system calls are slow, but reading data from a disk is slower.)

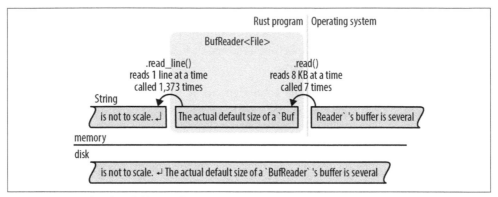

Figure 18-2. A buffered file reader

Buffered readers implement both `Read` and a second trait, `BufRead`, which adds the following methods:

`reader.read_line(&mut line)`

Reads a line of text and appends it to `line`, which is a `String`. The newline character `'\n'` at the end of the line is included in `line`. If the input has Windows-style line endings, `"\r\n"`, both characters are included in `line`.

The return value is an `io::Result<usize>`, the number of bytes read, including the line ending, if any.

If the reader is at the end of the input, this leaves `line` unchanged and returns `Ok(0)`.

`reader.lines()`

Returns an iterator over the lines of the input. The item type is `io::Result<String>`. Newline characters are *not* included in the strings. If the input has Windows-style line endings, `"\r\n"`, both characters are stripped.

This method is almost always what you want for text input. The next two sections show some examples of its use.

`reader.read_until(stop_byte, &mut byte_vec)`, `reader.split(stop_byte)`

These are just like `.read_line()` and `.lines()`, but byte-oriented, producing `Vec<u8>`s instead of `String`s. You choose the delimiter `stop_byte`.

`BufRead` also provides a pair of low-level methods, `.fill_buf()` and `.consume(n)`, for direct access to the reader's internal buffer. For more about these methods, see the online documentation.

The next two sections cover buffered readers in more detail.

Reading Lines

Here is a function that implements the Unix `grep` utility. It searches many lines of text, typically piped in from another command, for a given string:

```
use std::io;
use std::io::prelude::*;

fn grep(target: &str) -> io::Result<()> {
    let stdin = io::stdin();
    for line_result in stdin.lock().lines() {
        let line = line_result?;
        if line.contains(target) {
            println!("{}", line);
        }
    }
    Ok(())
}
```

Since we want to call `.lines()`, we need a source of input that implements `BufRead`. In this case, we call `io::stdin()` to get the data that's being piped to us. However, the Rust standard library protects `stdin` with a mutex. We call `.lock()` to lock `stdin` for the current thread's exclusive use; it returns an `StdinLock` value that implements `BufRead`. At the end of the loop, the `StdinLock` is dropped, releasing the mutex. (Without a mutex, two threads trying to read from `stdin` at the same time would cause undefined behavior. C has the same issue and solves it the same way: all of the C standard input and output functions obtain a lock behind the scenes. The only difference is that in Rust, the lock is part of the API.)

The rest of the function is straightforward: it calls `.lines()` and loops over the resulting iterator. Because this iterator produces `Result` values, we use the `?` operator to check for errors.

Suppose we want to take our `grep` program a step further and add support for searching files on disk. We can make this function generic:

```
fn grep<R>(target: &str, reader: R) -> io::Result<()>
    where R: BufRead
{
    for line_result in reader.lines() {
        let line = line_result?;
        if line.contains(target) {
            println!("{}", line);
        }
    }
    Ok(())
}
```

Now we can pass it either an `StdinLock` or a buffered `File`:

```
let stdin = io::stdin();
grep(&target, stdin.lock())?;  // ok

let f = File::open(file)?;
grep(&target, BufReader::new(f))?;  // also ok
```

Note that a `File` is not automatically buffered. `File` implements `Read` but not `BufRead`. However, it's easy to create a buffered reader for a `File`, or any other unbuffered reader. `BufReader::new(reader)` does this. (To set the size of the buffer, use `BufReader::with_capacity(size, reader)`.)

In most languages, files are buffered by default. If you want unbuffered input or output, you have to figure out how to turn buffering off. In Rust, `File` and `BufReader` are two separate library features, because sometimes you want files without buffering, and sometimes you want buffering without files (for example, you may want to buffer input from the network).

The full program, including error handling and some crude argument parsing, is shown here:

```
// grep - Search stdin or some files for lines matching a given string.

use std::error::Error;
use std::io::{self, BufReader};
use std::io::prelude::*;
use std::fs::File;
use std::path::PathBuf;

fn grep<R>(target: &str, reader: R) -> io::Result<()>
    where R: BufRead
{
    for line_result in reader.lines() {
        let line = line_result?;
        if line.contains(target) {
            println!("{}", line);
        }
    }
    Ok(())
}

fn grep_main() -> Result<(), Box<dyn Error>> {
    // Get the command-line arguments. The first argument is the
    // string to search for; the rest are filenames.
    let mut args = std::env::args().skip(1);
    let target = match args.next() {
        Some(s) => s,
        None => Err("usage: grep PATTERN FILE...")?
    };
    let files: Vec<PathBuf> = args.map(PathBuf::from).collect();
```

```
    if files.is_empty() {
        let stdin = io::stdin();
        grep(&target, stdin.lock())?;
    } else {
        for file in files {
            let f = File::open(file)?;
            grep(&target, BufReader::new(f))?;
        }
    }

    Ok(())
}

fn main() {
    let result = grep_main();
    if let Err(err) = result {
        eprintln!("{}", err);
        std::process::exit(1);
    }
}
```

Collecting Lines

Several reader methods, including `.lines()`, return iterators that produce `Result` values. The first time you want to collect all the lines of a file into one big vector, you'll run into a problem getting rid of the `Result`s:

```
// ok, but not what you want
let results: Vec<io::Result<String>> = reader.lines().collect();

// error: can't convert collection of Results to Vec<String>
let lines: Vec<String> = reader.lines().collect();
```

The second try doesn't compile: what would happen to the errors? The straightforward solution is to write a `for` loop and check each item for errors:

```
let mut lines = vec![];
for line_result in reader.lines() {
    lines.push(line_result?);
}
```

Not bad; but it would be nice to use `.collect()` here, and it turns out that we can. We just have to know which type to ask for:

```
let lines = reader.lines().collect::<io::Result<Vec<String>>>()?;
```

How does this work? The standard library contains an implementation of `FromIterator` for `Result`—easy to overlook in the online documentation—that makes this possible:

```
impl<T, E, C> FromIterator<Result<T, E>> for Result<C, E>
    where C: FromIterator<T>
{
    ...
}
```

This requires some careful reading, but it's a nice trick. Assume C is any collection type, like Vec or HashSet. As long we already know how to build a C from an iterator of T values, we can build a Result<C, E> from an iterator producing Result<T, E> values. We just need to draw values from the iterator and build the collection from the Ok results, but if we ever see an Err, stop and pass that along.

In other words, io::Result<Vec<String>> is a collection type, so the .collect() method can create and populate values of that type.

Writers

As we've seen, input is mostly done using methods. Output is a bit different.

Throughout the book, we've used println!() to produce plain-text output:

```
println!("Hello, world!");

println!("The greatest common divisor of {:?} is {}",
         numbers, d);

println!();   // print a blank line
```

There's also a print!() macro, which does not add a newline character at the end, and eprintln! and eprint! macros that write to the standard error stream. The formatting codes for all of these are the same as those for the format! macro, described in "Formatting Values" on page 454.

To send output to a writer, use the write!() and writeln!() macros. They are the same as print!() and println!(), except for two differences:

```
writeln!(io::stderr(), "error: world not helloable")?;

writeln!(&mut byte_vec, "The greatest common divisor of {:?} is {}",
         numbers, d)?;
```

One difference is that the write macros each take an extra first argument, a writer. The other is that they return a Result, so errors must be handled. That's why we used the ? operator at the end of each line.

The print macros don't return a Result; they simply panic if the write fails. Since they write to the terminal, this is rare.

The Write trait has these methods:

```
writer.write(&buf)
```
Writes some of the bytes in the slice buf to the underlying stream. It returns an io::Result<usize>. On success, this gives the number of bytes written, which may be less than buf.len(), at the whim of the stream.

Like Reader::read(), this is a low-level method that you should avoid using directly.

```
writer.write_all(&buf)
```
Writes all the bytes in the slice buf. Returns Result<()>.

```
writer.flush()
```
Flushes any buffered data to the underlying stream. Returns Result<()>.

Note that while the println! and eprintln! macros automatically flush the stdout and stderr stream, the print! and eprint! macros do not. You may have to call flush() manually when using them.

Like readers, writers are closed automatically when they are dropped.

Just as BufReader::new(reader) adds a buffer to any reader, BufWriter::new(writer) adds a buffer to any writer:

```
let file = File::create("tmp.txt")?;
let writer = BufWriter::new(file);
```

To set the size of the buffer, use BufWriter::with_capacity(size, writer).

When a BufWriter is dropped, all remaining buffered data is written to the underlying writer. However, if an error occurs during this write, the error is *ignored*. (Since this happens inside BufWriter's .drop() method, there is no useful place to report the error.) To make sure your application notices all output errors, manually .flush() buffered writers before dropping them.

Files

We've already seen two ways to open a file:

```
File::open(filename)
```
Opens an existing file for reading. It returns an io::Result<File>, and it's an error if the file doesn't exist.

```
File::create(filename)
```
Creates a new file for writing. If a file exists with the given filename, it is truncated.

Note that the File type is in the filesystem module, std::fs, not std::io.

When neither of these fits the bill, you can use `OpenOptions` to specify the exact desired behavior:

```
use std::fs::OpenOptions;

let log = OpenOptions::new()
    .append(true)  // if file exists, add to the end
    .open("server.log")?;

let file = OpenOptions::new()
    .write(true)
    .create_new(true)  // fail if file exists
    .open("new_file.txt")?;
```

The methods `.append()`, `.write()`, `.create_new()`, and so on are designed to be chained like this: each one returns `self`. This method-chaining design pattern is common enough to have a name in Rust: it's called a *builder*. `std::process::Command` is another example. For more details on `OpenOptions`, see the online documentation.

Once a `File` has been opened, it behaves like any other reader or writer. You can add a buffer if needed. The `File` will be closed automatically when you drop it.

Seeking

`File` also implements the `Seek` trait, which means you can hop around within a `File` rather than reading or writing in a single pass from the beginning to the end. `Seek` is defined like this:

```
pub trait Seek {
    fn seek(&mut self, pos: SeekFrom) -> io::Result<u64>;
}

pub enum SeekFrom {
    Start(u64),
    End(i64),
    Current(i64)
}
```

Thanks to the enum, the `seek` method is nicely expressive: use `file.seek(SeekFrom::Start(0))` to rewind to the beginning and use `file.seek(SeekFrom::Current(-8))` to go back a few bytes, and so on.

Seeking within a file is slow. Whether you're using a hard disk or a solid-state drive (SSD), a seek takes as long as reading several megabytes of data.

Other Reader and Writer Types

So far, this chapter has used File as its example workhorse, but there are many other useful reader and writer types:

io::stdin()

> Returns a reader for the standard input stream. Its type is io::Stdin. Since this is shared by all threads, each read acquires and releases a mutex.
>
> Stdin has a .lock() method that acquires the mutex and returns an io::StdinLock, a buffered reader that holds the mutex until it's dropped. Individual operations on the StdinLock therefore avoid the mutex overhead. We showed example code using this method in "Reading Lines" on page 479.
>
> For technical reasons, io::stdin().lock() doesn't work. The lock holds a reference to the Stdin value, and that means the Stdin value must be stored somewhere so that it lives long enough:
>
> ```
> let stdin = io::stdin();
> let lines = stdin.lock().lines();  // ok
> ```

io::stdout(), io::stderr()

> Return Stdout and Stderr writer types for the standard output and standard error streams. These too have mutexes and .lock() methods.

Vec<u8>

> Implements Write. Writing to a Vec<u8> extends the vector with the new data.
>
> (String, however, does *not* implement Write. To build a string using Write, first write to a Vec<u8>, and then use String::from_utf8(vec) to convert the vector to a string.)

Cursor::new(buf)

> Creates a Cursor, a buffered reader that reads from buf. This is how you create a reader that reads from a String. The argument buf can be any type that implements AsRef<[u8]>, so you can also pass a &[u8], &str, or Vec<u8>.
>
> Cursors are trivial internally. They have just two fields: buf itself and an integer, the offset in buf where the next read will start. The position is initially 0.
>
> Cursors implement Read, BufRead, and Seek. If the type of buf is &mut [u8] or Vec<u8>, then the Cursor also implements Write. Writing to a cursor overwrites bytes in buf starting at the current position. If you try to write past the end of a &mut [u8], you'll get a partial write or an io::Error. Using a cursor to write past the end of a Vec<u8> is fine, though: it grows the vector. Cursor<&mut [u8]> and Cursor<Vec<u8>> thus implement all four of the std::io::prelude traits.

`std::net::TcpStream`
Represents a TCP network connection. Since TCP enables two-way communication, it's both a reader and a writer.

The type-associated function `TcpStream::connect(("hostname", PORT))` tries to connect to a server and returns an `io::Result<TcpStream>`.

`std::process::Command`
Supports spawning a child process and piping data to its standard input, like so:

```
use std::process::{Command, Stdio};

let mut child =
    Command::new("grep")
    .arg("-e")
    .arg("a.*e.*i.*o.*u")
    .stdin(Stdio::piped())
    .spawn()?;

let mut to_child = child.stdin.take().unwrap();
for word in my_words {
    writeln!(to_child, "{}", word)?;
}
drop(to_child);  // close grep's stdin, so it will exit
child.wait()?;
```

The type of `child.stdin` is `Option<std::process::ChildStdin>`; here we've used `.stdin(Stdio::piped())` when setting up the child process, so `child.stdin` is definitely populated when `.spawn()` succeeds. If we hadn't, `child.stdin` would be `None`.

`Command` also has similar methods `.stdout()` and `.stderr()`, which can be used to request readers in `child.stdout` and `child.stderr`.

The `std::io` module also offers a handful of functions that return trivial readers and writers:

`io::sink()`
This is the no-op writer. All the write methods return `Ok`, but the data is just discarded.

`io::empty()`
This is the no-op reader. Reading always succeeds, but returns end-of-input.

`io::repeat(byte)`
Returns a reader that repeats the given byte endlessly.

Binary Data, Compression, and Serialization

Many open source crates build on the `std::io` framework to offer extra features.

The `byteorder` crate offers `ReadBytesExt` and `WriteBytesExt` traits that add methods to all readers and writers for binary input and output:

```
use byteorder::{ReadBytesExt, WriteBytesExt, LittleEndian};

let n = reader.read_u32::<LittleEndian>()?;
writer.write_i64::<LittleEndian>(n as i64)?;
```

The `flate2` crate provides adapter methods for reading and writing `gzipped` data:

```
use flate2::read::GzDecoder;
let file = File::open("access.log.gz")?;
let mut gzip_reader = GzDecoder::new(file);
```

The `serde` crate, and its associated format crates such as `serde_json`, implement serialization and deserialization: they convert back and forth between Rust structs and bytes. We mentioned this once before, in "Traits and Other People's Types" on page 268. Now we can take a closer look.

Suppose we have some data—the map for a text adventure game—stored in a `HashMap`:

```
type RoomId = String;                     // each room has a unique name
type RoomExits = Vec<(char, RoomId)>;     // ...and a list of exits
type RoomMap = HashMap<RoomId, RoomExits>; // room names and exits, simple

// Create a simple map.
let mut map = RoomMap::new();
map.insert("Cobble Crawl".to_string(),
           vec![('W', "Debris Room".to_string())]);
map.insert("Debris Room".to_string(),
           vec![('E', "Cobble Crawl".to_string()),
                ('W', "Sloping Canyon".to_string())]);
...
```

Turning this data into JSON for output is a single line of code:

```
serde_json::to_writer(&mut std::io::stdout(), &map)?;
```

Internally, `serde_json::to_writer` uses the `serialize` method of the `serde::Serialize` trait. The library attaches this trait to all types that it knows how to serialize, and that includes all of the types that appear in our data: strings, characters, tuples, vectors, and `HashMaps`.

`serde` is flexible. In this program, the output is JSON data, because we chose the `serde_json` serializer. Other formats, like MessagePack, are also available. Likewise, you could send this output to a file, a `Vec<u8>`, or any other writer. The preceding code prints the data on `stdout`. Here it is:

```
{"Debris Room":[["E","Cobble Crawl"],["W","Sloping Canyon"]],"Cobble Crawl":
[["W","Debris Room"]]}
```

serde also includes support for deriving the two key serde traits:

```
#[derive(Serialize, Deserialize)]
struct Player {
    location: String,
    items: Vec<String>,
    health: u32
}
```

This `#[derive]` attribute can make your compiles take a bit longer, so you need to explicitly ask serde to support it when you list it as a dependency in your *Cargo.toml* file. Here's what we used for the preceding code:

```
[dependencies]
serde = { version = "1.0", features = ["derive"] }
serde_json = "1.0"
```

See the serde documentation for more details. In short, the build system autogenerates implementations of serde::Serialize and serde::Deserialize for Player, so that serializing a Player value is simple:

```
serde_json::to_writer(&mut std::io::stdout(), &player)?;
```

The output looks like this:

```
{"location":"Cobble Crawl","items":["a wand"],"health":3}
```

Files and Directories

Now that we've shown how to work with readers and writers, the next few sections cover Rust's features for working with files and directories, which live in the std::path and std::fs modules. All of these features involve working with filenames, so we'll start with the filename types.

OsStr and Path

Inconveniently, your operating system does not force filenames to be valid Unicode. Here are two Linux shell commands that create text files. Only the first uses a valid UTF-8 filename:

```
$ echo "hello world" > ô.txt
$ echo "O brave new world, that has such filenames in't" > $'\xf4'.txt
```

Both commands pass without comment, because the Linux kernel doesn't know UTF-8 from Ogg Vorbis. To the kernel, any string of bytes (excluding null bytes and slashes) is an acceptable filename. It's a similar story on Windows: almost any string of 16-bit "wide characters" is an acceptable filename, even strings that are not valid

UTF-16. The same is true of other strings the operating system handles, like command-line arguments and environment variables.

Rust strings are always valid Unicode. Filenames are *almost* always Unicode in practice, but Rust has to cope somehow with the rare case where they aren't. This is why Rust has `std::ffi::OsStr` and `OsString`.

`OsStr` is a string type that's a superset of UTF-8. Its job is to be able to represent all filenames, command-line arguments, and environment variables on the current system, *whether they're valid Unicode or not*. On Unix, an `OsStr` can hold any sequence of bytes. On Windows, an `OsStr` is stored using an extension of UTF-8 that can encode any sequence of 16-bit values, including unmatched surrogates.

So we have two string types: `str` for actual Unicode strings; and `OsStr` for whatever nonsense your operating system can dish out. We'll introduce one more: `std::path::Path`, for filenames. This one is purely a convenience. `Path` is exactly like `OsStr`, but it adds many handy filename-related methods, which we'll cover in the next section. Use `Path` for both absolute and relative paths. For an individual component of a path, use `OsStr`.

Lastly, for each string type, there's a corresponding *owning* type: a `String` owns a heap-allocated `str`, a `std::ffi::OsString` owns a heap-allocated `OsStr`, and a `std::path::PathBuf` owns a heap-allocated `Path`. Table 18-1 outlines some of the features of each type.

Table 18-1. Filename types

	str	OsStr	Path
Unsized type, always passed by reference	Yes	Yes	Yes
Can contain any Unicode text	Yes	Yes	Yes
Looks just like UTF-8, normally	Yes	Yes	Yes
Can contain non-Unicode data	No	Yes	Yes
Text processing methods	Yes	No	No
Filename-related methods	No	No	Yes
Owned, growable, heap-allocated equivalent	String	OsString	PathBuf
Convert to owned type	.to_string()	.to_os_string()	.to_path_buf()

All three of these types implement a common trait, `AsRef<Path>`, so we can easily declare a generic function that accepts "any filename type" as an argument. This uses a technique we showed in "AsRef and AsMut" on page 317:

```
use std::path::Path;
use std::io;

fn swizzle_file<P>(path_arg: P) -> io::Result<()>
    where P: AsRef<Path>
```

```
    {
        let path = path_arg.as_ref();
        ...
    }
```

All the standard functions and methods that take path arguments use this technique, so you can freely pass string literals to any of them.

Path and PathBuf Methods

Path offers the following methods, among others:

`Path::new(str)`
Converts a &str or &OsStr to a &Path. This doesn't copy the string. The new &Path points to the same bytes as the original &str or &OsStr:

```
use std::path::Path;
let home_dir = Path::new("/home/fwolfe");
```

(The similar method OsStr::new(str) converts a &str to a &OsStr.)

`path.parent()`
Returns the path's parent directory, if any. The return type is Option<&Path>.

This doesn't copy the path. The parent directory of path is always a substring of path:

```
assert_eq!(Path::new("/home/fwolfe/program.txt").parent(),
           Some(Path::new("/home/fwolfe")));
```

`path.file_name()`
Returns the last component of path, if any. The return type is Option<&OsStr>.

In the typical case, where path consists of a directory, then a slash, and then a filename, this returns the filename:

```
use std::ffi::OsStr;
assert_eq!(Path::new("/home/fwolfe/program.txt").file_name(),
           Some(OsStr::new("program.txt")));
```

`path.is_absolute()`, `path.is_relative()`
These tell whether the file is absolute, like the Unix path */usr/bin/advent* or the Windows path *C:\Program Files*, or relative, like *src/main.rs*.

`path1.join(path2)`
Joins two paths, returning a new PathBuf:

```
let path1 = Path::new("/usr/share/dict");
assert_eq!(path1.join("words"),
           Path::new("/usr/share/dict/words"));
```

If `path2` is an absolute path, this just returns a copy of `path2`, so this method can be used to convert any path to an absolute path:

```
let abs_path = std::env::current_dir()?.join(any_path);
```

`path.components()`

Returns an iterator over the components of the given path, from left to right. The item type of this iterator is `std::path::Component`, an enum that can represent all the different pieces that can appear in filenames:

```
pub enum Component<'a> {
    Prefix(PrefixComponent<'a>),  // a drive letter or share (on Windows)
    RootDir,                      // the root directory, `/` or `\`
    CurDir,                       // the `.` special directory
    ParentDir,                    // the `..` special directory
    Normal(&'a OsStr)             // plain file and directory names
}
```

For example, the Windows path \\venice\Music\A Love Supreme\04-Psalm.mp3 consists of a `Prefix` representing \\venice\Music, followed by a `RootDir`, and then two `Normal` components representing *A Love Supreme* and *04-Psalm.mp3*.

For details, see the online documentation (*https://oreil.ly/mtHCk*).

`path.ancestors()`

Returns an iterator that walks from `path` up to the root. Each item produced is a `Path`: first `path` itself, then its parent, then its grandparent, and so on:

```
let file = Path::new("/home/jimb/calendars/calendar-18x18.pdf");
assert_eq!(file.ancestors().collect::<Vec<_>>(),
           vec![Path::new("/home/jimb/calendars/calendar-18x18.pdf"),
                Path::new("/home/jimb/calendars"),
                Path::new("/home/jimb"),
                Path::new("/home"),
                Path::new("/")]);
```

This is much like calling `parent` repeatedly until it returns `None`. The final item is always a root or prefix path.

These methods work on strings in memory. `Paths` also have some methods that query the filesystem: `.exists()`, `.is_file()`, `.is_dir()`, `.read_dir()`, `.canonicalize()`, and so on. See the online documentation to learn more.

There are three methods for converting `Paths` to strings. Each one allows for the possibility of invalid UTF-8 in the `Path`:

`path.to_str()`

Converts a `Path` to a string, as an `Option<&str>`. If `path` isn't valid UTF-8, this returns `None`:

```
    if let Some(file_str) = path.to_str() {
        println!("{}", file_str);
    } // ...otherwise skip this weirdly named file
```

`path.to_string_lossy()`

This is basically the same thing, but it manages to return some sort of string in all cases. If `path` isn't valid UTF-8, these methods make a copy, replacing each invalid byte sequence with the Unicode replacement character, U+FFFD ('�').

The return type is `std::borrow::Cow<str>`: an either borrowed or owned string. To get a `String` from this value, use its `.to_owned()` method. (For more about Cow, see "Borrow and ToOwned at Work: The Humble Cow" on page 325.)

`path.display()`

This is for printing paths:

```
    println!("Download found. You put it in: {}", dir_path.display());
```

The value this returns isn't a string, but it implements `std::fmt::Display`, so it can be used with `format!()`, `println!()`, and friends. If the path isn't valid UTF-8, the output may contain the � character.

Filesystem Access Functions

Table 18-2 shows some of the functions in `std::fs` and their approximate equivalents on Unix and Windows. All of these functions return `io::Result` values. They are `Result<()>` unless otherwise noted.

Table 18-2. Summary of filesystem access functions

	Rust function	Unix	Windows
Creating and deleting	`create_dir(path)`	`mkdir()`	`CreateDirectory()`
	`create_dir_all(path)`	like `mkdir -p`	like `mkdir`
	`remove_dir(path)`	`rmdir()`	`RemoveDirectory()`
	`remove_dir_all(path)`	like `rm -r`	like `rmdir /s`
	`remove_file(path)`	`unlink()`	`DeleteFile()`
Copying, moving, and linking	`copy(src_path, dest_path) -> Result<u64>`	like `cp -p`	`CopyFileEx()`
	`rename(src_path, dest_path)`	`rename()`	`MoveFileEx()`
	`hard_link(src_path, dest_path)`	`link()`	`CreateHardLink()`

	Rust function	Unix	Windows
Inspecting	canonicalize(path) -> Result<PathBuf>	realpath()	GetFinalPathNameByHandle()
	metadata(path) -> Result<Metadata>	stat()	GetFileInformationByHandle()
	symlink_metadata(path) -> Result<Metadata>	lstat()	GetFileInformationByHandle()
	read_dir(path) -> Result<ReadDir>	opendir()	FindFirstFile()
	read_link(path) -> Result<PathBuf>	readlink()	FSCTL_GET_REPARSE_POINT
Permissions	set_permissions(path, perm)	chmod()	SetFileAttributes()

(The number returned by copy() is the size of the copied file, in bytes. For creating symbolic links, see "Platform-Specific Features" on page 495.)

As you can see, Rust strives to provide portable functions that work predictably on Windows as well as macOS, Linux, and other Unix systems.

A full tutorial on filesystems is beyond the scope of this book, but if you're curious about any of these functions, you can easily find more about them online. We'll show some examples in the next section.

All of these functions are implemented by calling out to the operating system. For example, std::fs::canonicalize(path) does not merely use string processing to eliminate . and .. from the given path. It resolves relative paths using the current working directory, and it chases symbolic links. It's an error if the path doesn't exist.

The Metadata type that's produced by std::fs::metadata(path) and std::fs::symlink_metadata(path) contains such information as the file type and size, permissions, and timestamps. As always, consult the documentation for details.

As a convenience, the Path type has a few of these built in as methods: path.metadata(), for example, is the same thing as std::fs::metadata(path).

Reading Directories

To list the contents of a directory, use std::fs::read_dir or, equivalently, the .read_dir() method of a Path:

```
for entry_result in path.read_dir()? {
    let entry = entry_result?;
    println!("{}", entry.file_name().to_string_lossy());
}
```

Note the two uses of ? in this code. The first line checks for errors opening the directory. The second line checks for errors reading the next entry.

The type of entry is `std::fs::DirEntry`, and it's a struct with just a few methods:

`entry.file_name()`
  The name of the file or directory, as an `OsString`.

`entry.path()`
  This is the same, but with the original path joined to it, producing a new
  `PathBuf`. If the directory we're listing is `"/home/jimb"`, and `entry.file_name()`
  is `".emacs"`, then `entry.path()` would return `PathBuf::from("/home/
  jimb/.emacs")`.

`entry.file_type()`
  Returns an `io::Result<FileType>`. `FileType` has `.is_file()`, `.is_dir()`, and
  `.is_symlink()` methods.

`entry.metadata()`
  Gets the rest of the metadata about this entry.

The special directories . and .. are *not* listed when reading a directory.

Here's a more substantial example. The following code recursively copies a directory
tree from one place to another on disk:

```
use std::fs;
use std::io;
use std::path::Path;

/// Copy the existing directory `src` to the target path `dst`.
fn copy_dir_to(src: &Path, dst: &Path) -> io::Result<()> {
    if !dst.is_dir() {
        fs::create_dir(dst)?;
    }

    for entry_result in src.read_dir()? {
        let entry = entry_result?;
        let file_type = entry.file_type()?;
        copy_to(&entry.path(), &file_type, &dst.join(entry.file_name()))?;
    }

    Ok(())
}
```

A separate function, `copy_to`, copies individual directory entries:

```
/// Copy whatever is at `src` to the target path `dst`.
fn copy_to(src: &Path, src_type: &fs::FileType, dst: &Path)
    -> io::Result<()>
{
```

```
    if src_type.is_file() {
        fs::copy(src, dst)?;
    } else if src_type.is_dir() {
        copy_dir_to(src, dst)?;
    } else {
        return Err(io::Error::new(io::ErrorKind::Other,
                               format!("don't know how to copy: {}",
                                       src.display())));
    }
    Ok(())
}
```

Platform-Specific Features

So far, our copy_to function can copy files and directories. Suppose we also want to support symbolic links on Unix.

There is no portable way to create symbolic links that work on both Unix and Windows, but the standard library offers a Unix-specific symlink function:

```
use std::os::unix::fs::symlink;
```

With this, our job is easy. We need only add a branch to the if expression in copy_to:

```
    ...
    } else if src_type.is_symlink() {
        let target = src.read_link()?;
        symlink(target, dst)?;
    ...
```

This will work as long as we compile our program only for Unix systems, such as Linux and macOS.

The std::os module contains various platform-specific features, like symlink. The actual body of std::os in the standard library looks like this (taking some poetic license):

```
//! OS-specific functionality.

#[cfg(unix)]                    pub mod unix;
#[cfg(windows)]                 pub mod windows;
#[cfg(target_os = "ios")]       pub mod ios;
#[cfg(target_os = "linux")]     pub mod linux;
#[cfg(target_os = "macos")]     pub mod macos;
...
```

The #[cfg] attribute indicates conditional compilation: each of these modules exists only on some platforms. This is why our modified program, using std::os::unix, will successfully compile only for Unix: on other platforms, std::os::unix doesn't exist.

If we want our code to compile on all platforms, with support for symbolic links on Unix, we must use `#[cfg]` in our program as well. In this case, it's easiest to import `symlink` on Unix, while defining our own `symlink` stub on other systems:

```
#[cfg(unix)]
use std::os::unix::fs::symlink;

/// Stub implementation of `symlink` for platforms that don't provide it.
#[cfg(not(unix))]
fn symlink<P: AsRef<Path>, Q: AsRef<Path>>(src: P, _dst: Q)
    -> std::io::Result<()>
{
    Err(io::Error::new(io::ErrorKind::Other,
                       format!("can't copy symbolic link: {}",
                               src.as_ref().display())))
}
```

It turns out that `symlink` is something of a special case. Most Unix-specific features are not standalone functions but rather extension traits that add new methods to standard library types. (We covered extension traits in "Traits and Other People's Types" on page 268.) There's a `prelude` module that can be used to enable all of these extensions at once:

```
use std::os::unix::prelude::*;
```

For example, on Unix, this adds a `.mode()` method to `std::fs::Permissions`, providing access to the underlying u32 value that represents permissions on Unix. Similarly, it extends `std::fs::Metadata` with accessors for the fields of the underlying `struct stat` value—such as `.uid()`, the user ID of the file's owner.

All told, what's in `std::os` is pretty basic. Much more platform-specific functionality is available via third-party crates, like `winreg` (*https://oreil.ly/UkEzd*) for accessing the Windows registry.

Networking

A tutorial on networking is well beyond the scope of this book. However, if you already know a bit about network programming this section will help you get started with networking in Rust.

For low-level networking code, start with the `std::net` module, which provides cross-platform support for TCP and UDP networking. Use the `native_tls` crate for SSL/TLS support.

These modules provide the building blocks for straightforward, blocking input and output over the network. You can write a simple server in a few lines of code, using `std::net` and spawning a thread for each connection. For example, here's an "echo" server:

```
use std::net::TcpListener;
use std::io;
use std::thread::spawn;

/// Accept connections forever, spawning a thread for each one.
fn echo_main(addr: &str) -> io::Result<()> {
    let listener = TcpListener::bind(addr)?;
    println!("listening on {}", addr);
    loop {
        // Wait for a client to connect.
        let (mut stream, addr) = listener.accept()?;
        println!("connection received from {}", addr);

        // Spawn a thread to handle this client.
        let mut write_stream = stream.try_clone()?;
        spawn(move || {
            // Echo everything we receive from `stream` back to it.
            io::copy(&mut stream, &mut write_stream)
                .expect("error in client thread: ");
            println!("connection closed");
        });
    }
}

fn main() {
    echo_main("127.0.0.1:17007").expect("error: ");
}
```

An echo server simply repeats back everything you send to it. This kind of code is not so different from what you'd write in Java or Python. (We'll cover std::thread::spawn() in the next chapter.)

However, for high-performance servers, you'll need to use asynchronous input and output. Chapter 20 covers Rust's support for asynchronous programming, and shows the full code for a network client and server.

Higher-level protocols are supported by third-party crates. For example, the reqwest crate offers a beautiful API for HTTP clients. Here is a complete command-line program that fetches any document with an http: or https: URL and dumps it to your terminal. This code was written using reqwest = "0.11", with its "blocking" feature enabled. reqwest also provides an asynchronous interface.

```
use std::error::Error;
use std::io;

fn http_get_main(url: &str) -> Result<(), Box<dyn Error>> {
    // Send the HTTP request and get a response.
    let mut response = reqwest::blocking::get(url)?;
    if !response.status().is_success() {
        Err(format!("{}", response.status()))?;
    }
```

```
    // Read the response body and write it to stdout.
    let stdout = io::stdout();
    io::copy(&mut response, &mut stdout.lock())?;

    Ok(())
}

fn main() {
    let args: Vec<String> = std::env::args().collect();
    if args.len() != 2 {
        eprintln!("usage: http-get URL");
        return;
    }

    if let Err(err) = http_get_main(&args[1]) {
        eprintln!("error: {}", err);
    }
}
```

The `actix-web` framework for HTTP servers offers high-level touches such as the `Service` and `Transform` traits, which help you compose an app from pluggable parts. The `websocket` crate implements the WebSocket protocol. And so on. Rust is a young language with a busy open source ecosystem. Support for networking is rapidly expanding.

## CHAPTER 19

Concurrency

In the long run it is not advisable to write large concurrent programs in machine-oriented languages that permit unrestricted use of store locations and their addresses. There is just no way we will be able to make such programs reliable (even with the help of complicated hardware mechanisms).
—Per Brinch Hansen (1977)

Patterns for communication are patterns for parallelism.
—Whit Morriss

If your attitude toward concurrency has changed over the course of your career, you're not alone. It's a common story.

At first, writing concurrent code is easy and fun. The tools—threads, locks, queues, and so on—are a snap to pick up and use. There are a lot of pitfalls, it's true, but fortunately you know what they all are, and you are careful not to make mistakes.

At some point, you have to debug someone else's multithreaded code, and you're forced to conclude that *some* people really should not be using these tools.

Then at some point you have to debug your own multithreaded code.

Experience inculcates a healthy skepticism, if not outright cynicism, toward all multi-threaded code. This is helped along by the occasional article explaining in mind-numbing detail why some obviously correct multithreading idiom does not work at all. (It has to do with "the memory model.") But you eventually find one approach to concurrency that you think you can realistically use without constantly making mistakes. You can shoehorn pretty much everything into that idiom, and (if you're *really* good) you learn to say "no" to added complexity.

Of course, there are rather lots of idioms. Approaches that systems programmers commonly use include the following:

- A *background thread* that has a single job and periodically wakes up to do it.
- General-purpose *worker pools* that communicate with clients via *task queues*.
- *Pipelines* where data flows from one thread to the next, with each thread doing a little of the work.
- *Data parallelism*, where it is assumed (rightly or wrongly) that the whole computer will mainly just be doing one large computation, which is therefore split into *n* pieces and run on *n* threads in the hopes of putting all *n* of the machine's cores to work at once.
- A *sea of synchronized objects*, where multiple threads have access to the same data, and races are avoided using ad hoc *locking* schemes based on low-level primitives like mutexes. (Java includes built-in support for this model, which was quite popular during the 1990s and 2000s.)
- *Atomic integer operations* allow multiple cores to communicate by passing information through fields the size of one machine word. (This is even harder to get right than all the others, unless the data being exchanged is literally just integer values. In practice, it's usually pointers.)

In time, you may come to be able to use several of these approaches and combine them safely. You are a master of the art. And things would be great, if only nobody else were ever allowed to modify the system in any way. Programs that use threads well are full of unwritten rules.

Rust offers a better way to use concurrency, not by forcing all programs to adopt a single style (which for systems programmers would be no solution at all), but by supporting multiple styles safely. The unwritten rules are written down—in code—and enforced by the compiler.

You've heard that Rust lets you write safe, fast, concurrent programs. This is the chapter where we show you how it's done. We'll cover three ways to use Rust threads:

- Fork-join parallelism
- Channels
- Shared mutable state

Along the way, you're going to use everything you've learned so far about the Rust language. The care Rust takes with references, mutability, and lifetimes is valuable enough in single-threaded programs, but it is in concurrent programming that the true significance of those rules becomes apparent. They make it possible to expand

your toolbox, to hack multiple styles of multithreaded code quickly and correctly—
without skepticism, without cynicism, without fear.

Fork-Join Parallelism

The simplest use cases for threads arise when we have several completely independent
tasks that we'd like to do at once.

For example, suppose we're doing natural language processing on a large corpus of
documents. We could write a loop:

```
fn process_files(filenames: Vec<String>) -> io::Result<()> {
    for document in filenames {
        let text = load(&document)?;      // read source file
        let results = process(text);      // compute statistics
        save(&document, results)?;        // write output file
    }
    Ok(())
}
```

The program would run as shown in Figure 19-1.

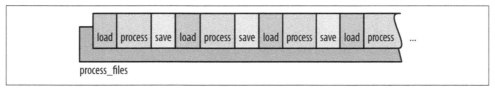

Figure 19-1. Single-threaded execution of `process_files()`

Since each document is processed separately, it's relatively easy to speed this task up
by splitting the corpus into chunks and processing each chunk on a separate thread,
as shown in Figure 19-2.

This pattern is called *fork-join parallelism*. To *fork* is to start a new thread, and to *join*
a thread is to wait for it to finish. We've already seen this technique: we used it to
speed up the Mandelbrot program in Chapter 2.

Fork-join parallelism is attractive for a few reasons:

- It's dead simple. Fork-join is easy to implement, and Rust makes it easy to get
  right.

- It avoids bottlenecks. There's no locking of shared resources in fork-join. The
  only time any thread has to wait for another is at the end. In the meantime, each
  thread can run freely. This helps keep task-switching overhead low.

- The performance math is straightforward. In the best case, by starting four
  threads, we can finish our work in a quarter of the time. Figure 19-2 shows one
  reason we shouldn't expect this ideal speedup: we might not be able to distribute

the work evenly across all threads. Another reason for caution is that sometimes fork-join programs must spend some time after the threads join *combining* the results computed by the threads. That is, isolating the tasks completely may make some extra work. Still, apart from those two things, any CPU-bound program with isolated units of work can expect a significant boost.

- It's easy to reason about program correctness. A fork-join program is *deterministic* as long as the threads are really isolated, like the compute threads in the Mandelbrot program. The program always produces the same result, regardless of variations in thread speed. It's a concurrency model without race conditions.

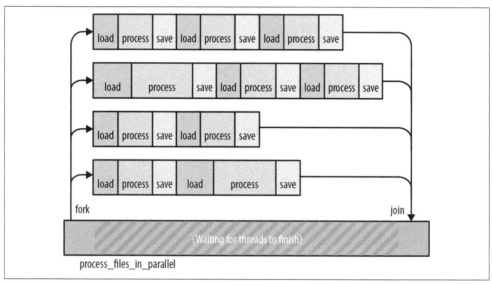

Figure 19-2. Multithreaded file processing using a fork-join approach

The main disadvantage of fork-join is that it requires isolated units of work. Later in this chapter, we'll consider some problems that don't split up so cleanly.

For now, let's stick with the natural language processing example. We'll show a few ways of applying the fork-join pattern to the process_files function.

spawn and join

The function std::thread::spawn starts a new thread:

```
use std::thread;

thread::spawn(|| {
    println!("hello from a child thread");
});
```

It takes one argument, an FnOnce closure or function. Rust starts a new thread to run the code of that closure or function. The new thread is a real operating system thread with its own stack, just like threads in C++, C#, and Java.

Here's a more substantial example, using spawn to implement a parallel version of the process_files function from before:

```
use std::{thread, io};

fn process_files_in_parallel(filenames: Vec<String>) -> io::Result<()> {
    // Divide the work into several chunks.
    const NTHREADS: usize = 8;
    let worklists = split_vec_into_chunks(filenames, NTHREADS);

    // Fork: Spawn a thread to handle each chunk.
    let mut thread_handles = vec![];
    for worklist in worklists {
        thread_handles.push(
            thread::spawn(move || process_files(worklist))
        );
    }

    // Join: Wait for all threads to finish.
    for handle in thread_handles {
        handle.join().unwrap()?;
    }

    Ok(())
}
```

Let's take this function line by line.

```
fn process_files_in_parallel(filenames: Vec<String>) -> io::Result<()> {
```

Our new function has the same type signature as the original process_files, making it a handy drop-in replacement.

```
    // Divide the work into several chunks.
    const NTHREADS: usize = 8;
    let worklists = split_vec_into_chunks(filenames, NTHREADS);
```

We use a utility function split_vec_into_chunks, not shown here, to divide up the work. The result, worklists, is a vector of vectors. It contains eight evenly sized portions of the original vector filenames.

```
    // Fork: Spawn a thread to handle each chunk.
    let mut thread_handles = vec![];
    for worklist in worklists {
        thread_handles.push(
            thread::spawn(move || process_files(worklist))
        );
    }
```

We spawn a thread for each `worklist`. `spawn()` returns a value called a `JoinHandle`, which we'll use later. For now, we put all the `JoinHandle`s into a vector.

Note how we get the list of filenames into the worker thread:

- `worklist` is defined and populated by the `for` loop, in the parent thread.
- As soon as the `move` closure is created, `worklist` is moved into the closure.
- `spawn` then moves the closure (including the `worklist` vector) over to the new child thread.

These moves are cheap. Like the `Vec<String>` moves we discussed in Chapter 4, the `String`s are not cloned. In fact, nothing is allocated or freed. The only data moved is the `Vec` itself: three machine words.

Most every thread you create needs both code and data to get started. Rust closures, conveniently, contain whatever code you want and whatever data you want.

Moving on:

```
// Join: Wait for all threads to finish.
for handle in thread_handles {
    handle.join().unwrap()?;
}
```

We use the `.join()` method of the `JoinHandle`s we collected earlier to wait for all eight threads to finish. Joining threads is often necessary for correctness, because a Rust program exits as soon as `main` returns, even if other threads are still running. Destructors are not called; the extra threads are just killed. If this isn't what you want, be sure to join any threads you care about before returning from `main`.

If we manage to get through this loop, it means all eight child threads finished successfully. Our function therefore ends by returning `Ok(())`:

```
    Ok(())
}
```

Error Handling Across Threads

The code we used to join the child threads in our example is trickier than it looks, because of error handling. Let's revisit that line of code:

```
handle.join().unwrap()?;
```

The `.join()` method does two neat things for us.

First, `handle.join()` returns a `std::thread::Result` that's an error *if the child thread panicked*. This makes threading in Rust dramatically more robust than in C++. In C++, an out-of-bounds array access is undefined behavior, and there's no protecting the rest of the system from the consequences. In Rust, panic is safe and per thread. The boundaries between threads serve as a firewall for panic; panic doesn't automatically spread from one thread to the threads that depend on it. Instead, a panic in one thread is reported as an error `Result` in other threads. The program as a whole can easily recover.

In our program, though, we don't attempt any fancy panic handling. Instead, we immediately use `.unwrap()` on this `Result`, asserting that it is an `Ok` result and not an `Err` result. If a child thread *did* panic, then this assertion would fail, so the parent thread would panic too. We're explicitly propagating panic from the child threads to the parent thread.

Second, `handle.join()` passes the return value from the child thread back to the parent thread. The closure we passed to `spawn` has a return type of `io::Result<()>`, because that's what `process_files` returns. This return value isn't discarded. When the child thread is finished, its return value is saved, and `JoinHandle::join()` transfers that value back to the parent thread.

The full type that's returned by `handle.join()` in this program is `std::thread::Result<std::io::Result<()>>`. The `thread::Result` is part of the `spawn`/`join` API; the `io::Result` is part of our app.

In our case, after unwrapping the `thread::Result`, we use the ? operator on the `io::Result`, explicitly propagating I/O errors from the child threads to the parent thread.

All of this may seem rather intricate. But consider that it's just one line of code, and then compare this with other languages. The default behavior in Java and C# is for exceptions in child threads to be dumped to the terminal and then forgotten. In C++, the default is to abort the process. In Rust, errors are `Result` values (data) instead of exceptions (control flow). They're delivered across threads just like any other value. Any time you use low-level threading APIs, you end up having to write careful error-handling code, but *given that you have to write it,* `Result` is very nice to have around.

Sharing Immutable Data Across Threads

Suppose the analysis we're doing requires a large database of English words and phrases:

```
// before
fn process_files(filenames: Vec<String>)

// after
fn process_files(filenames: Vec<String>, glossary: &GigabyteMap)
```

This `glossary` is going to be big, so we're passing it in by reference. How can we update `process_files_in_parallel` to pass the glossary through to the worker threads?

The obvious change does not work:

```
fn process_files_in_parallel(filenames: Vec<String>,
                             glossary: &GigabyteMap)
    -> io::Result<()>
{
    ...
    for worklist in worklists {
        thread_handles.push(
            spawn(move || process_files(worklist, glossary))  // error
        );
    }
    ...
}
```

We've simply added a `glossary` argument to our function and passed it along to `process_files`. Rust complains:

```
error: explicit lifetime required in the type of `glossary`
   |
38 |             spawn(move || process_files(worklist, glossary))  // error
   |             ^^^^^ lifetime `'static` required
```

Rust is complaining about the lifetime of the closure we're passing to `spawn`, and the "helpful" message the compiler presents here is actually no help at all.

`spawn` launches independent threads. Rust has no way of knowing how long the child thread will run, so it assumes the worst: it assumes the child thread may keep running even after the parent thread has finished and all values in the parent thread are gone. Obviously, if the child thread is going to last that long, the closure it's running needs to last that long too. But this closure has a bounded lifetime: it depends on the reference `glossary`, and references don't last forever.

Note that Rust is right to reject this code! The way we've written this function, it *is* possible for one thread to hit an I/O error, causing `process_files_in_parallel` to bail out before the other threads are finished. Child threads could end up trying to use the glossary after the main thread has freed it. It would be a race—with undefined behavior as the prize, if the main thread should win. Rust can't allow this.

It seems `spawn` is too open-ended to support sharing references across threads. Indeed, we already saw a case like this, in "Closures That Steal" on page 330. There, our solution was to transfer ownership of the data to the new thread, using a `move` closure. That won't work here, since we have many threads that all need to use the same data. One safe alternative is to `clone` the whole glossary for each thread, but since it's large, we want to avoid that. Fortunately, the standard library provides another way: atomic reference counting.

We described `Arc` in "Rc and Arc: Shared Ownership" on page 97. It's time to put it to use:

```
use std::sync::Arc;

fn process_files_in_parallel(filenames: Vec<String>,
                             glossary: Arc<GigabyteMap>)
    -> io::Result<()>
{
    ...
    for worklist in worklists {
        // This call to .clone() only clones the Arc and bumps the
        // reference count. It does not clone the GigabyteMap.
        let glossary_for_child = glossary.clone();
        thread_handles.push(
            spawn(move || process_files(worklist, &glossary_for_child))
        );
    }
    ...
}
```

We have changed the type of `glossary`: to run the analysis in parallel, the caller must pass in an `Arc<GigabyteMap>`, a smart pointer to a `GigabyteMap` that's been moved into the heap, by using `Arc::new(giga_map)`.

When we call `glossary.clone()`, we are making a copy of the `Arc` smart pointer, not the whole `GigabyteMap`. This amounts to incrementing a reference count.

With this change, the program compiles and runs, because it no longer depends on reference lifetimes. As long as *any* thread owns an `Arc<GigabyteMap>`, it will keep the map alive, even if the parent thread bails out early. There won't be any data races, because data in an `Arc` is immutable.

Rayon

The standard library's `spawn` function is an important primitive, but it's not designed specifically for fork-join parallelism. Better fork-join APIs have been built on top of it. For example, in Chapter 2 we used the Crossbeam library to split some work across eight threads. Crossbeam's *scoped threads* support fork-join parallelism quite naturally.

The Rayon library, by Niko Matsakis and Josh Stone, is another example. It provides two ways of running tasks concurrently:

```
use rayon::prelude::*;

// "do 2 things in parallel"
let (v1, v2) = rayon::join(fn1, fn2);

// "do N things in parallel"
giant_vector.par_iter().for_each(|value| {
    do_thing_with_value(value);
});
```

`rayon::join(fn1, fn2)` simply calls both functions and returns both results. The `.par_iter()` method creates a `ParallelIterator`, a value with `map`, `filter`, and other methods, much like a Rust `Iterator`. In both cases, Rayon uses its own pool of worker threads to spread out the work when possible. You simply tell Rayon what tasks *can* be done in parallel; Rayon manages threads and distributes the work as best it can.

The diagrams in Figure 19-3 illustrate two ways of thinking about the call `giant_vector.par_iter().for_each(...)`. (a) Rayon acts as though it spawns one thread per element in the vector. (b) Behind the scenes, Rayon has one worker thread per CPU core, which is more efficient. This pool of worker threads is shared by all your program's threads. When thousands of tasks come in at once, Rayon divides the work.

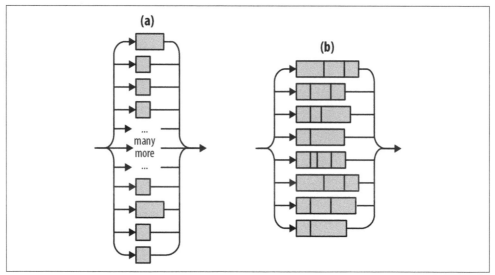

Figure 19-3. Rayon in theory and practice

Here's a version of `process_files_in_parallel` using Rayon and a `process_file` that takes, rather than `Vec<String>`, just a `&str`:

```
use rayon::prelude::*;

fn process_files_in_parallel(filenames: Vec<String>, glossary: &GigabyteMap)
    -> io::Result<()>
{
    filenames.par_iter()
        .map(|filename| process_file(filename, glossary))
        .reduce_with(|r1, r2| {
            if r1.is_err() { r1 } else { r2 }
        })
        .unwrap_or(Ok(()))
}
```

This code is shorter and less tricky than the version using `std::thread::spawn`. Let's look at it line by line:

- First, we use `filenames.par_iter()` to create a parallel iterator.
- We use `.map()` to call `process_file` on each filename. This produces a `ParallelIterator` over a sequence of `io::Result<()>` values.
- We use `.reduce_with()` to combine the results. Here we're keeping the first error, if any, and discarding the rest. If we wanted to accumulate all the errors, or print them, we could do that here.

  The `.reduce_with()` method is also handy when you pass a `.map()` closure that returns a useful value on success. Then you can pass `.reduce_with()` a closure that knows how to combine two success results.

- `reduce_with` returns an `Option` that is `None` only if `filenames` was empty. We use the `Option`'s `.unwrap_or()` method to make the result `Ok(())` in that case.

Behind the scenes, Rayon balances workloads across threads dynamically, using a technique called *work-stealing*. It will typically do a better job keeping all the CPUs busy than we can do by manually dividing the work in advance, as in "spawn and join" on page 502.

As a bonus, Rayon supports sharing references across threads. Any parallel processing that happens behind the scenes is guaranteed to be finished by the time `reduce_with` returns. This explains why we were able to pass `glossary` to `process_file` even though that closure will be called on multiple threads.

(Incidentally, it's no coincidence that we've used a `map` method and a `reduce` method. The MapReduce programming model, popularized by Google and Apache Hadoop, has a lot in common with fork-join. It can be seen as a fork-join approach to querying distributed data.)

Revisiting the Mandelbrot Set

Back in Chapter 2, we used fork-join concurrency to render the Mandelbrot set. This made rendering four times as fast—impressive, but not as impressive as it could be, considering that we had the program spawn eight worker threads and ran it on an eight-core machine!

The problem is that we didn't distribute the workload evenly. Computing one pixel of the image amounts to running a loop (see "What the Mandelbrot Set Actually Is" on page 23). It turns out that the pale gray parts of the image, where the loop quickly exits, are much faster to render than the black parts, where the loop runs the full 255 iterations. So although we split the area into equal-sized horizontal bands, we were creating unequal workloads, as Figure 19-4 shows.

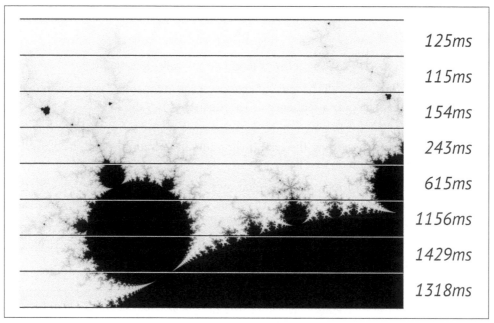

Figure 19-4. Uneven work distribution in the Mandelbrot program

This is easy to fix using Rayon. We can just fire off a parallel task for each row of pixels in the output. This creates several hundred tasks that Rayon can distribute across its threads. Thanks to work-stealing, it won't matter that the tasks vary in size. Rayon will balance the work as it goes.

Here is the code. The first line and the last line are part of the main function we showed back in "A Concurrent Mandelbrot Program" on page 35, but we've changed the rendering code, which is everything in between:

```
    let mut pixels = vec![0; bounds.0 * bounds.1];

    // Scope of slicing up `pixels` into horizontal bands.
    {
        let bands: Vec<(usize, &mut [u8])> = pixels
            .chunks_mut(bounds.0)
            .enumerate()
            .collect();

        bands.into_par_iter()
            .for_each(|(i, band)| {
                let top = i;
                let band_bounds = (bounds.0, 1);
                let band_upper_left = pixel_to_point(bounds, (0, top),
                                                     upper_left, lower_right);
                let band_lower_right = pixel_to_point(bounds, (bounds.0, top + 1),
                                                      upper_left, lower_right);
                render(band, band_bounds, band_upper_left, band_lower_right);
            });
    }

    write_image(&args[1], &pixels, bounds).expect("error writing PNG file");
```

First, we create `bands`, the collection of tasks that we will be passing to Rayon. Each task is just a tuple of type (`usize, &mut [u8]`): the row number, since the computation requires that, and the slice of `pixels` to fill in. We use the `chunks_mut` method to break the image buffer into rows, `enumerate` to attach a row number to each row, and `collect` to slurp all the number-slice pairs into a vector. (We need a vector because Rayon creates parallel iterators only out of arrays and vectors.)

Next, we turn `bands` into a parallel iterator, and use the `.for_each()` method to tell Rayon what work we want done.

Since we're using Rayon, we must add this line to *main.rs*:

```
use rayon::prelude::*;
```

and this to *Cargo.toml*:

```
[dependencies]
rayon = "1"
```

With these changes, the program now uses about 7.75 cores on an 8-core machine. It's 75% faster than before, when we were dividing the work manually. And the code is a little shorter, reflecting the benefits of letting a crate do a job (work distribution) rather than doing it ourselves.

Channels

A *channel* is a one-way conduit for sending values from one thread to another. In other words, it's a thread-safe queue.

Figure 19-5 illustrates how channels are used. They're something like Unix pipes: one end is for sending data, and the other is for receiving. The two ends are typically owned by two different threads. But whereas Unix pipes are for sending bytes, channels are for sending Rust values. `sender.send(item)` puts a single value into the channel; `receiver.recv()` removes one. Ownership is transferred from the sending thread to the receiving thread. If the channel is empty, `receiver.recv()` blocks until a value is sent.

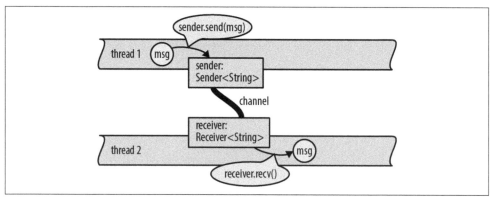

Figure 19-5. A channel for `Strings`: ownership of the string msg is transferred from thread 1 to thread 2.

With channels, threads can communicate by passing values to one another. It's a very simple way for threads to work together without using locking or shared memory.

This is not a new technique. Erlang has had isolated processes and message passing for 30 years now. Unix pipes have been around for almost 50 years. We tend to think of pipes as providing flexibility and composability, not concurrency, but in fact, they do all of the above. An example of a Unix pipeline is shown in Figure 19-6. It is certainly possible for all three programs to be working at the same time.

Rust channels are faster than Unix pipes. Sending a value moves it rather than copying it, and moves are fast even when you're moving data structures that contain many megabytes of data.

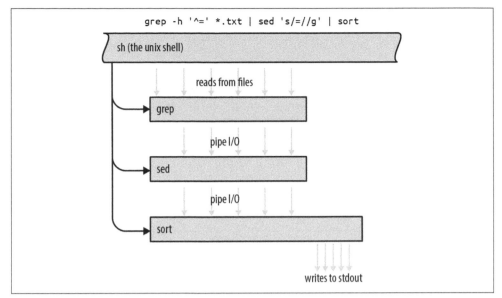

Figure 19-6. Execution of a Unix pipeline

Sending Values

Over the next few sections, we'll use channels to build a concurrent program that creates an *inverted index,* one of the key ingredients of a search engine. Every search engine works on a particular collection of documents. The inverted index is the database that tells which words appear where.

We'll show the parts of the code that have to do with threads and channels. The complete program (*https://oreil.ly/yF3me*) is short, about a thousand lines of code all told.

Our program is structured as a pipeline, as shown in Figure 19-7. Pipelines are only one of the many ways to use channels—we'll discuss a few other uses later—but they're a straightforward way to introduce concurrency into an existing single-threaded program.

We'll use a total of five threads, each doing a distinct task. Each thread produces output continually over the lifetime of the program. The first thread, for example, simply reads the source documents from disk into memory, one by one. (We want a thread to do this because we'll be writing the simplest possible code here, using `fs::read_to_string`, which is a blocking API. We don't want the CPU to sit idle whenever the disk is working.) The output of this stage is one long `String` per document, so this thread is connected to the next thread by a channel of `Strings`.

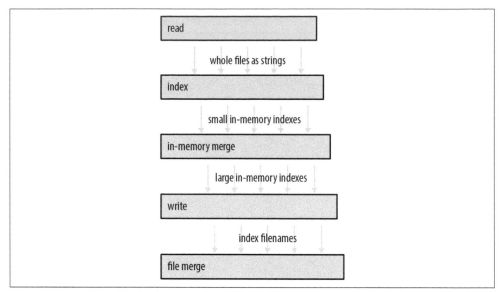

Figure 19-7. The index builder pipeline, where the arrows represent values sent via a channel from one thread to another (disk I/O is not shown)

Our program will begin by spawning the thread that reads files. Suppose `documents` is a `Vec<PathBuf>`, a vector of filenames. The code to start our file-reading thread looks like this:

```
use std::{fs, thread};
use std::sync::mpsc;

let (sender, receiver) = mpsc::channel();

let handle = thread::spawn(move || {
    for filename in documents {
        let text = fs::read_to_string(filename)?;

        if sender.send(text).is_err() {
            break;
        }
    }
    Ok(())
});
```

Channels are part of the `std::sync::mpsc` module. We'll explain what this name means later; first, let's look at how this code works. We start by creating a channel:

```
let (sender, receiver) = mpsc::channel();
```

The channel function returns a pair of values: a sender and a receiver. The underlying queue data structure is an implementation detail that the standard library does not expose.

Channels are typed. We're going to use this channel to send the text of each file, so we have a sender of type Sender<String> and a receiver of type Receiver<String>. We could have explicitly asked for a channel of strings, by writing mpsc::channel::<String>(). Instead, we let Rust's type inference figure it out.

```
let handle = thread::spawn(move || {
```

As before, we're using std::thread::spawn to start a thread. Ownership of sender (but not receiver) is transferred to the new thread via this move closure.

The next few lines of code simply read files from disk:

```
for filename in documents {
    let text = fs::read_to_string(filename)?;
```

After successfully reading a file, we send its text into the channel:

```
if sender.send(text).is_err() {
            break;
        }
    }
```

sender.send(text) moves the value text into the channel. Ultimately, it will be moved again to whoever receives the value. Whether text contains 10 lines of text or 10 megabytes, this operation copies three machine words (the size of a String struct), and the corresponding receiver.recv() call will also copy three machine words.

The send and recv methods both return Results, but these methods fail only if the other end of the channel has been dropped. A send call fails if the Receiver has been dropped, because otherwise the value would sit in the channel forever: without a Receiver, there's no way for any thread to receive it. Likewise, a recv call fails if there are no values waiting in the channel and the Sender has been dropped, because otherwise recv would wait forever: without a Sender, there's no way for any thread to send the next value. Dropping your end of a channel is the normal way of "hanging up," closing the connection when you're done with it.

In our code, sender.send(text) will fail only if the receiver's thread has exited early. This is typical for code that uses channels. Whether that happened deliberately or due to an error, it's OK for our reader thread to quietly shut itself down.

When that happens, or the thread finishes reading all the documents, it returns Ok(()):

```
    Ok(())
});
```

Note that this closure returns a `Result`. If the thread encounters an I/O error, it exits immediately, and the error is stored in the thread's `JoinHandle`.

Of course, just like any other programming language, Rust admits many other possibilities when it comes to error handling. When an error happens, we could just print it out using `println!` and move on to the next file. We could pass errors along via the same channel that we're using for data, making it a channel of `Result`s—or create a second channel just for errors. The approach we've chosen here is both lightweight and responsible: we get to use the ? operator, so there's not a bunch of boilerplate code, or even an explicit `try/catch` as you might see in Java, and yet errors won't pass silently.

For convenience, our program wraps all of this code in a function that returns both the `receiver` (which we haven't used yet) and the new thread's `JoinHandle`:

```
fn start_file_reader_thread(documents: Vec<PathBuf>)
    -> (mpsc::Receiver<String>, thread::JoinHandle<io::Result<()>>)
{
    let (sender, receiver) = mpsc::channel();

    let handle = thread::spawn(move || {
        ...
    });

    (receiver, handle)
}
```

Note that this function launches the new thread and immediately returns. We'll write a function like this for each stage of our pipeline.

Receiving Values

Now we have a thread running a loop that sends values. We can spawn a second thread running a loop that calls `receiver.recv()`:

```
while let Ok(text) = receiver.recv() {
    do_something_with(text);
}
```

But `Receiver`s are iterable, so there's a nicer way to write this:

```
for text in receiver {
    do_something_with(text);
}
```

These two loops are equivalent. Either way we write it, if the channel happens to be empty when control reaches the top of the loop, the receiving thread will block until some other thread sends a value. The loop will exit normally when the channel is empty and the `Sender` has been dropped. In our program, that happens naturally when the reader thread exits. That thread is running a closure that owns the variable sender; when the closure exits, sender is dropped.

Now we can write code for the second stage of the pipeline:

```
fn start_file_indexing_thread(texts: mpsc::Receiver<String>)
    -> (mpsc::Receiver<InMemoryIndex>, thread::JoinHandle<()>)
{
    let (sender, receiver) = mpsc::channel();

    let handle = thread::spawn(move || {
        for (doc_id, text) in texts.into_iter().enumerate() {
            let index = InMemoryIndex::from_single_document(doc_id, text);
            if sender.send(index).is_err() {
                break;
            }
        }
    });

    (receiver, handle)
}
```

This function spawns a thread that receives String values from one channel (texts) and sends InMemoryIndex values to another channel (sender/receiver). This thread's job is to take each of the files loaded in the first stage and turn each document into a little one-file, in-memory inverted index.

The main loop of this thread is straightforward. All the work of indexing a document is done by the function InMemoryIndex::from_single_document. We won't show its source code here, but it splits the input string at word boundaries and then produces a map from words to lists of positions.

This stage doesn't perform I/O, so it doesn't have to deal with io::Errors. Instead of an io::Result<()>, it returns ().

Running the Pipeline

The remaining three stages are similar in design. Each one consumes a Receiver created by the previous stage. Our goal for the rest of the pipeline is to merge all the small indexes into a single large index file on disk. The fastest way we found to do this is in three stages. We won't show the code here, just the type signatures of these three functions. The full source is online.

First, we merge indexes in memory until they get unwieldy (stage 3):

```
fn start_in_memory_merge_thread(file_indexes: mpsc::Receiver<InMemoryIndex>)
    -> (mpsc::Receiver<InMemoryIndex>, thread::JoinHandle<()>)
```

We write these large indexes to disk (stage 4):

```
fn start_index_writer_thread(big_indexes: mpsc::Receiver<InMemoryIndex>,
                             output_dir: &Path)
    -> (mpsc::Receiver<PathBuf>, thread::JoinHandle<io::Result<()>>)
```

Finally, if we have multiple large files, we merge them using a file-based merging algorithm (stage 5):

```
fn merge_index_files(files: mpsc::Receiver<PathBuf>, output_dir: &Path)
    -> io::Result<()>
```

This last stage does not return a `Receiver`, because it's the end of the line. It produces a single output file on disk. It doesn't return a `JoinHandle`, because we don't bother spawning a thread for this stage. The work is done on the caller's thread.

Now we come to the code that launches the threads and checks for errors:

```
fn run_pipeline(documents: Vec<PathBuf>, output_dir: PathBuf)
    -> io::Result<()>
{
    // Launch all five stages of the pipeline.
    let (texts,   h1) = start_file_reader_thread(documents);
    let (pints,   h2) = start_file_indexing_thread(texts);
    let (gallons, h3) = start_in_memory_merge_thread(pints);
    let (files,   h4) = start_index_writer_thread(gallons, &output_dir);
    let result = merge_index_files(files, &output_dir);

    // Wait for threads to finish, holding on to any errors that they encounter.
    let r1 = h1.join().unwrap();
    h2.join().unwrap();
    h3.join().unwrap();
    let r4 = h4.join().unwrap();

    // Return the first error encountered, if any.
    // (As it happens, h2 and h3 can't fail: those threads
    // are pure in-memory data processing.)
    r1?;
    r4?;
    result
}
```

As before, we use `.join().unwrap()` to explicitly propagate panics from child threads to the main thread. The only other unusual thing here is that instead of using ? right away, we set aside the `io::Result` values until we've joined all four threads.

This pipeline is 40% faster than the single-threaded equivalent. That's not bad for an afternoon's work, but paltry looking next to the 675% boost we got for the Mandelbrot program. We clearly haven't saturated either the system's I/O capacity or all the CPU cores. What's going on?

Pipelines are like assembly lines in a manufacturing plant: performance is limited by the throughput of the slowest stage. A brand-new, untuned assembly line may be as slow as unit production, but assembly lines reward targeted tuning. In our case, measurement shows that the second stage is the bottleneck. Our indexing thread uses `.to_lowercase()` and `.is_alphanumeric()`, so it spends a lot of time poking around in Unicode tables. The other stages downstream from indexing spend most of their time asleep in `Receiver::recv`, waiting for input.

This means we should be able to go faster. As we address the bottlenecks, the degree of parallelism will rise. Now that you know how to use channels and our program is made of isolated pieces of code, it's easy to see ways to address this first bottleneck. We could hand-optimize the code for the second stage, just like any other code; break up the work into two or more stages; or run multiple file-indexing threads at once.

Channel Features and Performance

The `mpsc` part of `std::sync::mpsc` stands for *multiproducer, single-consumer,* a terse description of the kind of communication Rust's channels provide.

The channels in our sample program carry values from a single sender to a single receiver. This is a fairly common case. But Rust channels also support multiple senders, in case you need, say, a single thread that handles requests from many client threads, as shown in Figure 19-8.

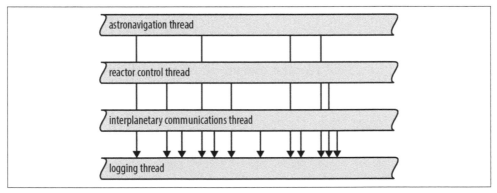

Figure 19-8. A single channel receiving requests from many senders

`Sender<T>` implements the `Clone` trait. To get a channel with multiple senders, simply create a regular channel and clone the sender as many times as you like. You can move each `Sender` value to a different thread.

A `Receiver<T>` can't be cloned, so if you need to have multiple threads receiving values from the same channel, you need a `Mutex`. We'll show how to do it later in this chapter.

Rust channels are carefully optimized. When a channel is first created, Rust uses a special "one-shot" queue implementation. If you only ever send one object through the channel, the overhead is minimal. If you send a second value, Rust switches to a different queue implementation. It's settling in for the long haul, really, preparing the channel to transfer many values while minimizing allocation overhead. And if you clone the `Sender`, Rust must fall back on yet another implementation, one that is safe when multiple threads are trying to send values at once. But even the slowest of these three implementations is a lock-free queue, so sending or receiving a value is at most a few atomic operations and a heap allocation, plus the move itself. System calls are needed only when the queue is empty and the receiving thread therefore needs to put itself to sleep. In this case, of course, traffic through your channel is not maxed out anyway.

Despite all that optimization work, there is one mistake that's very easy for applications to make around channel performance: sending values faster than they can be received and processed. This causes an ever-growing backlog of values to accumulate in the channel. For example, in our program, we found that the file reader thread (stage 1) could load files much faster than the file indexing thread (stage 2) could index them. The result is that hundreds of megabytes of raw data would be read from disk and stuffed in the queue at once.

This kind of misbehavior costs memory and hurts locality. Even worse, the sending thread keeps running, using up CPU and other system resources to send ever more values just when those resources are most needed on the receiving end.

Here Rust again takes a page from Unix pipes. Unix uses an elegant trick to provide some *backpressure* so that fast senders are forced to slow down: each pipe on a Unix system has a fixed size, and if a process tries to write to a pipe that's momentarily full, the system simply blocks that process until there's room in the pipe. The Rust equivalent is called a *synchronous channel*:

```
use std::sync::mpsc;

let (sender, receiver) = mpsc::sync_channel(1000);
```

A synchronous channel is exactly like a regular channel except that when you create it, you specify how many values it can hold. For a synchronous channel, `sender.send(value)` is potentially a blocking operation. After all, the idea is that blocking is not always bad. In our example program, changing the `channel` in `start_file_reader_thread` to a `sync_channel` with room for 32 values cut memory usage by two-thirds on our benchmark data set, without decreasing throughput.

Thread Safety: Send and Sync

So far we've been acting as though all values can be freely moved and shared across threads. This is mostly true, but Rust's full thread safety story hinges on two built-in traits, std::marker::Send and std::marker::Sync.

- Types that implement Send are safe to pass by value to another thread. They can be moved across threads.

- Types that implement Sync are safe to pass by non-mut reference to another thread. They can be shared across threads.

By *safe* here, we mean the same thing we always mean: free from data races and other undefined behavior.

For example, in the process_files_in_parallel example on page 502, we used a closure to pass a Vec<String> from the parent thread to each child thread. We didn't point it out at the time, but this means the vector and its strings are allocated in the parent thread, but freed in the child thread. The fact that Vec<String> implements Send is an API promise that this is OK: the allocator used internally by Vec and String is thread-safe.

(If you were to write your own Vec and String types with fast but non-thread-safe allocators, you would have to implement them using types that are not Send, such as unsafe pointers. Rust would then infer that your NonThreadSafeVec and NonThreadSafeString types are not Send and restrict them to single-threaded use. But that's a rare case.)

As Figure 19-9 illustrates, most types are both Send and Sync. You don't even have to use #[derive] to get these traits on structs and enums in your program. Rust does it for you. A struct or enum is Send if its fields are Send, and Sync if its fields are Sync.

Some types are Send, but not Sync. This is generally on purpose, as in the case of mpsc::Receiver, where it guarantees that the receiving end of an mpsc channel is used by only one thread at a time.

The few types that are neither Send nor Sync are mostly those that use mutability in a way that isn't thread-safe. For example, consider std::rc::Rc<T>, the type of reference-counting smart pointers.

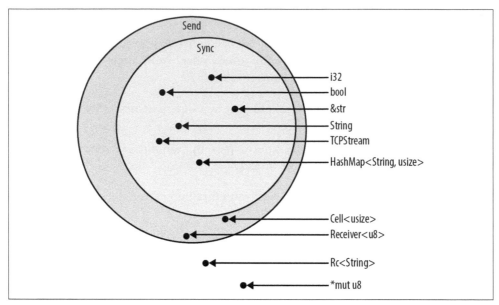

Figure 19-9. Send and Sync types

What would happen if `Rc<String>` were `Sync`, allowing threads to share a single `Rc` via shared references? If both threads happen to try to clone the `Rc` at the same time, as shown in Figure 19-10, we have a data race as both threads increment the shared reference count. The reference count could become inaccurate, leading to a use-after-free or double free later—undefined behavior.

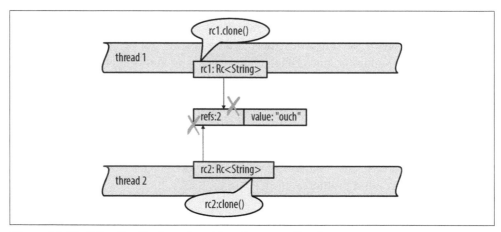

Figure 19-10. Why `Rc<String>` is neither `Sync` nor `Send`

Of course, Rust prevents this. Here's the code to set up this data race:

```
use std::thread;
use std::rc::Rc;

fn main() {
    let rc1 = Rc::new("ouch".to_string());
    let rc2 = rc1.clone();
    thread::spawn(move || {  // error
        rc2.clone();
    });
    rc1.clone();
}
```

Rust refuses to compile it, giving a detailed error message:

```
error: `Rc<String>` cannot be sent between threads safely
   |
10 |     thread::spawn(move || {  // error
   |                   ^^^^^ `Rc<String>` cannot be sent between threads safely
   |
   = help: the trait `std::marker::Send` is not implemented for `Rc<String>`
   = note: required because it appears within the type `[closure@...]`
   = note: required by `std::thread::spawn`
```

Now you can see how Send and Sync help Rust enforce thread safety. They appear as bounds in the type signature of functions that transfer data across thread boundaries. When you spawn a thread, the closure you pass must be Send, which means all the values it contains must be Send. Similarly, if you want to send values through a channel to another thread, the values must be Send.

Piping Almost Any Iterator to a Channel

Our inverted index builder is built as a pipeline. The code is clear enough, but it has us manually setting up channels and launching threads. By contrast, the iterator pipelines we built in Chapter 15 seemed to pack a lot more work into just a few lines of code. Can we build something like that for thread pipelines?

In fact, it would be nice if we could unify iterator pipelines and thread pipelines. Then our index builder could be written as an iterator pipeline. It might start like this:

```
documents.into_iter()
    .map(read_whole_file)
    .errors_to(error_sender)    // filter out error results
    .off_thread()               // spawn a thread for the above work
    .map(make_single_file_index)
    .off_thread()               // spawn another thread for stage 2
    ...
```

Traits allow us to add methods to standard library types, so we can actually do this. We start by writing a trait that declares the method we want:

```
use std::sync::mpsc;

pub trait OffThreadExt: Iterator {
    /// Transform this iterator into an off-thread iterator: the
    /// `next()` calls happen on a separate worker thread, so the
    /// iterator and the body of your loop run concurrently.
    fn off_thread(self) -> mpsc::IntoIter<Self::Item>;
}
```

Then we implement this trait for iterator types. It helps that `mpsc::Receiver` is already iterable:

```
use std::thread;

impl<T> OffThreadExt for T
    where T: Iterator + Send + 'static,
          T::Item: Send + 'static
{
    fn off_thread(self) -> mpsc::IntoIter<Self::Item> {
        // Create a channel to transfer items from the worker thread.
        let (sender, receiver) = mpsc::sync_channel(1024);

        // Move this iterator to a new worker thread and run it there.
        thread::spawn(move || {
            for item in self {
                if sender.send(item).is_err() {
                    break;
                }
            }
        });

        // Return an iterator that pulls values from the channel.
        receiver.into_iter()
    }
}
```

The `where` clause in this code was determined via a process much like the one described in "Reverse-Engineering Bounds" on page 283. At first, we just had this:

```
impl<T> OffThreadExt for T
```

That is, we wanted the implementation to work for all iterators. Rust was having none of it. Because we're using `spawn` to move an iterator of type `T` to a new thread, we must specify `T: Iterator + Send + 'static`. Because we're sending the items back over a channel, we must specify `T::Item: Send + 'static`. With these changes, Rust was satisfied.

This is Rust's character in a nutshell: we're free to add a concurrency power tool to almost every iterator in the language—but not without first understanding and documenting the restrictions that make it safe to use.

Beyond Pipelines

In this section, we used pipelines as our examples because pipelines are a nice, obvious way to use channels. Everyone understands them. They're concrete, practical, and deterministic. Channels are useful for more than just pipelines, though. They're also a quick, easy way to offer any asynchronous service to other threads in the same process.

For example, suppose you'd like to do logging on its own thread, as in Figure 19-8. Other threads could send log messages to the logging thread over a channel; since you can clone the channel's Sender, many client threads can have senders that ship log messages to the same logging thread.

Running a service like logging on its own thread has advantages. The logging thread can rotate log files whenever it needs to. It doesn't have to do any fancy coordination with the other threads. Those threads won't be blocked. Messages will accumulate harmlessly in the channel for a moment until the logging thread gets back to work.

Channels can also be used for cases where one thread sends a request to another thread and needs to get some sort of response back. The first thread's request can be a struct or tuple that includes a Sender, a sort of self-addressed envelope that the second thread uses to send its reply. This doesn't mean the interaction must be synchronous. The first thread gets to decide whether to block and wait for the response or use the .try_recv() method to poll for it.

The tools we've presented so far—fork-join for highly parallel computation, channels for loosely connecting components—are sufficient for a wide range of applications. But we're not done.

Shared Mutable State

In the months since you published the fern_sim crate in Chapter 8, your fern simulation software has really taken off. Now you're creating a multiplayer real-time strategy game in which eight players compete to grow mostly authentic period ferns in a simulated Jurassic landscape. The server for this game is a massively parallel app, with requests pouring in on many threads. How can these threads coordinate to start a game as soon as eight players are available?

The problem to be solved here is that many threads need access to a shared list of players who are waiting to join a game. This data is necessarily both mutable and shared across all threads. If Rust doesn't have shared mutable state, where does that leave us?

You could solve this by creating a new thread whose whole job is to manage this list. Other threads would communicate with it via channels. Of course, this costs a thread, which has some operating system overhead.

Another option is to use the tools Rust provides for safely sharing mutable data. Such things do exist. They're low-level primitives that will be familiar to any system programmer who's worked with threads. In this section, we'll cover mutexes, read/write locks, condition variables, and atomic integers. Lastly, we'll show how to implement global mutable variables in Rust.

What Is a Mutex?

A *mutex* (or *lock*) is used to force multiple threads to take turns when accessing certain data. We'll introduce Rust's mutexes in the next section. First, it makes sense to recall what mutexes are like in other languages. A simple use of a mutex in C++ might look like this:

```
// C++ code, not Rust
void FernEmpireApp::JoinWaitingList(PlayerId player) {
    mutex.Acquire();

    waitingList.push_back(player);

    // Start a game if we have enough players waiting.
    if (waitingList.size() >= GAME_SIZE) {
        vector<PlayerId> players;
        waitingList.swap(players);
        StartGame(players);
    }

    mutex.Release();
}
```

The calls `mutex.Acquire()` and `mutex.Release()` mark the beginning and end of a *critical section* in this code. For each `mutex` in a program, only one thread can be running inside a critical section at a time. If one thread is in a critical section, all other threads that call `mutex.Acquire()` will block until the first thread reaches `mutex.Release()`.

We say that the mutex *protects* the data: in this case, `mutex` protects `waitingList`. It is the programmer's responsibility, though, to make sure every thread always acquires the mutex before accessing the data, and releases it afterward.

Mutexes are helpful for several reasons:

- They prevent *data races,* situations where racing threads concurrently read and write the same memory. Data races are undefined behavior in C++ and Go. Managed languages like Java and C# promise not to crash, but the results of data races are still (to summarize) nonsense.

- Even if data races didn't exist, even if all reads and writes happened one by one in program order, without a mutex the actions of different threads could interleave in arbitrary ways. Imagine trying to write code that works even if other threads modify its data while it's running. Imagine trying to debug it. It would be like your program was haunted.

- Mutexes support programming with *invariants,* rules about the protected data that are true by construction when you set it up and maintained by every critical section.

Of course, all of these are really the same reason: uncontrolled race conditions make programming intractable. Mutexes bring some order to the chaos (though not as much order as channels or fork-join).

However, in most languages, mutexes are very easy to mess up. In C++, as in most languages, the data and the lock are separate objects. Ideally, comments explain that every thread must acquire the mutex before touching the data:

```
class FernEmpireApp {
    ...

private:
    // List of players waiting to join a game. Protected by `mutex`.
    vector<PlayerId> waitingList;

    // Lock to acquire before reading or writing `waitingList`.
    Mutex mutex;
    ...
};
```

But even with such nice comments, the compiler can't enforce safe access here. When a piece of code neglects to acquire the mutex, we get undefined behavior. In practice, this means bugs that are extremely hard to reproduce and fix.

Even in Java, where there is some notional association between objects and mutexes, the relationship does not run very deep. The compiler makes no attempt to enforce it, and in practice, the data protected by a lock is rarely exactly the associated object's fields. It often includes data in several objects. Locking schemes are still tricky. Comments are still the main tool for enforcing them.

Mutex<T>

Now we'll show an implementation of the waiting list in Rust. In our Fern Empire game server, each player has a unique ID:

```
type PlayerId = u32;
```

The waiting list is just a collection of players:

```
const GAME_SIZE: usize = 8;

/// A waiting list never grows to more than GAME_SIZE players.
type WaitingList = Vec<PlayerId>;
```

The waiting list is stored as a field of the `FernEmpireApp`, a singleton that's set up in an `Arc` during server startup. Each thread has an `Arc` pointing to it. It contains all the shared configuration and other flotsam our program needs. Most of that is read-only. Since the waiting list is both shared and mutable, it must be protected by a `Mutex`:

```
use std::sync::Mutex;

/// All threads have shared access to this big context struct.
struct FernEmpireApp {
    ...
    waiting_list: Mutex<WaitingList>,
    ...
}
```

Unlike C++, in Rust the protected data is stored *inside* the `Mutex`. Setting up the `Mutex` looks like this:

```
use std::sync::Arc;

let app = Arc::new(FernEmpireApp {
    ...
    waiting_list: Mutex::new(vec![]),
    ...
});
```

Creating a new `Mutex` looks like creating a new `Box` or `Arc`, but while `Box` and `Arc` signify heap allocation, `Mutex` is solely about locking. If you want your `Mutex` to be allocated in the heap, you have to say so, as we've done here by using `Arc::new` for the whole app and `Mutex::new` just for the protected data. These types are commonly used together: `Arc` is handy for sharing things across threads, and `Mutex` is handy for mutable data that's shared across threads.

Now we can implement the `join_waiting_list` method that uses the mutex:

```
impl FernEmpireApp {
    /// Add a player to the waiting list for the next game.
    /// Start a new game immediately if enough players are waiting.
    fn join_waiting_list(&self, player: PlayerId) {
```

```
        // Lock the mutex and gain access to the data inside.
        // The scope of `guard` is a critical section.
        let mut guard = self.waiting_list.lock().unwrap();

        // Now do the game logic.
        guard.push(player);
        if guard.len() == GAME_SIZE {
            let players = guard.split_off(0);
            self.start_game(players);
        }
    }
}
```

The only way to get at the data is to call the `.lock()` method:

```
let mut guard = self.waiting_list.lock().unwrap();
```

`self.waiting_list.lock()` blocks until the mutex can be obtained. The `MutexGuard<WaitingList>` value returned by this method call is a thin wrapper around a `&mut WaitingList`. Thanks to deref coercions, discussed on page 312, we can call `WaitingList` methods directly on the guard:

```
guard.push(player);
```

The guard even lets us borrow direct references to the underlying data. Rust's lifetime system ensures those references can't outlive the guard itself. There is no way to access the data in a `Mutex` without holding the lock.

When `guard` is dropped, the lock is released. Ordinarily that happens at the end of the block, but you can also drop it manually:

```
if guard.len() == GAME_SIZE {
    let players = guard.split_off(0);
    drop(guard);  // don't keep the list locked while starting a game
    self.start_game(players);
}
```

mut and Mutex

It may seem odd—certainly it seemed odd to us at first—that our `join_waiting_list` method doesn't take `self` by `mut` reference. Its type signature is:

```
fn join_waiting_list(&self, player: PlayerId)
```

The underlying collection, `Vec<PlayerId>`, *does* require a `mut` reference when you call its `push` method. Its type signature is:

```
pub fn push(&mut self, item: T)
```

And yet this code compiles and runs fine. What's going on here?

In Rust, `&mut` means *exclusive access*. Plain `&` means *shared access*.

We're used to types passing &mut access along from the parent to the child, from the container to the contents. You only expect to be able to call &mut self methods on starships[id].engine if you have a &mut reference to starships to begin with (or you own starships, in which case congratulations on being Elon Musk). That's the default, because if you don't have exclusive access to the parent, Rust generally has no way of ensuring that you have exclusive access to the child.

But Mutex does have a way: the lock. In fact, a mutex is little more than a way to do exactly this, to provide *exclusive* (mut) access to the data inside, even though many threads may have *shared* (non-mut) access to the Mutex itself.

Rust's type system is telling us what Mutex does. It dynamically enforces exclusive access, something that's usually done statically, at compile time, by the Rust compiler.

(You may recall that std::cell::RefCell does the same, except without trying to support multiple threads. Mutex and RefCell are both flavors of interior mutability, which we covered on page 225.)

Why Mutexes Are Not Always a Good Idea

Before we started on mutexes, we presented some approaches to concurrency that might have seemed weirdly easy to use correctly if you're coming from C++. This is no coincidence: these approaches are designed to provide strong guarantees against the most confusing aspects of concurrent programming. Programs that exclusively use fork-join parallelism are deterministic and can't deadlock. Programs that use channels are almost as well-behaved. Those that use channels exclusively for pipelining, like our index builder, are deterministic: the timing of message delivery can vary, but it won't affect the output. And so on. Guarantees about multithreaded programs are nice!

The design of Rust's Mutex will almost certainly have you using mutexes more systematically and more sensibly than you ever have before. But it's worth pausing and thinking about what Rust's safety guarantees can and can't help with.

Safe Rust code cannot trigger a *data race*, a specific kind of bug where multiple threads read and write the same memory concurrently, producing meaningless results. This is great: data races are always bugs, and they are not rare in real multithreaded programs.

However, threads that use mutexes are subject to some other problems that Rust doesn't fix for you:

- Valid Rust programs can't have data races, but they can still have other *race conditions*—situations where a program's behavior depends on timing among threads and may therefore vary from run to run. Some race conditions are benign. Some manifest as general flakiness and incredibly hard-to-fix bugs. Using mutexes in an unstructured way invites race conditions. It's up to you to make sure they're benign.

- Shared mutable state also affects program design. Where channels serve as an abstraction boundary in your code, making it easy to separate isolated components for testing, mutexes encourage a "just-add-a-method" way of working that can lead to a monolithic blob of interrelated code.

- Lastly, mutexes are just not as simple as they seem at first, as the next two sections will show.

All of these problems are inherent in the tools. Use a more structured approach when you can; use a `Mutex` when you must.

Deadlock

A thread can deadlock itself by trying to acquire a lock that it's already holding:

```
let mut guard1 = self.waiting_list.lock().unwrap();
let mut guard2 = self.waiting_list.lock().unwrap();  // deadlock
```

Suppose the first call to `self.waiting_list.lock()` succeeds, taking the lock. The second call sees that the lock is held, so it blocks, waiting for it to be released. It will be waiting forever. The waiting thread is the one that's holding the lock.

To put it another way, the lock in a `Mutex` is not a recursive lock.

Here the bug is obvious. In a real program, the two `lock()` calls might be in two different methods, one of which calls the other. The code for each method, taken separately, would look fine. There are other ways to get deadlock, too, involving multiple threads that each acquire multiple mutexes at once. Rust's borrow system can't protect you from deadlock. The best protection is to keep critical sections small: get in, do your work, and get out.

It's also possible to get deadlock with channels. For example, two threads might block, each one waiting to receive a message from the other. However, again, good program design can give you high confidence that this won't happen in practice. In a pipeline, like our inverted index builder, data flow is acyclic. Deadlock is as unlikely in such a program as in a Unix shell pipeline.

Poisoned Mutexes

`Mutex::lock()` returns a `Result` for the same reason that `JoinHandle::join()` does: to fail gracefully if another thread has panicked. When we write `handle.join().unwrap()`, we're telling Rust to propagate panic from one thread to another. The idiom `mutex.lock().unwrap()` is similar.

If a thread panics while holding a `Mutex`, Rust marks the `Mutex` as *poisoned*. Any subsequent attempt to `lock` the poisoned `Mutex` will get an error result. Our `.unwrap()` call tells Rust to panic if that happens, propagating panic from the other thread to this one.

How bad is it to have a poisoned mutex? Poison sounds deadly, but this scenario is not necessarily fatal. As we said in Chapter 7, panic is safe. One panicking thread leaves the rest of the program in a safe state.

The reason mutexes are poisoned on panic, then, is not for fear of undefined behavior. Rather, the concern is that you've probably been programming with invariants. Since your program panicked and bailed out of a critical section without finishing what it was doing, perhaps having updated some fields of the protected data but not others, it's possible that the invariants are now broken. Rust poisons the mutex to prevent other threads from blundering unwittingly into this broken situation and making it worse. You *can* still lock a poisoned mutex and access the data inside, with mutual exclusion fully enforced; see the documentation for `PoisonError::into_inner()`. But you won't do it by accident.

Multiconsumer Channels Using Mutexes

We mentioned earlier that Rust's channels are multiple producer, single consumer. Or to put it more concretely, a channel has only one `Receiver`. We can't have a thread pool where many threads use a single `mpsc` channel as a shared worklist.

However, it turns out there is a very simple workaround, using only standard library pieces. We can add a `Mutex` around the `Receiver` and share it anyway. Here is a module that does so:

```
pub mod shared_channel {
    use std::sync::{Arc, Mutex};
    use std::sync::mpsc::{channel, Sender, Receiver};

    /// A thread-safe wrapper around a `Receiver`.
    #[derive(Clone)]
    pub struct SharedReceiver<T>(Arc<Mutex<Receiver<T>>>);

    impl<T> Iterator for SharedReceiver<T> {
        type Item = T;

        /// Get the next item from the wrapped receiver.
        fn next(&mut self) -> Option<T> {
            let guard = self.0.lock().unwrap();
            guard.recv().ok()
        }
    }

    /// Create a new channel whose receiver can be shared across threads.
```

```
    /// This returns a sender and a receiver, just like the stdlib's
    /// `channel()`, and sometimes works as a drop-in replacement.
    pub fn shared_channel<T>() -> (Sender<T>, SharedReceiver<T>) {
        let (sender, receiver) = channel();
        (sender, SharedReceiver(Arc::new(Mutex::new(receiver))))
    }
}
```

We're using an `Arc<Mutex<Receiver<T>>>`. The generics have really piled up. This happens more often in Rust than in C++. It might seem this would get confusing, but often, as in this case, just reading off the names can help explain what's going on, as shown in Figure 19-11.

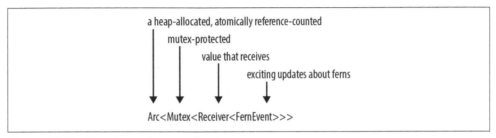

Figure 19-11. How to read a complex type

Read/Write Locks (RwLock<T>)

Now let's move on from mutexes to the other tools provided in `std::sync`, Rust's standard library thread synchronization toolkit. We'll move quickly, since a complete discussion of these tools is beyond the scope of this book.

Server programs often have configuration information that is loaded once and rarely ever changes. Most threads only query the configuration, but since the configuration *can* change—it may be possible to ask the server to reload its configuration from disk, for example—it must be protected by a lock anyway. In cases like this, a mutex can work, but it's an unnecessary bottleneck. Threads shouldn't have to take turns querying the configuration if it's not changing. This is a case for a *read/write lock*, or `RwLock`.

Whereas a mutex has a single `lock` method, a read/write lock has two locking methods, `read` and `write`. The `RwLock::write` method is like `Mutex::lock`. It waits for exclusive, `mut` access to the protected data. The `RwLock::read` method provides non-`mut` access, with the advantage that it is less likely to have to wait, because many threads can safely read at once. With a mutex, at any given moment, the protected data has only one reader or writer (or none). With a read/write lock, it can have either one writer or many readers, much like Rust references generally.

FernEmpireApp might have a struct for configuration, protected by an RwLock:

```
use std::sync::RwLock;

struct FernEmpireApp {
    ...
    config: RwLock<AppConfig>,
    ...
}
```

Methods that read the configuration would use RwLock::read():

```
/// True if experimental fungus code should be used.
fn mushrooms_enabled(&self) -> bool {
    let config_guard = self.config.read().unwrap();
    config_guard.mushrooms_enabled
}
```

The method to reload the configuration would use RwLock::write():

```
fn reload_config(&self) -> io::Result<()> {
    let new_config = AppConfig::load()?;
    let mut config_guard = self.config.write().unwrap();
    *config_guard = new_config;
    Ok(())
}
```

Rust, of course, is uniquely well suited to enforce the safety rules on RwLock data. The single-writer-or-multiple-reader concept is the core of Rust's borrow system. self.config.read() returns a guard that provides non-mut (shared) access to the AppConfig; self.config.write() returns a different type of guard that provides mut (exclusive) access.

Condition Variables (Condvar)

Often a thread needs to wait until a certain condition becomes true:

- During server shutdown, the main thread may need to wait until all other threads are finished exiting.
- When a worker thread has nothing to do, it needs to wait until there is some data to process.
- A thread implementing a distributed consensus protocol may need to wait until a quorum of peers have responded.

Sometimes, there's a convenient blocking API for the exact condition we want to wait on, like JoinHandle::join for the server shutdown example. In other cases, there is no built-in blocking API. Programs can use *condition variables* to build their own. In Rust, the std::sync::Condvar type implements condition variables. A Condvar has methods `.wait()` and `.notify_all()`; `.wait()` blocks until some other thread calls `.notify_all()`.

There's a bit more to it than that, since a condition variable is always about a particular true-or-false condition about some data protected by a particular `Mutex`. This `Mutex` and the `Condvar` are therefore related. A full explanation is more than we have room for here, but for the benefit of programmers who have used condition variables before, we'll show the two key bits of code.

When the desired condition becomes true, we call `Condvar::notify_all` (or `notify_one`) to wake up any waiting threads:

```
self.has_data_condvar.notify_all();
```

To go to sleep and wait for a condition to become true, we use `Condvar::wait()`:

```
while !guard.has_data() {
    guard = self.has_data_condvar.wait(guard).unwrap();
}
```

This `while` loop is a standard idiom for condition variables. However, the signature of `Condvar::wait` is unusual. It takes a `MutexGuard` object by value, consumes it, and returns a new `MutexGuard` on success. This captures the intuition that the `wait` method releases the mutex and then reacquires it before returning. Passing the `MutexGuard` by value is a way of saying, "I bestow upon you, `.wait()` method, my exclusive authority to release the mutex."

Atomics

The `std::sync::atomic` module contains atomic types for lock-free concurrent programming. These types are basically the same as Standard C++ atomics, with some extras:

- `AtomicIsize` and `AtomicUsize` are shared integer types corresponding to the single-threaded `isize` and `usize` types.

- `AtomicI8`, `AtomicI16`, `AtomicI32`, `AtomicI64`, and their unsigned variants like `AtomicU8` are shared integer types that correspond to the single-threaded types `i8`, `i16`, etc.

- An `AtomicBool` is a shared `bool` value.

- An `AtomicPtr<T>` is a shared value of the unsafe pointer type `*mut T`.

The proper use of atomic data is beyond the scope of this book. Suffice it to say that multiple threads can read and write an atomic value at once without causing data races.

Instead of the usual arithmetic and logical operators, atomic types expose methods that perform *atomic operations,* individual loads, stores, exchanges, and arithmetic operations that happen safely, as a unit, even if other threads are also performing atomic operations that touch the same memory location. Incrementing an `AtomicIsize` named `atom` looks like this:

```
use std::sync::atomic::{AtomicIsize, Ordering};

let atom = AtomicIsize::new(0);
atom.fetch_add(1, Ordering::SeqCst);
```

These methods may compile to specialized machine language instructions. On the x86-64 architecture, this `.fetch_add()` call compiles to a `lock incq` instruction, where an ordinary `n += 1` might compile to a plain `incq` instruction or any number of variations on that theme. The Rust compiler also has to forgo some optimizations around the atomic operation, since—unlike a normal load or store—it can legitimately affect or be affected by other threads right away.

The argument `Ordering::SeqCst` is a *memory ordering.* Memory orderings are something like transaction isolation levels in a database. They tell the system how much you care about such philosophical notions as causes preceding effects and time not having loops, as opposed to performance. Memory orderings are crucial to program correctness, and they are tricky to understand and reason about. Happily, the performance penalty for choosing sequential consistency, the strictest memory ordering, is often quite low—unlike the performance penalty for putting a SQL database into `SERIALIZABLE` mode. So when in doubt, use `Ordering::SeqCst`. Rust inherits several other memory orderings from Standard C++ atomics, with various weaker guarantees about the nature of existence and causality. We won't discuss them here.

One simple use of atomics is for cancellation. Suppose we have a thread that's doing some long-running computation, such as rendering a video, and we would like to be able to cancel it asynchronously. The problem is to communicate to the thread that we want it to shut down. We can do this via a shared `AtomicBool`:

```
use std::sync::Arc;
use std::sync::atomic::AtomicBool;

let cancel_flag = Arc::new(AtomicBool::new(false));
let worker_cancel_flag = cancel_flag.clone();
```

This code creates two `Arc<AtomicBool>` smart pointers that point to the same heap-allocated `AtomicBool`, whose initial value is `false`. The first, named `cancel_flag`, will stay in the main thread. The second, `worker_cancel_flag`, will be moved to the worker thread.

Here is the code for the worker:

```
use std::thread;
use std::sync::atomic::Ordering;

let worker_handle = thread::spawn(move || {
    for pixel in animation.pixels_mut() {
        render(pixel); // ray-tracing - this takes a few microseconds
        if worker_cancel_flag.load(Ordering::SeqCst) {
            return None;
        }
    }
    Some(animation)
});
```

After rendering each pixel, the thread checks the value of the flag by calling its `.load()` method:

```
worker_cancel_flag.load(Ordering::SeqCst)
```

If in the main thread we decide to cancel the worker thread, we store `true` in the `AtomicBool` and then wait for the thread to exit:

```
// Cancel rendering.
cancel_flag.store(true, Ordering::SeqCst);

// Discard the result, which is probably `None`.
worker_handle.join().unwrap();
```

Of course, there are other ways to implement this. The `AtomicBool` here could be replaced with a `Mutex<bool>` or a channel. The main difference is that atomics have minimal overhead. Atomic operations never use system calls. A load or store often compiles to a single CPU instruction.

Atomics are a form of interior mutability, like `Mutex` or `RwLock`, so their methods take `self` by shared (non-`mut`) reference. This makes them useful as simple global variables.

Global Variables

Suppose we are writing networking code. We would like to have a global variable, a counter that we increment every time we serve a packet:

```
/// Number of packets the server has successfully handled.
static PACKETS_SERVED: usize = 0;
```

This compiles fine. There's just one problem. `PACKETS_SERVED` is not mutable, so we can never change it.

Rust does everything it reasonably can to discourage global mutable state. Constants declared with `const` are, of course, immutable. Static variables are also immutable by default, so there is no way to get a mut reference to one. A static can be declared mut, but then accessing it is unsafe. Rust's insistence on thread safety is a major reason for all of these rules.

Global mutable state also has unfortunate software engineering consequences: it tends to make the various parts of a program more tightly coupled, harder to test, and harder to change later. Still, in some cases there's just no reasonable alternative, so we had better find a safe way to declare mutable static variables.

The simplest way to support incrementing PACKETS_SERVED, while keeping it thread-safe, is to make it an atomic integer:

```
use std::sync::atomic::AtomicUsize;

static PACKETS_SERVED: AtomicUsize = AtomicUsize::new(0);
```

Once this static is declared, incrementing the packet count is straightforward:

```
use std::sync::atomic::Ordering;

PACKETS_SERVED.fetch_add(1, Ordering::SeqCst);
```

Atomic globals are limited to simple integers and Booleans. Still, creating a global variable of any other type amounts to solving two problems.

First, the variable must be made thread-safe somehow, because otherwise it can't be global: for safety, static variables must be both Sync and non-mut. Fortunately, we've already seen the solution for this problem. Rust has types for safely sharing values that change: Mutex, RwLock, and the atomic types. These types can be modified even when declared as non-mut. It's what they do. (See "mut and Mutex" on page 529.)

Second, static initializers can only call functions specifically marked as const, which the compiler can evaluate during compile time. Put another way, their output is deterministic; it depends only on their arguments, not any other state or I/O. That way, the compiler can embed the results of that computation as a compile-time constant. This is similar to C++ constexpr.

The constructors for the Atomic types (AtomicUsize, AtomicBool, and so on) are all const functions, which allowed us to create a static AtomicUsize earlier. A few other types, like String, Ipv4Addr, and Ipv6Addr, have simple constructors that are const as well.

You can also define your own const functions by simply prefixing the function's signature with const. Rust limits what const functions can do to a small set of operations, which are enough to be useful while still not allowing any nondeterministic results. const functions can't take types as generic arguments, only lifetimes, and it's not possible to allocate memory or operate on raw pointers, even in unsafe blocks. We can, however, use arithmetic operations (including wrapping and saturating arithmetic), logical operations that don't short-circuit, and other `const` functions. For example, we can create convenience functions to make defining `statics` and `consts` easier and reduce code duplication:

```
const fn mono_to_rgba(level: u8) -> Color {
    Color {
        red: level,
        green: level,
        blue: level,
        alpha: 0xFF
    }
}

const WHITE: Color = mono_to_rgba(255);
const BLACK: Color = mono_to_rgba(000);
```

Combining these techniques, we might be tempted to write:

```
static HOSTNAME: Mutex<String> =
    Mutex::new(String::new());  // error: calls in statics are limited to
                                // constant functions, tuple structs, and
                                // tuple variants
```

Unfortunately, while `AtomicUsize::new()` and `String::new()` are const `fn`, `Mutex::new()` is not. In order to get around these limitations, we need to use the `lazy_static` crate.

We introduced the `lazy_static` crate in "Building Regex Values Lazily" on page 467. Defining a variable with the `lazy_static!` macro lets you use any expression you like to initialize it; it runs the first time the variable is dereferenced, and the value is saved for all subsequent uses.

We can declare a global `Mutex`-controlled `HashMap` with `lazy_static` like this:

```
use lazy_static::lazy_static;

use std::sync::Mutex;

lazy_static! {
    static ref HOSTNAME: Mutex<String> = Mutex::new(String::new());
}
```

The same technique works for other complex data structures like `HashMaps` and `Deques`. It's also quite handy for statics that are not mutable at all, but simply require nontrivial initialization.

Using `lazy_static!` imposes a tiny performance cost on each access to the static data. The implementation uses `std::sync::Once`, a low-level synchronization primitive designed for one-time initialization. Behind the scenes, each time a lazy static is accessed, the program executes an atomic load instruction to check that initialization has already occurred. (`Once` is rather special purpose, so we will not cover it in detail here. It is usually more convenient to use `lazy_static!` instead. However, it is handy for initializing non-Rust libraries; for an example, see "A Safe Interface to libgit2" on page 681.)

What Hacking Concurrent Code in Rust Is Like

We've shown three techniques for using threads in Rust: fork-join parallelism, channels, and shared mutable state with locks. Our aim has been to provide a good introduction to the pieces Rust provides, with a focus on how they can fit together into real programs.

Rust insists on safety, so from the moment you decide to write a multithreaded program, the focus is on building safe, structured communication. Keeping threads mostly isolated is a good way to convince Rust that what you're doing is safe. It happens that isolation is also a good way to make sure what you're doing is correct and maintainable. Again, Rust guides you toward good programs.

More importantly, Rust lets you combine techniques and experiment. You can iterate fast: arguing with the compiler gets you up and running correctly a lot faster than debugging data races.

## CHAPTER 20

Asynchronous Programming

Suppose you're writing a chat server. For each network connection, there are incoming packets to parse, outgoing packets to assemble, security parameters to manage, chat group subscriptions to track, and so on. Managing all this for many connections simultaneously is going to take some organization.

Ideally, you could just start a separate thread for each incoming connection:

```
use std::{net, thread};

let listener = net::TcpListener::bind(address)?;

for socket_result in listener.incoming() {
    let socket = socket_result?;
    let groups = chat_group_table.clone();
    thread::spawn(|| {
        log_error(serve(socket, groups));
    });
}
```

For each new connection, this spawns a fresh thread running the serve function, which is able to focus on managing a single connection's needs.

This works well, until everything goes much better than planned and suddenly you have tens of thousands of users. It's not unusual for a thread's stack to grow to 100 KiB or more, and that is probably not how you want to spend gigabytes of server memory. Threads are good and necessary for distributing work across multiple processors, but their memory demands are such that we often need complementary ways, used together with threads, to break the work down.

You can use Rust *asynchronous tasks* to interleave many independent activities on a single thread or a pool of worker threads. Asynchronous tasks are similar to threads, but are much quicker to create, pass control amongst themselves more efficiently, and have memory overhead an order of magnitude less than that of a thread. It is perfectly feasible to have hundreds of thousands of asynchronous tasks running simultaneously in a single program. Of course, your application may still be limited by other factors like network bandwidth, database speed, computation, or the work's inherent memory requirements, but the memory overhead inherent in the use of tasks is much less significant than that of threads.

Generally, asynchronous Rust code looks very much like ordinary multithreaded code, except that operations that might block, like I/O or acquiring mutexes, need to be handled a bit differently. Treating these specially gives Rust more information about how your code will behave, which is what makes the improved performance possible. The asynchronous version of the previous code looks like this:

```
use async_std::{net, task};

let listener = net::TcpListener::bind(address).await?;

let mut new_connections = listener.incoming();
while let Some(socket_result) = new_connections.next().await {
    let socket = socket_result?;
    let groups = chat_group_table.clone();
    task::spawn(async {
        log_error(serve(socket, groups).await);
    });
}
```

This uses the `async_std` crate's networking and task modules and adds `.await` after the calls that may block. But the overall structure is the same as the thread-based version.

The goal of this chapter is not only to help you write asynchronous code, but also to show how it works in enough detail that you can anticipate how it will perform in your applications and see where it can be most valuable.

- To show the mechanics of asynchronous programming, we lay out a minimal set of language features that covers all the core concepts: futures, asynchronous functions, `await` expressions, tasks, and the `block_on` and `spawn_local` executors.

- Then we present asynchronous blocks and the `spawn` executor. These are essential to getting real work done, but conceptually, they're just variants on the features we just mentioned. In the process, we point out a few issues you're likely to encounter that are unique to asynchronous programming and explain how to handle them.

- To show all these pieces working together, we walk through the complete code for a chat server and client, of which the preceding code fragment is a part.

- To illustrate how primitive futures and executors work, we present simple but functional implementations of `spawn_blocking` and `block_on`.

- Finally, we explain the `Pin` type, which appears from time to time in asynchronous interfaces to ensure that asynchronous function and block futures are used safely.

From Synchronous to Asynchronous

Consider what happens when you call the following (not async, completely traditional) function:

```
use std::io::prelude::*;
use std::net;

fn cheapo_request(host: &str, port: u16, path: &str)
                      -> std::io::Result<String>
{
    let mut socket = net::TcpStream::connect((host, port))?;

    let request = format!("GET {} HTTP/1.1\r\nHost: {}\r\n\r\n", path, host);
    socket.write_all(request.as_bytes())?;
    socket.shutdown(net::Shutdown::Write)?;

    let mut response = String::new();
    socket.read_to_string(&mut response)?;

    Ok(response)
}
```

This opens a TCP connection to a web server, sends it a bare-bones HTTP request in an outdated protocol,[1] and then reads the response. Figure 20-1 shows this function's execution over time.

This diagram shows how the function call stack behaves as time runs from left to right. Each function call is a box, placed atop its caller. Obviously, the `cheapo_request` function runs throughout the entire execution. It calls functions from the Rust standard library like `TcpStream::connect` and `TcpStream`'s implementations of `write_all` and `read_to_string`. These call other functions in turn, but eventually the program makes *system calls*, requests to the operating system to actually get something done, like open a TCP connection, or read or write some data.

---

1 If you actually need an HTTP client, consider using any one of the many excellent crates like `surf` or `reqwest` that will do the job properly and asynchronously. This client mostly just manages to get HTTPS redirects.

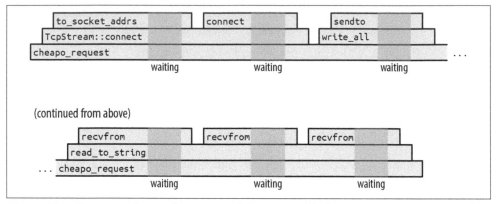

Figure 20-1. Progress of a synchronous HTTP request (darker gray areas are waiting for the operating system)

The darker gray backgrounds mark the times when the program is waiting for the operating system to finish the system call. We didn't draw these times to scale. If we had, the entire diagram would be darker gray: in practice, this function spends almost all of its time waiting for the operating system. The execution of the preceding code would be narrow slivers between the system calls.

While this function is waiting for the system calls to return, its single thread is blocked: it can't do anything else until the system call finishes. It's not unusual for a thread's stack to be tens or hundreds of kilobytes in size, so if this were a fragment of some larger system, with many threads working away at similar jobs, locking down those threads' resources to do nothing but wait could become quite expensive.

To get around this, a thread needs to be able to take up other work while it waits for system calls to complete. But it's not obvious how to accomplish this. For example, the signature of the function we're using to read the response from the socket is:

```
fn read_to_string(&mut self, buf: &mut String) -> std::io::Result<usize>;
```

It's written right into the type: this function doesn't return until the job is done, or something goes wrong. This function is *synchronous*: the caller resumes when the operation is complete. If we want to use our thread for other things while the operating system does its work, we're going need a new I/O library that provides an *asynchronous* version of this function.

Futures

Rust's approach to supporting asynchronous operations is to introduce a trait, `std::future::Future`:

```
trait Future {
    type Output;
```

```
    // For now, read `Pin<&mut Self>` as `&mut Self`.
    fn poll(self: Pin<&mut Self>, cx: &mut Context<'_>) -> Poll<Self::Output>;
}

enum Poll<T> {
    Ready(T),
    Pending,
}
```

A Future represents an operation that you can test for completion. A future's poll method never waits for the operation to finish: it always returns immediately. If the operation is complete, poll returns Poll::Ready(output), where output is its final result. Otherwise, it returns Pending. If and when the future is worth polling again, it promises to let us know by invoking a *waker*, a callback function supplied in the Context. We call this the "piñata model" of asynchronous programming: the only thing you can do with a future is whack it with a poll until a value falls out.

All modern operating systems include variants of their system calls that we can use to implement this sort of polling interface. On Unix and Windows, for example, if you put a network socket in nonblocking mode, then reads and writes return an error if they would block; you have to try again later.

So an asynchronous version of read_to_string would have a signature roughly like this:

```
fn read_to_string(&mut self, buf: &mut String)
    -> impl Future<Output = Result<usize>>;
```

This is the same as the signature we showed earlier, except for the return type: the asynchronous version returns *a future of* a Result<usize>. You'll need to poll this future until you get a Ready(result) from it. Each time it's polled, the read proceeds as far as it can. The final result gives you the success value or an error value, just like an ordinary I/O operation. This is the general pattern: the asynchronous version of any function takes the same arguments as the synchronous version, but the return type has a Future wrapped around it.

Calling this version of read_to_string doesn't actually read anything; its sole responsibility is to construct and return a future that will do the real work when polled. This future must hold all the information necessary to carry out the request made by the call. For example, the future returned by this read_to_string must remember the input stream it was called on, and the String to which it should append the incoming data. In fact, since the future holds the references self and buf, the proper signature for read_to_string must be:

```
fn read_to_string<'a>(&'a mut self, buf: &'a mut String)
    -> impl Future<Output = Result<usize>> + 'a;
```

This adds lifetimes to indicate that the future returned can live only as long as the values that self and buf are borrowing.

The async-std crate provides asynchronous versions of all of std's I/O facilities, including an asynchronous Read trait with a read_to_string method. async-std closely follows the design of std, reusing std's types in its own interfaces whenever possible, so errors, results, network addresses, and most of the other associated data are compatible between the two worlds. Familiarity with std helps you use async-std, and vice versa.

One of the rules of the Future trait is that, once a future has returned Poll::Ready, it may assume it will never be polled again. Some futures just return Poll::Pending forever if they are overpolled; others may panic or hang. (They must not, however, violate memory or thread safety, or otherwise cause undefined behavior.) The fuse adaptor method on the Future trait turns any future into one that simply returns Poll::Pending forever. But all the usual ways of consuming futures respect this rule, so fuse is usually not necessary.

If polling sounds inefficient, don't worry. Rust's asynchronous architecture is carefully designed so that, as long as your basic I/O functions like read_to_string are implemented correctly, you'll only poll a future when it's worthwhile. Every time poll is called, something somewhere should return Ready, or at least make progress toward that goal. We'll explain how this works in "Primitive Futures and Executors: When Is a Future Worth Polling Again?" on page 584.

But using futures seems like a challenge: when you poll, what should you do when you get Poll::Pending? You'll have to scrounge around for some other work this thread can do for the time being, without forgetting to come back to this future later and poll it again. Your entire program will be overgrown with plumbing keeping track of who's pending and what should be done once they're ready. The simplicity of our cheapo_request function is ruined.

Good news! It isn't.

Async Functions and Await Expressions

Here's a version of cheapo_request written as an *asynchronous function*:

```
use async_std::io::prelude::*;
use async_std::net;

async fn cheapo_request(host: &str, port: u16, path: &str)
                        -> std::io::Result<String>
{
    let mut socket = net::TcpStream::connect((host, port)).await?;

    let request = format!("GET {} HTTP/1.1\r\nHost: {}\r\n\r\n", path, host);
```

```
    socket.write_all(request.as_bytes()).await?;
    socket.shutdown(net::Shutdown::Write)?;

    let mut response = String::new();
    socket.read_to_string(&mut response).await?;

    Ok(response)
}
```

This is token for token the same as our original version, except:

- The function starts with `async fn` instead of `fn`.

- It uses the `async_std` crate's asynchronous versions of `TcpStream::connect`, `write_all`, and `read_to_string`. These all return futures of their results. (The examples in this section use version 1.7 of `async_std`.)

- After each call that returns a future, the code says `.await`. Although this looks like a reference to a struct field named `await`, it is actually special syntax built into the language for waiting until a future is ready. An `await` expression evaluates to the final value of the future. This is how the function obtains the results from `connect`, `write_all`, and `read_to_string`.

Unlike an ordinary function, when you call an asynchronous function, it returns immediately, before the body begins execution at all. Obviously, the call's final return value hasn't been computed yet; what you get is a *future of* its final value. So if you execute this code:

```
let response = cheapo_request(host, port, path);
```

then `response` will be a future of a `std::io::Result<String>`, and the body of `cheapo_request` has not yet begun execution. You don't need to adjust an asynchronous function's return type; Rust automatically treats `async fn f(...) -> T` as a function that returns a future of a T, not a T directly.

The future returned by an async function wraps up all the information the function body will need to run: the function's arguments, space for its local variables, and so on. (It's as if you'd captured the call's stack frame as an ordinary Rust value.) So `response` must hold the values passed for `host`, `port`, and `path`, since `cheapo_request`'s body is going to need those to run.

The future's specific type is generated automatically by the compiler, based on the function's body and arguments. This type doesn't have a name; all you know about it is that it implements `Future<Output=R>`, where R is the async function's return type. In this sense, futures of asynchronous functions are like closures: closures also have anonymous types, generated by the compiler, that implement the `FnOnce`, `Fn`, and `FnMut` traits.

When you first poll the future returned by `cheapo_request`, execution begins at the top of the function body and runs until the first `await` of the future returned by `TcpStream::connect`. The `await` expression polls the connect future, and if it is not ready, then it returns `Poll::Pending` to its own caller: polling `cheapo_request`'s future cannot proceed past that first `await` until a poll of `TcpStream::connect`'s future returns `Poll::Ready`. So a rough equivalent of the expression `TcpStream::connect(...).await` might be:

```
{
    // Note: this is pseudocode, not valid Rust
    let connect_future = TcpStream::connect(...);
    'retry_point:
    match connect_future.poll(cx) {
        Poll::Ready(value) => value,
        Poll::Pending => {
            // Arrange for the next `poll` of `cheapo_request`'s
            // future to resume execution at 'retry_point.
            ...
            return Poll::Pending;
        }
    }
}
```

An `await` expression takes ownership of the future and then polls it. If it's ready, then the future's final value is the value of the `await` expression, and execution continues. Otherwise, it returns the `Poll::Pending` to its own caller.

But crucially, the next poll of `cheapo_request`'s future doesn't start at the top of the function again: instead, it *resumes* execution mid-function at the point where it is about to poll `connect_future`. We don't progress to the rest of the async function until that future is ready.

As `cheapo_request`'s future continues to be polled, it will work its way through the function body from one `await` to the next, moving on only when the subfuture it's awaiting is ready. Thus, how many times `cheapo_request`'s future must be polled depends on both the behavior of the subfutures and the function's own control flow. `cheapo_request`'s future tracks the point at which the next `poll` should resume, and all the local state—variables, arguments, temporaries—that resumption will need.

The ability to suspend execution mid-function and then resume later is unique to async functions. When an ordinary function returns, its stack frame is gone for good. Since `await` expressions depend on the ability to resume, you can only use them inside async functions.

As of this writing, Rust does not yet allow traits to have asynchronous methods. Only free functions and functions inherent to a specific type can be asynchronous. Lifting this restriction will require a number of changes to the language. In the meantime, if you need to define traits that include async functions, consider using the `async-trait` crate, which provides a macro-based workaround.

Calling Async Functions from Synchronous Code: block_on

In a sense, async functions just pass the buck. True, it's easy to get a future's value in an async function: just `await` it. But the async function *itself* returns a future, so it's now the caller's job to do the polling somehow. Ultimately, someone has to actually wait for a value.

We can call `cheapo_request` from an ordinary, synchronous function (like `main`, for example) using `async_std`'s `task::block_on` function, which takes a future and polls it until it produces a value:

```
fn main() -> std::io::Result<()> {
    use async_std::task;

    let response = task::block_on(cheapo_request("example.com", 80, "/"))?;
    println!("{}", response);
    Ok(())
}
```

Since `block_on` is a synchronous function that produces the final value of an asynchronous function, you can think of it as an adapter from the asynchronous world to the synchronous world. But its blocking character also means that you should never use `block_on` within an async function: it would block the entire thread until the value is ready. Use `await` instead.

Figure 20-2 shows one possible execution of `main`.

The upper timeline, "Simplified view," shows an abstracted view of the program's asynchronous calls: `cheapo_request` first calls `TcpStream::connect` to obtain a socket and then calls `write_all` and `read_to_string` on that socket. Then it returns. This is very similar to the timeline for the synchronous version of `cheapo_request` earlier in this chapter.

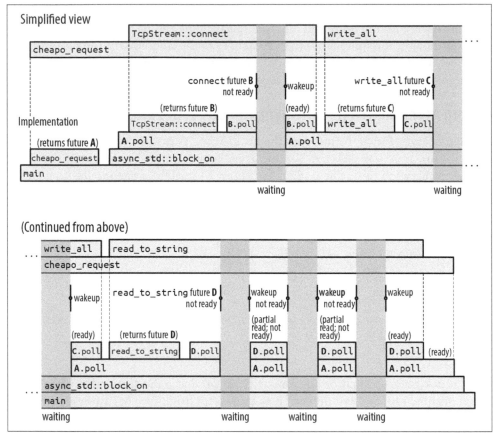

Figure 20-2. Blocking on an asynchronous function

But each of those asynchronous calls is a multistep process: a future is created and then polled until it's ready, perhaps creating and polling other subfutures in the process. The lower timeline, "Implementation," shows the actual synchronous calls that implement this asynchronous behavior. This is a good opportunity to walk through exactly what's going on in ordinary asynchronous execution:

- First, `main` calls `cheapo_request`, which returns future A of its final result. Then `main` passes that future to `async_std::block_on`, which polls it.

- Polling future A allows the body of `cheapo_request` to begin execution. It calls `TcpStream::connect` to obtain a future B of a socket and then awaits that. More precisely, since `TcpStream::connect` might encounter an error, B is a future of a `Result<TcpStream, std::io::Error>`.

- Future B gets polled by the await. Since the network connection is not yet established, B.poll returns Poll::Pending, but arranges to wake up the calling task once the socket is ready.

- Since future B wasn't ready, A.poll returns Poll::Pending to its own caller, block_on.

- Since block_on has nothing better to do, it goes to sleep. The entire thread is blocked now.

- When B's connection is ready to use, it wakes up the task that polled it. This stirs block_on into action, and it tries polling the future A again.

- Polling A causes cheapo_request to resume in its first await, where it polls B again.

- This time, B is ready: socket creation is complete, so it returns Poll::Ready(Ok(socket)) to A.poll.

- The asynchronous call to TcpStream::connect is now complete. The value of the TcpStream::connect(...).await expression is thus Ok(socket).

- The execution of cheapo_request's body proceeds normally, building the request string using the format! macro and passing it to socket.write_all.

- Since socket.write_all is an asynchronous function, it returns a future C of its result, which cheapo_request duly awaits.

The rest of the story is similar. In the execution shown in Figure 20-2, the future of socket.read_to_string gets polled four times before it is ready; each of these wake-ups reads *some* data from the socket, but read_to_string is specified to read all the way to the end of the input, and this takes several operations.

It doesn't sound too hard to just write a loop that calls poll over and over. But what makes async_std::task::block_on valuable is that it knows how to go to sleep until the future is actually worth polling again, rather than wasting your processor time and battery life making billions of fruitless poll calls. The futures returned by basic I/O functions like connect and read_to_string retain the waker supplied by the Context passed to poll and invoke it when block_on should wake up and try polling again. We'll show exactly how this works by implementing a simple version of block_on ourselves in "Primitive Futures and Executors: When Is a Future Worth Polling Again?" on page 584.

Like the original, synchronous version we presented earlier, this asynchronous version of cheapo_request spends almost all of its time waiting for operations to complete. If the time axis were drawn to scale, the diagram would be almost entirely dark gray, with tiny slivers of computation occurring when the program gets woken up.

This is a lot of detail. Fortunately, you can usually just think in terms of the simplified upper timeline: some function calls are sync, others are async and need an `await`, but they're all just function calls. The success of Rust's asynchronous support depends on helping programmers work with the simplified view in practice, without being distracted by the back-and-forth of the implementation.

Spawning Async Tasks

The `async_std::task::block_on` function blocks until a future's value is ready. But blocking a thread completely on a single future is no better than a synchronous call: the goal of this chapter is to get the thread *doing other work* while it's waiting.

For this, you can use `async_std::task::spawn_local`. This function takes a future and adds it to a pool that `block_on` will try polling whenever the future it's blocking on isn't ready. So if you pass a bunch of futures to `spawn_local` and then apply `block_on` to a future of your final result, `block_on` will poll each spawned future whenever it is able to make progress, running the entire pool concurrently until your result is ready.

As of this writing, `spawn_local` is available in `async-std` only if you enable that crate's `unstable` feature. To do this, you'll need to refer to `async-std` in your *Cargo.toml* with a line like this:

```
async-std = { version = "1", features = ["unstable"] }
```

The `spawn_local` function is an asynchronous analogue of the standard library's `std::thread::spawn` function for starting threads:

- `std::thread::spawn(c)` takes a closure c and starts a thread running it, returning a `std::thread::JoinHandle` whose `join` method waits for the thread to finish and returns whatever c returned.

- `async_std::task::spawn_local(f)` takes the future f and adds it to the pool to be polled when the current thread calls `block_on`. `spawn_local` returns its own `async_std::task::JoinHandle` type, itself a future that you can await to retrieve f's final value.

For example, suppose we want to make a whole set of HTTP requests concurrently. Here's a first attempt:

```
pub async fn many_requests(requests: Vec<(String, u16, String)>)
                           -> Vec<std::io::Result<String>>
{
    use async_std::task;

    let mut handles = vec![];
    for (host, port, path) in requests {
```

```
    handles.push(task::spawn_local(cheapo_request(&host, port, &path)));
}

let mut results = vec![];
for handle in handles {
    results.push(handle.await);
}

results
}
```

This function calls `cheapo_request` on each element of `requests`, passing each call's future to `spawn_local`. It collects the resulting `JoinHandles` in a vector and then awaits each of them. It's fine to await the join handles in any order: since the requests are already spawned, their futures will be polled as needed whenever this thread calls `block_on` and has nothing better to do. All the requests will run concurrently. Once they're complete, `many_requests` returns the results to its caller.

The previous code is almost correct, but Rust's borrow checker is worried about the lifetime of `cheapo_request`'s future:

```
error: `host` does not live long enough

    handles.push(task::spawn_local(cheapo_request(&host, port, &path)));
                    ---------------^^^^^--------------
                           |                |
                           |          borrowed value does not
                           |          live long enough
             argument requires that `host` is borrowed for `'static`
}
- `host` dropped here while still borrowed
```

There's a similar error for `path` as well.

Naturally, if we pass references to an asynchronous function, the future it returns must hold those references, so the future cannot safely outlive the values they borrow. This is the same restriction that applies to any value that holds references.

The problem is that `spawn_local` can't be sure you'll wait for the task to finish before `host` and `path` are dropped. In fact, `spawn_local` only accepts futures whose lifetimes are `'static`, because you could simply ignore the `JoinHandle` it returns and let the task continue to run for the rest of the program's execution. This isn't unique to asynchronous tasks: you'll get a similar error if you try to use `std::thread::spawn` to start a thread whose closure captures references to local variables.

One way to fix this is to create another asynchronous function that takes owned versions of the arguments:

```
async fn cheapo_owning_request(host: String, port: u16, path: String)
                               -> std::io::Result<String> {
    cheapo_request(&host, port, &path).await
}
```

This function takes `String`s instead of `&str` references, so its future owns the `host` and `path` strings itself, and its lifetime is `'static`. The borrow checker can see that it immediately awaits `cheapo_request`'s future, and hence, if that future is getting polled at all, the `host` and `path` variables it borrows must still be around. All is well.

Using `cheapo_owning_request`, you can spawn off all your requests like so:

```
for (host, port, path) in requests {
    handles.push(task::spawn_local(cheapo_owning_request(host, port, path)));
}
```

You can call `many_requests` from your synchronous `main` function, with `block_on`:

```
let requests = vec![
    ("example.com".to_string(),      80, "/".to_string()),
    ("www.red-bean.com".to_string(), 80, "/".to_string()),
    ("en.wikipedia.org".to_string(), 80, "/".to_string()),
];

let results = async_std::task::block_on(many_requests(requests));
for result in results {
    match result {
        Ok(response) => println!("{}", response),
        Err(err) => eprintln!("error: {}", err),
    }
}
```

This code runs all three requests concurrently from within the call to `block_on`. Each one makes progress as the opportunity arises while the others are blocked, all on the calling thread. Figure 20-3 shows one possible execution of the three calls to `cheapo_request`.

(We encourage you to try running this code yourself, with `eprintln!` calls added at the top of `cheapo_request` and after each `await` expression so that you can see how the calls interleave differently from one execution to the next.)

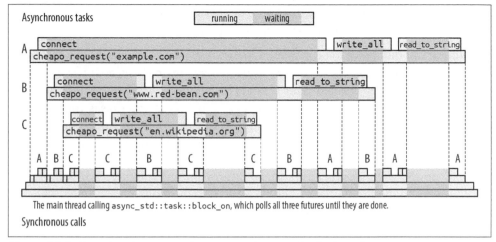

Figure 20-3. Running three asynchronous tasks on a single thread

The call to `many_requests` (not shown, for simplicity) has spawned three asynchronous tasks, which we've labeled A, B, and C. block_on begins by polling A, which starts connecting to `example.com`. As soon as this returns `Poll::Pending`, block_on turns its attention to the next spawned task, polling future B, and eventually C, which each begin connecting to their respective servers.

When all the pollable futures have returned `Poll::Pending`, block_on goes to sleep until one of the `TcpStream::connect` futures indicates that its task is worth polling again.

In this execution, the server `en.wikipedia.org` responds more quickly than the others, so that task finishes first. When a spawned task is done, it saves its value in its `JoinHandle` and marks it as ready, so that `many_requests` can proceed when it awaits it. Eventually, the other calls to `cheapo_request` will either succeed or return an error, and `many_requests` itself can return. Finally, `main` receives the vector of results from `block_on`.

All this execution takes place on a single thread, the three calls to `cheapo_request` being interleaved with each other through successive polls of their futures. An asynchronous call offers the appearance of a single function call running to completion, but this asynchronous call is realized by a series of synchronous calls to the future's `poll` method. Each individual `poll` call returns quickly, yielding the thread so that another async call can take a turn.

We have finally achieved the goal we set out at the beginning of the chapter: letting a thread take on other work while it waits for I/O to complete so that the thread's resources aren't tied up doing nothing. Even better, this goal was met with code that looks very much like ordinary Rust code: some of the functions are marked `async`, some of the function calls are followed by `.await`, and we use functions from `async_std` instead of `std`, but otherwise, it's ordinary Rust code.

One important difference to keep in mind between asynchronous tasks and threads is that switching from one async task to another happens only at `await` expressions, when the future being awaited returns `Poll::Pending`. This means that if you put a long-running computation in `cheapo_request`, none of the other tasks you passed to `spawn_local` will get a chance to run until it's done. With threads, this problem doesn't arise: the operating system can suspend any thread at any point and sets timers to ensure that no thread monopolizes the processor. Asynchronous code depends on the willing cooperation of the futures sharing the thread. If you need to have long-running computations coexist with asynchronous code, "Long Running Computations: yield_now and spawn_blocking" on page 563 later in this chapter describes some options.

Async Blocks

In addition to asynchronous functions, Rust also supports *asynchronous blocks*. Whereas an ordinary block statement returns the value of its last expression, an async block returns *a future of* the value of its last expression. You can use `await` expressions within an async block.

An async block looks like an ordinary block statement, preceded by the `async` keyword:

```
let serve_one = async {
    use async_std::net;

    // Listen for connections, and accept one.
    let listener = net::TcpListener::bind("localhost:8087").await?;
    let (mut socket, _addr) = listener.accept().await?;

    // Talk to client on `socket`.
    ...
};
```

This initializes `serve_one` with a future that, when polled, listens for and handles a single TCP connection. The block's body does not begin execution until `serve_one` gets polled, just as an async function call doesn't begin execution until its future is polled.

If you apply the `?` operator to an error in an async block, it just returns from the block, not from the surrounding function. For example, if the preceding `bind` call returns an error, the `?` operator returns it as `serve_one`'s final value. Similarly, `return` expressions return from the async block, not the enclosing function.

If an async block refers to variables defined in the surrounding code, its future captures their values, just as a closure would. And just like move closures (see "Closures That Steal" on page 330), you can start the block with async move to take ownership of the captured values, rather than just holding references to them.

Async blocks provide a concise way to separate out a section of code you'd like to run asynchronously. For example, in the previous section, spawn_local required a 'static future, so we defined the cheapo_owning_request wrapper function to give us a future that took ownership of its arguments. You can get the same effect without the distraction of a wrapper function simply by calling cheapo_request from an async block:

```rust
pub async fn many_requests(requests: Vec<(String, u16, String)>)
                            -> Vec<std::io::Result<String>>
{
    use async_std::task;

    let mut handles = vec![];
    for (host, port, path) in requests {
        handles.push(task::spawn_local(async move {
            cheapo_request(&host, port, &path).await
        }));
    }
    ...
}
```

Since this is an async move block, its future takes ownership of the String values host and path, just the way a move closure would. It then passes references to cheapo_request. The borrow checker can see that the block's await expression takes ownership of cheapo_request's future, so the references to host and path cannot outlive the captured variables they borrow. The async block accomplishes the same thing as cheapo_owning_request, but with less boilerplate.

One rough edge you may encounter is that there is no syntax for specifying the return type of an async block, analogous to the -> T following the arguments of an async function. This can cause problems when using the ? operator:

```rust
let input = async_std::io::stdin();
let future = async {
    let mut line = String::new();

    // This returns `std::io::Result<usize>`.
    input.read_line(&mut line).await?;

    println!("Read line: {}", line);

    Ok(())
};
```

This fails with the following error:

```
error: type annotations needed
  |
48 |     let future = async {
  |         ------ consider giving `future` a type
...
60 |         Ok(())
  |         ^^ cannot infer type for type parameter `E` declared
  |             on the enum `Result`
```

Rust can't tell what the return type of the async block should be. The read_line method returns Result<(), std::io::Error>, but because the ? operator uses the From trait to convert the error type at hand to whatever the situation requires, the async block's return type could be Result<(), E> for any type E that implements From<std::io::Error>.

Future versions of Rust will probably add syntax for indicating an async block's return type. For now, you can work around the problem by spelling out the type of the block's final Ok:

```
let future = async {
    ...
    Ok::<(), std::io::Error>(())
};
```

Since Result is a generic type that expects the success and error types as its parameters, we can specify those type parameters when using Ok or Err as shown here.

Building Async Functions from Async Blocks

Asynchronous blocks give us another way to get the same effect as an asynchronous function, with a little more flexibility. For example, we could write our cheapo_request example as an ordinary, synchronous function that returns the future of an async block:

```
use std::io;
use std::future::Future;

fn cheapo_request<'a>(host: &'a str, port: u16, path: &'a str)
    -> impl Future<Output = io::Result<String>> + 'a
{
    async move {
        ... function body ...
    }
}
```

When you call this version of the function, it immediately returns the future of the async block's value. This captures the function's arguments and behaves just like the future the asynchronous function would have returned. Since we're not using the async fn syntax, we need to write out the impl Future in the return type, but as far as callers are concerned, these two definitions are interchangeable implementations of the same function signature.

This second approach can be useful when you want to do some computation immediately when the function is called, before creating the future of its result. For example, yet another way to reconcile cheapo_request with spawn_local would be to make it into a synchronous function returning a 'static future that captures fully owned copies of its arguments:

```
fn cheapo_request(host: &str, port: u16, path: &str)
    -> impl Future<Output = io::Result<String>> + 'static
{
    let host = host.to_string();
    let path = path.to_string();

    async move {
        ... use &*host, port, and path ...
    }
}
```

This version lets the async block capture host and path as owned String values, not &str references. Since the future owns all the data it needs to run, it is valid for the 'static lifetime. (We've spelled out + 'static in the signature shown earlier, but 'static is the default for -> impl return types, so omitting it would have no effect.)

Since this version of cheapo_request returns futures that are 'static, we can pass them directly to spawn_local:

```
let join_handle = async_std::task::spawn_local(
    cheapo_request("areweasyncyet.rs", 80, "/")
);

... other work ...

let response = join_handle.await?;
```

Spawning Async Tasks on a Thread Pool

The examples we've shown so far spend almost all their time waiting for I/O, but some workloads are more of a mix of processor work and blocking. When you have enough computation to do that a single processor can't keep up, you can use async_std::task::spawn to spawn a future onto a pool of worker threads dedicated to polling futures that are ready to make progress.

async_std::task::spawn is used like async_std::task::spawn_local:

```
use async_std::task;

let mut handles = vec![];
```

```
    for (host, port, path) in requests {
        handles.push(task::spawn(async move {
            cheapo_request(&host, port, &path).await
        }));
    }
    ...
```

Like `spawn_local`, `spawn` returns a `JoinHandle` value you can await to get the future's final value. But unlike `spawn_local`, the future doesn't have to wait for you to call `block_on` before it gets polled. As soon as one of the threads from the thread pool is free, it will try polling it.

In practice, `spawn` is more widely used than `spawn_local`, simply because people like to know that their workload, no matter what its mix of computation and blocking, is balanced across the machine's resources.

One thing to keep in mind when using `spawn` is that the thread pool tries to stay busy, so your future gets polled by whichever thread gets around to it first. An async call may begin execution on one thread, block on an `await` expression, and get resumed in a different thread. So while it's a reasonable simplification to view an async function call as a single, connected execution of code (indeed, the purpose of asynchronous functions and `await` expressions is to encourage you to think of it that way), the call may actually be carried out by many different threads.

If you're using thread-local storage, it may be surprising to see the data you put there before an `await` expression replaced by something entirely different afterward, because your task is now being polled by a different thread from the pool. If this is a problem, you should instead use *task-local storage*; see the `async-std` crate's documentation for the `task_local!` macro for details.

But Does Your Future Implement Send?

There is one restriction `spawn` imposes that `spawn_local` does not. Since the future is being sent off to another thread to run, the future must implement the `Send` marker trait. We presented `Send` in "Thread Safety: Send and Sync" on page 521. A future is `Send` only if all the values it contains are `Send`: all the function arguments, local variables, and even anonymous temporary values must be safe to move to another thread.

As before, this requirement isn't unique to asynchronous tasks: you'll get a similar error if you try to use `std::thread::spawn` to start a thread whose closure captures non-`Send` values. The difference is that, whereas the closure passed to `std::thread::spawn` stays on the thread that was created to run it, a future spawned on a thread pool can move from one thread to another any time it awaits.

This restriction is easy to trip over by accident. For example, the following code looks innocent enough:

```
use async_std::task;
use std::rc::Rc;

async fn reluctant() -> String {
    let string = Rc::new("ref-counted string".to_string());

    some_asynchronous_thing().await;

    format!("Your splendid string: {}", string)
}

task::spawn(reluctant());
```

An asynchronous function's future needs to hold enough information for the function to continue from an `await` expression. In this case, `reluctant`'s future must use `string` after the `await`, so the future will, at least sometimes, contain an `Rc<String>` value. Since `Rc` pointers cannot be safely shared between threads, the future itself cannot be `Send`. And since `spawn` only accepts futures that are `Send`, Rust objects:

```
error: future cannot be sent between threads safely
     |
17   |         task::spawn(reluctant());
     |         ^^^^^^^^^^^ future returned by `reluctant` is not `Send`
     |


     |
127  | T: Future + Send + 'static,
     |              ---- required by this bound in `async_std::task::spawn`
     |
     = help: within `impl Future`, the trait `Send` is not implemented
             for `Rc<String>`
note: future is not `Send` as this value is used across an await
     |
10   |         let string = Rc::new("ref-counted string".to_string());
     |             ------ has type `Rc<String>` which is not `Send`
11   |
12   |         some_asynchronous_thing().await;
     |         ^^^^^^^^^^^^^^^^^^^^^^^^^^^^^^^^^
                 await occurs here, with `string` maybe used later
...
15   |     }
     |     - `string` is later dropped here
```

This error message is long, but it has a lot of helpful detail:

- It explains why the future needs to be `Send`: `task::spawn` requires it.

- It explains which value is not `Send`: the local variable `string`, whose type is `Rc<String>`.

- It explains why `string` affects the future: it is in scope across the indicated `await`.

There are two ways to fix this problem. One is to restrict the scope of the non-Send value so that it doesn't cover any await expressions and thus doesn't need to be saved in the function's future:

```
async fn reluctant() -> String {
    let return_value = {
        let string = Rc::new("ref-counted string".to_string());
        format!("Your splendid string: {}", string)
        // The `Rc<String>` goes out of scope here...
    };

    // ... and thus is not around when we suspend here.
    some_asynchronous_thing().await;

    return_value
}
```

Another solution is simply to use std::sync::Arc instead of Rc. Arc uses atomic updates to manage its reference counts, which makes it a bit slower, but Arc pointers are Send.

Although eventually you'll learn to recognize and avoid non-Send types, they can be a bit surprising at first. (At least, your authors were often surprised.) For example, older Rust code sometimes uses generic result types like this:

```
// Not recommended!
type GenericError = Box<dyn std::error::Error>;
type GenericResult<T> = Result<T, GenericError>;
```

This GenericError type uses a boxed trait object to hold a value of any type that implements std::error::Error. But it doesn't place any further restrictions on it: if someone had a non-Send type that implemented Error, they could convert a boxed value of that type to a GenericError. Because of this possibility, GenericError is not Send, and the following code won't work:

```
fn some_fallible_thing() -> GenericResult<i32> {
    ...
}

// This function's future is not `Send`...
async fn unfortunate() {
    // ... because this call's value ...
    match some_fallible_thing() {
        Err(error) => {
            report_error(error);
        }
        Ok(output) => {
            // ... is alive across this await ...
            use_output(output).await;
        }
    }
}
```

```
    }
    // ... and thus this `spawn` is an error.
    async_std::task::spawn(unfortunate());
```

As with the earlier example, the error message from the compiler explains what's going on, pointing to the Result type as the culprit. Since Rust considers the result of some_fallible_thing to be present for the entire match statement, including the await expression, it determines that the future of unfortunate is not Send. This error is overcautious on Rust's part: although it's true that GenericError is not safe to send to another thread, the await only occurs when the result is Ok, so the error value never actually exists when we await use_output's future.

The ideal solution is to use stricter generic error types like the ones we suggested in "Working with Multiple Error Types" on page 166:

```
    type GenericError = Box<dyn std::error::Error + Send + Sync + 'static>;
    type GenericResult<T> = Result<T, GenericError>;
```

This trait object explicitly requires the underlying error type to implement Send, and all is well.

If your future is not Send and you cannot conveniently make it so, then you can still use spawn_local to run it on the current thread. Of course, you'll need to make sure the thread calls block_on at some point, to give it a chance to run, and you won't benefit from distributing the work across multiple processors.

Long Running Computations: yield_now and spawn_blocking

For a future to share its thread nicely with other tasks, its poll method should always return as quickly as possible. But if you're carrying out a long computation, it could take a long time to reach the next await, making other asynchronous tasks wait longer than you'd like for their turn on the thread.

One way to avoid this is simply to await something occasionally. The async_std::task::yield_now function returns a simple future designed for this:

```
    while computation_not_done() {
        ... do one medium-sized step of computation ...
        async_std::task::yield_now().await;
    }
```

The first time the yield_now future is polled, it returns Poll::Pending, but says it's worth polling again soon. The effect is that your asynchronous call gives up the thread and other tasks get a chance to run, but your call will get another turn soon. The second time yield_now's future is polled, it returns Poll::Ready(()), and your async function can resume execution.

This approach isn't always feasible, however. If you're using an external crate to do the long-running computation or calling out to C or C++, it may not be convenient to change that code to be more async-friendly. Or it may be difficult to ensure that every path through the computation is sure to hit the `await` from time to time.

For cases like this, you can use `async_std::task::spawn_blocking`. This function takes a closure, starts it running on its own thread, and returns a future of its return value. Asynchronous code can await that future, yielding its thread to other tasks until the computation is ready. By putting the hard work on a separate thread, you can let the operating system take care of making it share the processor nicely.

For example, suppose we need to check passwords supplied by users against the hashed versions we've stored in our authentication database. For security, verifying a password needs to be computationally intensive so that even if attackers get a copy of our database, they can't simply try trillions of possible passwords to see if any match. The `argonautica` crate provides a hash function designed specifically for storing passwords: a properly generated `argonautica` hash takes a significant fraction of a second to verify. We can use `argonautica` (version `0.2`) in our asynchronous application like this:

```
async fn verify_password(password: &str, hash: &str, key: &str)
                     -> Result<bool, argonautica::Error>
{
    // Make copies of the arguments, so the closure can be 'static.
    let password = password.to_string();
    let hash = hash.to_string();
    let key = key.to_string();

    async_std::task::spawn_blocking(move || {
        argonautica::Verifier::default()
            .with_hash(hash)
            .with_password(password)
            .with_secret_key(key)
            .verify()
    }).await
}
```

This returns `Ok(true)` if `password` matches `hash`, given `key`, a key for the database as a whole. By doing the verification in the closure passed to `spawn_blocking`, we push the expensive computation onto its own thread, ensuring that it will not affect our responsiveness to other users' requests.

Comparing Asynchronous Designs

In many ways Rust's approach to asynchronous programming resembles that taken by other languages. For example, JavaScript, C#, and Rust all have asynchronous functions with `await` expressions. And all these languages have values that represent incomplete computations: Rust calls them "futures," JavaScript calls them "promises," and C# calls them "tasks," but they all represent a value that you may have to wait for.

Rust's use of polling, however, is unusual. In JavaScript and C#, an asynchronous function begins running as soon as it is called, and there is a global event loop built into the system library that resumes suspended async function calls when the values they were awaiting become available. In Rust, however, an async call does nothing until you pass it to a function like block_on, spawn, or spawn_local that will poll it and drive the work to completion. These functions, called *executors*, play the role that other languages cover with a global event loop.

Because Rust makes you, the programmer, choose an executor to poll your futures, Rust has no need for a global event loop built into the system. The async-std crate offers the executor functions we've used in this chapter so far, but the tokio crate, which we'll use later in this chapter, defines its own set of similar executor functions. And toward the end of this chapter, we'll implement our own executor. You can use all three in the same program.

A Real Asynchronous HTTP Client

We would be remiss if we did not show an example of using a proper asynchronous HTTP client crate, since it is so easy, and there are several good crates to choose from, including reqwest and surf.

Here's a rewrite of many_requests, even simpler than the one based on cheapo_request, that uses surf to run a series of requests concurrently. You'll need these dependencies in your *Cargo.toml* file:

```
[dependencies]
async-std = "1.7"
surf = "1.0"
```

Then, we can define many_requests as follows:

```
pub async fn many_requests(urls: &[String])
                           -> Vec<Result<String, surf::Exception>>
{
    let client = surf::Client::new();

    let mut handles = vec![];
    for url in urls {
        let request = client.get(&url).recv_string();
        handles.push(async_std::task::spawn(request));
    }

    let mut results = vec![];
    for handle in handles {
        results.push(handle.await);
    }
```

```
        results
    }

    fn main() {
        let requests = &["http://example.com".to_string(),
                         "https://www.red-bean.com".to_string(),
                         "https://en.wikipedia.org/wiki/Main_Page".to_string()];

        let results = async_std::task::block_on(many_requests(requests));
        for result in results {
            match result {
                Ok(response) => println!("*** {}\n", response),
                Err(err) => eprintln!("error: {}\n", err),
            }
        }
    }
```

Using a single surf::Client to make all our requests lets us reuse HTTP connections if several of them are directed at the same server. And no async block is needed: since recv_string is an asynchronous method that returns a Send + 'static future, we can pass its future directly to spawn.

An Asynchronous Client and Server

It's time to take the key ideas we've discussed so far and assemble them into a working program. To a large extent, asynchronous applications resemble ordinary multi-threaded applications, but there are new opportunities for compact and expressive code that you can look out for.

This section's example is a chat server and client. Check out the complete code (*https://oreil.ly/QFSUS*). Real chat systems are complicated, with concerns ranging from security and reconnection to privacy and moderation, but we've pared ours down to an austere set of features in order to focus on a few points of interest.

In particular, we want to handle *backpressure* well. By this we mean that if one client has a slow net connection or drops its connection entirely, that must never affect other clients' ability to exchange messages at their own pace. And since a slow client should not make the server spend unbounded memory holding on to its ever-growing backlog of messages, our server should drop messages for clients that can't keep up, but notify them that their stream is incomplete. (A real chat server would log messages to disk and let clients retrieve those they've missed, but we've left that out.)

We start the project with the command cargo new --lib async-chat and put the following text in *async-chat/Cargo.toml*:

```
[package]
name = "async-chat"
version = "0.1.0"
authors = ["You <you@example.com>"]
edition = "2021"

[dependencies]
async-std = { version = "1.7", features = ["unstable"] }
tokio = { version = "1.0", features = ["sync"] }
serde = { version = "1.0", features = ["derive", "rc"] }
serde_json = "1.0"
```

We're depending on four crates:

- The `async-std` crate is the collection of asynchronous I/O primitives and utilities we've been using throughout the chapter.

- The `tokio` crate is another collection of asynchronous primitives like `async-std`, one of the oldest and most mature. It's widely used and holds its design and implementation to high standards, but requires a bit more care to use than `async-std`.

  `tokio` is a large crate, but we need only one component from it, so the `features = ["sync"]` field in the *Cargo.toml* dependency line pares `tokio` down to the parts that we need, making this a light dependency.

  When the asynchronous library ecosystem was less mature, people avoided using both `tokio` and `async-std` in the same program, but the two projects have been cooperating to make sure this works, as long as each crate's documented rules are followed.

- The `serde` and `serde_json` crates we've seen before, in Chapter 18. These give us convenient and efficient tools for generating and parsing JSON, which our chat protocol uses to represent data on the network. We want to use some optional features from `serde`, so we select those when we give the dependency.

The entire structure of our chat application, client and server, looks like this:

```
async-chat
├── Cargo.toml
└── src
    ├── lib.rs
    ├── utils.rs
    └── bin
        ├── client.rs
        └── server
            ├── main.rs
            ├── connection.rs
            ├── group.rs
            └── group_table.rs
```

This package layout uses a Cargo feature we touched on in "The src/bin Directory" on page 189: in addition to the main library crate, *src/lib.rs*, with its submodule *src/utils.rs*, it also includes two executables:

- *src/bin/client.rs* is a single-file executable for the chat client.
- *src/bin/server* is the server executable, spread across four files: *main.rs* holds the `main` function, and there are three submodules, *connection.rs*, *group.rs*, and *group_table.rs*.

We'll present the contents of each source file over the course of the chapter, but once they're all in place, if you type `cargo build` in this tree, that compiles the library crate and then builds both executables. Cargo automatically includes the library crate as a dependency, making it a convenient place to put definitions shared by the client and server. Similarly, `cargo check` checks the entire source tree. To run either of the executables, you can use commands like these:

```
$ cargo run --release --bin server -- localhost:8088
$ cargo run --release --bin client -- localhost:8088
```

The `--bin` option indicates which executable to run, and any arguments following the `--` option get passed to the executable itself. Our client and server just want to know the server's address and TCP port.

Error and Result Types

The library crate's `utils` module defines the result and error types we'll use throughout the application. From *src/utils.rs*:

```
use std::error::Error;

pub type ChatError = Box<dyn Error + Send + Sync + 'static>;
pub type ChatResult<T> = Result<T, ChatError>;
```

These are the general-purpose error types we suggested in "Working with Multiple Error Types" on page 166. The `async_std`, `serde_json`, and `tokio` crates each define their own error types, but the `?` operator can automatically convert them all into a `ChatError`, using the standard library's implementation of the `From` trait that can convert any suitable error type to `Box<dyn Error + Send + Sync + 'static>`. The `Send` and `Sync` bounds ensure that if a task spawned onto another thread fails, it can safely report the error to the main thread.

In a real application, consider using the `anyhow` crate, which provides `Error` and `Result` types similar to these. The anyhow crate is easy to use and provides some nice features beyond what our `ChatError` and `ChatResult` can offer.

The Protocol

The library crate captures our entire chat protocol in these two types, defined in *lib.rs*:

```
use serde::{Deserialize, Serialize};
use std::sync::Arc;

pub mod utils;

#[derive(Debug, Deserialize, Serialize, PartialEq)]
pub enum FromClient {
    Join { group_name: Arc<String> },
    Post {
        group_name: Arc<String>,
        message: Arc<String>,
    },
}

#[derive(Debug, Deserialize, Serialize, PartialEq)]
pub enum FromServer {
    Message {
        group_name: Arc<String>,
        message: Arc<String>,
    },
    Error(String),
}


#[test]
fn test_fromclient_json() {
    use std::sync::Arc;

    let from_client = FromClient::Post {
        group_name: Arc::new("Dogs".to_string()),
        message: Arc::new("Samoyeds rock!".to_string()),
    };

    let json = serde_json::to_string(&from_client).unwrap();
    assert_eq!(json,
               r#"{"Post":{"group_name":"Dogs","message":"Samoyeds rock!"}}"#);

    assert_eq!(serde_json::from_str::<FromClient>(&json).unwrap(),
               from_client);
}
```

The FromClient enum represents the packets a client can send to the server: it can ask to join a group and post messages to any group it has joined. FromServer represents what the server can send back: messages posted to some group, and error messages. Using a reference-counted Arc<String> instead of a plain String helps the server avoid making copies of strings as it manages groups and distributes messages.

The #[derive] attributes tell the serde crate to generate implementations of its Serialize and Deserialize traits for FromClient and FromServer. This lets us call serde_json::to_string to convert them to JSON values, send them across the network, and finally call serde_json::from_str to convert them back into their Rust forms.

The test_fromclient_json unit test illustrates how this is used. Given the Serialize implementation derived by serde, we can call serde_json::to_string to turn the given FromClient value into this JSON:

```
{"Post":{"group_name":"Dogs","message":"Samoyeds rock!"}}
```

Then the derived Deserialize implementation parses that back into an equivalent FromClient value. Note that the Arc pointers in FromClient have no effect on the serialized form: the reference-counted strings appear directly as JSON object member values.

Taking User Input: Asynchronous Streams

Our chat client's first responsibility is to read commands from the user and send the corresponding packets to the server. Managing a proper user interface is beyond the scope of this chapter, so we're going to do the simplest possible thing that works: reading lines directly from standard input. The following code goes in *src/bin/client.rs*:

```
use async_std::prelude::*;
use async_chat::utils::{self, ChatResult};
use async_std::io;
use async_std::net;

async fn send_commands(mut to_server: net::TcpStream) -> ChatResult<()> {
    println!("Commands:\n\
                 join GROUP\n\
                 post GROUP MESSAGE...\n\
                 Type Control-D (on Unix) or Control-Z (on Windows) \
                 to close the connection.");

    let mut command_lines = io::BufReader::new(io::stdin()).lines();
    while let Some(command_result) = command_lines.next().await {
        let command = command_result?;
        // See the GitHub repo for the definition of `parse_command`.
        let request = match parse_command(&command) {
            Some(request) => request,
            None => continue,
        };

        utils::send_as_json(&mut to_server, &request).await?;
        to_server.flush().await?;
    }
}
```

```
        Ok(())
    }
```

This calls `async_std::io::stdin` to get an asynchronous handle on the client's standard input, wraps it in an `async_std::io::BufReader` to buffer it, and then calls `lines` to process the user's input line by line. It tries to parse each line as a command corresponding to some `FromClient` value and, if it succeeds, sends that value to the server. If the user enters an unrecognized command, `parse_command` prints an error message and returns `None`, so `send_commands` can go around the loop again. If the user types an end-of-file indication, then the `lines` stream returns `None`, and `send_commands` returns. This is very much like the code you would write in an ordinary, synchronous program, except that it uses `async_std`'s versions of the library features.

The asynchronous `BufReader`'s `lines` method is interesting. It can't return an iterator, the way the standard library does: the `Iterator::next` method is an ordinary synchronous function, so calling `command_lines.next()` would block the thread until the next line was ready. Instead, `lines` returns a *stream* of `Result<String>` values. A stream is the asynchronous analogue of an iterator: it produces a sequence of values on demand, in an async-friendly fashion. Here's the definition of the `Stream` trait, from the `async_std::stream` module:

```
trait Stream {
    type Item;

    // For now, read `Pin<&mut Self>` as `&mut Self`.
    fn poll_next(self: Pin<&mut Self>, cx: &mut Context<'_>)
        -> Poll<Option<Self::Item>>;
}
```

You can look at this as a hybrid of the `Iterator` and `Future` traits. Like an iterator, a `Stream` has an associated `Item` type and uses `Option` to indicate when the sequence has ended. But like a future, a stream must be polled: to get the next item (or learn that the stream has ended), you must call `poll_next` until it returns `Poll::Ready`. A stream's `poll_next` implementation should always return quickly, without blocking. And if a stream returns `Poll::Pending`, it must notify the caller when it's worth polling again via the `Context`.

The `poll_next` method is awkward to use directly, but you won't generally need to do that. Like iterators, streams have a broad collection of utility methods like `filter` and `map`. Among these is a `next` method, which returns a future of the stream's next `Option<Self::Item>`. Rather than polling the stream explicitly, you can call `next` and await the future it returns instead.

Putting these pieces together, `send_commands` consumes the stream of input lines by looping over the values produced by a stream using `next` with `while let`:

```
while let Some(item) = stream.next().await {
    ... use item ...
}
```

(Future versions of Rust will probably introduce an asynchronous variant of the `for` loop syntax for consuming streams, just as an ordinary `for` loop consumes `Iterator` values.)

Polling a stream after it has ended—that is, after it has returned `Poll::Ready(None)` to indicate the end of the stream—is like calling `next` on an iterator after it has returned `None`, or polling a future after it has returned `Poll::Ready`: the `Stream` trait doesn't specify what the stream should do, and some streams may misbehave. Like futures and iterators, streams have a `fuse` method to ensure such calls behave predictably, when that's needed; see the documentation for details.

When working with streams, it's important to remember to use the `async_std` prelude:

```
use async_std::prelude::*;
```

This is because the utility methods for the `Stream` trait, like `next`, `map`, `filter`, and so on, are actually not defined on `Stream` itself. Instead, they are default methods of a separate trait, `StreamExt`, which is automatically implemented for all `Stream`s:

```
pub trait StreamExt: Stream {
    ... define utility methods as default methods ...
}

impl<T: Stream> StreamExt for T { }
```

This is an example of the *extension trait* pattern we described in "Traits and Other People's Types" on page 268. The `async_std::prelude` module brings the `StreamExt` methods into scope, so using the prelude ensures its methods are visible in your code.

Sending Packets

For transmitting packets on a network socket, our client and server use the `send_as_json` function from our library crate's `utils` module:

```
use async_std::prelude::*;
use serde::Serialize;
use std::marker::Unpin;

pub async fn send_as_json<S, P>(outbound: &mut S, packet: &P) -> ChatResult<()>
where
    S: async_std::io::Write + Unpin,
    P: Serialize,
```

```
    {
        let mut json = serde_json::to_string(&packet)?;
        json.push('\n');
        outbound.write_all(json.as_bytes()).await?;
        Ok(())
    }
```

This function builds the JSON representation of `packet` as a `String`, adds a newline to the end, and then writes it all to `outbound`.

From its `where` clause, you can see that `send_as_json` is quite flexible. The type of packet to be sent, P, can be anything that implements `serde::Serialize`. The output stream S can be anything that implements `async_std::io::Write`, the asynchronous version of the `std::io::Write` trait for output streams. This is sufficient for us to send `FromClient` and `FromServer` values on an asynchronous `TcpStream`. Keeping the definition of `send_as_json` generic ensures that it doesn't depend on the details of the stream or packet types in surprising ways: `send_as_json` can only use methods from those traits.

The `Unpin` constraint on S is required to use the `write_all` method. We'll cover pinning and unpinning later in this chapter, but for the time being, it should suffice to just add `Unpin` constraints to type variables where required; the Rust compiler will point these cases out if you forget.

Rather than serializing the packet directly to the `outbound` stream, `send_as_json` serializes it to a temporary `String` and then writes that to `outbound`. The `serde_json` crate does provide functions to serialize values directly to output streams, but those functions only support synchronous streams. Writing to asynchronous streams would require fundamental changes to both `serde_json` and the `serde` crate's format-independent core, since the traits they are designed around have synchronous methods.

As with streams, many of the methods of `async_std`'s I/O traits are actually defined on extension traits, so it's important to remember to `use async_std::prelude::*` whenever you are using them.

Receiving Packets: More Asynchronous Streams

For receiving packets, our server and client will use this function from the `utils` module to receive `FromClient` and `FromServer` values from an asynchronous buffered TCP socket, an `async_std::io::BufReader<TcpStream>`:

```
use serde::de::DeserializeOwned;

pub fn receive_as_json<S, P>(inbound: S) -> impl Stream<Item = ChatResult<P>>
    where S: async_std::io::BufRead + Unpin,
          P: DeserializeOwned,
```

```
{
    inbound.lines()
        .map(|line_result| -> ChatResult<P> {
            let line = line_result?;
            let parsed = serde_json::from_str::<P>(&line)?;
            Ok(parsed)
        })
}
```

Like `send_as_json`, this function is generic in the input stream and packet types:

- The stream type S must implement `async_std::io::BufRead`, the asynchronous analogue of `std::io::BufRead`, representing a buffered input byte stream.

- The packet type P must implement `DeserializeOwned`, a stricter variant of serde's `Deserialize` trait. For efficiency, `Deserialize` can produce `&str` and `&[u8]` values that borrow their contents directly from the buffer they were deserialized from, to avoid copying data. In our case, however, that's no good: we need to return the deserialized values to our caller, so they must be able to outlive the buffers we parsed them from. A type that implements `DeserializeOwned` is always independent of the buffer it was deserialized from.

Calling `inbound.lines()` gives us a `Stream` of `std::io::Result<String>` values. We then use the stream's `map` adapter to apply a closure to each item, handling errors and parsing each line as the JSON form of a value of type P. This gives us a stream of `ChatResult<P>` values, which we return directly. The function's return type is:

```
impl Stream<Item = ChatResult<P>>
```

This indicates that we return *some* type that produces a sequence of `ChatResult<P>` values asynchronously, but our caller can't tell exactly which type that is. Since the closure we pass to `map` has an anonymous type anyway, this is the most specific type `receive_as_json` could possibly return.

Notice that `receive_as_json` is not, itself, an asynchronous function. It is an ordinary function that returns an async value, a stream. Understanding the mechanics of Rust's asynchronous support more deeply than "just add `async` and `.await` everywhere" opens up the potential for clear, flexible, and efficient definitions like this one that take full advantage of the language.

To see how `receive_as_json` gets used, here is our chat client's `handle_replies` function from *src/bin/client.rs*, which receives a stream of `FromServer` values from the network and prints them out for the user to see:

```
use async_chat::FromServer;

async fn handle_replies(from_server: net::TcpStream) -> ChatResult<()> {
    let buffered = io::BufReader::new(from_server);
```

```
        let mut reply_stream = utils::receive_as_json(buffered);

        while let Some(reply) = reply_stream.next().await {
            match reply? {
                FromServer::Message { group_name, message } => {
                    println!("message posted to {}: {}", group_name, message);
                }
                FromServer::Error(message) => {
                    println!("error from server: {}", message);
                }
            }
        }

        Ok(())
    }
```

This function takes a socket receiving data from the server, wraps a `BufReader` around it (note well, the `async_std` version), and then passes that to `receive_as_json` to obtain a stream of incoming `FromServer` values. Then it uses a `while let` loop to handle incoming replies, checking for error results and printing each server reply for the user to see.

The Client's Main Function

Since we've presented both `send_commands` and `handle_replies`, we can show the chat client's main function, from *src/bin/client.rs*:

```
use async_std::task;

fn main() -> ChatResult<()> {
    let address = std::env::args().nth(1)
        .expect("Usage: client ADDRESS:PORT");

    task::block_on(async {
        let socket = net::TcpStream::connect(address).await?;
        socket.set_nodelay(true)?;

        let to_server = send_commands(socket.clone());
        let from_server = handle_replies(socket);

        from_server.race(to_server).await?;

        Ok(())
    })
}
```

Having obtained the server's address from the command line, `main` has a series of asynchronous functions it would like to call, so it wraps the remainder of the function in an asynchronous block and passes the block's future to `async_std::task::block_on` to run.

Once the connection is established, we want the `send_commands` and `handle_replies` functions to run in tandem, so we can see others' messages arrive while we type. If we enter the end-of-file indicator or if the connection to the server drops, the program should exit.

Given what we've done elsewhere in the chapter, you might expect code like this:

```
let to_server = task::spawn(send_commands(socket.clone()));
let from_server = task::spawn(handle_replies(socket));

to_server.await?;
from_server.await?;
```

But since we await both of the join handles, that gives us a program that exits once *both* tasks have finished. We want to exit as soon as *either* one has finished. The `race` method on futures accomplishes this. The call `from_server.race(to_server)` returns a new future that polls both `from_server` and `to_server` and returns `Poll::Ready(v)` as soon as either of them is ready. Both futures must have the same output type: the final value is that of whichever future finished first. The uncompleted future is dropped.

The `race` method, along with many other handy utilities, is defined on the `async_std::prelude::FutureExt` trait, which `async_std::prelude` makes visible to us.

At this point, the only part of the client's code that we haven't shown is the `parse_command` function. That's pretty straightforward text-handling code, so we won't show its definition here. See the complete code in the Git repository for details.

The Server's Main Function

Here are the entire contents of the main file for the server, *src/bin/server/main.rs*:

```
use async_std::prelude::*;
use async_chat::utils::ChatResult;
use std::sync::Arc;

mod connection;
mod group;
mod group_table;

use connection::serve;

fn main() -> ChatResult<()> {
    let address = std::env::args().nth(1).expect("Usage: server ADDRESS");

    let chat_group_table = Arc::new(group_table::GroupTable::new());

    async_std::task::block_on(async {
        // This code was shown in the chapter introduction.
```

```
        use async_std::{net, task};

        let listener = net::TcpListener::bind(address).await?;

        let mut new_connections = listener.incoming();
        while let Some(socket_result) = new_connections.next().await {
            let socket = socket_result?;
            let groups = chat_group_table.clone();
            task::spawn(async {
                log_error(serve(socket, groups).await);
            });
        }

        Ok(())
    })
}

fn log_error(result: ChatResult<()>) {
    if let Err(error) = result {
        eprintln!("Error: {}", error);
    }
}
```

The server's `main` function resembles the client's: it does a little bit of setup and then calls `block_on` to run an async block that does the real work. To handle incoming connections from clients, it creates a `TcpListener` socket, whose `incoming` method returns a stream of `std::io::Result<TcpStream>` values.

For each incoming connection, we spawn an asynchronous task running the `connection::serve` function. Each task also receives a reference to a `GroupTable` value representing our server's current list of chat groups, shared by all the connections via an `Arc` reference-counted pointer.

If `connection::serve` returns an error, we log a message to the standard error output and let the task exit. Other connections continue to run as usual.

Handling Chat Connections: Async Mutexes

Here's the server's workhorse: the `serve` function from the `connection` module in *src/bin/server/connection.rs*:

```
use async_chat::{FromClient, FromServer};
use async_chat::utils::{self, ChatResult};
use async_std::prelude::*;
use async_std::io::BufReader;
use async_std::net::TcpStream;
use async_std::sync::Arc;

use crate::group_table::GroupTable;
```

```rust
pub async fn serve(socket: TcpStream, groups: Arc<GroupTable>)
                 -> ChatResult<()>
{
    let outbound = Arc::new(Outbound::new(socket.clone()));

    let buffered = BufReader::new(socket);
    let mut from_client = utils::receive_as_json(buffered);
    while let Some(request_result) = from_client.next().await {
        let request = request_result?;

        let result = match request {
            FromClient::Join { group_name } => {
                let group = groups.get_or_create(group_name);
                group.join(outbound.clone());
                Ok(())
            }

            FromClient::Post { group_name, message } => {
                match groups.get(&group_name) {
                    Some(group) => {
                        group.post(message);
                        Ok(())
                    }
                    None => {
                        Err(format!("Group '{}' does not exist", group_name))
                    }
                }
            }
        };

        if let Err(message) = result {
            let report = FromServer::Error(message);
            outbound.send(report).await?;
        }
    }

    Ok(())
}
```

This is almost a mirror image of the client's `handle_replies` function: the bulk of the code is a loop handling an incoming stream of `FromClient` values, built from a buffered TCP stream with `receive_as_json`. If an error occurs, we generate a `FromServer::Error` packet to convey the bad news back to the client.

In addition to error messages, clients would also like to receive messages from the chat groups they've joined, so the connection to the client needs to be shared with each group. We could simply give everyone a clone of the `TcpStream`, but if two of these sources try to write a packet to the socket at the same time, their output might be interleaved, and the client would end up receiving garbled JSON. We need to arrange safe concurrent access to the connection.

This is managed with the `Outbound` type, defined in *src/bin/server/connection.rs* as follows:

```
use async_std::sync::Mutex;

pub struct Outbound(Mutex<TcpStream>);

impl Outbound {
    pub fn new(to_client: TcpStream) -> Outbound {
        Outbound(Mutex::new(to_client))
    }

    pub async fn send(&self, packet: FromServer) -> ChatResult<()> {
        let mut guard = self.0.lock().await;
        utils::send_as_json(&mut *guard, &packet).await?;
        guard.flush().await?;
        Ok(())
    }
}
```

When created, an `Outbound` value takes ownership of a `TcpStream` and wraps it in a `Mutex` to ensure that only one task can use it at a time. The `serve` function wraps each `Outbound` in an `Arc` reference-counted pointer so that all the groups the client joins can point to the same shared `Outbound` instance.

A call to `Outbound::send` first locks the mutex, returning a guard value that dereferences to the `TcpStream` inside. We use `send_as_json` to transmit `packet`, and then finally we call `guard.flush()` to ensure it won't languish half-transmitted in some buffer somewhere. (To our knowledge, `TcpStream` doesn't actually buffer data, but the `Write` trait permits its implementations to do so, so we shouldn't take any chances.)

The expression `&mut *guard` lets us work around the fact that Rust doesn't apply deref coercions to meet trait bounds. Instead, we explicitly dereference the mutex guard and then borrow a mutable reference to the `TcpStream` it protects, producing the `&mut TcpStream` that `send_as_json` requires.

Note that `Outbound` uses the `async_std::sync::Mutex` type, not the standard library's `Mutex`. There are three reasons for this.

First, the standard library's `Mutex` may misbehave if a task is suspended while holding a mutex guard. If the thread that had been running that task picks up another task that tries to lock the same `Mutex`, trouble ensues: from the `Mutex`'s point of view, the thread that already owns it is trying to lock it again. The standard `Mutex` isn't designed to handle this case, so it panics or deadlocks. (It will never grant the lock inappropriately.) There is work underway to make Rust detect this problem at compile time and issue a warning whenever a `std::sync::Mutex` guard is live across an await expression. Since `Outbound::send` needs to hold the lock while it awaits the futures of `send_as_json` and `guard.flush`, it must use async_std's `Mutex`.

Second, the asynchronous `Mutex`'s `lock` method returns a future of a guard, so a task waiting to lock a mutex yields its thread for other tasks to use until the mutex is ready. (If the mutex is already available, the `lock` future is ready immediately, and the task doesn't suspend itself at all.) The standard `Mutex`'s `lock` method, on the other hand, pins down the entire thread while it waits to acquire the lock. Since the preceding code holds the mutex while it transmits a packet across the network, that might take quite a while.

Finally, the standard `Mutex` must only be unlocked by the same thread that locked it. To enforce this, the standard mutex's guard type does not implement `Send`: it cannot be transmitted to other threads. This means that a future holding such a guard does not itself implement `Send`, and cannot be passed to `spawn` to run on a thread pool; it can only be run with `block_on` or `spawn_local`. The guard for an async_std `Mutex` does implement `Send` so there's no problem using it in spawned tasks.

The Group Table: Synchronous Mutexes

But the moral of the story is not as simple as, "Always use `async_std::sync::Mutex` in asynchronous code." Often there is no need to await anything while holding a mutex, and the lock is not held for long. In such cases, the standard library's `Mutex` can be much more efficient. Our chat server's `GroupTable` type illustrates this case. Here are the full contents of *src/bin/server/group_table.rs*:

```
use crate::group::Group;
use std::collections::HashMap;
use std::sync::{Arc, Mutex};

pub struct GroupTable(Mutex<HashMap<Arc<String>, Arc<Group>>>);

impl GroupTable {
    pub fn new() -> GroupTable {
        GroupTable(Mutex::new(HashMap::new()))
    }

    pub fn get(&self, name: &String) -> Option<Arc<Group>> {
        self.0.lock()
            .unwrap()
            .get(name)
            .cloned()
    }

    pub fn get_or_create(&self, name: Arc<String>) -> Arc<Group> {
        self.0.lock()
            .unwrap()
            .entry(name.clone())
```

```
            .or_insert_with(|| Arc::new(Group::new(name)))
            .clone()
    }
}
```

A `GroupTable` is simply a mutex-protected hash table, mapping chat group names to actual groups, both managed using reference-counted pointers. The `get` and `get_or_create` methods lock the mutex, perform a few hash table operations, perhaps some allocations, and return.

In `GroupTable`, we use a plain old `std::sync::Mutex`. There is no asynchronous code in this module at all, so there are no `awaits` to avoid. Indeed, if we wanted to use `async_std::sync::Mutex` here, we would need to make `get` and `get_or_create` into asynchronous functions, which introduces the overhead of future creation, suspensions, and resumptions for little benefit: the mutex is locked only for some hash operations and perhaps a few allocations.

If our chat server found itself with millions of users, and the `GroupTable` mutex did become a bottleneck, making it asynchronous wouldn't address that problem. It would probably be better to use some sort of collection type specialized for concurrent access instead of `HashMap`. For example, the `dashmap` crate provides such a type.

Chat Groups: tokio's Broadcast Channels

In our server, the `group::Group` type represents a chat group. This type only needs to support the two methods that `connection::serve` calls: `join`, to add a new member, and `post`, to post a message. Each message posted needs to be distributed to all the members.

This is where we address the challenge mentioned earlier of *backpressure*. There are several needs in tension with each other:

- If one member can't keep up with the messages being posted to the group—if they have a slow network connection, for example—other members in the group should not be affected.

- Even if a member falls behind, there should be means for them to rejoin the conversation and continue to participate somehow.

- Memory spent buffering messages should not grow without bound.

Because these challenges are common when implementing many-to-many communication patterns, the `tokio` crate provides a *broadcast channel* type that implements one reasonable set of tradeoffs. A `tokio` broadcast channel is a queue of values (in our case, chat messages) that allows any number of different threads or tasks to send and receive values. It's called a "broadcast" channel because every consumer gets its own copy of each value sent. (The value type must implement `Clone`.)

Normally, a broadcast channel retains a message in the queue until every consumer has gotten their copy. But if the length of the queue would exceed the channel's maximum capacity, specified when it is created, the oldest messages get dropped. Any consumers who couldn't keep up get an error the next time they try to get their next message, and the channel catches them up to the oldest message still available.

For example, Figure 20-4 shows a broadcast channel with a maximum capacity of 16 values.

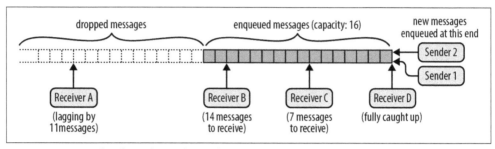

Figure 20-4. A tokio broadcast channel

There are two senders enqueuing messages and four receivers dequeueing them—or more precisely, copying messages out of the queue. Receiver B has 14 messages still to receive, receiver C has 7, and receiver D is fully caught up. Receiver A has fallen behind, and 11 messages were dropped before it could see them. Its next attempt to receive a message will fail, returning an error indicating the situation, and it will be caught up to the current end of the queue.

Our chat server represents each chat group as a broadcast channel carrying Arc<String> values: posting a message to the group broadcasts it to all current members. Here's the definition of the group::Group type, defined in *src/bin/server/group.rs*:

```
use async_std::task;
use crate::connection::Outbound;
use std::sync::Arc;
use tokio::sync::broadcast;

pub struct Group {
    name: Arc<String>,
    sender: broadcast::Sender<Arc<String>>
}

impl Group {
    pub fn new(name: Arc<String>) -> Group {
        let (sender, _receiver) = broadcast::channel(1000);
        Group { name, sender }
    }
```

```
    pub fn join(&self, outbound: Arc<Outbound>) {
        let receiver = self.sender.subscribe();

        task::spawn(handle_subscriber(self.name.clone(),
                                      receiver,
                                      outbound));
    }

    pub fn post(&self, message: Arc<String>) {
        // This only returns an error when there are no subscribers. A
        // connection's outgoing side can exit, dropping its subscription,
        // slightly before its incoming side, which may end up trying to send a
        // message to an empty group.
        let _ignored = self.sender.send(message);
    }
}
```

A Group struct holds the name of the chat group, together with a broadcast::Sender representing the sending end of the group's broadcast channel. The Group::new function calls broadcast::channel to create a broadcast channel with a maximum capacity of 1,000 messages. The channel function returns both a sender and a receiver, but we have no need for the receiver at this point, since the group doesn't have any members yet.

To add a new member to the group, the Group::join method calls the sender's subscribe method to create a new receiver for the channel. Then it spawns a new asynchronous task to monitor that receiver for messages and write them back to the client, in the handle_subscribe function.

With those details in hand, the Group::post method is straightforward: it simply sends the message to the broadcast channel. Since the values carried by the channel are Arc<String> values, giving each receiver its own copy of a message just increases the message's reference count, without any copies or heap allocation. Once all the subscribers have transmitted the message, the reference count drops to zero, and the message is freed.

Here's the definition of handle_subscriber:

```
use async_chat::FromServer;
use tokio::sync::broadcast::error::RecvError;

async fn handle_subscriber(group_name: Arc<String>,
                           mut receiver: broadcast::Receiver<Arc<String>>,
                           outbound: Arc<Outbound>)
{
    loop {
        let packet = match receiver.recv().await {
            Ok(message) => FromServer::Message {
                group_name: group_name.clone(),
                message: message.clone(),
```

```
        },

        Err(RecvError::Lagged(n)) => FromServer::Error(
            format!("Dropped {} messages from {}.", n, group_name)
        ),

        Err(RecvError::Closed) => break,
    };

    if outbound.send(packet).await.is_err() {
        break;
    }
    }
}
```

Although the details are different, the form of this function is familiar: it's a loop that receives messages from the broadcast channel and transmits them back to the client via the shared Outbound value. If the loop can't keep up with the broadcast channel, it receives a Lagged error, which it dutifully reports to the client.

If sending a packet back to the client fails completely, perhaps because the connection has closed, handle_subscriber exits its loop and returns, causing the asynchronous task to exit. This drops the broadcast channel's Receiver, unsubscribing it from the channel. This way, when a connection is dropped, each of its group memberships is cleaned up the next time the group tries to send it a message.

Our chat groups never close down, since we never remove a group from the group table, but just for completeness, handle_subscriber is ready to handle a Closed error by exiting the task.

Note that we're creating a new asynchronous task for every group membership of every client. This is feasible because asynchronous tasks use so much less memory than threads and because switching from one asynchronous task to another within a process is quite efficient.

This, then, is the complete code for the chat server. It is a bit spartan, and there are many more valuable features in the async_std, tokio, and futures crates than we can cover in this book, but ideally this extended example manages to illustrate how some of the features of asynchronous ecosystem work together: asynchronous tasks, streams, the asynchronous I/O traits, channels, and mutexes of both flavors.

Primitive Futures and Executors: When Is a Future Worth Polling Again?

The chat server shows how we can write code using asynchronous primitives like TcpListener and the broadcast channel, and use executors like block_on and spawn to drive their execution. Now we can take a look at how these things are implemented. The key question is, when a future returns `Poll::Pending`, how does it coordinate with the executor to poll it again at the right time?

Think about what happens when we run code like this, from the chat client's `main` function:

```
task::block_on(async {
    let socket = net::TcpStream::connect(address).await?;
    ...
})
```

The first time `block_on` polls the async block's future, the network connection is almost certainly not ready immediately, so `block_on` goes to sleep. But when should it wake up? Somehow, once the network connection is ready, `TcpStream` needs to tell `block_on` that it should try polling the async block's future again, because it knows that this time, the `await` will complete, and execution of the async block can make progress.

When an executor like `block_on` polls a future, it must pass in a callback called a *waker*. If the future is not ready yet, the rules of the `Future` trait say that it must return `Poll::Pending` for now, and arrange for the waker to be invoked later, if and when the future is worth polling again.

So a handwritten implementation of `Future` often looks something like this:

```
use std::task::Waker;

struct MyPrimitiveFuture {
    ...
    waker: Option<Waker>,
}

impl Future for MyPrimitiveFuture {
    type Output = ...;

    fn poll(mut self: Pin<&mut Self>, cx: &mut Context<'_>) -> Poll<...> {
        ...

        if ... future is ready ... {
            return Poll::Ready(final_value);
        }

        // Save the waker for later.
        self.waker = Some(cx.waker().clone());
        Poll::Pending
    }
}
```

In other words, if the future's value is ready, return it. Otherwise, stash a clone of the `Context`'s waker somewhere, and return `Poll::Pending`.

When the future is worth polling again, the future must notify the last executor that polled it by calling its waker's `wake` method:

```
// If we have a waker, invoke it, and clear `self.waker`.
if let Some(waker) = self.waker.take() {
    waker.wake();
}
```

Ideally, the executor and the future take turns polling and waking: the executor polls the future and goes to sleep, then the future invokes the waker, so the executor wakes up and polls the future again.

Futures of async functions and blocks don't deal with wakers themselves. They simply pass along the context they're given to the subfutures they await, delegating to them the obligation to save and invoke wakers. In our chat client, the first poll of the async block's future just passes the context along when it awaits `TcpStream::connect`'s future. Subsequent polls similarly pass their context through to whatever future the block awaits next.

`TcpStream::connect`'s future handles being polled as shown in the preceding example: it hands the waker over to a helper thread that waits for the connection to be ready and then invokes the waker.

`Waker` implements `Clone` and `Send`, so a future can always make its own copy of the waker and send it to other threads as needed. The `Waker::wake` method consumes the waker. There is also a `wake_by_ref` method that does not, but some executors can implement the consuming version a bit more efficiently. (The difference is at most a `clone`.)

It's harmless for an executor to overpoll a future, just inefficient. Futures, however, should be careful to invoke a waker only when polling would make actual progress: a cycle of spurious wakeups and polls can prevent an executor from ever sleeping at all, wasting power and leaving the processor less responsive to other tasks.

Now that we have shown how executors and primitive futures communicate, we'll implement a primitive future ourselves and then walk through an implementation of the `block_on` executor.

Invoking Wakers: spawn_blocking

Earlier in the chapter, we described the `spawn_blocking` function, which starts a given closure running on another thread and returns a future of its return value. We now have all the pieces we need to implement `spawn_blocking` ourselves. For simplicity, our version creates a fresh thread for each closure, rather than using a thread pool, as `async_std`'s version does.

Although `spawn_blocking` returns a future, we're not going to write it as an `async fn`. Rather, it'll be an ordinary, synchronous function that returns a struct, `SpawnBlocking`, on which we'll implement `Future` ourselves.

The signature of our `spawn_blocking` is as follows:

```
pub fn spawn_blocking<T, F>(closure: F) -> SpawnBlocking<T>
where F: FnOnce() -> T,
      F: Send + 'static,
      T: Send + 'static,
```

Since we need to send the closure to another thread and bring the return value back, both the closure `F` and its return value `T` must implement `Send`. And since we don't have any idea how long the thread will run, they must both be `'static` as well. These are the same bounds that `std::thread::spawn` itself imposes.

`SpawnBlocking<T>` is a future of the closure's return value. Here is its definition:

```
use std::sync::{Arc, Mutex};
use std::task::Waker;

pub struct SpawnBlocking<T>(Arc<Mutex<Shared<T>>>);

struct Shared<T> {
    value: Option<T>,
    waker: Option<Waker>,
}
```

The `Shared` struct must serve as a rendezvous between the future and the thread running the closure, so it is owned by an `Arc` and protected with a `Mutex`. (A synchronous mutex is fine here.) Polling the future checks whether `value` is present and saves the waker in `waker` if not. The thread that runs the closure saves its return value in `value` and then invokes `waker`, if present.

Here's the full definition of `spawn_blocking`:

```
pub fn spawn_blocking<T, F>(closure: F) -> SpawnBlocking<T>
where F: FnOnce() -> T,
      F: Send + 'static,
      T: Send + 'static,
{
    let inner = Arc::new(Mutex::new(Shared {
        value: None,
        waker: None,
    }));

    std::thread::spawn({
        let inner = inner.clone();
        move || {
            let value = closure();
```

```
            let maybe_waker = {
                let mut guard = inner.lock().unwrap();
                guard.value = Some(value);
                guard.waker.take()
            };

            if let Some(waker) = maybe_waker {
                waker.wake();
            }
        }
    });

    SpawnBlocking(inner)
}
```

After creating the Shared value, this spawns a thread to run the closure, store the result in the Shared's value field, and invoke the waker, if any.

We can implement Future for SpawnBlocking as follows:

```
use std::future::Future;
use std::pin::Pin;
use std::task::{Context, Poll};

impl<T: Send> Future for SpawnBlocking<T> {
    type Output = T;

    fn poll(self: Pin<&mut Self>, cx: &mut Context<'_>) -> Poll<T> {
        let mut guard = self.0.lock().unwrap();
        if let Some(value) = guard.value.take() {
            return Poll::Ready(value);
        }

        guard.waker = Some(cx.waker().clone());
        Poll::Pending
    }
}
```

Polling a SpawnBlocking checks if the closure's value is ready, taking ownership and returning it if so. Otherwise, the future is still pending, so it saves a clone of the context's waker in the future's waker field.

Once a Future has returned Poll::Ready, you're not supposed to poll it again. The usual ways of consuming futures, like await and block_on, all respect this rule. If a SpawnBlocking future is overpolled, nothing especially terrible happens, but it doesn't go to any effort to handle that case, either. This is typical for handwritten futures.

Implementing block_on

In addition to being able to implement primitive futures, we also have all the pieces we need to build a simple executor. In this section, we'll write our own version of block_on. It will be quite a bit simpler than async_std's version; for example, it won't support spawn_local, task-local variables, or nested invocations (calling block_on from asynchronous code). But it is sufficient to run our chat client and server.

Here's the code:

```
use waker_fn::waker_fn;        // Cargo.toml: waker-fn = "1.1"
use futures_lite::pin;         // Cargo.toml: futures-lite = "1.11"
use crossbeam::sync::Parker;   // Cargo.toml: crossbeam = "0.8"
use std::future::Future;
use std::task::{Context, Poll};

fn block_on<F: Future>(future: F) -> F::Output {
    let parker = Parker::new();
    let unparker = parker.unparker().clone();
    let waker = waker_fn(move || unparker.unpark());
    let mut context = Context::from_waker(&waker);

    pin!(future);

    loop {
        match future.as_mut().poll(&mut context) {
            Poll::Ready(value) => return value,
            Poll::Pending => parker.park(),
        }
    }
}
```

This is pretty short, but there's a lot going on, so let's take it one piece at a time.

```
let parker = Parker::new();
let unparker = parker.unparker().clone();
```

The crossbeam crate's Parker type is a simple blocking primitive: calling parker.park() blocks the thread until someone else calls .unpark() on the corresponding Unparker, which you obtain beforehand by calling parker.unparker(). If you unpark a thread that isn't parked yet, its next call to park returns immediately, without blocking. Our block_on will use the Parker to wait whenever the future isn't ready, and the waker we pass to futures will unpark it.

```
let waker = waker_fn(move || unparker.unpark());
```

The waker_fn function, from the crate of the same name, creates a Waker from a given closure. Here, we make a Waker that, when invoked, calls the closure move || unparker.unpark(). You can also create wakers by implementing the std::task::Wake trait, but waker_fn is a bit more convenient here.

```
pin!(future);
```

Given a variable holding a future of type F, the pin! macro takes ownership of the future and declares a new variable of the same name whose type is Pin<&mut F> and that borrows the future. This gives us the `Pin<&mut Self>` required by the `poll` method. For reasons we'll explain in the next section, futures of asynchronous functions and blocks must be referenced via a `Pin` before they can be polled.

```
loop {
    match future.as_mut().poll(&mut context) {
        Poll::Ready(value) => return value,
        Poll::Pending => parker.park(),
    }
}
```

Finally, the polling loop is quite simple. Passing a context carrying our waker, we poll the future until it returns `Poll::Ready`. If it returns `Poll::Pending`, we park the thread, which blocks until `waker` is invoked. Then we try again.

The `as_mut` call lets us poll `future` without giving up ownership; we'll explain this more in the next section.

Pinning

Although asynchronous functions and blocks are essential for writing clear asynchronous code, handling their futures requires a bit of care. The `Pin` type helps Rust ensure they're used safely.

In this section, we'll show why futures of asynchronous function calls and blocks can't be handled as freely as ordinary Rust values. Then we'll show how `Pin` serves as a "seal of approval" on pointers that can be counted on to manage such futures safely. Finally, we'll show a few ways to work with `Pin` values.

The Two Life Stages of a Future

Consider this simple asynchronous function:

```
use async_std::io::prelude::*;
use async_std::{io, net};

async fn fetch_string(address: &str) -> io::Result<String> {
    ❶
    let mut socket = net::TcpStream::connect(address).await❷?;
    let mut buf = String::new();
    socket.read_to_string(&mut buf).await❸?;
    Ok(buf)
}
```

This opens a TCP connection to the given address and returns, as a `String`, whatever the server there wants to send. The points labeled ❶, ❷, and ❸ are the *resumption points*, the points in the asynchronous function's code at which execution may be suspended.

Suppose you call it, without awaiting, like so:

```
let response = fetch_string("localhost:6502");
```

Now `response` is a future ready to begin execution at the start of `fetch_string`, with the given argument. In memory, the future looks something like Figure 20-5.

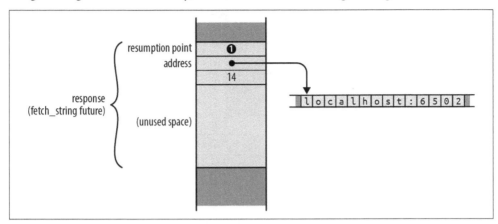

Figure 20-5. The future constructed for a call to `fetch_string`

Since we just created this future, it says that execution should begin at resumption point ❶, at the top of the function body. In this state, the only values a future needs to proceed are the function arguments.

Now suppose that you poll `response` a few times and it reaches this point in the function's body:

```
socket.read_to_string(&mut buf).await❸?;
```

Suppose further that the result of `read_to_string` isn't ready, so the poll returns `Poll::Pending`. At this point, the future looks like Figure 20-6.

A future must always hold all the information needed to resume execution the next time it is polled. In this case that is:

- Resumption point ❸, saying that execution should resume in the `await` polling `read_to_string`'s future.
- The variables that are alive at that resumption point: `socket` and `buf`. The value of `address` is no longer present in the future, since the function no longer needs it.
- The `read_to_string` subfuture, which the `await` expression is in the midst of polling.

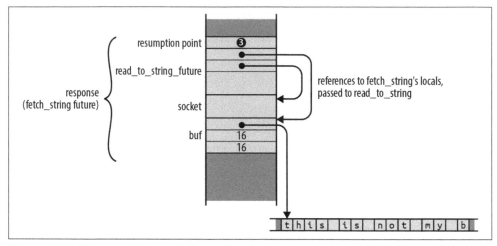

Figure 20-6. The same future, in the midst of awaiting `read_to_string`

Note that the call to `read_to_string` has borrowed references to `socket` and `buf`. In a synchronous function, all local variables live on the stack, but in an asynchronous function, local variables that are alive across an `await` must be located in the future, so they'll be available when it is polled again. Borrowing a reference to such a variable borrows a part of the future.

However, Rust requires that values not be moved while they are borrowed. Suppose you were to move this future to a new location:

```
let new_variable = response;
```

Rust has no means to find all the active references and adjust them accordingly. Instead of pointing to `socket` and `buf` at their new locations, the references continue to point at their old locations in the now-uninitialized `response`. They have become dangling pointers, as shown in Figure 20-7.

Preventing borrowed values from being moved is generally the borrow checker's responsibility. The borrow checker treats variables as the roots of ownership trees, but unlike variables stored on the stack, variables stored in futures get moved if the future itself moves. This means the borrows of `socket` and `buf` affect not just what `fetch_string` can do with its own variables, but what its caller can safely do with `response`, the future that holds them. Futures of async functions are a blind spot for the borrow checker, which Rust must cover somehow if it wants to keep its memory safety promises.

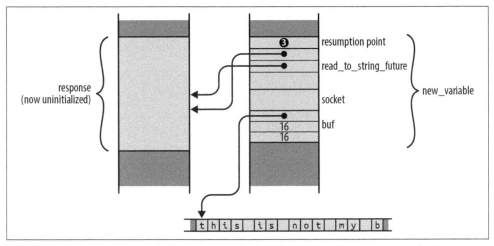

Figure 20-7. fetch_string's future, moved while borrowed (Rust prevents this)

Rust's solution to this problem rests on the insight that futures are always safe to move when they are first created, and only become unsafe to move when they are polled. A future that has just been created by calling an asynchronous function simply holds a resumption point and the argument values. These are only in scope for the asynchronous function's body, which has not yet begun execution. Only polling a future can borrow its contents.

From this, we can see that every future has two life stages:

- The first stage begins when the future is created. Because the function's body hasn't begun execution, no part of it could possibly be borrowed yet. At this point, it's as safe to move as any other Rust value.

- The second stage begins the first time the future is polled. Once the function's body has begun execution, it could borrow references to variables stored in the future and then await, leaving that part of the future borrowed. Starting after its first poll, we must assume the future may not be safe to move.

The flexibility of the first life stage is what lets us pass futures to block_on and spawn and call adapter methods like race and fuse, all of which take futures by value. In fact, even the asynchronous function call that created the future in the first place had to return it to the caller; that was a move as well.

To enter its second life stage, the future must be polled. The poll method requires the future be passed as a Pin<&mut Self> value. Pin is a wrapper for pointer types (like &mut Self) that restricts how the pointers can be used, ensuring that their referents (like Self) cannot ever be moved again. So you must produce a Pin-wrapped pointer to the future before you can poll it.

This, then, is Rust's strategy for keeping futures safe: a future can't become dangerous to move until it's polled; you can't poll a future until you've constructed a `Pin`-wrapped pointer to it; and once you've done that, the future can't be moved.

"A value you can't move" sounds impossible: moves are everywhere in Rust. We'll explain exactly how `Pin` protects futures in the next section.

Although this section has discussed asynchronous functions, everything here applies to asynchronous blocks as well. A freshly created future of an asynchronous block simply captures the variables it will use from the surrounding code, like a closure. Only polling the future can create references to its contents, rendering it unsafe to move.

Keep in mind that this move fragility is limited to futures of asynchronous functions and blocks, with their special compiler-generated `Future` implementations. If you implement `Future` by hand for your own types, as we did for our `SpawnBlocking` type in "Invoking Wakers: spawn_blocking" on page 586, such futures are perfectly safe to move both before and after they've been polled. In any handwritten `poll` implementation, the borrow checker ensures that whatever references you had borrowed to parts of `self` are gone by the time `poll` returns. It is only because asynchronous functions and blocks have the power to suspend execution in the midst of a function call, with borrows in progress, that we must handle their futures with care.

Pinned Pointers

The `Pin` type is a wrapper for pointers to futures that restricts how the pointers may be used to make sure that futures can't be moved once they've been polled. These restrictions can be lifted for futures that don't mind being moved, but they are essential to safely polling futures of asynchronous functions and blocks.

By *pointer*, we mean any type that implements `Deref`, and possibly `DerefMut`. A `Pin` wrapped around a pointer is called a *pinned pointer*. `Pin<&mut T>` and `Pin<Box<T>>` are typical.

The definition of `Pin` in the standard library is simple:

```
pub struct Pin<P> {
    pointer: P,
}
```

Note that the `pointer` field is *not* `pub`. This means that the only way to construct or use a `Pin` is through the carefully chosen methods the type provides.

Given a future of an asynchronous function or block, there are only a few ways to get a pinned pointer to it:

- The `pin!` macro, from the `futures-lite` crate, shadows a variable of type T with a new one of type `Pin<&mut T>`. The new variable points to the original's value, which has been moved to an anonymous temporary location on the stack. When the variable goes out of scope, the value is dropped. We used `pin!` in our `block_on` implementation to pin the future we wanted to poll.

- The standard library's `Box::pin` constructor takes ownership of a value of any type T, moves it into the heap, and returns a `Pin<Box<T>>`.

- `Pin<Box<T>>` implements `From<Box<T>>`, so `Pin::from(boxed)` takes ownership of boxed and gives you back a pinned box pointing at the same T on the heap.

Every way to obtain a pinned pointer to these futures entails giving up ownership of the future, and there is no way to get it back out. The pinned pointer itself can be moved in any way you please, of course, but moving a pointer doesn't move its referent. So possession of a pinned pointer to a future serves as proof that you have permanently given up the ability to move that future. This is all we need to know that it can be polled safely.

Once you've pinned a future, if you'd like to poll it, all `Pin<pointer to T>` types have an `as_mut` method that dereferences the pointer and returns the `Pin<&mut T>` that poll requires.

The `as_mut` method can also help you poll a future without giving up ownership. Our `block_on` implementation used it in this role:

```
pin!(future);

loop {
    match future.as_mut().poll(&mut context) {
        Poll::Ready(value) => return value,
        Poll::Pending => parker.park(),
    }
}
```

Here, the `pin!` macro has redeclared `future` as a `Pin<&mut F>`, so we could just pass that to poll. But mutable references are not Copy, so `Pin<&mut F>` cannot be Copy either, meaning that calling `future.poll()` directly would take ownership of `future`, leaving the next iteration of the loop with an uninitialized variable. To avoid this, we call `future.as_mut()` to reborrow a fresh `Pin<&mut F>` for each loop iteration.

There is no way to get a `&mut` reference to a pinned future: if you could, you could use `std::mem::replace` or `std::mem::swap` to move it out and put a different future in its place.

The reason we don't have to worry about pinning futures in ordinary asynchronous code is that the most common ways to obtain a future's value—awaiting it or passing to an executor—all take ownership of the future and manage the pinning internally. For example, our `block_on` implementation takes ownership of the future and uses the `pin!` macro to produce the `Pin<&mut F>` needed to poll. An `await` expression also takes ownership of the future and uses an approach similar to the `pin!` macro internally.

The Unpin Trait

However, not all futures require this kind of careful handling. For any handwritten implementation of `Future` for an ordinary type, like our `SpawnBlocking` type mentioned earlier, the restrictions on constructing and using pinned pointers are unnecessary.

Such durable types implement the `Unpin` marker trait:

```
trait Unpin { }
```

Almost all types in Rust automatically implement `Unpin`, using special support in the compiler. Asynchronous function and block futures are the exceptions to this rule.

For `Unpin` types, `Pin` imposes no restrictions whatsoever. You can make a pinned pointer from an ordinary pointer with `Pin::new` and get the pointer back out with `Pin::into_inner`. The `Pin` itself passes along the pointer's own `Deref` and `DerefMut` implementations.

For example, `String` implements `Unpin`, so we can write:

```
let mut string = "Pinned?".to_string();
let mut pinned: Pin<&mut String> = Pin::new(&mut string);

pinned.push_str(" Not");
Pin::into_inner(pinned).push_str(" so much.");

let new_home = string;
assert_eq!(new_home, "Pinned? Not so much.");
```

Even after making a `Pin<&mut String>`, we have full mutable access to the string and can move it to a new variable once the `Pin` has been consumed by `into_inner` and the mutable reference is gone. So for types that are `Unpin`—which is almost all of them—`Pin` is a boring wrapper around pointers to that type.

This means that when you implement `Future` for your own `Unpin` types, your `poll` implementation can treat `self` as if it were `&mut Self`, not `Pin<&mut Self>`. Pinning becomes something you can mostly ignore.

It may be surprising to learn that `Pin<&mut F>` and `Pin<Box<F>>` implement `Unpin`, even if F does not. This doesn't read well—how can a `Pin` be `Unpin`?—but if you think carefully about what each term means, it does make sense. Even if F is not safe to move once it has been polled, a pointer to it is always safe to move, polled or not. Only the pointer moves; its fragile referent stays put.

This is useful to know when you would like to pass the future of an asynchronous function or block to a function that only accepts `Unpin` futures. (Such functions are rare in `async_std`, but less so elsewhere in the async ecosystem.) `Pin<Box<F>>` is `Unpin` even if F is not, so applying `Box::pin` to an asynchronous function or block future gives you a future you can use anywhere, at the cost of a heap allocation.

There are various unsafe methods for working with `Pin` that let you do whatever you like with the pointer and its target, even for target types that are not `Unpin`. But as explained in Chapter 22, Rust cannot check that these methods are being used correctly; you become responsible for ensuring the safety of the code that uses them.

When Is Asynchronous Code Helpful?

Asynchronous code is trickier to write than multithreaded code. You have to use the right I/O and synchronization primitives, break up long-running computations by hand or spin them off on other threads, and manage other details like pinning that don't arise in threaded code. So what specific advantages does asynchronous code offer?

Two claims you'll often hear don't stand up to careful inspection:

- "Async code is great for I/O." This is not quite correct. If your application is spending its time waiting for I/O, making it async will not make that I/O run faster. There is nothing about the asynchronous I/O interfaces generally used today that makes them more efficient than their synchronous counterparts. The operating system has the same work to do either way. (In fact, an asynchronous I/O operation that isn't ready must be tried again later, so it takes two system calls to complete instead of one.)

- "Async code is easier to write than multithreaded code." In languages like JavaScript and Python, this may well be true. In those languages, programmers use async/await as well-behaved form of concurrency: there's a single thread of execution, and interruptions only occur at `await` expressions, so there's often no need for a mutex to keep data consistent: just don't await while you're in the midst of using it! It's much easier to understand your code when task switches occur only with your explicit permission.

  But this argument doesn't carry over to Rust, where threads aren't nearly as troublesome. Once your program compiles, it is free of data races. Nondeterministic behavior is confined to synchronization features like mutexes, channels, atomics, and so on, which were designed to cope with it. So asynchronous code has no unique advantage at helping you see when other threads might impact you; that's clear in *all* safe Rust code.

And of course, Rust's asynchronous support really shines when used in combination with threads. It would be a pity to give that up.

So, what are the real advantages of asynchronous code?

- *Asynchronous tasks can use less memory.* On Linux, a thread's memory use starts at 20 KiB, counting both user and kernel space.[2] Futures can be much smaller: our chat server's futures are a few hundred bytes in size and have been getting smaller as the Rust compiler improves.

- *Asynchronous tasks are faster to create.* On Linux, creating a thread takes around 15 µs. Spawning an asynchronous task takes around 300 ns, about one-fiftieth the time.

- *Context switches are faster between asynchronous tasks than between operating system threads*, 0.2 µs versus 1.7 µs on Linux.[3] However, these are best-case numbers for each: if the switch is due to I/O readiness, both costs rise to 1.7 µs. Whether the switch is between threads or tasks on different processor cores also makes a big difference: communication between cores is very slow.

This gives us a hint as to what sorts of problems asynchronous code can solve. For example, an asynchronous server might use less memory per task and thus be able to handle more simultaneous connections. (This is probably where asynchronous code gets its reputation for being "good for I/O.") Or, if your design is naturally organized as many independent tasks communicating with each other, then low per-task costs, short creation times, and quick context switches are all important advantages. This is why chat servers are the classic example for asynchronous programming, but multiplayer games and network routers would probably be good uses too.

In other situations, the case for using async is less clear. If your program has a pool of threads doing heavy computations or sitting idle waiting for I/O to finish, the advantages listed earlier are probably not a big influence on its performance. You'll have to optimize your computation, find a faster net connection, or do something else that actually affects the limiting factor.

---

2 This includes kernel memory and counts physical pages allocated for the thread, not virtual, yet-to-be-allocated pages. The numbers are similar on macOS and Windows.

3 Linux context switches used to be in the 0.2 µs range, too, until the kernel was forced to use slower techniques due to processor security flaws.

In practice, every account of implementing high-volume servers that we could find emphasized the importance of measurement, tuning, and a relentless campaign to identify and remove sources of contention between tasks. An asynchronous architecture won't let you skip any of this work. In fact, while there are plenty of off-the-shelf tools for assessing the behavior of multithreaded programs, Rust asynchronous tasks are invisible to those tools and thus require tooling of their own. (As a wise elder once said, "Now you have *two* problems.")

Even if you don't use asynchronous code now, it's nice to know that the option is there if you ever have the good fortune to be vastly busier than you are now.

## CHAPTER 21

Macros

A cento (from the Latin for "patchwork") is a poem made up entirely of lines quoted from another poet.

    —Matt Madden

Rust supports *macros*, a way to extend the language in ways that go beyond what you can do with functions alone. For example, we've seen the `assert_eq!` macro, which is handy for tests:

```
assert_eq!(gcd(6, 10), 2);
```

This could have been written as a generic function, but the `assert_eq!` macro does several things that functions can't do. One is that when an assertion fails, `assert_eq!` generates an error message containing the filename and line number of the assertion. Functions have no way of getting that information. Macros can, because the way they work is completely different.

Macros are a kind of shorthand. During compilation, before types are checked and long before any machine code is generated, each macro call is *expanded*—that is, it's replaced with some Rust code. The preceding macro call expands to something roughly like this:

```
match (&gcd(6, 10), &2) {
    (left_val, right_val) => {
        if !(*left_val == *right_val) {
            panic!("assertion failed: `(left == right)`, \
                    (left: `{:?}`, right: `{:?}`)", left_val, right_val);
        }
    }
}
```

`panic!` is also a macro, which itself expands to yet more Rust code (not shown here). That code uses two other macros, `file!()` and `line!()`. Once every macro call in the crate is fully expanded, Rust moves on to the next phase of compilation.

At run time, an assertion failure would look like this (and would indicate a bug in the `gcd()` function, since 2 is the correct answer):

```
thread 'main' panicked at 'assertion failed: `(left == right)`, (left: `17`,
right: `2`)', gcd.rs:7
```

If you're coming from C++, you may have had some bad experiences with macros. Rust macros take a different approach, similar to Scheme's `syntax-rules`. Compared to C++ macros, Rust macros are better integrated with the rest of the language and therefore less error prone. Macro calls are always marked with an exclamation point, so they stand out when you're reading code, and they can't be called accidentally when you meant to call a function. Rust macros never insert unmatched brackets or parentheses. And Rust macros come with pattern matching, making it easier to write macros that are both maintainable and appealing to use.

In this chapter, we'll show how to write macros using several simple examples. But like much of Rust, macros reward deep understanding, so we'll walk through the design of a more complicated macro that lets us embed JSON literals directly in our programs. But there's more to macros than we can cover in this book, so we'll end with some pointers for further study, both of advanced techniques for the tools we've shown you here, and for an even more powerful facility called *procedural macros*.

Macro Basics

Figure 21-1 shows part of the source code for the `assert_eq!` macro.

`macro_rules!` is the main way to define macros in Rust. Note that there is no `!` after `assert_eq` in this macro definition: the `!` is only included when calling a macro, not when defining it.

Not all macros are defined this way: a few, like `file!`, `line!`, and `macro_rules!` itself, are built into the compiler, and we'll talk about another approach, called procedural macros, at the end of this chapter. But for the most part, we'll focus on `macro_rules!`, which is (so far) the easiest way to write your own.

A macro defined with `macro_rules!` works entirely by pattern matching. The body of a macro is just a series of rules:

```
( pattern1 ) => ( template1 );

( pattern2 ) => ( template2 );

...
```

```
                              pattern        template
                                 /              /
                                /              /
macro_rules! assert_eq {       /              /
    ($left:expr , $right:expr) => ({
        match (&$left, &$right) {
            (left_val, right_val) => {
                if !(*left_val == *right_val) {
                    panic!("assertion failed: `(left == right)` \
                            (left: `{:?}`, right: `{:?}`)",
                            left_val, right_val)
                }
            }
        }
    });
}
```

Figure 21-1. The `assert_eq!` macro

The version of `assert_eq!` in Figure 21-1 has just one pattern and one template.

Incidentally, you can use square brackets or curly braces instead of parentheses around the pattern or the template; it makes no difference to Rust. Likewise, when you call a macro, these are all equivalent:

```
assert_eq!(gcd(6, 10), 2);
assert_eq![gcd(6, 10), 2];
assert_eq!{gcd(6, 10), 2}
```

The only difference is that semicolons are usually optional after curly braces. By convention, we use parentheses when calling `assert_eq!`, square brackets for `vec!`, and curly braces for `macro_rules!`.

Now that we've shown a simple example of a macro's expansion and the definition that generated it, we can get into the details necessary to put this to work:

- We'll explain exactly how Rust goes about finding and expanding macro definitions in your program.
- We'll point out some subtleties inherent in the process of generating code from macro templates.
- Finally, we'll show how patterns handle repetitive structure.

Basics of Macro Expansion

Rust expands macros very early during compilation. The compiler reads your source code from beginning to end, defining and expanding macros as it goes. You can't call a macro before it is defined, because Rust expands each macro call before it even looks at the rest of the program. (By contrast, functions and other items don't have to be in any particular order. It's OK to call a function that won't be defined until later in the crate.)

When Rust expands an `assert_eq!` macro call, what happens is a lot like evaluating a `match` expression. Rust first matches the arguments against the pattern, as shown in Figure 21-2.

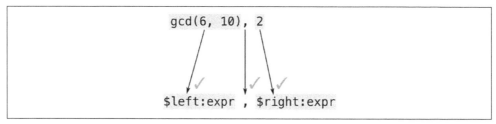

Figure 21-2. Expanding a macro, part 1: pattern-matching the arguments

Macro patterns are a mini-language within Rust. They're essentially regular expressions for matching code. But where regular expressions operate on characters, patterns operate on *tokens*—the numbers, names, punctuation marks, and so forth that are the building blocks of Rust programs. This means you can use comments and whitespace freely in macro patterns to make them as readable as possible. Comments and whitespace aren't tokens, so they don't affect matching.

Another important difference between regular expressions and macro patterns is that parentheses, brackets, and braces always occur in matched pairs in Rust. This is checked before macros are expanded, not only in macro patterns but throughout the language.

In this example, our pattern contains the *fragment* `$left:expr`, which tells Rust to match an expression (in this case, `gcd(6, 10)`) and assign it the name `$left`. Rust then matches the comma in the pattern with the comma following gcd's arguments. Just like regular expressions, patterns have only a few special characters that trigger interesting matching behavior; everything else, like this comma, has to match verbatim or else matching fails. Lastly, Rust matches the expression 2 and gives it the name `$right`.

Both code fragments in this pattern are of type `expr`: they expect expressions. We'll see other types of code fragments in "Fragment Types" on page 613.

Since this pattern matched all of the arguments, Rust expands the corresponding *template* (Figure 21-3).

```
                                    ┌──────────── replace with gcd(6, 10)
                                    │   ┌──────── replace with 2
    {                               │   │
        match (&$left, &$right) {   ▼   ▼
            (left_val, right_val) => {
                if !(*left_val == *right_val) {
                    panic!("assertion failed: `(left == right)` \
                        (left: `{:?}`, right: `{:?}`)",
                        left_val, right_val)
                }
            }
        }
    }
}
```

Figure 21-3. Expanding a macro, part 2: filling in the template

Rust replaces $left and $right with the code fragments it found during matching.

It's a common mistake to include the fragment type in the output template: writing $left:expr rather than just $left. Rust does not immediately detect this kind of error. It sees $left as a substitution, and then it treats :expr just like everything else in the template: tokens to be included in the macro's output. So the errors won't happen until you *call* the macro; then it will generate bogus output that won't compile. If you get error messages like cannot find type `expr` in this scope and help: maybe you meant to use a path separator here when using a new macro, check it for this mistake. ("Debugging Macros" on page 611 offers more general advice for situations like this.)

Macro templates aren't much different from any of a dozen template languages commonly used in web programming. The only difference—and it's a significant one—is that the output is Rust code.

Unintended Consequences

Plugging fragments of code into templates is subtly different from regular code that works with values. These differences aren't always obvious at first. The macro we've been looking at, assert_eq!, contains some slightly strange bits of code for reasons that say a lot about macro programming. Let's look at two funny bits in particular.

First, why does this macro create the variables `left_val` and `right_val`? Is there some reason we can't simplify the template to look like this?

```
if !($left == $right) {
    panic!("assertion failed: `(left == right)` \
            (left: `{:?}`, right: `{:?}`)", $left, $right)
}
```

To answer this question, try mentally expanding the macro call `assert_eq!` `(letters.pop(), Some('z'))`. What would the output be? Naturally, Rust would plug the matched expressions into the template in multiple places. It seems like a bad idea to evaluate the expressions all over again when building the error message, though, and not just because it would take twice as long: since `letters.pop()` removes a value from a vector, it'll produce a different value the second time we call it! That's why the real macro computes `$left` and `$right` only once and stores their values.

Moving on to the second question: why does this macro borrow references to the values of `$left` and `$right`? Why not just store the values in variables, like this?

```
macro_rules! bad_assert_eq {
    ($left:expr, $right:expr) => ({
        match ($left, $right) {
            (left_val, right_val) => {
                if !(left_val == right_val) {
                    panic!("assertion failed" /* ... */);
                }
            }
        }
    });
}
```

For the particular case we've been considering, where the macro arguments are integers, this would work fine. But if the caller passed, say, a `String` variable as `$left` or `$right`, this code would move the value out of the variable!

```
fn main() {
    let s = "a rose".to_string();
    bad_assert_eq!(s, "a rose");
    println!("confirmed: {} is a rose", s);  // error: use of moved value "s"
}
```

Since we don't want assertions to move values, the macro borrows references instead.

(You may have wondered why the macro uses `match` rather than `let` to define the variables. We wondered too. It turns out there's no particular reason for this. `let` would have been equivalent.)

In short, macros can do surprising things. If strange things happen around a macro you've written, it's a good bet that the macro is to blame.

One bug that you *won't* see is this classic C++ macro bug:

```
// buggy C++ macro to add 1 to a number
#define ADD_ONE(n)  n + 1
```

For reasons familiar to most C++ programmers, and not worth explaining fully here, unremarkable code like ADD_ONE(1) * 10 or ADD_ONE(1 << 4) produces very surprising results with this macro. To fix it, you'd add more parentheses to the macro definition. This isn't necessary in Rust, because Rust macros are better integrated with the language. Rust knows when it's handling expressions, so it effectively adds parentheses whenever it pastes one expression into another.

Repetition

The standard vec! macro comes in two forms:

```
// Repeat a value N times
let buffer = vec![0_u8; 1000];

// A list of values, separated by commas
let numbers = vec!["udon", "ramen", "soba"];
```

It can be implemented like this:

```
macro_rules! vec {
    ($elem:expr ; $n:expr) => {
        ::std::vec::from_elem($elem, $n)
    };
    ( $( $x:expr ),* ) => {
        <[_]>::into_vec(Box::new([ $( $x ),* ]))
    };
    ( $( $x:expr ),+ ,) => {
        vec![ $( $x ),* ]
    };
}
```

There are three rules here. We'll explain how multiple rules work and then look at each rule in turn.

When Rust expands a macro call like vec![1, 2, 3], it starts by trying to match the arguments 1, 2, 3 with the pattern for the first rule, in this case $elem:expr ; $n:expr. This fails to match: 1 is an expression, but the pattern requires a semicolon after that, and we don't have one. So Rust then moves on to the second rule, and so on. If no rules match, it's an error.

The first rule handles uses like vec![0u8; 1000]. It happens that there is a standard (but undocumented) function, std::vec::from_elem, that does exactly what's needed here, so this rule is straightforward.

The second rule handles vec!["udon", "ramen", "soba"]. The pattern, $
($x:expr),*, uses a feature we haven't seen before: repetition. It matches 0 or more
expressions, separated by commas. More generally, the syntax $(PATTERN),* is
used to match any comma-separated list, where each item in the list matches
PATTERN.

The * here has the same meaning as in regular expressions ("0 or more") although
admittedly regexps do not have a special ,* repeater. You can also use + to require at
least one match, or ? for zero or one match. Table 21-1 gives the full suite of repetition patterns.

Table 21-1. Repetition patterns

Pattern	Meaning
$(...)*	Match 0 or more times with no separator
$(...),*	Match 0 or more times, separated by commas
$(...);*	Match 0 or more times, separated by semicolons
$(...)+	Match 1 or more times with no separator
$(...),+	Match 1 or more times, separated by commas
$(...);+	Match 1 or more times, separated by semicolons
$(...)?	Match 0 or 1 times with no separator
$(...),?	Match 0 or 1 times, separated by commas
$(...);?	Match 0 or 1 times, separated by semicolons

The code fragment $x is not just a single expression but a list of expressions. The
template for this rule uses repetition syntax too:

```
<[_]>::into_vec(Box::new([ $( $x ),* ]))
```

Again, there are standard methods that do exactly what we need. This code creates a
boxed array and then uses the [T]::into_vec method to convert the boxed array to a
vector.

The first bit, <[_]>, is an unusual way to write the type "slice of something," while
expecting Rust to infer the element type. Types whose names are plain identifiers can
be used in expressions without any fuss, but types like fn(), &str, or [_] must be
wrapped in angle brackets.

Repetition comes in at the end of the template, where we have $($x),*. This $ (...),* is the same syntax we saw in the pattern. It iterates over the list of expressions that we matched for $x and inserts them all into the template, separated by commas.

In this case, the repeated output looks just like the input. But that doesn't have to be the case. We could have written the rule like this:

```
( $( $x:expr ),* ) => {
    {
        let mut v = Vec::new();
        $( v.push($x); )*
        v
    }
};
```

Here, the part of the template that reads $(v.push($x);)* inserts a call to v.push() for each expression in $x. A macro arm can expand to a sequence of expressions, but here we need just a single expression, so we wrap the assembly of the vector in a block.

Unlike the rest of Rust, patterns using $(...),* do not automatically support an optional trailing comma. However, there's a standard trick for supporting trailing commas by adding an extra rule. That is what the third rule of our vec! macro does:

```
( $( $x:expr ),+ ,) => {  // if trailing comma is present,
    vec![ $( $x ),* ]     // retry without it
};
```

We use $(...),+ , to match a list with an extra comma. Then, in the template, we call vec! recursively, leaving the extra comma out. This time the second rule will match.

Built-In Macros

The Rust compiler supplies several macros that are helpful when you're defining your own macros. None of these could be implemented using macro_rules! alone. They're hardcoded in rustc:

file!(), line!(), column!()
 file!() expands to a string literal: the current filename. line!() and column!() expand to u32 literals giving the current line and column (counting from 1).

 If one macro calls another, which calls another, all in different files, and the last macro calls file!(), line!(), or column!(), it will expand to indicate the location of the *first* macro call.

```
stringify!(...tokens...)
```
Expands to a string literal containing the given tokens. The `assert!` macro uses this to generate an error message that includes the code of the assertion.

Macro calls in the argument are *not* expanded: `stringify!(line!())` expands to the string `"line!()"`.

Rust constructs the string from the tokens, so there are no line breaks or comments in the string.

```
concat!(str0, str1, ...)
```
Expands to a single string literal made by concatenating its arguments.

Rust also defines these macros for querying the build environment:

```
cfg!(...)
```
Expands to a Boolean constant, `true` if the current build configuration matches the condition in parentheses. For example, `cfg!(debug_assertions)` is true if you're compiling with debug assertions enabled.

This macro supports exactly the same syntax as the `#[cfg(...)]` attribute described in "Attributes" on page 191 but instead of conditional compilation, you get a true or false answer.

```
env!("VAR_NAME")
```
Expands to a string: the value of the specified environment variable at compile time. If the variable doesn't exist, it's a compilation error.

This would be fairly worthless except that Cargo sets several interesting environment variables when it compiles a crate. For example, to get your crate's current version string, you can write:

```
let version = env!("CARGO_PKG_VERSION");
```

A full list of these environment variables is included in the Cargo documentation (*https://oreil.ly/CQyuz*).

```
option_env!("VAR_NAME")
```
This is the same as `env!` except that it returns an `Option<&'static str>` that is `None` if the specified variable is not set.

Three more built-in macros let you bring in code or data from another file:

```
include!("file.rs")
```
Expands to the contents of the specified file, which must be valid Rust code—either an expression or a sequence of items.

```
include_str!("file.txt")
```
Expands to a &'static str containing the text of the specified file. You can use it like this:

```
const COMPOSITOR_SHADER: &str =
    include_str!("../resources/compositor.glsl");
```

If the file doesn't exist or is not valid UTF-8, you'll get a compilation error.

```
include_bytes!("file.dat")
```
This is the same except the file is treated as binary data, not UTF-8 text. The result is a &'static [u8].

Like all macros, these are processed at compile time. If the file doesn't exist or can't be read, compilation fails. They can't fail at run time. In all cases, if the filename is a relative path, it's resolved relative to the directory that contains the current file.

Rust also provides several convenient macros we haven't covered previously:

```
todo!(), unimplemented!()
```
These are equivalent to panic!(), but convey a different intent. unimplemented!() goes in if clauses, match arms, and other cases that are not yet handled. It always panics. todo!() is much the same, but conveys the idea that this code simply has yet to be written; some IDEs flag it for notice.

```
matches!(value, pattern)
```
Compares a value to a pattern, and returns true if it matches, or false otherwise. It's equivalent to writing:

```
match value {
    pattern => true,
    _ => false
}
```

If you're looking for an exercise in basic macro-writing, this is a good macro to replicate—especially since the real implementation, which you can see in the standard library documentation, is quite simple.

Debugging Macros

Debugging a wayward macro can be challenging. The biggest problem is the lack of visibility into the process of macro expansion. Rust will often expand all macros, find some kind of error, and then print an error message that does not show the fully expanded code that contains the error!

Here are three tools to help troubleshoot macros. (These features are all unstable, but since they're really designed to be used during development, not in code that you'd check in, that isn't a big problem in practice.)

First and simplest, you can ask `rustc` to show what your code looks like after expanding all macros. Use `cargo build --verbose` to see how Cargo is invoking `rustc`. Copy the `rustc` command line and add `-Z unstable-options --pretty expanded` as options. The fully expanded code is dumped to your terminal. Unfortunately, this works only if your code is free of syntax errors.

Second, Rust provides a `log_syntax!()` macro that simply prints its arguments to the terminal at compile time. You can use this for `println!`-style debugging. This macro requires the `#![feature(log_syntax)]` feature flag.

Third, you can ask the Rust compiler to log all macro calls to the terminal. Insert `trace_macros!(true);` somewhere in your code. From that point on, each time Rust expands a macro, it will print the macro name and arguments. For example, consider this program:

```
#![feature(trace_macros)]

fn main() {
    trace_macros!(true);
    let numbers = vec![1, 2, 3];
    trace_macros!(false);
    println!("total: {}", numbers.iter().sum::<u64>());
}
```

It produces this output:

```
$ rustup override set nightly
...
$ rustc trace_example.rs
note: trace_macro
 --> trace_example.rs:5:19
  |
5 |     let numbers = vec![1, 2, 3];
  |                   ^^^^^^^^^^^^^
  |
  = note: expanding `vec! { 1 , 2 , 3 }`
  = note: to `< [ _ ] > :: into_vec ( box [ 1 , 2 , 3 ] )`
```

The compiler shows the code of each macro call, both before and after expansion. The line `trace_macros!(false);` turns tracing off again, so the call to `println!()` is not traced.

Building the json! Macro

We've now discussed the core features of `macro_rules!`. In this section, we'll incrementally develop a macro for building JSON data. We'll use this example to show what it's like to develop a macro, present the few remaining pieces of `macro_rules!`, and offer some advice on how to make sure your macros behave as desired.

Back in Chapter 10, we presented this enum for representing JSON data:

```
#[derive(Clone, PartialEq, Debug)]
enum Json {
    Null,
    Boolean(bool),
    Number(f64),
    String(String),
    Array(Vec<Json>),
    Object(Box<HashMap<String, Json>>)
}
```

The syntax for writing out Json values is unfortunately rather verbose:

```
let students = Json::Array(vec![
    Json::Object(Box::new(vec![
        ("name".to_string(), Json::String("Jim Blandy".to_string())),
        ("class_of".to_string(), Json::Number(1926.0)),
        ("major".to_string(), Json::String("Tibetan throat singing".to_string()))
    ].into_iter().collect())),
    Json::Object(Box::new(vec![
        ("name".to_string(), Json::String("Jason Orendorff".to_string())),
        ("class_of".to_string(), Json::Number(1702.0)),
        ("major".to_string(), Json::String("Knots".to_string()))
    ].into_iter().collect()))
]);
```

We would like to be able to write this using a more JSON-like syntax:

```
let students = json!([
    {
        "name": "Jim Blandy",
        "class_of": 1926,
        "major": "Tibetan throat singing"
    },
    {
        "name": "Jason Orendorff",
        "class_of": 1702,
        "major": "Knots"
    }
]);
```

What we want is a json! macro that takes a JSON value as an argument and expands to a Rust expression like the one in the previous example.

Fragment Types

The first job in writing any complex macro is figuring out how to match, or *parse*, the desired input.

We can already see that the macro will have several rules, because there are several different sorts of things in JSON data: objects, arrays, numbers, and so forth. In fact, we might guess that we'll have one rule for each JSON type:

```
macro_rules! json {
    (null)      => { Json::Null };
    ([ ... ])   => { Json::Array(...) };
    ({ ... })   => { Json::Object(...) };
    (???)       => { Json::Boolean(...) };
    (???)       => { Json::Number(...) };
    (???)       => { Json::String(...) };
}
```

This is not quite correct, as macro patterns offer no way to tease apart the last three cases, but we'll see how to deal with that later. The first three cases, at least, clearly begin with different tokens, so let's start with those.

The first rule already works:

```
macro_rules! json {
    (null) => {
        Json::Null
    }
}

#[test]
fn json_null() {
    assert_eq!(json!(null), Json::Null);  // passes!
}
```

To add support for JSON arrays, we might try matching the elements as exprs:

```
macro_rules! json {
    (null) => {
        Json::Null
    };
    ([ $( $element:expr ),* ]) => {
        Json::Array(vec![ $( $element ),* ])
    };
}
```

Unfortunately, this does not match all JSON arrays. Here's a test that illustrates the problem:

```
#[test]
fn json_array_with_json_element() {
    let macro_generated_value = json!(
        [
            // valid JSON that doesn't match `$element:expr`
            {
                "pitch": 440.0
            }
        ]
    );
    let hand_coded_value =
        Json::Array(vec![
            Json::Object(Box::new(vec![
                ("pitch".to_string(), Json::Number(440.0))
```

```
            ].into_iter().collect()))
        ]);
    assert_eq!(macro_generated_value, hand_coded_value);
}
```

The pattern `$( $element:expr ),*` means "a comma-separated list of Rust expressions." But many JSON values, particularly objects, aren't valid Rust expressions. They won't match.

Since not every bit of code you want to match is an expression, Rust supports several other fragment types, listed in Table 21-2.

Table 21-2. Fragment types supported by `macro_rules!`

Fragment type	Matches (with examples)	Can be followed by...
expr	An expression: `2 + 2, "udon", x.len()`	`=> , ;`
stmt	An expression or declaration, not including any trailing semicolon (hard to use; try expr or block instead)	`=> , ;`
ty	A type: `String, Vec<u8>, (&str, bool), dyn Read + Send`	`=> , ; = | { [ : > as where`
path	A path (discussed on page 183): `ferns, ::std::sync::mpsc`	`=> , ; = | { [ : > as where`
pat	A pattern (discussed on page 241): `_, Some(ref x)`	`=> , = | if in`
item	An item (discussed on page 138): `struct Point { x: f64, y: f64 }, mod ferns;`	Anything
block	A block (discussed on page 137): `{ s += "ok\n"; true }`	Anything
meta	The body of an attribute (discussed on page 191): `inline, derive(Copy, Clone), doc="3D models."`	Anything
literal	A literal value: `1024, "Hello, world!", 1_000_000f64`	Anything
lifetime	A lifetime: `'a, 'item, 'static`	Anything
vis	A visibility specifier: `pub, pub(crate), pub(in module::submodule)`	Anything
ident	An identifier: `std, Json, longish_variable_name`	Anything

Fragment type	Matches (with examples)	Can be followed by...
tt	A token tree (see text): ;, >=, {}, [0 1 (+ 0 1)]	Anything

Most of the options in this table strictly enforce Rust syntax. The `expr` type matches only Rust expressions (not JSON values), `ty` matches only Rust types, and so on. They're not extensible: there's no way to define new arithmetic operators or new keywords that `expr` would recognize. We won't be able to make any of these match arbitrary JSON data.

The last two, `ident` and `tt`, support matching macro arguments that don't look like Rust code. `ident` matches any identifier. `tt` matches a single *token tree*: either a properly matched pair of brackets, `(...)`, `[...]`, or `{...}`, and everything in between, including nested token trees, or a single token that isn't a bracket, like `1926` or `"Knots"`.

Token trees are exactly what we need for our `json!` macro. Every JSON value is a single token tree: numbers, strings, Boolean values, and `null` are all single tokens; objects and arrays are bracketed. So we can write the patterns like this:

```
macro_rules! json {
    (null) => {
        Json::Null
    };
    ([ $( $element:tt ),* ]) => {
        Json::Array(...)
    };
    ({ $( $key:tt : $value:tt ),* }) => {
        Json::Object(...)
    };
    ($other:tt) => {
        ... // TODO: Return Number, String, or Boolean
    };
}
```

This version of the `json!` macro can match all JSON data. Now we just need to produce correct Rust code.

To make sure Rust can gain new syntactic features in the future without breaking any macros you write today, Rust restricts tokens that appear in patterns right after a fragment. The "Can be followed by..." column of Table 21-2 shows which tokens are allowed. For example, the pattern `$x:expr ~ $y:expr` is an error, because `~` isn't allowed after an `expr`. The pattern `$vars:pat => $handler:expr` is OK, because `$vars:pat` is followed by the arrow `=>`, one of the allowed tokens for a `pat`, and `$handler:expr` is followed by nothing, which is always allowed.

Recursion in Macros

You've already seen one trivial case of a macro calling itself: our implementation of `vec!` uses recursion to support trailing commas. Here we can show a more significant example: `json!` needs to call itself recursively.

We might try supporting JSON arrays without using recursion, like this:

```
([ $( $element:tt ),* ]) => {
    Json::Array(vec![ $( $element ),* ])
};
```

But this wouldn't work. We'd be pasting JSON data (the `$element` token trees) right into a Rust expression. They're two different languages.

We need to convert each element of the array from JSON form to Rust. Fortunately, there's a macro that does this: the one we're writing!

```
([ $( $element:tt ),* ]) => {
    Json::Array(vec![ $( json!($element) ),* ])
};
```

Objects can be supported in the same way:

```
({ $( $key:tt : $value:tt ),* }) => {
    Json::Object(Box::new(vec![
        $( ($key.to_string(), json!($value)) ),*
    ].into_iter().collect()))
};
```

The compiler imposes a recursion limit on macros: 64 calls, by default. That's more than enough for normal uses of `json!`, but complex recursive macros sometimes hit the limit. You can adjust it by adding this attribute at the top of the crate where the macro is used:

```
#![recursion_limit = "256"]
```

Our `json!` macro is nearly complete. All that remains is to support Boolean, number, and string values.

Using Traits with Macros

Writing complex macros always poses puzzles. It's important to remember that macros themselves are not the only puzzle-solving tool at your disposal.

Here, we need to support `json!(true)`, `json!(1.0)`, and `json!("yes")`, converting the value, whatever it may be, to the appropriate kind of `Json` value. But macros are not good at distinguishing types. We can imagine writing:

```
macro_rules! json {
    (true) => {
        Json::Boolean(true)
```

```
    };
    (false) => {
        Json::Boolean(false)
    };
    ...
}
```

This approach breaks down right away. There are only two Boolean values, but rather more numbers than that, and even more strings.

Fortunately, there is a standard way to convert values of various types to one specified type: the From trait, covered on page 320. We simply need to implement this trait for a few types:

```
impl From<bool> for Json {
    fn from(b: bool) -> Json {
        Json::Boolean(b)
    }
}

impl From<i32> for Json {
    fn from(i: i32) -> Json {
        Json::Number(i as f64)
    }
}

impl From<String> for Json {
    fn from(s: String) -> Json {
        Json::String(s)
    }
}

impl<'a> From<&'a str> for Json {
    fn from(s: &'a str) -> Json {
        Json::String(s.to_string())
    }
}
...
```

In fact, all 12 numeric types should have very similar implementations, so it might make sense to write a macro, just to avoid the copy and paste:

```
macro_rules! impl_from_num_for_json {
    ( $( $t:ident )* ) => {
        $(
            impl From<$t> for Json {
                fn from(n: $t) -> Json {
                    Json::Number(n as f64)
                }
            }
        )*
    };
}
```

```
impl_from_num_for_json!(u8 i8 u16 i16 u32 i32 u64 i64 u128 i128
                        usize isize f32 f64);
```

Now we can use `Json::from(value)` to convert a `value` of any supported type to Json. In our macro, it'll look like this:

```
( $other:tt ) => {
    Json::from($other)  // Handle Boolean/number/string
};
```

Adding this rule to our `json!` macro makes it pass all the tests we've written so far. Putting together all the pieces, it currently looks like this:

```
macro_rules! json {
    (null) => {
        Json::Null
    };
    ([ $( $element:tt ),* ]) => {
        Json::Array(vec![ $( json!($element) ),* ])
    };
    ({ $( $key:tt : $value:tt ),* }) => {
        Json::Object(Box::new(vec![
            $( ($key.to_string(), json!($value)) ),*
        ].into_iter().collect()))
    };
    ( $other:tt ) => {
        Json::from($other)  // Handle Boolean/number/string
    };
}
```

As it turns out, the macro unexpectedly supports the use of variables and even arbitrary Rust expressions inside the JSON data, a handy extra feature:

```
let width = 4.0;
let desc =
    json!({
        "width": width,
        "height": (width * 9.0 / 4.0)
    });
```

Because `(width * 9.0 / 4.0)` is parenthesized, it's a single token tree, so the macro successfully matches it with `$value:tt` when parsing the object.

Scoping and Hygiene

A surprisingly tricky aspect of writing macros is that they involve pasting code from different scopes together. So the next few pages cover the two ways Rust handles scoping: one way for local variables and arguments, and another way for everything else.

To show why this matters, let's rewrite our rule for parsing JSON objects (the third rule in the json! macro shown previously) to eliminate the temporary vector. We can write it like this:

```
({ $($key:tt : $value:tt),* }) => {
    {
        let mut fields = Box::new(HashMap::new());
        $( fields.insert($key.to_string(), json!($value)); )*
        Json::Object(fields)
    }
};
```

Now we're populating the HashMap not by using collect() but by repeatedly calling the .insert() method. This means we need to store the map in a temporary variable, which we've called fields.

But then what happens if the code that calls json! happens to use a variable of its own, also named fields?

```
let fields = "Fields, W.C.";
let role = json!({
    "name": "Larson E. Whipsnade",
    "actor": fields
});
```

Expanding the macro would paste together two bits of code, both using the name fields for different things!

```
let fields = "Fields, W.C.";
let role = {
    let mut fields = Box::new(HashMap::new());
    fields.insert("name".to_string(), Json::from("Larson E. Whipsnade"));
    fields.insert("actor".to_string(), Json::from(fields));
    Json::Object(fields)
};
```

This may seem like an unavoidable pitfall whenever macros use temporary variables, and you may already be thinking through the possible fixes. Perhaps we should rename the variable that the json! macro defines to something that its callers aren't likely to pass in: instead of fields, we could call it __json$fields.

The surprise here is that *the macro works as is*. Rust renames the variable for you! This feature, first implemented in Scheme macros, is called *hygiene*, and so Rust is said to have *hygienic macros*.

The easiest way to understand macro hygiene is to imagine that every time a macro is expanded, the parts of the expansion that come from the macro itself are painted a different color.

Variables of different colors, then, are treated as if they had different names:

```
let fields = "Fields, W.C.";
let role = {
    let mut fields = Box::new(HashMap::new());
    fields.insert("name".to_string(), Json::from("Larson E. Whipsnade"));
    fields.insert("actor".to_string(), Json::from(fields));
    Json::Object(fields)
};
```

Note that bits of code that were passed in by the macro caller and pasted into the output, such as "name" and "actor", keep their original color (black). Only tokens that originate from the macro template are painted.

Now there's one variable named fields (declared in the caller) and a separate variable named fields (introduced by the macro). Since the names are different colors, the two variables don't get confused.

If a macro really does need to refer to a variable in the caller's scope, the caller has to pass the name of the variable to the macro.

(The paint metaphor isn't meant to be an exact description of how hygiene works. The real mechanism is even a little smarter than that, recognizing two identifiers as the same, regardless of "paint," if they refer to a common variable that's in scope for both the macro and its caller. But cases like this are rare in Rust. If you understand the preceding example, you know enough to use hygienic macros.)

You may have noticed that many other identifiers were painted one or more colors as the macros were expanded: Box, HashMap, and Json, for example. Despite the paint, Rust had no trouble recognizing these type names. That's because hygiene in Rust is limited to local variables and arguments. When it comes to constants, types, methods, modules, statics, and macro names, Rust is "colorblind."

This means that if our json! macro is used in a module where Box, HashMap, or Json is not in scope, the macro won't work. We'll show how to avoid this problem in the next section.

First, we'll consider a case where Rust's strict hygiene gets in the way, and we need to work around it. Suppose we have many functions that contain this line of code:

```
let req = ServerRequest::new(server_socket.session());
```

Copying and pasting that line is a pain. Can we use a macro instead?

```
macro_rules! setup_req {
    () => {
        let req = ServerRequest::new(server_socket.session());
    }
}
```

```
fn handle_http_request(server_socket: &ServerSocket) {
    setup_req!();  // declares `req`, uses `server_socket`
    ... // code that uses `req`
}
```

As written, this doesn't work. It would require the name `server_socket` in the macro to refer to the local `server_socket` declared in the function, and vice versa for the variable `req`. But hygiene prevents names in macros from "colliding" with names in other scopes—even in cases like this, where that's what you want.

The solution is to pass the macro any identifiers you plan on using both inside and outside the macro code:

```
macro_rules! setup_req {
    ($req:ident, $server_socket:ident) => {
        let $req = ServerRequest::new($server_socket.session());
    }
}

fn handle_http_request(server_socket: &ServerSocket) {
    setup_req!(req, server_socket);
    ... // code that uses `req`
}
```

Since `req` and `server_socket` are now provided by the function, they're the right "color" for that scope.

Hygiene makes this macro a little wordier to use, but that's a feature, not a bug: it's easier to reason about hygienic macros knowing that they can't mess with local variables behind your back. If you search for an identifier like `server_socket` in a function, you'll find all the places where it's used, including macro calls.

Importing and Exporting Macros

Since macros are expanded early in compilation, before Rust knows the full module structure of your project, the compiler has special affordances for exporting and importing them.

Macros that are visible in one module are automatically visible in its child modules. To export macros from a module "upward" to its parent module, use the #[macro_use] attribute. For example, suppose our *lib.rs* looks like this:

```
#[macro_use] mod macros;
mod client;
mod server;
```

All macros defined in the `macros` module are imported into *lib.rs* and therefore visible throughout the rest of the crate, including in `client` and `server`.

Macros marked with #[macro_export] are automatically pub and can be referred to by path, like other items.

For example, the lazy_static crate provides a macro called lazy_static, which is marked with #[macro_export]. To use this macro in your own crate, you would write:

```
use lazy_static::lazy_static;
lazy_static!{ }
```

Once a macro is imported, it can be used like any other item:

```
use lazy_static::lazy_static;

mod m {
    crate::lazy_static!{ }
}
```

Of course, actually doing any of these things means your macro may be called in other modules. An exported macro therefore shouldn't rely on anything being in scope—there's no telling what will be in scope where it's used. Even features of the standard prelude can be shadowed.

Instead, the macro should use absolute paths to any names it uses. macro_rules! provides the special fragment $crate to help with this. This is not the same as crate, which is a keyword that can be used in paths anywhere, not just in macros. $crate acts like an absolute path to the root module of the crate where the macro was defined. Instead of saying Json, we can write $crate::Json, which works even if Json was not imported. HashMap can be changed to either ::std::collections::HashMap or $crate::macros::HashMap. In the latter case, we'll have to re-export HashMap, because $crate can't be used to access private features of a crate. It really just expands to something like ::jsonlib, an ordinary path. Visibility rules are unaffected.

After moving the macro to its own module macros and modifying it to use $crate, it looks like this. This is the final version:

```
// macros.rs
pub use std::collections::HashMap;
pub use std::boxed::Box;
pub use std::string::ToString;

#[macro_export]
macro_rules! json {
    (null) => {
        $crate::Json::Null
    };
    ([ $( $element:tt ),* ]) => {
        $crate::Json::Array(vec![ $( json!($element) ),* ])
    };
```

```
({ $( $key:tt : $value:tt ),* }) => {
    {
        let mut fields = $crate::macros::Box::new(
            $crate::macros::HashMap::new());
        $(
            fields.insert($crate::macros::ToString::to_string($key),
                          json!($value));
        )*
        $crate::Json::Object(fields)
    }
};
($other:tt) => {
    $crate::Json::from($other)
};
}
```

Since the `.to_string()` method is part of the standard `ToString` trait, we use `$crate` to refer to that as well, using syntax we introduced in "Fully Qualified Method Calls" on page 274: `$crate::macros::ToString::to_string($key)`. In our case, this isn't strictly necessary to make the macro work, because `ToString` is in the standard prelude. But if you're calling methods of a trait that may not be in scope at the point where the macro is called, a fully qualified method call is the best way to do it.

Avoiding Syntax Errors During Matching

The following macro seems reasonable, but it gives Rust some trouble:

```
macro_rules! complain {
    ($msg:expr) => {
        println!("Complaint filed: {}", $msg)
    };
    (user : $userid:tt , $msg:expr) => {
        println!("Complaint from user {}: {}", $userid, $msg)
    };
}
```

Suppose we call it like this:

```
complain!(user: "jimb", "the AI lab's chatbots keep picking on me");
```

To human eyes, this obviously matches the second pattern. But Rust tries the first rule first, attempting to match all of the input with `$msg:expr`. This is where things start to go badly for us. `user: "jimb"` is not an expression, of course, so we get a syntax error. Rust refuses to sweep a syntax error under the rug—macros are already hard enough to debug. Instead, it's reported immediately and compilation halts.

If any other token in a pattern fails to match, Rust moves on the next rule. Only syntax errors are fatal, and they happen only when trying to match fragments.

The problem here is not so hard to understand: we're attempting to match a fragment, $msg:expr, in the wrong rule. It's not going to match because we're not even supposed to be here. The caller wanted the other rule. There are two easy ways to avoid this.

First, avoid confusable rules. We could, for example, change the macro so that every pattern starts with a different identifier:

```
macro_rules! complain {
    (msg : $msg:expr) => {
        println!("Complaint filed: {}", $msg);
    };
    (user : $userid:tt , msg : $msg:expr) => {
        println!("Complaint from user {}: {}", $userid, $msg);
    };
}
```

When the macro arguments start with msg, we'll get rule 1. When they start with user, we'll get rule 2. Either way, we know we've got the right rule before we try to match a fragment.

The other way to avoid spurious syntax errors is by putting more specific rules first. Putting the user: rule first fixes the problem with complain!, because the rule that causes the syntax error is never reached.

Beyond macro_rules!

Macro patterns can parse input that's even more intricate than JSON, but we've found that the complexity quickly gets out of hand.

The Little Book of Rust Macros (*https://oreil.ly/nZ2HP*), by Daniel Keep et al., is an excellent handbook of advanced macro_rules! programming. The book is clear and smart, and it describes every aspect of macro expansion in more detail than we have here. It also presents several very clever techniques for pressing macro_rules! patterns into service as a sort of esoteric programming language, to parse complex input. This we're less enthusiastic about. Use with care.

Rust 1.15 introduced a separate mechanism called *procedural macros*. Procedural macros support extending the #[derive] attribute to handle custom derivations, as shown in Figure 21-4, as well as creating custom attributes and new macros that are invoked just like the macro_rules! macros discussed earlier.

```
#[derive(Copy, Clone, PartialEq, Eq, IntoJson)]
struct Money {
    dollars: u32,                           custom derive
    cents: u16,
}
```

Figure 21-4. Invoking a hypothetical `IntoJson` procedural macro via a `#[derive]` attribute

There is no `IntoJson` trait, but it doesn't matter: a procedural macro can use this hook to insert whatever code it wants (in this case, probably `impl From<Money> for Json { ... }`).

What makes a procedural macro "procedural" is that it's implemented as a Rust function, not a declarative rule set. This function interacts with the compiler through a thin layer of abstraction and can be arbitrarily complex. For example, the `diesel` database library uses procedural macros to connect to a database and generate code based on the schema of that database at compile time.

Because procedural macros interact with compiler internals, writing effective macros requires an understanding of how the compiler operates that is out of the scope of this book. It is, however, extensively covered in the online documentation (*https://oreil.ly/0xB2x*).

Perhaps, having read all this, you've decided that you hate macros. What then? An alternative is to generate Rust code using a build script. The Cargo documentation (*https://oreil.ly/42irF*) shows how to do it step by step. It involves writing a program that generates the Rust code you want, adding a line to *Cargo.toml* to run that program as part of the build process and using `include!` to get the generated code into your crate.

## CHAPTER 22

Unsafe Code

Let no one think of me that I am humble or weak or passive;
Let them understand I am of a different kind:
dangerous to my enemies, loyal to my friends.
To such a life glory belongs.
   —Euripides, *Medea*

The secret joy of systems programming is that, underneath every single safe language and carefully designed abstraction is a swirling maelstrom of wildly unsafe machine language and bit fiddling. You can write that in Rust, too.

The language we've presented up to this point in the book ensures your programs are free of memory errors and data races entirely automatically, through types, lifetimes, bounds checks, and so on. But this sort of automated reasoning has its limits; there are many valuable techniques that Rust cannot recognize as safe.

Unsafe code lets you tell Rust, "I am opting to use features whose safety you cannot guarantee." By marking off a block or function as unsafe, you acquire the ability to call `unsafe` functions in the standard library, dereference unsafe pointers, and call functions written in other languages like C and C++, among other powers. Rust's other safety checks still apply: type checks, lifetime checks, and bounds checks on indices all occur normally. Unsafe code just enables a small set of additional features.

This ability to step outside the boundaries of safe Rust is what makes it possible to implement many of Rust's most fundamental features in Rust itself, just as C and C++ are used to implement their own standard libraries. Unsafe code is what allows the Vec type to manage its buffer efficiently; the `std::io` module to talk to the operating system; and the `std::thread` and `std::sync` modules to provide concurrency primitives.

This chapter covers the essentials of working with unsafe features:

- Rust's unsafe blocks establish the boundary between ordinary, safe Rust code and code that uses unsafe features.

- You can mark functions as unsafe, alerting callers to the presence of extra contracts they must follow to avoid undefined behavior.

- Raw pointers and their methods allow unconstrained access to memory, and let you build data structures Rust's type system would otherwise forbid. Whereas Rust's references are safe but constrained, raw pointers, as any C or C++ programmer knows, are a powerful, sharp tool.

- Understanding the definition of undefined behavior will help you appreciate why it can have consequences far more serious than just getting incorrect results.

- Unsafe traits, analogous to unsafe functions, impose a contract that each implementation (rather than each caller) must follow.

Unsafe from What?

At the start of this book, we showed a C program that crashes in a surprising way because it fails to follow one of the rules prescribed by the C standard. You can do the same in Rust:

```
$ cat crash.rs
fn main() {
    let mut a: usize = 0;
    let ptr = &mut a as *mut usize;
    unsafe {
        *ptr.offset(3) = 0x7ffff72f484c;
    }
}
$ cargo build
   Compiling unsafe-samples v0.1.0
    Finished debug [unoptimized + debuginfo] target(s) in 0.44s
$ ../../target/debug/crash
crash: Error: .netrc file is readable by others.
crash: Remove password or make file unreadable by others.
Segmentation fault (core dumped)
$
```

This program borrows a mutable reference to the local variable a, casts it to a raw pointer of type *mut usize, and then uses the offset method to produce a pointer three words further along in memory. This happens to be where main's return address is stored. The program overwrites the return address with a constant, such that returning from main behaves in a surprising way. What makes this crash possible is the program's incorrect use of unsafe features—in this case, the ability to dereference raw pointers.

An unsafe feature is one that imposes a *contract*: rules that Rust cannot enforce automatically, but which you must nonetheless follow to avoid *undefined behavior*.

A contract goes beyond the usual type checks and lifetime checks, imposing further rules specific to that unsafe feature. Typically, Rust itself doesn't know about the contract at all; it's just explained in the feature's documentation. For example, the raw pointer type has a contract forbidding you to dereference a pointer that has been advanced beyond the end of its original referent. The expression `*ptr.offset(3) = ...` in this example breaks this contract. But, as the transcript shows, Rust compiles the program without complaint: its safety checks do not detect this violation. When you use unsafe features, you, as the programmer, bear the responsibility for checking that your code adheres to their contracts.

Lots of features have rules you should follow to use them correctly, but such rules are not contracts in the sense we mean here unless the possible consequences include undefined behavior. Undefined behavior is behavior Rust firmly assumes your code could never exhibit. For example, Rust assumes you will not overwrite a function call's return address with something else. Code that passes Rust's usual safety checks and complies with the contracts of the unsafe features it uses cannot possibly do such a thing. Since the program violates the raw pointer contract, its behavior is undefined, and it goes off the rails.

If your code exhibits undefined behavior, you have broken your half of your bargain with Rust, and Rust declines to predict the consequences. Dredging up irrelevant error messages from the depths of system libraries and crashing is one possible consequence; handing control of your computer over to an attacker is another. The effects could vary from one release of Rust to the next, without warning. Sometimes, however, undefined behavior has no visible consequences. For example, if the `main` function never returns (perhaps it calls `std::process::exit` to terminate the program early), then the corrupted return address probably won't matter.

You may only use unsafe features within an `unsafe` block or an `unsafe` function; we'll explain both in the sections that follow. This makes it harder to use unsafe features unknowingly: by forcing you to write an `unsafe` block or function, Rust makes sure you have acknowledged that your code may have additional rules to follow.

Unsafe Blocks

An `unsafe` block looks just like an ordinary Rust block preceded by the `unsafe` keyword, with the difference that you can use unsafe features in the block:

```
unsafe {
    String::from_utf8_unchecked(ascii)
}
```

Without the `unsafe` keyword in front of the block, Rust would object to the use of `from_utf8_unchecked`, which is an `unsafe` function. With the `unsafe` block around it, you can use this code anywhere.

Like an ordinary Rust block, the value of an `unsafe` block is that of its final expression, or `()` if it doesn't have one. The call to `String::from_utf8_unchecked` shown earlier provides the value of the block.

An `unsafe` block unlocks five additional options for you:

- You can call `unsafe` functions. Each `unsafe` function must specify its own contract, depending on its purpose.

- You can dereference raw pointers. Safe code can pass raw pointers around, compare them, and create them by conversion from references (or even from integers), but only unsafe code can actually use them to access memory. We'll cover raw pointers in detail and explain how to use them safely in "Raw Pointers" on page 640.

- You can access the fields of `unions`, which the compiler can't be sure contain valid bit patterns for their respective types.

- You can access mutable `static` variables. As explained in "Global Variables" on page 537, Rust can't be sure when threads are using mutable `static` variables, so their contract requires you to ensure all access is properly synchronized.

- You can access functions and variables declared through Rust's foreign function interface. These are considered `unsafe` even when immutable, since they are visible to code written in other languages that may not respect Rust's safety rules.

Restricting unsafe features to `unsafe` blocks doesn't really prevent you from doing whatever you want. It's perfectly possible to just stick an `unsafe` block into your code and move on. The benefit of the rule lies mainly in drawing human attention to code whose safety Rust can't guarantee:

- You won't accidentally use unsafe features and then discover you were responsible for contracts you didn't even know existed.

- An `unsafe` block attracts more attention from reviewers. Some projects even have automation to ensure this, flagging code changes that affect `unsafe` blocks for special attention.

- When you're considering writing an `unsafe` block, you can take a moment to ask yourself whether your task really requires such measures. If it's for performance, do you have measurements to show that this is actually a bottleneck? Perhaps there is a good way to accomplish the same thing in safe Rust.

Example: An Efficient ASCII String Type

Here's the definition of `Ascii`, a string type that ensures its contents are always valid ASCII. This type uses an unsafe feature to provide zero-cost conversion into `String`:

```rust
mod my_ascii {
    /// An ASCII-encoded string.
    #[derive(Debug, Eq, PartialEq)]
    pub struct Ascii(
        // This must hold only well-formed ASCII text:
        // bytes from `0` to `0x7f`.
        Vec<u8>
    );

    impl Ascii {
        /// Create an `Ascii` from the ASCII text in `bytes`. Return a
        /// `NotAsciiError` error if `bytes` contains any non-ASCII
        /// characters.
        pub fn from_bytes(bytes: Vec<u8>) -> Result<Ascii, NotAsciiError> {
            if bytes.iter().any(|&byte| !byte.is_ascii()) {
                return Err(NotAsciiError(bytes));
            }
            Ok(Ascii(bytes))
        }
    }

    // When conversion fails, we give back the vector we couldn't convert.
    // This should implement `std::error::Error`; omitted for brevity.
    #[derive(Debug, Eq, PartialEq)]
    pub struct NotAsciiError(pub Vec<u8>);

    // Safe, efficient conversion, implemented using unsafe code.
    impl From<Ascii> for String {
        fn from(ascii: Ascii) -> String {
            // If this module has no bugs, this is safe, because
            // well-formed ASCII text is also well-formed UTF-8.
            unsafe { String::from_utf8_unchecked(ascii.0) }
        }
    }
    ...
}
```

The key to this module is the definition of the `Ascii` type. The type itself is marked `pub`, to make it visible outside the `my_ascii` module. But the type's `Vec<u8>` element is *not* public, so only the `my_ascii` module can construct an `Ascii` value or refer to its element. This leaves the module's code in complete control over what may or may not appear there. As long as the public constructors and methods ensure that freshly created `Ascii` values are well-formed and remain so throughout their lives, then the rest of the program cannot violate that rule. And indeed, the public constructor `Ascii::from_bytes` carefully checks the vector it's given before agreeing to construct an `Ascii` from it. For brevity's sake, we don't show any methods, but you can imagine a set of text-handling methods that ensure `Ascii` values always contain proper ASCII text, just as a `String`'s methods ensure that its contents remain well-formed UTF-8.

This arrangement lets us implement `From<Ascii>` for `String` very efficiently. The unsafe function `String::from_utf8_unchecked` takes a byte vector and builds a `String` from it without checking whether its contents are well-formed UTF-8 text; the function's contract holds its caller responsible for that. Fortunately, the rules enforced by the `Ascii` type are exactly what we need to satisfy `from_utf8_unchecked`'s contract. As we explained in "UTF-8" on page 430, any block of ASCII text is also well-formed UTF-8, so an `Ascii`'s underlying `Vec<u8>` is immediately ready to serve as a `String`'s buffer.

With these definitions in place, you can write:

```
use my_ascii::Ascii;

let bytes: Vec<u8> = b"ASCII and ye shall receive".to_vec();

// This call entails no allocation or text copies, just a scan.
let ascii: Ascii = Ascii::from_bytes(bytes)
    .unwrap(); // We know these chosen bytes are ok.

// This call is zero-cost: no allocation, copies, or scans.
let string = String::from(ascii);

assert_eq!(string, "ASCII and ye shall receive");
```

No `unsafe` blocks are required to use `Ascii`. We have implemented a safe interface using unsafe operations and arranged to meet their contracts depending only on the module's own code, not on its users' behavior.

An `Ascii` is nothing more than a wrapper around a `Vec<u8>`, hidden inside a module that enforces extra rules about its contents. A type of this sort is called a *newtype*, a common pattern in Rust. Rust's own `String` type is defined in exactly the same way, except that its contents are restricted to be UTF-8, not ASCII. In fact, here's the definition of `String` from the standard library:

```
pub struct String {
    vec: Vec<u8>,
}
```

At the machine level, with Rust's types out of the picture, a newtype and its element have identical representations in memory, so constructing a newtype doesn't require any machine instructions at all. In `Ascii::from_bytes`, the expression `Ascii(bytes)` simply deems the `Vec<u8>`'s representation to now hold an `Ascii` value. Similarly, `String::from_utf8_unchecked` probably requires no machine instructions when inlined: the `Vec<u8>` is now considered to be a `String`.

Unsafe Functions

An `unsafe` function definition looks like an ordinary function definition preceded by the `unsafe` keyword. The body of an `unsafe` function is automatically considered an `unsafe` block.

You may call `unsafe` functions only within `unsafe` blocks. This means that marking a function `unsafe` warns its callers that the function has a contract they must satisfy to avoid undefined behavior.

For example, here's a new constructor for the `Ascii` type we introduced before that builds an `Ascii` from a byte vector without checking if its contents are valid ASCII:

```
// This must be placed inside the `my_ascii` module.
impl Ascii {
    /// Construct an `Ascii` value from `bytes`, without checking
    /// whether `bytes` actually contains well-formed ASCII.
    ///
    /// This constructor is infallible, and returns an `Ascii` directly,
    /// rather than a `Result<Ascii, NotAsciiError>` as the `from_bytes`
    /// constructor does.
    ///
    /// # Safety
    ///
    /// The caller must ensure that `bytes` contains only ASCII
    /// characters: bytes no greater than 0x7f. Otherwise, the effect is
    /// undefined.
    pub unsafe fn from_bytes_unchecked(bytes: Vec<u8>) -> Ascii {
        Ascii(bytes)
    }
}
```

Presumably, code calling `Ascii::from_bytes_unchecked` already knows somehow that the vector in hand contains only ASCII characters, so the check that `Ascii::from_bytes` insists on carrying out would be a waste of time, and the caller would have to write code to handle `Err` results that it knows will never occur.

`Ascii::from_bytes_unchecked` lets such a caller sidestep the checks and the error handling.

But earlier we emphasized the importance of `Ascii`'s public constructors and methods ensuring that `Ascii` values are well-formed. Doesn't `from_bytes_unchecked` fail to meet that responsibility?

Not quite: `from_bytes_unchecked` meets its obligations by passing them on to its caller via its contract. The presence of this contract is what makes it correct to mark this function `unsafe`: despite the fact that the function itself carries out no unsafe operations, its callers must follow rules Rust cannot enforce automatically to avoid undefined behavior.

Can you really cause undefined behavior by breaking the contract of `Ascii::from_bytes_unchecked`? Yes. You can construct a `String` holding ill-formed UTF-8 as follows:

```
// Imagine that this vector is the result of some complicated process
// that we expected to produce ASCII. Something went wrong!
let bytes = vec![0xf7, 0xbf, 0xbf, 0xbf];

let ascii = unsafe {
    // This unsafe function's contract is violated
    // when `bytes` holds non-ASCII bytes.
    Ascii::from_bytes_unchecked(bytes)
};

let bogus: String = ascii.into();

// `bogus` now holds ill-formed UTF-8. Parsing its first character produces
// a `char` that is not a valid Unicode code point. That's undefined
// behavior, so the language doesn't say how this assertion should behave.
assert_eq!(bogus.chars().next().unwrap() as u32, 0x1fffff);
```

In certain versions of Rust, on certain platforms, this assertion was observed to fail with the following entertaining error message:

```
thread 'main' panicked at 'assertion failed: `(left == right)`
  left: `2097151`,
 right: `2097151`', src/main.rs:42:5
```

Those two numbers seem equal to us, but this is not Rust's fault; it's the fault of the previous `unsafe` block. When we say that undefined behavior leads to unpredictable results, this is the kind of thing we mean.

This illustrates two critical facts about bugs and unsafe code:

- *Bugs that occur before the `unsafe` block can break contracts.* Whether an `unsafe` block causes undefined behavior can depend not just on the code in the block itself, but also on the code that supplies the values it operates on. Everything that your `unsafe` code relies on to satisfy contracts is safety-critical. The conversion from `Ascii` to `String` based on `String::from_utf8_unchecked` is well-defined only if the rest of the module properly maintains `Ascii`'s invariants.

- *The consequences of breaking a contract may appear after you leave the `unsafe` block.* The undefined behavior courted by failing to comply with an unsafe feature's contract often does not occur within the `unsafe` block itself. Constructing a bogus `String` as shown before may not cause problems until much later in the program's execution.

Essentially, Rust's type checker, borrow checker, and other static checks are inspecting your program and trying to construct proof that it cannot exhibit undefined behavior. When Rust compiles your program successfully, that means it succeeded in proving your code sound. An `unsafe` block is a gap in this proof: "This code," you are saying to Rust, "is fine, trust me." Whether your claim is true could depend on any part of the program that influences what happens in the `unsafe` block, and the consequences of being wrong could appear anywhere influenced by the `unsafe` block. Writing the `unsafe` keyword amounts to a reminder that you are not getting the full benefit of the language's safety checks.

Given the choice, you should naturally prefer to create safe interfaces, without contracts. These are much easier to work with, since users can count on Rust's safety checks to ensure their code is free of undefined behavior. Even if your implementation uses unsafe features, it's best to use Rust's types, lifetimes, and module system to meet their contracts while using only what you can guarantee yourself, rather than passing responsibilities on to your callers.

Unfortunately, it's not unusual to come across unsafe functions in the wild whose documentation does not bother to explain their contracts. You are expected to infer the rules yourself, based on your experience and knowledge of how the code behaves. If you've ever uneasily wondered whether what you're doing with a C or C++ API is OK, then you know what that's like.

Unsafe Block or Unsafe Function?

You may find yourself wondering whether to use an `unsafe` block or just mark the whole function unsafe. The approach we recommend is to first make a decision about the function:

- If it's possible to misuse the function in a way that compiles fine but still causes undefined behavior, you must mark it as unsafe. The rules for using the function correctly are its contract; the existence of a contract is what makes the function unsafe.

- Otherwise, the function is safe: no well-typed call to it can cause undefined behavior. It should not be marked `unsafe`.

Whether the function uses unsafe features in its body is irrelevant; what matters is the presence of a contract. Before, we showed an unsafe function that uses no unsafe features, and a safe function that does use unsafe features.

Don't mark a safe function `unsafe` just because you use unsafe features in its body. This makes the function harder to use and confuses readers who will (correctly) expect to find a contract explained somewhere. Instead, use an `unsafe` block, even if it's the function's entire body.

Undefined Behavior

In the introduction, we said that the term *undefined behavior* means "behavior that Rust firmly assumes your code could never exhibit." This is a strange turn of phrase, especially since we know from our experience with other languages that these behaviors *do* occur by accident with some frequency. Why is this concept helpful in setting out the obligations of unsafe code?

A compiler is a translator from one programming language to another. The Rust compiler takes a Rust program and translates it into an equivalent machine language program. But what does it mean to say that two programs in such completely different languages are equivalent?

Fortunately, this question is easier for programmers than it is for linguists. We usually say that two programs are equivalent if they will always have the same visible behavior when executed: they make the same system calls, interact with foreign libraries in equivalent ways, and so on. It's a bit like a Turing test for programs: if you can't tell whether you're interacting with the original or the translation, then they're equivalent.

Now consider the following code:

```
let i = 10;
very_trustworthy(&i);
println!("{}", i * 100);
```

Even knowing nothing about the definition of `very_trustworthy`, we can see that it receives only a shared reference to `i`, so the call cannot change `i`'s value. Since the value passed to `println!` will always be 1000, Rust can translate this code into machine language as if we had written:

```
very_trustworthy(&10);
println!("{}", 1000);
```

This transformed version has the same visible behavior as the original, and it's probably a bit faster. But it makes sense to consider the performance of this version only if we agree it has the same meaning as the original. What if `very_trustworthy` were defined as follows?

```
fn very_trustworthy(shared: &i32) {
    unsafe {
        // Turn the shared reference into a mutable pointer.
        // This is undefined behavior.
        let mutable = shared as *const i32 as *mut i32;
        *mutable = 20;
    }
}
```

This code breaks the rules for shared references: it changes the value of i to 20, even though it should be frozen because i is borrowed for sharing. As a result, the transformation we made to the caller now has a very visible effect: if Rust transforms the code, the program prints 1000; if it leaves the code alone and uses the new value of i, it prints 2000. Breaking the rules for shared references in `very_trustworthy` means that shared references won't behave as expected in its callers.

This sort of problem arises with almost every kind of transformation Rust might attempt. Even inlining a function into its call site assumes, among other things, that when the callee finishes, control flow returns to the call site. But we opened the chapter with an example of ill-behaved code that violates even that assumption.

It's basically impossible for Rust (or any other language) to assess whether a transformation to a program preserves its meaning unless it can trust the fundamental features of the language to behave as designed. And whether they do or not can depend not just on the code at hand, but on other, potentially distant, parts of the program. In order to do anything at all with your code, Rust must assume that the rest of your program is well-behaved.

Here, then, are Rust's rules for well-behaved programs:

- The program must not read uninitialized memory.
- The program must not create invalid primitive values:
  — References, boxes, or fn pointers that are null
  — bool values that are not either a 0 or 1
  — enum values with invalid discriminant values
  — char values that are not valid, nonsurrogate Unicode code points
  — str values that are not well-formed UTF-8
  — Fat pointers with invalid vtables/slice lengths
  — Any value of the "never" type, written !, for functions that don't return

- The rules for references explained in Chapter 5 must be followed. No reference may outlive its referent; shared access is read-only access; and mutable access is exclusive access.

- The program must not dereference null, incorrectly aligned, or dangling pointers.

- The program must not use a pointer to access memory outside the allocation with which the pointer is associated. We will explain this rule in detail in "Dereferencing Raw Pointers Safely" on page 643.

- The program must be free of data races. A data race occurs when two threads access the same memory location without synchronization, and at least one of the accesses is a write.

- The program must not unwind across a call made from another language, via the foreign function interface, as explained in "Unwinding" on page 158.

- The program must comply with the contracts of standard library functions.

Since we don't yet have a thorough model of Rust's semantics for `unsafe` code, this list will probably evolve over time, but these are likely to remain forbidden.

Any violation of these rules constitutes undefined behavior and renders Rust's efforts to optimize your program and translate it into machine language untrustworthy. If you break the last rule and pass ill-formed UTF-8 to `String::from_utf8_unchecked`, perhaps 2097151 is not so equal to 2097151 after all.

Rust code that does not use unsafe features is guaranteed to follow all of the preceding rules, once it compiles (assuming the compiler has no bugs; we're getting there, but the curve will never intersect the asymptote). Only when you use unsafe features do these rules become your responsibility.

In C and C++, the fact that your program compiles without errors or warnings means much less; as we mentioned in the introduction to this book, even the best C and C++ programs written by well-respected projects that hold their code to high standards exhibit undefined behavior in practice.

Unsafe Traits

An *unsafe trait* is a trait that has a contract Rust cannot check or enforce that implementers must satisfy to avoid undefined behavior. To implement an unsafe trait, you must mark the implementation as unsafe. It is up to you to understand the trait's contract and make sure your type satisfies it.

A function that bounds its type variables with an unsafe trait is typically one that uses unsafe features itself, and satisfies their contracts only by depending on the unsafe trait's contract. An incorrect implementation of the trait could cause such a function to exhibit undefined behavior.

`std::marker::Send` and `std::marker::Sync` are the classic examples of unsafe traits. These traits don't define any methods, so they're trivial to implement for any type you like. But they do have contracts: `Send` requires implementers to be safe to move to another thread, and `Sync` requires them to be safe to share among threads via shared references. Implementing `Send` for an inappropriate type, for example, would make `std::sync::Mutex` no longer safe from data races.

As a simple example, the Rust standard library used to include an unsafe trait, `core::nonzero::Zeroable`, for types that can be safely initialized by setting all their bytes to zero. Clearly, zeroing a `usize` is fine, but zeroing a `&T` gives you a null reference, which will cause a crash if dereferenced. For types that were `Zeroable`, some optimizations were possible: you could initialize an array of them quickly with `std::ptr::write_bytes` (Rust's equivalent of `memset`) or use operating system calls that allocate zeroed pages. (`Zeroable` was unstable and moved to internal-only use in the `num` crate in Rust 1.26, but it's a good, simple, real-world example.)

`Zeroable` was a typical marker trait, lacking methods or associated types:

```
pub unsafe trait Zeroable {}
```

The implementations for appropriate types were similarly straightforward:

```
unsafe impl Zeroable for u8 {}
unsafe impl Zeroable for i32 {}
unsafe impl Zeroable for usize {}
// and so on for all the integer types
```

With these definitions, we could write a function that quickly allocates a vector of a given length containing a `Zeroable` type:

```
use core::nonzero::Zeroable;

fn zeroed_vector<T>(len: usize) -> Vec<T>
    where T: Zeroable
{
    let mut vec = Vec::with_capacity(len);
    unsafe {
        std::ptr::write_bytes(vec.as_mut_ptr(), 0, len);
        vec.set_len(len);
    }
    vec
}
```

This function starts by creating an empty `Vec` with the required capacity and then calls `write_bytes` to fill the unoccupied buffer with zeros. (The `write_byte` function treats `len` as a number of `T` elements, not a number of bytes, so this call does fill the entire buffer.) A vector's `set_len` method changes its length without doing anything to the buffer; this is unsafe, because you must ensure that the newly enclosed buffer space actually contains properly initialized values of type T. But this is exactly what the `T: Zeroable` bound establishes: a block of zero bytes represents a valid T value. Our use of `set_len` was safe.

Here, we put it to use:

```
let v: Vec<usize> = zeroed_vector(100_000);
assert!(v.iter().all(|&u| u == 0));
```

Clearly, `Zeroable` must be an unsafe trait, since an implementation that doesn't respect its contract can lead to undefined behavior:

```
struct HoldsRef<'a>(&'a mut i32);

unsafe impl<'a> Zeroable for HoldsRef<'a> { }

let mut v: Vec<HoldsRef> = zeroed_vector(1);
*v[0].0 = 1;    // crashes: dereferences null pointer
```

Rust has no idea what `Zeroable` is meant to signify, so it can't tell when it's being implemented for an inappropriate type. As with any other unsafe feature, it's up to you to understand and adhere to an unsafe trait's contract.

Note that unsafe code must not depend on ordinary, safe traits being implemented correctly. For example, suppose there were an implementation of the `std::hash::Hasher` trait that simply returned a random hash value, with no relation to the values being hashed. The trait requires that hashing the same bits twice must produce the same hash value, but this implementation doesn't meet that requirement; it's simply incorrect. But because `Hasher` is not an unsafe trait, unsafe code must not exhibit undefined behavior when it uses this hasher. The `std::collections::HashMap` type is carefully written to respect the contracts of the unsafe features it uses regardless of how the hasher behaves. Certainly, the table won't function correctly: lookups will fail, and entries will appear and disappear at random. But the table will not exhibit undefined behavior.

Raw Pointers

A *raw pointer* in Rust is an unconstrained pointer. You can use raw pointers to form all sorts of structures that Rust's checked pointer types cannot, like doubly linked lists or arbitrary graphs of objects. But because raw pointers are so flexible, Rust cannot tell whether you are using them safely or not, so you can dereference them only in an `unsafe` block.

Raw pointers are essentially equivalent to C or C++ pointers, so they're also useful for interacting with code written in those languages.

There are two kinds of raw pointers:

- A *mut T is a raw pointer to a T that permits modifying its referent.
- A *const T is a raw pointer to a T that only permits reading its referent.

(There is no plain *T type; you must always specify either const or mut.)

You can create a raw pointer by conversion from a reference, and dereference it with the * operator:

```
let mut x = 10;
let ptr_x = &mut x as *mut i32;

let y = Box::new(20);
let ptr_y = &*y as *const i32;

unsafe {
    *ptr_x += *ptr_y;
}
assert_eq!(x, 30);
```

Unlike boxes and references, raw pointers can be null, like NULL in C or nullptr in C++:

```
fn option_to_raw<T>(opt: Option<&T>) -> *const T {
    match opt {
        None => std::ptr::null(),
        Some(r) => r as *const T
    }
}

assert!(!option_to_raw(Some(&("pea", "pod"))).is_null());
assert_eq!(option_to_raw::<i32>(None), std::ptr::null());
```

This example has no unsafe blocks: creating raw pointers, passing them around, and comparing them are all safe. Only dereferencing a raw pointer is unsafe.

A raw pointer to an unsized type is a fat pointer, just as the corresponding reference or Box type would be. A *const [u8] pointer includes a length along with the address, and a trait object like a *mut dyn std::io::Write pointer carries a vtable.

Although Rust implicitly dereferences safe pointer types in various situations, raw pointer dereferences must be explicit:

- The . operator will not implicitly dereference a raw pointer; you must write (*raw).field or (*raw).method(...).
- Raw pointers do not implement Deref, so deref coercions do not apply to them.

- Operators like == and < compare raw pointers as addresses: two raw pointers are equal if they point to the same location in memory. Similarly, hashing a raw pointer hashes the address it points to, not the value of its referent.

- Formatting traits like `std::fmt::Display` follow references automatically, but don't handle raw pointers at all. The exceptions are `std::fmt::Debug` and `std::fmt::Pointer`, which show raw pointers as hexadecimal addresses, without dereferencing them.

Unlike the + operator in C and C++, Rust's + does not handle raw pointers, but you can perform pointer arithmetic via their `offset` and `wrapping_offset` methods, or the more convenient `add`, `sub`, `wrapping_add`, and `wrapping_sub` methods. Inversely, the `offset_from` method gives the distance between two pointers in bytes, though we're responsible for making sure the beginning and end are in the same memory region (the same `Vec`, for instance):

```
let trucks = vec!["garbage truck", "dump truck", "moonstruck"];
let first: *const &str = &trucks[0];
let last: *const &str = &trucks[2];
assert_eq!(unsafe { last.offset_from(first) }, 2);
assert_eq!(unsafe { first.offset_from(last) }, -2);
```

No explicit conversion is needed for `first` and `last`; just specifying the type is enough. Rust implicitly coerces references to raw pointers (but not the other way around, of course).

The `as` operator permits almost every plausible conversion from references to raw pointers or between two raw pointer types. However, you may need to break up a complex conversion into a series of simpler steps. For example:

```
&vec![42_u8] as *const String;  // error: invalid conversion
&vec![42_u8] as *const Vec<u8> as *const String;  // permitted
```

Note that `as` will not convert raw pointers to references. Such conversions would be unsafe, and `as` should remain a safe operation. Instead, you must dereference the raw pointer (in an `unsafe` block) and then borrow the resulting value.

Be very careful when you do this: a reference produced this way has an unconstrained lifetime: there's no limit on how long it can live, since the raw pointer gives Rust nothing to base such a decision on. In "A Safe Interface to libgit2" on page 681 later in this chapter, we show several examples of how to properly constrain lifetimes.

Many types have `as_ptr` and `as_mut_ptr` methods that return a raw pointer to their contents. For example, array slices and strings return pointers to their first elements, and some iterators return a pointer to the next element they will produce. Owning pointer types like `Box`, `Rc`, and `Arc` have `into_raw` and `from_raw` functions that convert to and from raw pointers. Some of these methods' contracts impose surprising requirements, so check their documentation before using them.

You can also construct raw pointers by conversion from integers, although the only integers you can trust for this are generally those you got from a pointer in the first place. "Example: RefWithFlag" on page 644 uses raw pointers this way.

Unlike references, raw pointers are neither Send nor Sync. As a result, any type that includes raw pointers does not implement these traits by default. There is nothing inherently unsafe about sending or sharing raw pointers between threads; after all, wherever they go, you still need an unsafe block to dereference them. But given the roles raw pointers typically play, the language designers considered this behavior to be the more helpful default. We already discussed how to implement Send and Sync yourself in "Unsafe Traits" on page 638.

Dereferencing Raw Pointers Safely

Here are some common-sense guidelines for using raw pointers safely:

- Dereferencing null pointers or dangling pointers is undefined behavior, as is referring to uninitialized memory or values that have gone out of scope.

- Dereferencing pointers that are not properly aligned for their referent type is undefined behavior.

- You may borrow values out of a dereferenced raw pointer only if doing so obeys the rules for reference safety explained in Chapter 5: no reference may outlive its referent, shared access is read-only access, and mutable access is exclusive access. (This rule is easy to violate by accident, since raw pointers are often used to create data structures with nonstandard sharing or ownership.)

- You may use a raw pointer's referent only if it is a well-formed value of its type. For example, you must ensure that dereferencing a *const char yields a proper, nonsurrogate Unicode code point.

- You may use the offset and wrapping_offset methods on raw pointers only to point to bytes within the variable or heap-allocated block of memory that the original pointer referred to, or to the first byte beyond such a region.

    If you do pointer arithmetic by converting the pointer to an integer, doing arithmetic on the integer, and then converting it back to a pointer, the result must be a pointer that the rules for the offset method would have allowed you to produce.

- If you assign to a raw pointer's referent, you must not violate the invariants of any type of which the referent is a part. For example, if you have a *mut u8 pointing to a byte of a String, you may only store values in that u8 that leave the String holding well-formed UTF-8.

The borrowing rule aside, these are essentially the same rules you must follow when using pointers in C or C++.

The reason for not violating types' invariants should be clear. Many of Rust's standard types use unsafe code in their implementation, but still provide safe interfaces on the assumption that Rust's safety checks, module system, and visibility rules will be respected. Using raw pointers to circumvent these protective measures can lead to undefined behavior.

The complete, exact contract for raw pointers is not easily stated and may change as the language evolves. But the principles outlined here should keep you in safe territory.

Example: RefWithFlag

Here's an example of how to take a classic[1] bit-level hack made possible by raw pointers and wrap it up as a completely safe Rust type. This module defines a type, RefWithFlag<'a, T>, that holds both a &'a T and a bool, like the tuple (&'a T, bool) and yet still manages to occupy only one machine word instead of two. This sort of technique is used regularly in garbage collectors and virtual machines, where certain types—say, the type representing an object—are so numerous that adding even a single word to each value would drastically increase memory use:

```
mod ref_with_flag {
    use std::marker::PhantomData;
    use std::mem::align_of;

    /// A `&T` and a `bool`, wrapped up in a single word.
    /// The type `T` must require at least two-byte alignment.
    ///
    /// If you're the kind of programmer who's never met a pointer whose
    /// 2⁰-bit you didn't want to steal, well, now you can do it safely!
    /// ("But it's not nearly as exciting this way...")
    pub struct RefWithFlag<'a, T> {
        ptr_and_bit: usize,
        behaves_like: PhantomData<&'a T> // occupies no space
    }

    impl<'a, T: 'a> RefWithFlag<'a, T> {
        pub fn new(ptr: &'a T, flag: bool) -> RefWithFlag<T> {
            assert!(align_of::<T>() % 2 == 0);
            RefWithFlag {
                ptr_and_bit: ptr as *const T as usize | flag as usize,
                behaves_like: PhantomData
            }
        }
    }
```

---

1 Well, it's a classic where we come from.

```
pub fn get_ref(&self) -> &'a T {
    unsafe {
        let ptr = (self.ptr_and_bit & !1) as *const T;
        &*ptr
    }
}

pub fn get_flag(&self) -> bool {
    self.ptr_and_bit & 1 != 0
}
}
}
```

This code takes advantage of the fact that many types must be placed at even addresses in memory: since an even address's least significant bit is always zero, we can store something else there and then reliably reconstruct the original address just by masking off the bottom bit. Not all types qualify; for example, the types u8 and (bool, [i8; 2]) can be placed at any address. But we can check the type's alignment on construction and refuse types that won't work.

You can use RefWithFlag like this:

```
use ref_with_flag::RefWithFlag;

let vec = vec![10, 20, 30];
let flagged = RefWithFlag::new(&vec, true);
assert_eq!(flagged.get_ref()[1], 20);
assert_eq!(flagged.get_flag(), true);
```

The constructor RefWithFlag::new takes a reference and a bool value, asserts that the reference's type is suitable, and then converts the reference to a raw pointer and then a usize. The usize type is defined to be large enough to hold a pointer on whatever processor we're compiling for, so converting a raw pointer to a usize and back is well-defined. Once we have a usize, we know it must be even, so we can use the | bitwise-or operator to combine it with the bool, which we've converted to an integer 0 or 1.

The get_flag method extracts the bool component of a RefWithFlag. It's simple: just mask off the bottom bit and check if it's nonzero.

The get_ref method extracts the reference from a RefWithFlag. First, it masks off the usize's bottom bit and converts it to a raw pointer. The as operator will not convert raw pointers to references, but we can dereference the raw pointer (in an unsafe block, naturally) and borrow that. Borrowing a raw pointer's referent gives you a reference with an unbounded lifetime: Rust will accord the reference whatever lifetime would make the code around it check, if there is one. Usually, though, there is some specific lifetime that is more accurate and would thus catch more mistakes. In this case, since `get_ref`'s return type is `&'a T`, Rust sees that the reference's lifetime is the same as RefWithFlag's lifetime parameter `'a`, which is just what we want: that's the lifetime of the reference we started with.

In memory, a `RefWithFlag` looks just like a `usize`: since `PhantomData` is a zero-sized type, the `behaves_like` field takes up no space in the structure. But the `PhantomData` is necessary for Rust to know how to treat lifetimes in code that uses `RefWithFlag`. Imagine what the type would look like without the `behaves_like` field:

```
// This won't compile.
pub struct RefWithFlag<'a, T: 'a> {
    ptr_and_bit: usize
}
```

In Chapter 5, we pointed out that any structure containing references must not outlive the values they borrow, lest the references become dangling pointers. The structure must abide by the restrictions that apply to its fields. This certainly applies to `RefWithFlag`: in the example code we just looked at, `flagged` must not outlive `vec`, since `flagged.get_ref()` returns a reference to it. But our reduced `RefWithFlag` type contains no references at all and never uses its lifetime parameter `'a`. It's just a `usize`. How should Rust know that any restrictions apply to `flagged`'s lifetime? Including a `PhantomData<&'a T>` field tells Rust to treat `RefWithFlag<'a, T>` *as if* it contained a `&'a T`, without actually affecting the struct's representation.

Although Rust doesn't really know what's going on (that's what makes `RefWithFlag` unsafe), it will do its best to help you out with this. If you omit the `behaves_like` field, Rust will complain that the parameters `'a` and `T` are unused and suggest using a `PhantomData`.

`RefWithFlag` uses the same tactics as the `Ascii` type we presented earlier to avoid undefined behavior in its `unsafe` block. The type itself is `pub`, but its fields are not, meaning that only code within the `ref_with_flag` module can create or look inside a `RefWithFlag` value. You don't have to inspect much code to have confidence that the `ptr_and_bit` field is well constructed.

Nullable Pointers

A null raw pointer in Rust is a zero address, just as in C and C++. For any type `T`, the `std::ptr::null<T>` function returns a `*const T` null pointer, and `std::ptr::null_mut<T>` returns a `*mut T` null pointer.

There are a few ways to check whether a raw pointer is null. The simplest is the `is_null` method, but the `as_ref` method may be more convenient: it takes a `*const T` pointer and returns an `Option<&'a T>`, turning a null pointer into a `None`. Similarly, the `as_mut` method converts `*mut T` pointers into `Option<&'a mut T>` values.

Type Sizes and Alignments

A value of any `Sized` type occupies a constant number of bytes in memory and must be placed at an address that is a multiple of some *alignment* value, determined by the machine architecture. For example, an (`i32`, `i32`) tuple occupies eight bytes, and most processors prefer it to be placed at an address that is a multiple of four.

The call `std::mem::size_of::<T>()` returns the size of a value of type T, in bytes, and `std::mem::align_of::<T>()` returns its required alignment. For example:

```
assert_eq!(std::mem::size_of::<i64>(), 8);
assert_eq!(std::mem::align_of::<(i32, i32)>(), 4);
```

Any type's alignment is always a power of two.

A type's size is always rounded up to a multiple of its alignment, even if it technically could fit in less space. For example, even though a tuple like (`f32`, `u8`) requires only five bytes, `size_of::<(f32, u8)>()` is 8, because `align_of::<(f32, u8)>()` is 4. This ensures that if you have an array, the size of the element type always reflects the spacing between one element and the next.

For unsized types, the size and alignment depend on the value at hand. Given a reference to an unsized value, the `std::mem::size_of_val` and `std::mem::align_of_val` functions return the value's size and alignment. These functions can operate on references to both `Sized` and unsized types:

```
// Fat pointers to slices carry their referent's length.
let slice: &[i32] = &[1, 3, 9, 27, 81];
assert_eq!(std::mem::size_of_val(slice), 20);

let text: &str = "alligator";
assert_eq!(std::mem::size_of_val(text), 9);

use std::fmt::Display;
let unremarkable: &dyn Display = &193_u8;
let remarkable: &dyn Display = &0.0072973525664;

// These return the size/alignment of the value the
// trait object points to, not those of the trait object
// itself. This information comes from the vtable the
// trait object refers to.
assert_eq!(std::mem::size_of_val(unremarkable), 1);
assert_eq!(std::mem::align_of_val(remarkable), 8);
```

Pointer Arithmetic

Rust lays out the elements of an array, slice, or vector as a single contiguous block of memory, as shown in Figure 22-1. Elements are regularly spaced, so that if each element occupies `size` bytes, then the ith element starts with the i * size th byte.

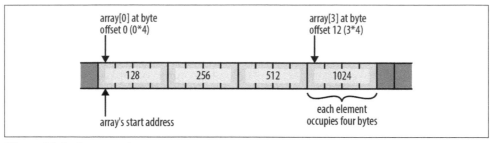

Figure 22-1. An array in memory

One nice consequence of this is that if you have two raw pointers to elements of an array, comparing the pointers gives the same results as comparing the elements' indices: if i < j, then a raw pointer to the ith element is less than a raw pointer to the jth element. This makes raw pointers useful as bounds on array traversals. In fact, the standard library's simple iterator over a slice was originally defined like this:

```
struct Iter<'a, T> {
    ptr: *const T,
    end: *const T,
    ...
}
```

The ptr field points to the next element iteration should produce, and the end field serves as the limit: when ptr == end, the iteration is complete.

Another nice consequence of array layout: if element_ptr is a *const T or *mut T raw pointer to the ith element of some array, then element_ptr.offset(o) is a raw pointer to the (i + o)th element. Its definition is equivalent to this:

```
fn offset<T>(ptr: *const T, count: isize) -> *const T
    where T: Sized
{
    let bytes_per_element = std::mem::size_of::<T>() as isize;
    let byte_offset = count * bytes_per_element;
    (ptr as isize).checked_add(byte_offset).unwrap() as *const T
}
```

The std::mem::size_of::<T> function returns the size of the type T in bytes. Since isize is, by definition, large enough to hold an address, you can convert the base pointer to an isize, do arithmetic on that value, and then convert the result back to a pointer.

It's fine to produce a pointer to the first byte after the end of an array. You cannot dereference such a pointer, but it can be useful to represent the limit of a loop or for bounds checks.

However, it is undefined behavior to use offset to produce a pointer beyond that point or before the start of the array, even if you never dereference it. For the sake of optimization, Rust would like to assume that `ptr.offset(i) > ptr` when `i` is positive and that `ptr.offset(i) < ptr` when `i` is negative. This assumption seems safe, but it may not hold if the arithmetic in `offset` overflows an `isize` value. If `i` is constrained to stay within the same array as `ptr`, no overflow can occur: after all, the array itself does not overflow the bounds of the address space. (To make pointers to the first byte after the end safe, Rust never places values at the upper end of the address space.)

If you do need to offset pointers beyond the limits of the array they are associated with, you can use the `wrapping_offset` method. This is equivalent to `offset`, but Rust makes no assumptions about the relative ordering of `ptr.wrapping_offset(i)` and `ptr` itself. Of course, you still can't dereference such pointers unless they fall within the array.

Moving into and out of Memory

If you are implementing a type that manages its own memory, you will need to track which parts of your memory hold live values and which are uninitialized, just as Rust does with local variables. Consider this code:

```
let pot = "pasta".to_string();
let plate = pot;
```

After this code has run, the situation looks like Figure 22-2.

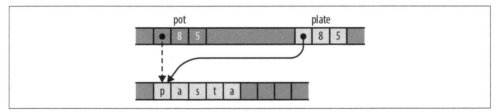

Figure 22-2. Moving a string from one local variable to another

After the assignment, `pot` is uninitialized, and `plate` is the owner of the string.

At the machine level, it's not specified what a move does to the source, but in practice it usually does nothing at all. The assignment probably leaves `pot` still holding a pointer, capacity, and length for the string. Naturally, it would be disastrous to treat this as a live value, and Rust ensures that you don't.

The same considerations apply to data structures that manage their own memory. Suppose you run this code:

```
let mut noodles = vec!["udon".to_string()];
let soba = "soba".to_string();
let last;
```

In memory, the state looks like Figure 22-3.

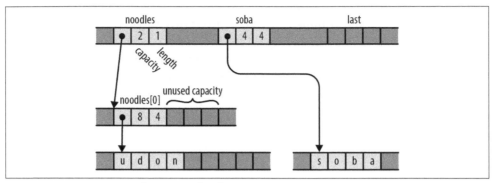

Figure 22-3. A vector with uninitialized, spare capacity

The vector has the spare capacity to hold one more element, but its contents are junk, probably whatever that memory held previously. Suppose you then run this code:

```
noodles.push(soba);
```

Pushing the string onto the vector transforms that uninitialized memory into a new element, as illustrated in Figure 22-4.

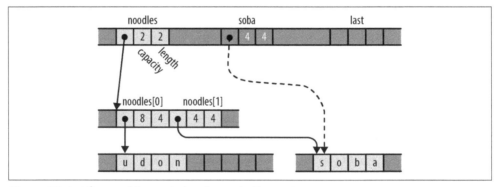

Figure 22-4. After pushing soba's value onto the vector

The vector has initialized its empty space to own the string and incremented its length to mark this as a new, live element. The vector is now the owner of the string; you can refer to its second element, and dropping the vector would free both strings. And soba is now uninitialized.

Finally, consider what happens when we pop a value from the vector:

```
last = noodles.pop().unwrap();
```

In memory, things now look like Figure 22-5.

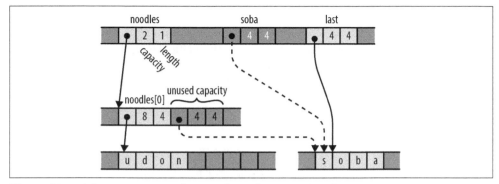

Figure 22-5. After popping an element from the vector into `last`

The variable `last` has taken ownership of the string. The vector has decremented its length to indicate that the space that used to hold the string is now uninitialized.

Just as with `pot` and `pasta` earlier, all three of `soba`, `last`, and the vector's free space probably hold identical bit patterns. But only `last` is considered to own the value. Treating either of the other two locations as live would be a mistake.

The true definition of an initialized value is one that is *treated as live*. Writing to a value's bytes is usually a necessary part of initialization, but only because doing so prepares the value to be treated as live. A move and a copy both have the same effect on memory; the difference between the two is that, after a move, the source is no longer treated as live, whereas after a copy, both the source and the destination are live.

Rust tracks which local variables are live at compile time and prevents you from using variables whose values have been moved elsewhere. Types like `Vec`, `HashMap`, `Box`, and so on track their buffers dynamically. If you implement a type that manages its own memory, you will need to do the same.

Rust provides two essential operations for implementing such types:

`std::ptr::read(src)`

Moves a value out of the location `src` points to, transferring ownership to the caller. The `src` argument should be a `*const T` raw pointer, where `T` is a sized type. After calling this function, the contents of `*src` are unaffected, but unless `T` is `Copy`, you must ensure that your program treats them as uninitialized memory.

This is the operation behind `Vec::pop`. Popping a value calls `read` to move the value out of the buffer and then decrements the length to mark that space as uninitialized capacity.

```
std::ptr::write(dest, value)
```
Moves `value` into the location `dest` points to, which must be uninitialized memory before the call. The referent now owns the value. Here, `dest` must be a `*mut T` raw pointer and `value` a `T` value, where `T` is a sized type.

This is the operation behind `Vec::push`. Pushing a value calls `write` to move the value into the next available space and then increments the length to mark that space as a valid element.

Both are free functions, not methods on the raw pointer types.

Note that you cannot do these things with any of Rust's safe pointer types. They all require their referents to be initialized at all times, so transforming uninitialized memory into a value, or vice versa, is outside their reach. Raw pointers fit the bill.

The standard library also provides functions for moving arrays of values from one block of memory to another:

```
std::ptr::copy(src, dst, count)
```
Moves the array of `count` values in memory starting at `src` to the memory at `dst`, just as if you had written a loop of `read` and `write` calls to move them one at a time. The destination memory must be uninitialized before the call, and afterward the source memory is left uninitialized. The `src` and `dest` arguments must be `*const T` and `*mut T` raw pointers, and `count` must be a `usize`.

ptr.copy_to(dst, count)
A more convenient version of `copy` that moves the array of `count` values in memory starting at `ptr` to `dst`, rather than taking its start point as an argument.

```
std::ptr::copy_nonoverlapping(src, dst, count)
```
Like the corresponding call to `copy`, except that its contract further requires that the source and destination blocks of memory must not overlap. This may be slightly faster than calling `copy`.

```
ptr.copy_to_nonoverlapping(dst, count)
```
A more convenient version of `copy_nonoverlapping`, like `copy_to`.

There are two other families of `read` and `write` functions, also in the `std::ptr` module:

```
read_unaligned, write_unaligned
```
These functions are like `read` and `write`, except that the pointer need not be aligned as normally required for the referent type. These functions may be slower than the plain `read` and `write` functions.

```
read_volatile, write_volatile
```
These functions are the equivalent of volatile reads and writes in C or C++.

Example: GapBuffer

Here's an example that puts the raw pointer functions just described to use.

Suppose you're writing a text editor, and you're looking for a type to represent the text. You could choose `String` and use the `insert` and `remove` methods to insert and delete characters as the user types. But if they're editing text at the beginning of a large file, those methods can be expensive: inserting a new character involves shifting the entire rest of the string to the right in memory, and deletion shifts it all back to the left. You'd like such common operations to be cheaper.

The Emacs text editor uses a simple data structure called a *gap buffer* that can insert and delete characters in constant time. Whereas a `String` keeps all its spare capacity at the end of the text, which makes `push` and `pop` cheap, a gap buffer keeps its spare capacity in the midst of the text, at the point where editing is taking place. This spare capacity is called the *gap*. Inserting or deleting elements at the gap is cheap: you simply shrink or enlarge the gap as needed. You can move the gap to any location you like by shifting text from one side of the gap to the other. When the gap is empty, you migrate to a larger buffer.

While insertion and deletion in a gap buffer are fast, changing the position at which they take place entails moving the gap to the new position. Shifting the elements requires time proportional to the distance being moved. Fortunately, typical editing activity involves making a bunch of changes in one neighborhood of the buffer before going off and fiddling with text someplace else.

In this section we'll implement a gap buffer in Rust. To avoid being distracted by UTF-8, we'll make our buffer store `char` values directly, but the principles of operation would be the same if we stored the text in some other form.

First, we'll show a gap buffer in action. This code creates a `GapBuffer`, inserts some text in it, and then moves the insertion point to sit just before the last word:

```
let mut buf = GapBuffer::new();
buf.insert_iter("Lord of the Rings".chars());
buf.set_position(12);
```

After running this code, the buffer looks as shown in Figure 22-6.

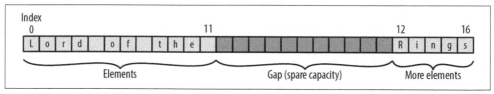

Figure 22-6. A gap buffer containing some text

Insertion is a matter of filling in the gap with new text. This code adds a word and ruins the film:

```
buf.insert_iter("Onion ".chars());
```

This results in the state shown in Figure 22-7.

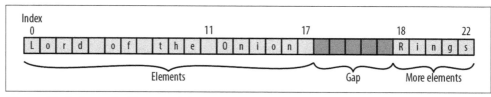

Figure 22-7. A gap buffer containing some more text

Here's our `GapBuffer` type:

```
use std;
use std::ops::Range;

pub struct GapBuffer<T> {
    // Storage for elements. This has the capacity we need, but its length
    // always remains zero. GapBuffer puts its elements and the gap in this
    // `Vec`'s "unused" capacity.
    storage: Vec<T>,

    // Range of uninitialized elements in the middle of `storage`.
    // Elements before and after this range are always initialized.
    gap: Range<usize>
}
```

`GapBuffer` uses its `storage` field in a strange way.[2] It never actually stores any elements in the vector—or not quite. It simply calls `Vec::with_capacity(n)` to get a block of memory large enough to hold n values, obtains raw pointers to that memory via the vector's `as_ptr` and `as_mut_ptr` methods, and then uses the buffer directly for its own purposes. The vector's length always remains zero. When the `Vec` gets dropped, the `Vec` doesn't try to free its elements, because it doesn't know it has any, but it

---

2 There are better ways to handle this using the `RawVec` type from the compiler-internal `alloc` crate, but that crate is still unstable.

does free the block of memory. This is what `GapBuffer` wants; it has its own `Drop` implementation that knows where the live elements are and drops them correctly.

`GapBuffer`'s simplest methods are what you'd expect:

```
impl<T> GapBuffer<T> {
    pub fn new() -> GapBuffer<T> {
        GapBuffer { storage: Vec::new(), gap: 0..0 }
    }

    /// Return the number of elements this GapBuffer could hold without
    /// reallocation.
    pub fn capacity(&self) -> usize {
        self.storage.capacity()
    }

    /// Return the number of elements this GapBuffer currently holds.
    pub fn len(&self) -> usize {
        self.capacity() - self.gap.len()
    }

    /// Return the current insertion position.
    pub fn position(&self) -> usize {
        self.gap.start
    }

    ...
}
```

It cleans up many of the following functions to have a utility method that returns a raw pointer to the buffer element at a given index. This being Rust, we end up needing one method for `mut` pointers and one for `const`. Unlike the preceding methods, these are not public. Continuing this `impl` block:

```
    /// Return a pointer to the `index`'th element of the underlying storage,
    /// regardless of the gap.
    ///
    /// Safety: `index` must be a valid index into `self.storage`.
    unsafe fn space(&self, index: usize) -> *const T {
        self.storage.as_ptr().offset(index as isize)
    }

    /// Return a mutable pointer to the `index`'th element of the underlying
    /// storage, regardless of the gap.
    ///
    /// Safety: `index` must be a valid index into `self.storage`.
    unsafe fn space_mut(&mut self, index: usize) -> *mut T {
        self.storage.as_mut_ptr().offset(index as isize)
    }
```

To find the element at a given index, you must consider whether the index falls before or after the gap and adjust appropriately:

```
/// Return the offset in the buffer of the `index`th element, taking
/// the gap into account. This does not check whether index is in range,
/// but it never returns an index in the gap.
fn index_to_raw(&self, index: usize) -> usize {
    if index < self.gap.start {
        index
    } else {
        index + self.gap.len()
    }
}

/// Return a reference to the `index`th element,
/// or `None` if `index` is out of bounds.
pub fn get(&self, index: usize) -> Option<&T> {
    let raw = self.index_to_raw(index);
    if raw < self.capacity() {
        unsafe {
            // We just checked `raw` against self.capacity(),
            // and index_to_raw skips the gap, so this is safe.
            Some(&*self.space(raw))
        }
    } else {
        None
    }
}
```

When we start making insertions and deletions in a different part of the buffer, we
need to move the gap to the new location. Moving the gap to the right entails shifting
elements to the left, and vice versa, just as the bubble in a spirit level moves in one
direction when the fluid flows in the other:

```
/// Set the current insertion position to `pos`.
/// If `pos` is out of bounds, panic.
pub fn set_position(&mut self, pos: usize) {
    if pos > self.len() {
        panic!("index {} out of range for GapBuffer", pos);
    }

    unsafe {
        let gap = self.gap.clone();
        if pos > gap.start {
            // `pos` falls after the gap. Move the gap right
            // by shifting elements after the gap to before it.
            let distance = pos - gap.start;
            std::ptr::copy(self.space(gap.end),
                           self.space_mut(gap.start),
                           distance);
        } else if pos < gap.start {
            // `pos` falls before the gap. Move the gap left
            // by shifting elements before the gap to after it.
            let distance = gap.start - pos;
            std::ptr::copy(self.space(pos),
```

```
                self.space_mut(gap.end - distance),
                distance);
        }

        self.gap = pos .. pos + gap.len();
    }
}
```

This function uses the `std::ptr::copy` method to shift the elements; `copy` requires that the destination be uninitialized and leaves the source uninitialized. The source and destination ranges may overlap, but `copy` handles that case correctly. Since the gap is uninitialized memory before the call and the function adjusts the gap's position to cover space vacated by the copy, the `copy` function's contract is satisfied.

Element insertion and removal are relatively simple. Insertion takes over one space from the gap for the new element, whereas removal moves one value out and enlarges the gap to cover the space it used to occupy:

```
/// Insert `elt` at the current insertion position,
/// and leave the insertion position after it.
pub fn insert(&mut self, elt: T) {
    if self.gap.len() == 0 {
        self.enlarge_gap();
    }

    unsafe {
        let index = self.gap.start;
        std::ptr::write(self.space_mut(index), elt);
    }
    self.gap.start += 1;
}

/// Insert the elements produced by `iter` at the current insertion
/// position, and leave the insertion position after them.
pub fn insert_iter<I>(&mut self, iterable: I)
    where I: IntoIterator<Item=T>
{
    for item in iterable {
        self.insert(item)
    }
}

/// Remove the element just after the insertion position
/// and return it, or return `None` if the insertion position
/// is at the end of the GapBuffer.
pub fn remove(&mut self) -> Option<T> {
    if self.gap.end == self.capacity() {
        return None;
    }

    let element = unsafe {
        std::ptr::read(self.space(self.gap.end))
```

```
        };
        self.gap.end += 1;
        Some(element)
    }
```

Similar to the way Vec uses `std::ptr::write` for push and `std::ptr::read` for pop, GapBuffer uses `write` for `insert` and `read` for `remove`. And just as Vec must adjust its length to maintain the boundary between initialized elements and spare capacity, GapBuffer adjusts its gap.

When the gap has been filled in, the `insert` method must grow the buffer to acquire more free space. The `enlarge_gap` method (the last in the `impl` block) handles this:

```
/// Double the capacity of `self.storage`.
fn enlarge_gap(&mut self) {
    let mut new_capacity = self.capacity() * 2;
    if new_capacity == 0 {
        // The existing vector is empty.
        // Choose a reasonable starting capacity.
        new_capacity = 4;
    }

    // We have no idea what resizing a Vec does with its "unused"
    // capacity. So just create a new vector and move over the elements.
    let mut new = Vec::with_capacity(new_capacity);
    let after_gap = self.capacity() - self.gap.end;
    let new_gap = self.gap.start .. new.capacity() - after_gap;

    unsafe {
        // Move the elements that fall before the gap.
        std::ptr::copy_nonoverlapping(self.space(0),
                                      new.as_mut_ptr(),
                                      self.gap.start);

        // Move the elements that fall after the gap.
        let new_gap_end = new.as_mut_ptr().offset(new_gap.end as isize);
        std::ptr::copy_nonoverlapping(self.space(self.gap.end),
                                      new_gap_end,
                                      after_gap);
    }

    // This frees the old Vec, but drops no elements,
    // because the Vec's length is zero.
    self.storage = new;
    self.gap = new_gap;
}
```

Whereas `set_position` must use `copy` to move elements back and forth in the gap, `enlarge_gap` can use `copy_nonoverlapping`, since it is moving elements to an entirely new buffer.

Moving the new vector into `self.storage` drops the old vector. Since its length is zero, the old vector believes it has no elements to drop and simply frees its buffer. Neatly, `copy_nonoverlapping` leaves its source uninitialized, so the old vector is correct in this belief: all the elements are now owned by the new vector.

Finally, we need to make sure that dropping a `GapBuffer` drops all its elements:

```
impl<T> Drop for GapBuffer<T> {
    fn drop(&mut self) {
        unsafe {
            for i in 0 .. self.gap.start {
                std::ptr::drop_in_place(self.space_mut(i));
            }
            for i in self.gap.end .. self.capacity() {
                std::ptr::drop_in_place(self.space_mut(i));
            }
        }
    }
}
```

The elements lie before and after the gap, so we iterate over each region and use the `std::ptr::drop_in_place` function to drop each one. The `drop_in_place` function is a utility that behaves like `drop(std::ptr::read(ptr))`, but doesn't bother moving the value to its caller (and hence works on unsized types). And just as in `enlarge_gap`, by the time the vector `self.storage` is dropped, its buffer really is uninitialized.

Like the other types we've shown in this chapter, `GapBuffer` ensures that its own invariants are sufficient to ensure that the contract of every unsafe feature it uses is followed, so none of its public methods needs to be marked unsafe. `GapBuffer` implements a safe interface for a feature that cannot be written efficiently in safe code.

Panic Safety in Unsafe Code

In Rust, panics can't usually cause undefined behavior; the `panic!` macro is not an unsafe feature. But when you decide to work with unsafe code, panic safety becomes part of your job.

Consider the `GapBuffer::remove` method from the previous section:

```
pub fn remove(&mut self) -> Option<T> {
    if self.gap.end == self.capacity() {
        return None;
    }

    let element = unsafe {
        std::ptr::read(self.space(self.gap.end))
    };
    self.gap.end += 1;
    Some(element)
}
```

The call to `read` moves the element immediately following the gap out of the buffer, leaving behind uninitialized space. At this point, the `GapBuffer` is in an inconsistent state: we've broken the invariant that all elements outside the gap must be initialized. Fortunately, the very next statement enlarges the gap to cover that space, so by the time we return, the invariant holds again.

But consider what would happen if, after the call to `read` but before the adjustment to `self.gap.end`, this code tried to use a feature that might panic—say, indexing a slice. Exiting the method abruptly anywhere between those two actions would leave the `GapBuffer` with an uninitialized element outside the gap. The next call to `remove` could try to `read` it again; even simply dropping the `GapBuffer` would try to drop it. Both are undefined behavior, because they access uninitialized memory.

It's all but unavoidable for a type's methods to momentarily relax the type's invariants while they do their job and then put everything back to rights before they return. A panic mid-method could cut that cleanup process short, leaving the type in an inconsistent state.

If the type uses only safe code, then this inconsistency may make the type misbehave, but it can't introduce undefined behavior. But code using unsafe features is usually counting on its invariants to meet the contracts of those features. Broken invariants lead to broken contracts, which lead to undefined behavior.

When working with unsafe features, you must take special care to identify these sensitive regions of code where invariants are temporarily relaxed, and ensure that they do nothing that might panic.

Reinterpreting Memory with Unions

Rust provides many useful abstractions, but ultimately, the software you write is just pushing bytes around. Unions are one of Rust's most powerful features for manipulating those bytes and choosing how they are interpreted. For instance, any collection of 32 bits—4 bytes—can be interpreted as an integer or as a floating-point number.

Either interpretation is valid, though interpreting data meant for one as the other will likely result in nonsense.

A union representing a collection of bytes that can be interpreted as either an integer or a floating-point number would be written as follows:

```
union FloatOrInt {
    f: f32,
    i: i32,
}
```

This is a union with two fields, f and i. They can be assigned to just like the fields of a struct, but when constructing a union, unlike a struct, you must choose exactly one. Where the fields of a struct refer to different positions in memory, the fields of a union refer to different interpretations of the same sequence of bits. Assigning to a different field simply means overwriting some or all of those bits, in accordance with an appropriate type. Here, one refers to a single 32-bit memory span, which first stores 1 encoded as a simple integer, then 1.0 as an IEEE 754 floating-point number. As soon as f is written to, the value previously written to the FloatOrInt is overwritten:

```
let mut one = FloatOrInt { i: 1 };
assert_eq!(unsafe { one.i }, 0x00_00_00_01);
one.f = 1.0;
assert_eq!(unsafe { one.i }, 0x3F_80_00_00);
```

For the same reason, the size of a union is determined by its largest field. For example, this union is 64 bits in size, even though SmallOrLarge::s is just a bool:

```
union SmallOrLarge {
    s: bool,
    l: u64
}
```

While constructing a union or assigning to its fields is completely safe, reading from any field of a union is always unsafe:

```
let u = SmallOrLarge { l: 1337 };
println!("{}", unsafe {u.l}); // prints 1337
```

This is because, unlike enums, unions don't have a tag. The compiler adds no additional bits to tell variants apart. There is no way to tell at run time whether a SmallOrLarge is meant to be interpreted as a u64 or a bool, unless the program has some extra context.

There is also no built-in guarantee that a given field's bit pattern is valid. For instance, writing to a SmallOrLarge value's l field will overwrite its s field, creating a bit pattern that definitely doesn't mean anything useful and is most likely not a valid bool. Therefore, while writing to union fields is safe, every read requires unsafe. Reading from u.s is permitted only when the bits of the s field form a valid bool; otherwise, this is undefined behavior.

With these restrictions in mind, unions can be a useful way to temporarily reinterpret some data, especially when doing computations on the representation of values rather than the values themselves. For instance, the previously mentioned FloatOrInt type can easily be used to print out the individual bits of a floating-point number, even though f32 doesn't implement the Binary formatter:

```
let float = FloatOrInt { f: 31337.0 };
// prints 1000110111101001101001000000000
println!("{:b}", unsafe { float.i });
```

While these simple examples will almost certainly work as expected on any version of the compiler, there is no guarantee that any field starts at a specific place unless an attribute is added to the union definition telling the compiler how to lay out the data in memory. Adding the attribute #[repr(C)] guarantees that all fields start at offset 0, rather than wherever the compiler likes. With that guarantee in place, the overwriting behavior can be used to extract individual bits, like the sign bit of an integer:

```
#[repr(C)]
union SignExtractor {
    value: i64,
    bytes: [u8; 8]
}

fn sign(int: i64) -> bool {
    let se = SignExtractor { value: int};
    println!( "{:b} ({:?})", unsafe { se.value }, unsafe { se.bytes });
    unsafe { se.bytes[7] >= 0b10000000 }
}

assert_eq!(sign(-1), true);
assert_eq!(sign(1), false);
assert_eq!(sign(i64::MAX), false);
assert_eq!(sign(i64::MIN), true);
```

Here, the sign bit is the most significant bit of the most significant byte. Because x86 processors are little-endian, the order of those bytes is reversed; the most significant byte is not bytes[0], but bytes[7]. Normally, this is not something Rust code has to deal with, but because this code is directly working with the in-memory representation of the i64, these low-level details become important.

Because unions can't tell how to drop their contents, all their fields must be Copy. However, if you simply must store a String in a union, there is a workaround; consult the standard library documentation for std::mem::ManuallyDrop.

Matching Unions

Matching on a Rust union is like matching on a struct, except that each pattern has to specify exactly one field:

```
unsafe {
    match u {
        SmallOrLarge { s: true } => { println!("boolean true"); }
        SmallOrLarge { l: 2 } => { println!("integer 2"); }
        _ => { println!("something else"); }
    }
}
```

A match arm that matches against a union variant without specifying a value will always succeed. The following code will cause undefined behavior if the last written field of u was u.i:

```
// Undefined behavior!
unsafe {
    match u {
        FloatOrInt { f } => { println!("float {}", f) },
        // warning: unreachable pattern
        FloatOrInt { i } => { println!("int {}", i) }
    }
}
```

Borrowing Unions

Borrowing one field of a union borrows the entire union. This means that, following the normal borrowing rules, borrowing one field as mutable precludes any additional borrows on it or other fields, and borrowing one field as immutable means there can be no mutable borrows on any fields.

As we'll see in the next chapter, Rust helps you build safe interfaces not only for your own unsafe code but also for code written in other languages. Unsafe is, as the name implies, fraught, but used with care it can empower you to build highly performant code that retains the guarantees Rust programmers enjoy.

CHAPTER 23

Foreign Functions

Cyberspace. Unthinkable complexity. Lines of light ranged in the non-space of the mind, clusters and constellations of data. Like city lights, receding . . .
—William Gibson, *Neuromancer*

Tragically, not every program in the world is written in Rust. There are many critical libraries and interfaces implemented in other languages that we would like to be able to use in our Rust programs. Rust's *foreign function interface* (FFI) lets Rust code call functions written in C, and in some cases C++. Since most operating systems offer C interfaces, Rust's foreign function interface allows immediate access to all sorts of low-level facilities.

In this chapter, we'll write a program that links with libgit2, a C library for working with the Git version control system. First, we'll show what it's like to use C functions directly from Rust, using the unsafe features demonstrated in the previous chapter. Then, we'll show how to construct a safe interface to libgit2, taking inspiration from the open source git2-rs crate, which does exactly that.

We'll assume that you're familiar with C and the mechanics of compiling and linking C programs. Working with C++ is similar. We'll also assume that you're somewhat familiar with the Git version control system.

There do exist Rust crates for communicating with many other languages, including Python, JavaScript, Lua, and Java. We don't have room to cover them here, but ultimately, all these interfaces are built using the C foreign function interface, so this chapter should give you a head start no matter which language you need to work with.

Finding Common Data Representations

The common denominator of Rust and C is machine language, so in order to anticipate what Rust values look like to C code, or vice versa, you need to consider their machine-level representations. Throughout the book, we've made a point of showing how values are actually represented in memory, so you've probably noticed that the data worlds of C and Rust have a lot in common: a Rust `usize` and a C `size_t` are identical, for example, and structs are fundamentally the same idea in both languages. To establish a correspondence between Rust and C types, we'll start with primitives and then work our way up to more complicated types.

Given its primary use as a systems programming language, C has always been surprisingly loose about its types' representations: an `int` is typically 32 bits long, but could be longer, or as short as 16 bits; a C `char` may be signed or unsigned; and so on. To cope with this variability, Rust's `std::os::raw` module defines a set of Rust types that are guaranteed to have the same representation as certain C types (Table 23-1). These cover the primitive integer and character types.

Table 23-1. `std::os::raw` types in Rust

C type	Corresponding `std::os::raw` type
short	c_short
int	c_int
long	c_long
long long	c_longlong
unsigned short	c_ushort
unsigned, unsigned int	c_uint
unsigned long	c_ulong
unsigned long long	c_ulonglong
char	c_char
signed char	c_schar
unsigned char	c_uchar
float	c_float
double	c_double
void *, const void *	*mut c_void, *const c_void

Some notes about Table 23-1:

- Except for `c_void`, all the Rust types here are aliases for some primitive Rust type: `c_char`, for example, is either `i8` or `u8`.
- A Rust `bool` is equivalent to a C or C++ `bool`.

- Rust's 32-bit char type is not the analogue of wchar_t, whose width and encoding vary from one implementation to another. C's char32_t type is closer, but its encoding is still not guaranteed to be Unicode.

- Rust's primitive usize and isize types have the same representations as C's size_t and ptrdiff_t.

- C and C++ pointers and C++ references correspond to Rust's raw pointer types, *mut T and *const T.

- Technically, the C standard permits implementations to use representations for which Rust has no corresponding type: 36-bit integers, sign-and-magnitude representations for signed values, and so on. In practice, on every platform Rust has been ported to, every common C integer type has a match in Rust.

For defining Rust struct types compatible with C structs, you can use the #[repr(C)] attribute. Placing #[repr(C)] above a struct definition asks Rust to lay out the struct's fields in memory the same way a C compiler would lay out the analogous C struct type. For example, libgit2's *git2/errors.h* header file defines the following C struct to provide details about a previously reported error:

```
typedef struct {
    char *message;
    int klass;
} git_error;
```

You can define a Rust type with an identical representation as follows:

```
use std::os::raw::{c_char, c_int};

#[repr(C)]
pub struct git_error {
    pub message: *const c_char,
    pub klass: c_int
}
```

The #[repr(C)] attribute affects only the layout of the struct itself, not the representations of its individual fields, so to match the C struct, each field must use the C-like type as well: *const c_char for char *, c_int for int, and so on.

In this particular case, the #[repr(C)] attribute probably doesn't change the layout of git_error. There really aren't too many interesting ways to lay out a pointer and an integer. But whereas C and C++ guarantee that a structure's members appear in memory in the order they're declared, each at a distinct address, Rust reorders fields to minimize the overall size of the struct, and zero-sized types take up no space. The #[repr(C)] attribute tells Rust to follow C's rules for the given type.

You can also use #[repr(C)] to control the representation of C-style enums:

```
#[repr(C)]
#[allow(non_camel_case_types)]
enum git_error_code {
    GIT_OK          =  0,
    GIT_ERROR       = -1,
    GIT_ENOTFOUND   = -3,
    GIT_EEXISTS     = -4,
    ...
}
```

Normally, Rust plays all sorts of games when choosing how to represent enums. For example, we mentioned the trick Rust uses to store Option<&T> in a single word (if T is sized). Without #[repr(C)], Rust would use a single byte to represent the git_error_code enum; with #[repr(C)], Rust uses a value the size of a C int, just as C would.

You can also ask Rust to give an enum the same representation as some integer type. Starting the preceding definition with #[repr(i16)] would give you a 16-bit type with the same representation as the following C++ enum:

```
#include <stdint.h>

enum git_error_code: int16_t {
    GIT_OK          =  0,
    GIT_ERROR       = -1,
    GIT_ENOTFOUND   = -3,
    GIT_EEXISTS     = -4,
    ...
};
```

As mentioned earlier, #[repr(C)] applies to unions as well. Fields of #[repr(C)] unions always start at the first bit of the union's memory—index 0.

Suppose you have a C struct that uses a union to hold some data and a tag value to indicate which field of the union should be used, similar to a Rust enum.

```
enum tag {
    FLOAT = 0,
    INT   = 1,
};

union number {
    float f;
    short i;
};

struct tagged_number {
    tag t;
    number n;
};
```

Rust code can interoperate with this structure by applying #[repr(C)] to the enum, structure, and union types, and using a match statement that selects a union field within a larger struct based on the tag:

```rust
#[repr(C)]
enum Tag {
    Float = 0,
    Int = 1
}

#[repr(C)]
union FloatOrInt {
    f: f32,
    i: i32,
}

#[repr(C)]
struct Value {
    tag: Tag,
    union: FloatOrInt
}

fn is_zero(v: Value) -> bool {
    use self::Tag::*;
    unsafe {
        match v {
            Value { tag: Int, union: FloatOrInt { i: 0 } } => true,
            Value { tag: Float, union: FloatOrInt { f: num } } => (num == 0.0),
            _ => false
        }
    }
}
```

Even complex structures can be easily used across the FFI boundary using this kind of technique.

Passing strings between Rust and C is a little harder. C represents a string as a pointer to an array of characters, terminated by a null character. Rust, on the other hand, stores the length of a string explicitly, either as a field of a String or as the second word of a fat reference &str. Rust strings are not null-terminated; in fact, they may include null characters in their contents, like any other character.

This means that you can't borrow a Rust string as a C string: if you pass C code a pointer into a Rust string, it could mistake an embedded null character for the end of the string or run off the end looking for a terminating null that isn't there. Going the other direction, you may be able to borrow a C string as a Rust &str, as long as its contents are well-formed UTF-8.

This situation effectively forces Rust to treat C strings as types entirely distinct from String and &str. In the std::ffi module, the CString and CStr types represent owned and borrowed null-terminated arrays of bytes. Compared to String and str, the methods on CString and CStr are quite limited, restricted to construction and conversion to other types. We'll show these types in action in the next section.

Declaring Foreign Functions and Variables

An extern block declares functions or variables defined in some other library that the final Rust executable will be linked with. For example, on most platforms, every Rust program is linked against the standard C library, so we can tell Rust about the C library's strlen function like this:

```
use std::os::raw::c_char;

extern {
    fn strlen(s: *const c_char) -> usize;
}
```

This gives Rust the function's name and type, while leaving the definition to be linked in later.

Rust assumes that functions declared inside extern blocks use C conventions for passing arguments and accepting return values. They are defined as unsafe functions. These are the right choices for strlen: it is indeed a C function, and its specification in C requires that you pass it a valid pointer to a properly terminated string, which is a contract that Rust cannot enforce. (Almost any function that takes a raw pointer must be unsafe: safe Rust can construct raw pointers from arbitrary integers, and dereferencing such a pointer would be undefined behavior.)

With this extern block, we can call strlen like any other Rust function, although its type gives it away as a tourist:

```
use std::ffi::CString;

let rust_str = "I'll be back";
let null_terminated = CString::new(rust_str).unwrap();
unsafe {
    assert_eq!(strlen(null_terminated.as_ptr()), 12);
}
```

The CString::new function builds a null-terminated C string. It first checks its argument for embedded null characters, since those cannot be represented in a C string, and returns an error if it finds any (hence the need to unwrap the result). Otherwise, it adds a null byte to the end and returns a CString owning the resulting characters.

The cost of CString::new depends on what type you pass it. It accepts anything that implements Into<Vec<u8>>. Passing a &str entails an allocation and a copy, as the conversion to Vec<u8> builds a heap-allocated copy of the string for the vector to own. But passing a String by value simply consumes the string and takes over its buffer, so unless appending the null character forces the buffer to be resized, the conversion requires no copying of text or allocation at all.

CString dereferences to CStr, whose as_ptr method returns a *const c_char pointing at the start of the string. This is the type that strlen expects. In the example, strlen runs down the string, finds the null character that CString::new placed there, and returns the length, as a byte count.

You can also declare global variables in extern blocks. POSIX systems have a global variable named environ that holds the values of the process's environment variables. In C, it's declared:

```
extern char **environ;
```

In Rust, you would say:

```
use std::ffi::CStr;
use std::os::raw::c_char;

extern {
    static environ: *mut *mut c_char;
}
```

To print the environment's first element, you could write:

```
unsafe {
    if !environ.is_null() && !(*environ).is_null() {
        let var = CStr::from_ptr(*environ);
        println!("first environment variable: {}",
                var.to_string_lossy())
    }
}
```

After making sure environ has a first element, the code calls CStr::from_ptr to build a CStr that borrows it. The to_string_lossy method returns a Cow<str>: if the C string contains well-formed UTF-8, the Cow borrows its content as a &str, not including the terminating null byte. Otherwise, to_string_lossy makes a copy of the text in the heap, replaces the ill-formed UTF-8 sequences with the official Unicode replacement character, �, and builds an owning Cow from that. Either way, the result implements Display, so you can print it with the {} format parameter.

Using Functions from Libraries

To use functions provided by a particular library, you can place a #[link] attribute atop the extern block that names the library Rust should link the executable with. For example, here's a program that calls libgit2's initialization and shutdown methods, but does nothing else:

```
use std::os::raw::c_int;

#[link(name = "git2")]
extern {
    pub fn git_libgit2_init() -> c_int;
    pub fn git_libgit2_shutdown() -> c_int;
}

fn main() {
    unsafe {
        git_libgit2_init();
        git_libgit2_shutdown();
    }
}
```

The `extern` block declares the extern functions as before. The `#[link(name = "git2")]` attribute leaves a note in the crate to the effect that, when Rust creates the final executable or shared library, it should link against the `git2` library. Rust uses the system linker to build executables; on Unix, this passes the argument `-lgit2` on the linker command line; on Windows, it passes `git2.LIB`.

`#[link]` attributes work in library crates, too. When you build a program that depends on other crates, Cargo gathers together the link notes from the entire dependency graph and includes them all in the final link.

In this example, if you would like to follow along on your own machine, you'll need to build `libgit2` for yourself. We used `libgit2` (*https://oreil.ly/T1dPr*) version 0.25.1. To compile `libgit2`, you will need to install the CMake build tool and the Python language; we used CMake (*https://cmake.org*) version 3.8.0 and Python (*https://www.python.org*) version 2.7.13.

The full instructions for building `libgit2` are available on its website, but they're simple enough that we'll show the essentials here. On Linux, assume you've already unzipped the library's source into the directory */home/jimb/libgit2-0.25.1*:

```
$ cd /home/jimb/libgit2-0.25.1
$ mkdir build
$ cd build
$ cmake ..
$ cmake --build .
```

On Linux, this produces a shared library */home/jimb/libgit2-0.25.1/build/libgit2.so .0.25.1* with the usual nest of symlinks pointing to it, including one named *libgit2.so*. On macOS, the results are similar, but the library is named *libgit2.dylib*.

On Windows, things are also straightforward. Assume you've unzipped the source into the directory *C:\Users\JimB\libgit2-0.25.1*. In a Visual Studio command prompt:

```
> cd C:\Users\JimB\libgit2-0.25.1
> mkdir build
> cd build
> cmake -A x64 ..
> cmake --build .
```

These are the same commands as used on Linux, except that you must request a 64-bit build when you run CMake the first time to match your Rust compiler. (If you have installed the 32-bit Rust toolchain, then you should omit the -A x64 flag to the first cmake command.) This produces an import library *git2.LIB* and a dynamic-link library *git2.DLL*, both in the directory *C:\Users\JimB\libgit2-0.25.1\build\Debug*. (The remaining instructions are shown for Unix, except where Windows is substantially different.)

Create the Rust program in a separate directory:

```
$ cd /home/jimb
$ cargo new --bin git-toy
    Created binary (application) `git-toy` package
```

Take the code shown earlier and put it in *src/main.rs*. Naturally, if you try to build this, Rust has no idea where to find the libgit2 you built:

```
$ cd git-toy
$ cargo run
   Compiling git-toy v0.1.0 (/home/jimb/git-toy)
error: linking with `cc` failed: exit status: 1
  |
  = note: /usr/bin/ld: error: cannot find -lgit2
          src/main.rs:11: error: undefined reference to 'git_libgit2_init'
          src/main.rs:12: error: undefined reference to 'git_libgit2_shutdown'
          collect2: error: ld returned 1 exit status


error: could not compile `git-toy` due to previous error
```

You can tell Rust where to search for libraries by writing a *build script*, Rust code that Cargo compiles and runs at build time. Build scripts can do all sorts of things: generate code dynamically, compile C code to be included in the crate, and so on. In this case, all you need is to add a library search path to the executable's link command. When Cargo runs the build script, it parses the build script's output for information of this sort, so the build script simply needs to print the right magic to its standard output.

To create your build script, add a file named *build.rs* in the same directory as the *Cargo.toml* file, with the following contents:

```
fn main() {
    println!(r"cargo:rustc-link-search=native=/home/jimb/libgit2-0.25.1/build");
}
```

This is the right path for Linux; on Windows, you would change the path following the text `native=` to `C:\Users\JimB\libgit2-0.25.1\build\Debug`. (We're cutting some corners to keep this example simple; in a real application, you should avoid using absolute paths in your build script. We cite documentation that shows how to do it right at the end of this section.)

Now you can almost run the program. On macOS it may work immediately; on a Linux system you will probably see something like the following:

```
$ cargo run
    Compiling git-toy v0.1.0 (/tmp/rustbook-transcript-tests/git-toy)
     Finished dev [unoptimized + debuginfo] target(s)
       Running `target/debug/git-toy`
target/debug/git-toy: error while loading shared libraries:
libgit2.so.25: cannot open shared object file: No such file or directory
```

This means that, although Cargo succeeded in linking the executable against the library, it doesn't know where to find the shared library at run time. Windows reports this failure by popping up a dialog box. On Linux, you must set the `LD_LIBRARY_PATH` environment variable:

```
$ export LD_LIBRARY_PATH=/home/jimb/libgit2-0.25.1/build:$LD_LIBRARY_PATH
$ cargo run
     Finished dev [unoptimized + debuginfo] target(s) in 0.0 secs
       Running `target/debug/git-toy`
```

On macOS, you may need to set `DYLD_LIBRARY_PATH` instead.

On Windows, you must set the `PATH` environment variable:

```
> set PATH=C:\Users\JimB\libgit2-0.25.1\build\Debug;%PATH%
> cargo run
     Finished dev [unoptimized + debuginfo] target(s) in 0.0 secs
       Running `target/debug/git-toy`
>
```

Naturally, in a deployed application you'd want to avoid having to set environment variables just to find your library's code. One alternative is to statically link the C library into your crate. This copies the library's object files into the crate's *.rlib* file, alongside the object files and metadata for the crate's Rust code. The entire collection then participates in the final link.

It is a Cargo convention that a crate that provides access to a C library should be named `LIB-sys`, where `LIB` is the name of the C library. A `-sys` crate should contain nothing but the statically linked library and Rust modules containing `extern` blocks and type definitions. Higher-level interfaces then belong in crates that depend on the `-sys` crate. This allows multiple upstream crates to depend on the same `-sys` crate, assuming there is a single version of the `-sys` crate that meets everyone's needs.

For the full details on Cargo's support for build scripts and linking with system libraries, see the online Cargo documentation (*https://oreil.ly/Rxa1D*). It shows how to avoid absolute paths in build scripts, control compilation flags, use tools like pkg-config, and so on. The git2-rs crate also provides good examples to emulate; its build script handles some complex situations.

A Raw Interface to libgit2

Figuring out how to use libgit2 properly breaks down into two questions:

- What does it take to use libgit2 functions in Rust?
- How can we build a safe Rust interface around them?

We'll take these questions one at a time. In this section, we'll write a program that's essentially a single giant unsafe block filled with nonidiomatic Rust code, reflecting the clash of type systems and conventions that is inherent in mixing languages. We'll call this the *raw* interface. The code will be messy, but it will make plain all the steps that must occur for Rust code to use libgit2.

Then, in the next section, we'll build a safe interface to libgit2 that puts Rust's types to use enforcing the rules libgit2 imposes on its users. Fortunately, libgit2 is an exceptionally well-designed C library, so the questions that Rust's safety requirements force us to ask all have pretty good answers, and we can construct an idiomatic Rust interface with no unsafe functions.

The program we'll write is very simple: it takes a path as a command-line argument, opens the Git repository there, and prints out the head commit. But this is enough to illustrate the key strategies for building safe and idiomatic Rust interfaces.

For the raw interface, the program will end up needing a somewhat larger collection of functions and types from libgit2 than we used before, so it makes sense to move the extern block into its own module. We'll create a file named *raw.rs* in *git-toy/src* whose contents are as follows:

```
#![allow(non_camel_case_types)]

use std::os::raw::{c_int, c_char, c_uchar};

#[link(name = "git2")]
extern {
    pub fn git_libgit2_init() -> c_int;
    pub fn git_libgit2_shutdown() -> c_int;
    pub fn giterr_last() -> *const git_error;

    pub fn git_repository_open(out: *mut *mut git_repository,
                              path: *const c_char) -> c_int;
```

```
        pub fn git_repository_free(repo: *mut git_repository);

        pub fn git_reference_name_to_id(out: *mut git_oid,
                                        repo: *mut git_repository,
                                        reference: *const c_char) -> c_int;

        pub fn git_commit_lookup(out: *mut *mut git_commit,
                                 repo: *mut git_repository,
                                 id: *const git_oid) -> c_int;

        pub fn git_commit_author(commit: *const git_commit) -> *const git_signature;
        pub fn git_commit_message(commit: *const git_commit) -> *const c_char;
        pub fn git_commit_free(commit: *mut git_commit);
    }

    #[repr(C)] pub struct git_repository { _private: [u8; 0] }
    #[repr(C)] pub struct git_commit { _private: [u8; 0] }

    #[repr(C)]
    pub struct git_error {
        pub message: *const c_char,
        pub klass: c_int
    }

    pub const GIT_OID_RAWSZ: usize = 20;

    #[repr(C)]
    pub struct git_oid {
        pub id: [c_uchar; GIT_OID_RAWSZ]
    }

    pub type git_time_t = i64;

    #[repr(C)]
    pub struct git_time {
        pub time: git_time_t,
        pub offset: c_int
    }

    #[repr(C)]
    pub struct git_signature {
        pub name: *const c_char,
        pub email: *const c_char,
        pub when: git_time
    }
```

Each item here is modeled on a declaration from libgit2's own header files. For example, *libgit2-0.25.1/include/git2/repository.h* includes this declaration:

```
extern int git_repository_open(git_repository **out, const char *path);
```

This function tries to open the Git repository at `path`. If all goes well, it creates a `git_repository` object and stores a pointer to it in the location pointed to by `out`. The equivalent Rust declaration is the following:

```
pub fn git_repository_open(out: *mut *mut git_repository,
                           path: *const c_char) -> c_int;
```

The `libgit2` public header files define the `git_repository` type as a typedef for an incomplete struct type:

```
typedef struct git_repository git_repository;
```

Since the details of this type are private to the library, the public headers never define `struct git_repository`, ensuring that the library's users can never build an instance of this type themselves. One possible analogue to an incomplete struct type in Rust is this:

```
#[repr(C)] pub struct git_repository { _private: [u8; 0] }
```

This is a struct type containing an array with no elements. Since the `_private` field isn't `pub`, values of this type cannot be constructed outside this module, which is perfect as the reflection of a C type that only `libgit2` should ever construct, and which is manipulated solely through raw pointers.

Writing large `extern` blocks by hand can be a chore. If you are creating a Rust interface to a complex C library, you may want to try using the `bindgen` crate, which has functions you can use from your build script to parse C header files and generate the corresponding Rust declarations automatically. We don't have space to show `bindgen` in action here, but `bindgen`'s page on crates.io (*https://oreil.ly/sr8rS*) includes links to its documentation.

Next we'll rewrite *main.rs* completely. First, we need to declare the `raw` module:

```
mod raw;
```

According to `libgit2`'s conventions, fallible functions return an integer code that is positive or zero on success, and negative on failure. If an error occurs, the `giterr_last` function will return a pointer to a `git_error` structure providing more details about what went wrong. `libgit2` owns this structure, so we don't need to free it ourselves, but it could be overwritten by the next library call we make. A proper Rust interface would use `Result`, but in the raw version, we want to use the `libgit2` functions just as they are, so we'll have to roll our own function for handling errors:

```
use std::ffi::CStr;
use std::os::raw::c_int;

fn check(activity: &'static str, status: c_int) -> c_int {
    if status < 0 {
        unsafe {
            let error = &*raw::giterr_last();
```

```
            println!("error while {}: {} ({})",
                     activity,
                     CStr::from_ptr(error.message).to_string_lossy(),
                     error.klass);
            std::process::exit(1);
        }
    }

    status
}
```

We'll use this function to check the results of `libgit2` calls like this:

```
check("initializing library", raw::git_libgit2_init());
```

This uses the same `CStr` methods used earlier: `from_ptr` to construct the `CStr` from a C string and `to_string_lossy` to turn that into something Rust can print.

Next, we need a function to print out a commit:

```
unsafe fn show_commit(commit: *const raw::git_commit) {
    let author = raw::git_commit_author(commit);

    let name = CStr::from_ptr((*author).name).to_string_lossy();
    let email = CStr::from_ptr((*author).email).to_string_lossy();
    println!("{} <{}>\n", name, email);

    let message = raw::git_commit_message(commit);
    println!("{}", CStr::from_ptr(message).to_string_lossy());
}
```

Given a pointer to a `git_commit`, `show_commit` calls `git_commit_author` and `git_commit_message` to retrieve the information it needs. These two functions follow a convention that the `libgit2` documentation explains as follows:

> If a function returns an object as a return value, that function is a getter and the object's lifetime is tied to the parent object.

In Rust terms, `author` and `message` are borrowed from `commit`: `show_commit` doesn't need to free them itself, but it must not hold on to them after `commit` is freed. Since this API uses raw pointers, Rust won't check their lifetimes for us: if we do accidentally create dangling pointers, we probably won't find out about it until the program crashes.

The preceding code assumes these fields hold UTF-8 text, which is not always correct. Git permits other encodings as well. Interpreting these strings properly would probably entail using the `encoding` crate. For brevity's sake, we'll gloss over those issues here.

Our program's `main` function reads as follows:

```
use std::ffi::CString;
use std::mem;
use std::ptr;
use std::os::raw::c_char;

fn main() {
    let path = std::env::args().skip(1).next()
        .expect("usage: git-toy PATH");
    let path = CString::new(path)
        .expect("path contains null characters");

    unsafe {
        check("initializing library", raw::git_libgit2_init());

        let mut repo = ptr::null_mut();
        check("opening repository",
                raw::git_repository_open(&mut repo, path.as_ptr()));

        let c_name = b"HEAD\0".as_ptr() as *const c_char;
        let oid = {
            let mut oid = mem::MaybeUninit::uninit();
            check("looking up HEAD",
                    raw::git_reference_name_to_id(oid.as_mut_ptr(), repo, c_name));
            oid.assume_init()
        };

        let mut commit = ptr::null_mut();
        check("looking up commit",
                raw::git_commit_lookup(&mut commit, repo, &oid));

        show_commit(commit);

        raw::git_commit_free(commit);

        raw::git_repository_free(repo);

        check("shutting down library", raw::git_libgit2_shutdown());
    }
}
```

This starts with code to handle the path argument and initialize the library, all of which we've seen before. The first novel code is this:

```
let mut repo = ptr::null_mut();
check("opening repository",
        raw::git_repository_open(&mut repo, path.as_ptr()));
```

The call to git_repository_open tries to open the Git repository at the given path. If it succeeds, it allocates a new git_repository object for it and sets repo to point to that. Rust implicitly coerces references into raw pointers, so passing &mut repo here provides the *mut *mut git_repository the call expects.

This shows another `libgit2` convention in use (from the `libgit2` documentation):

> Objects which are returned via the first argument as a pointer-to-pointer are owned by the caller and it is responsible for freeing them.

In Rust terms, functions like `git_repository_open` pass ownership of the new value to the caller.

Next, consider the code that looks up the object hash of the repository's current head commit:

```
let oid = {
    let mut oid = mem::MaybeUninit::uninit();
    check("looking up HEAD",
          raw::git_reference_name_to_id(oid.as_mut_ptr(), repo, c_name));
    oid.assume_init()
};
```

The `git_oid` type stores an object identifier—a 160-bit hash code that Git uses internally (and throughout its delightful user interface) to identify commits, individual versions of files, and so on. This call to `git_reference_name_to_id` looks up the object identifier of the current `"HEAD"` commit.

In C it's perfectly normal to initialize a variable by passing a pointer to it to some function that fills in its value; this is how `git_reference_name_to_id` expects to treat its first argument. But Rust won't let us borrow a reference to an uninitialized variable. We could initialize `oid` with zeros, but this is a waste: any value stored there will simply be overwritten.

It is possible to ask Rust to give us uninitialized memory, but because reading uninitialized memory at any time is instant undefined behavior, Rust provides an abstraction, `MaybeUninit`, to ease its use. `MaybeUninit<T>` tells the compiler to set aside enough memory for your type `T`, but not to touch it until you say that it's safe to do so. While this memory is owned by the `MaybeUninit`, the compiler will also avoid certain optimizations that could otherwise cause undefined behavior even without any explicit access to the uninitialized memory in your code.

`MaybeUninit` provides a method, `as_mut_ptr()`, that produces a `*mut T` pointing to the potentially uninitialized memory it wraps. By passing that pointer to a foreign function that initializes the memory and then calling the unsafe method `assume_init` on the `MaybeUninit` to produce a fully initialized `T`, you can avoid undefined behavior without the additional overhead that comes from initializing and immediately throwing away a value. `assume_init` is unsafe because calling it on a `MaybeUninit` without being certain that the memory is actually initialized will immediately cause undefined behavior.

In this case, it is safe because `git_reference_name_to_id` initializes the memory owned by the `MaybeUninit`. We could use `MaybeUninit` for the `repo` and `commit` variables as well, but since these are just single words, we just go ahead and initialize them to null:

```
let mut commit = ptr::null_mut();
check("looking up commit",
        raw::git_commit_lookup(&mut commit, repo, &oid));
```

This takes the commit's object identifier and looks up the actual commit, storing a `git_commit` pointer in `commit` on success.

The remainder of the `main` function should be self-explanatory. It calls the `show_commit` function defined earlier, frees the commit and repository objects, and shuts down the library.

Now we can try out the program on any Git repository ready at hand:

```
$ cargo run /home/jimb/rbattle
    Finished dev [unoptimized + debuginfo] target(s) in 0.0 secs
      Running `target/debug/git-toy /home/jimb/rbattle`
Jim Blandy <jimb@red-bean.com>

Animate goop a bit.
```

A Safe Interface to libgit2

The raw interface to `libgit2` is a perfect example of an unsafe feature: it certainly can be used correctly (as we do here, so far as we know), but Rust can't enforce the rules you must follow. Designing a safe API for a library like this is a matter of identifying all these rules and then finding ways to turn any violation of them into a type or borrow-checking error.

Here, then, are `libgit2`'s rules for the features the program uses:

- You must call `git_libgit2_init` before using any other library function. You must not use any library function after calling `git_libgit2_shutdown`.

- All values passed to `libgit2` functions must be fully initialized, except for output parameters.

- When a call fails, output parameters passed to hold the results of the call are left uninitialized, and you must not use their values.

- A `git_commit` object refers to the `git_repository` object it is derived from, so the former must not outlive the latter. (This isn't spelled out in the `libgit2` documentation; we inferred it from the presence of certain functions in the interface and then verified it by reading the source code.)

- Similarly, a `git_signature` is always borrowed from a given `git_commit`, and the former must not outlive the latter. (The documentation does cover this case.)

- The message associated with a commit and the name and email address of the author are all borrowed from the commit and must not be used after the commit is freed.

- Once a `libgit2` object has been freed, it must never be used again.

As it turns out, you can build a Rust interface to `libgit2` that enforces all of these rules, either through Rust's type system or by managing details internally.

Before we get started, let's restructure the project a little bit. We'd like to have a `git` module that exports the safe interface, of which the raw interface from the previous program is a private submodule.

The whole source tree will look like this:

```
git-toy/
├── Cargo.toml
├── build.rs
└── src/
    ├── main.rs
    └── git/
        ├── mod.rs
        └── raw.rs
```

Following the rules we explained in "Modules in Separate Files" on page 180, the source for the `git` module appears in *git/mod.rs*, and the source for its `git::raw` submodule goes in *git/raw.rs*.

Once again, we're going to rewrite *main.rs* completely. It should start with a declaration of the `git` module:

```
mod git;
```

Then, we'll need to create the *git* subdirectory and move *raw.rs* into it:

```
$ cd /home/jimb/git-toy
$ mkdir src/git
$ mv src/raw.rs src/git/raw.rs
```

The `git` module needs to declare its `raw` submodule. The file *src/git/mod.rs* must say:

```
mod raw;
```

Since it's not `pub`, this submodule is not visible to the main program.

In a bit we'll need to use some functions from the `libc` crate, so we must add a dependency in *Cargo.toml*. The full file now reads:

```
[package]
name = "git-toy"
version = "0.1.0"
authors = ["You <you@example.com>"]
edition = "2021"

[dependencies]
libc = "0.2"
```

Now that we've restructured our modules, let's consider error handling. Even libgit2's initialization function can return an error code, so we'll need to have this sorted out before we can get started. An idiomatic Rust interface needs its own Error type that captures the libgit2 failure code as well as the error message and class from giterr_last. A proper error type must implement the usual Error, Debug, and Display traits. Then, it needs its own Result type that uses this Error type. Here are the necessary definitions in *src/git/mod.rs*:

```
use std::error;
use std::fmt;
use std::result;

#[derive(Debug)]
pub struct Error {
    code: i32,
    message: String,
    class: i32
}

impl fmt::Display for Error {
    fn fmt(&self, f: &mut fmt::Formatter) -> result::Result<(), fmt::Error> {
        // Displaying an `Error` simply displays the message from libgit2.
        self.message.fmt(f)
    }
}

impl error::Error for Error { }

pub type Result<T> = result::Result<T, Error>;
```

To check the result from raw library calls, the module needs a function that turns a libgit2 return code into a Result:

```
use std::os::raw::c_int;
use std::ffi::CStr;

fn check(code: c_int) -> Result<c_int> {
    if code >= 0 {
        return Ok(code);
    }

    unsafe {
        let error = raw::giterr_last();
```

```
    // libgit2 ensures that (*error).message is always non-null and null
    // terminated, so this call is safe.
    let message = CStr::from_ptr((*error).message)
        .to_string_lossy()
        .into_owned();

    Err(Error {
        code: code as i32,
        message,
        class: (*error).klass as i32
    })
    }
}
```

The main difference between this and the check function from the raw version is that this constructs an Error value instead of printing an error message and exiting immediately.

Now we're ready to tackle libgit2 initialization. The safe interface will provide a Repository type that represents an open Git repository, with methods for resolving references, looking up commits, and so on. Continuing in *git/mod.rs*, here's the definition of Repository:

```
/// A Git repository.
pub struct Repository {
    // This must always be a pointer to a live `git_repository` structure.
    // No other `Repository` may point to it.
    raw: *mut raw::git_repository
}
```

A Repository's raw field is not public. Since only code in this module can access the raw::git_repository pointer, getting this module right should ensure the pointer is always used correctly.

If the only way to create a Repository is to successfully open a fresh Git repository, that will ensure that each Repository points to a distinct git_repository object:

```
use std::path::Path;
use std::ptr;

impl Repository {
    pub fn open<P: AsRef<Path>>(path: P) -> Result<Repository> {
        ensure_initialized();

        let path = path_to_cstring(path.as_ref())?;
        let mut repo = ptr::null_mut();
        unsafe {
            check(raw::git_repository_open(&mut repo, path.as_ptr()))?;
        }
        Ok(Repository { raw: repo })
```

```
        }
    }
```

Since the only way to do anything with the safe interface is to start with a `Repository` value, and `Repository::open` starts with a call to `ensure_initialized`, we can be confident that `ensure_initialized` will be called before any `libgit2` functions. Its definition is as follows:

```
fn ensure_initialized() {
    static ONCE: std::sync::Once = std::sync::Once::new();
    ONCE.call_once(|| {
        unsafe {
            check(raw::git_libgit2_init())
                .expect("initializing libgit2 failed");
            assert_eq!(libc::atexit(shutdown), 0);
        }
    });
}

extern fn shutdown() {
    unsafe {
        if let Err(e) = check(raw::git_libgit2_shutdown()) {
            eprintln!("shutting down libgit2 failed: {}", e);
            std::process::abort();
        }
    }
}
```

The `std::sync::Once` type helps run initialization code in a thread-safe way. Only the first thread to call `ONCE.call_once` runs the given closure. Any subsequent calls, by this thread or any other, block until the first has completed and then return immediately, without running the closure again. Once the closure has finished, calling `ONCE.call_once` is cheap, requiring nothing more than an atomic load of a flag stored in `ONCE`.

In the preceding code, the initialization closure calls `git_libgit2_init` and checks the result. It punts a bit and just uses `expect` to make sure initialization succeeded, instead of trying to propagate errors back to the caller.

To make sure the program calls `git_libgit2_shutdown`, the initialization closure uses the C library's `atexit` function, which takes a pointer to a function to invoke before the process exits. Rust closures cannot serve as C function pointers: a closure is a value of some anonymous type carrying the values of whatever variables it captures or references to them; a C function pointer is just a pointer. However, Rust `fn` types work fine, as long as you declare them `extern` so that Rust knows to use the C calling conventions. The local function `shutdown` fits the bill and ensures `libgit2` gets shut down properly.

In "Unwinding" on page 158, we mentioned that it is undefined behavior for a panic to cross language boundaries. The call from `atexit` to `shutdown` is such a boundary, so it is essential that `shutdown` not panic. This is why `shutdown` can't simply use `.expect` to handle errors reported from `raw::git_libgit2_shutdown`. Instead, it must report the error and terminate the process itself. POSIX forbids calling `exit` within an `atexit` handler, so `shutdown` calls `std::process::abort` to terminate the program abruptly.

It might be possible to arrange to call `git_libgit2_shutdown` sooner—say, when the last `Repository` value is dropped. But no matter how we arrange things, calling `git_libgit2_shutdown` must be the safe API's responsibility. The moment it is called, any extant `libgit2` objects become unsafe to use, so a safe API must not expose this function directly.

A `Repository`'s raw pointer must always point to a live `git_repository` object. This implies that the only way to close a repository is to drop the `Repository` value that owns it:

```
impl Drop for Repository {
    fn drop(&mut self) {
        unsafe {
            raw::git_repository_free(self.raw);
        }
    }
}
```

By calling `git_repository_free` only when the sole pointer to the `raw::git_repository` is about to go away, the `Repository` type also ensures the pointer will never be used after it's freed.

The `Repository::open` method uses a private function called `path_to_cstring`, which has two definitions—one for Unix-like systems and one for Windows:

```
use std::ffi::CString;

#[cfg(unix)]
fn path_to_cstring(path: &Path) -> Result<CString> {
    // The `as_bytes` method exists only on Unix-like systems.
    use std::os::unix::ffi::OsStrExt;

    Ok(CString::new(path.as_os_str().as_bytes())?)
}

#[cfg(windows)]
fn path_to_cstring(path: &Path) -> Result<CString> {
    // Try to convert to UTF-8. If this fails, libgit2 can't handle the path
    // anyway.
    match path.to_str() {
        Some(s) => Ok(CString::new(s)?),
```

```
            None => {
                let message = format!("Couldn't convert path '{}' to UTF-8",
                                      path.display());
                Err(message.into())
            }
        }
    }
}
```

The `libgit2` interface makes this code a little tricky. On all platforms, `libgit2` accepts paths as null-terminated C strings. On Windows, `libgit2` assumes these C strings hold well-formed UTF-8 and converts them internally to the 16-bit paths Windows actually requires. This usually works, but it's not ideal. Windows permits filenames that are not well-formed Unicode and thus cannot be represented in UTF-8. If you have such a file, it's impossible to pass its name to `libgit2`.

In Rust, the proper representation of a filesystem path is a `std::path::Path`, carefully designed to handle any path that can appear on Windows or POSIX. This means that there are `Path` values on Windows that one cannot pass to `libgit2`, because they are not well-formed UTF-8. So although `path_to_cstring`'s behavior is less than ideal, it's actually the best we can do given `libgit2`'s interface.

The two `path_to_cstring` definitions just shown rely on conversions to our `Error` type: the `?` operator attempts such conversions, and the Windows version explicitly calls `.into()`. These conversions are unremarkable:

```
impl From<String> for Error {
    fn from(message: String) -> Error {
        Error { code: -1, message, class: 0 }
    }
}

// NulError is what `CString::new` returns if a string
// has embedded zero bytes.
impl From<std::ffi::NulError> for Error {
    fn from(e: std::ffi::NulError) -> Error {
        Error { code: -1, message: e.to_string(), class: 0 }
    }
}
```

Next, let's figure out how to resolve a Git reference to an object identifier. Since an object identifier is just a 20-byte hash value, it's perfectly fine to expose it in the safe API:

```
/// The identifier of some sort of object stored in the Git object
/// database: a commit, tree, blob, tag, etc. This is a wide hash of the
/// object's contents.
pub struct Oid {
    pub raw: raw::git_oid
}
```

We'll add a method to `Repository` to perform the lookup:

```
use std::mem;
use std::os::raw::c_char;

impl Repository {
    pub fn reference_name_to_id(&self, name: &str) -> Result<Oid> {
        let name = CString::new(name)?;
        unsafe {
            let oid = {
                let mut oid = mem::MaybeUninit::uninit();
                check(raw::git_reference_name_to_id(
                        oid.as_mut_ptr(), self.raw,
                        name.as_ptr() as *const c_char))?;
                oid.assume_init()
            };
            Ok(Oid { raw: oid })
        }
    }
}
```

Although `oid` is left uninitialized when the lookup fails, this function guarantees that its caller can never see the uninitialized value simply by following Rust's `Result` idiom: either the caller gets an `Ok` carrying a properly initialized `Oid` value, or it gets an `Err`.

Next, the module needs a way to retrieve commits from the repository. We'll define a `Commit` type as follows:

```
use std::marker::PhantomData;

pub struct Commit<'repo> {
    // This must always be a pointer to a usable `git_commit` structure.
    raw: *mut raw::git_commit,
    _marker: PhantomData<&'repo Repository>
}
```

As we mentioned earlier, a `git_commit` object must never outlive the `git_repository` object it was retrieved from. Rust's lifetimes let the code capture this rule precisely.

The `RefWithFlag` example earlier in this chapter used a `PhantomData` field to tell Rust to treat a type as if it contained a reference with a given lifetime, even though the type apparently contained no such reference. The `Commit` type needs to do something similar. In this case, the `_marker` field's type is `PhantomData<&'repo Repository>`, indicating that Rust should treat `Commit<'repo>` as if it held a reference with lifetime `'repo` to some `Repository`.

The method for looking up a commit is as follows:

```
impl Repository {
    pub fn find_commit(&self, oid: &Oid) -> Result<Commit> {
        let mut commit = ptr::null_mut();
        unsafe {
            check(raw::git_commit_lookup(&mut commit, self.raw, &oid.raw))?;
        }
        Ok(Commit { raw: commit, _marker: PhantomData })
    }
}
```

How does this relate the `Commit`'s lifetime to the `Repository`'s? The signature of `find_commit` omits the lifetimes of the references involved according to the rules outlined in "Omitting Lifetime Parameters" on page 121. If we were to write the lifetimes out, the full signature would read:

```
fn find_commit<'repo, 'id>(&'repo self, oid: &'id Oid)
    -> Result<Commit<'repo>>
```

This is exactly what we want: Rust treats the returned `Commit` as if it borrows something from `self`, which is the `Repository`.

When a `Commit` is dropped, it must free its `raw::git_commit`:

```
impl<'repo> Drop for Commit<'repo> {
    fn drop(&mut self) {
        unsafe {
            raw::git_commit_free(self.raw);
        }
    }
}
```

From a `Commit`, you can borrow a `Signature` (a name and email address) and the text of the commit message:

```
impl<'repo> Commit<'repo> {
    pub fn author(&self) -> Signature {
        unsafe {
            Signature {
                raw: raw::git_commit_author(self.raw),
                _marker: PhantomData
            }
        }
    }

    pub fn message(&self) -> Option<&str> {
        unsafe {
            let message = raw::git_commit_message(self.raw);
            char_ptr_to_str(self, message)
        }
    }
}
```

Here's the Signature type:

```
pub struct Signature<'text> {
    raw: *const raw::git_signature,
    _marker: PhantomData<&'text str>
}
```

A git_signature object always borrows its text from elsewhere; in particular, signatures returned by git_commit_author borrow their text from the git_commit. So our safe Signature type includes a PhantomData<&'text str> to tell Rust to behave as if it contained a &str with a lifetime of 'text. Just as before, Commit::author properly connects this 'text lifetime of the Signature it returns to that of the Commit without us needing to write a thing. The Commit::message method does the same with the Option<&str> holding the commit message.

A Signature includes methods for retrieving the author's name and email address:

```
impl<'text> Signature<'text> {
    /// Return the author's name as a `&str`,
    /// or `None` if it is not well-formed UTF-8.
    pub fn name(&self) -> Option<&str> {
        unsafe {
            char_ptr_to_str(self, (*self.raw).name)
        }
    }

    /// Return the author's email as a `&str`,
    /// or `None` if it is not well-formed UTF-8.
    pub fn email(&self) -> Option<&str> {
        unsafe {
            char_ptr_to_str(self, (*self.raw).email)
        }
    }
}
```

The preceding methods depend on a private utility function char_ptr_to_str:

```
/// Try to borrow a `&str` from `ptr`, given that `ptr` may be null or
/// refer to ill-formed UTF-8. Give the result a lifetime as if it were
/// borrowed from `_owner`.
///
/// Safety: if `ptr` is non-null, it must point to a null-terminated C
/// string that is safe to access for at least as long as the lifetime of
/// `_owner`.
unsafe fn char_ptr_to_str<T>(_owner: &T, ptr: *const c_char) -> Option<&str> {
    if ptr.is_null() {
        return None;
    } else {
        CStr::from_ptr(ptr).to_str().ok()
    }
}
```

The _owner parameter's value is never used, but its lifetime is. Making the lifetimes in this function's signature explicit gives us:

```
fn char_ptr_to_str<'o, T: 'o>(_owner: &'o T, ptr: *const c_char)
    -> Option<&'o str>
```

The CStr::from_ptr function returns a &CStr whose lifetime is completely unbounded, since it was borrowed from a dereferenced raw pointer. Unbounded lifetimes are almost always inaccurate, so it's good to constrain them as soon as possible. Including the _owner parameter causes Rust to attribute its lifetime to the return value's type, so callers can receive a more accurately bounded reference.

It is not clear from the libgit2 documentation whether a git_signature's email and author pointers can be null, despite the documentation for libgit2 being quite good. Your authors dug around in the source code for some time without being able to persuade themselves one way or the other and finally decided that char_ptr_to_str had better be prepared for null pointers just in case. In Rust, this sort of question is answered immediately by the type: if it's &str, you can count on the string to be there; if it's Option<&str>, it's optional.

Finally, we've provided safe interfaces for all the functionality we need. The new main function in *src/main.rs* is slimmed down quite a bit and looks like real Rust code:

```
fn main() {
    let path = std::env::args_os().skip(1).next()
        .expect("usage: git-toy PATH");

    let repo = git::Repository::open(&path)
        .expect("opening repository");

    let commit_oid = repo.reference_name_to_id("HEAD")
        .expect("looking up 'HEAD' reference");

    let commit = repo.find_commit(&commit_oid)
        .expect("looking up commit");

    let author = commit.author();
    println!("{} <{}>\n",
             author.name().unwrap_or("(none)"),
             author.email().unwrap_or("none"));

    println!("{}", commit.message().unwrap_or("(none)"));
}
```

In this chapter, we've gone from simplistic interfaces that don't provide many safety guarantees to a safe API wrapping an inherently unsafe API by arranging for any violation of the latter's contract to be a Rust type error. The result is an interface that Rust can ensure you use correctly. For the most part, the rules we've made Rust enforce are the sorts of rules that C and C++ programmers end up imposing on themselves anyway. What makes Rust feel so much stricter than C and C++ is not that the rules are so foreign, but that this enforcement is mechanical and comprehensive.

Conclusion

Rust is not a simple language. Its goal is to span two very different worlds. It's a modern programming language, safe by design, with conveniences like closures and iterators, yet it aims to put you in control of the raw capabilities of the machine it runs on, with minimal run-time overhead.

The contours of the language are determined by these goals. Rust manages to bridge most of the gap with safe code. Its borrow checker and zero-cost abstractions put you as close to the bare metal as possible without risking undefined behavior. When that's not enough or when you want to leverage existing C code, unsafe code and the foreign function interface stand ready. But again, the language doesn't just offer you these unsafe features and wish you luck. The goal is always to use unsafe features to build safe APIs. That's what we did with `libgit2`. It's also what the Rust team has done with `Box`, `Vec`, the other collections, channels, and more: the standard library is full of safe abstractions, implemented with some unsafe code behind the scenes.

A language with Rust's ambitions was, perhaps, not destined to be the simplest of tools. But Rust is safe, fast, concurrent—and effective. Use it to build large, fast, secure, robust systems that take advantage of the full power of the hardware they run on. Use it to make software better.

Index

Symbols

! operator, 151, 291
!= operator, 152, 294
#![feature] attribute, 193
#[allow] attribute, 191
#[cfg] attribute, 191, 495
#[derive] attribute, 19
#[inline] attribute, 192
#[link] attribute, 671
#[repr(C)] attribute, 667
#[repr(i16)] attribute, 668
#[should_panic] attribute, 194
#[test] attribute, 192
$ (command prompt), 6
% operator, 151
& operator, 14, 103, 151, 248
& pattern, 248
&& operator, 152
&mut operator, 103
&mut type, 529
&mut [T] type, 66
&str (string slice), 75
&[T] type, 65
* operator
    accessing referenced value, 151
    dereferencing, 14, 105, 312, 641
    multiplication, 151
    overloading of, 312
    pattern matching and, 248
* wildcard, for crate versions, 203
*const T, 641
*mut T, 641
+ operator, 151, 292, 440
- operator, 151, 291

. operator, 106, 149, 312
.. operator, 150
..= operator, 150
/ operator, 151
/// (documentation comments), 27, 197
:: operator, 183
::<...> (turbofish symbol), 149, 221
< operator, 152, 297, 642
<< operator, 151
<= operator, 152, 297
= operator, 152
== operator, 152, 294, 642
=> operator, 152
> operator, 152, 297
>= operator, 297
>> operator, 151
? operator, 164
@ patterns, 250
^ operator, 151
{:?} format parameter, 459
{:p} format parameter, 460
| (vertical bar) in matching patterns, 250
| operator, 151
|| operator, 152
~ operator, 151

A

aborting, 159
absolute path, 185
"Abstraction and the C++ Machine Model"
    (Stroustrup), 4
accumulation methods for iterators, 375, 379
actix-web framework, 15-21, 341, 498
adapter methods

enumerate, 39
fuse, 546
adapter methods for iterators, 358-375
 by_ref, 372-373
 chain, 370
 cloned, 373
 copied, 374
 cycle, 374
 enumerate, 371, 372
 filter_map and flat_map, 361-363
 flatten, 363-364
 fuse, 368
 inspect, 369
 map and filter, 358-360
 peekable, 366
 reversible iterators and rev, 368-369
 skip and skip_while, 365
 take and take_while, 365, 372
 zip, 372
adapter methods for readers
 bytes method, 477
 chain method, 477
 take method, 477
algebraic data types, 231
alignment value, required by types, 647
align_of function, 647
align_of_val function, 647
all, iterator method, 378
#[allow] attribute, 191
any, iterator method, 378
anyhow error handling crate, 166, 568
Arc pointer type, 98-100, 217-217, 507, 528
args function, 12, 366
Arguments type, for string formatting, 464
arithmetic operators, 151, 288-290
 compound assignment operators, 293-294
 overloading, 292
arithmetic, pointer, 647-649
array patterns, 246
arrays, 67
 concatenating arrays of, 402
 raw pointers to, 647-649
 slices and, 71
 tuples versus, 63
arrays, joining arrays of, 402
as operator, 436
ASCII characters, 54, 430, 433, 434
Ascii string type, unsafe code for conversion
 into String, 631-634

AsMut trait, 317
AsRef trait, 317, 489
assert! macro, 9, 194
assert_eq! macro, 194, 601, 602-603
assignment
 C++ versus Rust, 87-90
 compound assignment operators, 152,
  293-294
 expressions, 152
 moves and (see moves)
 Python versus Rust, 86-90
 references, 107
 in Rust, 90-94
 to a variable, 90
assignment operators, 152
associated consts, 218, 282
associated functions, 215
associated types, 276-279
associativity, 134
async functions, 546-552, 558
async move blocks, 557
async streams, 573-575
async-std crate, 542, 546, 547, 552
asynchronous programming, 541-599
 async blocks, 542, 556-559
 async functions, 546-552, 558
 client and server, 566-584
 compared with synchronous programming,
  543-566
 futures and executors, coordinating,
  584-590
 HTTP client crate, 565
 pinning futures, 590-597
 tasks versus traditional threads, 541
 useful situations for, 597-599
as_mut_ptr method, 642
as_ptr method, 642
atomic integer operations, 538
atomic reference count (see Arc pointer type)
Atomic types and operations, 535, 538
attributes, 10, 191-193
await expressions, 546-552, 553-556

B

background thread, 500
backpressure
 asynchronous client and chat server,
  581-584
 pipeline approach, 520

bat command, 42
binary input/output, 487
binary numeric literal, 54
binary operators, 151, 292
binary, formatting numbers in, 457
BinaryHeap, 395, 412-413
BinaryTree type, 240, 252, 389-392
bindgen crate, 677
bitwise operators, 151, 293-294
blocks, 137-140
    asynchronous, 542, 556-559
    declarations in, 138
    extern block, 670-671
    impl block, 214-218
    unsafe, 66, 628, 630-633, 635
block_on, 549-552, 585, 588-590
Boolean type (bool), 61, 459
Borrow trait, 318-320
Borrow<str> trait, 449
borrowing, 101
    futures and, 553, 592-594
    iteration and, 14, 372
    local variables and, 110-113
    unions, 663
    values of arbitrary expressions, 109
BorrowMut trait, 318-320
bounds, reverse-engineering, 283-286
Box type, 66, 83, 217-217
break expressions, 144
broadcast channel, 581-584
BTreeMap<K, V> collection type, 413-420
BTreeSet collection type, 420-424
BTreeSet::new, 421
buffered readers, 477-482
BufRead trait, 478
    consume method, 478
    fill_buf method, 478
    read_line method, 478
    read_until method, 478
    split method, 478
BufReader type, 477
BufReader<TcpStream>, 573
BufWriter::with_capacity, 483
bugs, unsafe code and, 634
build profiles, 177
build script, 673
BuildHasher trait, 425
by value/by reference
    passing a collection, 352, 393

passing function arguments, 104-105
byte literals, 54
byte strings, 74
byteorder crate, 487
by_ref iterator adapter, 372-373

C

C, 2
    (see also foreign functions)
    enums, 232-234
    passing strings between Rust and, 669
    pointers in, 640, 642
    rules for avoiding undefined behavior, 2
    type representations, 666-670
C#
    asynchronous functions, 565
    enums, 231-234
    traits versus virtual methods, 258
C++, 2
    (see also foreign functions)
    assignment in, 87-90
    constexpr, 538
    enums, 231-234
    invalidation errors and, 125, 393, 409
    macros, 602, 607
    mutexes in, 526-527
    ownership in, 81-84
    pointers in, 640, 642
    pointers to const versus shared references,
        130
    reference creation in, 105
    rules for avoiding undefined behavior, 2
    traits versus virtual methods, 258
calculate_tides method, 170
callbacks, closures and, 341-345
cancellation, atomics and, 536
capacity of a vector, 69, 398
captures_iter method on Regex type, 467
Cargo, 4
    build script, 673
    documentation, 197-202
    rustup and, 6-8
    src/bin directory, 189-191
    versioning, 202
cargo build, 174-176
cargo command, 6
cargo doc command, 197
cargo package command, 205
cargo test command, 194-196

Cargo.lock, 204
case conversion
    for characters, 435
    for strings, 447
casts, 153
catch_unwind function, 159
Cell type, 226
#[cfg] attribute, 191, 495
cfg! macro, 610
ch.to_digit method, 434
chain adapter, 370
channels, 512-525
    broadcast channel, 582-584
    deadlock with, 531
    features and performance, 519-520
    multiconsumer channels using mutex, 532
    non-pipeline uses, 525
    piping iterator to, 523-525
    receiving values, 516
    Send and Sync for thread safety, 521-523
    sending values, 512-525
character literals, 61
characters (char), 61-63, 432-436
    case conversion, 435
    classifying, 433-434
    digits, 434
    integer conversion, 436
    is_digit method, 435
    is_lowercase method, 435
    is_uppercase method, 435
    numeric types versus, 61
    Rust and C type commonalities, 667
    to_digit method, 435
    to_lowercase method, 435
    to_uppercase method, 435
chat groups, tokio's broadcast channels,
    581-584
checked operations, 57
child process, 486
ChildStdin type, 486
client and server, asynchronous chat, 566-584
    chat connections with async mutexes,
        577-580
    chat groups, tokio's broadcast channels,
        581-584
    client's main function, 575-576
    error and result types, 568
    protocol, 569-570
    receiving packets, 573-575

sending packets, 572
server's main function, 576
streams to take user input, 570-572
clone method, 90, 258
Clone trait, 310, 340, 397
cloned adapter method for iterators, 373
closed (end-inclusive) ranges, 150
closures, 39, 154, 327-346
    borrowing references, 330
    callbacks, 341-345
    capturing variables, 329
    Clone for, 340
    Copy for, 340
    dropping values, 336-338
    effective use of, 345
    FnMut, 338-340
    FnOnce, 336-338
    inspect adapter and, 369
    layout in memory, 335
    move keyword, 331
    performance, 334
    safety, 335-341
    "that kill", 336
    types, 332-334
    in web server example, 17
code fragments, macros, 604-607
collaboration, Rust and, 4
collect method, 39, 44, 384-385, 386, 481
collections, 393-427
    BinaryHeap<T>collection type, 412-413
    BTreeMap<K, V>, 413-420
    BTreeSet<T>, 420-424
    custom, 427
    hashing, 424-426
    HashMap<K, V>, 413-420
    HashSet<T>, 420-424
    iterating over by value, 352, 393
    iterators and, 350
    strings as generic, 453
    Vec<T>, 395-410
    VecDeque<T>, 410-412
column! macro, 609
command prompt ($), 6
Command type, 486
command-line arguments, 11-15, 28-30
command-line interface, 42-44
community, Rust, 208
comparison operators, 61, 152
    with iterators, 377

overloading, 297
references and, 108
with strings, 77
compatibility equivalence for Unicode characters, 470
complex numbers, 30
composed versus decomposed Unicode characters, 468
compound assignment operators, 152, 293-294
compression, 487
concat method, 76
concat! macro, 610
concurrency, 3, 499-540
    channels, 512-525
    fork-join parallelism, 501-511
    Mandelbrot set, 35-40
    Rust's support for, 22-41, 80
    shared mutable state, 525-539
condition (with if statement), 140
condition variables (Condvar), 534
const function, 538
const generics, 222, 263
constants, 179, 187, 538
consts, 187
    *const T, 641
    associated, 218, 282
    shared references versus pointers to, 130
consume method, 478
consuming iterators, 375-387
    accumulation methods, 375
    any and all methods, 378
    collect method, 384-385
    comparing item sequences, 377
    count method, 375
    ExactSizeIterator, 379
    Extend trait, 385
    find, rfind, and find_map methods, 382
    fold method, 379
    for_each method, 387
    FromIterator trait, 384
    last method, 382
    max_by and min_by methods, 376
    max_by_key and min_by_key methods, 377
    min and max methods, 376
    nth and nth_back methods, 382
    partition method, 386
    position method, 378
    product method, 375
    rfind method, 383

rfold method, 380
rposition method, 378
sum method, 375
try_fold and try_rfold methods, 380-382
try_for_each method, 387
contracts
    unsafe feature and, 629
    unsafe functions and, 634
    unsafe traits and, 638
copied adapter, 374
copy method, 475
Copy type, 94-97, 311, 340
count method, 375
Cow (clone on write) type, 325, 451-453
crates, 173-178
    #[inline] attribute, 192
    $crate fragment versus crate keyword, 623
    doc-tests, 199-202
    publishing to crates.io, 205
    specifying dependencies, 202-205
    src/bin directory and, 189-191
    workspaces, 207
crates.io, 205
critical section in code, 526
crossbeam crate, 38
Cursor::new, 485
cycle adapter, 374

D

dangling pointer, 79, 123
data parallelism, 500
data races, 22, 41, 527, 530
deadlock, 531
Debug formatting trait, 449, 642
debugging
    formatting values for, 459-461
    macros, 611-612
debug_assert! macro, 9, 194
debug_assert_eq! macro, 194
declarations, 138, 670-675
decomposed versus composed Unicode characters, 468
Default trait, 315-317, 387
default trait implementation, 267
dependencies
    Cargo.lock, 204
    in crate context, 175
    specifying, 202-205
    versions and, 202

dependency graph, 175
Deref coercions, 154, 313, 641
Deref trait, 312-315
dereferencing
    * operator, 14, 105, 641
    raw pointers, 66, 629, 630, 643-646
DerefMut trait, 312-315
#[derive] attribute, 19
Deserialize trait, 574
digits, handling, 434
directionality of text, 432
directories
    modules and, 181
    reading, 493-494
    src/bin, 189-191
DirEntry struct, 494
    file_name method, 494
    file_type method, 494
    metadata method, 494
    path method, 494
discriminated unions, 231
Display formatting trait, 448, 642
divergent function, 147
doc comments, 197
doc-tests, 199-202
documentation, 197-202
documentation comments (///), 27, 197
double quotes, 18
DoubleEndedIterator trait, 368
drain method, 355
Drop trait, 304-307, 477
dropping values
    in closures, 336-338
    FnOnce, 336-338
    ownership and, 82
    in Rust, 85
duck typing, 50
dynamic widths and precisions, 461

E

editions, 176
elapsed method, 169
elements
    tuple-like struct values, 212
    Vec<T> collection type, 396-397, 408
embarrassingly parallel algorithm, 22
end-exclusive (half-open) ranges, 150, 250
end-inclusive (closed) ranges, 150
entries, map key-value pairs as, 413

Entry type, HashMap and BTreeMap, 417-420
enumerate adapter, 39, 371, 372
enumerated type (enum), 27, 231-254
    C-style, 232-234
    with data, 234
    generic, 238-241
    hash implementation, 424
    in memory, 235
    rich data structures with, 236-238
env module, 12
env! macro, 610
eprintln! macro, 13
Eq trait, 424
equality operators, 152, 294-297
error handling, 157-172
    across threads, 504
    anyhow crate, 166
    asynchronous chat, 568
    avoiding syntax errors in macro matching,
        624
    catching errors, 160-162
    channels and, 515
    declaring a custom error type, 171
    errors that "can't happen", 168
    formatting error types, 459
    ignoring errors, 169
    invalidation errors, 393, 409
    in main function, 169
    with multiple error types, 166-167
    panic, 157-160
    PoisonError::into_inner, 532
    printing errors, 163-164
    propagating errors, 164
    Result type, 160-172, 568
    unsafe code and, 683
Error trait
    source method, 163
    to_string method, 163
escape_time function, 354
ExactSizeIterator trait, 379
exceptions, Result versus, 172
exclusive (half-open) ranges, 150
executors (asynchronous)
    block_on, 549-552, 585, 588-590
    spawn function, 502-504, 505, 552, 560
    spawn_local, 552-556, 560
expect method, 13, 34, 169
expressions, 133-155
    assignment, 152

blocks and semicolons, 137-140
closures, 154
declarations, 138
fields and elements, 149
function/method calls, 148
if and match, 140-142
if let, 142
loops, 144-145
precedence and associativity, 134
reference operators, 151
regular expressions, 466-468
return, 145
Rust as expression language, 133
statements versus, 133
struct, 210
type casts, 153
extend function, 124
Extend trait, 385
extend_from_slice method, 124
extension traits, 269, 572
extern block, 670-671

F

fat pointer, 71, 110, 641
#![feature] attribute, 193
FFI (see foreign functions)
fields, expressions and, 149
File type, 465, 484
file! macro, 609
File::create, 483
File::open, 483
filename types, 489
files, 488-496
    filesystem access functions, 492-493
    OsStr and Path, 488-490
    Path and PathBuf types, 490-492
    platform-specific features, 495-496
    reading and writing, 45, 483
    reading directories, 493-494
filesystems, 42-48, 492
fill_buf method, 478
filter adapter, 358-360
filter_map adapter, 361-363
find and replace, 46
find method, 29, 382
find_iter iterator, 467
find_map method, 383
fixed-width numeric types, 52-60
flate2 crate, 487

flatten adapter, 363-364
flat_map adapter, 361-363
floating-point literals, 59
floating-point types, 58-60, 376, 458
flow-sensitive analyses, 146
flush method, 268
Flux architecture, 346
fmt module, 462
fn keyword, 9, 139
Fn trait, 339
fn type, 344
FnMut trait, 338-340, 355
FnOnce trait, 336-338
fnv crate, 426
fold method, 348, 379
for loop, 12
    control flow in, 145
    IntoIterator, 350, 352, 353
foreign functions, 665-692
    declaring foreign functions and variables,
        670-671
    finding common data representations,
        666-670
    from libraries, 671-675
    raw interface to libgit2, 675-681
    safe interface to libgit2, 681-691
    unsafe code and, 630
fork-join parallelism, 501-511
    error handling across threads, 504
    Mandelbrot set rendering, 510-511
    Rayon library, 508-509
    shared immutable data across threads,
        505-507
    spawn and join, 502-504
format parameters, 454
format! macro, 76, 454
formatting arguments, by index or name, 461
formatting numbers, 457-458
formatting values, 454-465
    Boolean values, 459
    for debugging, 459-461
    Display trait, 448, 642
    dynamic widths and precisions, 461
    error types, 459
    format string directive notation, 462
    formatting language in your own code,
        464-465
    implementing traits for your own types,
        462-464

internet protocol address types, 459
Pointer trait, 642
referring to arguments by index or name,
461
string examples, 454
text values, 455-456
format_args! macro, 454, 464
for_each method, 387
free functions, 215
From trait, 320-323, 618
FromIterator trait, 384, 386, 437
FromStr trait, 447
from_digit method, 434
from_fn method, 353-355
from_slice function, 273
from_str method, 12
fs module, 492
fully qualified method calls, 274-275
function arguments, receiving references as,
113-115
function pointers (fn type), 344
functional language, 71
functions
    associated, 215
    async, 546-552, 558
    calling, 148
    const, 538
    filesystem access, 492-493
    foreign (see foreign functions)
    free, 215
    generic, 28, 50, 260-264
    passing references to, 115
    syntax for, 8-10
    type-associated, 217, 272
    types, 332-334
    unsafe, 628, 633-635
fuse adapter, 368, 546
Future trait, 544-546
FutureExt trait, 576
futures, 543-566, 584-590
    async blocks, 556-559
    async functions, 546-552, 558
    asynchronous HTTP client crate, 565
    await expression, 548
    block_on, 549-552, 588-590
    borrowing and, 553
    comparing asynchronous designs, 564
    implementing Send, 560-563
    long-running computations, 563-564

pinning, 590-597
spawning async tasks, 552-556, 559
spawn_blocking, 586-588

G
GapBuffer, 653-660
garbage collection, 65, 79, 329
gcd function, 9, 21
generic code, 255, 256
    associated types and, 276-279
    consts, 282
    generic functions, 28, 50, 260-264
    generic traits, 279-282
    IntoIterator and, 353
    reverse-engineering bounds, 283-286
    trait objects versus, 264-266
generic collections, strings as, 453
generic enums, 238-241
generic functions
    with constant parameters, 263
generic parameters
    constants, 222, 263
generic structs, 25, 219-221
generic swaps, 64
generic types
    with constant parameters, 222
get method, 227
get_form function, 22
get_index function, 18
git2-rs crate, 665
global event loop versus Rust executors, 565
global variables, 537-540
grep utility, 479
guards, 249

H
half-open (end-exclusive) ranges, 150
half-open ranges, 250
handle.join method, 504
hash method, 425
Hash trait, 424-426
Hasher, 425
HashMap trait, 237
HashMap::with_capacity, 415
HashMap<K, V> collection type, 413-420
HashSet::new, 421
HashSet::with_capacity, 421
HashSet<T> collection type, 420-424
Hashtable, 125

heap.peek method, 412
heap.peek_mut method, 412
heap.pop method, 412
heap.push method, 412
hexadecimal numeric literal, 54, 62
hexadecimal, formatting numbers in, 457
HTTP client crate, 565
hygienic macros, 620

I

if expression, 9, 140-142
if let expressions, 142
image files, for Mandelbrot set, 33-34
image space, mapping to complex number
    plane, 30
immutable references, 65
impl block, 214-218
impl trait, 280-282
imports, 183
inbound.lines method, 574
include! macro, 610
include_bytes! macro, 611
include_str! macro, 611
Index trait, 300-302
indexed content, 92-94, 461, 513-519, 523-525
IndexMut trait, 300-302
infinite loops, 143
#[inline] attribute, 192
inlining, 334
input and output, 473-498
    files and directories, 488-496
    networking, 496-498
    readers and writers, 474-488
inspect adapter, 369
installation, Rust, 6-8
integer literals, 54, 59, 244
integer types, 53-56, 457
integers, 9
    converting characters to/from, 436
    converting to raw pointers, 643
    division by zero panic, 151
    Rust and C type commonalities, 666
integration tests, 196
interior mutability, 99, 225-229
internet protocol address types, formatting, 459
Into trait, 320-323
IntoIter, associated type of, 349
IntoIterator trait, 349-350, 351-353, 388
into_iter iterator, 39

into_iter method, 350
invalidation errors, 393, 409
invariants, mutexes and, 527, 532
inverted index, 513-519, 523-525
invoking wakers, in spawn_blocking, 586-588
io module, 475
IpAddr type, 448, 459
irrefutable patterns, 251
isize type, 54
item declarations, 139
items, 178, 191-193
iter method, 350, 353
iter.collect method, 415, 421, 437
iterable type, 349
iterating
    borrowing and, 372
    over a map, 420
    over sets, 422
    over text, 444-446
iterator adapters (see adapter methods)
Iterator methods, 349
Iterator trait, 275, 349, 388
iterators, 12, 347-392
    adapter methods, 358-375
    associated types and, 276-279
    consuming (see consuming iterators)
    creating, 350-356
    implementing for your own types, 388-392
    in standard library, 356
    traits, 349-350
iter_mut method, 350, 353

J

Java
    ConcurrentModificationException, 125
    object-mutex relationship in, 527
JavaScript, asynchronous function, 565
join method
    combining strings, 76
    on rayon parallel iterators, 508
    waiting for thread, 504
JSON (JavaScript Object Notation), 236
json! macro, 612-624
    fragment types, 613-616
    importing and exporting, 622-624
    recursion in, 617
    scoping and hygiene, 619-622
    using traits with, 617-619

K

Keep, Daniel
    The Little Book of Rust Macros, 625
key argument, map, 417

L

language extension traits, 303
last method, 382
Latin-1 character set, 430
lazy_static crate, 467, 539
len method, 70, 75, 379
let statement, 9, 90, 138
Li, Peng, 2
libgit2, 665, 671-675
    raw interface to, 675-681
    safe interface to, 681-691
libraries, 188-189
    doc-tests, 199-202
    documentation, 197-202
    foreign functions from, 671-675
    src/bin directory, 189-191
    third-party (see crates)
lifetime
    parameters for generic functions, 262
    parameters for references, 110, 114-123
    reference constraints, 642
    structs with, 221
line! macro, 609
lines method, on input streams, 381, 571
#[link] attribute, 671
Linux
    Rust package for, 6
    using functions from libraries, 672
literals, in patterns, 244
The Little Book of Rust Macros (Keep), 625
lock method, 529
locking data
    mutexes, 528-533
    read/write locks, 533
logging
    channels for, 525
    formatting pointers for, 464
    formatting values for, 459
logical operators, 152
log_syntax! macro, 612
long-running computations, asynchronous
    programming, 563-564
loop (for infinite loops), 143
looping expressions, 142-145

lvalues, 149

M

machine language, 666
machine types, integer types, 53-56
machine word, 53
macOS
    Rust package for, 6
    using functions from libraries, 672
macros, 601-626
    built-in, 609-611
    debugging, 611-612
    expansion, 601, 603-605
    fragment types, 613-616
    importing and exporting, 622-624
    json!, 612-624
    procedural, 625
    recursion in, 617
    repetition, 607-609
    scoping and hygiene, 619-622
    unintended consequences, 605-607
    using traits with, 617-619
macro_rules!, 602, 615
main function, 12, 17, 169
Mandelbrot set, 22-27
    concurrent implementation, 22-41
    mapping from pixels to complex numbers,
      30
    parsing pair command-line arguments,
      28-30
    plotting, 32
    rendering with fork-join parallelism,
      510-511
    running the plotter, 40
    writing image files, 33-34
map (HashMap and BTreeMap) methods
    append method, 416
    btree_map.split_off method, 417
    clear method, 417
    contains_key method, 416
    entry(key) method, 418
    entry(key).and_modify method, 419
    entry(key).or_default method, 418
    entry(key).or_insert method, 418
    entry(key).or_insert_with method, 419
    extend method, 416
    get method, 416
    get_mut method, 416
    insert method, 416

into_iter method, 420
into_keys method, 420
into_values method, 420
is_empty method, 416
keys method, 420
len method, 415
remove method, 416
remove_entry method, 416
retain method, 416
values method, 420
values_mut method, 420
map adapter, 358-360
map and mapping, 30
    BTreeMap<K, V>, 395, 413-420
    filter_map and flat_map adapters, 360-363
    find_map method, 383
    HashMap trait, 237
    HashMap<K, V>, 395, 413-420
    map and filter, 358-360
marker traits, 303, 521-523, 560-563, 596-597, 639
match expression, 29, 140, 241-242
match statement, 34
matches! macro, 611
matching unions, 663
Matsakis, Niko, 508
max method, 376
max_by method, 376
max_by_key method, 377
MaybeUninit type, 680
memory, 79
    (see also ownership)
    closure layout in, 335
    enums in, 235
    raw pointers and, 649-653
    reinterpreting with unions, 660-663
    strings in, 74-76
    types for representing sequence of values in, 67-72
memory ordering, for atomic operations, 536
methods
    calling, 148
    defining with impl, 214-218
    fully qualified method calls, 274-275
min method, 376
min_by method, 376
min_by_key method, 377
Model-View-Controller (see MVC)
modules, 178-187

libraries and, 188-189
    nested, 179
    paths and imports, 183-185
    prelude, 179
    in separate files, 180
    standard prelude, 186
monomorphization, 261
Morris worm, 2
moves, 85-94
    closures and, 331
    constructing new values, 91
    control flow and, 91
    Copy types as exception to, 94-97
    indexed content and, 92-94
    passing values to a function, 91
    returning values to a function, 91
    assigning to a variable, 90
mpsc (multiproducer, single-consumer) module, 514, 519, 532
Mul (multiplication trait), 279
multiple readers, 104
multithreaded programming, 499-501, 521
    (see also asynchronous programming; concurrency)
mut (mutable) keyword, 9
mut (mutable) reference, 530
mutability, interior, 225-229
mutable references (&mut T), 66, 103
    FnMut, 338-340
    IntoIterator implementation, 352
    Mutex and, 529
    rules for, 126
    shared references versus, 103, 123-129
    splitting and, 402-405
mutable slice, 67
mutable state, shared, 525-539
mutable statics, 113, 187, 630
Mutex type, 580-581
Mutex::new, 528
mutexes, 526-527
    chat connections with async mutexes, 577-580
    creating with Mutex<T>, 528-529
    deadlocks and, 531
    invariants and, 527, 532
    limitations, 530
    multiconsumer channels using, 532
    mut reference and, 530
    poisoned, 531

MVC (Model-View-Controller), 345

N

named-field structs, 209-212
namespaces (see modules)
NaN (not-a-number) values, 296
native_tls crate, 496
nested modules, 179
net module, 496
networking, 496-498
newtypes, 213, 632
next method, 276, 373, 572
non-mut references, splitting, 402-405
normalization, Unicode, 468-471
not-a-number (NaN) values, 296
nth and nth_back methods, 382
nth triangle number, 347
null pointers, 109
null raw pointers, 641, 646
null references not allowed, 65, 109
numbers, complex, 30
numeric types
    fixed-width, 52-60
    floating-point types, 58-60
    integer types, 53-56, 457

O

OccupiedEntry type, HashMap and BTreeMap, 419
octal numeric literal, 54
octal, formatting numbers in, 457
offset method, 628, 642, 643, 648
One Definition Rule, 270
OpenOptions struct, 484
operator overloading, 287-302
    arithmetic/bitwise operators, 288-294
    binary operators, 292
    compound assignment operators, 293-294
    equality tests, 294-297
    generic traits and, 279
    Index and IndexMut, 300-302
    limitations on, 302
    ordered comparisons, 297-299
    unary operators, 291
operator precedence, 134
operators
    arithmetic, 151, 288-290, 293-294
    as operator, 436
    binary, 151, 292
    bitwise, 151, 293-294
    comparison, 61, 77, 108, 152, 376
    equality, 294-297
    reference, 151
    unary, 291
Option<&T>, 109
option_env! macro, 610
ordered comparison operators, 297-299
Ordering::SeqCst, atomic memory ordering, 536
orphan rule, 270
os module, 495
OsStr string type, 488-490
Outbound type, 579
overflowing operations, 58
ownership, 79-100
    Arc, 97-100
    C++ versus Rust, 81-85
    Cow, 325
    iteration and, 14
    moves, 85-94
    Rc, 97-100
    shared, 97-100
owning type, 489

P

panic, 9, 157-160
    aborting, 159
    poisoned mutexes, 532
    safety in unsafe code, 659
    unwinding, 158-159
panic! macro, 158, 454, 602
parallel programming, 3
    (see also concurrency)
ParallelIterator, 508
parameters
    formatting, 454, 459, 461
    lifetime, 110, 114-123, 262
    type, 29, 220, 261, 295
parse method, 448
parse_args function, 45
parse_complex function, 30
parse_pair function, 29
PartialEq trait, 294-297
PartialOrd trait, 297-299
partition method, 386
part_iter method, 508
Path type, 351, 456, 488-492
    ancestors method, 491

components method, 491
display method, 492
file_name method, 490
is_absolute method, 490
is_relative method, 490
join method, 490
parent method, 490
to_str method, 491
to_string_lossy method, 492
Path::new method, 490
PathBuf type, 490
paths, standard library, 183-185
patterns, 241-254
 @ patterns, 250
 array, 246
 avoiding syntax errors during matching in
  macros, 624
 guards, 249
 literals in, 244
 match expressions and, 141
 matching multiple possibilities with, 250
 populating a binary tree, 252
 reference, 247-249
 searching and replacing, 442-443
 situations that allow, 251
 slice, 246
 struct, 245
 tuple, 245
 variables in, 244
 wildcards in, 244
peek method, 367
Peekable iterator, 367
Pin type, 594
pinned pointer, 594-596
pinning futures, 590-597
pipeline approach
 concurrent programming, 500
 iterator stages, 348, 350
 multiple threads, 513-519, 520, 523-525
pixel_to_point function, 40
plotting, Mandelbrot set, 32, 40
Pointer formatting trait, 642
pointer types, 65-66
 boxes, 66
 non-owning, 104
 pinned pointer, 594-596
 raw pointers, 66, 640-660
 references (see references (pointer type))
pointers, Rust's restrictions on, 80

PoisonError::into_inner, 532
poll method, 545, 563
polling interface, asynchronous programming,
 545-546, 565, 585-590
polymorphism, 255
position method, 378
post_gcd function, 20, 22
precedence, operator, 134
prelude module, 179, 496, 572
print! macro, 454, 482
println! macro, 20, 76, 454, 482
println! method, 163
print_error function, 169
print_padovan function, 83
print_usage function, 43
procedural macros, 625
process_files function, 502
product method, 375
profiler, 177
propagating errors, 164
protocol
 client and server as asynchronous, 569-570
 internet protocol address types, formatting,
  459
ptr module, 651
ptr.copy_to, 652
ptr.copy_to_nonoverlapping, 652
ptr::copy, 652
ptr::copy_nonoverlapping, 652
ptr::read, 651
ptr::write , 652
public vocabulary traits, 303
Python, assignment in, 86-90

R

race method, 576
rand crate, 408
rand::thread_rng method, 409
ranges
 closed, 150
 end-exclusive, 250
 half-open, 150, 250
 in loop expressions, 143
 unbounded, 250
raw module, 666, 675-681
raw pointers, 66, 628, 640-660
 dereferencing, 66, 629, 630, 643-646
 GapBuffer example, 653-659
 moving into/out of memory, 649-653

nullable pointers, 646
panic safety in unsafe code, 659
pointer arithmetic, 647-649
RefWithFlag example, 644-646
type sizes and alignments, 647
raw strings, 73
Rayon library (Matsakis and Stone), 508-509
Rc pointer type, 98-100, 217-217
Read trait, 473, 474
    bytes method, 477
    chain method, 477
    lines method, 478
    read method, 476
    read_exact method, 477
    read_to_end method, 476
    read_to_string method, 476
    take method, 477
read-only access, shared access as, 126
read/write locks (RwLock), 533
ReadBytesExt trait, 487
readers, 475-482
    binary data, compression, serialization,
        487-488
    buffered, 477-482
    collecting lines, 481
    files, 483
    other types, 485-486
    reading lines, 479-480
    Seek trait, 484
read_dir method, 493
read_numbers function, 166
read_to_string function, 45
read_unaligned, 652
read_volatile, 653
Receiver type, 532
receiving packets, asynchronous chat, 573-575
recursion, macros, 617
RefCell type
    borrow methid, 228
    borrow_mut method, 228
    try_borrow method, 228
    try_borrow_mut method, 228
RefCell::new(value), 227
RefCell<T> struct, 227
reference (ref) patterns, 247-249
reference operators, 151
reference-counted (Rc) pointer type, 98-100
references (pointer type), 65, 101-131
    assigning, 107

borrowing, 109, 110-113, 330
C++ versus Rust, 105
comparing, 108
constraints on, 110-120, 642
immutable, 65
IntoIterator implementation, 352
iteration and, 14
lifetime parameters and, 110, 114-123
mutable (see mutable references)
null, 65
null pointers and, 109
passing references to functions, 115
receiving as function arguments, 113-115
returning, 116
safety of, 110-123
"sea of objects" and, 130-131
shared versus mutable, 103, 123-129
structs containing, 117-120
to references, 107
to slices and trait objects, 110
to values, 102-105
refutable patterns, 252
RefWithFlag<'a, T>, 644-646
Regex struct, 46
Regex::captures method, 466
Regex::new constructor, 467-468
regular expressions (regex), 466-468
    basic use, 466-467
    building values on demand, 467
    macros versus, 604
relational operators, 152
replace_all method, 46
#[repr(C)] attribute, 667
#[repr(i16)] attribute, 668
reqwest crate, 497
resource-constrained programming, xvi
Result type, 13, 160-172
    as_mut method, 162
    as_ref method, 162
    catching errors, 157, 160-162
    dealing with errors that "can't happen", 168
    declaring a custom error type, 171
    err method, 161
    error handling across threads, 504
    expect method, 161
    handling errors in main function, 169
    ignoring errors, 169
    is_err method, 161
    is_ok method, 161

key points of design, 172
with multiple error types, 166-167
ok method, 161
printing errors, 163-164
propagating errors, 164
type aliases, 162
unwrap method, 161
unwrap_or method, 161
unwrap_or_else method, 161
return expressions, 10, 10, 145
rev adapter, 368-369
reverse method, 69
reversible iterators, 368-369
rfind method, 383
rfold method, 380
Rhs type parameter, 295
root module, 189
route method, 18
routers, callbacks and, 341-345
rposition method, 378
Rust, 5-48
    command-line arguments, 11-15
    command-line interface, 42-44
    community, 208
    concurrency, 22-41
    filesystems, 42-48
    find and replace, 46
    functions in, 8-10
    installation, 6-8
    reading files, 45
    reasons for using, 2-4
    rules for well-behaved program, 637
    simple web server, 15-21
    unit testing in, 10
    website, 6
rustc command, 6, 175, 612
rustdoc command, 6
rustup, 6-8
RwLock, 533

S

safe interface to libgit2, 681-691
safety
    closures and, 335-341
    invisibility of, 41
    with references, 110-123
    thread safety with Send and Sync, 521-523
saturating operations, 58
say_hello function, 260

scopes and scoping, 507, 619-622
searching
    slices, 407, 443
    text, 441-443
Seek trait, 484
self argument, 217-217
self keyword, 184
Self type, 270-271
semicolons following expressions, 137
SEMVER variable, 468
Send marker trait, 521-523, 560-563, 639
send_as_json, 572
serde library/crate, 269, 487, 567
serde_json crate, 236, 487, 567
serialization, 487
set method, 227
set types (HashMap and BTreeMap)
    contains method, 421
    difference method, 423
    get method, 422
    insert method, 421
    intersection method, 423
    is_disjoint method, 424
    is_empty method, 421
    is_subset method, 424
    is_superset method, 424
    iter method, 422
    len method, 421
    remove method, 421
    replace method, 423
    retain method, 421
    symmetric_difference method, 423
    take method, 422
    union method, 423
sets, 420
    (see also Mandelbrot set)
    BTreeSet<T>, 420-424
    HashSet<T> type, 420-424
shadowing, 139
shared access, 126
shared immutable data across threads, 505-507
shared mutable state, 525-539
    atomics, 535, 538
    condition variables (Condvar), 534
    deadlock, 531
    global variables, 537-540
    multiconsumer channels using mutex, 532
    mut and Mutex, 529
    mutex limitations, 530

Mutex<T>, 528-529
poisoned mutexes, 531
read/write locks (RwLock), 533
shared references (&T), 103
C's pointers to const values versus, 130
IntoIterator implementation, 352
mutable references versus, 123-129
rules for, 126, 130
shared slice of Ts, 67
Shared struct, spawn_blocking, 587
#[should_panic] attribute, 194
show_it function, 314
signed integer types, 53
single writer, multiple readers rule, 104
SipHash-1-3, 426
Sized trait, 307-310, 647
size_hint method, 373, 385
size_of_val function, 647
skip and skip_while adapters, 365
slice patterns, 246
slices, 71
&str (string slice), 76
binary_search method, 407
binary_search_by method, 407
binary_search_by_key method, 407
borrowing as other text-like types, 449
bytes method, 445
case conversion for strings, 447
chars method, 444
char_indices method, 444
choose method, 408
chunks method, 404
chunks_exact method, 405
chunks_exact_mut method, 405
chunks_mut method, 404
comparing, 408
concat method, 402
contains method, 408, 443
ends_with method, 408, 443
find method, 443
first method, 397
first_mut method, 397
get method, 397
get_mut method, 397
IntoIterator implementation, 353
is_char_boundary method, 438
is_empty method, 398, 438
iter method, 403
iterating over text, 444-446

iter_mut method, 403
join method, 402
joining in arrays of arrays, 402
last method, 397
last_mut method, 397
len method, 398, 438
lines method, 445
matches method, 446
match_indices method, 446
random output, 408
rchunks method, 404
rchunks_exact method, 405
rchunks_exact_mut method, 405
rchunks_mut method, 404
references to, 110
replace method, 443
replacen method, 443
reverse method, 407
rfind method, 443
rmatch_indices method, 446
rsplit method, 404, 445
rsplitn method, 404, 445
rsplitn_mut method, 404
rsplit_mut method, 404
rsplit_terminator method, 445
searching, 407, 443
shuffle method, 409
slice[range], 438
sort method, 406
sorting, 406
sort_by method, 406
sort_by_key method, 406
split method, 404, 445
splitn method, 404, 445
splitn_mut method, 404
splitting non-mut references, 402-405
split_ascii_whitespace method, 446
split_at method, 403, 438
split_at_mut method, 403
split_first method, 404
split_first_mut method, 404
split_last method, 404
split_last_mut method, 404
split_mut method, 404
split_terminator method, 445
split_whitespace method, 446
starts_with method, 408, 443
strip_prefix method, 447
strip_suffix method, 447

swap method, 405
swapping contents of, 405
to_lowercase method, 447
to_owned method, 438
to_string method, 437
to_uppercase method, 447
to_vec method, 397
trim method, 446
trimming strings, 446
trim_matches method, 447
UTF-8 and, 449-451
windows method, 405
snake-case, 210
SocketAddr type, 459
sorting slices, 406
spawn function
    for asynchronous tasks, 542, 552, 560
    for creating threads, 502-504, 505
spawning async tasks, 552-556, 559
spawn_blocking, 563-564, 586-588
spawn_local, 552-556, 560
splice method, 271
src/bin directory, 189-191
stack unwinding, 158-159
standard prelude, 186
statements, expressions versus, 133
static keyword, 187, 630
static methods, 148
static values (statics), 113, 179
std (standard library), 183
Stderr type, 485
Stdin type, 485
StdinLock type, 485
Stdout type, 485
Stone, Josh, 508
str::from_utf8, 450
str::from_utf8_unchecked, 451
Stream trait, 571
streams
    async streams, 573-575
    client and server as asynchronous, 570-572
    TcpStream, 486, 573
String and str types, 29, 73-78, 436-453
    appending text, 439-440
    Ascii, 631-634
    borrowing slice's content, 449
    byte strings, 74
    case conversion, 447
    clear method, 440

converting nontextual values to, 448-449
creating String values, 437
drain method, 441
extend method, 439
filename types, 489
from_utf8, 450
from_utf8_lossy, 450
from_utf8_unchecked, 451
as generic collections, 453
insert method, 439
inserting text, 439-440
insert_str method, 439
iterating over text, 441, 444-446
non-Unicode strings, 77
parsing values from, 447
pop method, 440
producing text from UTF-8 data, 450
push method, 439
push_str method, 439
putting off allocation, 451-453
remove method, 441
removing and replacing text, 440
replace_range method, 441
searching text, 441-443
simple inspection, 438
strings in memory, 74-76
trimming text, 446
truncate method, 440
UTF-8 and, 61, 449-451
string literals, 73, 74, 77
string slice (&str), 76
String::new, 437
String::with_capacity, 437, 440
stringify! macro, 610
strings and text, 429-471
    characters (char), 432-436
    formatting values, 454-465
    normalization, 468-471
    passing between Rust and C, 669
    regular expressions, 466-468
    Unicode background, 430-432
    unsafe code for conversion of Ascii into
        String, 631-634
Stroustrup, Bjarne
    "Abstraction and the C++ Machine Model",
        4
struct expression, 210
struct patterns, 245
structs, 186, 209-229

defining methods with impl, 214-218
deriving common traits for struct types, 225
generic, 219-221
hash implementation, 424
interior mutability, 225-229
layout, 213
with lifetime parameters, 221
named-field, 209-212
references in, 117-120
tuple-like, 212
unit-like, 213
submodules, 179
subtraits, 271
successors method, 353-355
sum method, 375
sum types, 231
supertrait, 272
switch statement, 244
symlink method, 495-496
Sync type, 521-523, 639
synchronized objects, 500
synchronous channel, concurrency, 520
synchronous to asynchronous programming,
543-566
async blocks, 556-559
async functions, 546-552, 558
asynchronous HTTP client crate, 565
await expression, 548
comparing asynchronous designs, 564
futures (see futures)
implementing Send, 560-563
long-running computations, 563-564
spawning async tasks, 552-556, 559
thread pool, spawning async tasks from, 559
syntax errors, macros and, 624
system calls, 543
systems programming, xv, 1

T

<T>, 64
[T] slices, 71
(see also slices)
take and take_while adapters, 365, 372
task_local! macro, 560
TcpStream, 486, 573
templates, macro, 604
#[test] attribute, 192
tests, 193-202
doc-tests, 199-202

integration tests, 196
text, 430
(see also strings and text; UTF-8)
appending and inserting, 439-440
ASCII, 430, 433, 434, 631-634
case conversion, 435, 447
conventions for searching/iterating, 441
directionality of, 432
GapBuffer example, 653-660
iterating over, 444
removing and replacing, 440
searching, 441-443
trimming, 446
text values, formatting, 455-456
thread pool, spawning async tasks on, 559
threads
asynchronous tasks versus, 541
background thread, 500
channels and, 512-525
deadlock, 531
error handling across, 504
safety with Send and Sync, 521-523
shared immutable data across, 505-507
todo! macro, 611
token tree, 616
tokens, macro patterns, 604
tokio crate, 565, 567, 581-584
ToOwned trait, 324-326
to_owned method, 76
to_string method, 46, 76
trace_macros! macro, 612
trait objects, 258-260
generic code versus, 264-266
layout, 259
references to, 110
unsized types and, 308
traits, 12, 97, 255-286
associated consts, 282
defining and implementing, 266-273
for defining relationships between types,
275-283
fully qualified method calls, 274-275
impl, 280-282
implementing for your own types, 462-464
iterators and associated types, 276-279
with macros, 617-619
for operator overloading, 279, 287
other people's types and, 268-270
reverse-engineering bounds, 283-286

Self as type, 270-271
    for struct types, 225
    subtraits, 271
    type-associated functions, 272
    unsafe, 638-640
    utility (see utility traits)
transitive dependencies, 175
Travis CI, 208
trees, 84
trimming string text, 446
try! macro, 165
TryFrom trait, 323
TryInto trait, 323
try_fold and try_rfold methods, 380-382
try_for_each method, 387
tuple patterns, 245
tuple-like structs, 212
tuples, 63-64
type aliases, 78, 162, 186
type alignment, raw pointers and, 647
type inference, 49
type parameters, 29, 220, 261, 295
type size, raw pointers and, 647
type-associated functions, 217, 272
types, 49-78
    arrays, 67
    associated, 276-279
    casts and, 153
    of closures and functions, 332-334
    error handling, 160-172, 459, 568
    filename, 489
    floating-point, 58-60, 376, 458
    formatting values, 458, 462-464
    implementing iterators for your own,
        388-392
    IntoIterator implementation, 351-353
    numeric, 52-60, 457
    operator overloading and, 287
    parameters, 220, 261, 295
    pointers (see pointer types)
    for representing sequence of values in mem-
        ory, 67-72
    Sized, 307-310
    slices, 71
    String and str (see String and str types)
    traits for adding methods to, 268
    traits for defining relationships between,
        275-283
    tuples, 63-64

unsized, 308-310
user-defined, 186
vectors, 68-71

U
unary operators, 291
unbounded ranges, 250
undefined behavior, 2, 629, 636-638
Unicode, 430-432
    ASCII and, 430
    character literals, 61
    Latin-1 and, 430
    normalization, 468-471
    OsStr and, 489
    text directionality, 432
    UTF-8, 430-432
unicode-normalization crate, 471-471
unimplemented! macro, 611
unions, 231, 630, 660-663
unit testing, 10
unit type, 64
unit-like structs, 213
Unix
    files and directories, 495-496
    pipes, 512-516
Unpin marker trait, 596-597
Unpin trait, 573
unsafe blocks, 66, 628, 630-633, 635
unsafe code, 627-663
    foreign functions (see foreign functions)
    libgit2 raw interface, 675-681
    raw pointers (see raw pointers)
    undefined behavior, 636-638
    unions, 660-663
    unsafe blocks, 66, 628, 630-633, 635
    unsafe feature, 628-629
    unsafe functions, 628, 633-635
    unsafe traits, 638-640
unsafe functions, 628, 633-635
unsafe traits, 638-640
unsigned integer types, 53
unsized types, 308-310
unwinding, 158-159
unwrap method, 34, 505
use declarations, 183, 186
user-defined types, 186
usize type, 54, 396
UTF-8, 430-432
    accessing text as, 449

ASCII methods with, 434
char type and, 61
OsStr and, 488-490
producing text from data, 450
String and str handling, 436
strings in memory, 74
unsafe code and, 631-633
utility traits, 303-326
    AsRef and AsMut, 317
    Borrow and BorrowMut, 318-320
    Clone, 310, 340, 397
    Copy, 311, 340
    Cow, 325, 451-453
    Default, 315-317, 387
    Deref and DerefMut, 312-315
    Drop, 304-307
    From and Into, 320-323, 618
    Sized, 307-310
    ToOwned, 324-326
    TryFrom and TryInto, 323
utils module, 568

V
VacantEntry type, HashMap and BTreeMap,
    419
values
    building on demand, 467
    dropping, 82, 85, 336-338
    formatting, 454-465, 642
    fundamental types for representing, 49-78
    moves, 91
    passing by, 105, 352, 393
    receiving via channels, 516
    references and, 102-110
    sending via channels, 513-516
    sets and differences in "equal" values, 422
    static, 113, 179, 187
    String and str types, 447-449
variable capture, 329
variables
    assigning to, 90
    borrowing local, 110-113
    condition, 534
    declaring from foreign libraries, 670-671
    global, 537-540
    ownership, 14, 79-100, 325
    in patterns, 244
    static, 537
Vec type, 12

append method, 400
building from VecDeque, 412
capacity method, 398
clear method, 400
dedup method, 401
dedup_by method, 401
dedup_by_key method, 402
drain method, 401
extend method, 400
insert method, 399
pop method, 399
push method, 399
remove method, 399
reserve method, 399
reserve_exact method, 399
resize method, 400
resize_with method, 400
retain method, 401
shrink_to_fit method, 399
split_off method, 400
swap_remove method, 406
truncate method, 400
with_capacity method, 398
vec! macro, 68, 395, 607-609
Vec<T> collection type, 67, 69, 394, 395-410
    accessing elements, 396-397
    comparing slices, 408
    growing/shrinking vectors, 398-402
    invalidation errors, ruling out, 409
    iteration, 398
    joining, 402
    random elements, 408
    searching, 407
    sorting, 406
    splitting, 402-405
    swapping, 405
Vec<u8>, 485
VecDeque, 394, 410-412
    back method, 410
    back_mut method, 410
    front method, 410
    front_mut method, 410
    make_contiguous method, 411
    pop_back method, 410
    pop_front method, 410
    push_back method, 410
    push_front method, 410
VecDeque::from(vec), 412
vector of Ts, 67

vectors, 68-71, 398-402
versions, file, 202
vertical bar (|), 250
virtual table (vtable), 260

W

waker, 545, 585-590
weak pointers, 100
web server, creating with Rust, 15-21
well-behaved program, Rust's rules for, 637
while let loop, 143
while loop, 9, 143, 145
whole-set operations, 423
wildcards, 183, 203, 244
Windows
    files and directories, 495
    OsStr and, 488
    Rust package for, 6
    using functions from libraries, 672
work-stealing, 509
worker pools, 500
workspaces, 207
wrapping operations, 56, 57
wrapping_offset method, 642, 643
write function, 45
write method, 255, 268
Write trait, 473

appending and inserting text, 439
    flush method, 483
    using formatting language in your code, 465
    write method, 483
    write_all method, 483
write! macro, 292, 439, 454, 482
WriteBytesExt trait, 487
writeln! macro, 164, 439, 454, 482
writers, 474, 482-483
    binary data, compression, serialization,
        487-488
    files, 483
    other types, 485-486
    Seek trait, 484
write_image function, 34
write_unaligned, 652
write_volatile, 653

Y

yield_now, 563-564

Z

zero-overhead principle, 4
zero-tuple, 64
Zeroable trait, 639
zip adapter, 372

About the Authors

Jim Blandy has been programming since 1981 and writing free software since 1990. He has been the maintainer of GNU Emacs and GNU Guile, and a maintainer of GDB, the GNU Debugger. He is one of the original designers of the Subversion version control system. Jim now works on Firefox's graphics and renderiing for Mozilla.

Jason Orendorff works on undisclosed Rust projects at GitHub. He previously worked on the SpiderMonkey JavaScript engine at Mozilla. He is interested in grammar, baking, time travel, and helping people learn about complicated topics.

Leonora Tindall is a type system enthusiast and software engineer who uses Rust, Elixir, and other advanced languages to build robust and resilient systems software in high-impact areas like healthcare and data ownership. She works on a variety of open source projects, from genetic algorithms that evolve programs in strange languages to the Rust core libraries and crate ecosystem, and enjoys the experience of contributing to supportive and diverse community projects. In her free time, Leonora builds electronics for audio synthesis and is an avid radio hobbyist. Her love of hardware extends to her software engineering practice as well. She has built applications software for LoRa radios in Rust and Python and uses software and DIY hardware to create experimental electronic music on a Eurorack synthesizer.

Colophon

The animal on the cover of *Programming Rust* is a Montagu's crab (*Xantho hydrophilus*). Montagu's crab has been found in the northeastern Atlantic Ocean and in the Mediterranean Sea. It lives under rocks and boulders during low tide. If one is exposed when a rock is lifted, it will aggressively hold its pincers up and spread them wide open to make itself appear bigger.

This robust-looking crab has a muscly appearance with a broad carapace about 70 mm wide. The edge of the carapace is furrowed, and the color is yellowish or reddish-brown. It has 10 legs: the front pair (the chelipeds) are equal in size with black-tipped claws or pincers; then there are three pairs of walking legs that are stout and relatively short; and the last pair of legs are for swimming. They walk and swim sideways.

This crab is an omnivore. They eat mostly algae, snails, and crabs of other species. They are mostly active at night. Egg-bearing females are found from March through July, and the larvae are present in plankton for most of the summer.

Many of the animals on O'Reilly covers are endangered; all of them are important to the world.

The cover illustration is by Karen Montgomery, based on an image from *Wood's Natural History*. The cover fonts are Gilroy Semibold and Guardian Sans. The text font is Adobe Minion Pro; the heading font is Adobe Myriad Condensed; and the code font is Dalton Maag's Ubuntu Mono.

O'REILLY®

There's much more where this came from.

Experience books, videos, live online training courses, and more from O'Reilly and our 200+ partners—all in one place.

Learn more at oreilly.com/online-learning

Milton Keynes UK
Ingram Content Group UK Ltd.
UKHW052111061023
429951UK00007B/11